MW00652488

Basic
American Government

Other Books
by
Clarence Carson

The Fateful Turn
The American Tradition
The Flight from Reality
The War on the Poor
Throttling the Railroads
The Rebirth of Liberty
The World in the Grip of an Idea
Organized Against Whom? The Labor Union in America
The Colonial Experience
The Beginning of the Republic
The Sections and the Civil War
The Growth of America
The Welfare State
America: From Gridlock to Deadlock
A Teacher's Guide to A Basic History of the United States
Basic Economics
Basic Communism
Swimming Against the Tide

Basic American Government

by
Clarence B. Carson

American Textbook Committee
www.americantextbookcommittee.org

ISBN 1-931789-19-3

CONTENTS

Section I
Introduction and Examination
of American Government

Section II
Background of Political Thought
and Practice

Section III
American Government in the 19th Century

Section IV
Leviathan:
American Government in the 20th Century

Preface

It would be a considerable fraud to do a book on American government which talked as if the constitution were still being substantially observed, that pretended that when Presidents took the oath of office they intended to observe the bounds set by the Constitution, that Congressmen recited their pledges with the same intent, and that Federal judges were still construing the Constitution as it was written. In sum, any book on American government worthy of the name ought to make clear how remote from the Constitution the government has become. Every effort has been made to do so in this book.

This book is not, then, simply a manual on the nuts and bolts of government which accepts whatever it is that government does without reference to constitutional authorization. It is not a manual on how to live under its authority and operate the government in the year of our Lord 1993. There are manuals aplenty that provide such information. On the contrary, this is a work addressed to potential citizens, who wish to constrain and control their government by constitutional means, not to conforming servants, beggars for portions of its loot, nor employees or operators of a leviathon-sized government.

This book contains an account of the general government as established by the Constitution, of the state governments which preceded it and came after it and their constitutions. More, it details the Ancient and modern foundations, scriptural and secular, on which these constitutions and governments rested. The Founders of the United States built on a great foundation, and the story of that is told in these pages. The story is told, too, how the Constitution of 1787 became the Higher Law for many Americans, including most of those who governed them, in the 19th century. It ends with a detailed account of the massive departures from the Constitution in the 20th century on the way to constructing a Leviathon, in which government is now out of control.

This is a work intended for citizens and potential citizens of the United States of all ages and conditions. Can such a work be intended for young people? Indeed, it can and is, for however shameful the departures from and betrayal of the Constitution have been, the knowledge of them is not something from which anyone should be protected.

I am grateful to those who have helped in many ways to make this work possible, and especially to the Directors of American Textbook Committee, who have maintained a lively interest in it during the considerable while it was in preparation. My special thanks, too, go to my wife, Myrtice Sears Carson, who has not only done much to make the way of a writer smooth but also read copy, corrected proofs, and otherwise helped to produce this book. But my dependence upon these and other people in no way relieves me of responsibility for the accuracy of the facts and fidelity to the truth of the material contained herein. That responsibility is mine alone, and I accept it, albeit with more than a little misgiving.

Clarence B. Carson
Wadley, Alabama, 1993

Section I

Introduction and Examination of American Government

Chapter 1

Introduction:
The Political Crisis

We might suppose that because of the means available for communicating with and informing one another that people are better informed in this day than they have ever been and in closer communion with one another than ever before in all of history. It is indeed the case that the means of communication have increased in number, variety, speed, and precision in the 20th century. It is now possible to transmit pictures and sound from almost anywhere on earth to anywhere else virtually instantaneously via satellite. Commercial and cable television brings these wonders to many of the peoples on earth. Not only can we speak to people by telephone but also transmit letters and copies of documents long distances and almost instantaneously by Fax machines. Older means of informing people survive, such as in bookmaking, but have been made much more effective in disseminating their messages by the rapidity of transportation and swiftness and scale of printing. In short, means of communicating and informing people abound in our time.

Yet it is most doubtful that we are thereby better informed or more adept at or successful at communicating with one another than in earlier eras. There are some obvious senses, of course, in which we are better informed, if we wish to be, and cases in which we can and do communicate more expeditiously than in earlier times. We get reports of sports events, for example, in many cases while the events are still in progress, but in any case within hours of their completion. Nor is it only frivolous events that we learn about swiftly. We often hear of catastrophes within minutes of the time they occur. That one country has gone to war with another is information brought all too swiftly over the airwaves, by satellite, and in the daily newspaper. At the private level, we can often get almost instantaneous notice of the illness, accident or death befalling relatives and friends by telephone or other swift means of communication. Or, to take another tack, there surely is vastly more information available about a great variety of matters in our day than there has ever been. Computers, data disks, and retrieval systems are making more and more such information available.

3

Yet in the midst of this great abundance of information, it is possible for us to be grossly ignorant or grotesquely misinformed about matters of great moment to us. The situation is analogous to people lost at sea who die of thirst afloat upon an ocean of water. Or again, amidst all the devices of communication it is possible to be very lonely for want of real communion with others because they are so busily engaged in superficial exchanges. In a similar fashion, it is possible in the midst of a wonderful variety of highly advanced instruments of communication to be alienated because the bonds that link individuals to one another, families and communities together, and make possible societies, can be so loosened or broken that less effective communication takes place. Thus, the means to communicate abound but the state of human relations that make effective communication safe and rewarding become rarer and rarer. The best contemporary example of this condition can be readily conceived in the breakup (or break down) of the family, especially in widespread divorce. Clearly, divorces do not ordinarily occur because there are any shortage of devices by which husbands and wives may communicate. Indeed, there has never been a time in all of history when mates who spend time separate from one another have had so many instruments with which to communicate. They can communicate in writing by first class and express packages, by telephonic fax machines, and by courier (as a last resort). Orally, they can communicate by shouting, telephones, both stationary and mobile, by short wave radio, and by closed circuit television. But no one supposes that the great incidence of divorce was brought on by the lack of means of communication. Still, to speak of the matters this way may help us to see more clearly the fact that the presence of facilities in no way assures us that they are being used for the highest and best ends.

There are undoubtedly points at which the matters on which we are grossly ignorant and the failure to communicate have intersected and inter-acted with one another. That, however, is not the main concern at this stage. Let us, instead, focus on the arena in which we are grossly ignorant or grotesquely misinformed. Such a focus should bring us to the political crisis of our times.

The political crisis of our times has been caused by the fact that peoples have been grotesquely misinformed about the nature and character of gov-ernment. They have not had clearly in mind the inherent limits of govern-ment as a beneficent instrument for the concentration and exercise of power. They have not been well informed about how to limit, restrict, and restrain government. On the contrary, the main means of informing people have been used to convey distorted notions about the potentialities and possibil-ities of the use of government. This has, of course, been the message of numerous politicians, of many classes in schools, of the major media of communication, and so on. Although this story needs to be told in more detail, the fact of the crisis needs first to be made clear.

The political crisis of our times is the result of governments becoming gorged with power and running amok with the undisciplined exercise of power. It has probably been the most universally observable phenomenon in the 20th century. Hardly a country in the world has escaped a great growth and concentration of power and the unleashing of power in new directions, though there have been major differences in degree both in the concentration of power and the extent to which it was unleashed. Some countries aggressively expanded, making conquests of territory in other lands. Most countries, however, used the accretions of powers of government upon their own inhabitants.

Nazi Germany provided a grotesque example of the concentration of power in the hands of a central government ruled by a dictator and the aggressive bent to conquest in the 1930s and early 1940s. Hitler first conquered the people within Germany. He subdued or abolished all organized potential sources of opposition to his rule. As soon as he had removed potential opposition, he began large scale building programs, expanded the military force, mechanized it, and provided it with a major air force. As this rearming proceeded, Hitler became increasingly belligerent in foreign relations, making demands on adjoining foreign countries, eventually dispatching military force to carry on undeclared wars with his erstwhile neighbors. World War II was largely the result of Hitler's aggressive foreign thrusts and the responses of other countries to them.

A calm and dispassionate account of Hitler's concentration of power and loosing it upon surrounding countries does not, however, begin to capture the barbarity, oppression, and destruction which followed in its wake. Hitler came to be Chancellor of Germany legally, even though his tactics as an aspirant to office were hardly civilized. He was not only demagogic from the outset but surrounded himself with bullies and moved about in an undercurrent of violence which frequently erupted at his meetings. Once in power, he wasted little time in seizing the funds and shutting down the operations of labor unions, purging his organizations and jailing or killing his enemies, seizing the major means of communications, turning news into propaganda, and putting those whom he feared or despised into concentration camps, i.e., Communists, Jews, those people who call themselves Jehovah's Witnesses, Gypsies, and others who incurred his wrath from time to time. In lands which he conquered, he virtually destroyed them as nations, ruled by military government, and with puppet regimes. All restraints on his power to use the government as he would were removed. Hitler's was indeed a government run rampant.

But Nazi Germany has only been the best publicized and anathematized example of the tendency toward despotic and unrestrained government power in the 20th century. The Bolshevik (i.e., Communist) government which began to take over what it could of the Russian Empire in late 1917 not only antedated the rule of Hitler in Germany but showed him the way to concentrate power, subdue the people, establish one party dictatorships, and use government power as a battering ram. Hitler learned much of the pattern he was to follow from the Soviet rulers, as did Benito Mussolini, and many other less well known tyrants. Indeed, Soviet Communism is much the better example of government powers swollen to the bursting point and employed in the unholy enterprise of subduing and transforming whole peoples. Communism's ideology was much more ample than that of Nazism or Italian Fascism. Its vision of transforming people was much more thoroughgoing and totalitarian than any other in this or any other century. Moreover, Nazism was only in power for about a dozen years; while Soviet Communism lasted for about 73 years, at least. Although the slaughter by the Nazis was of millions of people, the probability is that Soviet Communists may have killed—murdered is the appropriate term in both cases—five times as many, though there is some conjecture involved in both cases.

In any case, the tyranny of a government cut loose from all restraint was much longer, more sustained, more thorough, and more general in the Soviet Union than in Nazi Germany. The terror eventually applied to the Jews in Germany and in Europe generally during World War II was applied almost indiscriminately to whole peoples in the Soviet Union under Stalin. Virtually the whole population of the vast Soviet Empire was impoverished for well over a half century. All private property in land, buildings, and means of production was taken away from people. The possessions of millions were seized and virtually confiscated. Monasteries were suppressed, seminaries were greatly restricted, thousands of churches were either demolished or seized and used for state and secular purposes. Concentration camps were first operated by Communists during the rule of Lenin and greatly increased in number and expanded in population under Stalin. The suffering of millions of people sentenced to these slave labor camps, often located in parts of the Soviet Union with the greatest extremes of temperature and the most inhospitable locales, often beggars the imagination both of those who have undertaken to relate it and those fortunate enough only to read about it.

The Soviet Union was, of course, only one land in which Communism was more or less deeply established in the years during and after World War II. There have been many other countries where Communist rule has been imposed on more or less unwilling populations: Poland, Czechoslovakia, Hungary, Latvia, Estonia, Lithuania, Yugoslavia, Rumania, Bulgaria, Albania, North Korea, mainland China, North Vietnam (then all of Vietnam), Cuba, Cambodia, Laos, Nicaragua, Ethiopia, South Yemen, Afghanistan, Benin, Angola, Guyana, and in several other countries, such as Libya, Algeria, and Syria, to greater or less degrees. In the 1950s through the 1970s, Russia and China became competitive centers for the spread of Communism around the world.

Everywhere Communism was established, the government was characterized by one party rule, dictatorship, an unbridled government security force, the taking over by government of most productive private property, and vast efforts by government action to make over the people. Religious persecution has been commonplace in Communist regimes. Government control and direction of the media of communication always follows or precedes Communist rule. Concentration (work or slave labor) camps are usually adjuncts to the power of monolithic totalitarian Communist states. Communism is a prescription for the most extensive and intensive use of government power to dominate and control populaces. The vision that activated Communist rulers from the outset was that every country in the world would eventually be Communist. Until that had been accomplished, the aim of Communist parties within virtually all the countries in the world was to undermine existing governments in preparation for Communist takeovers.

It would be a mistake, however, to focus attention exclusively on the totalitarian governments of the 20th century, whether Nazi, Fascist, or Communist. Indeed, dictatorship has been much more widespread than in the countries with ideologies of those distinct flavors. There have been many "right wing," dictatorships, as Communists and their camp followers tend to style anti-Communist dictatorships. Among the better known of these have been Franco in Spain, Juan Peron in Argentina, Salazar in Portugal, Fulgencio Batista in Cuba, and so on. These dictators frequently have one party rule, often persecute their political enemies, and develop surprisingly large Swiss bank accounts before they fall from power. They are in some measure the fall-out from the assault upon monarchy and hereditary aristocracies, particularly in Latin countries. Even so, they exemplify, often to a less frightening degree, the loss of legitimacy in governments, the concentration of power in them, and the lack of restraint (as well as corruption) in its exercise.

It would be a mistake, however, to suppose that countries that generally steered clear of outright dictatorship and one party rule have escaped the concentration of power in government and its increasingly unrestricted use to make over populations. No country in the world has been free of the movement or tendencies in this direction. The major impetus to this concentration, expansion, and exercise of government power has been one or another variety of socialism, though it has not necessarily been called by that name. Some sort of latent animus to the building of a perfect society has been the source of the effort. In practice, governments have used much of this energy in redistributing wealth and in restraining and regulating economic activity. Countries that have retained the outward form of popular rule—commonly referred to as "democracies"—have generally loosened the restraints on government and extended the use of their power. This has been the case in the United States, the United Kingdom, Canada, Australia, Sweden, Norway, France, Italy, and virtually every such country in the world since World War II, if not before.

Sweden took the lead in the 1930s in establishing what has since come to be called a "welfare state." Its main characteristics are government provision of all sorts of services and payments to people from funds acquired by virtually confiscatory taxation. Indeed, the government in Sweden early took on many, most, or, in some instances, virtually all, of the functions once provided by fathers; it is a paternal ("father-like") state. As soon as conception takes place, the state is ready to step in. Free maternity clinics were established for expectant mothers and their unborn children. The state even pays three-fourths of the cost of the mother's dental care. If the expectant mother should prefer a midwife to deliver the baby, the state will pay the fee. If she goes to a hospital, the state will pay the taxi-fare as well as the cost of the stay in the hospital. In addition, the state provides a substantial monetary award to the new mother after the birth of her child. There is then a supplement for cost of housing to mother and child and for the father as well, should he decide to live with them. Should the mother be a "single parent," the state has caused to be built and set aside for their special use apartments for unmarried mothers. Special support is provided for each child regardless of the status of his parents. If one or both parents dies, the children receive pensions from the government. Especially needy families can apply for and get additional supplements for each child. Of course, nurseries are provided for small children, and schools, books, dental and psychiatric as well as medical care, are provided for the children. In short, Sweden early established all sorts of aids and supplements to relieve parents of much of the cost and responsibility of childbearing, as well as for many other exigencies of living.

Of course, these amenities provided by government come at a high price indeed in individual taxes on working people. In times past, it has not been unusual for a workman to pay more than 50 percent of his income in taxes. Local and national income taxes have ordinarily taken away about a third of their pay. Those with higher incomes are taxed at much higher rates. A general sales tax is levied on the cost of most items bought. Unusually high taxes are levied on gasoline, liquor, beer, cigarettes, and chocolates. While businesses are usually privately owned, they are heavily taxed and closely controlled in Sweden. The people of Sweden have progressively lost control of their own affairs as the power of government has expanded.

Sweden was one of the earliest and most thorough examples of a "democratic" government focusing on redistributing wealth. Productive property remained in private hands generally, but great pressures were brought to bear for maximum productivity. Thus, the wealth to redistribute might be available in large quantity. By contrast, the United Kingdom of England, Scotland, and Wales may have been the best (or worst) example of a "democratic" government rushing headlong into socialism. In July, 1945, an election was held throughout the United Kingdom. The Labour Party won overwhelmingly, electing 393 members to the House of Commons to 189 for the Conservatives and 58 for all other parties. In its election manifesto for 1945, the Labour Party proclaimed that it was "a socialist party and proud of it."[1] And, the British Labourites went to work with a right good will to impose a system of socialism on the country.

In contrast to the Swedes, the British proceeded to take-over, i.e., "nationalize," major industries. The broad categories of industries nationalized were banking, power and light, transport, and iron and steel. The first nationalization was authorized by the Bank of England Act passed in 1946; the last major one was authorized by the Iron and Steel Act of 1949. A fairly typical nationalization measure was the Coal Industry Nationalization Act passed in 1946, to go into effect January 1, 1947. "The act provided for a National Coal Board appointed by the minister of fuel and power and consisting of nine representatives of various functions within the industry (such as finance, technology, labor, marketing) who were to operate all coal mines subject to the general supervision of the ministry. The public corporation replaced more than eight hundred private companies which surrendered their assets for a compensation. . . ."[2] However little the British Labourites might know about actually running an economy, they did know generally what industries comprise the main arteries of a modern economy, and they had nationalized them.

But the Labourites were hardly content with the nationalization of major industries. A vast network of controls, subsidies, priorities, prescriptions, proscriptions, and regulations were extended over the remainder of industry and agriculture. All that could be was done to give the government as complete control over the economy as possible without actually taking over every sort of business. The production that those in power judged desirable "was encouraged; luxury production was limited. Licenses were required to export raw materials and any manufactured articles needed at home. Domestic consumption was regulated by rationing subsidies and price controls. . . . New industrial enterprises seeking capital had to be approved by a government committee. . . . Treasury budgets were drafted with a view to controlling investment. . . ."[3] As for agriculture, it was decided not to nationalize the land but to regulate and control activity in this area. The Ministry of Food was authorized to buy agricultural produce and became, in effect, the sole market in which farmers were to sell. Agriculture was controlled "by a range of other measures, such as the giving of acreage grants for particular crops, financial aid for improvements, loans to agricultural workers. . . ." Power was authorized to "give directions to farmers to plough up land and grow particular crops."[4]

Of course, the Labourites set up their own particular variety of the welfare state in Britain. And to pay for all this, steeply graduated income taxes were imposed. How steep it was is made clear by the following: "[A] big American business which had decided to pay the head of its English subsidiary a salary of 20,000 dollars (£5,000) was informed that, owing to the Income

Tax, the recipient would in fact touch half only. Not to be put off, the American business asked how much it would need to pay its servant to ensure him £5,000 net. The answer came back—£50,000, the figure which will, after taxation, leave £5,093 10s. 0d.''[5]

Perhaps, the British Labour government in the years immediately after World War II was not completely out of control. After all, there were things it did not, perhaps could not, do. Freedom of speech and press still existed, and ancient rights to protect the individual from arbitrary imprisonment, and the like, were still in operation. But the government had ridden rough shod over long standing economic principles and the right of people to the product of their labor. The rights to own and operate productive property had been severely reduced, if not entirely abandoned. In short order, socialism in England came close to destroying the relics of a once great economy which had already been rigorously put to the test by two world wars and the government intervention of the 1930s.

That socialism in England was a failure, so far as nationalization of industry and government planning was concerned, was widely accepted by the 1950s. Until the British experiment with nationalization had failed so signally, socialists in the West had generally believed that was the way to go. Opinion now shifted more strongly toward government regulation and manipulation of an economy in which the forms of private property still existed. The Swedes had already shown the way toward the welfare state within a framework of private property. The United States moved that way before, during, and since World War II.

Blatant, aggressive socialism has been widely discredited over the past several decades. Over the past five years, Communism in the Soviet Union and Eastern Europe has disintegrated. Internationally, Communism is generally in retreat as well. The number of avowed socialists has rapidly declined, and may well be at an all time low for this century, or at least for the past 60 years. If the retreat from avowed socialism (including Communism) continues apace for the remainder of this decade, the ideology, as such, will have sunken from view.

Why, then, is there a political crisis in the world? Surely, the decline of socialism does not make a crisis, at least not one of government run amok. After all, by the preceding analysis, it would appear that socialism (in all its varieties) was a major source of out of control government. That is correct, so far as it goes. It does not follow, however, that the decline of avowed socialism will make any large inroads in the concentration and expansion of government power. After all, the United States has never had an avowed socialist government. Avowed socialist parties have never received more than a relatively small minority vote in the United States.

Even so, America has been gradually moving toward socialism for much of this century. Twenty-five years ago, Earl Browder, a former head of the

Communist Party of the United States, described how it came about this way:

> America is getting socialism on the installment plan through the programs of the welfare state. . . .
>
> Americans may not be willing to vote for a program under the name of "socialism," but put it under another party label—whether liberal Republican or Democrat—and they're by and large in favor of the idea. . . .
>
> We have no real socialist party, no socialist ideology, but we have a large—and growing—degree of what 50 years ago would have been recognized as socialism.[6]

And, accompanying what Browder referred to as "socialism on the installment plan," there has been a great concentration of power in the central government and expansion of the exercise of power upon the people. It is true that during the Presidency of Ronald Reagan there was some talk, but much less action, of reducing the role of government in American lives. But the welfare state is still very much in place, and the Federal government is extended far beyond constitutional bounds.

The political crisis arises because the decline of avowed socialism has not been accompanied by any committed effort to circumscribe and limit government. The disintegration of Communism in Eastern Europe and the Soviet Union provides an opening for establishing much needed restraints upon the exercise of government power. But in their undeserved pride (and clear ignorance of the extent of the problem) Western leaders are not prepared to offer even advice about how to contain and restrain the exercise of government power. (Most of them are too busy exercising to the fullest extent any power they can get their hands on to even think about limiting power.) The most they have done is to urge that former Communist lands become what they are pleased to call "democracies." If they do that and adopt what is being called "capitalism" for an economy, they will presumably have solved all political and economic problems and can live happily ever after. In the current state of our political language, these terms are little more than "buzz" words. As the British political philosopher, Michael Oakeshott admonished us, "we must stop hiding behind such irrelevant expressions as 'democracy' and 'capitalism'. . . ."[7]

"Irrelevant" is precisely the right term for the place of "democracy" and "capitalism" in the present situation. The critical problem facing us, as noted above, is one of government broken loose from its moorings and running amok. What is wanted are effective means of restraining governments, of holding them to their main, if not only proper, function of keeping the peace. Popularly elected officials and representatives, which is about all that can be precisely meant by the term "democracy," may well legitimize a government by providing authority for its actions, but it hardly restrains government in our day. Why this is so is explained, at least in part, by reference again to Oakeshott:

> To some people, "government" appears as a vast reservoir of power which inspires them to dream of what use might be made of it. They have favorite projects, of various dimensions, which they sincerely believe are for the benefit of mankind, and to capture this source of power, if necessary to increase it, and to use it for imposing their favorite projects upon their fellows is what they understand as the adventure of governing men. They are, thus, disposed to recognize government as an instrument of passion; the art of politics is to inflame and direct desire. . . .[8]

What a marvelous description—"to inflame and direct desire"—of what politics has largely become in modern "democracies." In such a setting, popular government does not restrain government but rather tends to expand government power to satisfy the desires the politicians have aroused. To put it somewhat more bluntly, politicians buy the votes of the electorate by promising them goodies to be provided by government. Rather than restraining government, this practice makes government into a ravenous scavenger preying on producers within its jurisdiction.

Nor is it readily apparent how or why "capitalism" would limit or restrain government. There are, of course, those who use the term to refer to an economic system in which there is private ownership of the means of production and freedom of enterprise within a free market. The late Ludwig von Mises used the term that way, or at least claimed that he did. There is a linguistic violation in using the term to signify such a system. "Capital" is a term with a fairly precise meaning in economics. It refers to one of the three basic elements of production. The other two are land and labor. "Capital" is most commonly defined as wealth used to produce commodities or goods. It can be most easily made concrete and visualized as tools used in the production of goods. When "ism" is added to "capital", the resulting term should refer to an ideology or system of some sort. Most plausibly, it should refer to an economic system or ideology in which capital is given a preferential or dominant role in the economy, dominant over the other two elements of production. Governments often intervene to give such a preference, and a system such as that would clearly be "capitalism." To make this term stand for private ownership and a free market, it is necessary to divest the term of its actual meaning and assign it a purely arbitrary one.

"Capitalism" is suspect on other grounds as well. If Karl Marx did not coin the term, which he is often credited with doing, he certainly gave currency to it. It cannot readily be separated from the usage he assigned to it, nor is it clear why anyone would want to borrow from his weighted and heated language base. Marx rarely, if ever, contributed to clarity, and he sowed confusion with "capitalism." In any case, "capitalism" hardly solves the problem of governments out of control.

The main point of the discussion of these terms and their centrality in contemporary political and economic discourse is to emphasize how much political philosophy and thought has declined in our time. Confronted, as we are, by governments bloated by accretions of political power and prone to abusive use of it, all we can propose as a remedy is more "democracy." To illustrate the point, the following example is submitted. A journalist proposed in a recent newspaper column that what the United States needs is an entirely new Constitution. He says, "Like a broken watch, we should return the government for repair. This time, though, no mere tinkering. The whole inside has to come out and be discarded, to be replaced by something that works." He explains at more length how this is to be accomplished:

> This means convening a constitutional convention to scrap the present Constitution, or most of it, and substitute a new document for today and tomorrow. The old Constitution worked remarkably well for two centuries but it no longer applies to the way the United States lives or to the people Americans have become. It can't be held together by glue and baling wire much longer. It's past time for a new model.[9]

The writer went on to outline some of what he considers failures of the various branches of government, but he does not link these to the Constitution in such a way as to show that they arise from that document. Instead, he makes his one concrete proposal to correct matters by way of a constitutional convention. His concern is with the racial, ethnic, and sexual composition of delegates to the convention. In his own words, "All delegates to the 1787 convention were white males. This time, the delegates must include females, African-Americans, Hispanic-Americans, Asian Americans and the usually forgotten Native Americans. And every other kind of American, hyphenated or not."[10] He does not tell us by what electoral scheme such a diverse and presumably balanced group might be chosen for his convention, nor why, if it were, it would be likely to produce a constitution that would deal effectively with the ills which beset us. Obviously, however, the writer has absolute faith in "democracy," and is certain that if only a convention could be assembled that would be sufficiently representative, i. e., democratic, enough, it would be sure to produce a masterpiece. In sum, to him, and many others, "democracy" is the sufficient cure for all our political ills.

Here is some further evidence that this fixation on "democracy" indicates a decline in political philosophy. Some years back, a British political philosopher made the point that political philosophy had so far declined that such political ideas as were alluded to generally were grotesque simplifications. He said, by way of example, ''The dominant political idea in the modern world is democracy. . . . And where are the political theorists of democracy today? Instead of a rational theory it has become a sort of incantation. It is the open sesame of political treasure hunters everywhere." He explains his thought further, ''Liberal democratic principles, evolved in the seventeenth and eighteenth centuries, dominated the nineteenth century, which however failed to refashion and think out anew, for the benefit of its successors, the ideas that it was living on. . . . Meanwhile democracy, for lack of thought, ceased to be a living political idea. It became a shibboleth, and is now not even serviceable as such. . . . Politicians, like the princess in the fairy-tale condemned to the oracular utterances of frogs, seem scarcely able to open their mouths without some platitude about democracy flopping out. . . .''[11]

The book in which these words appeared was published in 1960. At about the same time, the present writer published an article in which he concluded that ''twentieth-century America is a wasteland so far as political thought is concerned. In part, at least, this absence of thought can be laid to the fact that thinkers have been mesmerized by the pleasing sound of the word democracy.''[12] The article was mainly concerned with exploring how the educational philosopher, John Dewey, had used the word with so many connotations and meanings, trying to make it evoke a whole philosophical outlook. In consequence, the word ''has lost most if not all of its descriptive value. Contrariwise, it has picked up meanings in some kind of inverse proportion to its loss of descriptive accuracy. . . . It is so full of meanings that it has the long distance accuracy of a shotgun, as it were, in precise expression. It has become a loaded word.''[13] The current bemusement with ''democracy'' owes much to Dewey's obfuscations.

The present low state of political thought and ignorance of our political heritage and terminology is currently being illustrated by the professed amazement of Senators and journalists over the candidacy of Judge Clarence Thomas to become a justice on the Supreme Court. Thomas has made known his attachment to the natural law philosophy. That should augment his qualifications for the post to which the President would appoint him, for the Founders of the United States were generally devotees of the natural law. Jefferson had written of the ''laws of nature and of nature's God.'' The great documents of our founding years, including the Constitution, can hardly be understood or correctly interpreted without a considerable grasp of natural law doctrine. That is not to say that natural laws themselves are directly written into the Constitution. So far as there are natural laws, they operate without our acknowledgement, and it would be ludicrous to set them forth in a document prescribing the form, powers, and limits upon a government. But they nonetheless undergird and make the Constitution as written workable.

There is potential guidance in the United States Constitution both for those who may be looking for ways to limit and restrain government in lands where Communism has lately been repudiated. Even more important, there is guidance in our Constitution for Americans to bring their government under control once again, as well as for those in similar condition elsewhere. But to get that guidance, it is necessary to understand the political system that we inherited in its full richness and complexity. To do that, our understanding of politics and government has to go much beyond some vague and largely incorrect notion that the United States is, or was, a democracy. To do that, it is necessary first to study the Constitution and get clearly in mind the government authorized by that document. That will be done in the chapter that follows this one.

The book is written in this fashion because there may be those concerned in getting this summary knowledge only, or focusing on it. Then, the remainder of the book will fill in the background to the Constitution, its development, the departures from it, and how we have reached our current pass of bloated and ineffective government. Students may read chapter 2 first to get the Constitutional form and content of American government clearly in mind before studying its background and development. Or, they may read it last as a summary and review. Or, they may read it both first and last.

At any rate, the placement of chapter 2 should make clear the present writer's view, i. e., that the Constitution is the centerpiece of American government. More precisely, it became the basis and foundation of the general government of the United States—the government of the Union, so to speak. It is the foundation, the starting point, the guide to development, due north on our national compass, so to speak, the point of departure, and the place of return. That is its rightful place in American history, and this book will give it that central role.

That is not to say that the United States government is the only government in the country. Each of the states has its own constitution and its own government. These state governments are not constitutionally inferior to the United States government, though acts of the United States in accord with the Constitution do occupy a superior position at law. Even so, state governments have an origin and existence distinct from that of the United States. Some states preceded the Constitution, and all of them were brought into being by their citizenry before being admitted to the Union. All this, of course, will be taken up in its place. It needed to be stated generally here, however, to make clear the centrality of the Constitution to American government.

Chapter 2
American Government: Sum and Substance

The United States is not a democracy. It is a Constitutional Federated Republic. These three terms constitute the most summary manner in which it can begin to be comprehended. Indeed, the government of the United States is much more complex and broad than this phrase can fully cover. The United States government is a part of a federal system of government which includes the states as well, though with our contemporary bent for reductionism, it has become customary now to refer only to the general government as being "federal." It is a limited government. It is in form a mixed government, though few people are any longer aware of that. But to call it a "constitutional federated republic" can be made to suggest much of this.

The important thing, however, is not to have some word or phrase which captures the essence of the American form of government. Such things are apt to be most useful in making bumper sticker slogans or battle cries at pep rallies than they are in advancing our understanding and giving a fuller grasp of subjects. Our stock of words is not so short nor time for the matter so brief that we are restricted to one word or a brief phrase in discussing our government. What *is* important from the outset is to understand that there are many facets to our government, that its nature cannot be comprehended in a word or phrase, that as a form it is the result of the long heritage of political thought developed during the emergence of Western Civilization, and though the popular base from which the government of the United States operates is highly important the populace as such has only an indirect impact on the government as constituted.

a. A Constitutional Government

There is a sense in which it would be true to say that any government that holds sway for more than the briefest of spans will have a constitution of sorts. That is, they will have some regular ways of conducting the business of government. Laws will be promulgated in one way or another by those who rule a country. Certain people have it as one or more of their duties to enforce the laws. If a country is very large it will almost certainly have some sort of armed force, either in reserve or in the field. The force will have commanders, and these may be arranged in some sort of hierarchy from top to bottom. It is generally more convenient that a government be organized according to some regular pattern, and that the various regularities in government be observed as a rule. Tyrants may act arbitrarily, of course, and despots may not observe many of the rules. Even so, to the extent that there are regularities usually observed, a country could be said to have a constitution.

Sometimes a constitution may assume a firmer shape than what we conceive of as generally recognized ways of doing things. That was the case with the British Constitution. It comprises customary ways of carrying on the business of government, hereditary, appointive, and elective means of choosing those who are to govern, documents in which the monarch has recognized certain rights belonging to the citizenry, such as Magna Carta, the Petition of Rights, and the Bill of Rights, as well as some acts of Parliament. Still, it is not quite a written constitution, not in the American sense, anyhow, nor does it have quite the fixity of the United States Constitution.

Americans may not have invented the written constitution, but they certainly made important innovations in the form, strengthened its image, and broadened its coverage. The fact that it is written gives a fixity to it that it would not otherwise have. Moreover, the United States has the oldest written constitution still in operation in the world. It became the model for written constitutions after its success, as republics emerged in other countries. Perhaps its most important feature is that it not only prescribes the form and operation of the government, but it places substantive restrictions and limitations on the exercise of government power both by the United States and the states. It has been a bulwark both of stability and of individual liberty.

(1) Significance of Written Constitution

In 1803, Thomas Jefferson wrote the following to a friend, "I had rather ask an enlargement of power from the nation, where it is found necessary, than to assume it by a construction which would make our powers boundless. Our peculiar security is in the possession of a written Constitution. Let us not make it a blank paper by construction."[14] George Washington spoke to much the same point when he wrote in his "Farewell Address," "If in the opinion of the people . . . the constitutional powers be in any particular wrong, let it be corrected by an amendment in the way which the Constitution designates. But let there be no change by usurpation; for though this in one instance may be the instrument of good, it is the customary weapon by which free governments are destroyed." Washington was saying that those in authority should abide by the Constitution as written and seek to change it only by amendment. Jefferson even more explicitly claimed that having a written Constitution should provide some security against its being changed by interpretation.

It is obvious that the written word is superior in important ways to the spoken word. The written word can become a fixed text, which can be re-examined from time to time and referred to again and again over the years. So long as the original text is preserved, what was said is not simply a matter of opinion; anyone may satisfy himself as to what was said by referring to it. The written word has occupied an especially lofty place in the minds and affections of Americans. We have been by and large a people of "the book," the Holy Bible. This has been especially so for the predominant Protestant portion of the population, who may well accord the greatest authority to the original Scriptures, but it is only to a lesser degree, if any, true of Catholics and Jews as well. In time, Americans found it easy to especially revere the original Constitution (plus the first ten Amendments) and to strongly favor a strict adherence to it.

"Law" also occupied an important role in the thought of those who drew up, adopted, and supported the Constitution as well. They especially favored having a "government of laws and not of men." They feared the rule of men unrestrained by law because it would be an arbitrary rule. Laws written down and codified were very important for a government of laws, for it provided much greater certainty as to what was the law in any particular case. There were two kinds of ordinary law known to the Founders of the United States. They were *statutory* law and *common* law. Statutory law is that law resulting from *statutes* passed by legislatures. It exists in a formal document, and is thus referred to as *written* law. Common law, on the other hand—the law recognized by Americans in the Constitution as well as in courts—is law built on custom and court decision. It is also referred to as *unwritten* law. Statutory law prevails over common law when the two deal with the same subject.

It was within this frame that Jefferson's observation about "Our peculiar security is in the possession of a written Constitution" is to be understood. What he was saying was that the United States Constitution did not arise out of age old custom and legal usage or court decisions. It was not a common law instrument. Hence, it was not legally subject to change by construction or changes in custom. It could be changed only by formal amendment. The Constitution bears this out. Article V specifies the ways in which the Constitution may be amended. One way is for two-thirds of the members of both Houses (the House of Representatives and the Senate) to propose amendments which are then submitted to the states, and when three-fourths of the states approve such amendments they become a part of the Constitution. The other way to start an amendment would be for two-thirds of the states to call a constitutional convention. Any changes the convention might propose would require approval of three-fourths of the states to go into effect. Congress has the option to prescribe whether the approval of the states shall be determined by the legislatures of the states or by conventions held in the respective states. In two matters, the Constitution was placed beyond the amending process. One of these restrictions has long since expired, since it was in effect only until 1808, but the other—that no state shall be denied its equal suffrage (having the votes of two Senators) without its consent—is still in effect.

In certain respects, the provisions of the Constitution have the standing of statutory law, as noted above, but as the above paragraph implies, if it does not make it entirely clear, the Constitution is not on the level of *ordinary* law. Statutory law can be changed by the legislature competent to pass it in the first place. Thus, for example, Congress may pass laws with the standing of statutes (with the approval of the President, or over his veto with extraordinary majorities). But Congress cannot by itself amend or change the provisions of the Constitution. The Constitution was brought into being initially by extraordinary proceedings—by the calling and assembling of a Convention made up of delegates from all participating states—and went into operation by the concurrence of three-fourths of the participating states. As already noted, it can only be amended by analogous extraordinary measures.

In a word, the Constitution is a kind of *higher* law. Although the provisions of the Constitution are like statutes in that they are written, contained in a document and do not come into being by way of custom or court decisions, they are not statutes in being enacted or subject to nullification by legislatures alone. Nor do they apply directly to the generality of the inhabitants or citizenry in the ordinary course of going about their private business. The provisions of the Constitution are a law for the lawmakers, so to speak, or, more broadly, a law for those who govern. The Constitution prescribes the branches and major offices of government, how the officers are to be chosen, what qualifications may properly apply, how long their tenure in office may be, and what the powers, duties, and jurisdiction of these offices may be. It also lays restrictions on the power to be exercised by both state governments and the United States government. The Constitution is, then, so far as it is a law, a law for government.

It is higher than statutory law within its jurisdiction, either the statutes of state governments or those of Congress. That it is higher than state laws and constitutions in matters to which its authority reaches is stated explicitly in Article VI of the Constitution. Specifically:

> This Constitution, and the Laws of the United States which shall be made in pursuance thereof; and all Treaties made, or which shall be made under the Authority of the United States, shall be the supreme Law of the Land; and the Judges in every State shall be bound thereby, any Thing in the Constitution or Laws of any State to the Contrary notwithstanding.

In sum, laws enacted by Congress and treaties made by lawful authority, that is, in both cases, in accord with the Constitution, are supreme over anything in state laws or constitutions.

The Constitution does not explicitly state that statutes or other acts of those within any branch of the United States that are contrary to Constitution are null and void and of no effect. Nor does it designate a branch or body of the government which would make such decisions and give them force. Yet it is the logic of the situation that acts of anyone or body of the United States government contrary to the provisions of the Constitution should have no effect. The most direct evidence of this may be the oath prescribed for the President as he takes office. It reads, ''I do solemnly swear (or affirm) that I will faithfully execute the Office of President of the United States, and will, to the best of my Ability, preserve, protect, and defend the Constitution of the United States.'' Other major officers of the United States, whether elected or appointed, take similar oaths, though the terminology is not specifically prescribed by the Constitution.

Beyond that, though, the logic of the situation is that since the Constitution prescribes the powers of those who govern, if they exceed those prescribed they are acting without warrant and their acts are of no effect. Alexander Hamilton explained the case this way:

> There is no position which depends on clearer principles than that every act of a delegated authority, contrary to the tenor of the commission under which it is exercised is void. No legislative act, therefore, contrary to the Constitution, can be valid. To deny this would be to affirm that the deputy is greater than his principal; that the servant is above his master, the representatives of the people are superior to the people themselves, that men acting by virtue of powers may do not only what their powers do not authorize, but what they forbid.[15]

Hamilton was not suggesting, of course, that each man may decide for himself whether a statute passed by Congress, for example, is authorized by the Constitution or not, and whether he will obey it or not. That would be anarchy. What Hamilton argued was that the courts must resolve this question, though they are not specifically so empowered by the Constitution. He noted that judges in the ordinary course of carrying on their jobs decide what laws to apply and how to construe them. It will fall to them in the course of their work, then, to discover whether a statute is in conflict with the Constitution. ''The interpretation of the laws is the Proper and peculiar province of the courts,'' Hamilton said. More, ''A constitution is, in fact, and must be regarded by the judges as, a fundamental law. It therefore belongs to them to ascertain its meaning as well as the meaning of any particular act proceeding from the legislative body. If there should happen to be an irreconcilable variance between the two, that which has superior obligation and validity ought, of course to be preferred; or, in other words, the Constitution ought, of course, to be preferred to the statute, the intention of the people to the intention of their agents.''[16] Again, Hamilton was saying that the Constitution is superior to ordinary law, and that courts are duty bound to make the superior prevail over the inferior by their rulings.

John Marshall had not served for long as Chief Justice of the Supreme Court before a case came before him involving a statute, one of whose provisions appeared to be contrary to a provision of the Constitution. The case was *Marbury vs. Madison,* and Marshall composed the decision in 1803. William Marbury had been appointed justice of the peace in the District of Columbia in 1801 by President John Adams. Marshall, who was then Secretary of State, neglected to deliver the commission to Marbury. When he became President, Thomas Jefferson ordered his Secretary of State, James Madison, not to deliver the commission to Marbury. Marbury went directly to the Supreme Court, as was provided by the statutory Judiciary Act of 1789, suing for a writ of mandamus compelling Madison to deliver the commission. A problem arose because the Constitution lists kinds of cases over which the Supreme Court has original jurisdiction and says that ''In all other cases, the supreme court shall have appellate jurisdiction.'' Justices of the peace and the like did not come under any of the cases listed for original jurisdiction for the court. There was, then, Marshall said, a conflict between the relevant portion of the Constitution and the applicable portion of an act of Congress.

As Marshall laid matters out in his decision, there was no doubt that Marbury was entitled to his commission and that some court should afford him relief. But had he come to the right place to get it? Marshall said no. When a statute conflicts with the Constitution, he maintained that the Supreme Court was bound by the Constitution. He put it this way:

> Certainly all those who have framed written constitutions contemplate them as forming the fundamental and paramount law of the nation, and consequently the theory of every such government must be that an act of the legislature contrary to the Constitution is void. . . .
> If, then, the courts are to regard the constitution, and the constitution is superior to any ordinary act of the legislature, the constitution, and not such ordinary act, must govern the case to which they both apply.[17]

Thus, he held the Supreme Court lacked jurisdiction and denied the mandamus to William Marbury.

The main point, however, is that Marshall, speaking for the court, had affirmed the superiority of the written Constitution to ordinary statutes. In effect, he had held that the Constitution was a kind of higher law. Hamilton, as quoted earlier, suggested that constitutional law was superior to statute because it stems from the people, whereas statutes proceeds from their agents. A better statement of the case might be that the United States Constitution and amendments to it require broader support and more extensive approval than legislative acts. We can also concur with the idea that a written constitution, as Marshall said, is intended to be and is adopted under the claim that it is superior to ordinary law. That might be enough to give it a special place of respect and veneration for people generally, which has certainly been the case for the United States Constitution during much of its history. It might have been enough, but there was more undergirding the veneration of the United States Constitution than that.

American belief in the superiority of constitutional law nestled in and was supported by a broader and deeper belief in higher law. At the mundane level, they had been subjected to British law, which was superior to the laws of their legislatures when the two were in conflict. For example, the charter which authorized the settlement and government in Maryland specified that "laws be made with the consent of the freemen and agreeable to the laws of England." Most colonies had charters or grants with similar provisions. Moreover, laws passed in the colonies were reviewed from time to time in England, and some of them were nullified as being in conflict with British law.

But the Founders also believed that there were laws higher than those of nations, that transcended the will of men and people, and with which human law must accord to be effective. William Blackstone, the British legal authority much admired by Americans, stated this view of higher law in 1765: "Upon these two foundations, the law of nature and the law of revelation, depend all human laws. . . . And herein it is that human laws have their greatest force and efficacy: for, with regard to such points as are not indifferent, human laws are only declaratory of, and act in subordination to the former."[18] Blackstone was referring to natural law and that which comes to us more directly from God by way of revelation. An American, Nathaniel Ward, writing in the early 17th century, declared: "Moral laws, royal prerogatives, popular liberties are not of man's making or giving, but God's. Man is but to measure them out by God's rule: which if man's wisdom cannot reach, man's experience must mend."[19] Elsewhere he says, "The truths of God are the pillars of the world whereon states and churches may stand. . . ."[20] In the middle of the 18th century, Jonathan Mayhew said: "We may safely assert . . . that no civil rulers are to be obeyed when they enjoin things that are inconsistent with the commands of God. . . . All commands running counter to the declared will of the supreme legislator of heaven and earth are null and void. . . ."[21]

The belief in a higher law was affirmed and alluded to by many Americans contemporary with the making of the Constitution. On the matter of the right of expatriation (to leave one's native country and take up residence elsewhere), Jefferson exclaimed: "We do not claim these under the charters of kings or legislators, but under the King of kings."[22] Alexander Hamilton, writing in 1775, said: "Good and wise men, in all ages, have embraced . . . [this] theory. They have supposed that the Deity . . . has constituted an eternal and immutable law, which is indispensably obligatory upon all mankind, prior to any institution whatever."[23]

None of this is meant to suggest that the Constitution is a compilation of either natural laws or the laws of God. It is rather to say that it was drawn within a framework in which men believed generally in these higher laws, that it derived from and in ways reflected what these laws would hold is appropriate to government. This gave the Constitution some claim to be treated as a special document and a kind of higher law. Many Americans have shared that view of it and might well agree with James Madison's observation after remarking upon the fact that so many difficulties had been surmounted in the Constitutional Convention with such unanimity: "It is impossible for a man of pious reflection not to perceive in it a finger of that Almighty hand which has been so frequently and signally extended to our relief in the critical stages of the revolution."[24]

Having discussed Hamilton's views on the interpretation of the Constitution by the courts, some qualifications about this need to be noted. While Hamilton did not argue for an exclusive role for the courts in interpretation, those familiar with present day notions about the monopoly of the courts in the matter may suppose that he was pointing in that direction. Whatever Hamilton's unexpressed views on the extent of the court's role, most of his contemporaries did not hold anything like the present day popularized idea on the subject. The Jeffersonians believed very strongly that those in all three branches were bound both to interpret the Constitution and observe its limits. Before passing laws the members of Congress should satisfy themselves as to their constitutionality. Before approving measures passed by Congress, the President should decide for himself about the constitutionality of them, and if they were not, he should veto them on the grounds of their unconstitutionality. It was agreed, of course, that measures understood to be unconstitutional by the courts should not be applied or enforced. This is a far cry, of course, from the present day attitude of many Congressmen which is the highly irresponsible view that they will go ahead and approve the bill before them and leave to the courts the question of constitutionality.

(2) The Powers of Congress

The powers granted to Congress in the Constitution may be considered the innovative powers of the government of the United States.* The Constitu-

*The United States government has been described by a variety of phrases throughout its history. In addition to the phrase just used, it has been described as the government of the Union, the general government, the central government, and the federal government. Since both the state governments and the general government comprise our federal system of government, the phrase is inaccurate. When it

tion itself says that all legislative powers are "vested" in Congress. Since "to legislate" means to "make laws," the technical meaning is that all law-making power is conferred on Congress. The Constitution authorizes three branches of government—the legislative, executive, and judicial. This was in accord with the view that the powers of government should be separate, so as to guard against the abuse of powers that would likely occur if they were concentrated in any one branch. The Congress, then, was to make the laws, the executive to put them into operation, and the judiciary to enforce them with punishments and decrees.

It should be noticed as the account proceeds that the powers granted are not entirely separate. In fact, they are frequently intertwined so to require the joint efforts of two or more of the branches to carry out or place in operation some action. For example, the President must approve an act of Congress before it can become a law. Otherwise, extraordinary majorities must be obtained in both houses. The effect of requiring the participation of two or more branches is an added guarantee against tyrannical action, because it is supposed to make it that much more difficult for government to act arbitrarily.

The major inner check in the Congress is that it is divided into two houses: the House of Representatives and the Senate. Each house must concur by at least a majority of those present for a bill to be passed. Moreover, the two houses are differently constituted. Representatives are elected for a term of only two years. From the beginning, they were popularly elected. By contrast, the Senators serve six year terms (except for the first ones elected after the ratification of the Constitution: one-third of these were elected for two years, one-third for four years, and the other third for six years). Madison noted that the longer terms for Senators gave greater stability and provided much greater experience to the national legislature. He said, "A good government implies two things: first, fidelity to the object of government, which is the happiness of the people; secondly, a knowledge of the means by which that object can be best attained. Some governments are deficient in both these qualities. . . . The federal Constitution avoids this error. . . ."[25] That is, it provides for both stability and experience in the longer terms of its members. Another provision which has much the same effect is that Senators must be at least thirty years old, while Representatives have to be only twenty-five.

Another difference between the two bodies was that while the House of Representatives was elected by popular vote and the number apportioned to each state was to be based on population, Senators were elected by their state legislatures, and each state was allotted two Senators. Thus, the states had equality of representation in the Senate. Madison argued for that provision this way:

is used to describe the general government in this work, the first letter will be capitalized, i. e., Federal government.

> In this spirit it may be remarked that the equal vote allowed to each
> state is at once a constitutional recognition of the portion of sover-
> eignty remaining in the individual States and an instrument for pre-
> serving that residuary sovereignty. . . .
>
> Another advantage accruing from this ingredient in the constitution
> of the Senate is the additional impediment it must prove against im-
> proper acts of legislation. No law or resolution can now be passed
> without the concurrence, first, of a majority of the people, and then of
> a majority of the States. . . .[26]

With somewhat more precision, it could be said that the state governments
had their representation in the Senate.

There are some differences between the two bodies of Congress in regard
to the powers to be exercised also. All revenue measures have to originate
in the House of Representatives. This was an attempt to give additional
power to the popularly elected body over taxing and spending. The power
of impeachment of officers of the United States, including the President,
belongs to the House.** The Senate tries all cases of impeachment, and
upon conviction by two-thirds of the Senators present, may remove the
convicted person from office and deny him any future office of trust within
the United States government. When the President is tried by the Senate, the
Chief Justice of the Supreme Court presides. The Senate is empowered to
give its consent to treaties and presidential appointments such as of ambassadors, justices of the Supreme Court, and other major officers as determined by law. In the case of treaties, Senate concurrence must be by at least
two-thirds of those Senators voting.

The independence of the houses of Congress is safeguarded in several
ways. Both may chose their own officers, such as majority leaders, speaker
of the House, and the like, except that the Vice President of the United
States is constitutionally charged with being President of the Senate. "Each
House shall be the Judge of the Elections, Returns and qualifications of its
own Members. . . ." Each house is permitted to set its own rules for
proceeding, punish members for disorderly conduct, and the like. They can
determine the amount they are to be paid, but this must be ascertained by
law, that is, by a bill which passes each of the houses by a majority and is
either approved by the President or passed over his veto. They are free from
arrest while attending a session of Congress, or going to and from one,
except for "Treason, Felony and Breach of the Peace." And, they are not
subject to investigation by any body for any vote or participation in debate
in their respective bodies.

The general powers of Congress are listed in Article I, Section 8. These
are, in effect, the general legislative powers of Congress, that is, as noted

---

**"Impeachment," as used in the Constitution, is the equivalent of a grand jury indictment in ordinary
trials, for what the House does is to bring charges of wrongdoing against an officer of the government.

earlier, the innovative powers of the government. Although the point will be made in more detail later, it needs to be emphasized from the beginning. The United States is a limited government. It shares the powers of government over the people within its bounds with the state governments. More, it is limited to the exercise of its enumerated powers. And most of those powers are enumerated in Article I, Section 8 of the Constitution. This section, along with the following Section 9, and the first ten amendments surely constitute the most important parts of the Constitution, for it is in the innovative powers of the government and the limits and restraints upon them that the major protections of the liberty of the people are to be found.

Section 8 is the main enumeration of powers in the Constitution. Congress is authorized to levy a variety of taxes, including excises and duties on imports; to borrow money; to regulate commerce with foreign countries, among the states, and with Indian tribes; to establish rules of naturalization for foreigners and for bankruptcies within the United States; to coin money and fix standards of weights and measures; to make laws prohibiting and punishing the counterfeiting of the coin and securities of the United States; to establish post offices and post roads; to pass patent and copyright laws; to set up a system of courts below the Supreme Court; to deal with piracy and other crimes on the high seas; to declare war and rules for conducting war at sea; to raise and support armies; to establish a navy; to regulate land and naval forces; to organize, arm, and establish discipline for a militia which may ordinarily be under the control of the states; to exercise exclusive legislation over a district which will be the seat of the United States government and all lands and buildings acquired elsewhere by the United States government, such as for forts, arsenals, dockyards, and the like; for calling out the militia to execute the laws of the union, suppress insurrections and repel invasions. Then, lest there be any doubt, Congress is authorized ''To make all Laws which shall be necessary and proper for carrying into Execution the foregoing Powers, and all other Powers vested by the Constitution in the Government of the United States, or in any Department or Officer thereof.''

Some of these powers as listed are circumscribed and limited by further particulars. This is especially so for the taxing powers. In addition, Section 9 carries a number of specific restrictions and limitations on the powers of Congress. However, all these restrictions will be discussed in connection with limitations on government discussed below.

(3) The Powers of the President

Just as the legislative power was vested in Congress the executive power was vested in the President of the United States. But whereas the legislative power was distributed among more than ninety legislators, comprising two distinct houses, with a number of built-in safeguards against the abuse of power, the executive power was concentrated in the hands of a single person. That is not to say that one man would actually put into effect and operate the whole government structure—i. e., execute the laws. That would be done by several departments, each with its own head and personnel. Still, the responsibility for execution would lie with the President, and he was vested with the authority to move the machinery of government, or much of it, by his own commands.

Even so, the Founders tried to make the President independent of the other branches, both in his selection and in his actions. At the Constitutional Convention, much consideration was given to having the President elected by the Congress or one or the other of the houses. After much consideration, however, this notion was shifted to a backup role for dealing with ties should they occur. To have elected the President by vote of the Congress or one of the Houses would have made him too dependent on that body. Instead, the Convention decided to have the President and Vice President elected by an electoral college. This was purely an expedient so as to make the President independent of any continuing body and to give him a source of selection distinct from either of the other two branches.

The electoral college was to be made up in this fashion. Each state has as many electors as it has Senators and Representatives combined. The electors of each state can be appointed in whatever manner the state legislature directs. In the several elections of the late 18th and early 19th century they were appointed by the state legislatures. By the time of the Civil War most states had shifted to direct election of the electors. Probably, the Founders expected that electors would make their votes for President and Vice President according to their own wishes or determinations, without regard to any outside influences. That was not how it happened, not beyond the first election, anyway. Political parties arose early, and before long electors were voting by party for candidates.

That bid fair to play havoc with one provision of the Constitution. It instructed electors each to vote for two persons, one of whom, at least, was not to be from the same state as the elector. The vote would not distinguish between which vote might have been cast for President and which for Vice President. Then, the person who received the most votes would be President, and the one receiving the next highest number would be Vice President. That might have worked well enough if votes were not cast along party lines, but once that happened, as it had by 1800, there were likely to be frequent ties between the candidates for the two offices. The Constitution prescribed that in the case of ties the decision would go to the House of Representatives. If two persons had a majority of the vote, the House should choose one of them for President, the vote being by states rather than as individual members. If no person had a majority, the House would choose one from among the five highest on the list, and so on. However, this provision was altered by the 12th Amendment which was ratified in 1804, which required that electors designate one of their votes for President and one for Vice President, among other minor changes.

As for qualifications for office, the President must be at least thirty-five years old, a natural born citizen of the United States, and have been a resident within the United States for fourteen years. To secure him further from the influence of Congress or of any states, he is to be compensated for his services by the United States government at a rate of pay that is not to be increased or diminished during the period for which he was elected. Beyond that, he is to accept no compensation from the United States or any state.

Most of his powers are over the military, over the conduct of foreign affairs, or stem from his appointments. He is commander-in-chief of the armed forces of the United States, including the militia (now national guard) when it is called into the service of the United States. He is empowered on his own motion to grant pardons and reprieves for offenses against the United States except in cases of impeachment. His control over the departments of government is secured by his appointive power, by the fact that he can require the opinion in writing of department heads on their conduct of their offices, and that he can, in effect, remove disobedient officers from their positions. (The last power has sometimes been questioned, but ordinarily and by custom Presidents may require resignations from officers under them. In fact, the Constitution only specifically provides for the removal of officers by the route of impeachment.)

The President can influence legislation by his constitutional powers, but he has no powers of compulsion regarding it. He is granted authority to and the responsibility is placed upon him to inform the Congress from time to time about the state of the Union. By custom, he makes a "State of the Union Address" at the beginning of each session of Congress. He is authorized to recommend measures to Congress, and he can call Congress into special session if he sees fit, and if there is disagreement between Congress and the President as to when they should adjourn, the President may adjourn the Congress for a specified time. He is, of course, charged with faithfully executing the laws and is authorized to commission all military officers. This last consolidates his power as commander-in-chief of the armed forces.

(4) The Authority of the Courts

The judicial power of the United States is vested in the Supreme Court and whatever inferior courts the Congress may establish. As noted earlier, the power of appointment of judges is given to the President acting with the advice and consent of the Senate. Once appointed, the judges are supposed to be free of political influence and control. The appointments are indefinite, dependent only upon their continued "good Behavior." They can be removed from office during their lifetime only by the process of impeachment.

Their compensation is not to be diminished during their continuance in office. Thus, there is no handle with which to punish justices for the conduct of their offices except by impeachment.

The jurisdiction of the courts of the United States is an extensive one. The opening clause describing it reads: "The judicial Power shall extend to all Cases, in Law and Equity, arising under this Constitution, the Laws of the United States, and treaties made, or which shall be made under their Authority. . . ." Particular kinds of cases over which the courts have jurisdiction are then elaborated. They include the following: Ambassadors, consuls, and other officers in what are now called the Foreign Service; maritime cases; cases in which the United States is a party; controversies between two or more states; and so on. The general rule is that the jurisdiction extends to all cases involving the Constitution and laws or treaties made in pursuance of its provisions, to all cases involving officers of the United States in pursuance of their duties, and all matters involving the United States beyond the jurisdiction of the states.

As noted earlier, the instances in which the Supreme Court has original jurisdiction are enumerated. They are: "all cases affecting Ambassadors, other public Ministers and Consuls, and those in which a State shall be a Party. . . ." Any other cases which come before the Supreme Court must come by way of appeal. The court, is not necessarily the sole judge of what types of cases can be appealed to it, however, for Congress can direct much of this by making exceptions or otherwise regulating the appeal process. The other main restraint on the power of the judges is that jury trials are required in the courts of the United States for all cases involving crimes.

(5) A Mixed Government

Perhaps the least understood aspect of the United States government is that it is a mixed government. This may have been generally understood at the time of the founding of the country, but it has since disappeared from view. The main reason over the past century has been the heady emphasis upon our government's either being or supposed to be a democracy. At any rate, it is a mixed government in form. There are three basic forms of government. They are government by one; government by a few; or government by many. Government by one is most often described as a *monarchy*, though any sort of dictatorship will also qualify. Government by a few is often described as an *aristocracy*. In both monarchy and aristocracy the rulers may have inherited their positions, but that is not necessary to the classification. Government, or rule, by many, or the people, is sometimes described as democracy. At the time of the founding of the United States, a democracy was understood as a system in which the people ruled by assembling and acting as legislature or even a court, as the situation might require.

The United States was not founded as a monarchy, an aristocracy, or a democracy. Instead it combined, as it still combines, elements from each of these. It was monarchical, aristocratical, and democratical without being purely any one of these.

(a) The Monarchical Principle

The monarchical principle in the American government is embodied in the office of the President. That is, the presidency entails rule by one person. There was much concern about this fact during the Constitutional Convention. Most Americans did not like monarchy at that time; they associated it with the rule of such hereditary rulers as King George III. The delegates at the Convention discussed the possibility of placing the executive powers in the hands of two or more persons to guard against creating a tyrant by placing the power in the hands of a single person. They could set up a dyarchy, rule by two, or a triarchy, rule by three, and so on. Such experiments had been tried or practices had been followed in the past. But there was no great enthusiasm for having the executive powers shared in this fashion.

In *The Federalist Papers,* no. 70, Alexander Hamilton explained that unity was virtually essential to the effective exercise of executive power, and that the way to achieve unity was to have a single person as executive. Hamilton wrote:

> That unity is conducive to energy will not be disputed. Decision, activity, secrecy, and dispatch will generally characterize the proceedings of one man in a much more eminent degree than the proceedings of any greater number; and in proportion as the number is increased, these qualities will be diminished.[27]

Hamilton went on to point out that there were two ways to destroy unity in the executive: one was to have plural executives; the other was to make a single executive dependent upon the concurrence of a council. He gives examples of such practices from ancient and modern history. And he goes on to say that common sense and reason should make it clear that a plurality of people are not likely to rule well. Men often disagree over what is best to be done. They may become so divided as to make concerted action difficult, if not impossible. If that should happen, he wrote, it "might impede or frustrate the most important measures of the government in the most critical emergencies of the state. And what is still worse, they might split the community into the most violent factions, adhering differently to the different individuals who composed the magistracy."[28]

Such arguments induced many Americans to overcome their fears of monarchy to the extent of accepting the monarchical principle in the presidency. That is not at all to say that the President is a monarch in the usual acceptance of the term. Hamilton went to some trouble in *The Federalist Papers* to show the presidency differs from monarchy in England, pointing out that the President is elected for four years, while the king is hereditary ruler for life, that the President can be removed from office by impeachment, while there is no regular means of removing an unfit king, and that the powers of the President are circumscribed in various ways that the king's were not. Still, it is true that the presidency is monarchical in principle, that he does exercise the executive powers as rule by one, that he does have the power of pardon, however circumscribed, that he is commander-in-chief of the armed forces, that he can make treaties, albeit with the support of extraordinary majorities in the Senate, that he does have considerable powers of appointment, though this power is hedged around by the necessity for the concurrence of the Senate for high officers, and so forth. These powers in most instances have their origin in powers allotted to monarchs and are monarchical in principle.

(b) The Aristocratical Principle

The Senate is less an aristocracy than the President is a monarch. The share which the members have of ruling power is not great enough to maintain that the Senate is rule by a few. The trappings of aristocracy, as we ordinarily think of them, are generally missing. There are no lords temporal or spiritual, no dukes or earls, no bishops and archbishops, none who hold their position by hereditary right, or by appointment from the monarch.

Yet the Senate does represent the aristocratical principle in our government. It is the upper house of our national legislature. The members are relatively few in number, only two from each state. Its most immediate antecedents were the governor's council in the colonial period and the British House of Lords. Its namesakes were the Roman Senate in antiquity, and ecclesiastical and other synods. The United States Senate is territorially based rather than on population as was the British House of Lords. Senators were conceived as a select group in age, experience, and in their appointment by state legislatures. Senators not only comprise an upper house of the legislature but also serve as a council to the President. They are supposed to advise and consent to the treaties and appointments made by the President. They serve to limit the powers of the President in these matters. While their position is not hereditary, they have the longest terms of anyone in government except judges. And, the Senate originally represented states in Congress and only indirectly the people in their states.

(c) The Democratical Principle

As originally conceived, the House of Representatives was based on the democratical principle. It was based upon the *demos,* the people. The number of representatives a state could have was based on population. Districts within which they are elected are based on a portion of the population arrived at by dividing the population of the state by the number of representatives. Representatives were and are elected by the direct votes of the people in the districts. The most direct principle at work is representation or agency. Given that, however, the make-up of the House is democratical.

Thus, the United States is not a monarchy. It is not an aristocracy. It is not a democracy. It has a mixed government, which combines monarchical, aristocratical, and democratical principles.

b. A Republic

The United States is a republic. More completely—to repeat an earlier formula—, the United States is a constitutional federated republic. But if its character must be reduced to one word, it is a republic. A part of the difficulty with that is that the word does not go very far in distinguishing one country from another in our day. It was different at the time the United States attained its independence from Britain. At that time, most countries were monarchies, empires or some variant of that, such as duchies, principalities, and the like. Republics belonged to history mostly, especially early Rome in ancient times. Probably, the most distinctive feature of a republic at the time of the founding of the United States was that it was not a monarchy. In practice, a republic was likely to be any country that did not have an hereditary ruler.

The above is not, of course, a definition of a republic; it only gives the historical setting for that. Aside from not having an hereditary ruler, there are two things which distinguish a republic. They are: (1) the origin of the powers of a government; (2) the manner in which the powers are exercised. That is, they come from the *public* (or people), that is one; and they are exercised by representatives, that is the other. An *American College Dictionary* defines a republic as "a state in which the supreme power rests in the body of citizens entitled to vote and is exercised by representatives chosen directly or indirectly by them." The meaning has not changed since the time of the founding of the American Republic. James Madison said that "we may define a republic to be . . . a government which derives all its powers directly or indirectly from the great body of the people, and is administered by persons holding their offices during pleasure, for a limited period, or during good behavior."[29] Patrick Henry focused attention on representation in his definition: "The delegation of power to an adequate number of representatives, and an unimpeded reversion of it back to the people, at short periods, form the principal traits of a republican government."[30] In short, republican government is popular representative government.

There was widespread, perhaps nearly universal, agreement among Americans at the time about the desirability of having republican government. As James Madison said in 1788: "The first question that offers itself is, whether the general form and aspect of the government be strictly republican? It is evident that no other form would be reconcilable with the genius of the people of America; with the fundamental principles of the revolution; or with that honorable determination which animates every votary of Freedom, to rest all our political experiments on the capacity of mankind for self-government."[31]

When the Constitution of 1787—"the Constitution" to later Americans—was in the making and being pushed for ratification, the idea was advanced that what was wanted was a more effective government, one that would secure the happiness and well being of the people. They wanted a government to conduct foreign affairs, to settle disputes among the states, and in the words of the Preamble, "secure the Blessings of Liberty to ourselves and our Posterity. . . ." Many wanted a dependable government, a "regular government," as Edmund Pendleton put it in a speech favoring ratification made before the Virginia Convention. What he had to say on this head is worth quoting at some length:

> I wish, sir, for a regular government, in order to secure and protect those honest citizens who have been distinguished—I mean the *industrious* farmer and planter. I wish them to be protected in the enjoyment of their honestly and industriously acquired property. I wish commerce to be fully protected and encouraged, that the people may have an opportunity of disposing of their crops at market, and of procuring such supplies as they may be in want of. I presume that there can be no political happiness, unless industry be cherished and protected, and property secured. . . . In my mind the true principle of republicanism, and the greatest security of liberty, is regular government.[32]

For some Americans, at least, republican government was apparently linked with good government.

By definition, republican government is government by the consent of the people. But it is not obvious why popular government should be thought likely to produce the ends that the Founders sought. Conceivably, they might have believed that the people are naturally good and virtuous, that they are by nature bent to justice and order, that a majority will always make the right decision, and that the voice of the people is the voice of God. Had they started with these assumptions, it would be clear why they favored popular government.

But these emphatically were not the assumptions of most of the men who produced and favored the ratification of the United States Constitution. On the contrary, Alexander Hamilton said, "The voice of the people has been said to be the voice of God; and, however generally this maxim has been quoted and believed, it is not true to fact. The people are turbulent and changing; they seldom judge or determine right."[33] John Adams approved Machiavelli's contention "that whoever would found a state, and make proper laws for the government of it, must presume that all men are bad by nature; that they will not fail to show that natural depravity of heart whenever they have a fair opportunity."[34] Moses Ames, speaking in the Massachusetts Convention called to consider ratification of the Constitution, said about popular government: "It has been said that a pure democracy is the best government for a small people who assemble in person. . . . It may be of some use in this argument . . . to consider, that it would be very burdensome, subject to faction and violence; decisions would often be made by surprise, in the precipitancy of passion, by men who either understand nothing about the subject; or by interested men, or those who vote for their own indemnity. It would be a government not by laws, but by men."[35] James Madison said that "on a candid examination of history, we shall find that turbulence, violence, and abuse of power, by the majority trampling on the rights of the minority, have produced factions and commotions, which, in republics, have more frequently than any other cause, produced despotism."[36] In a similar vein, though written some years later, John C. Calhoun said that the "truth is,—the Government of the uncontrolled numerical majority, is but the *absolute and despotic form of popular governments. . . .*"[37]

Yet some of these same men, and others of similar views, professed themselves to favor popularly based government. Alexander Hamilton declared: "The fabric of American Empire ought to rest on the solid basis of THE CONSENT OF THE PEOPLE. The streams of national power ought to flow immediately from that pure, original fountain of all legitimate authority."[38] Elbridge Gerry maintained that "it must be admitted that a free people are the proper guardians of their rights and liberties. . . ."[39] Moses Ames said, "The people must govern by a majority with whom all power resides."[40] A Mr. Lee of Westmoreland in Virginia took a similar position: "I say that this new system [the Constitution] shows, in stronger terms than words could declare, that the liberties of the people are secure. It goes on the principle that all power is in the people, and that rulers have no power but what are enumerated in that paper [the Constitution]."[41] John Marshall "conceived that, as the government was drawn from the people, the feelings and interests of the people would be attended to. . . ."[42] James Madison asked, "Who but the people have a right to form government? The expression [We the People] is a common one, and a favorite one with me."[43]

There is an apparent contradiction in the above. On the one hand, man is a flawed creature, both individually, and when he acts in concert with others. On the other hand, these men were bent on having a republican government, a government based on the general consent of the people, and one which will utilize people as governors. Rather than seeing this as a contradiction, the Founders generally saw it as a reality within which they had to work in establishing as good a government as possible. That, as they saw it, was one which could establish and enforce laws making social life and social intercourse possible, but which would also allow for individual liberty. After all, as James Madison pointed out, "what is government itself but the greatest of all reflections on human nature? If men were angels, no government would be necessary. If angels were to govern men, neither external nor internal controls on government would be necessary." But that is obviously not the case. Men are not angels either individually or corporately. Kings are not angels; aristocrats are not angels, and men when they act in concert, as in democracies, are hardly purified in their motives or altered in their bent to trespass and trample upon the rights of others. So it is, as Madison said further, that "In framing a government which is to be administered by men over men, the great difficulty lies in this: you must first enable the government to control the governed; and in the next place oblige it to control itself."[44] In short, since all men are by nature flawed, it is necessary to limit both those who are governed and those who govern in the exercise of their faculties and their powers. To put it yet another way, to have a government of laws and not of men both those who govern and those who are governed must be ruled by law. The law for governments should be their constitution.

Madison went on to say that the government's dependence upon the people for the selection of its political officers would restrain those who govern to some extent. The Constitution as drawn limits both the governors and the governed. The substantive limits will be discussed in another section below, but the organizational limits need to be covered here. The people must have some power directly over those who govern to exercise their restraint as well as to authorize the government use of power. Under the United States Constitution, the direct popular impact was in the voting for members of the House of Representatives. But the populace might come under the sway of some unworthy motive or divide into factions, some of which might gain control of government for their own ends. One of the ways to thwart this was by the diffusion of power in the government and to have different sets of electors for different branches. That was done as has already been explained. By having authority exercised by representatives, and most of those chosen by a winnowing process, the hope was to obtain reasonable government rather than one based upon passion or self-interest narrowly conceived. Representation was conceived as the best hope for getting reason to prevail in political affairs. By selection, a considerable number of the most reasonable men might be chosen; by making it cumbersome to take action the delays would give men time to "come to their senses"; by counterpoising branch against branch men might have to recur to persuasion. Thus, men might be restrained in their actions but also induced to rise toward that level where the public good might more likely prevail over self-interest narrowly conceived. A republic offered that prospect.

c. A Federal System of Government

The United States government is further limited in that it is part of a federal system of government. The other parts of that system are the state governments. As regards the inhabitants of the fifty states, everyone lives under the distinct jurisdictions of the general government and of the state in which he resides or happens to be at the moment.* They may limit one another since either may try to extend its powers** at the expense of the other, and it is expected that each government will be jealous of its powers and resist the extension of the other. That this would tend to limit the United States government was strongly suggested at the time of the founding. Alexander Hamilton noted at the New York convention to consider the ratification of the Constitution that

> This balance between the nation and state governments ought to be dwelt on with peculiar attention, as it is of the utmost importance. It forms a double security to the people. If one encroaches on their rights, they will find a powerful protection in the other. Indeed they will both be prevented from overpassing their constitutional limits, by a certain rivalship, which will ever subsist between them. . . .[45]

James Madison described some of the particular ways in which the general government was dependent on the states and thus limited it:

> The State governments may be regarded as constituent and essential parts of the federal government; whilst the latter is nowise essential to the operation or organization of the former. Without the intervention of the State legislatures, the President of the United States cannot be elected at all. They must in all cases have a great share in his appointment, and will, perhaps, in most cases, of themselves determine it. The Senate will be elected absolutely and exclusively by the state legislature [changed to direct election by the 17th Amendment]. Even the House of Representatives, though drawn immediately from the people, will be

---

*Those residing in the District of Columbia live only under the jurisdiction of the United States government by special provision of the Constitution. It might be supposed that local governments such as those of counties and towns and cities would constitute further governments with their own distinct jurisdictions, but that is not the case. They are creatures of the states and are permitted to share in the jurisdiction of the state.

**The phrase "State's Rights" came into use over the years to describe the powers and the jurisdiction of the state. That is a misnomer, however, because neither states nor governments have rights strictly speaking. They have powers; individuals have rights and privileges, however derived.

chosen very much under the influence of that class of men, whose influence over the people obtains for themselves an election into the State legislatures. Thus, each of the principal branches of the federal government will owe its existence more or less to the favor of the State governments, and must consequently feel a dependence. . . .[46]

The members of the Senate originally served to defend the powers of the state governments. Hamilton also pointed out that the state governments by their major role in administering criminal and civil justice should have a large sway over their citizens and a counterpoise to the power of the United States. It is well to keep in mind, too, that the Constitution of the United States specifically limits the powers of the states. Thus, both are limited.

But we have proceeded with the discussion without defining and clarifying the nature of a federal system of government. It can be defined as a "form of government of which the essential principle is that there is a union of two or more states under one central body for certain permanent objects." Although nothing much was made of it at the time, the American system of federalism was almost certainly a new system. Leagues and confederations have a much longer lineage, since they were known in ancient times. Leagues were the result of a close alliance between or among independent states for military or defense purposes. They were usually short-lived and were subject to dominance by the most populous or dominant state within the league. Confederations could have much longer existence. For example, the Swiss Confederation existed in one way or another from the Middle Ages to the mid-19th century. Of this Confederation, the *Encyclopedia Britannica* says that in the 18th century "Every form of government existed side by side. . . . Every state . . . ruled subject territories; there was little sense of nationality and no common language, coinage, system of weights and measures, army or law courts." In short, it was a loose confederation of independent states until the mid-19th century. The United States was first described as a confederation under the Articles of Confederation. The Articles also described it as a league.

The major distinction between a federal system and a confederation is that under a federal system the central government may act directly upon the inhabitants of all the constituent states. As noted earlier, both the states and the United States government have a *jurisdiction* within which they may act upon the inhabitants. Anyone who will read the Constitution should be able to see that this is clearly what the Founders intended, that the central government should act upon all inhabitants in certain ways, and that in others the states retain their authority over the inhabitants.

Commentators at the time of the ratification of the Constitution emphasized that this was the character of the new federal system of government. John Jay, arguing for adoption before the convention held in New York state, said that the general government was very limited in scope, and had but few objects. "They comprehend the interests of the states in relation to each other and in relation to foreign powers."[47] In his argument for a national judiciary, Edmund Randolph also indicated what he thought the national government would be. He said that "a national judiciary was needed as an auxiliary to the federal government, [to] support and maintain harmony between the United States and foreign powers, and between different states, and prevent a failure of justice in cases to which particular state courts are incompetent. . . . Self-defence is its first object. . . . Its next object is to perpetuate harmony between us and foreign powers."[48] James Madison observed that "the powers of the general government relate to external objects and are but few."[49] Edmund Pendleton declared that the "general government" was to act "in great national concerns, in which we are interested in common with other members of the Union. . . ."[50] Earlier he had heatedly denied that the Constitution authorized a consolidated government:

> I should understand a consolidated government to be that which should have the sole and exclusive power, legislative, executive, and judicial, without any limitation. Is this such a government? Or can it be changed to such a one? It only extends to the general purpose of the Union. It does not intermeddle with the local, particular affairs of the states.[51]

Some of the above may overstate the limits on the government of the United States even at the beginning. Even so, there should be no doubt that the states retained a large residue of the powers of government after the Constitution was ratified. No man of good sense in the 1780s would have proposed seriously that a unitary state be erected to embrace all English Americans. Almost every man's hand would have been against him. The states had obtained their independence before the Constitution of 1787 had gone into effect. Their existence as distinct entities had a long history during the colonial period. Many differences existed between them which could not readily be resolved. Some of these differences gave rise to regional and local cultures, each with its own particular flavor and ways. Men grew attached to particular colonies and took pride in those things which differentiated them from the inhabitants of other colonies. A Virginian writing in 1728 gave voice to this sentiment when he said: "If *New England* be called a Receptacle of Dissenters . . . , *Pensylvania* [sic] the Nursery of Quakers, *Maryland* the Retirement of *Roman Catholicks, North Carolina* the Refuge of Runaways, *South Carolina* the Delight of Buccaneers . . . , *Virginia* may be justly esteemed the happy Retreat of *true Britons* and true Churchmen."[52] Perhaps more important politically, in their contests with Britain over the years, many colonists had come to think of their particular colonies as the defender of their liberties. On the other hand, they feared government remote from them as being a potential source of tyranny.

In any case, Americans made it clear in the 10th Amendment to the Constitution that large powers were reserved to the states. It reads:

> The powers not delegated to the United States by the Constitution, nor prohibited by it to the States, are reserved to the States respectively, or to the people.

This amendment should make it clear also that the United States government has only delegated or enumerated powers.

The federal system is sometimes described also as one in which there is dual sovereignty. That is, the states have a portion of the sovereignty belonging to government, and the United States has a portion. "Sovereignty" is a mischievous, if not pernicious, notion, and the use of it is much more apt to distort rather than clarify the nature of our federal system. Even so, the term has been widely used throughout American history, so that it must at least be discussed.

The word "sovereignty" has absolutist origins. While the concept has been around for more than two thousand years, it was given a firm absolutist character in the 17th century of our era. It is generally defined as referring to the supreme, ultimate, or absolute seat of power and authority within the state. Two philosophers gave currency to this notion of sovereignty: Jean Bodin in the 16th century and Thomas Hobbes in the 17th. Both men were monarchists, holding that only kings are able to provide stable government. "Hence the best form of government," Bodin thought, "is unlimited and hereditary monarchy: it must be unlimited if it is not to end in chaos, and it must be hereditary to avoid wars of succession. Monarchy, like paternal authority, has prevailed over most of the earth and through the longest time; it has the sanction of history."[53] Hobbes had similar ideas of sovereignty. His ideas have been summarized this way: "However based, the sovereign, to be really sovereign must have absolute power, for without it he cannot ensure individual security and public peace. . . . Absolutism is necessary, for when power is shared, as between king and parliament, there will soon be conflict. . . . Consequently the only logical form of government is monarchy."[54]

There have been attempts from time to time to apply this concept of sovereignty, which tends to be absolutist in any case, to the United States. Some claim that the states are sovereign; some say the United States government is the locus of sovereignty; and some would locate sovereignty in the people. Indeed, over the last three or four decades, the notion seems to have gained ground that ultimate power in this country resides in the Supreme Court, though the idea has not as yet been linked with sovereignty. But at least three theories have been advanced.

The idea that the states are sovereign is probably the one having the greatest vintage. In fact, some states early annexed the term to their name, as in "the great sovereign state of Georgia," or something of the sort. Here is a summary statement of the theory from a contemporary writer. "Finality knows no degrees," he has said. "In law, as in mountain climbing, there comes a point at which the pinnacle is reached. . . . The argument here is that the states, in forming a new perpetual union to replace their old perpetual union, remained in essence what they had been before: separate, free, and independent states. They *surrendered* nothing to the federal government they created. *Some of their powers they delegated; all of their sovereignty they retained.*"[55]

On the other hand, historian C. M. Wiltse maintained that the government of the United States emerged supreme in the Civil War. Referring to the presidency of Abraham Lincoln, Wiltse wrote: "The sovereign power of the nation rested in his hands, and he exercised it. The rebellious South was beaten back into the Union, and the great debate was finally over. . . . A century after the Stamp Act had been rejected . . . the United States of America itself emerged as a true national state, whose sovereignty was undisputed and whose will was uncontrolled within the limits of its power."[56]

The following is a simple and direct statement of the concept "that the people are sovereign; that the people created both state and national governments and that therefore both levels of government are merely the agencies of the people."[57]

There is something to be said for each of these views. Some states did precede the United States, and they were the instruments by which powers were delegated to the United States government in the Constitution of 1787. It does not follow, however, that the powers were delegated by the states; they were delegated by representatives of the people meeting in conventions within the states and elected for this very purpose. In any case, when the United States government acts in accord with that Constitution, it is supreme within its realm. It is true also that the powers exercised by both state and national governments derive from the people and might conceivably be reclaimed. There is a sense, too, as Thomas Jefferson argued, that the people are the ultimate arbiters of the Constitution, since that document can be amended through more or less popular processes.

But neither the states nor the national government nor the people are the seats of sovereignty in our constitutional federated republic. The concept of sovereignty is alien to our system of government. The federal system is not absolutist. The Constitution does not envisage the concentration of power in any body such as is suggested by the word sovereignty. On the contrary, the genius of our constitutional federated republic is *limited government*. The state governments are limited by the United States Constitution and their own constitutions. The national government is limited, having only enumerated powers, by the jurisdictions of the states counterpoised against its expansion, by division into branches which tend to limit and restrain one another, and by specific provisions against some kinds of acts. The people, too, are limited by the constitutions they have adopted. They are limited by the fact that they do not act directly but rather through representatives and other ways to make their impact even more indirect. The courts are limited by procedural requirement, appellate courts above trial courts, by prescribed trials by jury, and by the fact that judges can be removed from office by impeachment. And, that is only the broad outline of limits on the various governments and branches.

Why have so many limits on government? Why have such a complicated system of government made up of local governments, state governments, and the United States government? Those are the questions we must now explore, plus describing some of the limits in detail.

d. A Limited Government

It is highly doubtful that the dispersal of power among two or more governments is necessary to effective government. In fact, the complex system of government in the United States probably is more productive of inefficiency than efficiency. Government enforcement of the laws could most likely be more expeditiously carried out if those charged with that task did not have to go through due process. Totalitarian governments have demonstrated in this century that standing laws may be a hindrance to the vigorous operation of government. Monarchies and aristocracies are even cumbersome when compared to dictatorship. All this is a way of pointing out that the American system of government was not devised to get the job of government done and over with, so to speak. The division and separation of powers into branches is to limit and restrain government. The federal system was also thought to have that effect, as was having a written constitution with substantive prohibitions against the exercise of certain kinds of power.

The ultimate purpose was to free people from government intrusive interference in their lives and trespass on their property. It was to enable people to manage their own affairs, to use their lives and property in constructive ways, and to provide for themselves and their own. The Founders believed, of course, that government was necessary and, when rightly used, beneficial. But they were acutely aware, too, that government power is dangerous to the lives, liberty, and property of the citizenry. Government may need to have a monopoly of the use of force in order to maintain the peace, but man is a weak vessel, or so they thought, and power in the hands of men is subject to be and is often abused.

The documents of the era of the founding of the United States abound with references to the dangers of government. John Dickinson, in his objections to British taxes, provided a primer in how governments gradually increase their powers until they become despotic. He said:

> Indeed, nations in general, are not apt to *think* until they feel; and therefore nations in general have lost their liberty: For as violations of the rights of the *governed,* are commonly not only specious, but small at the beginning, they spread over the multitude in such a manner, as to touch individuals but slightly. Thus they are disregarded. . . . They regularly increase the first injuries, till at length the inattentive people are compelled to perceive the heaviness of their burdens—They begin to complain and inquire—but too late. They find their oppressors so strengthened by success, and themselves so entangled in examples of express authority on the part of their rulers, and of tacit recognition on their own part, that they are quite confounded. . . .
>
> From these reflections I conclude that every free state should incessantly watch, and instantly take alarm on any addition being made to the power exercised over them. Innumerable instances might be produced to show from what slight beginnings the most extensive consequences have flowed. . . .[58]

The danger of government was palpable to Thomas Jefferson, and none exceeded him in their fears of it and desire to see it restrained. He even declared that "The natural progress of things is for liberty to yield and government to gain ground."[59] Richard Henry Lee, in his *Letters from the Federal Farmer,* expressed agreement with John Adams' view "that unbridled passions produce the same effect, whether in a king, nobility, or a mob. The experience of all mankind has proved the prevalence of a disposition to use power wantonly. It is therefore as necessary to defend an individual against the majority in a republick [*sic*] as against the king in a monarchy."[60]

The dangers of government were rehearsed in full measure in the Constitutional Convention. For example, Rufus King of Massachusetts objected to setting a date for Congress to meet each year because he "could not think there would be a necessity for meeting every year. A great vice of our system was that of legislating too much."[61] Roger Sherman of Connecticut wanted to make the President absolutely dependent on Congress because "An independence of the Executive . . . was in his opinion the very essence of tyranny. . . ."[62] Benjamin Franklin opposed salaries for those in the executive branch because, he said, "there are two passions which have a powerful influence on the affairs of men. These are ambition and avarice; the love of power, and the love of money. Separately each of these has great force in prompting men to action; but when united in view of the same object, they have in many minds the most violent effects. Place before the eyes of men, a post *honour* that shall be at the same time a place of *profit,* and they will move heaven and earth to obtain it."[63]

James Madison pointed up the dangers of unrestricted majority rule: "In all cases where a majority are united by a common interest or passion, the rights of the minority are in danger." Among others, he gave the following examples:

> We have seen the mere distinction of colour [i. e., black] made . . . a ground of the most oppressive dominion ever exercised by man over man. . . . Debtors have defrauded their creditors. The landed interest has borne hard on the mercantile interest. The holders of one species of property have thrown a disproportion of taxes on the holders of another species. The lesson we are to draw from the whole is that where a majority are united by a common sentiment, and have an opportunity, the rights of the minor party become insecure.[64]

Some feared that the Congress might be tyrannical. For example, Gouverneur Morris of Pennsylvania thought that "It is necessary then that the Executive Magistrate should be the guardian of the people, even of the lower classes, against Legislative tyranny, against the Great & wealthy who in the course of things will necessarily compose the Legislative body."[65] On the other hand, Madison pointed out the need for "defending the Community against the incapacity, negligence or perfidy of the chief Magistrate [President]. The limitation of the period of his service, was not a sufficient security. He might lose his capacity after his appointment. He might pervert his administration by a scheme of peculation [embezzling money] or oppression. He might betray his trust to foreign powers."[66]

Beyond all the particular dangers from branches or officers or in particular powers granted, there was a general danger which some saw. They often referred to it as the danger of centralized and consolidated government, the danger of a government remote from the people with large powers, the peril of such a power for the liberties of the people. Patrick Henry probably overstated the danger from the government provided for in the Constitution at that time, but this is the way he described it in the debates over ratification in the Virginia convention:

> . . . Had the delegates who were sent to Philadelphia a power to propose a consolidated government . . . ? Here is a resolution as radical as that which separated us from Great Britain. It is radical in this . . . ; our rights and privileges are endangered, and the sovereignty of the states will be relinquished. . . . The rights of conscience, trial by jury, liberty of the press, all pretensions to human rights and privileges are rendered insecure. . . . [This was, of course, before the Bill of Rights had been added to the Constitution.] A number of characters, of the greatest eminence in this country object to this government for its consolidating tendency. . . . The government will operate like an

ambuscade. It will destroy the state governments, and swallow the liberties of the people.[67]

The main point here is that the Founders were aware of the dangers of government to the life, liberty, and property of the people, and they took steps to limit and restrain those who governed so as to make the abuse of power and tyranny less likely. We have already examined the organizational devices set up in the Constitution to do that, and it is in order now to examine the substantive provisions.

The powers of Congress are most directly limited in Article I, Section 9 of the Constitution. The first provision of this character prohibits Congress to interfere with the migration or importation of such persons as the states might decide to allow to enter the country until the year 1808. The primary purpose of that was to allow those who wanted additional slaves to bring them in the country until that year. As soon as the time was up on this prohibition, the Congress did forbid further importation. The Constitution also prohibits the Congress to lay any tax of more than ten dollars per person on any persons imported into the country. Congress is not authorized to suspend the privilege of obtaining a writ of *habeas corpus* except in cases of rebellion or invasion. The availability of such a writ makes arbitrary imprisonment much more difficult for police and jailors. When a jailor is presented with such a writ he must either release the prisoner or charge him with the violation of some standing law along with alleging some of the particulars by which the accused might begin the preparation of a defense. This is a major protection of the *liberty* of the individual in the most rudimentary sense.

Congress is also prohibited to pass bills of attainder or *ex post facto* laws. These are, at bottom, laws passed to punish particular individuals. A bill of attainder would usually be passed to apply to a felon such as a traitor, murderer, or the like. Such a bill might result in the confiscation of his property. If it works "corruption of blood" it would mean that the felon could neither inherit nor transmit property to any heirs. Such a person was said to be attainted. An *ex post facto* law was a law passed after some sort of acts had been committed making something illegal which was not at the time they were committed and punishing the offenders. The effect of this was not only to deny arbitrary power to the national legislature but also prevent them from acting as a super court. This provision of the Constitution protected both the liberty and property of people from arbitrary types of legislative acts.

The Constitution prohibits Congress to pass any direct or capitation tax unless they are apportioned according to the census. This provision refers back to an earlier provision of the Constitution which says, "Representatives and direct Taxes shall be apportioned among the several States . . . , according to their respective numbers, which shall be determined by adding to the whole number of free Persons . . . , three fifths of all other Persons.'' The other persons referred to here were Negro slaves. The purpose of these provisions so far as they referred to taxes was to reduce the amount of taxes that would have to be paid on slaves in case a *capitation* tax was levied. A capitation tax is also referred to sometimes as a ''head'' tax or a ''poll'' tax. That is, it is a tax levied upon and to be paid on each inhabitant, and without the above provision slaves would have been taxed the same as free persons (since there is also a provision that all taxes are to be uniform). The other purpose would be to prevent any direct tax levied on individuals to be levied unequally.

Taxes on exports from states (including to foreign countries no doubt) are prohibited by the Constitution. The significance of this provision stems in part, at least, from the fact Congress was authorized to levy taxes, duties, and imposts, and that might have been assumed to include taxes on exports. This removed all doubt. The Founders not only wanted to be sure that trade among the states was as free as possible but also that manufacturers and farmers be able to compete on foreign markets. They were less concerned with encouraging imports. There was a further provision that Congress was to give no preference in regulation to ports of one state over those of another nor was one state to be permitted to control the traffic of another or force the payment of duties on the shipping of another.

Both executive and legislative branches are limited by the requirement that no money is to be drawn from the Treasury except that authorized by lawful appropriations, requiring that records be kept of receipts and expenditures, and made public from time to time. The United States government is prohibited to grant any title of nobility, nor are those having positions in the government to receive foreign titles, positions, or payments unless Congress consent to them.

Some of the limits on the Congress are not stated as prohibitions. Some are stated in the process of granting power. That is certainly the case with the granting of the taxing power to Congress in Article I, Section 8 of the Constitution. In the first place the taxing powers are to be used ''to pay the Debts and provide for the common Defence and general Welfare of the United States.'' Secondly, in the case of the taxation that is in the nature of ''Duties, Imposts, and Excises'' they are to be ''uniform throughout the United States.'' There should be no doubt that the requirement of uniformity is a limitation on the taxing power to which it applies. ''Imposts'' are tax rates as they are levied on goods from foreign countries. ''Duties'' are taxes due on foreign goods entering the country. Excises are taxes added to the price of goods before they are offered for sale. The meaning of the limitation was that rates on such items as these types of taxes were levied on would have to be uniform.

But the provision alluded to first has not always been and is not today generally seen as a limitation, particularly that part of it which reads ''to provide for the . . . general Welfare of the United States.'' It has been used since the 1930s as an authorization for a considerable variety of programs which are held to be for the welfare of the United States. Thus, the statement within its context must be examined more carefully and in some detail to see in what ways it was intended to limit the general government, or empower it, as the case might be. Let us note first that the government is authorized to levy taxes for the *general* welfare. That could be understood as a restrictive clause, approving taxation for the benefit of all, but not for any part or portion of the population or peoples in the country.

What was being guarded against by this restriction was the levying of taxes on the whole people to pay for benefits for some people in some class, locale, state, or region of the country. For example, by this reading, taxes could not be properly levied to pay for an undertaking such as the Tennessee Valley Authority, since it would entail taxing the whole country to pay for benefits to a region only. There was a definite interest in the Constitutional Convention to restrict such practices. For example, at one point in the proceedings, Benjamin Franklin proposed that the general government be given "a power to provide for cutting canals where deemed necessary." Roger Sherman objected. "The expence in such cases," he said, "will fall on the U[nited] States, and the benefit accrue to the places where the canals may be cut."[68] Franklin's motion was defeated by a vote of 8 states to 3.

The above interpretation is, however, open to the charge that its validity is a matter of semantics, that it hinges on the meaning of a word. Indeed, it does. Probably even more important is that it depends upon the proposition that the clause contains a grant of power to the government to tax *for* the *general* welfare. From other evidence, however, that is not the case; its restrictive sense holds sway. The clause in question does not authorize expenditures *for* the general welfare; it does not authorize taxing or spending for any program. Let us look at the general context of the clause under consideration.

It is contrary to the whole tenor of the Constitution that the power to provide for the general welfare should have been granted in the sentence authorizing taxation. In the very same clause, the men who drew the Constitution did not assume that by granting the power to tax in order to pay debts that they had authorized indebtedness. On the contrary, the very next sentence authorizes Congress "To borrow Money on the credit of the United States." Nor did they assume that by authorizing taxation to pay for the common defense that they had granted the power to bring into being a military establishment. On the contrary, again, the earlier authorization is followed by a list of powers to accomplish this purpose. In this enumeration, Congress is authorized

To raise and support Armies . . . ;
To provide and maintain a Navy;

To make rules for the Government and Regulation of the land and naval Forces. . . .

If the power to provide for the common defense had been granted in the taxing power, each of these powers would have been implied by it. The enumeration of powers which follow would have been redundant. Redundancies are commonplace in legal documents, of course; lawyers are notorious for piling them on one another, but the Constitution is remarkably free of redundancies. It is spare, lean, and once stated, repetition of a position is avoided.

Indeed, the powers which the Founders reckoned necessary to the general welfare of the United States are enumerated. Among them are the power of Congress to enact uniform laws on bankruptcies, to coin money, to fix standards of weights and measures, to establish post offices and post roads, to give authors and inventors exclusive rights for a time to their writings and discoveries, and the like. There are no omnibus grants of power in the Constitution; powers granted are described in specific detail so as to make reasonably clear their limits. Those not enumerated were reserved to the states or to the people by the 10th Amendment.

Even so, the phrases of the taxation clause were a fertile source of power for those seeking to extend the power of some branch or the whole of the Federal government, even in the early years of the Republic, when the principles informing the Constitution were still fresh in mind. The issue came up for President James Madison in 1817, when he was presented with a bill for making internal improvements such as roads and canals. He vetoed it on constitutional grounds.

In his veto, Madison said, in part: "The legislative powers vested in Congress are specified and enumerated in the eighth section of the first article of the Constitution, and it does not appear that the power proposed to be exercised by the bill is among the enumerated powers. . . ." Regarding the general welfare phrase specifically, he said: "To refer the power in question to the clause 'to provide for the common defense and general welfare' would be contrary to the established and consistent rules of interpretation, as rendering the special and careful enumeration of powers which follow the clause as nugatory [of no effect] and improper. Such a view of the Constitution would have the effect of giving to Congress a general power of legislation instead of the defined and limited one hitherto understood to belong to them. . . ."[69]

President James Monroe echoed Madison's analysis, and added some reservations of his own, in vetoing a bill for maintaining the Cumberland Road in 1822. He denied that Congress had the power to do this. "If the power exist," he said, "it must be either because it has been specifically granted to the United States or that it is incidental to some power which has been granted. If we examine the specific grants of power we do not find it among them, nor is it incidental to any power which has been specifically granted." Among those from which he could not trace the power, he declared, was the clause "to pay the debts and provide for the common defense and general welfare."[70] In an added paper to his veto message, Monroe included this thought: "Have Congress a right to raise and appropriate the money to any and to every purpose according to their will and pleasure? They certainly have not," he declared, "The Government of the United States is a limited Government, instituted for great national purposes, and for those only."[71]

The conclusion here, then, is that there is no general power granted in the Constitution to provide for the general welfare. The phrase in the taxation clause is restrictive instead of being a grant of power. It denies the use of the taxing power for local, regional, state, or class purposes. Authorized purposes are in the grants of enumerated powers which follow it.

The most basic, broadest, and most comprehensive limitation on the United States government was not mentioned in the original Constitution. It is spelled out to some extent in the 9th and 10th Amendments, but it was always implicit, as those who favored the ratification of the Constitution argued. The limitation is that those powers not specifically granted to the United States in the Constitution do not belong to it. In order for powers to be legitimately exercised by the government they must be derived from the Constitution.

Over the years, some interpreters of the Constitution have claimed that "implied powers" were granted to the United States by the "necessary and proper" clause. It reads as follows as a further statement of the powers of Congress:

> To make all Laws which shall be necessary and proper for carrying into Execution the foregoing Powers, and all other Powers vested by this Constitution in the Government of the United States, or in any Department or Officer thereof.

The language is clear enough that it is not a grant of additional or "implied" powers. Rather, the clause makes clear that those in the government empowered to do so may take the "necessary and proper" steps to exercise powers that have been granted. For example, Congress is authorized "To provide and maintain a Navy," and in doing so may purchase and commission ships and provide all those things "necessary and proper" to the task. There is nothing more to be read into the clause in question.

It may not be so easy to see, however, how the absence of a grant of power is supposed to work to limit the government. To get to a good example, let us turn to limitations upon the states. These are spelled out in Article I, Section 10. States are prohibited to enter into any treaty, make an alliance with, or join any confederation with other states or foreign countries. They are, among other things, prohibited to coin money, issue bills of credit, "make anything but gold and silver Coin a tender in Payment of Debts." In addition, and in keeping with the prohibitions on the United States government, the states are not to grant titles of nobility, pass bills of attainder, make *ex post facto* laws, or any law impairing the obligation of contracts. Nor are states permitted to levy taxes on imports or exports, except those necessary to pay for laws of inspection. In effect, Congress retains control over this whole area, for the consent of Congress is necessary for any action by state governments. States are only to engage in war-like acts on their own when they are invaded or the danger of their being invaded is so great as not to admit of delay.

The main point here is that states are limited in certain ways by the United States Constitution. As governments, the states are also limited by their own constitutions. The monetary prohibitions may not be entirely clear. It may be clear enough, however, that the states are prohibited to coin money. It may now be recalled that the Congress was authorized to do that, and the effect of the two provisions would be to give the United States government sole governmental authority to mint or coin money within the country. (Private mints were neither contemplated nor prohibited.) States are further prohibited to make anything but gold and silver coins *legal tender*. In general, to make anything legal tender is to make it a currency that has to be accepted in payment of debts. Anyone who refused such tenders of payment, then, would have no recourse at law in collecting the debts, though other sorts of penalties have also been levied. States are prohibited to emit bills of credit. "Bills of credit" are what is now often referred to as "paper money." States are prohibited to issue paper money, then, and, even if they could do that, they are prohibited to make it legal tender.

But what about the United States government? Was it authorized to "emit bills of credit?" No such power is granted in the Constitution. Was the United States government authorized to pass tender laws? No such power is granted in the Constitution, though the states are prohibited to make anything but gold or silver legal tender. The presumption in this case would be that in the absence of such a grant no such power exists. Nor need we speculate in this case whether or not there is some "implied power" among those granted for the Federal government to issue paper money and make it a tender in payment of debts. This is so because the matter was taken up during the Constitutional Convention.

The Congress under the Articles of Confederation had been authorized to "emit bills of credit," and had done so on a large scale to the detriment of the currency. Even so, as was the case with many of the powers granted under the Articles, the power "to emit bills on the credit of the United States" was proposed for inclusion in the Constitution. Gouverneur Morris of Pennsylvania moved to strike out this particular grant of power. Pierce Butler of South Carolina seconded his motion. This was followed by discussion on the floor where several delegates spoke out forcefully in favor of omitting the power, while a few indicated a reluctance to strike it.[72] Nine states voted to strike the grant of power from the Constitution, and two voted to retain. (Twelve states had sent delegates to the convention, but New York's delegates were not present at the time of this vote.)

It is reasonable to infer from what had been done that the government under the Constitution was granted no power to issue paper money. George Mason, who opposed the motion, admitted as much at the convention. Moreover, James Madison explained in a footnote that he "became satisfied that striking out the words would . . . cut off the pretext for a paper currency, and particularly for making the bills a tender for public or private debts."[73]

A good way to study the Constitution is to ask whether this or that power that is or has been exercised by some government is authorized in the Constitution. The way to find out is to examine the provisions, and given the premise that what is not enumerated is not granted, it is a good way, too, to learn how the United States government is limited by the Constitution.

Although there are other limitations of one sort or another in the original Constitution, it is time now to confront the best known limitations as they are found in the first ten Amendments to the Constitution.

e. The Bill of Rights

The ink was hardly dry on the Constitution before a hue and cry began to be raised that the document was severely defective because it lacked a bill of rights. The absence of a recognizable listing of the rights of the people became a bone of contention in a number of the state conventions called to consider ratification of the Constitution. Thomas Jefferson, though he was not in the country at the time, asserted his view on the matter this way: "Let me add that a bill of rights is what the people are entitled to against every government, general or particular, and what no just government should refuse. . . ."[74]

On the other hand, Alexander Hamilton argued that the Constitution, as it was, needed no such bill, and that it would be dangerous to add one. He wrote:

> I go further and affirm that bills of rights, in the sense and to the extent in which they are contended for, are not only unnecessary in the proposed Constitution but would even be dangerous. They would contain various exceptions to powers which are not granted; and, on this very account, would afford a colorable pretext to claim more than were granted. For why declare that things shall not be done which there is no power to do? Why, for instance, should it be said that the liberty of the press shall not be restrained, when no power is given by which

restrictions may be imposed? I will not contend that such a provision would confer a regulating power; but it is evident that it would furnish to men disposed to usurp, a plausible pretense for claiming that power. . . .[75]

But to those who argued that no powers were granted in the Constitution to invade the rights of the people, Patrick Henry gave this ringing rebuttal at the Virginia convention to consider ratification: "Mr. Chairman, the necessity of a bill of rights appears to me to be greater in this government than ever it was in any government before. I have observed already that the sense of European nations, and particularly Great Britain, is against the construction of rights being retained which are not expressly relinquished. I repeat, that all nations have adopted the construction, that all rights not expressly and unequivocally reserved to the people, are impliedly and incidentally relinquished to rulers, as necessarily inseparable from delegated powers. . . . If you intend to reserve your unalienable rights, you must have the most express stipulation; for, if implication be allowed, you are ousted of those rights."[76]

There is no way of knowing whether Hamilton or Henry was right. Probably both of them were and are. There is a tendency for governments, or rather the men in them, to assume all the powers not specifically denied them. On the other hand, amendments were added to the Constitution which have been referred to as a Bill of Rights. And, subsequent to that, the Federal government has claimed many of those powers neither granted nor specifically denied. There is no way of knowing now whether the addition of a "Bill of Rights" set the stage for that or not.

There is a related flaw in listing a few rights; there may be an implication that these are the only ones, or at least the main ones. That may not, however, be the case. Thomas Jefferson gave a memorable definition of liberty. "I would say," he said, "that, in the whole plenitude of its extent, it is unobstructed action according to our will, but rightful liberty is unobstructed according to our will within limits drawn around us by the equal rights of others."[77] He did, however, make a sort of list of what might be considered the "main" ones, or, as he claimed, the ones most likely to be threatened, which were, "the rights of thinking and publishing our thoughts by speaking or writing; the right of free commerce; the right of personal freedom."[78] But the "right of personal freedom" must surely entail a host of particular rights, such as, to go and come as we will, to select our clothing according to our taste, to own and dispose of our property at will, and so on and on. As we will see, the Bill of Rights tried to deal with this problem as well as to explicitly protect some particular rights.

At any rate, whatever was or could be said against it, a list of rights was brought forward and adopted as amendments to the Constitution. They appear as the first ten amendments and are sometimes referred to as the

"Bill of Rights." This came about because there had been widespread feeling that the absence of such a list was a serious flaw and defect in the Constitution. Ratification in several states was only achieved on the tacit understanding that such a list would be added to the Constitution. Two states—North Carolina and Rhode Island—had not ratified the Constitution when it went into effect in 1789. Anti-Federalists, as those opposed to ratification were called, were still eager to have another constitutional convention, or at least some of them were. The wiser ones among the Federalists—those favoring ratification—could see that the adoption of a Bill of Rights would be the most effective way of ending significant opposition to the Constitution.

James Madison took the lead in providing one. It was a major undertaking. A mass of material had come in from the states both during and after ratification. "Not counting the two states that still refused to ratify . . . , formal requests for a bill of rights had come in from five states. . . . In one way or another proposals for amendments had come in from nine states. In all, the various proposals encompassed 186 amendments, or 210 if the twenty-four preamble-type amendments offered by the New York convention are included."[79] There was, of course, much duplication and repetition in this mass of proposals. Madison reduced the number to 19 amendments, which he submitted to the House of Representatives, since he was a member from Virginia. The House reduced the number to seventeen, and having approved those submitted them to the Senate. By consolidation, the Senate reduced the proposed amendments to twelve, which were approved and submitted to the states for ratification. Two of the proposed amendments, which dealt with the number and salaries of congressmen, were not ratified. The other ten were ratified and became a part of the Constitution on December 15, 1791.

Before examining the Bill of Rights in detail, it may be well to make it clear the nature of the rights Americans understood themselves to be establishing. The Constitution does not hold that government grants these rights. On the contrary, they were understood to be natural rights. John Adams described them this way in the Massachusetts Declaration of Rights:

> All men are born free and independent, and have certain natural, essential, and unalienable rights, among which may be reckoned the right of enjoying and defending their lives and liberties; that of acquiring, possessing, and protecting property; in fine, that of seeking and obtaining their safety and happiness.[80]

These rights were generally understood to be a gift of God implanted in the nature of things. As Alexander Hamilton put it, "the Deity, from the relations we stand in to himself and to each other, has constituted an eternal and immutable law. . . . Upon this depend the natural rights of mankind. . . ."[81]

More to the point, "Civil liberty is only natural liberty modified and secured by the sanctions of civil society."[82] Thus, there is no suggestion in the Constitution that government grants or is the source of rights which men have.

These rights have usually been referred to as "natural" rights. They are natural because they are understood to arise from the nature of things. The nature of things, further, was generally understood to have been made a part of them by the Creator, hence the rights were God-given. That rights subsist in the nature of things can be illustrated by reference to those rights which the Founders usually alluded to as summarizing them all: the rights to life, liberty, and property.

The right to life is so fundamental that it is difficult to see what is meant. It means simply that a person has a right to his life, that no one else can rightfully claim his life as theirs. In effect, and ultimately, it means that he has the right to dispose of his life and energies as he will within the confines of such obligations as he undertakes.

The right to liberty has two dimensions. One dimension, as explained earlier, is the right not to be restrained (except as penalty for some offense). The second is the right to the constructive use of his faculties or capacities and abilities by a person. That this right arises from the nature of things can be made clear. He alone can will the use of his faculties and bring them into constructive use. True, a person may be induced by coercion to use his faculties against his will. But is there a right to use coercion on a person in that way? And, even if there were, such coercion would be effective only at the least creative levels of employment, and is notoriously inefficient.

As for the right to property, it may be best understood as the right to the fruits of one's labor. In the nature of things, that which one has produced with his own hands out of his own materials is surely his. It is his as the fruits of his labor as well as the fruits of his materials if honestly acquired. Some may suppose that because law deals with various rights in property, the rights themselves arise from government. But the right precedes government and law; it arises from the nature of things.

The Bill of Rights in the United States Constitution, then, is not a grant of rights to the American people. Instead, it is a series of prohibitions and limitations on government so that people can more fully exercise their rights. To make this clear, the First Amendment begins, "Congress shall make no law" and proceeds "respecting an establishment of religion, or prohibiting the free exercise thereof; or abridging the freedom of speech, or of the press; or the right of the people peaceably to assemble, and to petition the Government for a redress of grievances." The language is very specific that Congress shall make no law "respecting an establishment of religion." An established religion ordinarily involves government support of some particular church or denomination, frequently to the exclusion of all others. At the time of the adoption of the Constitution, several states had established churches or denominations, in varying degrees. In respect to these, the Constitution prohibits Congress to interfere with them. In regard to the United States, Congress is prohibited to establish any religion. On the other hand, it is prohibited to abridge the free exercise of religion in the country. The same prohibitions against abridgement are extended to speech, the press, the right of people to assemble peacefully, and to petition the government for a redress of grievances. This last must be understood to mean that any community within the country would be free to assemble and draw up a petition. Governments have often prohibited such activities.

The last part of the Second Amendment should be clear enough. It says that "the right of the people to keep and bear arms shall not be infringed." Originally, when Madison was working on these rights, the prohibitions had been extended to state governments as well as the United States. In the process of getting them through Congress, however, the prohibitions on the states were removed. Thus, the Second and later Amendments in the Bill of Rights should be read to have prohibited the United States government to infringe on rights. Thus, the above could be read "the right of the people to keep and bear arms shall not be infringed" by the United States government. (In the 20th century, the Supreme Court has held that at least some of these prohibitions extend to state governments as well by way of the 14th Amendment. But that will be taken up elsewhere.) The first part of the Second Amendment may pose some problem, however, for it says, "A well regulated Militia, being necessary to the security of a free State, the right of the people" etc., "shall not be infringed." This is apparently intended to justify the right to keep and bear arms, but if it has any effect today it is to confuse the matter. We no longer have a militia composed of all able-bodied men who provide their own weapons and garb. Instead, we have a paid National Guard whose weapons and training are provided by the United States government and whose men may well bear arms on orders from their commanders, but they do not ordinarily keep these arms in their own dwellings. The right to keep and bear arms is still relevant and important, but the constitutional justification is irrelevant to its defense.

The Third Amendment has had little attention since its ratification. It simply prohibits the quartering of troops in private buildings without the consent of the owner in time of peace, and only permits it in wartime when it is done in a manner prescribed by law. The United States does not appear to have been tempted very often to quarter troops in private buildings in time of peace and has had few occasions, except during the Civil War, to do so in time of war. Numerous violations occurred during the Civil War, but it was difficult for Southerners to invoke the protection of the amendment.

Note again that it is government that is supposed to be restrained by these amendments so that Americans may enjoy their natural rights. The Fourth Amendment provides major protection against arbitrary and despotic government. The first clause contains a general prohibition with no readily apparent teeth. It says, "The right of the people to be secure in their persons, houses, papers, and effects, against unreasonable searches and seizures, shall not be violated. . . ." The teeth come in the second clause, which reads, "and no Warrants shall issue, but upon probable cause, supported by Oath or affirmation, and particularly describing the place to be searched, and the persons or things to be seized." The assumption here is that in accord with received practice searches and seizures are to proceed only upon the presentation of a warrant, and that warrants are to be issued upon "probable cause," supported by legally sworn or affirmed assertion with particulars given.

The requirement of "due process of law" occurs in the Constitution. What meeting its requirement involves is more or less spelled out in the prohibitions in the Fourth, Fifth, Sixth, and possibly Eighth Amendments, in criminal cases. The Fourth Amendment deals with restraints upon government in seeking for evidence and in seizing (arresting) persons or evidence.

The Fifth and Sixth Amendments deal with what must, or must not, take place by way of trials and the like before a person can be deprived of life, liberty or property. The Fifth Amendment requires that in the case of major crimes before a person can be tried he must be indicted by a grand jury, except for those in the armed forces during wartime or periods of public peril. In general, it prohibits the trial of a person more than once for the same offense, prohibits making a person testify or be a witness against himself in a criminal case. It ends with a majestic prohibition against depriving a person "of life, liberty, or property, without due process of law; nor shall private property be taken for public use, without just compensation." In this clause, property is given the same legal standing in the Constitution as life and liberty. Moreover, not even due process of law is sufficient to alienate property from its owner, if the government is taking the property for public use. Then, the owner of the property must receive "just compensation" for surrendering it to the government.

This is as a good a place as any to point out, too, that an amendment takes precedence over anything appearing in the Constitution in regard to matters to which it may refer. For example, the original Constitution grants Congress the power to regulate interstate commerce. But that regulation has bounds, including, once the Fifth Amendment was ratified, that in making regulations property not be taken without due process of law. In short, every power granted to Congress, the Courts, and the executive branch in the original Constitution was circumscribed so far as it would apply to the restraint of the Fifth Amendment once it was ratified. Nor would later amendments alter those restraints unless they dealt in some way with life, liberty, and property so as to alter the Fifth Amendment. That rule applies to all other amendments to the Constitution, of course. Madison originally wished to make the Bill of Rights an integral part of the Constitution, rather than amendments added after it. If he had succeeded in doing so, the rights secured by them would not have had that precedence they have since held because of their standing as amendments.

The Sixth Amendment continues with even more specific protections of persons accused of crimes from the government. The accused has the right to a speedy, public trial "by an impartial jury," in the state and district where the crime was committed. He has the right to be notified as to what crime he is alleged to have committed, and why he is suspected of having committed it. The accused has the right to confront those who testify against him, to use the powers of government to compel witnesses in his favor to appear and testify in court, and to have an attorney defend him. In this manner is life and liberty protected in the Constitution. Property is also protected by these provisions, since crimes often carry fines as well as imprisonment or execution as their penalties.

Since the Seventh Amendment does not deal with criminal matters, and the Eighth does, they appear to be out of order. For that reason, the Eighth will be taken up before the Seventh. The Eighth Amendment restricts punishment that can be inflicted in the incarceration before trial or after one has been found guilty of crimes. It reads, "Excessive bail shall not be required, nor excessive fines imposed, nor cruel and unusual punishments inflicted." This is the vaguest of the amendments and probably of the provisions in the Constitution. What, after all, is an "excessive" fine or bail? How much is too much? What makes one kind of punishment "cruel" and another not? Nor does "unusual" tell us much more than that something is not commonly done. It is true that "cruel and unusual" are combined in such a way as to be mutually reinforcing restrictions. In any case, many sorts of punishments which we might now classify as "cruel and unusual," such as, disemboweling, drawing and quartering, stretching on the rack, disfiguring, the cutting off of ears, hands, and the like, have long since been discontinued. The Constitution does not set a precise standard by any means, but it provides language for appeals against what may come to be thought of as excesses.

The Seventh Amendment was a backhanded way of preserving the rules of common law as well as the use of the common law by the Federal judiciary. It also secures trial by jury in such cases "where the value in controversy shall exceed twenty dollars." A constitutional theorist has written that the "primary purpose of this amendment was to preserve the historic line separating the province of the jury from that of the judge in civil cases. . . ."[83] More precisely, it would keep the determination of facts in the hands of the jury. Judges might rule on the law, but facts were to be largely matters for the jury.

The Ninth Amendment was an attempt to deal with any damage that might result from listing some of the rights belonging to people. It reads, "The enumeration in the Constitution of certain rights shall not be construed to deny or disparage others retained by the people." It can probably be best interpreted to mean that the fact that some rights have been enumerated is not taken to mean that government may trample at will on other rights not mentioned. What it was saying, in effect, was that the United States government still only has the powers granted to it, despite the fact that some things have been prohibited to the government which it was not authorized to do in the first place.

The Tenth Amendment was a last major effort to make clear that the Federal government had only such powers as had been delegated to it. There is nothing backhanded about nor any reverse English on this amendment, which says, "The powers not delegated to the United States by the Constitution, nor prohibited by it to the States, are reserved to the States respectively, or to the people." Once again, the Federal government cannot rightfully claim powers that may be alleged to inhere in government. It is a government of delegated powers. Nor does this amendment make any blanket statement about what powers state governments may have. After all, state governments have constitutions as well, and various powers may be denied by their constitutions to state governments also. The limits on Federal power are succinctly restated in the Tenth Amendment.

It may be well to conclude the discussion of the Bill of Rights here by noting a major distinction the Founders made. In their usage, governments have *powers;* people have *rights*. Governments have power to make treaties with foreign countries, to levy taxes, to make laws, to regulate commerce, to declare and conduct wars, to enforce the laws and punish offenders, and so on through the various and sundry powers exercised by governments. They have their just powers as they have been delegated to them by the people. Rights are of an entirely different character. They should not entail power over others, which power always does. This distinction needs to be carefully observed so that we can think clearly about government.

The above is a summary account of American government, with particular attention to the constitutional provisions for the government of the United States, the enumeration of the powers of Congress and the other branches of government, of the separation of powers, the independence of the branches, and of the assorted limitations on both the government of the United States and state governments. The point has been vigorously emphasized that the United States has a constitutional federated republic, that the federal system comprises both the states and the United States government, that the control of the people over the government is indirect, and that ours is a mixed government with monarchical, aristocratical, and democratical elements, but that it is neither a monarchy, an aristocracy, nor democracy in form.

Now we must look back to the time before this government was formed to examine the traditions and principles, as well as the learning and experience, on which this government was based.

Section II

Background of Political Thought and Practice

Chapter 3
The Heritage of Political Thought

The roots of American government lie deep. To examine them even briefly, it is necessary to scan close to nearly 3,000 years of history, to look back to the Hebrew prophets, to ancient Greece and Rome and the Middle Ages. Our constitutions and institutions grew out of our Judeo-Christian heritage, the civilizations of Greece and Rome, the Medieval culture in which these were blended and given an admixture of Germanic culture, the Renaissance in which the memory of Ancient thought was greatly revived and redirected, the Protestant and Catholic reformations, the modern European and especially British background, and the American colonial experience. This chapter will try to give some account of that background up through the Middle Ages in Europe.

a. Judeo-Christian Background

It may seem strange to some Americans to start the examination of the roots of American government with religion. No doctrine is more widely pronounced than that in this country we have a separation of church and state. It is true, of course, that Congress is prohibited to establish any religion by the First Amendment. But that this separates church and state, whatever that may be taken to mean, is by no means so clear. The amendment does prohibit the government to control or interfere in religious matters. Nor is government permitted to impose any religious faith or beliefs on anyone. (Note again, that at the time of the ratification of the Constitution this restriction extended only to the Federal government.) The tendency of this amendment is to free people generally as well as churches from government interference in matters of religion. There is yet another restriction as regards religion in the original Constitution. It is found in Article VI, and the relevant portion reads: "but no religious Test shall ever be required to any Office or public Trust under the United States." What this means, in practice, is that it is not necessary to subscribe to any religious belief or faith in order to hold office in the United States government.

The above are limitations upon government, as are many other provisions of the Constitution. Religion and churches are freed to use persuasion and

influence (not force) upon people generally as well as on those who govern.
The Constitution does not proclaim that religion is simply a private matter
about which there can be no public concern. On the contrary, the Founders
of the United States believed that the support of religion was essential to the
well being of the state. As George Washington put it in his Farewell Address:

> Of all the dispositions and habits which lead to political prosperity,
> religion and morality are indispensable supports. In vain would that
> man claim the tribute of patriotism who should labor to subvert these
> great pillars of human happiness—these firmest props of the duties of
> men and citizens. The mere politician, equally with the pious man,
> ought to respect and cherish them. . . . Let it simply be asked, Where
> is the security for property, for reputation, for life, if the sense of
> religious obligation *desert* the oaths which are the instruments of in-
> vestigation in courts of justice? And let us with caution indulge the
> supposition that morality can be maintained without religion. What-
> ever may be conceded to the influence of refined education on minds
> of peculiar structure, reason and experience both forbid us to expect
> that national morality can prevail in exclusion of religious principle.

Organized religion as well as the faith that sustains men has both supported government, limited it, and held it up to high standards of conduct
and activity. To put it simply and directly, without faith in God, government
has no transcendental sanction or support for its exercise of authority. Scripture makes it abundantly clear in many places that not only is man dependent
upon God but also that government is sanctioned by God. Both religion and
history have resonated with the affirmations of the profound foundation of
government in religion. John Calvin, the great Protestant reformer, said that
even among heathen writers "not one of them has treated of the office of
magistrates, of legislation, and civil government without beginning with
religion and Divine worship."[84]

The Old Testament contains many affirmations that the earthly power of
government comes from God. From Proverbs, Scripture says, as with the
voice of God: "By me kings reign, and princes decree justice. By me
princes rule, and nobles, even all the judges of the earth."[85] Daniel affirmed
that God is the origin of the power of kings, when he said, "Blessed be the
name of God for ever and ever: for wisdom and might are his: and he
changeth the times and the seasons: he removeth kings and setteth up
kings. . . ." More, Daniel said to King Nebuchadnezzar: "Thou, O king art
a king of kings: for the God of heaven hath given thee a kingdom, power,
and strength, and glory. And wheresoever the children of men dwell, the
beasts of the field and the fowls of the heaven hath he given into thine hand,
made thee ruler over them all."[86]

Jesus made the same point about the origin of earthly power when he was being examined by Pontius Pilate. Pilate asked him: "Speakest thou not unto me? knowest thou not that I have power to crucify thee, and have power to release thee?" To which, Jesus replied: "Thou couldst have no power at all against me, except it were given thee from above. . . ."[87]

How did kings and others who govern come to possess the power to rule? Scripture gives a suggestive account of this in the annointing of Saul as king by Samuel. Samuel had been a prophet and leader of Israel, but in his old age he turned his powers over to his two sons. They abused their authority so badly that the elders of Israel approached Samuel, "And said unto him, Behold, thou art old, and thy sons walk not in thy ways: now make us a king to judge us like all nations."[88] Samuel was opposed to the idea. He knew that the power to rule over others, by kings or otherwise, could all too readily become the power to oppress. But he prayed about it, and the Lord made it clear to him that he should follow the wishes of the people and appoint a king. Before doing so, however, he should warn the people about how they would be oppressed, and to make it known also that they were rejecting God by following this course.

Samuel proceeded to point out in considerable detail to the people how they would be oppressed under a king. For example, "he will take the tenth of your seed, and of your vineyards . . . , and your menservants, and your maidservants, and your goodliest young men and asses, and put them to his work. And he will take the tenth of your sheep: and ye shall be his servants. And ye shall cry out in that day because of your king which ye shall have chosen you; and the Lord will not hear you in that day."[89] The people were still unmoved, still insisting that they wanted a king. After Samuel knew that Saul was to be the king, but before he had presented him to the people, he called them together, and said:

> . . . Thus saith the Lord God of Israel, I brought up Israel out of Egypt, and delivered you out of the hand of the Egyptians, and out of the hand of all kingdoms, and of them that oppressed you.
> And ye have this day rejected your God, who himself saved you out of all your adversities and your tribulations; and ye have said unto him, No, but set a king over us. . . .[90]

So, Samuel gave them Saul for a king.

If men would obey God freely, do His will, and live in peace and harmony with others, we may gather, they would need no king. Indeed, they would need no government. Well, perhaps, and perhaps not. Men might still disagree about the terms of agreements with one another, honestly disagree. In any case, that is hardly the situation. Man is a fallen creature, self-interested of necessity, and rebellious by nature. From the beginning, he disobeyed God, and when he is left to his own devices, he is apt to prey upon others, to trespass upon his neighbors, to steal, to disturb the peace, and do all manner of wrongful things. Thus, as in the above account, because they will have nothing less, God sets a king over them. To generalize, God recognizes the necessity of government to keep the peace among disobedient and rebellious people.

Rulers not only have their powers from God, then, but men are often exhorted in Scriptures to yield obedience to earthly powers. The Apostle Paul put it this way:

> Let every soul be subject unto the higher powers. For there is no power but of God: the powers that be are ordained of God.
>
> Whosoever therefore resisteth the power, resisteth the ordinance of God: and they that resist shall receive to themselves damnation.
>
> For rulers are not a terror to good works, but to the evil. Wilt thou then not be afraid of the power? do that which is good, and thou shalt have praise of the same.
>
> For he is the minister of God to thee for good. But if thou do that which is evil, be afraid; for he beareth not the sword in vain: for he is the minister of God, a revenger to execute wrath upon him that doeth evil.
>
> Wherefore ye must needs be subject, not only for wrath, but also for conscience sake.[91]

Paul was, of course, laying down general principles and speaking in the most general terms. The absence of exceptions or qualifications here should not be taken to mean that laws made by men are always just, that every particular decision by those in authority is correct, or that decisions are never to be appealed. (Indeed, Paul himself appealed from the Jewish authorities who accused him to the Roman rulers, claiming his rights as a citizen of Rome.[92]) In fact, Paul was not writing a treatise on political science or a book on government. Had he been doing so he might well have proceeded in a quite different fashion, noting exceptions, and making qualifications in many ways. Instead, he was writing instructions to the church at Rome and to Christians regarding their proper attitude toward the earthly powers that ruled over them. In the briefest scope, he set forth some general principles and alluded to reasons, both prudential and moral, for their validity. In the broadest sense, he was saying to Christians, do not rise up, revolt, or resist the authorities placed over you. They have a work ordained of God to perform; accept your subjection to them to that end; give them their due.

At any rate, the main point here is the Christian sanction for governmental authority. Many authorities affirmed it. For example Peter wrote, ''Submit yourselves to every ordinance of man for the Lord's sake: whether it be to the king, as supreme; Or unto governors as unto them are sent by him for the punishment of evildoers, and for the praise of them that do well.''[93]

There is a greater point than this, however, both for governments and for people generally. There is a law higher than man made law. There is right higher than the right proclaimed by government. There is a good greater than the good perceived by man. There is a justice higher than man's version. The ultimate role of religion is the limitation of the power and pretensions of government. Scripture makes clear that God's rule is antecedent to and superior to the rule of any man. The Psalmist says:

> Put not your trust in princes, nor in the son of man, in whom there is no help. . . .
> Happy is he that hath the God of Jacob for his help, whose hope is in the Lord his God:
> Which made heaven, and earth, the sea, and all that therein is; which keepeth truth for ever:
> Which executeth Judgment for the oppressed: which giveth food to the hungry. The Lord looseth the prisoners.
> The Lord openeth the eyes of the blind: the Lord raiseth them that are bowed down; the Lord loveth the righteous:
> The Lord preserveth the strangers; he relieveth the fatherless and widow: but the way of the wicked he turneth upside down.
> The Lord shall reign for ever, even thy God, O Zion, unto all generations. . . .[94]

This places government, its power, and its rule in true perspective. There is one other large point that needs to be made here about the relationship between Christianity and government. Are Christian churches to call on the use of government to advance their work? The clearest answer to this is found in the teachings of Jesus. After Jesus had been baptized, he went into the wilderness and had fasted for 40 days and nights. Then Satan tempted Him repeatedly. The third temptation speaks to the issue of the use of the power of government:

> Again, the devil taketh him up into an exceedingly high mountain, and sheweth him all the kingdoms of the world, and the glory of them; and saith unto him, All these things will I give thee, if thou wilt fall down and worship me.
> Then Said Jesus unto him, Get thee hence, Satan: for it is written, Thou shalt worship the Lord thy God, and him only shalt thou serve.[95]

Jesus was at the time of the above event about to set out upon his ministry. The above temptation and reply should obviously be interpreted in that light. He was surely pondering and planning how he was to expound and propagate the Good News that He had to tell. Would his work not be much easier and more effective if He could use the power of government to that end? Rather than going through the difficult business of trying to persuade men of beliefs and ways that were unfamiliar to them, they could be compelled by the force of government to accept his teachings and propagate them. Think how risky and uncertain it was to follow the course which he did: to choose 12 disciples, men neither of any great learning or influence, to go from place to place teaching and preaching, with no earthly authority behind him, and to preach only, or mostly, in a remote province of the Roman Empire. Yet, He rejected political power at the outset. Why? Because, as Scripture says, to get it he would have to worship Satan. He would, no doubt, have to use the devices of this world, to make the compromises by which power is gained and wielded. Ultimately, he would have to use force to propagate the Gospel. He would have to reveal God's love toward man with force. It was, of course, a contradiction revealed in the very terms. God's love could only be fully revealed through the way that Jesus chose, through service, through humility, through sacrifice. The force of government could only have been a hindrance in the work of Jesus.

Jesus explained the matter a different way when he was before Pontius Pilate. Pilate asked Him if He was the king of the Jews. Jesus asked Pilate where he had heard this idea, whether he had conceived it himself or been told it by others. Pilate answered, in effect, that the Jews had accused Jesus of making such a claim, and asked Him what he had done.

> Jesus answered, MY kingdom is not of this world: if my kingdom were of this world, then would my servants fight, that I should not be delivered to the Jews: but now is my kingdom not from hence.[96]

His kingdom, Jesus was maintaining, is of a different order and standing than earthly kingdoms. He made the point less dramatically and over a less important issue earlier in his ministry. Some men sent to spy on Him and hoping to catch Him in a contradiction asked Jesus: "Is it lawful to give tribute to Caesar, or not? But he perceived their craftiness, and said unto them, 'Why tempt ye me? Shew me a penny. Whose image and superscription hath it?' They answered and said, Caesar's. And he said unto them, 'Render therefore unto Caesar the things which be Caesar's, and unto God the things which be God's.'"[97] Not only did Jesus give an answer which could hardly be offensive but also once again made the vital distinction between what St. Augustine later described as the Earthly City and the Heavenly City.

There is much more in Scripture that could be alluded to or emphasized regarding government, but the major points for the later influence on Americans particularly have been made. A summary of these is now in order. First, the necessity for earthly government is affirmed in the Bible. Men are enjoined to obey its rule over them. That being the case, the authority of government within its realm is sanctioned by Judeo-Christian teachings. Second, the power exercised by earthly rulers comes originally from God. Third, it is man's disobedience to God—his sinfulness—that has made earthly rule necessary. Rulers are appointed to punish evil and see to it that it does not gain sway among peoples. Such a commission implies that those who govern should not punish for acts that are in their nature good or that God has laid upon men's consciences to do. Fourth, there is a higher authority than earthly rulers; it is his revealed truth and goodness, as these may be known through Scripture, experience, and reason. These place limits upon what governments may rightfully or effectively do. This may be easy enough to see where what are called natural laws are concerned, when we examine them elsewhere, but it is also true otherwise. Fifth, the force of government is not to be employed in spreading the Gospel. Force can properly be used to restrain and punish wrongdoers, but it is out of its realm in doing good and building the kingdom of God.

The Bible, as noted already, is not a political treatise. It does not deal with the subject exhaustively. Most often its references to kings and rulers is incidental, and even when it is not, the character and doings of the rulers is more apt to be the focus than discussions of the nature of government. There is considerable concern with justice and injustice in the Old Testament, which often entails rulers and governments, but not much of what we would call political theory. So it is that we turn to different sources for the rudiments of political theory.

b. Greek Rationalism

The Greeks may not have been the first to ponder the subject of government and politics at length and in depth. It is certain that highly organized governments over considerable realms antedated their known efforts by many hundreds, if not thousands, of years. But the Greeks were the first to record systematic political theory and to leave behind a considerable legacy of political thought. More important to the purpose here, some of their ideas were still bouncing around, so to speak, when the United States Constitution was conceived and written, well over two thousand years later. It can be said with considerable justification that the Greeks invented philosophy, and, in like manner, that they were the first to apply reason with some consistency to political thinking. Indeed, it is important to emphasize here that the best known of the Greek thinkers—Socrates, Plato, and Aristotle—relied primarily on reason for proof of their insights.

To understand the Greek, and later the Roman, contribution it may be helpful to look at some philosophical conceptions, particularly those that undergird reason. The validity of reason as a mode of arriving at truth or knowledge hinges upon the existence of an order in reality which can be reached by it. The use of reason will also be conditioned by what is reckoned to be real. There are at least three levels of reality, or to be more precise, three different orders of being, though they may be otherwise characterized. They are in ascending order of importance: the physical, the metaphysical, and the spiritual. It may be generally agreed that we cannot know the spiritual by way of reason. We may arrive at such knowledge as we have of the spiritual realm by Revelation as contained in Scriptures, by personal inward experience, by intimation, by intuition, and the like. Factual knowledge of the physical realm comes to us most directly by way of the senses of sight, hearing, smelling, tasting, and feeling (the sense of touch). Facts brought to us from the senses may be raw materials on which we may reason toward more general categories and natures of things. When it is used in this fashion it is called inductive reasoning. The other form is known as deductive reasoning, a method used to extend knowledge from established or self-evident premises. Such reasoning is described as syllogistic. The following is the classic example of the syllogism:

Major premise: All men are mortal
Minor premise: Socrates is a man
Conclusion: Socrates is mortal

The above syllogism takes us into another realm—the metaphysical. Mortality—that which is in the nature of beings which will die—is a metaphysical idea. It is something beyond the physical, something that we cannot perceive through any one or combination or all of the senses together. It's true that we can see the body of a person who has died, and can with the aid of the senses determine that death has taken place. But we cannot see, hear, taste, smell, or feel mortality. There are those, and have been for a long time, who have argued that such terms are only names or words, and have no other being or reality. (Those who believe in this way are called *nominalists.*) They are in error, for there is an order of being or level of reality in which they are real. It is best called the metaphysical, though it may be also known as the realm of essences or essentials.

The metaphysical is the realm that gives the regularity and order to things in the universe. It may become clearer if we think of regularities proceeding from the metaphysical realm. One of the earliest insights of man known to us is that there are regularities in the world about us. Things do not simply exist each in its peculiarity and individuality but also in patterns, common form, and in regularities which suggest an overall order. For example, the seasons of the year follow one another in predictable fashion, and, having completed the cycle, they recur. Seeds taken from a plant reproduce that plant when placed in the ground during the growing season. All animals, including man, go through a cycle of life: conception, birth, growth, maturity, death, decay, unless the cycle is interrupted by premature death. Night follows day and the two together constitute a 24 hour cycle corresponding to the rotation of the earth on its axis. "Then there are also the regular changes in the positions of the heavenly bodies, beginning with the sun and moon and after them the planets. The regular sequence . . . of the tides . . . , of eclipses of the sun and moon were observed at a very early date."[98] Indeed, the order in the universe appears in all sorts of regularities, sequences, and patterns. Some of them can be mathematically calculated, or even stated as laws.

There are those who refer to these, or some of them, as *physical* laws. For example, the law of the uniform acceleration of freely falling bodies, first stated by Gallileo, might be called a physical law. But that is incorrect. True, the law pertains to physical bodies, but the law itself is not physical. We cannot see, hear, feel, smell, or taste it. The law exists in another realm; it is metaphysical. It is a part of the underlying order of reality available to us through the process of reasoning both inductive and deductive. To put it another way, the metaphysical order is in the nature of things. That there is such an underlying and overarching order is a part of that natural law philosophy which has played so large a role in political theory, and especially American political theory. That things have a nature has been so crucial to political thought that it must be emphasized from the very beginning of our examination.

The key to this underlying order and natural laws is that they come into view when we focus our attention on the enduring features of reality. They are discovered by an act of the mind in stripping away all that changes, that is ephemeral (that belongs to the level of things that change), that is cultural, that is a result of history, that is peculiar to each individual thing or being. It is in this fashion that we discover the nature of things, the laws that govern or pertain to them, the way they are and can be. For example, if we would know the nature of men, we must remove everything that is accidental to any particular man (or woman), in any particular time or age: dress, language, size, girth, how hairy he is, what color his skin is, and anything peculiar to a particular man or people. Then, we ask what the distinctive features of his kind are. What are the potentialities of his being? What is the nature of man?

We have already observed that all men are mortal. This mortality, we know by both observation and reason combined, has nothing to do with his dress, his language, his customs, his traditions, his religion, where he grew up, what family he grew up in, or any of thousand differentiating features we might name for any given man. But mortality is not a distinctive feature of man among the animals of the earth. All animals are mortal as well. Indeed, to the best of our knowledge, and in the nature of things, all living beings are mortal. On the other hand, it has been widely held by those, thinking in terms of the nature of things, that the distinctive feature of man (as a species, including woman, of course), is that he is a rational, or reasoning being. That is, he has the *potential* to reason. That is not at all to say that he always reasons carefully, that he always draws his conclusions on the basis of reasoning, or that his actions are moved by the conclusions he has drawn from reasoning. It is rather to say that man by his nature is capable of extended reasoning, if his potential is developed and if he is not defective in some way that makes him less than fully human. Again, this potential or capacity for reasoning is not a matter of race, religion, nationality, sex, language, or any of those things that differentiate individuals and peoples from one another.

Some of the Greek thinkers who are best known to us, such as Socrates, believed in reason, especially deductive reason, as virtually the sole guide to the truth. They came very close to holding that if it was rational it was real and true. At any rate they were greatly taken with reason. But Socrates and those giants of philosophy who came after him were in a line of philosophers stretching backward into the Greek past. These included Thales, Anaximander, Anaximenes, Heraclitus, Parmenides, Pythagoras, Empedocles, Anaxagoras, Zeno, Protagoras, and others—mostly shadowy figures who either produced little that was written or little which has survived.

Even so, some of them had considerable influence on men who did become better known, and some of whose works have survived. They did so through followers and fragments of their thought, remembered or written down. Zeno's paradoxes eventually became famous throughout the Mediterranean. Pythagoras and his followers provided a philosophical concept which has had profound effect on the Western world, perhaps the whole world. The Pythagoreans held that the universe is not only an ordered one but also that the nature of that order is ultimately mathematical, and hence intelligible. As one historian of philosophy has said, "This idea, taken up by Plato and passed on to Christian theology, is one of the great heritages of the modern mind."[99] The belief that there is an underlying order which transcends and informs the real world around us has been a crucial belief for political thought for 2,500 years now. The Pythagoreans began the establishment of the philosophical premises for that belief.

But three Greek philosophers finally loom above all the others: Socrates, Plato, and Aristotle. Socrates taught Plato, and Plato taught Aristotle. The lives of these men in sequence span a considerable portion of the 5th and 4th centuries B. C.: Socrates (circa 470–399); Plato (circa 428–348); Aristotle (384–322). At their hands, Greek philosophy reached its peak. Their lives encompassed both the peak of Athenian dominance and its political decline. Though Aristotle was not an Athenian by birth—he was born in Stagira on the shores of the Aegean, and is sometimes referred to as the Stagirite—as the other two men were, he spent some of his best years in Athens. Each of these men is of sufficient importance in the development of political thought to be treated in some detail.

(1) Socrates

The city-state was the unitary political organization best known to ancient Greece. That was so because there were many city-states in what we know today as Greece. Athens and Sparta were the best known of these in ancient times. A city-state, in general, consisted of a city and however much of a surrounding countryside it might claim. The city was generally the center of the commercial, religious and political life of the inhabitants. Politics came to the fore in ancient Greece as the focus of the life of a people, possibly because a considerable portion of the people participated directly in the political life. Classical democracy reached its peak in ancient Greece, especially at Athens. The Greeks were, of course, familiar with empires, with leagues, and with confederations, but they prized, above all, the city-state.

Socrates was a man of the city, of the city-state of Athens. So central was it to his life that when he was given a choice between death and exile, he chose death. So far as is known, Socrates never wrote anything of consequence; if he did, it did not survive him. Much that we know of him, in fact, his philosophical reputation, is due mainly to the labors of his disciple, Plato. Plato made Socrates the main character of a whole series of dialogues, and especially dramatized the events and conversations which preceded the death of Socrates. That is not to say that Plato invented Socrates. In addition to Plato, other contemporary writers, such as Xenophon, Theophrastus, and Aristophanes, attest to the fact that Socrates was a philosopher in his own right to be reckoned with. The problem is that it is often difficult, if not impossible, to determine whether the ideas ascribed to Socrates in the dialogues were his or Plato's.

Judging by Plato's dialogues especially, Socrates developed and spread his philosophy by conversations held outdoors usually, in the streets, byways, and public places of Athens. On his walks he got involved in exchanges which attracted a gathering of men. Usually, Socrates acted as interlocutor and asked questions. One historian has described his approach this way:

> . . . His method was simple: he called for the definition of a large idea; he examined the definition, usually to reveal its incompleteness, its contradictoriness, or its absurdity; he led on, by question after question, to a fuller and juster definition. . . . Sometimes he proceeded to a general conception, or exposed another, by investigating a long series of particular instances, thereby introducing a measure of induction into Greek logic; sometimes . . . , he unveiled the ridiculous consequences of the definition or opinion he wished to destroy.[100]

Socrates appeared to be much more the fount of questions than the source of answers. Indeed, if anyone turned on him to demand answers, he was most

apt to profess his ignorance. He was, he said, a midwife of ideas, drawing
out what others knew rather than presenting his own ideas.

Yet there was a purpose behind the randomness of his method. He was
using the *dialectical* method to get a firmer grip on and a clearer view of
truth. He came to the fore in the wake of those teachers known as Sophists.
These were traveling men who plied their trade for money, so it was
charged, who taught young men how to get ahead, so they claimed. Sophists
believed that man is the measure of all things, that there are no universal
truths, that truth is relative, that there are no fixed rules of goodness and of
right. Justice, Thrasymachus, a well known Sophist, said to Socrates, "is
nothing but the advantage of the stronger." In short, as we would say, might
makes right. Thrasymachus went on to spell out the political implications of
his relativism:

> Is not the strong power in each the ruling power? And power lays
> down the laws so as to itself, a democracy democratic laws, and a
> despotism despotic laws, and so with the rest; and in laying them down
> they [do so for] their own advantage. . . . Then this is what I mean, my
> good friend; that the same thing is just in all states, the advantage of
> the established government . . . [which] has the power, so if you
> reason correctly, if follows that everywhere the same thing is just, the
> advantage of the stronger.[101]

Socrates would not have it so. He would question, probe, dig, define until
he was in sight, at least, of fixed principles and an enduring order. He was
grasping for evidence of universal truth beyond the opinions of men, an idea
some would already profess. There was a difference between the customs
and conventions of men and laws which transcended these. The playright
Sophocles had Antigone defend herself from the charge of violating the law
when she performed the funeral rites of her brother by laying claim to this
higher law. She said:

> Yea, for these laws were not ordained of Zeus,
> And she who sits enthroned with gods below,
> Justice, enacted not these human laws.
> Nor did I deem that thou, a mortal man,
> Could'st by a breath annul and override
> The immutable unwritten laws of Heaven,
> They were not born to-day nor yesterday;
> They die not; and none knoweth whence they sprung.[102]

It was some such vision as this that Socrates was attempting to keep alive
or restore. As one historian has said, "Socrates taught that beneath the
variety and confusion of laws and customs general and universal rules of

morality might be found." More, "he believed that fundamental principles of right and justice might be discovered . . . , that the state . . . and its laws, if based upon wisdom, would correspond to universal reason."[103] His philosophy is also called idealism sometimes, because of his emphasis upon the ideal of the good and the virtuous.

One of the greatest impacts of Socrates on political thought was not in something that he is supposed to have taught but rather in what happened to him. Athens was a democracy in which all male citizens participated directly. Socrates was charged with corrupting the young by impious and irreligious teachings. In consequence, he was tried before a jury of 500, selected from the populace at large. He was found guilty of the charges by a majority of the jury, though Socrates heatedly denied the truth of them, and his followers maintained his innocence. The jury imposed the death penalty, though there was no law requiring such a penalty. Whatever Socrates himself may have thought of democracy, the most famous of his followers certainly doubted that it was the best form of government. It is now time to turn to their thought.

(2) Plato

Plato was a student and follower of Socrates. While he did not invent philosophy, he brought it to such a level that he can be described as the founder of it as an intellectual discipline. Indeed, it has been well said that the history of philosophy is a series of footnotes to Plato. He casts a long shadow (or better perhaps, *bright light*) over philosophy as it has developed. Unlike his mentor Socrates, Plato was very much a writer. Thirty-five dialogues (more or less book length) and thirteen letters attributed to him have survived, though a few of them are not now recognized as authentic. Three of his dialogues, *The Republic, The Statesman*, and *Laws*, deal most directly with politics. The main character in most of the dialogues is Socrates. By contrast, Plato is never identified by name in any of them, nor did he otherwise distinguish between the ideas of Socrates and his own. Even so, the major ideas which are developed in the dialogues are treated as ones which Plato contributed to the development of philosophy and probably believed to be correct.

Plato also founded a school, the Academy, as an institution for the training of students. It specialized in the teaching of mathematics, which Plato thought was the proper foundation for logical thinking and philosophy. The Academy was the forerunner of the university, though it lacked either the extensive organization or diversity characteristic of the modern university. It might best be thought of as some sort of advanced school of philosophy of which Plato was the headmaster. So far as can be gathered from Aristotle's account, Plato lectured without notes. He propounded problems to be solved by the researches and other work of his students. Plato's students led

the way in the development of mathematics in the 4th century B. C.,
especially of solid geometry, and contributed to the work in other sciences
as well. Aristotle was undoubtedly the most productive of all Plato's students.

The Republic is not only the best known of Plato's political works but it
is also reckoned to be the greatest literary masterpiece of all the dialogues,
as well as being a major innovation in political thought. This long dialogue
is devoted to examining what the best or ideal form of society and government would be within a state. The ideal state, according to Plato (or
Socrates, as the case may have been), is one in which justice prevails and the
happiness of the whole reaches its peak. The reasoning goes this way:

> . . . [W]e thought that in a State which is ordered with a view to the
> good of the whole we should be most likely to find justice, and in the
> ill-ordered State injustice: and, having found them, we might then
> decide which of the two is happier. . . .[104]

In any case, Plato believed that it was a part of the business of the state
to establish justice. But his conception of justice was both more complex
and somewhat differently oriented than what has been most commonly
thought of as involved in justice. Justice has usually been thought of as
seeing that a man gets his due. That is, if he has earned something or
deserves it for what he has done, whether of good or evil, he should be
appropriately rewarded or punished. That is his due; that is justice. In some
measure, Plato seems to be saying the same thing, as when he asks, "And
are suits decided on any other ground but that a man may neither take what
is another's, nor be deprived of what is his own? . . ." More, he only slides
away from it slightly in this affirmative statement: "Then on this view also
justice will be admitted to be the having and *doing* what is a man's own, and
belongs to him. . . ."[105]

Nonetheless, Plato was shifting toward the view that justice consisted
mainly in a person's staying within his own class and performing his function there. He claimed that in an ideal society there would be three classes,
i.e., the producing class, the warrior class, and the ruling class. He further
claimed that each man by the nature of his talents belonged to one or the
other of these and that there should be no overlapping, moving back and
forth from one class to another, or belonging of a man by his occupation to
more than one of these classes. If such things happened, Plato declared, it
would be "the ruin of the State."[106]

It would be the ruin of the state because it would be an injustice, since he
had supposedly already established that for each man to stay in his "place"
or class was in accord with the ideal of justice. It was logical, of course, for
Plato to reach that conclusion, since a man should have his own to have
justice and that to have his own involved occupying his appointed place

within society. Logical, that is, given his premises, but not necessarily reasonable or in accord with any other reality. Plato had confused logic with reason or reality, or, at the least, with the ideal.

In any case, the class system he imagined provided him with an ideal class to serve as a ruling class. What Plato was leading up to was the rule of the state by philosophers, or as they have sometimes been called, philosopher-kings. Plato believed that the ideal form of government was an aristocracy. And for aristocrats or rulers, he wanted men versed in philosophy. Only men deeply imbued with philosophy, he thought, could rule justly and impose the sort of rule that would meet the ideal. Only men who spent their lives in preparation for and ruling would be up to the level Plato envisioned for the rulers of the ideal state.

The Republic was a utopian dialogue, then, though the word itself did not come into use until 2,000 years after Plato wrote. Some modern writers have charged Plato with being a totalitarian as well. Certainly, he did not believe in equality, and he did envision in *The Republic* a role of government in the lives of the populace that would verge on the oppressive, if not totalitarian. However Plato may have intended it, the dialogue might better be considered a cautionary tale rather than an account of a desirable state. Plato proposed to make men good and virtuous, and to do that a government would probably have totalitarian power, though it is doubtful even then it would accomplish its object. If *The Republic* had been all that Plato contributed to political thought, he would have done more toward stretching political imagination than altering political reality. Happily, that was not the case.

In *The Statesman* and *Laws,* believed to have been written in his later years, Plato turned his mind away from the ideal state to political matters both more practical and more familiar. While he turned away from the imaginary, Plato still utilized rational analysis in his writings. In *The Statesman,* he set forth what would be the classic understanding of the possible forms of government. They are rule by one, rule by a few, and rule by many. These are, indeed, the possible forms of rule, but with his ethical bent, Plato divided these into legitimate uses of the form and those which were perversions of the form. Thus, he considered monarchy to be the legitimate form of rule by one. Its perversion would be rule by a tyrant or tyranny. An aristocracy would be rule by the few and oligarchy its perversion. Democracy was rule by the many, and he gave no distinctive names to its illegitimate or its perverted forms.

In his later writings, Plato came down strongly in favor of rule by law, something he had not advocated in *The Republic.* In *Laws,* he made the arguments for this, saying, "Mankind must have laws, and conform to them or their life would be as bad as that of the most savage beast. And the reason of this is that no man's nature is able to know what is best for human society; or knowing, always able and willing to do what is best. . . ." He emphasized, too, that laws were not simply necessary to govern a people but especially in order to limit and constrain those who govern. For he maintained that though a man know that the public good is different from the private good and, that the art of politics has to do with the public good, "yet if he be possessed of absolute power, he will never remain firm in his principles. . . . Human nature will be always drawing him into avarice and selfishness, avoiding pain and pursuing pleasure without any reason, and will bring these to the front, obscuring the juster and better; and so working darkness in his soul will at last fill with evils both him and the whole city."[107] In sum, Plato realized that human nature was flawed, that man was so bent toward self-seeking, that it was necessary to restrain him by law. In *The Republic,* he had made the best argument he could devise that rulers should have the discretion to deal with every situation as it arose without reference to established laws. Chastened by age and experience, he now remarked the full impropriety of this approach.

He appears to have been leaning toward limiting those who governed in other ways in his later years. He at least considered the notion that the best form of government might be some sort of mixed one, such as in an aristocracy and democracy combined in some way. Even so, Plato always contemplated giving government more power than many of us would consider desirable. In an important sense, he was seeking a way to salvation through the use of government power in the city-state. That is not so different, after all, from the attitude of many intellectuals toward government in the 20th century of our era.

(3) Aristotle

Aristotle was not simply a philosopher, as we might think of one, a man who would be expected to spend much time in meditation, contemplation, and reasoning. On the contrary, he was, above all else, a compiler, arranger, and classifier of information. He was as fact-conscious as Socrates was idea-conscious. One writer describes his activities as fact gatherer and classifier in biology this way:

> He classifies the animal kingdom into . . . blooded and bloodless—
> approximately corresponding to our "vertebrates" and "invertebrates." He subdivides the bloodless animals into testaceans, crustaceans, mollusks, and insects; the sanguineous into fishes, amphibians, birds, and mammals. He covers an impressively vast and varied field: organs of digestion, excretion, sensation, locomotion, reproduction and defense. . . .[108]

Much of his work falls into what we would now call science. But his interests were well nigh universal: he ranged from politics to metaphysics and from logic to astronomy, covering a broad spectrum of fields. His emphasis upon facts led him to add inductive reasoning (reasoning from particulars to general statements and propositions) to our methods of getting knowledge. In the later Middle Ages, Aristotle was hailed as *the* philosopher, above all others.

He was not a native Athenian, as noted earlier, but was born in the Greek colony of Stagira in Thrace. His father was royal physician in the court of Philip of Macedon's father. Aristotle's later researches may have been influenced by his father's interests, but at the age of 17 he went to live and study at Plato's Academy in Athens. He remained at the Academy for twenty years until Plato himself died. If he had remained a student, that sounds like a long apprenticeship, but the evidence indicates that Aristotle had become a master in his own right long before Plato died. After Plato's death, Aristotle traveled from city to city and in other lands, teaching and studying. It was during these years that he tutored the son of Philip of Macedon, who went on to become a world conqueror and to be known as Alexander the Great. In the final stage of his life, Aristotle returned to Athens, founded his own school, the Lyceum, put together a large library, continued his nature studies, and spread his ideas by lecturing. "In the morning he taught advanced subjects to regular students; in the afternoon he lectured to a more popular audience. . . ."[109]

Aristotle was reputed to be a prolific writer who composed 400 works on a great variety of subjects. He was known to later Roman readers through his dialogues, of which there were 27, influenced no doubt by Plato. They did not, however, survive the Germanic invasions. Of his 400 works, only 40 have survived. These are believed to have been written during the last stage of his life when he was in Athens. They were probably assembled from Aristotle's lecture notes as well as from notes made by his students from the lectures. Thus, they are neither so well organized nor so lively as they might have been had they been polished for publication by the author.

Even so, the range of his work that survives is quite impressive, including the following titles, among others: *Prior Analytics, Physics, Mechanics, On the Heavens, Reproduction of Animals, On the Soul, Metaphysics, Nichomachean Ethics,* and *Politics.* It is doubtful that Aristotle had in mind creating a body of work for the ages, yet it worked out that way. From the late Middle Ages into the early modern era, until well into the 17th century, his was the authoritative voice in science and philosophy for European Civilization.

While the main concern here is with Aristotle's political thought, two of his premises are so essential to his thought that they should be put on record. The first was that there is one God who is the First and Final Cause of all things and their Prime Mover as well. He stated his premise and belief this way:

> . . . All causes at last go back to the First Cause Uncaused, all motions to the Prime Mover Unmoved; we must assume some origin

or beginning for the motion and power in the world, and this source is God. As God is the sum and source of all motion, so he is the sum and goal of all purposes in nature; he is the Final, as well as the First Cause. . . . As the tree is drawn by its inherent nature, power, and purposes toward the light, so the world is drawn by its inherent nature, power, and purposes, which are God. God is not the creator of the material world, but its energizing form; he moves it not from behind, but as an inner direction or goal, as something beloved moves the lover. . . . God is pure thought, rational soul, contemplating itself in the eternal forms that constitute at once the essence of the world and God.[110]

Not only does he posit, or reason to, the necessity for an uncaused Cause and an unmoved Mover, but he also attributes to all things a movement or development toward an end, which he says is the purpose of the energizing God. The whole universe and all that therein is, then, is unified and permeated by a presence beyond all the independent parts. This is indeed a potent intellectual concept.

Aristotle's other central premise was in his exposition of ethics, summarized in his *Nichomachean Ethics*. Indeed, *Nichomachean Ethics* and *Politics* composed one book originally, suggesting that the two were closely related to one another, but they were later divided. The concept that is crucial to his ethics is that of aiming for the "golden mean." As a general rule, he thought that a good and virtuous life would be one in which people avoided extremes and aimed at the middle ground between excesses. Aristotle called this the "mean," and explained it this way:

> It is a middle state between two faulty ones, in the way of excess on one side and of defect on the other: and it is so moreover, because the faulty states on one side fall short of, and the other exceed, what is right, both in the case of the feelings and the actions; but Virtue finds, and when found adopts, the mean.

For instance, he says:

> [I]t is possible . . . to feel the emotions of fear, confidence, lust, anger, compassion, and pleasure and pain generally, too much or too little, and in either case wrongly; but to feel them when we ought, on what occasions, towards whom, why, and as we should do, is the mean, or, in other words, the best state, and this is the property of Virtue.

Aristotle does go on to point out, however, that not every action or feeling has a golden mean which is in the middle between the most and the least. Some things are bad in whatever quantity, for example, adultery, theft, or murder, "for all these and such like are blamed because they are in themselves bad, not the having too much or too little of them."[111]

Aristotle's political thought was in some measure a reaction to Plato's *Republic* (as indeed Plato's own later political thought was). In any case, the search for the middle position was a strong current in his thought. He gave little to no attention to seeking for or describing an ideal state. Instead, he sought the mean between extremes, the best state possible under given conditions of usage, preference, experience, and local circumstances. It might be useful, he thought, to speculate occasionally about the best of all possible governments, but what was always necessary to know was what government was appropriate under particular conditions. "For the best is often unattainable . . . , for political writers, although they have excellent ideas, are often unpractical. We should consider, not what form of government is best, but also what is possible. . . ."[112]

Aristotle may well have been the first scholar to make a comparative study of governments or constitutions of states. He is reputed to have compiled 158 constitutions, but of these the *Constitution of Athens* is the only one that survives. Even so, his *Politics* contains many references to practices and constitutional provisions of other states. It was, of course, typical of Aristotle to collect as much information as possible on a subject before drawing his conclusions.

Aristotle held that the most basic association is that of the family; it is an association for the purpose of meeting the most basic needs. The next step in organization, he reckoned, was that of a village. The association of several villages might then provide the basis of a state, particularly a city-state, no doubt. Aristotle held that the state is by far the most important and essential human institution. Private organizations that often attract modern loyalties, such as churches, business organizations, fraternal organizations, if they existed at all, tended to be subservient to the state. The state was the organization which brought all the doings of men to their fruition and fulfillment. Man, Aristotle said, is a political animal and social being by nature. "And he who by nature and not by mere accident is without a state, is either a bad man or above humanity; he is like the 'Tribeless, lawless, heartless one. . . .' "[113] Justice, he says, is the bond of men in states, for the administration of justice, which is the determination of what is just, is the principle of order in political society." Man, he held, can be perfected by the state, but without its ministrations he would be "the most unholy and the most savage of animals, and the most full of lust and gluttony."[114] Whether Aristotle had imbibed these expectations from the state from the culture within which he lived, from Plato or Socrates, or whatever source, it could hardly have been arrived at inductively. In any case, the above indicates the great importance the Greeks tended to attribute to the state.

None of this is meant to suggest, however, that Aristotle held that all states are equally just, well constituted, and well run. On the contrary, they differ greatly in many, if not quite all, respects. We can gather from Aristotle's comments that man would be better off in the worst of states than to have none at all. But he was also greatly concerned that the rule over men be just, and to that end he sought to understand both the nature of government and which sorts of rule made for justice and which for injustice, despotism, and tyranny.

Like Plato, Aristotle noted that there are by nature three possible forms of government: rule by one, rule by a few, and rule by the many. Like Plato, Aristotle also distinguished between the proper and acceptable use of the form and its perversion in practice. Since Aristotle's distinctions would have much later influence, it is worthwhile to elaborate on them somewhat.

In theory, or ideally, Aristotle said that monarchy—rule by one—might be the best form of government. Thus, he said, "If . . . there be some one person, or more than one . . . , whose virtue is so pre-eminent that the virtues or the political capacity of all the rest admit of no comparison with his or theirs, he or they can be no longer regarded as part of a state. . . . Such an one may be truly deemed a God among men."[115] If there be such a person who stands so far above the others in the community, Aristotle argued that he must either become the absolute monarch or be cast out of the country. The reason being that none would exist who could justly rule over such a man. "The only alternative is that all should joyfully obey such a ruler, according to what seems to be the order of nature, and that men like him should be kings in their state for life."[116]

But Aristotle doubted that such a situation would occur except very rarely, or that if it did, it would be quite as good as might be imagined. In reality, the wisest and best intentioned would need the counsel of other men as well as their assistance in ruling, and law would be preferable to personal rule. Besides, the most likely result of rule by one would be tyranny. Tyranny is the perversion of rule by one. It occurs when a man rules in his own interest and for his own purposes rather than in the interest of those whom he governs. The tyrant governs "with a view to his own advantage, not that of [his] subjects, and therefore against their will. No freeman, if he can escape from it, will endure such a government."[117]

The rule of the few, if it is a good government, Aristotle called an aristocracy. It would be the rule of the best qualified men in the country, who would be expected to rule in the general interest of the people. In Aristotle's writings that have survived, however, he does not discuss aristocracies at length. Perhaps that is because there is little reason or experience to show that good governments emerge from the rule of a few. At any rate, Aristotle referred to the perversion of aristocracy as oligarchy. Oligarchy he inclined to define as rule by a few in their own interest. Also, he thought oligarchs were likely to be privileged by wealth or by birth. Aristotle distinguished several types of oligarchies, but the main point seems to be that oligarchies tend to keep power perpetually in the hands of a few who use the government as if it were their personal possession. They become despotic or tyrannical.

Rule by the many has the potentiality for being the best form of government, according to Aristotle. More precisely, he believed that the best government would be one which included both the few—men of wealth and other high attainments—as well as the many—including those from both the lower and middling ranks. The middle class provided the best hope for good government, Aristotle thought. He wrote to that effect, saying: "It is plain, then, that the most perfect political community must be amongst those who are in the middle rank, and those states are best instituted wherein these are a larger and more respectable part . . . ; or, if that cannot be, at least [greater than either of the other classes taken separately]; so that being thrown into the balance it may prevent either scale from preponderating."[118] There is more than a little of the "golden mean" in these political views, for Aristotle thought that if the middle class held sway they would be more likely to have a moderate government, one that avoided extremes, and followed the rule of law. Since the greater part of the populace would have some part in governing, the laws would be more readily obeyed. Such a government would be more precisely a *polity,* in Aristotle's phrase, or a constitutional government.

"Democracy" was the term Aristotle employed to describe the perverted form of rule by the many. It should be made clear that Aristotle did not object to rule by the many so long as it was rule by law and moderated by thoughtful and experienced men. However, the perversion occurs when "the multitude have the supreme power, and supersede the law by their decrees. This is a state of affairs brought about by the demagogues." For "where the laws are not supreme, there demagogues spring up. . . . This sort of democracy . . . grows into a despotism; the flatterer is held in honor . . . ; they exercise a despotic rule over the better citizens. The decrees of the demos [the people] correspond to the edicts of the tyrants. . . . The demagogues make the decrees of the people override the laws. . . ."[119] Such a government acts not in what is for the good of the country but what appeals to the worst inclinations of the people collectively. Its tendency is toward mob rule.

The impact of Greek thought and practice on the founding of the United States was more indirect than direct. The United States was never composed of city-states. Nor were Americans, except for some New Englanders, ever taken much with direct democracy. The American idea of rule by law was drawn more from the Roman and British example than that of Athens. Nor was the American republic an utopian experiment in the manner of Plato's *Republic.* But indirectly the influence of the classical Greeks was considerable on the United States as well as European civilization in general. By the end of the 4th century B. C., the Greek city-states had lost their independence to the thrust of empires in the Mediterranean. But the ideas survived in the Hellenistic Civilization that was spread around the Mediterranean in the 3rd and 2nd centuries B. C. And Rome took them up and expanded greatly on the Greek ideas for the ends of the Romans.

Greek thought supplied the foundations for natural law doctrines, which were to brook large in American insights which undergirded the Constitution. Constitutionalism began to take shape with the political thought of the Greeks. The Greek thinkers understood that law served to restrain and limit government. They made major contributions to the idea of rational examination and critical judgement of governments. They were aware and made known their views about the strength and weaknesses of various forms of government. While both Plato and Aristotle saw God as primal and providing a framework within which people lived and governments operated, their study of governments was basically rational and philosophical rather than religious. In many respects, the American constitution makers were in this line of thought.

c. Roman

The Roman influence on the political institutions and practices of the United States was great. Not only had many of the Founders cut their intellectual teeth on the heroes and villains of ancient Rome, but they had lately been mightily reminded of the glory and decline of Rome. The first volume of Edward Gibbon's *Decline and Fall of the Roman Empire* was published in 1776, the same year as our Declaration of Independence. Of its impact, Russell Kirk has written: "The grandeur that was Rome, suffusing Gibbon's chapters, worked strongly upon the imagination of the men who founded the United States. Between the Roman Republic and their own republican creation they perceived parallels."[120]

Whatever the influence of Gibbon's history, the Roman influence on the Constitution was great. Rome had a constitution going back to the Twelve Tablets in 450 B. C., and forward through many changes in arrangement until the very end of the Republic. The United States was styled a republic on the model of Rome, and the Constitution provides that the states are guaranteed republican governments as well. Rome was the prime example from the ancient world of a country having representative government and dispensing with a monarch. The territorial holdings of Rome had early become too extensive for a direct democracy, such as Athens had. It had begun as a city-state, but before long had conquered the surrounding city-states and was expanding around the Mediterranean. Thus, it had what amounted to a two-house legislature, a Senate and an assembly of Tribunes.

The United States Senate was certainly named after that of Rome, and had more than a few of the powers exercised by the earlier body. Membership in the Roman Senate was an appointment for life, and the powers of the Senate extended to "the conduct of foreign relations, the making of alliances and treaties, the waging of war, the government of the colonies and provinces, the management and distribution of the public lands, the control of the treasury. . . . It was legislature, executive, and judiciary in one [at least for certain functions]. It acted as judge in crimes like treason, conspiracy, or assassination. . . ."[121] While the Roman Senate had both more extensive and exclusive powers than does the United States Senate, there is a clear similarity between them.

Rome had a limited government, a constitutionally limited government, as does the United States. Its limitations existed in such division and separation of powers as it had. As earlier noted, the Roman Republic had a Senate and an assembly. Much of the executive power was vested in its chief magistrates, two consuls. Rome had a mixed government, then: it had the relics of monarchy in the consuls; the Senate was aristocratic, and the plebian assembly was democratical. The United States was more monarchical, with its powerful single executive, but its Senate is less aristocratic, and, in any case, the similarities stand out.

Rome's greatest political contribution to western civilization, however, was Roman law. Rome developed two bodies of law, the *jus civile* and the *jus gentium*. The first of these is the Roman civil law, the law that applied generally to Roman citizens. It might also be called the local law, for it had grown out of customary usage in Rome, not so much by legislative enactment as by common agreement and reflected in court decisions. As it became more complex, much of it was affirmed annually by the chief judicial officers of Rome. "Under the . . . civil law for Roman citizens," as one writer has said, "the Romans enjoyed immunities against arbitrary power, and protection of their property, that were rare in the ancient world: for all its severity, the Roman commonwealth knew ordered liberty."[122]

For a variety of reasons, however, the civil law for Romans was not readily applied to the conquered cities and territories. After all, as conquerors, the Romans had advantages they would not be eager to share with the conquered. Being a Roman was coming to mean something special in the Mediterranean world, and it was not likely the Romans would be inclined to give away their edge. But even if they had been in the matter of law, other cities and communities had their own laws, their own religions, and their own ways. The Romans came to understand that they needed a particular kind of law, not their own civil law, with which to administer the provinces over which they ruled. They called this law *jus gentium*, the law of nations.

As much as it might sound like it, it was not international law, which applies to sovereign nations in their dealings with one another. Rather, it was conceived as those rules and laws common to people generally. Its particular purpose under Roman rule was to settle disputes between people of different provinces or between provincials and Rome. As for disputes among people living in the same province and not involving Roman authority, these were left to local courts applying the local law.

Roman thinkers did not proceed far with their thought about a law of nations before that began to link the concept with natural law, a concept toward which some of the Greek thinkers had leaned. Natural law, if it be accepted as a valid concept, consisted of universal laws, laws that were everywhere applicable. When applied to actual cases in court, it would probably most resemble what *equity* courts are supposed to do. That is, they would not be positive laws passed by legislatures nor derived from court decisions or even local customs. They would, instead, be arrived at by reasoning upon what would be just in such a case. Such a law is conceivable as the ''law of nations,'' although it is doubtful that Rome could claim some sort of exclusive jurisdiction for applying such law. For further exposition of the natural law concept, however, it may be better to turn to a leading expositor of this law.

(1) Cicero

Marcus Tullius Cicero (106–43 B. C.) was one of the most versatile and impressive men in the age of Rome when it hung between Republic and Empire. A hint of his influence on America is contained in John Adams's tribute to him, ''As all the ages of the world have not produced a greater statesman and philosopher united than Cicero.''[123] In his own day, he was famed as an orator, was a popular and successful lawyer as a young man, a reluctant warrior, a Senator at Rome, a Consul who ruled Rome for a time, a literary figure in his own right, and at last a philosopher. He was a contemporary of Julius Caesar, whom he greatly liked personally, but he loved the Republic and its constitution too much to support him, or Pompey, and or Cataline. Marc Antony was virtually a contemporary as well. Cicero married a woman of great wealth and compiled a great fortune of his own as well. Of his literary outpouring, a biographical novelist has said: ''His letters to his publisher and dearest friend, Atticus, fill many books in the Vatican Library, and in other great libraries over the world. . . . His own books are voluminous, concerning law, old age, duty, consolation, morals, etc. . . . His law cases are famous. His orations constitute many volumes. . . .''[124] His most important works on political philosophy are *On Laws, On Offices,* and *On Republics.*

Cicero was the great champion of republican government, of constitutional government, and of the natural law. He supported his belief in universal natural law with a belief in God, who was surely not of the gods of Rome, or of Athens, or of any city, but the universal God, who made of all men one species, having a like nature, and subject to the same laws. Of God's Law, he wrote:

> Power and the law are not synonymous. In truth they are frequently in opposition and irreconcilable. There is God's Law from which all equitable laws of man emerge and by which men must live if they are

not to die in oppression, chaos and despair. Divorced from God's eternal and immutable Law, established before the founding of the suns, man's power is evil no matter the noble words with which it is employed or the motives urged when enforcing it.

Men of good will, mindful therefore of the Law laid down by God, will oppose governments whose rule is by men, and, if they wish to survive as a nation they will destroy that government which attempts to adjudicate by the whim or power of venal judges.[125]

Cicero believed in a government of laws not of men, believed that the highest law is God's Law, and identified that with natural law. More, he identified both with right reason. To wit:

True law is right reason conformable to nature, universal, unchangeable, eternal, whose commands urge us to duty, and whose prohibitions restrain us from evil. Whether it enjoins or forbids, the good respect its injunctions and the wicked treat them with indifference. This law cannot be contradicted by any other law, and is not liable either to derogation or abrogation. Neither the senate nor the people can give us any dispensation for not obeying this universal law of justice. . . . It is not one thing at Rome, and another at Athens; one thing today, and another tomorrow; but in all times and nations this universal law must for ever reign, eternal and imperishable. It is the sovereign master and emperor of all beings. God himself is its author, its promulgator, its enforcer, and he who does not obey it flies from himself, and does violence to the nature of man.[126]

The Romans, not the least of whom was Cicero, gave an impetus to the concept of natural law which it had not had before in political thought. It has had a checkered career since that time. There have been several revivals of it from Roman times to the time of the founding of the United States, especially during the High Middle Ages, the Renaissance, and the 17th and 18th centuries. It had great influence on American thinkers in the 18th century and played a significant role in constitution making in America.

Cicero summed up well another set of ideas which both suggests the great contribution of Classical thought to politics and brings us back to what government should be about. He said, "Those who design to be partakers in the government should be sure to remember those two precepts of Plato; first, to make the safety and interest of their citizens the great aim and design of all their thoughts and endeavors, without ever considering their own personal advantage; and secondly, so to take care of the whole collective body of the republic as not to serve the interest of any one party, to the prejudice or neglect of all the rest. For the government of a state is much-like the office of a guardian or trustee. . . ."[127] His second recommendation is very much like what the Founders meant by general welfare. The first takes into account what the best of the Greek and Romans left behind—the idea and practice of seeking for the best form of government. They also taught the use of reason in this quest.

(2) The Philosopher Kings

There are other Roman thinkers and writers whose works and sayings might be examined, Cato the Elder, Cato the Younger, Horace, Livy, Tacitus, Seneca, Juvenal, and so on. But the Romans were more often doers than thinkers. And Americans looked to Rome not only for the institutions which they imitated, such as constitutionalism, representative government, mixed government, and the great development of law, but also as exemplars of a variety of forms of government, good and bad, and to the virtues and vices of their assorted rulers as well. It is perhaps as well, then, that we turn to men who exemplified Roman virtue long after Cicero had despaired over the decay of virtue and who demonstrated that even emperors could seek justice in their rule.

Socrates and Plato had dreamed of rule by philosopher kings, and Roman emperors came close to fulfilling some aspects of that dream. Edward Gibbon wrote that "If a man were called upon to fix the period in the history of the world during which the condition of the human race was most happy and prosperous, he would without hesitation name that which elapsed from the accession of Nerva to the death of Aurelius. Their united reigns are possibly the only period of history in which the happiness of a great people was the sole object of government."[128] It may not have been the sole object of the government, but it was certainly a major one. The years involved were A.D. 96–180. The rulers were: Nerva, who ruled from 96–98; Trajan ruled from 98–117; Hadrian from 117 to 138; Antoninus Pius from 138–161; and Marcus Aurelius from 161–180. One of the reasons why these rulers may appear so benign and devoted to justice is the contrast between those who came before and immediately after them. Rome had to all intents and purposes become an empire by the middle of the first century B. C. Its territories extended from Asia Minor to North Africa to Spain and Britain and deep into the continent of Europe. Those who ruled could properly be called emperors, though in the period under consideration the rule was styled *principate*. In any case, they were monarchs or kings. Those who ruled from A.D. 14–96 were mostly despots; seven of the ten died violent deaths. Terror often held sway in Rome and parts of Italy during those years. Commodus, who followed the philosophical rule of Marcus Aurelius, was a despot, if not worse. He was a brutal and violent man, was said to beat men to death with his club for no apparent purpose, was lustful and licentious, feared assassination, and had many of those around him put to death because he claimed they were part of a conspiracy to kill him. As frequently happened to tyrants, Commodus was finally assassinated, strangled to death by an athlete he kept to wrestle with him.

None of the five philosopher kings died violently by assassination. Their rules were generally of such character that they did not make bitter enemies and were respected or beloved by those around them. Hadrian was in such poor health in his last days that he tried to get his servants to kill him, but none would oblige. Nerva did get into trouble with some of his subjects, but it was because of his generosity rather than any intended offense. Among other conciliatory acts, he recalled Roman citizens who had been exiled by the despot Domitian, who preceded Nerva, and restored their property. The Praetorian Guard, who did not like his policies anyway, used his clemency toward Domitian's exile as a pretext for attacking Nerva's palace and making demands on him. Nerva bade the Guards to kill him then, but they declined. He finished his brief reign of 16 months and died a natural death.

Trajan, who succeeded Nerva, was a soldier, a military commander, who so far continued in his ways that he made territorial conquests and expanded the empire. Even so, he was a just and honest ruler; he lowered taxes, kept, and made public, receipts and expenditures, consulted with the Senate before making significant changes, and took care not to punish innocent men who had been charged with offenses. He undertook a grandiose building program in the capital at Rome. His military struggles and administrative and building undertakings finally wore him down after 19 years, and he died a natural death.

Hadrian was probably the most versatile and brilliant of all the Roman emperors. He was much more a man of peace than his predecessor, and reduced and consolidated the boundaries of the empire rather than expanding them. His generosity was personal as well as state policy. "He visited the sick, helped the unfortunate, extended the existing charities to orphans and widows, and was a generous patron to artists, writers, and philosophers."[129] Among his many attainments, Hadrian was a singer, dancer, harpist, a writer, and something of an intellectual. In his many decrees, he tried to protect the weak from the strong, slaves from their masters, and tenants from their landlords.

Unlike most emperors, Hadrian vowed to visit all the numerous provinces in his empire. Thus, he visited what is now France and Germany, then took ship for Britain, from which he went on to spend the winter in Spain. Later, he journeyed to Ephesus in what is now Turkey, visited many cities on the eastern Mediterranean, and returned to Greece to winter in Athens. Hadrian then outdid himself in building. He refurbished the city of Athens, so to speak, and also built a number of new structures. Rome was also the scene of much building and restoration during his rule. He even visited the Holy City of Jerusalem, which had fallen into such desolation that he made large changes there in the hope of reviving it. It was said that the Roman Empire had never known such prosperity as during Hadrian's rule.

Antoninus Pius ruled for twenty-three years that were so free of major changes, of large scale warfare, or public disturbances that his rule was more like a period of rest and relaxation than a period of imperial grandeur. He was a man of such modest and retiring habits that he counted it a loss to become emperor and be surrounded by pomp and circumstance. When he became emperor, Antoninus gave all his wealth to the public treasury, and at the end of his reign there was a large surplus in the treasury. It was said of him that he had hundreds of friends and no enemies. Truth to tell, he was not a philosopher, for he did not have great learning, but the benevolent actions testified to his deep wisdom.

Marcus Aurelius, his successor, by contrast, was indeed a man of learning and a philosopher. In the course of growing up he had seventeen tutors: four in grammar, four in rhetoric, one in law, and eight in philosophy. He might have made a career of philosophy if he had not been chosen to rule an empire. One book by him, entitled *Meditations,* is ample proof that he was a Stoic in philosophy. Although he was a philosopher king, he made it clear that was not to be taken in quite the Platonic sense. "Never hope," he wrote, "to realize Plato's Republic. Let it be sufficient that you have in some degree ameliorated [made better the life of] mankind, and do not think such improvement a matter of small importance. Who can change the opinions of men? And without a change of sentiments what can you make but reluctant slaves and hypocrites?"[130] He said also that he had been taught (and presumably accepted) "the idea of a state in which there is the same law for all, a polity of equal rights and freedom of speech, and the idea of a kingly government that most of all respects the freedom of the governed."[131]

Marcus Aurelius proposed to rule by example, to treat all with dignity, and to bring justice to his empire. Much that he tried to do we would affirm was admirable, such as increasing the court days and shortening trials, requiring that gladiators use foils on their weapons, and reducing public expenditures on games, but it hardly increased his popularity. Moreover, his period of rule was made difficult by war in many places and the spread of a great pestilence or plague. In the wake of the plague which spread over much of the empire came famine to some provinces. Even so, Marcus continued the war on his frontiers successfully, and turned an empire virtually intact over to his son Commodus. The reigns of the philosopher kings had come to an end.

Just as the world could not permanently forget the legacy of Classical Greece, even the destruction of Barbarian armies could not exorcise the memory of Rome. The Greeks survived in their literature and architecture above everything else. The Romans survived in their rhetoric, the masterful Latin language, the idea of a republic, and the idea of a world unified under law. Greece bequeathed reason and the inception of natural law; Rome bequeathed the law of nations and a more vivid conception of natural law.

Both the Classical Greeks and Romans were pagans, at least through Christian eyes, but their best thinkers were reaching for a conception of one God, before whom their pagan deities were no account. The impact of Rome on the founding of the United States was almost as direct as if Rome had been a much admired contemporary country. They knew aspects of it well from history.

d. The Middle Ages

The impact of the Middle Ages on the formation of American government was much more indirect than was that of Rome, despite the fact that the Middle Ages were nearer in time. There were two main reasons for this. The first, perhaps the main one, was that Medieval Europe was Roman Catholic, and America was settled, and a government of the Union was formed, in the wake of the Protestant Reformation. Most Americans of the 18th century were Protestant, and their churches had taken shape out of a more or less profound rejection of Catholicism. Thus, they were little inclined to be taught by Catholics. On top of this, the Reformation had been preceded and accompanied by a Renaissance which exalted the learning of Greece and Rome above that of the Middle Ages, which were often referred to indiscriminately as the Dark Ages. Since the Renaissance had so revived the memories of Greece and Rome, they seemed almost to be more recent than the Middle Ages. At any rate they were better known, and more favorably, to the Founders of the United States.

Even so, the Middle Ages was a major link from the Ancient world to the modern one. Medieval culture was the result of a mingling of the Roman, Germanic, and Christian. All of Europe became or was Christian during the Middle Ages, formally, loosely, or devoutly, as the case might be. During its first three centuries, Christians were often persecuted by Roman rulers. Beyond that, they were sometimes persecuted under local laws and rulers. Nonetheless, Christianity continued to spread, and the number of Christians continued to increase. The Emperor Constantine of Rome adopted Christian symbols on his battle shields in A.D. 313, and in the ensuing years first established toleration of Christianity, apparently converted to Christianity himself, began to favor Christians at law. Constantine himself presided at the Council of Nicea in 325, and to all intents and purposes Christianity became the religion of the Roman Empire.

That was in the early 4th century. But the rise of Christianity was accompanied by the continuing decline of the Roman Empire. As the strength of Rome waned, the onslaught of Germanic and other armies from without became more pressing. It is now customary to say that Rome fell to the Barbarians in A.D. 476. In that year, the Roman emperor Romulus was replaced by the Barbarian ruler Odoacer. This event, however, was anticlimactic, for Italy had suffered invasion after invasion in the course of the 5th century, and Rome had been repeatedly sacked. The will no longer existed to rule from Rome. Since the time of Constantine, there had usually been two seats for the empire, one at Rome, the other at Constantinople. The relics of an empire in the east continued to be ruled from Constantinople for nearly a thousand years. It was known as the Byzantine Empire during the Middle Ages. The Roman Empire in the West, involving most of Europe, had now broken down.

The significance of all this for developments in government, and for modern thought, can be viewed mainly from the point of view of the institutions and ideas which took hold in the West in the following centuries. The breakup of the Roman Empire resulted in a quite different set of political arrangements. As the rule of law broke down and any kind of widespread political authority was uncertain, men reverted to self-defense and turned toward personal relationships with others to defend themselves and their property. The eventual result was the feudalism that prevailed generally in Europe from the 11th century onward. During the Dark Ages that preceded the 11th century the political situation was much too unstable for generalization. Under feudalism every man was supposed to have an overlord, in theory, at least. This overlord, whatever his title might be, owed protection to his vassals, who in turn owed him their military services, among other things. Much of political thought in the Middle Ages had to do with the duties, responsibilities and powers of those within the feudal system.

Of course, the memory of the unity, law, and greatness of Rome did not entirely die out in the Middle Ages. From time to time there were attempts to revive an empire on the order of Rome. Thus, Charlemagne—or Charles the Great—formed an empire in the 9th century. And there were periodic attempts to form a Holy Roman Empire in the High Middle Ages, but none ever succeeded fully or for very long. There was a logic in the feudal system for an emperor over all of Christian Europe. If everyone should have an overlord, then princes and kings should have an overlord as well. But logic never fully won out over power, if it ever does.

In any case, there was an institution which stood for the unity of Western Christendom during the Middle Ages. It was the Roman Catholic Church. Moreover, its unity was focused within a single head, that of the Bishop of Rome, the Pope. There were bishops of Rome, nay popes, of sorts, before, but they became increasingly important from the fourth century onward. It was a master stroke to locate the head of the Catholic Church at Rome, for the Western church thus inherited much of the prestige and glory that had been Rome. It was not surprising, either, that peoples used to looking to Rome for leadership should look there for church leadership as well. The Papacy may have been located there more to fill a vacuum than through any deliberate planning. However that may be, there were other reasons for churchmen to look to Rome for guidance. As one historian points out, "The church at Rome was the oldest and wealthiest in the West. Its founder was believed to be the apostle Peter, and its traditions included both Peter and Paul. . . . These factors were enough to make Rome a leading church whose bishops enjoyed great influence. In addition the personal ability of the Roman bishops was impressive. They were, with few exceptions, remarkably conservative and orthodox in doctrinal matters."[132] In addition, the Roman pontifs claimed their leading power from Peter, to whom Jesus had said: "Thou art Peter, and upon this rock I will build my church. . . ."

Two popes in the early Middle Ages went far toward establishing the dominance of the church by the bishop of Rome. The first of these was Pope Leo the Great (440–461). Leo had such presence that he turned back Attila the Hun from his march on Rome. He got the temporal ruler, Valentinian III, to issue an edict in 445 making it a matter of law that the pope had jurisdiction over all bishops in Western Europe. Imperial officials were ordered to enforce obedience to church authority from Rome. Gregory I, the Great (590–604), brought great administrative skill to the task of consolidating the leadership of Rome over Western Christendom.

Out of the prestige and influence of the Roman Catholic Church in the Middle Ages, and its contest with the temporal (earthly) powers, a doctrine may have been partly shaped which had great influence on America. The doctrine is that of the separation and balance of powers. Another doctrine less well articulated in America may also have had its inception in the Middle Ages, that of the independence of the church of the powers of the state. At any rate, there was no doctrine more influential on the makers of our Constitution than that of the separation and balance of powers. Pope Gelasius I (492–496) made one of the earliest formulations regarding the distinct powers of the church and the state. He held that spiritual powers belonged to the church and that temporal powers belonged to secular rulers. These constitute separate realms, but when either of them enters the other realm he comes under the authority of the rulers of that realm. However, Gelasius maintained, as later churchmen would, that spiritual authority is ultimately superior to temporal, though both owed their power to God.

It should come as no surprise, of course, that theoretical statements often did not govern in actual affairs. There was often contests and sometimes vigorous confrontations between the rulers of the two realms. There was hardly any doubt that in a contest of arms between the clergy and the temporal authority, the earthly rulers would win. After all, they had the armed forces, while the clergy were forbidden to draw blood. Even so, the church had powers, authority, and influence, which could sometimes bring force onto the battlefield on its behalf. It could ex-communicate rulers and lay their realms under interdict, as well as free their subjects from obedience to them. Unpopular kings might find themselves at war with their erstwhile vassals through the workings of the powers of the church.

There were many statements made about the powers of both church and state. For example, Charlemagne "commanded that every man in his whole

kingdom, whether ecclesiastic or layman, and each one according to his vow
and occupation, should now promise to him as emperor the fidelity which he
had previously promised to him as king; and all of those who had not yet
made their promise likewise, down to those who were twelve years old."[133]
Nor did Charlemagne leave much doubt that it was his view that his authority extended over the pope himself. He wrote to Pope Leo III that "It is
my part to defend everywhere the Holy Church of Christ by armed force, on
the one hand against pagan raids and devastation of the unbelievers; on the
other hand by the diffusion of the Catholic Faith. It is your part, most holy
father, . . . to help by your prayers the victory of our arms." Otherwise, he
instructed the pope to "live virtuously and . . . observe the holy canons."[134]

Popes in the High Middle Ages, however, often attempted to assert their
authority over kings and emperors or other princes. The most outspoken and
tenacious of these was Innocent III (1198–1216). He said, "Princes have
power in earth, priests over the soul. As much as the soul is worthier than
the body, so much worthier is the priesthood than the monarchy. . . . The
Lord Jesus Christ has set up one ruler over all things as his universal vicar,
and all things in heaven, earth and hell bow to the knee to Christ, so should
all obey Christ's vicar, that there be one flock and one shepherd."[135]

The most thoroughgoing claim that the spiritual power was superior to the
temporal and that the Church was over and above kings and emperors was
made by Pope Boniface VIII in 1302. He wrote: "Both swords, the spiritual
and the material . . . are in the power of the Church . . . ; the one by the hand
of the priest, the other by the hand of kings and knights, but at the will and
sufferance of the priest. One sword, moreover, ought to be under the other,
and the temporal authority to be subjected to the spiritual. . . . Therefore if
the earthly power err it shall be judged by the spiritual power. . . ." He went
on to affirm that if the highest spiritual power on earth shall err, it is to be
judged by God alone.[136]

Probably the most dramatic contest, though there were many others,
between spiritual and temporal authorities occurred between Pope Gregory
VII and the German emperor, Henry IV, in the mid-1070s. The main issue
that brought their dispute to a head was that of "lay investiture." Gregory
maintained that the authority to appoint and confer the symbols and authority of office on high churchmen, especially bishops, belonged to the pope.
By contrast, German emperors, as well as some other rulers, had long
appointed bishops and invested them with lands and other property, as well
as the symbols of their office. Rulers argued that these men were, in effect,
feudal vassals, and fell under their authority. Indeed, Henry argued that his
power came from God. Gregory VII set out to put an end to such lay
investiture and notified Henry to that effect. Henry IV gathered such of his
bishops as would come about him and got them to renounce obedience to the
pope. Henry sent him a message which was intended to depose Gregory VII,
addressing him in this way, "Henry king not through usurpation but through

the holy ordination of God . . . [bidding him to] descend, descend, to be damned throughout the ages."[137]

Gregory VII received the message in February, 1076, during a synod being held at Rome. The bishops there assembled excommunicated Henry's high churchmen who had issued their decree. Gregory then proceeded to excommunicate Henry, to anathematize and depose him, and to release his subjects from obedience to him. The influence of the papacy, or at least Gregory VII, was much greater than that of Henry IV. In any case, it was an Age of Faith, and the spiritual bonds were stronger than the temporal ones. Freed by the pope from their feudal obligations to Henry IV, many of his former subjects revolted, and he found little support anywhere. Thus, the once proud emperor of Germany set out in the winter 1076–1077 to reach the pope in Italy. In January, 1077, he found Gregory at Canossa, a castle in Tuscany. There on January 25, he stood outside the castle, and, according to Gregory's report, in the severest winter in memory, "He presented himself at the gate of the castle, barefoot and clad only in wretched woolen garments, beseeching us with tears to grant him absolution and forgiveness. This he continued to do for three days, while all those about us were moved to compassion at his plight and interceded for him with tears and prayers. . . . At length we removed the excommunication from him, and received him again into the bosom of Holy Mother Church."[138]

Gregory's victory was short lived, for Henry IV restored to power exacted his revenge through conquest. Innocent III exerted much more authority over kingly rulers a century later than would have been possible for Gregory. In any case, the claims to superiority of either popes or emperors is not the main point here. The point is that tension between these powers along with their claims served to balance and restrain both church and state. In fact, church rulers did in various ways limit kings and princes: they limited wars by establishing certain times when there should be no fighting. Religious leaders crowned and thus gave legitimacy to the rule of kings and princes. Church buildings served as a refuge from arbitrary kingly power. The Roman Catholic Church proclaimed its independence of temporal rulers, yet it called upon them to enforce many of its decisions. Kings could thus abate the activities of the Church refusing to enforce unjust decisions. The elements of the separation and balance of powers were there in this Medieval tension.

In general, though, the Middle Ages did not give rise to many political institutions which appealed to Americans. When men of the Middle Ages looked backward to ancient Rome, it was to the empire rather than the republic. Both direct democracy and representative government were very nearly foreign to the Medieval mind. Inequality was deeply imbedded in the hierarchical practices of the Middle Ages. Different classes had different rights and privileges, but ruling belonged to an hereditary aristocracy. Slavery had been commonplace both in Greece and Rome, and it was abolished in Christian Europe in the Middle Ages, but it was at least partially replaced by serfdom. Councils and synods of church leaders and of aristocrats provided the major examples of rule by a few in the Middle Ages. Monarchy was profoundly in accord with the spirit of the age.

The major intellectual challenge of Christian leaders in the later years of the Roman Empire and early Middle Ages was what to do about Greek and Roman thought. It was, after all, pagan, as already noted, as was virtually all of the existing literature and methods of learning. There were those, of course, who favored rejecting and avoiding all of pagan philosophy and learning as a snare and a delusion for Christians. For example, Turtullian, a prominent churchman in the early 3rd century, argued that Christians could obtain all knowledge from Scripture. But the most influential churchmen from the 4th century on were not of that persuasion. They tended to agree with the great Christian and Greek thinker, Origen, that Christians needed all the learning possible not only to explain their own faith but also to refute the pagans. Christians were, after all, engaged in capturing the minds of men as well as their hearts. In any case, Christians of the 4th century were often educated and trained in pagan philosophy before they became Christian. Their task was not to dispense with their learning, but to turn it to Christian ends.

That was the view of the three outstanding church leaders and mentors of the 4th century: St. Ambrose, St. Jerome, and St. Augustine. They were not only learned in pagan philosophy, but in Greek Christian thought which was far superior in intellectual content to that in the West, at least until these three men had their impact. Ambrose (around 340–407) came to the fore as Bishop of Milan. Born to an aristocratic Roman family, he had received an excellent education in earlier Roman thought before he became a Christian. In addition to turning his classical education to the service of Christianity through powerful sermons and hymns, he worked vigorously and effectively to establish the independence of the church from the Roman government. This was of critical importance, for the Roman government had traditionally used religion as an adjunct of the state. He freed Christianity from any such subservience by proclaiming that the authority of the church was superior to that of the state. He brought the Stoic ethics within the framework of Christianity while insisting that the first loyalty and duty of the Christian is to God and not to state. Such Christian teachers helped to break the hold of the state on the life of men, which had been the legacy of the ancient world.

Jerome (around 340–419) was born into a Christian family but was nonetheless well educated in pagan literature. Indeed, so attached did he become to pagan works that he says he had a vision in which he appeared before the throne of God where he asserted that he was a Christian, and was told, "Thou liest; thou art no Christian, but a Ciceronian; where thy treasure is, there thy heart is also."[139] He promised to give up the pagan classics, but while he never quite managed to do that he did use his great learning in the service of Christianity. His signal achievement was a new translation of the Bible into Latin, a version known as the Vulgate, which eventually became the approved Bible for Roman Catholics. He was also a scourge to ignorant Christians in his time. He said that "only doctors practice medicine and only carpenters build houses, but searching the meaning of Scripture is the one art that everybody is sure he possesses; it is bad enough to teach what you do not know, but worse not even to be aware of what you do not know."[140]

Augustine (354–430) was the greatest of the thinkers of the early Christian church and generally ranked as one of the major philosophers in Western Civilization. His studies as a youth and young man were more eclectic than thorough, though his intellectual interest was keen, and he did become well versed in the pagan thought of Classical Antiquity. Although his mother was a Christian, Augustine was quite a libertine in his youth and was only finally converted to Christianity in his thirties. He is best known for his *Confessions* and *The City of God*. *Confessions* deals with his early life of the flesh, as he would have called it, when he reveled in a sensual life, and his conversion to Christianity. So wild was his life before conversion, as he described it, and so shaking was his salvation, that he ever believed and taught that it was only by the grace of God that the will of man could be drawn to follow the right path. *The City of God* was especially written to refute the charge that Christianity undermined the Roman Empire and was responsible for its fall. But it is much more than this. It is a kind of universal history of struggle between good and evil, or between the City of God and the Earthly City.

In general, Augustine did not contribute much to political thought or institutions. He did labor mightily to defend Christian doctrine from various heresies as well as from pagans. Indeed, of Augustine, Ambrose, and Jerome, one historian has said: "the intellectual opposition of a waning paganism had not only been met, but many of its philosophical concepts, especially Stoic ethics and Neo-Platonic metaphysics, had been assimilated into Christian thought. The Church was heir to Rome not only in Ecclesiastical organization; the Fathers of the Church incorporated the intellectual heritage of Rome into Christian thought."[141]

Reason was already giving way to the dominance of faith, however, in the works of Ambrose, Jerome, and Augustine. In the ensuing centuries, faith would occupy the field. That is not to say that men ever entirely cease to use reason, but its use can become so simplified that it does not rise to capture complex thought. Nor did the men known as church fathers do much by way of passing on the conception of natural law. But from the 6th through the 10th centuries matters were much worse than that in Western Europe. The successive invasions of barbarians not only destroyed much of the literature, the institutions, and the achievements in general of the civilization which they overran. Those who had an interest in such things had only a couple of Plato's works and very little from Aristotle. Reading and writing became a rare accomplishment outside the clergy, and many of them had only a rudimentary knowledge. The culture in general reverted to such a primitive level that not only were there no advances in philosophy taking place, but what had earlier been developed was almost lost.

By the 11th century, Europe was on the rise once again: order over considerable kingdoms was widespread; trade was revived and spreading; interest in other places and other times was mounting; and there was prosperity here and there in the cities once more. At least, there were some cities emerging once again. A revival of learning took place in Europe in the 12th and 13th centuries. It would later be overshadowed, at least in the minds of moderns, by the Renaissance in Italy in the 15th and 16th century, but it was a renaissance in its own right, as a good many scholars in the 20th century have affirmed. The revival of towns and growth of trade and cities set the stage for this revival. Many works of ancient writers became available in the 12th and 13th centuries, from Moslem and other sources.

Some men began to assert the role of reason in the discovery and advancement of knowledge once again. The rise of great universities, such as the one at Paris, Bologna, and Oxford, provided centers for the honing of intellectual skills and the spread of new techniques. A key figure in working to revive the emphasis upon reason was Peter Abelard, who had his great success as a lecturer at the University of Paris. His most influential work is called *Yes and No* in English translation. He brought together the thought of the church fathers on a variety of philosophical questions and showed that they were often not in agreement with one another (hence, his yes and no). Thus, he raised doubts about the authorities that were usually relied upon to resolve theological questions. To raise doubts was clearly his intent, for he wrote that "By doubting we are led to inquiry; and from inquiry we perceive the truth."[142] In one way or another reason would probably have to be brought into play to resolve the difficulties.

Peter Lombard took the method beyond Abelard in his manual of philosophy, whose title translates into English as the *Four Books of Sentences*. Not only did Lombard list the various opinions of but he also attempted to harmonize these writers by the use of reason. This method—the citation of a variety of authorities on particular questions, the pointing out of apparent contradictions between them, and pointing out a way that was supposed to resolve the difficulties—became the Medieval mode for philosophical writing and lecturing. It is known as *scholasticism*, or the method of the school-men.

The political thought of at least two philosophers in the high Middle Ages needs to be discussed. The first of these was John of Salisbury, who was born around 1117 in England. He treats aspects of politics more or less fully in his book *Polycraticus*. His writings were in the Roman and Christian traditions, or, more precisely, Christianized Roman thought, but he was thoroughly Medieval in his emphasis upon monarchy as the proper form of government. He said that "The place of the head in the body of the commonwealth is filled by the prince, who is subject only to God and to those who exercise His office and represent Him on earth, even as in the human body the head is quickened and governed by the soul."[143] That is, the king, prince, or monarch is the head of the government, but in his rule he is subject to God and his representative, i.e., the pope, on earth.

However, John did not elaborate the means by which the king would be physically limited in the exercise of power. He believed that the monarch should, of course, rule with reason and moderation for the good of those whom he ruled. And, if a ruler should depart from these precepts, if he should become a tyrant, it might become necessary for people to take power into their own hands. Certainly, John said, "if the power of the ruler opposes the divine commandments, and wishes to make me share in its war against God, then with unrestrained voice I answer that God must be preferred before any man on earth. . . . To kill a tyrant is not merely lawful, but right and just." But he did later modify this claim by the proviso that "the slayer is not bound by fealty to the tyrant."[144] Since these were the people most likely to recognize and slay a tyrant, John of Salisbury was clearly guarding against widespread tyrannicide by his qualification. It should be recalled, however, that popes could and sometimes did relieve subjects from their oaths to kings and princes.

Thomas Aquinas (1225–1274) was the most important philosopher as well as political thinker since Augustine. The great influence on Thomas's work was Aristotle, but many of the works of other writers from Classical Antiquity were available to him in the 13th century also. Indeed, other enthusiasts about Aristotle and the Greek thinkers preceded Thomas in Europe. The most notable of these was Albertus Magnus or Albert the Great (the only philosopher ever honored by that adjective). He was called "great," in part at least, because of the sheer volume of his writings. He not only studied at length the surviving major works of Aristotle, but wrote extensive commentaries on them. His aim, no doubt, was to Christianize the thought of Aristotle and to bring Christian thought up to the level of Aristotle, if that was possible. Although Thomas was born in Italy and studied in college first at the University of Naples, he came eventually to Paris, where he studied under Albertus Magnus and was infused by his admiration for Aristotle. When Albert was transferred to Cologne, Thomas followed him there to continue his studies. But he returned to Paris later, this time to teach and to write.

The political thought of Thomas Aquinas was cast very much in the classical mode. Thus, like the Greeks, he held that rule may be by one, by the few, or by the many. He held, of course, that God is the source of all power, but that he has vested this power, originally, in those to be governed. They may, at least originally, have that power wielded by one, a few, or many. He thought monarchy might be best, since it was potentially the most efficient. He put it this way, in somewhat stilted terms:

The more efficacious [i.e., effective] . . . a government is in keeping the . . . peace, the more useful it will be. For we call that more useful which leads the better to the [desired] end. Now it is manifest that what is itself one can more efficaciously bring about unity than several: just as the most efficacious cause of heat is that which is by its nature hot. Therefore, the rule of one man is more useful than the rule of many.[145]

If what is wanted from government is determined by how efficient the affairs of government are managed, there is little doubt that monarchy would be best. Clearly, one person can make the decisions and direct affairs more efficiently than a few or many. But would it not be more likely that a government by one would be dictatorial, corrupt, despotic, and tyrannical? Might he not more readily use the government for his own selfish ends than taking care of the common well being of his subjects? Thomas was aware of these possibilities, but it did not appear to him to be so great a threat as it did to our Founding Fathers. First, he thought the power of the monarch would be limited because he did not have spiritual or religious matters in his care. These things were in the care of priests and ultimately of the Roman Pontiff, and they would limit monarchs.

Thomas thought that the people would limit the king also, since their approval was the immediate source of his power. And they could, if the situation warrants it, reclaim the power for themselves. Thomas said:

If to provide itself with a king belong to the right of any multitude, it is not unjust that the king set up by that multitude be destroyed or his power restricted, if he tyrannically abuse the royal power. It must not be thought that such a multitude is acting unfaithfully in deposing the tyrant, even though it had previously subjected itself to him in perpetuity; because he has deserved that the covenant with his subjects should not be kept, since in ruling the multitude, he did not act faithfully as the office of a king demands.[146]

Like John of Salisbury, Thomas Aquinas does not describe any mechanism by which the "multitude" might depose or restrict the power of the monarch. He may well have believed that the superior numbers of the multitude might be able to persuade, intimidate, or force a king to yield. It did happen a goodly number of times in the Middle Ages that the vassals of a king would take arms against him to limit his powers or force concessions from, or, indeed, to depose him.

There was, however, yet another means emphasized by Thomas by which monarchs might be limited, i.e., by the necessity of ruling by law. He gave renewed emphasis to natural law theory and made it central to his political theories. There are three kinds of law, according to Thomas: divine law, natural law, and man made laws, what are in our time referred to as positive law. Thomas relied heavily on reason in his thinking; thus, he defined law in its most general sense as "nothing else but an ordinance of reason for the common good, promulgated by him who has the care of the community."[147] While all enduring law issues from God, that which specifically is distinguished as divine is the law known by revelation, as in the Scriptures, or other more direct means. Natural law is the law found in the nature of things put there by the Creator and discernible by reason. Man made law is the particular law laid down by rulers to apply to a particular people in their situation and time, that is, positive law.

There is for Thomas Aquinas, as for the Greeks, especially Aristotle, whose thought he adapted to Christian ends, an underlying order informing all things. And there is an order by which men and things may move or be moved toward their ends. Man made law, to be just and proper, must be a reflection of this underlying order. Unjust laws are not truly laws at all, and are not binding upon people. Thus, if a ruler makes arbitrary decrees which are by their nature unjust, he exceeds the limits of his power once again and is properly subject to being deposed or restrained. One of the great debates of the Middle Ages was whether or not the king is under the law or above the law. Is the king subject to his own decrees? In Thomas's system, he is clearly subject to divine law and falls under the spiritual authority for its enforcement. He is clearly subject to natural law, as are all men and things. Decree as he will, his voice cannot still the waves of the ocean nor stay the sun in its course. He lies under the same requirements of achieving ends by reasonable methods as does everyone else. Moreover, since just laws are a reflection of the underlying order, they would apply to him as to the others in his kingdom.

Beyond Thomas Aquinas, there was a major revival of interest in law in the 12th and 13th centuries. "In the twelfth century a remarkable revival of the study of Roman law began at Bologna and soon spread elsewhere. The leading spirit was that of Irnerius (d. 1130), the first of a series of great commentators on the Code of Justinian. Irnerius' school . . . whose main interest was in achieving a correct understanding of Roman law, was followed, in the thirteenth century by a school . . . who . . . began to apply its principles to the social, political, and legal questions of their own time." In so doing, "the study of the Roman law began to modify the old ideas [Germanic] of law as custom, and this brought back the Roman idea that it was possible to create new law. Finally, it revived the Roman idea of natural law as a norm for the interpretation and enforcement of all positive law."[148] This latter is also much the same position as Thomas Aquinas had reached.

Chapter 4
The Development of Modern Political Thought

A great deal happened between the 14th and the 18th century to make Classical Antiquity seem more immediate and relevant to Americans than the Middle Ages. Indeed, to them, and so far as they considered the matter at all, the Middle Ages was hardly distinct from the Dark Ages, a backward time when people were dominated by superstition and religious idolatry. Papism, as they were inclined to refer to the Roman Catholic system, was generally something to be shunned rather than emulated or borrowed from. True, Americans became more tolerant in religious matters in the course of the 18th century, but they were still mostly descendants of Englishmen who had broken from the Catholic Church in the 16th century. Many of them had gone further, disavowing those relics of Catholicism they perceived in the Church of England, and forming or joining other denominations.

But there were more than simply religious changes in the early modern period. Moreover, as far as that goes, the Roman Catholic Church had made some signal changes in the middle of the 16th century, changes which have been well characterized as Counter-Reformation or Catholic Reformation. Beyond these, there were changes in outlook promoted by new emphases and new discoveries. It would be hard to overestimate the impact of the invention of the printing press in the mid-15th century, which made it so much easier to spread ideas and information. The horizons of Europe were greatly expanded by the discovery of the Americas and by sailing around the world. The thrust toward unity which held such sway over Medieval thought gave way to a quest for and reveling in diversity. The great changes of this era can be covered under the following topics: the Renaissance, the Reformation, and the Age of Reason.

a. The Renaissance

The Italian Renaissance, which was concentrated in the 15th and 16th centuries, was in some ways a continuation of the renaissance that had occurred in the 12th and 13th centuries. There had been a heightened interest in the language, manuscripts, and literature of ancient Greece and Rome in the earlier centuries. This interest continued and mounted in the 14th and later centuries. This latter interest can be well illustrated by the lives and activities of Francesco Petrarch (1304–1374) and Giovanni Boccaccio (1313–1375). Some would date the beginning of the Italian Renaissance with their meeting in 1350, but it is surely the case that something so imprecise as the Renaissance had no such precise beginning or end. Be that as it may, these two men were early exemplars of the outlook and activities associated with this movement.

Petrarch's interest in Roman and Greek materials is described in the following: "He inspired his friend to search for lost manuscripts of Latin or Greek literature, to copy ancient inscriptions, and collect ancient coins, as precious documents of history. . . . [O]n his travels he sought and bought classic texts . . . ; he transcribed unpurchasable manuscripts with his own hand; and at home he hired copyists to live with him. He gloried in a Homer sent him from Greece, begged the sender for a copy of Euripides . . . [and] knew from references in these works that numberless masterpieces had been forgotten or mislaid; and it became his passion to recover them."[149]

He inspired Boccaccio with a like passion for recovering ancient writings. "Urged on by Petrarch, [Boccaccio] collected classical manuscripts, rescued book XI–XVI from the *Annals,* and books I–V of the *Histories,* of Tacitus from their oblivion in the neglected library of Monte Cassino; restored the texts of Martial and Ausonius, and contrived to give Homer to the Western world."[150] In addition to recovering manuscripts, Boccaccio learned Greek and wrote many manuals and books to acquaint Europeans with the classics.

On the surface, the work of Boccaccio, Petrarch, and those who followed their lead may not appear to differ much from what had been going on in the Middle Ages. It did, however. For one thing the Medieval system was in decline and beginning to lose its hold and sway in the 14th and 15th century. Perhaps the best sign of this decline was that the reigning pope forsook Rome and took up residence at Avignon in France in the early 14th century. This continued for over a century, though in 1378 a competing pope was crowned and resided in Rome, so there were two popes from 1378 to 1417. During this period the unity of the Church was riven, since the pope at Avignon was under the sway of the French king. Also, the feudal unity of Europe was being broken by the rise of nation-states. What this meant, in effect, was that the rule of monarchs was becoming territorial rather than based on personal loyalties. One of the best illustrations of this was the war between England and France which lasted—intermittently—from 1337–1453, and has been called the Hundred Year's War. Undoubtedly, too, the Black Death contributed to breaking the hold of feudalism and the guild system. It was a plague which swept over Europe during the years 1348–1350—killing as much as a third or more of the population.

The major change in the attitude toward Classical Antiquity and its literature was that it was no longer being Christianized, so to speak. Albertus
Magnus and Thomas Aquinas had labored mightily to fit the thought of
ancient philosophers into a Christian framework, to make it subservient to
Christianity. By contrast, Petrarch, Boccaccio, and those who came after,
studied and learned from them in their historical and pagan framework, so
far as they could. From the ancient Greeks and Romans they learned to
focus on life in this world. It was not that people in the Middle Ages had not
had an interest in life in this world. It was rather that it had been a narrow
and confined interest; it hardly extended to their literature, their art, their
music. Their broader concerns were spiritual, and hence in their thrust were
other worldly. Medieval towns and cities were dominated by the churches
and cathedrals, often with their spires pointed heavenward. That is symbolic. (Just as it is symbolic of our materialism and earthliness that the great
buildings of our cities are office building and centers of banking, insurance,
and trade.) Some have called Petrarch the first modern man. Will Durant has
written: "By common consent he was the first humanist, the first writer to
express with clarity and force the right of man to concern himself with this
life, to enjoy and augment its beauties, and to labor to deserve well of
posterity. He was the Father of the Renaissance."[151]

The new outlook has well been called humanism, an emphasis on human
concerns, on human reason, on human potentiality, on human individuality,
and a renewed interest in learning of the world about them. That is not to
suggest that men of the Renaissance became full fledged pagans; that was
exceedingly rare, if it happened at all. By and large, they remained con-
fessing Christians, though, as is more usual than not, some were Christian
in name more than deed, some devoutly so, and many went through the
forms. Nor was Renaissance humanism an earlier version of "secular humanism," which has emerged in the past century or so, for the latter is more
or less blatant atheism. Renaissance humanism might be called Christian
humanism, but with the Christian no longer having so dominant a role. It did
give the secular a larger, and sometimes dominant, role in the affairs of
men.

At any rate, the Renaissance spirit was evinced in many ways. The age of
discovery in the late fifteenth and early 16th centuries flowed naturally from
it. There was great interest in other cultures, in other societies, and other
political ways. Trade took on a new life, as did travel. The focus on the
individual in people gave a new vitality to painting, sculpture, drama, and
literature as well. People who definitely evinced the Renaissance spirit in art
and literature included Leonardo da Vinci, Titian, Raphael, Michelangelo,
Erasmus, and Shakespeare. The ideal man of the Renaissance was a man of
a great variety of attainments and accomplishments. Probably, Leonardo da
Vinci approached as near to that ideal as anyone in this age of multifaceted
people. He was a superb painter, a prolific writer, though he started much

more than he ever finished, an inventor or conceiver of a great variety of devices, and had a consummate interest in the sciences. Most men, whether of the Renaissance or not, are not possessed of so much talent and ability as da Vinci, but we speak here of an ideal, of course.

The main concern here, however, is with developments in politics and political thought. In regard to changes in political institutions, it needs to be noted that the Protestant Reformation overlapped so much with the Renaissance that most of the political changes are in some degree also tied up with it. Nonetheless, some political developments more nearly belong to the Renaissance than with the Reformation. One of these, already mentioned in passing, was the breakup of what political unity there had been in Europe. France, England, and Spain had emerged as virtually sovereign nation-states by 1500. None of these admitted the exercise of temporal authority within their realm by any ruler from outside the territory of their kingdoms. Nor were they much inclined to allow the exercise of papal authority in their realms, as would be made clear within not too many years. As for German and Italian states, these were numerous and disinclined to attend to any imperial authority.

The other major Renaissance development was the absolutizing of the power and authority of the monarchs. The power of the nobles was broken in a number of realms. (That had been the result of the War of the Roses in England in the latter half of the 15th century.) This power was increasingly being replaced by appointees of the king, which resemble more a bureaucracy than what had gone before. This new bureaucracy was distinct not only in the skills men had for their office but in the fact that they were paid servants of those who ruled. One political writer gives an example of this in what happened when the Governor of Milan (who ruled for Charles V of Spain and the Empire) asked the officials to turn over a part of their earnings, or all of them, to make up for a deficiency in the treasury due to military reversals. "Their reply was curt and plain. We have only such wages for our offices as we deserve: they are not a bounty from His Majesty. If His Majesty and His Excellency the Governor are not satisfied with us and our work, our offices should be given to others. But so long as we hold them, we are receiving no more than is due us."[152] The main point, however, is that the power of the monarch was greatly enhanced by the dependence of his officials upon him.

The Renaissance was little noted for political thought during these years, and what there was did not have much direct impact on the founding of the United States, but there is a little that needs mentioning. It is even doubtful that Marsilius of Padua (1270–1342) would qualify as a man of the Renaissance, since his writings occurred in the first half of the 14th century. But they are not of a piece with Medieval writings either. He was greatly influenced by Aristotle in what he wrote, and he does not try to Christianize him either. He wrote a little book entitled *In Defence of Peace,* in which he advanced some ideas that have had great influence in the modern era, whether that influence came directly from him or not.

Marsilius argued that the authority for passing laws belongs "only to the whole body of the citizens or to the weightier part thereof." By this latter phrase, he says that "I mean to take into consideration the quantity and quality of the persons in that community over which the law is made."[153] In support of his argument, which seems to be that the greater part of the community should make the laws, is that those to whom they apply must be consulted and in some manner give their approval. If they have approved them, they will be most likely to observe the laws. He does not, however, ignore the fact that some men are more learned and discerning in the conceiving of laws. Instead, he affirms the truth of this, and says that such men should be assigned the "investigation, discovery, and examination of the . . . future laws or statutes. . . . After . . . the future laws have been discovered and diligently examined, they must be layed before the assembled whole body of citizens for their approval or disapproval, so that if any citizen thinks that something should be added, subtracted, changed, or completely rejected, he can say so, since in this way the law will be more usefully ordained. For . . . the less learned citizens can sometimes perceive something which must be corrected in a proposed law even though they could not have discovered the law itself. Also, the laws thus made by the hearing and consent of the entire multitude will be better observed, nor will anyone have any protest to make against them."[154] Thus, he proposes that the laws be approved and promulgated by the citizenry at large, or at least the "weightier" portion of them.

However, the people themselves do not directly rule, according to the plan of Marsilius. They do have the approval or disapproval of the laws by which they are to be governed. As to the execution of the laws, however, Marsilius agreed with Aristotle that monarchy would be best. Moreover, he thought it would be better if the monarch were elected by the vote of the citizenry, "for by the method of election alone is the best ruler obtained."[155] But whether the monarch was chosen by election or by heredity, he thought it would be a good rule if he applied and executed only the laws as they had been conceived and approved by the citizenry. "But since the ruler is a human being, he has understanding and desire, which may receive other forms, like false opinion or perverted desire or both, as a result of which he comes to the contraries of the things determined by the law."[156] In sum, if the ruler is allowed to do his will unchecked, he may well become arbitrary, despotic, and tyrannical.

That being the case, Marsilius saw clearly that there must be some power to restrain or punish, to bring him back to the observance of the laws. That power, he says, belongs to the legislator, which, for him, meant the citizenry or the "weightier" part of them. He appears to believe, however, that it would be better to appoint some one or a few persons (a court, perhaps, he does not say) to try him and decide his punishment. Marsilius does think to observe that it would be wise to suspend the ruler from his office during the time when he is being tried and corrected, so that there be no contest for dominance or power during this period.

Marsilius was aware, of course, that during the Middle Ages the rulers of the Catholic Church had stepped in to restrain and punish temporal rulers who were supposed to have exceeded their authority or become despotic. Not only did this occasion great disputes and disturbances, but Marsilius thought the spiritual powers were greatly exceeding their rightful authority. Regarding the power of the churchmen, Marsilius wrote: "For the office of coercive rulership over any individual of whatever condition he may be, or over any community or group, does not belong to the Roman or any other bishop, priest, or spiritual minister, as such."[157] It was both to remove the occasion for churchmen to intermeddle to restrain temporal rulers and to provide some authority which would have coercive authority to restrain rulers that Marsilius made the above proposals. It may be recalled that John of Salisbury had argued that it would be right to depose or kill a tyrant, he had not proposed any regular or legal way it might be done. Marsilius of Padua supplied that defect.

Marsilius did seem to be on the verge of promoting ideas remarkably similar to those that have occupied moderns. He clearly separated the legislative from executive function, though he had not conceived of an independent judiciary to deal with trials, nor did he exactly advance the idea of impeachment of public officials. The idea of a balance of powers, however, was clearly emerging. He did not, of course, invent the idea of the legislative power belonging to the citizenry, but he did advance it at a time when it had been largely abandoned. His ideas were closer to those of Aristotle than to those of John Locke, say, but the moderns could have claimed him at a later date.

Niccolo Machiavelli (1469–1527) was very much a man of the Renaissance, one that Marsilius could not have even conceived in his day. Machiavelli lived during the years when the Renaissance was at its peak in Italy; though in the last decade of his life the Protestant Reformation was sweeping over northern Europe, it had little or no impact on him. He was born in Florence, which had been the setting for the early flowering of the Renaissance, and he spent a goodly portion of his adult life officially involved in the intrigues and diplomacy of the city-states, principalities, and aspiring republics of a disunited Italy. A united Italy could only be a hope, an aspiration, or a dream during the lifetime of Machiavelli, but he did have a vision of how it might be accomplished. Indeed, as he turned to writing later in life, because his career in diplomacy had ended in charges of treason or something of the sort, he devoted himself to the task of describing the ways in which power might be exercised so as to unify Italy.

Machiavelli's two major works on politics were *The Prince* and *The*

Discourses on Titus Livy. It should be noted here that so far as he was influenced by the ancient classics, it was the Romans and not the Greeks. His political works are not in the least colored by either the metaphysics or idealism of the Greeks. More, he was so far gone in the character of Renaissance man that he repudiated Christian ethics. He accepted the ritual and liturgy of the Catholic Church and Christianity as providing the necessary religion for a successful state, but he thought the emphasis upon gentleness, humility and turning the other cheek was the opposite of what was needed to make a strong and resolute government.

The Discourses is the broader and more balanced work on statecraft, but *The Prince* is much the better known and almost certainly the more influential. *The Discourses* was an attempt to bring both ancient and modern history to bear on questions of how to govern effectively. The following is an example of how he did this:

> I believe it to be most true that it seldom happens that men rise from low condition to high rank without employing force or fraud. . . . Nor do I believe that force alone will ever be found to suffice. . . . Xenophon shows in his Life of Cyrus the necessity of deception to success; the first expedition of Cyrus against the king of Armenia is replete with fraud, and it was deceit alone, and not force, that enabled him to seize that kingdom. And Xenophon draws no other conclusion from it than that a prince who wishes to achieve great things must learn to deceive. Cyrus also practised a variety of deception upon Cyaxares, king of the Medes, his maternal uncle; and Xenophon shows that without these frauds Cyrus would never have achieved the greatness which he did attain. . . .[158]

He gives further examples from Italian and Roman history, and concludes that sometimes it may be possible to obtain power by deceit alone, it is never possible by the use of force alone.

The greater fame of *The Prince* may be owing to its directness and the absence of so many names and other historical references. In any case, both books have a similar message: that successful rulers are often deceitful, sometimes brutal, and whatever may appear to be the case, act for their own ends. Even so, Machiavelli held that it was necessary that a prince appear to have all sorts of good qualities. However,

> It is not essential that a Prince should have all the good qualities I have enumerated above, but it is most essential that he should seem to have them. As a matter of fact I will venture to affirm that if he has and invariably practises them all, they are hurtful, whereas the appearance of having them is useful. . . .
>
> And you are to understand that a Prince . . . cannot observe all those

rules of conduct in respect of which men are considered good; since he is often forced to act in opposition to good faith, charity, humanity, and religion in order to preserve his Princedom, he must therefore keep his mind ready to shift as the winds and tides of Fortune turn, and, as I have already said, ought not to leave good courses if he can help it but should know how to follow evil if he must.[159]

In short, a ruler must take whatever measures are necessary to gain and use power.

Did Machiavelli intend what he wrote to be taken literally and seriously? Or, was he merely satirizing the behavior of princes in Italy in the early 16th century? If he had written only *The Prince,* it might well be taken as a satire on contemporary political morality. After all, he did take as one of his exemplars Cesare Borgia, the illegitimate son of Pope Alexander VI, who was more than a little ill-famed for his underhanded behavior as a ruler. But he advanced similar ideas in *The Discourses,* which roamed over nearly all of history for examples and conclusions. Moreover, many rulers have taken him seriously over the centuries. As Will Durant has said: "Philosophers have been well nigh unanimous in condemning *The Prince* and statesmen in practising its precepts." This last may be an exaggeration, but as he points out further, "Charles V studied it carefully, Catherine de' Medici brought it to France, Henry III and Henry IV of France had it with them at their death, [Cardinal] Richelieu admired it, William of Orange kept it under his pillow as if to memorize it by osmosis."[160] Others who were drawn to his descriptions were the philosophers Francis Bacon and Spinoza, and the man who aspired to conquer much of the world, Napoleon Bonaparte.

If Machiavelli's political ideas affected directly the Founders of the United States, it has escaped the notice of historians. Whether they were aware of it or not, the Founders did set some of his ideas on their head. Machiavelli said, "Whoever would found a state and give it laws, must start by assuming that all men are bad and ever ready to display their vicious nature whenever they find occasion for it."[161] Some, perhaps many, of the Founders did not think so poorly of human nature as that, but they did incline to the view that the seductiveness of power and its corruption must be strenuously guarded against by limitations on the power itself. Thus, far from taking Machiavelli's prescriptions as the appropriate rules for statesmanship, they took them rather as a warning against entrusting overmuch power to those who govern.

Thomas More (1478–1535) was very much a man of the Renaissance, but his best known work, *Utopia,* differed much from what many would call the cynicism of Machievelli. He was born in London and came to manhood at a time when the Renaissance was in full flower in northern Europe. He was sent to Oxford University to study as a young man and there came in contact with such British Renaissance scholars as John Colet and Thomas Linacre.

Later, he became a good friend of the man who more than any other personified the Northern Renaissance, Erasmus, who was born a Dutchman but spent much of his life in England. It was these Renaissance influences, especially the interest in Classical Antiquity, which provided the background for More's *Utopia*.

Utopia means, literally, not a place, or rendered more freely, the land that is nowhere. More's *Utopia* was modeled after Plato's *Republic*, though, unlike Plato, who accepted men in general as they were, More imagined that they had been transformed by their changed conditions on his imaginary island. What has wrought the change in what men have supposed was human nature is the change in property ownership, and with it the changes in laws and government. More described the necessary change in conditions this way:

> I am persuaded, that till property is taken away there can be no equitable or just distribution of things, nor can the world be happily governed: for as long as that is maintained, the greatest and the far best part of mankind will be still oppressed with a load of cares and anxieties. [162]

How this will come about, he describes in more detail in the following:

> In all places it is visible, that while people talk of a commonwealth, every man seeks his own wealth; but there, where no man has any property, all men zealously pursue the good of the public: and, indeed, it is no wonder to see men act so differently; for in other commonwealths every man knows that unless he provides for himself, how flourishing so-ever the commonwealth may be, he must die of hunger; so that he sees the necessity of preferring his own concerns to the public; but in Utopia, where every man has a right to everything, they all know that if care is taken to keep the public stores full, no private man can want anything; for among them there is no unequal distribution, so that no man is poor, none in necessity; and though no man has anything, yet they are all rich; for what can make a man so rich as to lead a serene and cheerful life, free from anxieties. . . . [163]

It is difficult to believe at this remove that Thomas More truly believed that the abolition of private property, the holding of all goods in common, and equal distribution, could transform men and rulers and produce serenity. What is more likely is that he was seduced by an appealing idea into spinning it out into a lengthy romance or novel. Indeed, he puts into his own mouth the telling critique of the work. "I am of the opinion," he has himself say, "that men shall never live wealthily where all things are in common. For how can there be abundance of goods . . . where the regard of his own gains driveth not to work, but the hope that he hath in other men's travails maketh him slothful. . . . It is not possible for all things to be well unless all men were good—which I think will not be yet these many years."[164] Nor is it easy to believe that Thomas More was for long such a committed materialist as to believe that communism could transform man. After all, Henry VIII of England had More beheaded for his refusal to see the Church of England separated from Rome, and the Roman Catholic Church has finally proclaimed him as a martyr in the 20th century.

In any case, *Utopia* was so well received that it went through six Latin editions—the language in which it was at first published—and was then translated and printed in German, Italian, and French. It was the talk of the Continent in the 1520s, but it was not finally published in English until 1551. So influential was the work that "Utopia" became the generic word for a novel describing a perfect (albeit imaginary) society, although "utopian" also eventually became a derogatory term meaning impractical. There have been many utopian novels published since 1516, the greatest concentration of them being in the late 19th and early 20th centuries.

Utopianism has had considerable influence on the United States in the 20th century, but little if any of that came directly from More's *Utopia*. Nor were the Founders directly affected in their undertaking by that book. Still the conception of an ideal, if not perfect, republic or commonwealth did play some role in what they accomplished. They did conceive that they were attempting to form a polity in which justice might hold sway, and they surely sought to make it the best one they could conceive. The idea of doing that can be traced all the way from Plato's *Republic* through More's *Utopia* and beyond.

b. The Reformation

Neither the political thought nor practice common to the Renaissance had much more than a little indirect impact on the United States. By contrast, the Protestant Reformation had a crucial effect both on the founding of the colonies in America and through them upon the government of the United States. The spread of Protestant beliefs and practices broke up the religious unity of Europe and tended to undercut the political foundations of monarchy and aristocracy in Europe. The recognition by the Papacy of the legitimacy of successors to thrones was the basis of rule in Europe. In the wake of the Protestant Reformation, wars and contentions over succession were commonplace in the 17th and 18th centuries. There were major changes both in political practices and political theories during this unsettled era, as rulers and ruled sought adjustments to the situation.

The Protestant Reformation began around the year 1517, when Martin Luther nailed his 95 theses (propositions) on the church door at Wittenburg.

It might as well be dated from 1521, when Martin Luther repudiated Catholic teaching definitively at the Diet of Worms and proclaimed his right to determine religious matters by his own lights. He said, "Unless I am convicted by the testimony of Sacred Scriptures or by evident reason (I do not accept the authority of popes and councils, for they have contradicted each other), my conscience is captive to the Word of God. I cannot and I will not recant anything, for to go against my conscience is neither right nor safe."[165] In his decision, less than a month later, Emperor Charles V of Spain and the Holy Roman Empire made it clear that Luther's position undermined all authority in his realm. His edict said that "His teaching makes for rebellion, division, war, murder, robbery, arson, and the collapse of Christendom. . . . He does more harm to the civil than to the ecclesiastical power. We have labored with him, but he recognizes only the authority of Scripture, which he interprets in his own sense."[166] Or its beginning could be dated earlier, at various times over the past century.

In any case, one thing is clear: by the 1520s revolt and separation from the Catholic Church was welcomed by large numbers in many countries of Europe. Protestant clergy were advancing ideas whose time had come. Protestantism spread like a wild fire through western Europe, through Germany, to Switzerland, to the Scandinavian countries of Denmark, Norway, and Sweden, to Holland, to England, and Scotland. Its spread within two decades of 1517 made it appear that all Europe might go Protestant and the Roman Catholic Church might wither and fade away.

That was not to be, of course. Not all the countries and principalities in which Protestant teaching gained followers did go entirely Protestant. France did not, nor did some of the provinces in Germany. Neither Italy, Spain, nor Portugal were penetrated to any extent by Protestants. The Catholic Church made major reforms in the mid-16th century, and soon became the church militant once again under the leadership of Ignatius Loyola and the Society of Jesus (Jesuits), among others. Not only did a resurgent Catholicism compete with Protestants in the latter part of the 16th and in the 17th century but Protestant leaders and denominations competed with one another for members and followers. For example, Martin Luther denounced the Protestant Ulrich Zwingli in Switzerland with virtually the same fervor as he did Pope Leo X of Rome. In Frankfurt, Germany, it was observed in 1592 that "for several years past . . . the books written by Protestants against Protestants are three times as numerous as those of Protestants against Catholics." There were Lutherans and Calvinists, Anglicans and Separatists, Pietists and Anabaptists, Quakers and Puritans, and a spate of denominations. As one Protestant put it in 1610, "These raging theologians have so greatly aggravated and augmented the disastrous strife among the Christians who have seceded from the papacy, that there seems no hope of all of this screaming, slandering, abusing, damning, anathematizing, etc., coming to an end before the advent of the Last Day."[167] None of this should be taken to mean, however, that the contests between Protestants and Catholics were not often vicious during this period of history.

The initial impact of the Reformations was to augment the power of monarchy. The 16th and 17th centuries, or major portions of them, are referred to as the Age of Absolutism in Europe, when monarchs usually reigned with few technical restraints on their power and authority. The break from the Catholic Church by Protestants and the spate of religious denominations which emerged should not be taken to mean that people were free to worship as they pleased or to choose whichever denomination best suited them. At the Peace of Augsburg in 1555, the decision was reached for Germany that the religion of the prince would be the religion of the people. Indeed, that principle generally prevailed throughout Europe, excepting Switzerland, which had no monarch, and oases of toleration which existed here and there and from time to time. Hardly anyone in the 16th century could conceive of a political commonwealth or state which could be effectively ruled unless all the people were of the same religious faith. The necessity for religious cohesion came to modern Europe from ancient Rome, through the Middle Ages. It survived such secularization as there was in the Renaissance and was an article of faith for most Protestants and Catholics in the 16th and well into the 17th centuries.

Even so, few countries were blessed, if that is the right word, with people all of the same confession or denomination after the Protestant Reformation. Indeed, most provinces and countries had dissenters from the official religion, sometimes numerous, and often troublesome. Conflicts were often bitter, sometimes violent, and protracted. In England, for example, the conflict between Protestants and Catholics and the Church of England and other Protestant sects lasted off and on from the 1530s to 1689, sometimes coming to a head in war or dynastic changes, and leading to the migration of persecuted minorities to America or other lands.

Far and away the most violent and protracted of these conflicts, however, occurred in Germany from 1618–1648, a conflict known as the Thirty Year's War, or, sometimes, the Wars of Religion. The war was fought mainly on German soil, but the combatants came from all over Europe. There were armies that were German, Danish, Swedish, Bohemian (now in Czechoslovakia), Spanish, and French. The makeup of the armies was much more varied than that might suggest, however, for many of the troops were mercenaries. It was one of the most violent and destructive wars ever fought, and soldiers were often vindictive beyond all bounds. "To massacre any garrison that had refused to surrender, after surrender became inevitable, was a principle accepted by all combatants. Soldiers felt that civilians were legitimate prey; they shot at their feet in the streets, conscripted them as servants, kidnapped their children for ransom, fired their haystacks and burned their churches for fun."[168] It was officially a contest between Protestants and Catholics over who would prevail in Germany, but the issue in gravest doubt was whether Christianity or Germany could survive such barbaric and heedless destruction. It is probable that the population of Germany and Austria declined from 21 million to somewhat over 13 million people during the war. Whole villages were depopulated in some areas, and houses as well as people were destroyed.

Although the Peace of Westphalia which brought this horrendous war to an end was made up mainly of territorial changes and compromises, and neither Catholics nor Protestants made huge gains, the war may well have convinced many of the desirability of tempering their theological zeal. Certainly, some measure of religious toleration became more commonplace in the following century. It may be well to point out, too, that major colonial settlements were made in New England during the Thirty-Year's War, and Britain had its own war of religion, the English Civil War, toward the end of the Continental conflict. Undoubtedly, the Protestant Reformation had awakened a renewed interest and zeal about Christian doctrine and theology, about faith and works, and many other religious matters, but it had also aroused, as did the Catholic Counter-Reformation, hot tempers and loosed violent conflicts. The danger lay not so much with religious zeal as with the linkage of religion with government power and the determination of some to force religious beliefs or orthodoxy on others. Protestants had not originated this practice, but neither did they disassociate themselves from it effectively during their first century or so.

The best of Protestant political thought did lean, however, toward freedom in matters of faith. Martin Luther taught that Christians should obey temporal authority as regards earthly affairs. But that matters of faith and belief are beyond the power of government to effect or control. Governments should not try to exert force in these matters. As he said, "Since, then, belief or unbelief is a matter of every one's conscience, and since this is no lessening of the secular power, the latter should be content and attend to its own affairs and permit men to believe one thing or another, as they are able and willing, and constrain no one by force. For faith is a free work, to which no one can be forced. Nay, it is a divine work, done in the Spirit, certainly not a matter which outward authority should compel or create. Hence, arises the well-known saying, found also in Augustine, 'No one can or ought to be constrained to believe.'"[169] Luther's argument in the above was that temporal authority should not be used to root out heresy or to impose faith or doctrines. His argument was indeed a valid one, but he was much more impressed by it when he was contending against the Catholic position than when he got civil authority behind him.

Actually, Luther ranged over a variety of positions as to what the posture of government should be toward religion. At the least, he believed that the ruler should discover from Scripture which were the correct beliefs and use his temporal authority to support these. One writer describes Luther's position this way: "In *A Treatise of Good Works* (1520) he lays it down that a prince is an example to the people, for the simple folk will believe as he does. It is therefore his duty to believe and maintain the true religion. . . . In the *Commentary on Psalm 86* (1530) he discusses which heretics should be persecuted and concludes that the secular power should punish those who, on religious grounds, deny the dignity and authority of civil government and also those who deny doctrines which are found clearly in Scripture and are accepted throughout Christendom, for this is blasphemy.'' As to Roman Catholics, Luther thought that the ruler should try their doctrines by Scripture, and if he had, and the ruler found the Catholics in error, he should command them to be silent. "But often Luther is far more all-inclusive and bloodthirsty in his demands for the punishment of his opponents. Some times he speaks of the death penalty for papists and Anabaptists, but some-times he thinks banishment sufficient. But in any case the Word should be supported by the sword of the civil magistrate.''[170]

Luther had started his political analysis by maintaining that there were two kingdoms—an analysis reminiscent of Augustine's *City of* God—an earthly kingdom ruled over by princes directly under the authority of God, and a spiritual kingdom under God. Neither of these kingdoms was under the authority of the other. Thus, he broke the Medieval connection of the two maintained by the Roman Catholic Church. His theoretical position suited Luther well enough, but in practice he wanted an intertwined influence of church and state, and he was not above seeking the use of the force of government for his ends. Ultimately, Martin Luther was drawn to the prevailing view that in any particular nation the people must adhere to one religion which gave its support to the ruling powers. In practice, Lutheran churches were usually state supported churches where they prevailed.

Although there were many Protestant leaders in the early years, the influence of two men was greater than the others over the years: these were Martin Luther and John Calvin (1509–1564). Calvin was not a Protestant leader at the time of the onset of the Reformation; he was much too young for that if he had been so inclined. Indeed, he did not become a Protestant until sometime during or a little before or after 1533. Calvin was born and brought up in France. His early and youthful education was in the framework of the Roman Catholic Church, and it appeared for a time that he would become a priest. However, his father suggested that he study law instead, which he did for a time. In the wake of these studies, it looked as if he might become a scholar with primary interest in the humanist studies of the Renaissance. In the midst of this, he underwent a religious conversion and in short order became a leader in the reform movement in France.

Calvin differed decisively in temperament from Luther. Luther was emotional, passionate, volatile, sometimes erratic, but nonetheless a man of considerable learning and great skill in writing and translation. By contrast, Calvin was logical, systematic, dogmatic (even ideological), more dispassionate than not. His great work on theology was *Institutes of the Christian*

Religion. While Calvin held like Luther that there are the two distinct kingdoms, he never left any doubt that the earthly, or civil, authority has jurisdiction over the outward practice and observance of religion. He said that government "is equally as necessary to mankind as bread and water, light and air, and far more excellent. For it not only tends to secure accommodations arising from all these things, that men may breathe, eat, drink, and be sustained in life, though it comprehends all these things while it causes them to live together, yet I say this is not its only tendency; its objects also are that idolatry, sacrileges against the name of God, blasphemies against his truth, and other offenses against religion may not openly appear and be disseminated among the people; that the public tranquility may not be disturbed . . . ; that men may transact their business together without fraud or injustice; that integrity and modesty may be cultivated among them; in short, that there may be a public form of religion among Christians, and that humanity may be maintained among them."[171]

Calvin found opportunity in Geneva, Switzerland to put his political and religious ideas into effect so far as that was possible. He became the leading pastor in Geneva, which was at this time governed by a council. The council, in turn, gave over the governing of the city to a presbytery composed of clergymen and lay members. Under the leadership of Calvin, these imposed a governmental rule over the community at large which was supposed to be in accord with scripture. All households were required to attend worship in a recognized church on Sunday and were expected to attend other religious services during the rest of the week. The private lives of people were minutely regulated in great detail. Whatever the merits of this great effort, it is clear that Calvin intertwined religion and government, more completely than had usually been the case under Catholicism.

As regards the kinds or types of law, Luther and Calvin did not differ much in general with Thomas Aquinas. Indeed, it could be said they gave new life to earlier legal formulations. There is Divine law, which is revealed in Scriptures. This law is conceived as eternal and unchanging, but not all rules and prescriptions found in Scripture were held to be of this character. The ceremonial and ritual rules in the Old Testaments were held to be obsolete after the Advent of Christ. The Protestant reformers differed with Catholic teachers about another aspect of Divine law; they held that the council of perfection applied to all Christians alike, while Catholics taught that different men in different stations fell under the Divine law in varying degrees.

The second form of the law is Natural Law. It is God's law, too, not His law as revealed in Scripture, but His law as revealed in the universe and in the "uncorrupted" nature of man. Natural law is discoverable by the reason of man; it is universal in that all men are subject to it, whether they are aware of it or not, and there is ultimately no way of evading its requirements. "Its discovery requires careful thought and consideration of all the issues, for 'the noble gem called natural law and reason is a rare thing among the children of men.' ''[172]

Luther and Calvin also recognized the legitimacy of man-made or positive law. That is, they were aware that there is a need to supplement Divine revelation and natural law with particular laws for people in communities, nations, and the like. These laws are binding on the citizen generally and must be obeyed without question, except such as might trespass into the area of faith. This is so despite the fact that lawmaking is sometimes done ineptly. "Here one must patch and dar, and help oneself with the laws, sayings, and examples of heroes as they are recorded in books. Thus we must continue to be disciples of those speechless masters we call books. Yet we never do as well as it is written there; we crawl after it and cling to it as to a bench or to a cane."[173]

Neither Luther nor Calvin believed an ideal or utopian form of government was practical or possible. Man is a fallen creature, a "weak vessel," as it were. His powers of reasoning were flawed and his will was drawn astray by his weaknesses. Moreover, it was presumptuous for man to devote himself to such projects. Luther inclined to the view that monarchy was the best form of government. The alternatives that he foresaw were mob rule or monarchy. He appears to have believed that any sort of rule based on the populace would degenerate quickly into mob rule. Whereas, there was much greater likelihood of having a just and reasonable rule by a king. He might by good fortune even be a Christian. But even if a monarch should turn out to be a tyrant, he probably would not be so capricious and disorderly as mob rule. In any case, Luther thought that constitutional checks on the monarch would be helpful.

Calvin, on the other hand, was much more disposed toward elected legislators and governors. He especially favored the rule of several rather than of one, since they would restrain one another, for, as he said, "owing to the vices or defects of men it is safer and more tolerable when several bear rule, that they may mutually resist, instruct, and admonish each other, and should any one be disposed to go too far, the others are censors and masters to curb his excess."[174] Thus, Calvin opened the way for some sort of elected government, though he was by no means disposed to the direct rule of the populace.

Neither Luther nor Calvin contributed much directly to the development of popular government or individual liberty. It is true that Luther provided some theoretical basis for the liberty of the individual in his teaching of the priesthood of all believers and emphasizing the necessity of each person's studying and understanding the scriptures. But it is equally true that Luther labored mightily to close the door he had partly opened. In Lutheran realms, it was usually the princes, not individuals, who determined what religions the inhabitants would practice, and among Protestants generally, what was orthodox was determined by church and political leaders, not the man in the pew. Indeed, denominations did proliferate, and heroic individuals did choose their own faith, but this was only indirectly due to the influence of Luther and Calvin. Nor did popular government get much of a boost from Calvin.

The Protestant reformers were much more bent toward restoring the religious bent and intensity that was characteristic of the earlier Middle Ages than they were in making social and political changes. They taught that men should obey political authority virtually without question, and though they might rebuke temporal rulers for their pride and pretensions, most Protestant leaders hardly encouraged revolt. Unintentionally, perhaps, their more direct impact was to break down such restraint as the Catholic Church still placed on temporal rulers, to consolidate the power of nation-states, and to contribute more than a little to the absolute rule of monarchs.

Although he was not a Protestant or reformation thinker, *per se,* Jean Bodin (1530–1596) may be best discussed in the context of the political absolutism of these years and the Protestant Reformation which inadvertently gave it free rein. Bodin was born in France, trained in the law, and served the king and those under him. He was also one of the more innovative political thinkers of his day. The breakdown of the old Germanic (Holy Roman) Empire and the loss of sway of the Roman Catholic Church in the 16th century, coupled with the emergence of nation-states made much of Medieval political theory obsolete. What was wanted was a theory of the independent state beholden neither to popes, emperors nor to any other outside powers. Jean Bodin obliged by providing just such a theory. Its most important component was the doctrine of sovereignty. Bodin did not exactly invent the doctrine, but he defined it with precision, gave it currency, and fortified its standing as an instrument in political thought.

Bodin defined both sovereignty and the powers of the sovereign, though they refer to the same things. "Sovereignty," he said, "is the absolute and perpetual power of the state, that is, the greatest power to command."[175] What he appears to be saying is that there is within each independent state an absolute and perpetual power which is the greatest power in it. It is, in effect, the power to issue commands to those who live in the state and these commands cannot be lawfully countermanded. Sovereignty is something belonging to or residing in the state, as such, as a result of its independence of other powers.

Who, if anyone, may exercise this sovereign power is another matter. The state, as such, is not an animate being; it cannot exercise power at all. "Bodin . . . distinguish[ed] carefully between state and government, holding that the possession of sovereignty was the characteristic of the state, but that the system through which sovereignty was exercised determined the form of government. States were monarchic, aristocratic, or democratic, depending upon whether the sovereign power resided in one person, in a minority of the citizens, or in a majority."[176] However, his own preference was for monarchy, and his examples of the exercise of sovereign power usually entail that form of government.

"Only he is absolutely sovereign who, after God, acknowledges no one greater than himself," Bodin wrote. If citizens elect a person or persons to office for a specified period of time or subject to their recall, then such a person(s) does not possess absolute sovereignty. He is only an agent or trustee, according to Bodin. If a prince yield some of his power to an underling, the underling is not sovereign. To be sovereign, the prince must possess absolute power, subject only to "the laws of God and nature," for "all princes are in the world and are bound by them." His sovereignty is evinced ultimately in the making of laws. "We thus conclude that the principal aspect of sovereign rule and absolute power consists in making general laws for the subjects without their consent. . . . If the prince requires the consent of superiors, then he is a subject himself; if that of equals, he shares his authority with others; if that of his subjects, senate or people, he is not sovereign."[177]

Bodin was more than a little captive to the logic of his definitions. It may be true that there resides some ultimate power within an independent state, and that when push comes to shove, as we say, it must be exercisable by some body. But much of the rest makes little sense, at least to an American. Even so, it is important to understand the concept, because it has brooked large in modern political thought, including many pronouncements and claims in the United States. Much mischief has been done in its name, whether that should be charged to Bodin or not is often debatable. But that it was an absolutist concept conceived mainly to support absolute monarchy should not be in doubt.

c. The Age of Reason

It would not do to leave the account of the Protestant Reformation in Europe without emphasizing once again the importance of that movement for the settlement of America and establishment of the United States. America was settled during that first century not only by Anglicans (of the Church of England who had broken from Rome and undergone a reformation in the 16th century), but also by dissenters from a great variety of sects and denominations spawned out of the Protestant Reformation: Anabaptists and Pietists from Germany, Huguenots from France, Presbyterians from Scotland, Baptists, Puritans, Independents, Quakers, Mennonites, and so on. While Luther's influence tended to dominate in northern Europe, Calvin had by far the greater impact in Great Britain, France, the Netherlands, and Switzerland, and almost certainly in America. Even those Catholics who settled in America in the 17th century, mainly in Maryland, were English Catholics, dissenters, as it were, from the Church of England. They, too, were influenced by the Protestant Reformation by way of the Catholic Reformation as well as by more direct contacts with it. Americans of the Founding era still tended to look at past history through the lenses of the Reformation as well as learning from its more violent episodes a more genteel tolerance.

It should be noted, too, that to this point in surveying the background to political thought and practice, very little attention has been paid to British developments. That is because in the ensuing chapter, the English heritage will be surveyed, some of it going back to the Middle Ages, but it would have been repetitious to have covered it earlier.

Now to the Age of Reason. The chronological boundaries of this period are even less precise than those of the Renaissance, for example. Some would begin their account of it with the momentous claims of Nicolai Copernicus in the middle of the 16th century and extend it all the way to the latter part of the 18th century, to the death of Voltaire, say, in 1778. But whatever bounds different ones may set, there is more than a little agreement that somewhere in the course of the 17th century a new outlook began to gain hold of the minds of men in Europe and America. It was clearly beginning to happen by the middle of the 17th century and it was gaining sway by the end of that century.

The change has been described in a variety of ways. One way is to emphasize the shift of the quest for truth from looking back to ancient times into the present. Men of the Renaissance had looked to the ancient Greeks and Romans as a means of expanding their learning and increasing their knowledge. In that respect, the Medieval scholastics had a similar outlook, though they viewed Ancient thought from a somewhat different angle. The Protestant reformers looked back also, looked back to the early church practice and to the Scriptures as the guide for Christians. The Renaissance had aroused a sense of history and of the deterioration and falling away that occurs with the passage of time. Reformation leaders sought to restore an earlier and presumably purer Christianity. The Catholic Reformation also sought to purify the Church of superstitions and unbiblical practices which had grown over the years.

In the course of the 17th century, some men began to believe that they were beginning to discover truths that were unknown in the past, and thought that they had a method for discovering truth superior to the past. They thought they were making progress beyond what had taken place in earlier times. One way to describe this is to say that the idea of progress was replacing the idea of retrogression with the passage of time. Francis Bacon (1561–1626) was an early forerunner of this new outlook with what he claimed was a new and superior way to discover truth. It was, in essence, the inductive method (though Aristotle had preceded him with that by nearly two thousand years). No matter, he described the situation this way:

There are and can exist but two ways of investigation and discovering truth. The one hurries on rapidly from the senses and particulars to the most general axioms, and from them, as principles, and their supposed indisputable truth, derives and discovers the intermediate axioms. This is the way now in use. The other constructs its axioms from the senses and particulars, by ascending continually and gradually, till it finally arrives at the most general axioms, which is the true but unattempted way. . . .[178]

Whatever the exaggerations in Bacon's claims, he was setting forth his conception of the scientific method.

Some years later, René Descartes somewhat more philosophically set forth his idea about a new method to arrive at truth in his *Discourse on Method*. He not only proposed that clarity would be his test of truth, but that he would proceed toward truth using the methods of mathematics, especially those of geometry. Here is Descartes own description of it:

The long chains of simple and easy reasonings by means of which geometers are accustomed to reach the conclusions of their most difficult demonstrations, had led me to imagine that all things, to the knowledge of which man is competent, are mutually connected in the same way, and that there is nothing so far removed from us as to be beyond our reach, or so hidden that we cannot discover it, provided only we abstain from accepting the false for the true, and always preserve in our thoughts the order necessary for the deduction of one truth from another. And I had little difficulty in determining the objects with which it was necessary to commence, for I was already persuaded that it must be with the simplest and easiest to know, and considering that of all those who have hitherto sought truth in the Sciences, the mathematicians alone have been able to find any demonstrations, that is, any certain and evident reasons. I did not doubt but that such must have been the rule of their investigations.[179]

The kind of reality, hence truth, that Descartes sought was necessarily measurable and in essence statistical or mechanical. The impact of those of his persuasion in the modern world is indicated by the passion for precision and quantifying that abounds in everything from the avid gathering of statistics to the measuring of time down to the minute, second and tenth of a second, and so on. Such quantifications often pass for knowledge among us, and learning often consists of knowing how to make them. There are still poets, artists, cooks, orators, physicians, bakers, jewelers, and foresters among us, but they are inherited and continued from an earlier day. It is precision quantifiers who so much distinguish our age from past ones. But then, the ancient Greeks started us on that road, at least.

The point here, however, is not whether these ideas were something new under the sun or whether they were superior to other methods of acquiring knowledge. Rather, it is that men at the forefront of developments came increasingly under the sway of the belief that they had discovered and were using methods that would reveal the secrets and enable them to advance learning above what had been done in the past. There was indeed an explosion of discoveries concentrated in the 17th century and the surrounding years which has been called the Scientific Revolution. It includes such names as Copernicus, Johann Kepler, Galileo, Sir Isaac Newton, Thomas Boyle, Fahrenheit, Christian Huygens, Leibniz, Edmund Halley, William Harvey, and so on and on. And these scientific innovators were preceded or accompanied by such a variety of major philosophers as the world had hardly seen. There were Francis Bacon and René Descartes, already mentioned, Hugo Grotius, Baruch Spinoza, Thomas Hobbes, John Locke, George Berkeley, Leibniz, the Earl of Shaftesbury, Nicolas de Malebranche, and many more.

The great discoveries of this age are premised on the uniformity of nature and the regularity of the laws operating in nature. You can read that certainty of uniformity in the following statement of a law by Sir Isaac Newton:

> Thus the force of the same loadstone is greater at a less distance, and less at a greater: also the force of gravity is greater in valleys, less on tops of exceedingly high mounts; and yet less, at greater distances from the body of the earth, but at equal distances, it is the same everywhere; because (taking away, allowing for, the resistance of air), it equally accelerates all falling bodies, whether heavy or light, great or small. . . . [180]

Baruch Spinoza (1632–1677) stated the universality of law in philosophic rather than scientific terms when he wrote:

> Nothing comes to pass in nature in contravention to her universal laws, nay, everything agrees with them and follows from them, for whatever comes to pass comes to pass by the will and eternal decree of God; that is, whatever comes to pass comes to pass according to laws and rules which involve eternal necessity and truth; nature, therefore, always observes laws and rules which involve eternal necessity and truth, although they may not all be known to us, and therefore she keeps a fixed and immutable order. [181]

"The Age of Reason," writes one historian, "was an age of faith in the rational behavior of nature and in immutable scientific laws." [182]

What did all these philosophical and scientific developments have to do with political thought and practice? They provided the framework for new political ideas and practices as well as buttressing and giving fuller meaning to older ideas. Natural law theory had long been applied to some extent in the political realm. The Romans had based much of their conception of general laws upon it. It had been revived in the Middle Ages, renewed in the Renaissance, continued by Protestant reformers, but now it was given a huge boost by scientific and philosophic developments in the 17th century. Natural law theory had been around for, perhaps, two thousand years, at the least, but never had it gained such impressive support as it did from the discovery of exact relations, mathematically demonstrable, as in the 17th and 18th centuries. Increasingly, thinkers were coming to believe that nature would reveal her secrets if the methods used in the natural sciences were applied into every realm, including the political and economic.

An historian of ideas observes that "Under this conception the idea of natural law took on a new meaning. Locke spoke of a 'law antecedent and paramount to all positive laws of men.' John Wise thought that the rules of government were drawn up by a 'wise and provident nature, and by the dictates of right reason.' Montesquieu professed to draw his 'principles not from prejudices but from the nature of things.' Bolingbroke derived nationality and government from the universal laws of reason."[183]

As this movement moved into the 18th century and reached its peak, or, perhaps better, its extreme, it picked up another descriptive title, "The Enlightenment." Its presumption was much clearer now; men had come out of the darkness into the light; they were now enlightened. The movement called the Enlightenment reached its fruition in the first three-fourths of the 18th century, was concentrated in France and led by Frenchmen. Indeed, France had emerged as the leading country in Europe during the long reign of Louis XIV in the 17th century and continued its intellectual leadership in the eighteenth century. French had become the second language of people of learning throughout Europe, when it was not the first, and it had gone far to replace Latin as the language of learning. Among the Frenchmen who were at the forefront of the Enlightenment, after Voltaire, were Marquis de Condorcet, Denis Diderot, Charles Louis Montesquieu, Baron D'Holbach, Carolus Linnaeus, Etienne Condillac, Georges Louis Leclerc Buffon, Jean Jacques Rousseau, Jean Le Rond d'Alembert, Claude Adrien Helvetius, and Bernard Fontenelle, as well as such French Physiocrats as Francois Quesnay and Robert Jacques Turgot.

Paris was the center of the intellectual world, and the salons of Paris were the meeting places at which intellectuals—a new breed of men made possible by greater freedom, wealth, and the loss of the power to discipline effectively by churches—set forth their bold new ideas. These salons were presided over by women, who provided a setting, a sympathetic ear, and the attraction to draw men together. Probably, the most remarkable of these women to hold forth in Paris was Madame de Pompadour. In a land where beautiful women were almost commonplace, she was reckoned to be more attractive than all the rest. She was a person of wide reading and much learning, and gathered a library of 3,500 books in the course of her life.

Next to King Louis XV, she may well have been the most powerful person in France, for she was his mistress for many years. She became a patron of intellectuals, many of whom she entertained in her salon. "She brought Voltaire to court, gave him commissions, tried to protect him. She helped Montesquieu, Marmontel, Duclos, Buffon, Rousseau; she eased Voltaire and Duclos into the French Academy. . . . She chose as her personal physician Francois Quesnay, protagonist of the physiocrats, and assigned him a suite of rooms directly under her own at Versailles. There she entertained Diderot, d'Alembert, Duclos, Hélvetius, Turgot, and others whose ideas would have startled the king. . . ."[184] Such was the frame within which the Age of Reason both peaked and began the deterioration which resulted in the French Revolution.

There are three main political developments which grew out of the Age of Reason in continental Europe. One has already been noted, i. e., the renewed emphasis upon the natural law philosophy and its application to political thought. The major immediate political application has been described as Enlightened Despotism by historians. It was the attempt to impose the ideas of the French *philosophes* by way of monarchs upon their countries. Frederick the Great of Prussia was the prize pupil of Voltaire; Catherine the Great of Russia was drawn to the ideas but did not get far in applying them; and Louis XV of France was neither especially enlightened nor particularly despotic. It was not surprising, however, that intellectuals should conceive of the notion of putting their ideas into effect by strong monarchs.

Americans were hardly enamored of despots, enlightened or not, but they were strongly attracted to the discovery of new extended justifications for individual liberty. One French writer whose work was known to some of the American Founders, and whose *Spirit of the Laws* was greatly admired, was Baron de Montesquieu (1689–1755). He was an exponent of natural law and a careful student of it. He said that "all beings have their laws; the Deity his laws, the material world its laws . . . man his laws. . . ." He understood natural law as something residing in the nature of things. For example,

> Particular intelligent beings may have laws of their own making; but they have some likewise which they never made. Before they were intelligent beings, they were possible; they had therefore possible relations, and consequently possible laws. Before laws were made, there were relations of possible justice. To say that there is nothing just or unjust, but what is commanded or forbidden by positive laws, is the same as saying that, before the describing of a circle, all the radii were not equal.[185]

Some commentators on natural law claim that its exponents believed that man once lived under natural law at some time in the past. That is not at all what Montesquieu was saying. All men in all times are subject to natural law. Natural law, as such, has no history in human terms and is not to be conceived in that way.

But the most important part of Montesquieu's thought to Americans was his conception of the separation and balance of powers as essential to the liberty of the citizen. He said that "Political liberty is to be found only in moderate governments; and even in these it is not always found. It is there only when there is no abuse of power: but constant experience shows us that every man invested with power is apt to abuse it, and to carry his authority as far as it will go." Therefore, he said, "To prevent this abuse, it is necessary, from the very nature of things, power should be a check to power."[186] What particularly interested the American Founders was that he described how a government could be so constituted that power could be checked against power.

The main thing, Montesquieu thought, was that the three basic functions of government—the legislative, executive, and judicial be separated and independent of one another. He particularly admired the British system for the liberties it provided to its people in the 18th century and thought it due mainly to the separation of powers. Montesquieu, like Aristotle, recommended a mixed system of government—monarchic, aristocratic, and democratical. He was favorably disposed to representative government for the legislative branch, and in that regard thought that the "members . . . of the legislature should not be chosen from the general body of the nation; but it is proper, that, in every considerable place, a representative should be elected by the inhabitants."[187] Americans incorporated this into their Constitution as well.

The other major development for individual liberty was the economic theory advanced by the Physiocrats, especially Quesnay, Turgot, and Dupont de Nemours. The Physiocrats opposed government interference in the market place or in economic affairs generally. They said that there are natural laws which have to do with economy. As Dupont put it: "The social laws established by the supreme being prescribe only the preservation of the right of property, and of that liberty which is inseparable from it. . . . If the ordinances of sovereigns [those who govern] were contradictory to the laws of the social order, if they prohibited the respect of property, if they commanded men to burn crops, if they prescribed the sacrifice of little children, they would not be *laws,* they would be insane acts obligatory upon no one. Thus there is a natural judge, a court of final appeal, for the ordinances of sovereigns themselves, and this judge is the evidence of their conformity or their opposition to the natural laws of the social order."[188] The Physiocrats declared that the proper rule for government was *laissez-faire,* to keep hands off of the economy.

But the influence of British practice and thought was much greater and more direct upon the Americans than was that of continental Europe. Thus, we must turn now to an examination of that impact.

Chapter 5
The English Heritage

One of the major elements in the complex of experience and background which the Americans brought to their founding activities was their English heritage. The majority of the colonists were of English lineage, and they were preponderantly British in origin, since the latter designation would include those of Scotch and Irish descent. What the Americans constructed when they got the opportunity were mainly alterations and reshapings of their English heritage.

Nonetheless, there was considerable ambiguity in the attitude of the colonists toward their English background. Indeed, this ambiguity has attended the attitudes of those who have come from Europe over the centuries to settle in America. On the one hand, they have rejected the Old World, the most obvious sort of rejection being their very coming to the New World. Many who came have fled from one kind or another of persecution or oppression. The Old World has often been described by those who betook themselves to the New as a seat of persecution and corruption. Certainly, American colonists of the latter part of the eighteenth century readily identified the English Church and government with corruption—the Church with its pampered hierarchy and impoverished parish priests, and the government with its rotten boroughs and members of Parliament whose votes were bought by the monarch with sinecures.

And yet, however ambiguous their attitude toward it may have been at times, the Americans did not basically reject their English heritage. Instead, they valued it essentially, made great efforts to preserve it, treasured its outlines, and, when the time came, builded upon it. From first to last, over a colonial period of a little less than two hundred years these settlers showed their attachment to and dependence upon England. Fathers who could afford it frequently sent their sons to be educated in England. They read English books, watched English plays, if any, and consumed English-produced goods.

In many ways, the settlers showed their preference for things English, both in words and deeds. Professor Samuel E. Morison says that two early New England writers, Nathaniel Morton and Edward Winslow, declared that one of the main reasons the Pilgrims left Holland for the New World was the fear that their children would lose their language and nationality.[189] One historian has recently shown how devoted the Puritans were to their English background. He says, "They were hardly more worried that their laws should be 'scriptural,' that is approved by the Bible, than that they should be sufficiently English; and that any changes in English laws should have ample warrant in local needs."[190] Even more strongly, he declares:

> Scholarly dispute as to whether early New England law was primarily scriptural or primarily English is beside the point. For early New Englanders these two turned out to be pretty much the same. Very little of their early legal literature attempted to construct new institutions from Biblical materials. They were trying, for the most part, to demonstrate the coincidence between what the scriptures required and what English law had already provided.[191]

A case could be made, however, that the New Englanders were among the least devoted to their English heritage of the American colonists. They were dissenters from the Church, developed a considerable literature of their own, were opposed to such things as plays, had colleges of their own, and had more latitude than was usual in developing their governments. Certainly, many of the other colonies conformed much more closely to English ways. A Virginian, writing in 1728, contrasted that colony with others, and proclaimed that "Virginia may be justly esteemed the happy Retreat of *true Britons* and true Churchmen."[192] Statements affirming the connection between Britain and America can be found in abundance all the way up to the Declaration of Independence.

Not all the affirmations of admiration for things English nor all the reliance on Britain should be taken at face value as indicating the real state of sentiment or that everything that was done was voluntary. Colonists were under a variety of pressures and restraints which bent them toward such conformity. The charters under which they were supposed to operate usually required that their laws not be contrary to English law. For example, the General Court of Massachusetts was authorized by the charter to make laws for the inhabitants, with the proviso that they be "not contrairie to the Lawes of this our Realme of England."[193] The Maryland charter provided that the proprietor "was to make no laws incompatible with those of England, and none without the consent of the freemen or their representatives."[194] Since others usually had similar provisions, colonists found it in their interest not only to conform to the British pattern but to profess to do so as well.

A dependence on Britain for many things was engendered by British regulations. In general, they were encouraged over the years to buy various products from the mother country because of restrictions on their manufacture in the colonies. Such restriction definitely hampered the development of an American literature by limiting printing opportunities. An American printer could rarely undertake the publication of a book because of the scarcity of type. "In England the supply had been limited as part of the control of the press; a Star Chamber Decree of 1637 allowed only four persons, each with a limited number of apprentices, to operate type-foundries at any one time. Not until the Revolution could American printers buy type of American manufacture."[195] In the late seventeenth century, the King provided the Governor of Virginia with orders "that no person be permitted to use any press for printing upon any occasion whatsoever."[196] Not all the dependence of the colonies upon England was by choice, it is clear.

Even so, the Americans did revere the essentials of their English heritage. They could hardly have done otherwise; to reject it out of hand would have been to repudiate much of themselves as they were. The furniture of their minds was made up largely of British conceptions. Their angle of vision was set to see things the way one of such descendance would see them. The best proof that they revered the heritage, however, is that they kept so much of it when they had an opportunity following the revolt to dispense with it. To see that this was so, it will be useful to call up the outlines of the English systems and ways.

A profound ingredient of the English heritage is the conservative cast of mind. In a general sense, this may not distinguish British peoples from most others. It is quite likely that most peoples at most times have been preponderantly conservative, though not necessarily in a discriminating way. It could even be argued that man is by nature conservative (as are also the lower animals) in that he usually prefers to continue to do things in the same way he has done them. Small children tend to be conservative in insisting on ritualizing activities and in their intolerance toward things or people that are different. Such conservatism is undifferentiated in its posture toward things familiar, reveres them for their familiarity alone.

British conservatism is something different from and more than what might well be called "brute conservatism." If it were not, it should hardly have come to our attention, for it would only be a universal condition, one which would be no more worthwhile to announce than that Englishmen have two legs. The peculiarities of British conservatism took shape over many centuries of experience, took shape in the Middle Ages as a people defended their ways against Danish and Norman monarchs, as the classes battled against arbitrary and despotic kings, as the thrust of change was blunted by the persistent clinging to ancient rights and privileges.

There were two major developments in the High Middle Ages of what for Americans would be their English heritage. One of these is symbolized by the Magna Carta, or Great Charter, as the phrase translates in English. The signing of this charter took place at Runnymede in 1215 between King John and his barons, the great lords. It was an attempt by the barons to limit the power of the king, or perhaps better, to get him to acknowledge that his powers were limited. Was John an especially despotic king of England? The record is not clear about this, though his barons thought he was. In fact, his predecessors were a despotic and arbitrary lot, recognizing few limits on their authority. It wasn't so much that King John was more arbitrary and despotic than his predecessors as that he was not a success as a ruler. No, worse than that, his reign was punctuated by successive disasters.

His first major disaster was that he lost most of his French territory. Philip Augustus, who ruled France at this time, was a powerful monarch who got John to become his subject for his French fiefs, then hailed John before his court for misconduct and declared that his French fiefs were forfeit to France. Philip then proceeded to enforce his decree at arms, and one after another he took the French provinces from John. John's barons might not have been so concerned about his military losses on the continent had he not continued to make levies of troops and arms upon them to prosecute new wars against Philip. As if all this were not enough, John ran afoul of the most powerful pope in the Middle Ages, Pope Innocent III, over the appointment of an archbishop of Canterbury. This quarrel continued from 1206–1213, and came to a head when John refused to allow the man whom Pope Innocent declared to have been duly elected to enter England. "The pope laid the kingdom under interdict, and subsequently excommunicated the King. This interdict meant that all the churches were closed: no masses sung, no marriages or funerals conducted. Only baptism and confession for the dying were permitted. For seven years the churches were silent, while pope and king and archbishop wrangled. In 1213 peace was arranged: the King surrendered."[197] The king had been ignominiously defeated in a controversy with the Church. On top of that, in 1214 John tried again to recover the lost territory in France with the aid of a continental ally. To no avail, he was defeated and driven off the continent once more.

By early 1215 John's nobles had had enough; the king was clearly a failure, and his treasury was empty. The nobles rebelled, and King John yielded to them at Runnymede. They presented him with the Magna Carta or Great Charter which was drawn up in his name and therewith issued by him. By this remarkable document he affirmed that his powers were limited and that various classes and orders as well as free men in general were possessed of various rights and liberties which he was not supposed to violate. The charter is addressed to "the archbishops, bishops, abbots, earls, barons, justiciars [judges or administrators of justice], foresters, sheriffs, reeves, servants, and all baliffs and his faithful people. . . ." The provisions of the charter began by affirming that "the English church shall be free, and shall hold its rights entire and its liberties uninjured; and we will that it thus be observed. . . ." It goes on to give special affirmation to freedom of elections in the church. The second provision declares that "We have granted moreover to all free men of our kingdom and for us and our heirs forever all the written below, to be had and holden by themselves and their heirs from us and our heirs.'' There followed a long list of things either forbidden to the king to do or prescriptions as to the conditions under which he could do them.

The following are examples of these provisions:

> No free man shall be taken or imprisoned or dispossessed or outlawed or banished, or in any way destroyed, nor will we go upon him, nor send upon him except by the legal judgment of his peers or by the law of the land.
>
> And the city of London shall have all its ancient liberties and free customs, as well by land as by water. Moreover, we will and grant that all other cities and boroughs and villages and ports shall have all their liberties and free customs.
>
> To no one will we sell, to no one will we deny or delay right or justice.[198]

It may be objected that the rights, liberties, and customs are often not spelled out, and that some of them are rather vague. Those that were spelled out were apt to be feudal rather than modern in character. That is all quite true. It was nonetheless an important document for it did make it clear that the king was limited in what he could rightfully do, and it was one of those benchmarks on the way to establishing constitutional government in England.

The other major development in the Middle Ages was that of the Common Law. Common law, in its most general signification, means a law common to all England, and, as English rule and the English language extended to other lands in the 17th through 19th centuries, the common law also followed this expansion. Common law is contrasted with local law and custom, on the one hand, and to positive or legislative enacted law on the other. In some respects, it resembles the law of nations of Roman law, but they had best not be confused. It arose as the law which emerged from the king's court, as opposed to that in local or traditional courts.

The common law began to be shaped by the courts during the long reign of Henry II (1154–1189). During the course of his reign, the king's court was ever more widely used to provide justice in the land. These courts began to weave three different kinds of law—"mostly old Saxon local law, Norman local law, and feudal law"—into one law, the common law. Thus, as a constitutional history says, "itinerant justices, going from a single central court and carrying that court and its law into every county in turn, was making a common law for the whole kingdom. Before very long they began to call it, as we do, the common law, meaning the law which is alike everywhere. . . ."[199] Two names stand out in the early recording of this new common law. They are Ranulf Glanvill, who did his work in the 12th century and was a contemporary, more or less, of Henry II, and Henry

Bracton in the 13th century. His work was printed for the first time in the
16th century, and thus he became a kind of authority on Medieval English
law to moderns.

There was a third major development, the growth of parliament, but it
took place mainly in the late Middle Ages. It had its origin in the King's
Councils which met irregularly in the 13th century and were usually made
up of nobles. "After the magnates had insisted on it in the Provisions of
Oxford (1258), parliament met fairly regularly, generally about twice a year
in the earlier part of Edward I's reign. Its composition varied but it generally
included the king and his council and great individuals, such as earls and
bishops. . . ."[200] The most momentous changes took place in both the
composition and functions of parliament during the reign of Edward I
(1272–1307).

The major function of parliament as it first began to take shape was to
serve as a court, ultimately a supreme court. It settled major disputes which
arose in the land. As it grew in importance it became an instrument for
issuing the decrees of the king. "Edward I wrote to the pope in 1275 that he
would take counsel with his magnates in parliament and that he could not do
anything affecting the rights of realm without such counsel. Edward's chief
statutes were promulgated in parliaments."[201] This statement of the matter
may be a little misleading, however, since making major changes in the way
things were done by law was foreign to the Middle Ages. By such legal
theory as they operated on, men did not so much make law as discover what
the law was or had been in olden times. In that regard, parliament would
have been more inclined to guard against innovations by the king than to
assist him in making them. At any rate, the parliament did come to share
with the king in such legislative function as there was. And, parliament
came into its own as the body necessary to the approval of the levying of
taxes. It should be noted here that within the feudal system, the king was
ordinarily supposed to make do with the income from his estates and such
other dues or fees as came his way from time to time. Hence, there arose the
saying that "the king ought to live off his own." That was not so farfetched
as might be imagined, since kings at that time had no great bureaucracies to
support nor any vast systems of welfare to maintain. New taxes, then, were
likely to be extraordinary measures and greatly resented when they were
levied.

It was this ability to levy taxes by parliament which led kings to make the
body more representative by bringing commoners into it. As one historian
has said, "there is no doubt that the king's need to summon it for taxation
was the chief historical cause for the form and importance which it assumed
from the last decade of the thirteenth century."[202] Edward I issued a call for
a parliament to meet on November 13, 1295. The resulting body has been
known to history as the Model Parliament, because of the representative
character of the assemblage. King Edward set forth the basic principle in his

call, by declaring: "As the most righteous law established by the . . . sacred princes, exhorts and ordains that that which touches all shall be approved by all, it is very evident that common dangers must be met by measures concerted in common. . . ."[203] In short, King Edward argued both that all should give their approval or disapproval (through representatives) in matters which touch them, and also that military threats should be met by commonly approved action. In any case, his was an argument for broadly representative government. The parliament that he summoned was to be broadly representative, as follows: "the archbishops and bishops are to bring the heads of their chapters, their archdeacons, one proctor for the clergy of each cathedral, and two for the clergy of each diocese. Every sheriff is to cause two knights of each shire, two citizens of each city, and two burghers of each borough, to be elected and returned. Seven earls and forty one barons have special summons."[204] The assumption was that in this assemblage all free men were represented: the clergy, the nobility, city dwellers, townsmen, and folks living in rural areas. There is, of course, no pretense that serfs, vagabonds, and those with no estate or standing were represented.

During the reign of Edward III (1327–1377), parliament took the definite form of a legislature of two houses: the House of Lords and House of Commons. "After 1327 the Commons' right to be present in every parliament was recognised. In return for grants of money they expected their grievances to be listened to and they presented them in the form of the Commons Petition." The following was the usual procedure when parliament assembled. "It began with a solemn address, often from the Chancellor, explaining the king's needs. Then the whole body split up into two houses. One house consisted of the lords who had been individually summoned because of their personal importance—the earls, the barons, bishops, and the abbots of great abbeys. The Commons deliberated separately and negotiated with king and lords until agreement was reached over the grant of money to be made. It was generally over in a few weeks and the knights [townsmen and the like] went back to their shires. . . ."[205]

It could be said that in the 14th century England was ready for nationhood but had not attained it. Indeed, the disentanglement from France (by way of the Hundred Years' War) continued on for much of the 14th century and at least half of the 15th. Moreover, the ties to Rome were strengthened somewhat in the course of the 15th century. Parliament was established as an ongoing institution, which might have limited the power of the king. It did so from time to time, by way of the power of the purse, but the monarch still ruled the country largely unrestrained. Moreover, the nobility had provided the main restraints on the monarch in the Middle Ages and they were virtually wiped out in the middle third of the 15th century during the War of the Roses.

The War of the Roses is usually dated from about 1447 to 1485, though it reached its most ferocious pitch in the early 1480s. It was a struggle for the throne by a variety of claimants, mainly the House of York and House of Lancaster. How this conflict resulted in the decimation of the nobility is well illustrated by the death of Edward IV in 1483. Edward V, who was supposed to succeed him, was a boy of 12. The Queen was apparently expected to rule as regent with a cabal of nobles supporting her. It did not work out that way. Instead, Richard, Duke of Gloucester, a Yorkist noble, "joined forces with another substantial Yorkist magnate, Henry Stafford, Duke of Cunningham, encountered Rivers [an earl] bringing Edward V to London at Scony Stratford, and seized them both. Dorset fled the country, the Queen retired to sanctuary at Westminster, and . . . Richard was in control at London. . . ." But Richard was by no means satisfied; he wanted to remove all opposition. "In June, Hastings, the most prominent layman of Edward IV's intimates still in power, was suddenly arrested at a council meeting and executed." Richard then declared that Edward IV's marriage had been invalid and he, Richard, was the rightful claimant to the throne, which he then took by declaring himself Richard III. "Rivers was executed and Edward V and his younger brother placed in the tower, where they were probably murdered soon after."[206] Even so, the open season on the English nobility continued apace until 1485, when Richard III was slain in battle.

Henry Tudor succeeded Richard III as King Henry VII. He and his descendants ruled England from 1485 to 1603; they included Henry VIII, Edward VI (inherited the throne as a child, rule was by regents), Mary, and Elizabeth I. The long rules by Henry VIII (1509–1547) and Elizabeth I (1558–1603) were the most significant reigns, though Henry VII did bring peace to the country and firm up the control of the country by the monarch. The greatest constitutional change of the Tudor period was in the relation of the church to the state. Henry VIII took the church in England out of the Roman Catholic Church in the early 1530s with the aid of Parliament. Legislation was enacted prohibiting appeals from England to the papal court, stopping all payments from the English church to Rome, making the king supreme head of the English church. In the ensuing years the monasteries were suppressed, many of the church lands were seized, and many Protestant changes were made in the Church of England.

The king of England was now a full fledged sovereign, owing no allegiance to nor accepting any authority of any power outside of the country. As one historian has well said, "When the Crown in Parliament effected a series of revolutions in ecclesiastical and religious affairs, it was demonstrated beyond all question that the State had acquired unlimited sovereign authority." For "in the Tudor epoch the nation asserted its new strength, and, expelling all foreign authorities and suppressing all local immunities, claimed the right to do whatever it liked within its own frontiers. These novel claims . . . were embodied in the person of the Prince."[207] More precisely, they were embodied in the person of Henry VIII.

Clearly, the power of the king of England had been greatly augmented by taking the church in England out of the Roman church. Two related political developments during the Tudor era need to be discussed. One is that the Tudor monarchs exercised more or less absolute and arbitrary powers and ruled despotically. Henry VIII had both Protestants and Catholics put to death during his reign; whether it was arbitrarily done or not, it was nonetheless tyrannical. His daughter Mary (called "Bloody Mary" by Protestants) tried to return England to the Catholic fold and caused hundreds of Protestants to be put to death. Elizabeth I ruled much longer and more moderately, but she was a despot nonetheless, at least in the powers she wielded.

The other major development was that Parliament survived this era of concentrated royal rule and was reckoned to be a more important institution at the end than it was at the beginning of Tudor rule. While the Estates General in France and the Cortes in Spain and such parliamentary institutions as existed in other countries were falling into disuse, the English parliament was growing in prestige. This came about mainly because the Tudor monarchs were able to use Parliament to their ends. Henry VII had very little hereditary claim to the throne. Thus, after his victory over Richard III, he "summoned parliament and placed before it a claim to the throne based on the rights of conquest and heredity. Parliament granted him the crown, but was silent about his hereditary right which, as a matter of fact, did not exist."[208] In fact, his claim to rule, and thus that of the Tudors who succeeded him, rested upon a parliamentary grant. Henry VII tacitly allied himself with the merchants and gentry who were represented in the House of Commons and subjugated the Lords, whose prominent men had been killed off during the War of the Roses.

Henry VIII had an additional reason to that of legitimizing his claim to the throne for using parliament. He needed and used it to take England out of the Roman Catholic Church. "The instrument chosen by Henry to effect his Royal Reformation was Parliament. . . . The legislation that completed the breach with Rome, destroyed the monasteries, and established the supremacy of the State over the Church in England, was prepared by Privy Councillors and passed after discussion by both Houses. The Reformation Parliament . . . sat for seven years, and in the course of its eight sessions . . . built up the traditions of the modern House of Commons as a great instrument of government."[209] It should be emphasized, however, that Henry VIII valued parliament above all because it served as *his* instrument of government. Nor was he above flattering the members of parliament. In 1543 he told them:

> We be informed by our Judges that we at no time stand so high in our estate royal as in the time of Parliament, when we as head and you as members are conjoined and knit together in one body politic.[210]

Elizabeth I both courted and used parliament for her purposes, and when she died it was probably a stronger institution than when she had come to the throne. In one of her last messages to parliament she told the members that "Though God hath raised me high, yet this I count the glory of my crown, that I have reigned with your loves!"[211]

That the English parliament had survived and even gained in prestige at a time when absolute monarchies were the rule elsewhere in Europe had great bearing on American government, though its founding was still nearly 200 years off. Parliament was the nearest thing not only to a model upon which the Congress of the United States was based but also for the legislatures in the various colonies. That the Commons had gained in prestige was very important, too, for Commons would eventually become the symbol of popular government in England, as the lower houses of the legislature would in the United States.

It should be emphasized, however, that even at the end of the Tudor reign, parliament was still more a Medieval than a modern institution. Though it was representative in character, it represented the classes, not the populace, as such, of England. As an historian of the period has observed, "Parliament in the seventeenth century represented exclusively the propertied classes. The House of Lords was composed of the biggest landowners, together with the Bishops. . . . But the House of Commons also represented the wealth of the country. . . . The county electoral franchise, restricted to men having freehold land worth forty shillings a year, excluded smaller freeholders, copyholders, cottagers, leaseholders, and paupers, who probably formed eighty to ninety per cent of the rural population. . . ." Of those actually elected to the Commons from rural areas, they "were invariably drawn from the leading landed families below the rank of peer, . . . In towns the franchise [vote] was more varied . . . , but in most towns the propertied minority had a decisive voice."[212] It was also the case that liberty and right had not quite taken on its modern meaning as well. It was still largely something belonging to classes and orders rather than those freedoms which many came to speak of and venerate by the 18th century.

Changes in the 17th century were of much greater direct importance for American political institutions than those that had gone before. The main English settlements were made in America in the 17th century, of course. Great changes occurred both in political thought and practice in England in this century. At the beginning of the century, the monarch reigned supreme; by the end of the century, England had a constitutional monarchy, and parliament could and did limit the powers of the king. In the midst of the century, the English had the only revolution they ever suffered, the Puritan Revolution, and for eleven years they had no king, something that had not happened since the memory of man runneth not to the contrary. Major documents were added to the Constitution as well. But it is time now to take some of these changes up in more detail.

a. Political Changes of 17th Century

The century had hardly begun when Queen Elizabeth died and England got a new family dynasty and a new king. James Stuart, who had been King James VI of Scotland, became James I (1603–1625) of England. James I was a proud, stubborn and more than a little arrogant man who was determined to hold on to and exert all the powers inherent in his office. He may not have been more stubborn than most of the Tudor monarchs had been, but he was confronted by a sterner opposition. The main thing was that the Protestant Reformation had been partially contained in England—with the Church of England it had stopped somewhere between the Roman Catholic Church and full fledged Protestantism. Non-conforming Protestants had been restricted and persecuted in Elizabethan England as well as Catholics. Puritans—those bent on "purifying" the Church of England—had not only increased greatly in number by the time of James I but had also prospered particularly as merchants and tradesmen, and a goodly number of them had made their way into the House of Commons. There, they were at the forefront of the struggle between the king and parliament in the 17th century.

In Scotland, where the Presbyterian church was established, James was outwardly a Presbyterian. Thus, the Puritans were very hopeful at the outset of his rule that he would be favorably disposed to their effort to "purify" the church. They presented the king with what was called a "millenary petition," which had been signed by a thousand clergymen. James rejected their request and declared, "If you aim at a Scottish presbytery it agreeth as well with monarchy as God and the devil."[213] He suspected the Puritans of wanting to get rid of the hierarchy in the church, and his view was that "no bishop, no king," that a church hierarchy was necessary to support the institution of monarchy. This may have set the stage for the confrontations between king and parliament in the ensuing years.

The issue, put in its most adamant form, was whether the king's powers were absolute or whether they depended upon the determination and consent of parliament. Particular issues, however, dominated much of the confrontation between the two. The Commons took the initiative for the parliamentary side, insisting on "their right to give advice on foreign affairs and on the need to purify the Church, and they demanded that the King should abolish various traditional means by which the Crown raised money, such as 'purveyance'—the right to requisition goods and services for the royal use . . . —the right of the Crown to administer the lands of minors, and the sale of patents or monopolies. . . ."[214] As for King James I, his aim was to keep and exercise the Royal prerogatives as they had come down to him. For those he would have to contend with parliament. Undoubtedly, the king would have liked to be independent of parliament; as for parliament, or at least Commons, it would have liked to be independent of the king as well.

The House of Commons was not the only branch with such ideas either. Some of the judges felt that they should be independent of the monarch and be able to limit his powers as well. The greatest champion, both of the supremacy of the law and of the independence of judges during the reigns of the early Stuarts was Sir Edward Coke. Coke was above all a champion of the English common law. He made the greatest compilation and interpretation of the common law that had ever been made. He was the first man to be named Lord Chief Justice of England. He held that the king was under the law and did not share James's view that he could make law by his decrees. A group of judges were trying a case having to do with the king's power, and the king ordered them to consult with him. The other judges agreed to yield to the wishes of the king, but Coke said he would rule according to law. He was subsequently dismissed from his post as a judge, though he went on to serve in Commons, where he continued in his efforts to limit the power of the king. Nor did his courageous stand lead to the independence of the judiciary over the short term. Chief Justice Crew was dismissed in 1626, and during "the personal government of Charles I repeated dismissals reduced the judges to a state in which they enforced monopolies, abandoned Coke's attempt to restrict the jurisdiction of Church courts, and declared Ship Money legal."[215] In short, the judges became extensions of the will of the monarch.

Although James I contended frequently with parliament, particularly over finances, he maintained the bulk of his authority throughout his reign and died with his boots on, so to speak. It was not the case, however, for his son, Charles I (1625–1649). He was hardly crowned before he was embroiled in quarrels, with his wife, his ministers, France, Spain, and, above all, with parliament. He was soon at war with France and Spain, and badly in need of funds, else he would probably have ruled from the beginning without parliament. Parliament was little inclined to accommodate him by passing new taxes, but very much inclined to inquire into his policies and actions. When the king would not yield, parliament refused to vote taxes; the king dissolved it, and financed his undertakings as he would. It was in the midst of a series of confrontations between 1625–1628 that the House of Commons drew up and got Charles's consent to the Petition of Right. It is generally considered to have been a landmark document in affirming that the king must rule according to law.

The Petition begins by listing a variety of grievances against the king, grievances which it claims were in violation of the Great Charter and other statutes and charters over the years. The grievances include: forced loans, taxation without the consent of parliament, punishments imposed without trial by jury or without being charged with violating a definite law of the land, that soldiers and sailors have been quartered in private facilities without the consent and against the will of owners, that Commissioners have been appointed to proceed with the enforcement of martial law without regard to due process of law, and that some are exempt from the enforcement of the laws of the land. After rehearsing all these grievances comes the main clause of the Petition:

> They do humbly pray . . . that no man hereafter be compelled to make or yield any gift, loan, benevolence, tax, or such like charge, without common consent by Act of Parliament; and that none be called to make answer, or take such oath, or to give attendance, or be confined or otherwise molested or disquieted concerning the same, or for refusal thereof; and that no freeman, in any such manner as is before mentioned, be imprisoned or detained, and that your Majesty will be pleased to remove the said soldiers and mariners, and that your people may not be so burdened in time to come; and that the aforesaid commissions for proceeding by martial law, may be revoked and annulled; and that hereafter no commissions of like nature may issue forth to any person or persons whatsoever, to be executed as aforesaid, lest by colour of them any of your Majesty's subjects be destroyed or put to death, contrary to the laws and franchise of the land.

The following clause asks assurances that to protect the rights and liberties of the people the king and all who serve him be made to observe the "laws and statutes of the realm." Charles I made the following reply, which is also a part of the Petition of Right:

> The King willeth that right to be done according to the laws and customs of the realm; and that the statutes be put in due execution, that his subjects may have no cause to complain of any wrongs or oppressions, contrary to their just rights and liberties, to the preservation whereof he holds himself as well obliged as of his prerogative.[216]

Although this is reckoned to be an historic constitutional document in making the monarch subject to law, it had little immediate impact on Charles I. After Charles accepted the Petition of Right, parliament voted taxes, and the king dismissed it. However, he called parliament into session again in 1629. When it refused to pass the desired legislation and defied the king's wishes, he dissolved it, and ruled for the next eleven years without parliament. As Charles said, "Parliaments are altogether in my power for the calling, sitting and dissolution. Therefore, as I find the fruits of them to be good or evil, they are to continue or not to be."[217] That was true enough, but it hardly excused his becoming a despot. He had leading members of parliament imprisoned for nothing more than disagreeing with him. Sir John Eliot died in prison rather than recant for what he did not suppose to be wrongdoing. William Laud, Archbishop of Canterbury, enforced a rigorous and dogmatic Anglicanism on the populace, driving tens of thousands of

Puritans to America, and punishing dissenters severely. Moreover, Charles violated the spirit, if not the letter, of the Petition of Right with the taxes he imposed. As if all that were not enough, he withdrew on poor terms from his foreign wars because they would have required more taxes than he could personally impose to execute well. Whether the king was right or wrong, his withdrawal from an active foreign policy alienated many of the Protestant persuasion in the country. The Thirty Year's War (between Protestants and Catholics) was going on in Germany, and many Protestants in England wanted England to oppose the Catholic powers. There was more than a little suspicion, too, that Charles was a secret Catholic sympathizer.

In any case, Charles I stirred up resistance in Scotland by his attempt to impose Anglican ways on the Presbyterian church there. The Scotch took up arms and Charles called for a new parliament in 1640. Charles's popularity rating, if there had been one, would not have raised a blip on the Richter Scale, to name some sort of measure, and the country tended to favor those most strenuously opposed to him in the election. It was dubbed the "Short Parliament" because it lasted only three weeks before Charles dissolved it. The king demanded that parliament pass new taxes before it took up grievances, but the House of Commons was of no mind to be done out of their turn so easily. Charles would not have it and raised an uproar in the country by dissolving parliament. It was not long, however, before the Scots forced him to assemble parliament as a condition of their coming to terms with him. This assemblage was called the Long Parliament, for it lasted in one form or another for the better part of twenty years.

The Long Parliament acted almost immediately to pass constitutional reforms guaranteeing much greater independence for itself and giving parliament more complete control over taxation. It soon became clear, however, that no middle ground could be found on which the majority in parliament and King Charles could meet. Thus, war broke out between the king and such forces as he could muster and the parliamentary forces. What followed was the Civil War and the Puritan Revolution. Charles I was executed on orders of the House of Commons in 1649. Thereafter, England was governed for eleven years without a king.

Tremendous changes were made during these years, and revolution let loose forces that even scared the Puritans, but the revolution was only an *interregnum,* an interval between the reign of Charles I which ended in 1649 and Charles II (1660–1685), who took over when monarchy was restored in 1660. The basic governmental and religious establishment was restored after 1660; the King-in-Parliament ruled once again; the religious rule of bishops and the Church of England was restored as well. That is not to suggest that there were not some enduring changes as a result of the tumultuous events from 1640 to 1660.

One historian says that a great "revolution took place." He goes on to flesh out what had taken place, and his main points can be summarized this way:

1. The power of the monarch had been curtailed; it was now clear that he was not an absolute ruler.
2. Arbitrary courts, such as Star Chamber and the High Commission, were things of the past.
3. That parliament had to authorize taxation had been established by law.
4. Church courts had lost any legal standing.
5. "The country had managed to get on without King, Lords, and Bishops; but it could never henceforth be ruled without the willing co-operation of those whom the House of Commons represented."[218]
6. The common law emerged triumphant over legal claims of other kinds of law, with the exception of legislative enactments, perhaps.
7. Feudal tenures were abolished.
8. "In industry, monopolies and government interference were ended. . . ."[219]

Even with all these changes, the great constitutional changes of the 17th century were by no means completed. The crowning achievement of the century was the Bill of Rights adopted in 1689. But even before that a new Habeas Corpus Act was passed by parliament in 1679. Its purpose was to prevent arbitrary imprisonment and to require that those held in jails should be both charged and tried expeditiously. The availability of a writ of *habeas corpus* was not new to the 17th century, of course, nor did its availability get first affirmed by the above act. It was known prior to the issuance of the Magna Carta, and was affirmed in 1215 by that document. Moreover, such a writ was customarily available to courts in England. But it also deals with matters and provides protections to people generally that rulers and those who enforce their commands are ever inclined to evade. They can often think of all sorts of reasons why people ought to be held in jail on suspicion of having committed some crime, until they have confessed to something, as punishment for aggravating the powers that be, and so on. The Stuart monarchs and their officers were frequently guilty of evading the requirements of a writ of *habeas corpus*. If matters stood as the Habeas Corpus Act of 1679 claimed, it often happened that the issuance of a writ brought no activity from jailers and keepers of places of confinement. To remedy this situation the new Habeas Corpus Act prescribed that anyone receiving such a writ shall present the person before the court which issued the writ within three days, with exceptions for some major crimes, or be subject to fines. At which time, the person detaining him must show an acceptable cause why the man is being confined or release him. It seems, too, that sometimes people were sent into other jurisdictions to avoid their being

freed by such writs. This was specifically prohibited in some detail, as it
says in the act:

> And for preventing illegal imprisonments in prisons beyond the seas;
> be it further enacted . . . that no subject of this realm . . . shall or may
> be sent prisoner into Scotland, Ireland, Jersey, Guernsey, Tangier or
> into any ports, garrisons, islands or places beyond the seas . . . and that
> every such imprisonment is . . . adjudged to be illegal. . . .[220]

This last illustrates how determined parliament was to make the king and all
his officers abandon all efforts at arbitrary imprisonment.

This was but a prelude, and a small one at that, to that revolution known
as the Glorious Revolution when the English people got their Bill of Rights.
(The very phrase was almost sacred to Americans a hundred years later.)
There were two phases to the Glorious Revolution. The first was the driving
of King James II (1685–1688) from the throne in 1688 and replacing him
with William of Orange and his wife Mary. The second was the adoption in
1689 of the Bill of Rights. It was "glorious," as historian G. M. Trevelyan
has said, because the "Revolution . . . was bloodless, that there was no civil
war, no massacre, no proscription and above all that a settlement . . . was
reached of the religious and political differences that had so long and so
fiercely divided men and parties. The settlement of 1689 stood the test of
time. It led . . . to a new and wider liberty. . . ."[221]

The dispute that led to the fall of James II came about in this way. James
II was the younger brother of Charles II. While Charles II had leaned toward
the Catholic side, he did not openly tip his hand if he intended to restore
Catholicism to England. James, on the other hand, had occupied the throne
for only a very short time before he was defying parliament, overturning
laws, bringing known Catholics into his government. In short order, he had
alienated much of parliament, many of the leaders in the Church of England,
and many of the Puritans and Protestant dissenters. Perhaps, James did no
wrong in putting down the Monmouth Rebellion, but the highhanded way he
prosecuted those accused of participating in it made enemies of many Puritans. This might have been borne, since it affected only a portion of the
population, but when the king began suspending laws and surrounding
himself with Catholic advisers contrary to the law something had to be done.
There was a ray of hope, however, since both of James's children, his
daughters Mary and Anne, were Protestants, and the oldest, Mary, was
married to William of Orange, a prominent Dutch Protestant. That hope was
dashed, however, when James's second wife gave birth to a son, whose
claim would supercede that of his much older sisters to the throne. James's
second wife was a Catholic, and there was no doubt that the young Prince
of Wales would be brought up a Catholic.

Had James not taken the law into his own hands, had he acted in cooperation with parliament according to law, and had he not been so brazenly

pro-Catholic, much that he attempted to do was admirable. He moved forthrightly to establish religious toleration in England. ("Toleration" should not be confused with full fledged religious freedom. What it meant, most directly, was that those who disagreed with the established religion would be allowed to practice their faith.) "On August 4, 1687, James issued his first Declaration of Indulgence. . . . It suspended all penal laws affecting religion, abrogated all religious tests, allowed freedom of worship to all, and forbade interference with peaceable religious assemblies. It released all persons who were imprisoned for religious nonconformity."[222] Laudable as all this might be, it came from a tainted source as far as many Englishmen were concerned, for James was becoming ever more openly Catholic, and the birth of a son forecast a return to Catholicism (minus toleration) for England. When James reissued his Declaration a year later, required the bishops of the Church of England to have it read on successive Sundays, had those bishops who refused to comply imprisoned and brought to trial (at which they were found not guilty by a jury), and in the midst of which his wife gave birth to a male heir, his days as ruler of England were near to an end.

Prominent Englishmen, such as the Duke of Devonshire, the Earl of Shrewsbury, Admiral Edward Russell, and Bishop Henry Compton invited William to come to England to take over and assured him of their support. William assembled a considerable military force, an armada of fifty warships, many more transports, and sailed for England in November, 1688. James II intended to defend his throne, but his prospects were not good. The ships sent to prevent William's fleet from landing were scattered by a storm; the army with which he intended to contend with William was so unenthusiastic that James ordered a retreat immediately. William made it easy for James II to flee the country secretly, and he took refuge in France. In February, 1689, William and Mary were crowned king and queen of England, and technically jointly ruled the country thereafter. Those events comprised the Glorious Revolution so far as it involved the overthrow of a reigning king.

What was much more important for the later history of England (and of the United States as well) was the adoption of a declaration known to history as the English Bill of Rights. While it was originally presented in February, 1689, it was authoritatively reenacted by Parliament in December of that year. Aside from confirming the rule of William and Mary, it has two main parts: one is the list of grievances against James II; the other a considerable list of limitations on the power of the king.

The list of grievances against James II might well have been used as a model by Thomas Jefferson nearly a century later when he drew up his grievances against George III (1760–1820) in the Declaration of Independence, though the charges differ in particulars, of course. The grievances of 1689 declared that "Whereas the late King James the Second, by the assistance of divers evil Councellors, Judges, and Ministers employed by him, did endeavour to subert and extirpate the Protestant Religion, and the laws and liberties of this Kingdom. . . ." It then goes on to give particulars, such as: "1. By assuming and exercising a power of dispensing with and suspending of laws, and the execution of laws without the consent of Parliament. . . . 5. By raising and keeping a Standing Army within the Kingdom in time of Peace, without consent of Parliament, and quartering Soldiers contrary to law. . . ."[223]

But whatever doubt there may be that this list of grievances may have served as a model for those in the Declaration of Independence, there can be no reasonable doubt that some of the limitations on the power of the king were included in the United States Constitution and the First 10 Amendments, with appropriate adjustments. For example:

9. That the Freedom of Speech, and Debates and Proceedings in Parliament ought not to be impeached or questioned in any Court or place out of Parliament.
10. That excessive Bail ought not to be required, nor excessive Fines imposed, nor cruel and unusual punishments inflicted. . . .

But to understand the document better as limiting the power of the king and protecting Parliament and the people who choose its members, other provisions, not so closely resembling those in our Constitution, need to be mentioned. For example:

1. That the pretended power of suspending laws, or the execution of laws, by Regal authority, without consent of Parliament is illegal; . . .
4. That levying of money for the use of the Crown, by pretence of Prerogative, without grant of Parliament, for longer time, or in other manner, than the same is or shall be granted, is illegal;
5. That it is the right of the subjects to Petition the King, and Prosecutions for such petitioning are illegal; . . .
7. That the subjects which are Protestants, may have Arms for their defence suitable to their conditions, and as allowed by law; . . .
12. That all Grants and Promises of Fines and Forfeitures of particular persons before conviction are illegal and void;
13. And that for redress of all grievances, and for the amending strengthening and preserving of the laws, Parliaments ought to be held frequently. . . .[224]

The great constitutional documents were rounded out by the Act of Settlement of 1701, by which it was made clear by Parliament that all kings of England should thereafter be Protestants. More, it fixed the heirs to the throne in the House of Hanover, should King William or Queen Anne fail to produce a successor (which indeed occurred). Moreover, the writers and signers of the Act of Settlement fervently hoped, that since "the Laws of England are the birthright of the People thereof," that all "the Kings and Queens . . . ought to administer the Government of the same according to the said Laws. . . ."[225]

After these events, it should be clear that no doubt any longer existed that England had a limited and constitutional monarchy. Parliament had also indicated that in the final analysis it was the dominant branch of government. It could make and unmake monarchs, though this was ordinarily left to the workings of heredity and nature; it could prescribe what kings could and could not do; and it was the only branch of the government that could take property away from the people by levying taxes. An American might well ask, then, what were the constitutional limits on the powers of parliament? That is a good question, but not one which the members of parliament have been inclined to ask. There are no written constitutional authorizations or limits on what parliaments may or may not do. Indeed, it could be argued that there are no substantive limits on what parliaments may do. The limits, such as they are, are procedural, the existence of balancing powers, and popular influence and election (in the case of the House of Commons). Procedurally, it is expected that parliament must act by law and generally in accord with standing law. If the king is under the law, then it may be equally said that parliament is also under the law, though parliament may also change the law.

But parliament, even after the Glorious Revolution, was not independent of the king; it was only free in its debates and in its actions. The king still summoned parliament, and he could also dismiss a session of parliament or dissolve it. It was still the case, at least in the 18th century, that legislative acts were acts of the king-in-parliament. The having of two houses which voted and acted separately from one another provided interior restraints on parliament. Until the 20th century, acts had to be approved by both the House of Lords and Commons to become law. The executive power of the government rested in the hands of the monarch. All these things limited in one way or another the power of parliament.

Although little was said about the independence of the courts or the rights and liberties of people generally (in any concrete sense) in the great documents of this era, gains were being made in these matters as well, though less dramatically than in the adjustment of powers between king and parliament. As one historian has said: "Justice and humanity . . . gained greatly from the signal overthrow of James. . . . The Judges ceased to be removable at the will of the Crown. Trials were conducted with decency and on the whole with fairness. Cruel floggings and exorbitant fines ceased to be a usual weapon of party politics. In 1695 the Censorship of the Press was allowed to lapse. . . ."[226] The Toleration Act of 1689 brought to an end the attempt of the government to force everyone into the mold of the Church of England. It was still the established church, but it no longer had a monopoly over religious observance in the country.

b. British Political Thought

It may well be that English political forms and practices had a greater influence on Americans than did their political philosophy. If so, it was only by a matter of degree, for Americans of the Founding period were greatly influenced by English political thought as well as practice. This was so not simply because that thought was most apt to be available in the English language and that Americans relied on booksellers in London for most of their purchases but also because British thought was closest to their own. In fact, most American colonials with much learning could and did read books in several languages, including Latin and Greek.

It is important to note, too, that British constitutional change came to a halt for more than a century after 1689. That was not the case, however, with political thought. Not only did it continue to develop throughout the 18th century, but it also had a decided libertarian flavor from 1650 on. Thus, it is well at this time to turn to an examination of some influential British thinkers who preceded the making of the United States Constitution.

(1) Richard Hooker

A look at the work of Richard Hooker (1553–1600) takes us back to the 16th century. Even so, it is a necessary journey through time for it is a necessary starting point both for modern English political thought and for that which had a direct bearing on the work of the Founders of the United States. Hooker's work is at the crossroads between the Ancient, Medieval, Rennaisance, and modern worlds. He drew upon the great body of learning from the past—historical, philosophical, and theological—and brought it to the justification of English polity and the Church of England. His great work was the *Laws of Ecclesiastical Polity,* which was designed to consist of 8 books, only 5 of which were finished in his lifetime. The universality of his appeal is well illustrated by Pope Clement VIII after reading a portion of his work: "There is no learning that this man hath not searched into," he said. "This man indeed deserves the name of an author; his books will get reverence by age, for there is in them such seeds of eternity, that if the rest be like this, they shall last until the last fire shall consume all learning."[227] His impact on later Americans has been suggested by Russell Kirk, who says, "Hooker's arguments, like his prose style . . . would be familiar—if only in paraphrase sometimes—to nearly all educated men in eighteenth-century America." Among the ideas of "Hooker's that passed into American social assumptions," he says, "are his concepts of law, of continuity, of constitutional liberty, and of tolerance."[228]

Hooker forcefully brought the thoughts of Thomas Aquinas on eternal and natural laws into a Protestant, or at least Anglican, framework, and gave it his own authoritative statement. He held that the whole cosmos is permeated by law from God, which not only gives it order but moves it toward ends which are of the will of God. As one writer says, "The law laid down by God for Himself and all other things is the eternal law, and from it all other laws flow."[229] It may also be thought of as natural law so far as it applies to man and things. Hooker believed that this law is perfectly reasonable, as it comes from the hand of God. The laws can be known by man who is capable of discerning them by the use of his reason. Hooker believed that it was man's will rather than his ability to reason that was flawed.

Man must live under government because he is a fallen creature and requires a power from outside himself to discipline and restrain him. He believed that the power which government exercises comes from those who are ruled originally. Thus, the people are the origin of political power. Government may gain that power by conquest, by contractual consent (the social compact), or by willingly living under it. Hooker inclined to believe that constitutional monarchy was the best form of government, but he agreed that different peoples might have different forms of government in keeping with their traditions and experience. In any case, he thought that government should be by the consent of the governed, though that consent might be given by voting for representatives or in other ways.

(2) Thomas Hobbes

The American Founders were not given to referring to Thomas Hobbes (1588–1679) or otherwise citing him as an authority on government. There was good reason for this: he taught the absolute authority of the king, and virtual absolute obedience of the subject. He was cynical about the nature of man, and Machiavellian in his attitude about the appropriate behavior of a prince. On top of that, he was little, if any, short of being an atheist. Even so, Hobbes is an important figure in political thought because of his political theories about natural law and the state of nature. His best known work is *The Leviathon,* which to us is more or less synonymous with an all powerful state.

Hobbes began his political thought with man in a "state of nature." There has been considerable discussion over the past century or so whether there was ever such an historical state as a "state of nature." The question is irrelevant for Hobbes and for most natural law theorists. They are referring to a potential condition in which there is no political authority over a man, none which lays down and has the power to enforce the laws. The "state of nature" is, then, a condition of anarchy, when there is no government. Hobbes tells us that "during the time when men live without a common power to keep them all in awe, they are in that condition which is called war . . . , when every man is enemy to every man. . . ."

> . . . In such condition, there is no place for industry, because the fruit thereof is uncertain; and consequently no culture of the earth

[farming] no navigation, nor use of the commodities that may be
imported by sea . . . ; no knowledge of the face of the earth; no account
of time; no arts; no letters; no society and, which is the worst of all,
continual fear, and danger of violent death; and the life of man, soli-
tary, poor, nasty, brutish, and short.[230]

To those who doubt that such a condition would exist without government,
Hobbes reminds them that they lock their doors at night, go armed when
they make a journey, and lock their chests in their houses even when they
are home. And these they do, he says, even though they have laws to protect
them from aggression upon them and a government to enforce the laws. It
is to end this dire condition, or at least abate it, Hobbes says, that men leave
the state of nature and form governments.

Governments are properly instituted, Hobbes held, by the citizens of a
land entering into a *covenant*. "Covenant" was a word very much in vogue
in the 17th century. It meant a very firm commitment. It was a commitment,
however, in the Hobbes system only among the ruled, not between the ruled
and the sovereign. The sovereign is equipped with all those powers to
maintain the peace and protect the people from foreign invaders. Nor is the
sovereign limited in the powers he may exercise and as to how he may
exercise them. It is true, thought Hobbes, that a man may resist when
government forces him to do harm to himself. But otherwise, the man living
under a settled government should count himself fortunate regardless of
inconveniences, because his condition is so much better than it would be
without the peace government can bring. Those who complain of the yoke
of government only led Hobbes to conclude that "all men are by nature
provided of notable multiplying glasses, that is their passions and self love,
through which every little payment appears a great grievance, but are destitute
of those prospective glasses, [which enable them] to see afar off the miseries
that hang over them, and cannot without such payments be avoided."[231]

That is not to say that he did not suppose that men were usually possessed
with some liberties. If they are not in prison or otherwise physically restrained, they are in the most obvious sense at liberty. Otherwise, "The
liberty of a subject . . . lies only in those things which, in regulating their
actions the sovereign has disregarded: such as the liberty to buy, and sell,
and otherwise contract with one another; to choose their own abode, their
own diet, their own trade of life, and instruct their children as they themselves think fit; and the like."[232] Of course, if he should happen not to
"disregard" such things, there appears to be little recourse from the resulting tyranny for the citizen. He has yielded all power and virtually all rights
to the sovereign in yielding to a pact to have government.

Whatever the merits of the political thought of Thomas Hobbes, it is small
wonder that the American Founders did not appeal to him as an authority.
He did, however, make a good explanation of the state of nature concept.

(3) John Milton

His fame does not rest ultimately upon his political writings, for John Milton (1608–1674) was one of the greatest Protestant Christian poets of all time. Yet his political writings were not themselves without significance. As one American scholar has written: "Milton's works were early known in America and exercised their influence upon New England election sermons and political papers. 'They are indeed,' wrote Jonathan Mayhew in a letter, 'the principles which, God be thanked, generally prevail in New England.' "[233] In his writings, he defended mixed governments with elements of monarchy, aristocracy, and democracy in them, representative government, the freedoms of men in general, and especially freedom of the press. Milton was born in London in a Protestant household and spent most of the first three decades of his life in studies, formal and informal. He was inclined at one time to become a clergyman, but he was Puritan in his sympathies and knew that he would not be free to express his views in the Church of England. He wrote a few pieces during his twenties and thirties, some political polemics and some poems. When the Puritans came to power in the 1640s, Milton went into government work and served as secretary to Oliver Cromwell. It was during these years that he became almost totally blind. In the years after monarchy was restored, he retired to private life and produced those epic works on which his literary reputation rests: *Paradise Lost, Paradise Regained,* and *Samson Agonistes.*

Milton's best known political writing is *Areopagitica,* an argument for freedom of the press from government licensing. Indeed, his is the great classic argument for freedom of the press, made in an age when censorship was the rule and some degree of freedom the exception. Thus, he began his treatise by admitting that governments may well be concerned about what appears in books, for books, he admits, are very potent things and may indeed work mischief in the state. "And yet," he wrote, "on the other hand, unless wariness be used, as good almost kill a man as kill a good book; who kills a man kills a reasonable creature, God's image; but he who destroys a good book, kills reason itself, kills the image of God, as it were in the eye. Many a man lives a burden to the earth; but a good book is the precious life-blood of a master spirit, embalmed and treasured up on purpose to a life beyond life. . . ."[234]

The above was a somewhat impassioned plea, but Milton went on to buttress his position with reasoned arguments. He noted that the licenser or censor would need to be very learned himself to do a good job, and doubted very much that there were many fit for the task who would be willing to undertake it for long. Nor could he understand why a full grown man when he undertakes to write something must submit to a government busybody as censor as if he were a schoolchild. Nor is it clear to him how a man can be an authority in his own right if he must submit to the judgment of someone much less learned than himself on the subject. Moreover, who would want to read what a writer has to say knowing that he may be holding his best back in order to pass the censor. Milton points out that he has visited foreign lands where thought is ruled by censors. "There it was," he wrote, "that I visited the famous Galileo grown old, a prisoner to the Inquisition, for thinking otherwise than the Franciscan and Dominican licensers thought. . . ."

He concludes with these thoughts: "For who knows not that truth is strong, next to the Almighty; she needs no policies, nor strategems, nor licensings to make her victorious; those are the shifts and the defences that error uses against another power. . . . What great purchase is this Christian liberty which Paul so often boasts of? His doctrine is, that he who eats or eats not, regards a day or regards it not, may do either to the Lord. How many other things might be tolerated in peace, and left to conscience, had we but charity, and were it not the chief stronghold of our hypocrisy to be ever judging one another."[235] No doctrine became more hallowed in the United States than that of freedom of the press.

It has already been observed that Milton favored a mixed government, in which he originally accepted monarchy. But by 1651, he had come to doubt that a king was right for England and he justified not only deposing Charles I but also executing him. After that, he leaned more and more to a republican form of government. That was his view in *The Ready and Easy Way to Establish a Free Commonwealth* published in 1659. He wanted a representative government, something on the order of the House of Commons, to whom the authority to govern had been delegated. This body would then choose a Council which would exercise the executive powers of government. Both from his reading of classical authors and from experience, he feared both democracy and monarchy, and sought to put a buffer between the people and those who would exercise the power of government. He believed, as the Romans had, that for a republic to succeed those who rule and are ruled must have high standards of conduct. He said, "To make the people fittest to choose, and the chosen fittest to govern, will be to amend our corrupt and faulty education, to teach the people faith not without virtue, temperance, modesty, sobriety, parsimony, justice . . . , to place everyone his private welfare and happiness in the public peace, liberty and safety."[236] He also wanted an independent church separated from the power of the state. In this, too, his work foreshadowed what took place in the United States.

(4) John Locke

Seventeenth century England produced quite a crop of political thinkers, several of whom had considerable influence on later Americans. Among them are some who should be named here, though they cannot be discussed. James Harrington wrote his *Oceana* in the middle of the century; its main thesis was that the distribution of property had much to do with the political system in a country. Sir Algernon Sidney (1622–1683) had considerable impact on American thinkers with his *Discourses Concerning Government.* The titles of some of the chapters in this book suggest its message: "Mixed and popular governments preserve peace and manage wars better than absolute monarchies." "Mischiefs and cruelties proceeding from tyranny are greater than any that can come from popular or mixed governments." "The liberties of nations are from God and nature, not from Kings."[237] Others would include John Selden, Harry Vane, Henry Neville, and Benjamin Hoadly.

But John Locke (1632–1704) looms above all the others in his influence on Americans of the Founding era. His *Second Treatise on Civil Government* may well have been the most influential book on political theory ever written. It was probably the most lucid work explaining natural law ever written, and it came at a time when the attachment to and application of natural law was moving toward a peak. The *Two Treatises on Civil Government,* of which the *Second* is by far the most important, was published in the wake of the Glorious Revolution and is generally accepted as the philosophical justification of that event and the settlement which followed. His work was especially important to Americans because he justified revolution and Jefferson even used some of his phraseology in the Declaration of Independence. Locke was a major source of Whig thought, which was often dominant in Britain in the 18th century, and was universally accepted in America among the leaders of the movement for independence and the Founders of the United States.

Locke was born in Somersetshire, England, grew up in a mild Puritan household, and was educated at Oxford when the Puritans were coming to power in England. He retained his connections at Oxford afterward and had a living of sorts from his efforts as a tutor, and the like. He might have become a clergyman had there been greater toleration in his day, and he dabbled in medicine for a while, but his enduring reputation rests on his writings in political thought and philosophy. Indeed, Locke is known to philosophy mainly for his *Essay Concerning Human Understanding,* a speculative work on the psychology of the working of the mind. His political works are prized primarily for their support of popular government and individual liberty.

Undoubtedly, Locke's *Letters Concerning Toleration* had an impact on Americans in their efforts to limit and contain government from intervention in religious matters. Locke looks at both government and religion in terms of their distinct natures, which is the natural law approach to a subject. He concludes that it is "necessary to distinguish exactly the business of civil government from that of religion, and to settle the just bounds that lie between the one and the other." Government, he concludes, is properly concerned with such matters as the protection of life, liberty, and property.

But, he says, it has nothing to contribute to the salvation of souls, which is the principal business of religion. He argues that the "care of souls is not committed to the civil magistrate [government] any more than to other men. It is not committed unto him, I say, by God; because it appears not that God has ever given any such authority to one man over another, as to compel any one to his religion. Nor can any such power be vested in the magistrate by the consent of the people. . . ." Moreover, he points out, the civil magistrate (or government) operates as such only with the use of force, and force is ineffective in altering or fixing the beliefs of men. This argument is more broadly an argument for intellectual freedom in all areas. He goes on, "In the third place, the care of the salvation of men's souls cannot belong to the magistrate; because, though the rigour of laws and the force of penalties were capable [which he says they are not] to convince and change men's minds, yet would not that help at all to the salvation of their souls. . . ."[238]

Locke began his political theory by reasoning from a state of nature, just as Hobbes had done, though his view of man in a state of nature was not nearly so dismal. By "state of nature" thinkers generally meant that state in which man would be without government, whether such a state ever existed or not. The state of nature, Locke wrote, is a condition in which all men are in "a state of perfect freedom to order their actions and dispose of their possessions and persons as they think fit, within the bounds of the law of nature, without asking leave or depending upon the will of any other man."[239] (He did not suppose that children were in such a condition in a state of nature and could be so free, something he explained later on.) He also held that people in a state of nature would all be equal, though his argument for that is not very persuasive. He did not think that it would be a state in which men might *right*fully run rough shod over one another, since they would be subject to the law of nature which could be discovered by the effective use of reason.

Even so, men quit the state of nature and form political societies, and this is universally the case, as Locke himself observed. Why would he do so, if the state of nature was so delightful? Here, Locke gave the usual answer, although he did not put it so starkly as Hobbes had done. He submits to government for fear that others would molest his person, reduce his liberty, and take away his property. Men form or submit to government "for the mutual preservation of their lives, liberties, and estates." More bluntly, he said:

> The great and chief end, therefore, of men uniting into common-wealths, and putting themselves under government, is the preservation of their property; to which in a state of nature there are many things wanting.[240]

Among the things he said that were wanting in a state of nature were: a settled set of laws which all must accept, or at least be expected to know, someone to apply the law such as an impartial judge, power to enforce the law, and the like.

The powers which men have in a state of nature, such as self defense and the punishment of offenders, they either continue to exercise now jointly with others in a democratic assembly, or elect others to act for them in a legislature. The legislature, Locke thought, would usually be the most important branch of the government because it would make the laws under which people were to live. Locke held that the following four rules should be observed:

> First, they are to govern by promulgated established laws, not to be varied in particular cases, nor to have one rule for rich and poor, for the favorite at court, and the countryman at plough.
>
> Secondly: These laws also ought to be designed for no other end ultimately but the good of the people.
>
> Thirdly: They must not raise taxes on the property of the people without the consent of the people given by themselves or their deputies. . . .
>
> Fourthly: The legislative power neither must nor can transfer the power of making laws to anybody else, or place it anywhere but where the people have. . . . [241]

These principles were ones that the Founders of the United States generally accepted for legislatures also.

Locke was so devoted to natural law that he thought it ought to be the great guide for lawmakers as well. He said, "Thus the law of nature stands as an external rule to all men, legislators as well as others. The rules that they make for other men's actions must, as well as their own . . . , be conformable to the law of nature—i. e., to the will of God, of which that is a declaration, and the fundamental law of nature, being the preservation of mankind, no human sanction can be good or valid against it."[242]

In Locke's opinion, man did not give up any of his freedom or rights when he subjected himself to government. True, he is subject to taxation under government, and some portion of his property can thereby be taken from him. But, as Locke would have it, he has given his consent to this, either by participating in the election of representatives who tax him, or by subjecting himself to government.

Locke subscribed to the notion that governments are formed by a social compact or contract. It is not clear whether he is speaking ideally, potentially, or historically in taking this position. In any case, we do know that in many cases throughout history peoples have been governed by rulers who did not enter into any such compact. Be that as it may, Locke described how such a compact might be formed this way:

. . . The only way whereby any one . . . puts on the bonds of civil society, is by agreeing with other men to join and unite into a community, for their comfortable, safe, and peaceable living one amongst another, in a secure enjoyment of their properties, and a greater security against any that are not of it. . . .

For when any number of men have, by the consent of every individual, made a community, they have thereby made that community one body, with a power to act as one body, which is only by the will and determination of the majority. . . .

And thus every man, by consenting with others to make one body politic under one government, puts himself under an obligation to every one of that society to submit to the determination of the majority. . . .[243]

But whether what Locke's account describes is the universal method of forming governments or not, it was close enough to the American condition and methods to apply to and be applied by them to their formation of governments. That is roughly what they did.

Locke also wrote a justification for revolution in his *Second Treatise on Civil Government*. He says that when a legislature (or presumably, a government) becomes arbitrary, dictatorial, and acts in violation of the compact, it is the right of the people to dispose of it and install another in its place. While Locke may have been troubled by the objection that in saying these things he was encouraging people to revolt casually and frequently, he denied that this would be the case. He did not doubt that there might be people who would try to stir up rebellion or revolution. "It is true," said Locke, "such men stir whenever they please, but it will only be to their own just ruin and perdition. For till the mischief be grown general, and the ill designs of the rulers become visible, or their attempts sensible to the greater part, the people who are more disposed to suffer than right themselves by resistance, are not apt to stir. . . ."[244] This idea in some of the same words appears in the Declaration of Independence.

If Locke did not exactly announce and embrace a doctrine of natural rights, he set the stage for it. Clearly, the rights which he outlined in his writings were "unalienable," as men would say in the 18th century, and it was already clear that they proceeded from the nature of things. At any rate, some things were left for writers in the 18th century with greater directness and in more detail.

(5) Trenchard and Gordon

The English governmental system did not change much in the course of the 18th century. Great Britain—the island—became the United Kingdom of England, Wales, and Scotland in 1707. After the death of Queen Anne, the transition to the House of Hanover went off smoothly, though for George I and George II English was not their native language. In any case, "Georgian" more aptly described an architectural style than it did a system of government. Even so, England was getting more freedom by intellectual nuance and interpretation than by changes in institutions. English thought on restraining government and liberating men was moving toward that crescendo that would take place in the United States in the late 18th century.

John Trenchard and Thomas Gordon were two Englishmen who contributed much to this development in the first two or three decades of the 18th century. They did so mainly by their journalistic writings which appeared mainly in two publications, *The Independent Whig* and *Cato's Letters*. The *Independent Whig* dealt mainly with such religious matters as the relation of church and state, the intolerance of high churchmen, and religious liberty. *Cato's Letters* dealt more broadly with a whole range of political ideas. John Trenchard was educated at Dublin, trained as a lawyer, and admitted to the bar, but did not long trouble himself with that profession. Thomas Gordon's background is uncertain, although he may have had some university or legal training. Their main contribution, however, was their popularization of ideas on limited government and individual liberty.

Trenchard and Gordon's major journalistic contributions occurred mainly in the first quarter of the 18th century, but they continued to spread through the English-speaking world through much of the rest of the century through the printing of collections of their works. An American edition of their work appeared in New York in 1724 and another from Philadelphia in 1740. John Adams wrote in 1816 that in the early 1770s "Cato's Letters and the Independent Whig, and all the writings of Trenchard and Gordon . . . became fashionable reading." A 20th century American historian, Clinton Rossiter, wrote that "No one can spend any time in the newspapers, library inventories, and pamphlets of colonial America without realizing that *Cato's Letters* rather than Locke's *Civil Government* was the most popular, quotable, esteemed source of political ideas in the colonial period."[245] This last may be a slight exaggeration, but a look at some of their ideas should confirm the influence.

Here is their explanation of the unalienable right to liberty:

All men are born free; Liberty is a Gift which they receive from God; nor can they alienate the same by Consent, though possibly they may forfeit it by Crimes. . . .

The Right [i. e., power] of the Magistrate arises only from the Right of private Men to defend themselves, to repel Injuries, and to punish those who commit them: That Right being conveyed by the Society to their publick Representative, he can execute the same no further than the Benefit and Security of that Society requires that he should. When he exceeds his Commission, his Acts are as extrajudicial as are those of any private Officer usurping an unlawful Authority, that is, they are void. . . .[246]

Their definition of liberty is a classic one and was very similar to ones that some of the Founders later gave. They say that "Liberty" is the "power which every man has over his own Actions, and his Right to enjoy the Fruit of his Labour, Art, and Industry, as far as by it he hurts not the Society, or any Members of it, by taking from any Member, or by hindering him from enjoying what he himself enjoys. The Fruits of a Man's honest Industry are the just Rewards of it, ascertained to him by natural and eternal Equity, as is his Title to use them in the Manner which he thinks fit: And thus, with the above Limitations, every Man is sole Lord and Arbiter of his own private Actions and Property. . . ."[247] They also drive home the point once again that living in society under government does not substantially alter these rights. "The entering into political Society," they say, "is so far from a Departure from his natural Right, that to preserve it was the sole Reason why men did so; and mutual Protection and Assistance is the only reasonable Purpose of all reasonable Societies."[248]

With great insight, Trenchard and Gordon say that there are two constitutional means to limit and restrain government. One is to make the interests of those who govern and are governed the same. This might be done by having all those with any substantial interest in what government does assemble in person and vote on it. If representatives vote, they may be required to live under and in accord with the laws that they pass. The other constitutional means would be to deny to those who govern the power to do things contrary to the common good.

The titles of some of the essays will indicate the primary concern of the authors in limiting government and preserving individual liberty. For example: "Of Freedom of Speech: That the same is inseparable from Publick Liberty;" "What Measures are actually taken by wicked and desparate Ministers to ruin and enslave their Country;" "How free Governments are to be framed so as to last, and how they differ from such as are arbitrary;" "Of the Restraints which ought to be laid upon publick Rulers," and many more of a similar character. Trenchard and Gordon provided a primer, of sorts, for founding free governments, and it is small wonder then that Americans were influenced by it.

(6) Sir William Blackstone

The first volume of Blackstone's *Commentaries on the Laws of England* was published in London in 1765, and the succeeding volumes over the next several years. It is of more than a little interest that they were published in Philadelphia in 1771, and were ready to make their impact at just that time in American history when they could have the greatest influence. The material that went into the *Commentaries* had first been delivered as lectures at Oxford from 1753 onward, and their fame preceded their publication in book form. Blackstone's lectures were so well organized, so clear, expressed with such felicity, and carried such conviction that Blackstone's place in history was virtually assured by their publication. Nothing like them had ever appeared in English before, and little since.

William Blackstone (1723–1780) was born in England, the son of a London merchant who died before William was born. The boy had the best of education, going from school to Oxford and eventually to the study of the law. The practice of law did not satisfy him, and he returned to lecture at Oxford, where he did his best known writing and acquired his reputation. Given the system, he must and did stand for and get elected to Parliament, but he was an indifferent legislator, as it turned out. He spent the last ten years as a judge in the court of common pleas.

It was not, however, in the details of his life that his greatness lay but rather in the majesty of his *Commentaries on the Laws of England.* The impact of this work was great in England and other English-speaking lands, but especially in the United States. Of his influence on the United States, Russell Kirk has observed, "Although Blackstone was not quite the Solon of America, probably no other new nation-state has been so much governed by a single legal authority from abroad. Until the middle of the nineteenth century, there were not a few American judges whose chief source of legal knowledge was a copy of Blackstone. . . ." As his premier example, he says: "When John Marshall was a boy in the Blue Ridge Mountains, on Virginia's frontier, his father subscribed for him to the first American edition of Blackstone. . . . Father and son read those volumes together, the boy being intended for the bar. John Marshall would become the greatest of chief justices. . . . Like his more learned colleague, Joseph Story, Marshall accepted Blackstone as the best of guides in the labyrinth of the law."[249]

Two things Americans learned from Blackstone, the great importance of natural law and devotion to the Common Law as he had expounded it. In his writing he tended to cut through the contradictions and confusions of natural law and common law to their sensible essences, making them more available, believable, and useful. His definition of natural law may go all the way back to Cicero, but the economy with which he states it is remarkable:

> This law of nature, being co-eval with mankind and dictated by God himself, is of course superior in obligation to any other. It is binding over all the globe, and all countries, and at all times: no human laws are of any validity if contrary to this; and such of them as are valid derive all their force, and all their authority, mediately or immediately from this original.[250]

This last clause makes an especially strong claim; it says that all man-made laws, i. e., positive laws, must reflect natural law and be in accord with it to be valid and have the force of law. It may be more readily understood if we understand him to be saying that laws to be valid must be in accord with and reflect the nature of things. Otherwise, the law would be an attempt to change the very nature of things. But, of course, that is precisely what intellectuals have been increasingly bent on doing for more than a hundred years now—change the very nature of things. Or, on their way to that end, to deny that man or things have a nature. This bent explains why they have rejected and despised Blackstone for so long now.

Blackstone was also a vigorous adocate of the natural rights of man. He explained the position this way:

> For the principal aim of society is to protect individuals in the enjoyment of those absolute rights which were vested in them by the immutable laws of nature; but which could not be preserved in peace without that mutual assistance and intercourse which is gained by the institution . . . of communities. Hence it follows that the first and primary end of human laws is to maintain . . . those *absolute* rights of individuals. . . .
>
> The absolute rights of man . . . are usually summed up in one general appellation, and denominated the natural liberty of mankind. This natural liberty consists properly in a power of acting as one thinks fit, without any restraint or control, unless by the law of nature; being a right inherent in us by birth, and one of the gifts of God to man at his creation, when he endued him with the faculty of freewill. . . . [251]

Blackstone makes clear, however, that the "natural liberty" of man is set in a different and more restrained framework when he enters society and comes under government. Some rights, such as that of self defense, for example, are then regulated, and in other cases what Blackstone calls "civil privileges" may be provided "in lieu of the natural liberty so given up," which he lists as "the right of personal security, the right of personal liberty, and the right of private property." These, however, as best it can be interpreted, have the same character generally as natural rights under government protection.

Blackstone was also a great expounder and defender of the English common law. Americans, at the time of the founding of the United States, generally revered and incorporated it into our system by various references and provisions. That this was done owes more than a little to Blackstone's *Commentaries,* for he not only made the common law more comprehensible and readily available but also fitted it into a natural law framework. The common law had grown up over a period of nearly a thousand years, had incorporated custom and ancient usage, and underwent a continual winnowing which tended to leave a residue of man's legal wisdom over the ages.

That what remained vital would likely be closer to being in keeping with the nature of things than legislation contrived without its aid, seemed probable to Blackstone. The common law resisted change—hence, was conservative—yet yielded to reason with the passage of time. Reason was the touchstone of natural law, but reason tempered by knowledge and long experience.

(7) Adam Smith

One other thinker needs to be covered before we turn away from the British, *per se*. Adam Smith (1723–1790) was neither an Englishman by birth nor a political theorist or philosopher. He was born in Kirkcaldy, Scotland and made his most famous contribution in what was in earlier times referred to as political economy and is now generally called economics. Smith began his college education at the University of Glasgow, went on from there to study at Oxford, and then coming back to lecture for a goodly number of years at Glasgow. In his later years, he served as tutor to a young noble and traveled with him in southern Europe. In France, Smith met and had lengthy discussions with the Physiocrats Quesnay and Turgot, among others. He learned from them and became firm in his views about economics. His best known work, *The Wealth of Nations,* was published in 1776 and was very soon a classic in its own right. It may have been a coincidence that Smith's great book and the American Declaration of Independence were issued in the same year, but both are great landmarks of liberty.

The Wealth of Nations deserves discussion here, even though it is not primarily about government. Smith wrote from the vantage point of natural law and natural rights and applied these to the relationship between government and the economy. In the course of history, governments have often intervened in economic activity for the alleged benefit of society. At the time that Adam Smith wrote, governments in Western Europe had long been engaged in promoting manufacturing in their own countries and discouraging imports of manufactured goods into their own countries through subsidies and tariffs. Smith called this system "mercantilism," and proceeded to disprove its major premises. But the thrust of his work was broader than that, for he held that economic activity freed from government control, regulations, and prohibitions generally, would work best for the good of all people and nations.

Smith described the system of natural liberty for an economy this way:

> All systems either of preference or of restraint, therefore, being thus completely taken away, the obvious and simply system of natural liberty establishes itself of its own accord. Every man, as long as he does not violate the laws of justice, is left perfectly free to pursue his own interest his own way, and to bring his industry and capital into

competition with those of any other men or order of men. The sovereign is completely discharged from a duty, in the attempting to perform which he must always be exposed to innumerable delusions, and for the proper performance of which no human wisdom or knowledge could ever be sufficient; the duty of superintending the industry of private people, and of directing it towards the employments most suitable to the interest of society. According to the system of natural liberty, the sovereign has only three duties to attend to . . . : first, the duty of protecting the society from the violence and invasion of other independent societies; secondly, the duty of protecting . . . every member of the society from the injustice or oppression of every other member of it . . . ; and, thirdly, the duty of erecting and maintaining certain public works and certain public institutions. . . .[252]

In sum, Smith did not believe that government could or should intervene in the economy under whatever pretence it might do so. Of the mercantile regulations, he said:

It is the highest impertinence and presumption, therefore, in kings and ministers, to pretend to watch over the economy of private people, and to restrain their expence, either by sumptuary laws, or by prohibiting the importation of foreign luxuries. They are always themselves, and without any exception, the greatest spendthrifts in the society. Let them look well after their own expence, and they may safely trust private people with theirs.[253]

The truth was, Adam Smith thought, those who rule or govern us lack the know-how to manage and control an economy, not because of some deficiency in rulers but rather because man's abilities are not god-like. He put it this way:

The statesman, who should attempt to direct private people in what manner they ought to employ their capital, would not only load himself with a most unnecessary attention, but assume an authority which could safely be trusted, not only to no single person, but to no council or senate whatever, and would nowhere be so dangerous as in the hands of a man who had folly and presumption enough to fancy himself fit to exercise it.[254]

The reason Smith was so certain of what he was saying is that by attending to the nature of things he discovered both the springs of economic activity and an underlying harmony between the peaceful pursuit of self-interest and the general well-being of society. The key, he thought, lies in the individual's motives to produce as much as he can and the corresponding benefit to society of the greater quantity of goods available for consumption. The motive is described this way by Smith:

> Every individual is continually exerting himself to find out the most advantageous employment for whatever capital he can command. It is his own advantage, indeed, and not that of society, which he has in view. But the study of his own advantage naturally, or rather necessarily, leads him to prefer that employment which is most advantageous to the society.[255]

How this works in practice was described in considerable more detail by Smith:

> The produce of industry is what it adds to the subject or materials upon which it is employed. In proportion as the value of this produce is great or small, so will likewise be the profits of the employer. But it is only for the sake of profit that any man employs a capital in the support of industry; and he will always, therefore, endeavor to employ it in the support of that industry of which the produce is likely to be of the greatest value, or to exchange for the greatest quantity either of money or other goods.

In effect, Smith went on to point out that the produce of the country is the sum of that produced within its bounds by all individuals and companies. Now, he continues with his larger point:

> As every individual, therefore, endeavours as much as he can both to employ his capital in support of domestic industry, and so to direct that industry that its produce may be of the greatest value; every individual necessarily labours to render the annual revenue of the society as great as he can. He generally, indeed, neither intends to promote the public interest, nor knows how much he is promoting it. By preferring the support of domestic to that of foreign industry, he intends only his own security; and by directing that industry in such a manner as its produce may be of the greatest value, he intends only his own gain, and is in this, as in many other cases, led by an invisible hand to promote an end which was no part of his intention. Nor is it always the worse for society that it was no part of it. By pursuing his own interest he frequently promotes that of the society more effectually than when he really intends to promote it. I have never known much good done by those who affected to trade for the public good. It is an affectation, indeed, not very common among merchants, and few words need be employed in dissuading them from it.

Smith not only pointed out the futility and harmfulness of attempts of government to direct the economy within the country, but he thought it was in the interest of peoples everywhere that trade among peoples of different nations be free as well. He summed up the case for free trade this way: "The interest of a nation in its commercial relations to foreign nations is, like that of a merchant with regard to the different people with whom he deals, to buy as cheap and to sell as dear [high] as possible. But it will be most likely to buy cheap, when by the most perfect freedom of trade it encourages all nations to bring to it the goods which it has occasion to purchase; and, for the same reason, it will be most likely to sell dear, when its markets are thus filled with the greatest number of buyers."[256]

Adam Smith made the case for economic freedom, as John Milton had made the case for a free press, as Trenchard and Gordon made the case for religious freedom, and as Blackstone and others made the case for the rights to private property. Indeed, English statesmen had long since made the case for limited government, though they never went so far in practice with that as the Americans would. The British often appealed to their constitution, too, and there are many documents which give substance to it, though it falls short of being a written constitution in the American sense. In any case, there should be no doubt that Americans went to school, so to speak, to their English heritage in the 18th century, and learned many of its principles and lessons well.

Even so, Americans had a considerable experience of their own during the colonial period, and it was this experience which had the greatest immediacy at the time of the founding of the United States, though it, too, was derived, much of it anyway, from the British background.

Chapter 6
American Colonial Experience

The American experience as colonies of England was nearly as long as the experience under the Constitution has been to date. There were continuous English colonial settlements from 1607 to 1783, when Britain recognized by treaty the independence of the American states, though independence had been declared in 1776. The Constitution went into effect in 1789 and has provided the basic foundation for the United States government to the present. Although earlier efforts were made, the first successful colony was planted at Jamestown in 1607, and the last was made in Georgia in 1732. Initially, such settlements were commonly referred to as *plantations* rather than or in addition to being called colonies. In time, of course, the original term was applied to large rural estates, worked by slaves, and the settlements were called colonies. Most of the colonies were founded under the Stuart monarchs and in the 17th century. Most of them were founded and their patterns or forms of government set before the Glorious Revolution, and the changes which were made in England were not fully extended to the colonies.

At any rate, Americans had a long and fruitful colonial experience during which they got much familiarity with government. They learned to like local government and to fear and dislike government at great remove from them. They, of course, developed a bias in favor of self-government and an increasing distaste for monarchy and royal government. Their attachment for constitutional government was firmly fixed during this period, too. It may be well to note, too, that the forming of governments by the consent of (at least some of) the governed was a common experience of Americans during this period. Those who object to Locke's description on the grounds that it was unhistorical in its account of how governments have actually been formed have not read American colonial history with discernment.

The establishment of government in the colonies was usually done by charters, compacts, or other decrees or agreements. Since the Virginia colony was the first, it may be examined in some little detail for what it tells us about the form of colonial governments. The first charter, issued in 1606, authorized two colonies to be settled along the Atlantic coast of North America. The one authorized for the London Company is the one that

161

concerns us here, for that company undertook the settlement at Jamestown. The charter provided that the colony "shall have a Council, which shall govern and order all Matters and Causes, which shall arise, grow, or happen, to or within the . . . Colonies. . . ." These Councils were to reside within the colony for which they were appointed, to consist of thirteen persons, and were to act in accord with the laws of England, or, as the charter said, "according to such Laws, Ordinances, and Instructions" as shall come by the hand and seal of the King of England. The charter also provided that a Council of Thirteen was to be established of persons residing in England who would have the overseeing of these colonies. The council method of management or governing within the colony did not last long, because groups are not very effective rulers.

This first charter also provided potentially very important privileges and rights for those who would settle in America, and similar provisions were contained in most other charters. It provided that "all . . . Persons, being our Subjects, which shall dwell and inhabit within . . . any of the said Colonies and Plantations, and every [one] of their children, which shall happen to be born within any of the Limits and Precincts of the said several Colonies and Plantations, shall HAVE and enjoy all Liberties, Franchises, and Immunities, within any of our other Dominions, to all Intents and Purposes, as if they had been abiding and born, within this our Realm of *England*, or any other of our said Dominions. . . ."[257]

By July, 1619, Virginia had the basic forms of colonial government as they would take shape elsewhere as well. It had a governor, a council (to the governor), and a legislative assembly. The colony was still run under the auspices of the London Company, but that would change in 1624 when it became a royal colony. The fact that Virginia in 1619 had a legislative assembly is most important for the establishment of representative government in America. The document authorizing this change has been lost, but it is believed very similar to an Ordinance for Virginia issued in July, 1621. It refers to the governor, his council, and a legislative assembly. The council, the Ordinance said, would mainly be concerned with "assisting with their Care, Advice, and Circumspection, to the said Governor." The assembly, which came to be called the House of Burgesses, was to be elected from the towns, and other rural election districts, by the inhabitants of them. The governor was to call the assembly into session once a year, and on extraordinary occasions, and questions taken up by them were to be resolved by majority vote. The Ordinance says that the legislature "shall have free power to treat, consult, and conclude, as well of all emergent occasions concerning the Publick Weal of the said Colony and every part thereof, as also to make, ordain, and enact such general Laws and Orders, for the Behoof of the said Colony, and the good Government thereof as shall from time to time appear necessary or requisite. . . ." Such enactments were, of course, subject to the absolute veto of the governor and to the further restraint that they "follow the form of Government—Laws, Customs, and manner of trial, and other Administration of Justice, used in the Realm of England."[258]

Elsewhere, in 1620, an equally dramatic event had taken place in America. A group of people known as the Pilgrims landed at Plymouth in what is now Massachusetts (but was then reckoned to be in the northern part of Virginia). They did indeed form a covenant to provide for their government much in the manner that natural law theorists imagined. It was the Mayflower Compact. Since it is a brief document, it is in order to quote most of it:

> In the Name of God, Amen. We whose names are underwritten, the loyal subjects of our dread Sovereign Lord King James, by the Grace of God of Great Britain, France, and Ireland. . . .
>
> Having undertaken, for the Glory of God and advancement of the Christian Faith and Honour of our King and Country, a Voyage to plant the First Colony in the Northern Parts of Virginia, do by these presents solemnly and mutually in the presence of God and one of another, Covenant and Combine ourselves together into a Civil Body Politic, for our better ordering and preservation and furtherance of the ends aforesaid; and by virtue hereof to enact, constitute and frame such just and equal Laws, Ordinances, Acts, Constitutions and Offices, from time to time, as shall be thought most meet and convenient for the general good of the Colony, unto which we promise all due submission and obedience. . . .[259]

There followed a lengthy list of the signatures of the heads of households and grown men in the company. This document served the Pilgrims for such charter or constitution as they had during the early years.

Most of the colonies had charters that were grants of the territories they were to inhabit, usually from the king, and the charters also frequently spelled out the form of government they were to have and what powers the government would have as well as restraints upon it. Thus, the charters were constitutions of sorts. For example, the charter of the Massachusetts Bay Company, issued in 1629 (which was the charter under which the Puritans settled in Massachusetts in the 1630s and thereafter), served as a kind of constitution for that colony. It was issued by Charles I, but the organizing company came to Massachusetts, bringing the charter with them, and exercised their authority directly, giving them greater latitude in governing than most colonies had. The charter provided for a governor and assembly, referred to as a court, or general court, and that they were empowered "to make Laws and Ordinances for the Good and Welfare of the said Company, and for the Government and ordering of the said Lands and Plantation and People inhabiting . . . the same. . . ." These powers were granted with the limitation, of course, that all the subjects of the King of England who come to live in this territory "shall have and enjoy all liberties and Immunities of free natural subjects . . ." as if they still abided in Great Britain. And, it contained the obligatory provision that all laws and statutes made in the colonies should be "not contrary to the Laws of this our Realm of England."[260]

Of somewhat different order was the Fundamental Orders of Connecticut, adopted in 1639. It was drawn up and adopted by the settlers of the towns of Windsor, Hartford, and Wethersfield, without authorization of any charter from England directly. Although in character the Fundamental Orders of Connecticut most resembles the Mayflower Compact, it differs from that document in that it neither mentions King Charles I, nor the English government, nor pledges obedience to them. Thus, some describe it as "the first written constitution that created a government." That is, it was the first that brought a government into being without relation to any other, save that of God. The language of the Fundamental Orders makes it clear that "we the Inhabitants and Residents of Windsor, Hartford and Wethersfield . . . do therefore associate and conjoin our selves to be as one Public State or Commonwealth; and do, for our selves and our Successors . . . , enter into Combination and Confederation together to maintain and preserve the liberty and purity of the gospel of our Lord Jesus . . . ; As also in our Civil Affairs to be guided and governed according to such Laws, Rules, Orders and decrees as shall be made, ordered and decreed. . . ."

It made clear in the following paragraph that the laws were to be made by an assembly known as a General Court. The members chosen for this assembly "shall be chosen by all that are admitted Inhabitants of the several Towns and have taken the oath of fidelity; provided that none be chosen a Deputy for any General Court which is not a Freeman of this Commonwealth. . . ." Each town was to choose by this election four deputies to be sent to the General Court, "which deputies shall have the power of the whole Town to give their votes and allowance to all such laws and orders as may be for the public good, and unto which the said Towns are to be bound." In addition, a governor and several magistrates, chosen by a Court of Election, were to be a part of the General Court, along with the deputies elected directly by the towns. This last was probably an attempt to get some sort of balance of power in the legislature, as well as a little restraint.[261]

Other agreements and charters for other colonies could be examined, but perhaps the main points have been made with these. It should be clear that the American colonists had considerable experience with making and living under agreements, charters, and constitution-like documents. Indeed, from their earliest days here, it is clear that British Americans believed in having some sort of political compact describing a system of government and authorizing the passage of laws. They were politically naked, so to speak, until they had such a compact or charter, which was, in effect, some sort of constitution. Generally, too, they leaned toward having some sort of elected legislature and an appointive or otherwise chosen executive officer, which they frequently called a governor. Moreover, they were used to having their government restrained by having to act, in general, in accord with British customs and laws.

It is not surprising, then, that when the Americans broke from England and declared their independence they moved as quickly as they could to draw up, if necessary, and adopt constitutions. So it was that when independence was declared, the states either adopted some charter such as they had as their constitution or else drew up a new document and adopted it. So it was, too, that shortly after declaring independence, Congress put a committee to work on drawing up a constitution for the United States. The result of that effort was the Articles of Confederation which was finally ratified in 1781. With that background in mind, it is in order now to turn to their practical political experience during the colonial period.

a. Practical Political Experience

Americans in the colonial period had a goodly amount of practical political experience before they broke from England, experience with the uses and abuses of power.[262] They had it in what is probably the best way to gain experience with the use of power; the power at their disposal was limited and constrained. The colonists gained experience within the confines of the English constitution, in the first place. Their laws were supposed to conform to those of England. To make sure that they did, the system provided that court cases could be appealed to the Privy Council in England.

The colonists were restricted in what they could do also by their charters. Most of the colonies had originally been founded as commercial ventures, though a few were founded as proprietaries which harked back to the feudal system for models, and one—Georgia—was a trust. In any case, they were founded on the basis of charters. These spelled out the territory to be occupied, the financial arrangements, and the rights and privileges of the settlers. Ordinarily, the settlers were permitted to participate in the making of laws, and such laws as were passed had to be in keeping with and not contrary to English law. It would be correct to say that the colonists were both restrained and enfranchised by their charters.

The colonies were restricted also in that they were a part of the British Empire. In that capacity, they fell under the authority of the government of England (after 1707, the United Kingdom) and were subject to certain of the acts of the Crown-in-Parliament.

Before discussing this relationship, however, it will be useful to note some major changes that had occurred in the English government in the last years of the seventeenth century, the changes associated with the Glorious Revolution. These changes raised questions about the extent of parliamentary authority over the colonies under the constitution as it had developed, questions that were not finally pushed to the point of irreconcilable contradiction until the 1770's.

At the time when most of the colonies were chartered and founded, England was more or less of an absolute monarchy. Parliament was, for the Tudors and the early Stuarts, an auxiliary to them in the exercise of their power. In theory, and usually in practice, Parliament was that body which enabled the monarch to make alterations from time to time in the contract with his subjects whom he ruled by Divine right. Ordinarily, he could and did rule without consultations with Parliament. If some change were wanted by the monarch—e. g., a new tax measure—then he might call a session in order to get the needed legislation. If he could get by on established revenues and laws, he had usually foregone the nuisance of having Parliament meet.

The Stuart kings and Parliament were at odds for most of the seventeenth century over their respective powers. The issues were resolved by the Glorious Revolution and its aftermath, resolved in favor of Parliament. As one historian summarizes the consequences of this Revolution, it "demolished the doctrine of the divine right of kings. . . . After that momentous victory Parliament slowly and gradually, yet remorselessly and irresistibly, extended its power in all directions."[263] Another sums up the changes this way:

> William III began his reign with a clear recognition on his part that the royal office had been shorn of extensive powers. As it has been expressed by a distinguished historian of the constitution: "The king was distinctly below statute; he was to have no power to suspend statutes or to dispense with statutes; he could not by his proclamations create any new offence; he could not keep a standing army in the realm in time of peace without the consent of parliament; parliament had begun to appropriate supplies; the military tenures were gone; he had no powers of purveyance and preemption; he could not try men by martial law; the judges were no longer to hold office during his good pleasure. . . ." We may add: he could make no laws without the consent of the nation's representatives; he could lay no taxes; he could claim no kingship by divine right. . . .[264]

In short, Parliament had come to occupy much of the ground formerly held by the monarch and would in the course of the eighteenth century gain much more control over affairs. England had a constitutional monarchy.

These changes affected Americans in two most important ways. One of them is that Parliament's powers were neither clearly delineated nor restricted. The British had spent much energy over the centuries in limiting the king. This was now as well accomplished as it might be without making him impotent. In doing so, however, a new power had been loosed—Parliament.

It is true that the House of Commons is restrained by having its members stand for election. This was so, however, only for England and then the United Kingdom.

The other import of this for Americans was related, for it had to do with what the power of Parliament over colonials would be. The colonists had no representatives in the House of Commons, nor were there any American bishops or nobles sitting in the House of Lords. Moreover, nothing comparable to the Glorious Revolution occurred in the colonies. Parliament proceeded to pass acts affecting the colonies, though there was now doubtful constitutional, warrant for such measures. For a long time the issue was not pushed with vigor by either side; it lay dormant ready to spring to life when differences between the colonists and the mother country rose to the point where constitutional questions would come into focus.

One reason that the issue did not come to the fore was that Parliament exercised restraint in legislating for the colonies until the 1760's. Parliamentary acts known as statutes of the realm usually applied only to England, Wales, and to Scotland after 1707. "Inasmuch as both Parliament and the colonial assemblies exercised the lawmaking power, a rather indefinite distinction between internal and external legislation was allowed to develop. Parliament generally confined itself to the regulation of the external affairs of the colonies (trade, currency, etc.) and permitted the colonial assemblies to legislate for domestic concerns."[265] This policy is sometimes referred to as one of "salutary neglect." Why it should be so called except by a partisan of British rule and Parliament is not clear; it suggests that the colonies were neglected and that Parliament had the authority to impose its will over the colonies—both doubtful propositions.

If there was "neglect," it was in the neglectful manner of the founding of the colonies, not so much in their later governance. The Stuart kings probably had two prime motives in authorizing plantations. One was to benefit England commercially; the other was to be rid of troublesome, undesirable, or, in the case of Roman Catholics to whom they were sympathetic, persecuted elements. The latitude that many of them were given in matters of religion suggests that the monarchs did not expect the growth of large, peaceful societies under their dominion. At any rate, a strong case can be made that over the years the British government was less and less "neglectful" and more and more concerned to tie the colonies close to England and make them conform to the British pattern. It is certain that over the years more and more laws were passed, and more and more attention was given to imposing the British will over the colonies.

One way to see the trend toward greater British control is to look at the types of colonial governments and changes in them. There were three types of governments in the colonies: royal or crown, proprietary, and charter. A royal colony was one in which the colony fell directly under the king: the governor was appointed by the monarch; he was an agent of the king, in effect, acted in the place of the king, and he, in turn, appointed lesser officers. A proprietary colony was one in which the proprietor appointed the governor and otherwise had authority reminiscent of a feudal lord. He, in turn, was a kind of vassal of the king. A charter colony was one operating on the basis of a charter; in effect, the members of the colony were members of a corporation, and the electors among them controlled the government on the basis of the charter.

The trend over the years was for England to extinguish the charters and proprietorships, which the original colonies had been, and to make of them royal colonies. By the middle of the eighteenth century, there were only three proprietary colonies and two charter colonies. The meaning of this is made clearer by this contemporary comment on the power of the people in the charter colonies: "The people in these Colonies chuse their Governors, Judges, Assemblymen, Counsellors, and all the rest of their Officers; and the King and Parliament have as much influence there as in the wilds of Tartary."[266] This is an exaggeration, but it does indicate that the trend toward royal colonies was a trend toward greater British control.

Despite the fact that the colonies had grown up to considerable degree separate from one another, they had a similar form of government to one another and to that of England. Each of them had a governor, whose powers were modeled on those of the English monarch. The extent to which the English attempted to gain or maintain control of colonial development is indicated both by the fact that most colonies were made royal colonies and by the extensive powers of the governor. He "was the personal representative of the king and the symbol of the empire in the colony, 'endowed with vice-regal powers, analogous though inferior in degree to those of the monarch.' As such he was the commander-in-chief of the military forces in the colony and the chief among the agents of the crown. He had the power to appoint judges in the vice-admiralty court, where there was such a court in his colony, and judges, justices of the peace, and sheriffs in the administration of civil justice. He also had the power to nominate members of the executive council . . . , and the power to veto acts passed by the legislature. . . ."[267] He could summon, adjourn, and dissolve the legislature, and he could pardon those who had been convicted of offenses. "The governor's powers were thus fourfold, for he was at once a Crown agent and the effective head of the executive, the legislative, and the judicial arms of government."[268]

A colony ordinarily had one or more councils, but usually there was a single council which served in several capacities. These were men chosen from among natives who were usually men of wealth and position in their communities. In one of their capacities, they were a sort of governor's cabinet, assisting him in governing by advice and in other ways. In another capacity, they might serve as a court of appeals. And, they were the nearest thing to an upper house of the legislature that the colonies had. In this capacity, they were analogous to the House of Lords. Many colonials got experience in governing by serving on councils.

However, most of the colonial political experience was gained by serving in the legislative assembly. This body was known by different names from colony to colony—i. e., House of Delegates, General Court, House of Burgesses, and so forth—but each of the colonies had one. It was the fount of popular government in the colonies, the only body at the level of colony that was chosen by the freeholders. In theory, it was subordinate to the governor in royal and proprietary colonies, awaiting on his call, subject to his dismissal, even subject to being dissolved in favor of the election of a new one, and its acts subject to his absolute veto. It could almost be said that it existed at the pleasure of the governor.

Theory is often one thing, however, practice another, and this was certainly so for the colonial assemblies. In their service in assemblies colonials learned the subtleties by which power is counterbalanced and the maneuvers by which power can be gained. The way they worked, in general, is described by one scholar in this passage:

> One is impressed with the rather prosaic manner in which the lower houses went about the task of extending their authority, with the infrequency of dramatic conflict. They gained much of their power in the course of routine business, quietly and simply extending and consolidating their authority by passing laws and establishing practices, the implications of which escaped both colonial executive and imperial authorities and were not always fully recognized even by the lower houses themselves. In this way they gradually extended their financial authority to include the powers to audit accounts of all public officers, to share in disbursing public funds, and eventually even to appoint officials concerned in collecting and handling revenues.[269]

Some of the devices by which they gained power are interesting and were quite valuable experience for colonists. One position from which they gained leverage over governors was that the salary of most of the governors was paid by their respective colonies. This meant that the legislature had to appropriate it. If they would only appropriate it on an annual basis, the governor would find it expedient to call the legislature into session each year. If they made the appropriation of his salary the last item of business before they were ready to adjourn, he could be, and was, effectively stripped of his powers to prorogue the assembly. "Not content with reducing the governors' legislative power, the assemblies . . . used their control over the purse to usurp many executive functions, insisting that certain conditions be met before appropriation bills were sanctioned. Thus the assemblies extended their sway over financial matters by stating in detail how money was to be spent, by appointing provincial treasurers . . . , by naming collectors of the revenues . . . , and by setting up committees to supervise the spending of money appropriated."[270]

Colonists got political experience at two other levels than that of colony. One level that did not involve many people directly but was nonetheless important was as agent for a colony to the government in England. An agent was sent from most colonies toward the end of the colonial period to England to explain to various governing bodies the situation in the particular colony, the attitudes of the inhabitants, and the effects laws and other English actions might have. Sometimes both a governor and a legislature would send such an agent. He would have no official standing in England, but he would be valued for his service both by the mother country and the colonies and would gain much valuable experience. Benjamin Franklin undoubtedly got the most experience as agent, for he represented several colonies at one time; through this experience, he was prepared for the yeoman work he would later perform as diplomat for the United States.

The other level was local governments. Of their importance, Clinton Rossiter says: "In general, the central governments of the colonies exercised even less control over local institutions than did the mother country over the colonies." That is, they managed most governmental affairs locally by institutions that were in keeping with the locale. In New England, town government was the most important level, and the town meeting the device by which the electorate directed affairs. In other parts of the country, county and parish government handled most local affairs. These were the features of local governments Rossiter thought particularly worthy of note: "the broader suffrage for local than for colony-wide elections; the multiplicity of unpaid offices and duties, a system under which a much larger percentage of citizens performed some sort of public duty than is the case today. . . ."[271] In short, a large number of colonists had political experience while they were under nominal British control.

The British government did not neglect the colonists in the last hundred years or so of the colonial period. They set over most of them an arrangement that should, in theory, have brought them under the will of those who governed in England. There were governors with comprehensive appointive powers, numerous agents of a variety of boards and committees were sent to America, and Americans were in some ways more clearly under the dominion of the king than were the inhabitants of the United Kingdom. Short of taking from the Americans their institutions of government, it is not clear how they could have been prevented from developing as they did.

Nonetheless, the American colonies did evolve away from the British pattern, even as, to a lesser extent, the government in the homeland was evolving away from its older pattern. Americans today do not feel great unfamiliarity with colonial institutions and practices as they had developed by 1765. They would, however, if they understood them, find most of the institutions that were originally transplanted unfamiliar and foreign. Many of these institutions were medieval in character when they had been set up. For example, a town was a corporation with definite bounds, with privileges for its inhabitants, with powers to exclude others from them, with monopolistic powers, with an exclusive and delimited character. This had so far broken down by the end of the colonial period that men could generally come and go, move in or out, and go about their business without much onerous restriction.

In a similar and related manner, there was an attempt to maintain class arrangements and prescriptions in America. In the middle of the seventeenth century, the General Court of Massachusetts forbade the wearing of certain clothing to the lower orders. Yet, such efforts were of little avail, and long before the end of the colonial period it was commonly observed that respect for and distinctions among classes were disappearing.

When confronted with the Puritan demands for the abolition of episcopacy, James I declared, "No bishop, no king." His prophecy proved correct for America. Though there were several colonies in which the Anglican Church was established, there was never a bishop in America. The Bishop of London was appointed over the American colonies, and he was represented from time to time in particular colonies by a commissary, a man appointed to perform some of the overseeing functions of the bishop. But there was no clerical hierarchy that amounted to anything in America. Hence, even in Anglican colonies, the control of church affairs tended to slip out of the hands of the clergy and into that of the vestry. Of course, in several of the colonies, the prevailing denominations neither had any hierarchy nor approved of it as an institution. The religious supports for rule by an hierarchical order were missing.

In the same manner, there was never any titled nobility in the colonies to speak of. There is a saying that "Dukes don't migrate," and it is substantially true. For decades on end most Americans never saw a titled noble, and if they did, he was most likely a royal governor. No native Americans were ever raised to such rank, to my knowledge, nor is it likely that they aspired to it. Americans who acquired extensive possessions aspired to the life of a country gentleman, so far as we can tell, and would have been aliens in their own country had they been titled.

The effect of this is that Americans turned away from the old sources of authority and political power even more than did their counterparts in England. Authority, for them, did not extend from the top downward; it derived from the place they were accorded by their peers. Americans looked up to men who had acquired possessions by their own efforts or that of their immediate forebears and, among these, to those who showed ability at managing their affairs. Birth counted for little; achievement counted most.

Probably, Americans had more extensive experience in governing in legislatures, in towns, in counties, and as councilors than did any people anywhere in the world at that time. True, it was limited experience. They had little experience as chief executives or in foreign affairs, and they operated within the limitations of the British constitution and the empire. Even so, they were probably better prepared for popular government than anyone else, unless it was the English people themselves.

b. Development of Ideas on Liberty

The development of ideas in English America paralleled that in Britain. Indeed, it may well have been the case that by the 1760s Americans were more attuned to and attached to their natural rights and liberties, and more versed in them, than were those who still resided in the old country. When Thomas Paine called Americans to separate from England in his stirring book, *Common Sense,* he declared that "A government of our own is our natural right; and when a man seriously reflects on the precariousness of human affairs, he will become convinced that it is infinitely wiser and safer to form a Constitution of our own in a cool, deliberate manner while we have it in our power than to trust such an interesting event to time and chance."[272] Jefferson based his argument in the Declaration of Independence upon the "Laws of Nature and of Nature's God." State constitutions frequently listed a number of rights which were described as "natural." The United States Constitution was implicitly derived from an order explicit in the natural law philosophy. As Clinton Rossiter has said of the Americans of the founding era: "The principles in which they placed their special trust were . . . those of . . . the school of natural law." More, the limits they sought for political power were "more universal than those staked out in laws, charters, and constitutions." The great philosophy that preached the reality of moral restraints on power had always been part of their Anglo-Christian heritage. Now in their time of trial, the colonists summoned it to their defense.[273]

Up to the point where Americans declared their independence of Britain, they could and did cast their defense, in part at least, in terms of the British constitution, the charters granted by the king, the rights of Englishmen, and the like. But once they had made the break, none of this would do any more. They had to rest their case on something broader and more universal. The natural law philosophy was ready to hand, and they utilized it to the full.

Since it played such a crucial role in the establishment of American independence and the founding of the United States, it is in order to make a summary at this point of the main tenets of natural law as they had come to be viewed by many Americans.[274] The crucial feature of it was that conclusions were drawn by reasoning on the nature of things. The natural law doctrines which had arisen from this approach had been a staple of Western thought since the time of the Roman Stoics, and its antecedents go back even further than that, as has been pointed out earlier in this book.

Interest in and attachment to these doctrines was not constant, of course; it waxed and waned over the centuries. But every revival of learning (harking back to and rediscovering aspects of Ancient thought) brought renewed interest in natural law, up to and including the classical revival of the 17th and 18th centuries. Indeed, Otto Gierke declared that "The development of natural-law ideas . . . attained its culmination at the end of the eighteenth century. After that time," he continued, "we can begin to trace a process of collapse and disintegration in the natural-law system of thought."[275]

The impact of the natural law idea is suggested in this summary by a contemporary scholar: "It was a theory which culminated in the American Declaration of Independence in 1776 and the French Revolution in 1789. It was a theory adorned by many illustrious names—Hooker and Suarez; Althusius, Grotius and Pufendorf; Milton and Sidney; Hobbes, Locke and Rousseau; Spinoza and Leibnitz; Thomasius and Wolff . . . , Vico and Beccaria; Fichte and Kant."[276] But if we examine the extended impact of the concept, many more famous names should be included in the role: Newton, Gallileo, and Franklin; Haydn, Mozart, and Vivaldi; Jefferson, Adams, and Paine; Blackstone, Hume, Smith, Turgot, and Ricardo; Pope, Addison, and Steele.

Perhaps the natural law system can be best understood in terms of certain doctrines developed out of it. Underlying these doctrines was the belief that this is an orderly universe whose order is reasonable and can be understood by the application of reason. What makes it orderly is the underlying natural order. Undergirding this is the belief that there is a law for man and a law for things, that everything has its own nature imbedded in it, that these things account for perceived regularities, and there is a remarkable harmony pervading all of Creation. The following are some of the natural law doctrines: state of nature, the laws of nations, social contract, and natural rights.

The key to natural law doctrines is that they come into view when we focus our attention on the enduring features of reality. They are discovered by an act of the mind in stripping away all that changes, that is ephemeral, that is cultural, that is a result of history, that is peculiar to each individual thing. It is in this fashion that we discover the nature of things, the laws that govern or pertain to them, the way they are and can be. For example, if we would know the nature of man, then we must remove from our consideration everything that is incidental, peculiar, or accidental to any particular man (or woman) in any particular time or place: dress, language, size, height, girth, color of skin, afflictions, accents, odor, hairiness, and the like. Then we ask what the distinctive features are of man, *per se,* minus his warts, so to speak. What are the essences and potentialities of his being? By such methods and with such questions we may come to a grasp of the nature of man.

In like manner, it is possible to discover the nature of things that are institutions. What, for example, is the nature of government? Not this government, nor that government, nor any particular government, but of government *per se*. Thus, we are not concerned with whether or not the government is headed by an emperor, a king, a prime minister, a president, a governor, or whether it is ruled by one, three, six or a council of ten. Nor does it matter what the color of its flag may be, what color uniforms its police or soldiers may wear, where its capitol is located, whether it has a national anthem or not, and so on and on. All these things are irrelevant to the determination of the nature or essence of government. The nature of government, to answer the question, is that government is that organization with the exclusive authority to use force within a jurisdiction to maintain the peace, and, as the Founders would and did say, to protect the people in their rights to life, liberty and property.

Let us now examine the conception of natural rights as they were conceived in the 17th and 18th centuries within a framework of natural law. The common formulation at the time of the founding of the United States was that man has a natural right to life, liberty, and property. By focusing on the nature of things, we can arrive at a justification of the right to life this way. In the nature of things, who has a right to the life of a man? Who but himself could have established such a right? To put it another way, who but man himself can direct and control his life to constructive ends? In the final analysis, that is beyond the power, justly, of any and all other persons. It is his by right. Only he can justly forfeit his right to life by willing acts, such as by murder. We are discussing what is right and just, of course, not what may be done by tyrants, despots, murderers, outlaws, and thieves.

The right to liberty is most directly the right not to be restrained or imprisoned. To put it affirmatively, it is the right to go and come at will, without let or hindrance. In practice, it means the right to do this unless he must be restrained for some good reason, duly attested and proved. In its extended sense, the right to liberty is the right to use one's own faculties (abilities) as one wills for his own ends. This, too, is founded in the nature of things. Only the individual is situated so as to use his faculties for constructive purposes. He must command their use by his own mind, issue the signals through his nervous system, and concentrate on what he is doing with his various faculties. Only he can direct them to their highest and best use. The right to the use of one's faculties is actually an adjunct to the right to life, for it is by the employment of them to constructive purposes that life can be maintained.

The natural right to property arises in this way. That which a person has conceived in his own mind, made with his own tools from his materials, is his by right. In like manner, that which he has acquired from others by voluntary exchange or free gift is his as well by right. It is his by right to use, consume, save, exchange, bequeath, or dispose of as he will on mutually agreeable terms to others. The right to real property in land is somewhat more complex, as many writers have recognized. Obviously, none of us individually brought land into being or created it. Nor did all of us collectively create the land. Primordially, neither men individually, nor collectively in nations or however they may have existed, had any especial claim on the land. It might be supposed that in a "state of nature" a man or family might lay claim to such land as he could control and defend. In like manner, as social and political organizations came into being they might lay claim to such lands as they could conquer and successfully defend. It may well be that private property in land can be explained as being in the nature of things, but if so that explanation takes us well past a "state of nature."

It is probable, as many writers have thought, that the right to private property in land is secondary rather than primary. That is, it arises from man's actions upon and exchanges having to do with *real* property. Improvements upon land do indeed give secondary claims to the land. Thus, in the nature of things, a house built upon land becomes a fixture upon it. To have property in the house, it greatly facilitates matters to own the land upon which it is situated. Indeed, a deed commonly only describes the bounds of the property in detail and assumes that all improvements belong to him who owns the land. In the nature of things, the highest and best use of property by way of improvements and preservation virtually require private property in land. Another secondary right to real property arises from purchases from an owner by someone else. It is true that an owner cannot convey a greater right than he has, and thereby we reach the mass of legal research, activity, and laws surrounding the ownership and transfer of real property. Justice requires the continuation of real property in land as a right once it has been established. In the nature of things, all life—individual and social—depends upon being able to use land. Since no two bodies can occupy the same space at the same time, and no two persons can carry into effect the will to make contrary uses of any plot of land, some sort of distribution of land must be made. Justice requires that the person(s) having the best claim by tenure, through improvements made, by inheritance, or by purchase have title to particular plots of real property. That is apparently what most Americans thought, and they probably thought that it was consistent with the natural rights doctrine.[277]

Many advocates of natural law held that God reveals Himself and His purposes through nature's structure, order, and laws. To learn these, man uses his reason to discover both the underlying laws and the principles governing them. If, as many had come to believe by the middle of the 18th century, man is entitled by God to natural rights, then it is a duty and requirement to establish and defend them in society. They thought that man must live in accord with nature's laws if he is to achieve just and constructive purposes on earth. Most Americans of this time would have said that God not only reveals Himself through nature which is discoverable by reason but also through Scripture. Both are binding upon man. This was the greatest intellectual strength of the natural law doctrine.

It should be pointed out again in this summary that natural rights are not absolute; there are limits on their exercise and they may be forfeited. The rights to life, liberty and property are limited by the equal rights of others to theirs. When the rights of others are violated, the violator may suffer restrictions upon or loss of rights. For example, a man who takes the life of another may thereby forfeit the right to his own and have it taken from him. It goes further than that, however, as we can see by reference to the social contract.

Although we have examined instances of the formation of covenants, compacts, or other forms of agreements by people, in order to establish a government, the social contract has deeper roots than these. There is a more basic social contract that must exist for a peaceful and reasonably constructive society to exist, whether anyone has overtly or even consciously entered into it. It is that underlying agreement which is necessary, in the nature of things, to the existence of society. It is everyman's tacit agreement not to use violence to get his way, to leave others to the enjoyment of the fruits of their labor, not to trespass upon the property of others, to fulfill the terms of his individually entered into agreements, honor his parents, to succor his children, to keep his word, to meet his obligations. The social contract embraces, too, the obligation of the citizen to support the government—with a portion of his means and, if need be, with his personal service and even his life—which protects him and his in the enjoyment of their rights. Rights entail responsibilities, and, in the nature of things, men must assume their responsibilities if they are to be able to enjoy their rights.

It remains only now to show by some illustrations and examples that Americans were becoming more attached to natural law doctrines and becoming more sensitized to their rights. When the early English settlements were made in America, people tended to look primarily and almost exclusively to Scripture to discover God's will and purpose. The clergy were the men generally trained and skilled in explaining Scripture. Most Americans were, after all, Protestants and placed great emphasis upon Scripture. But by the 18th century, some of the leading thinkers were placing equal or greater emphasis upon the laws of nature discovered by reason.

A good example of a man at the forefront of this shift in emphasis was John Wise (1652–1725). He was born in Massachusetts, educated at Harvard, and though he was a clergyman by vocation, he was a learned advocate of natural law, natural rights, and individual liberty. His most important work in this regard was *A Vindication of the Government of New England Churches*. It was reprinted in 1772 as the movement for Independence was abuilding. Wise placed great emphasis upon man's rationality. It is this that enables him to discern the law of nature, which Wise says is what "is to be drawn from man's reason. . . ." And, having discovered the law of nature, it is man's duty to live according to it, for "God has established the law of nature. . . ."[278] As others had done before him, Wise argued that in a state of nature man was naturally at liberty. "And so every man must be conceived to be perfectly in his own power and disposal, and not controlled by the authority of any other."[279] Yet when he enters into civil society under government, he makes concessions in order to be protected from injury by others. But, he held, "It is certainly a great truth that man's original liberty . . . ought to be cherished in all wise governments; or otherwise a man in making himself a subject, he alters himself from a freeman into a slave, which to do is repugnant to the law of nature." Indeed, Wise argued, "The end of all good government is to cultivate humanity and promote the happiness of all, and the good of every man in all his rights, his life, liberty, estate, honor, etc., without injury or abuse done to any."[280]

John Wise did not contribute much to natural law doctrine. He did, however, give some publicity to these doctrines in America, and he made it clear that to observe and submit to natural law was to submit to the laws of God as planted in man and the universe.

One of the doctrines that was crucial for Americans was the right of people to revolt against and replace an oppressive regime. Jonathan Mayhew (1720–1766) delivered a famous sermon on the subject in 1750. He began by denying that the duty to submit to tyranny is unlimited. Here is a part of his argument on this score:

> If we calmly consider the nature of the thing itself, nothing can well be imagined more directly contrary to common sense than to suppose that millions of people should be subjected to the arbitrary, precarious pleasure of one single man (who has naturally no superiority over them in point of authority), so that everything that is valuable in life, even their lives also, shall be absolutely at his disposal, if he happens to be wanton and capricious enough to demand them. What unprejudiced man can think that God made all to be thus subservient to the lawless pleasure and frenzy of one, so that it shall always be a sin to resist him. . . .

Mayhew went on to deny that this notion could be justified from either Scripture or reason. On the contrary, he said, civil rulers are not to be obeyed when they command things contrary to what God has commanded. There is yet another reason for refusing to submit to civil authority, one that apparently lies in the nature of things. It is "that no government is to be submitted to at the expense of that which is the sole end of government: the common good and safety of society." When the government abandons its proper purpose and ends and acts contrary to these, oppression may be resisted. "For a nation thus abused to arise unanimously, and to resist their prince, even to dethroning him, is not criminal, but a reasonable way of vindicating their liberties and their just rights; it is making use of the means, and the only means, which God has put into their power, for mutual and self-defense. . . .''[281] Clearly, Mayhew had gone beyond Scripture in making this last argument and based it upon reason and natural law.

The life of Benjamin Franklin (1706–1790) spanned most of the 18th century, and he was touched by or particated in the main developments of those years ranging from the Albany Plan for a union of the colonies in 1754 to the Constitutional Convention of 1787. Although he was born in Massachusetts and lived most of his life in Philadelphia, Franklin was truly a man of the world in both his travels and activities. Although his formal schooling ended at the age of ten, he received honorary doctorates from the universities of St. Andrews and Oxford, was reckoned to be one of the leading scientists of his age, was a printer and publisher, legislator, foreign diplomat, and famous writer. His beliefs were suffused with the natural law ideas, he applied them to arguments for religious tolerance and various freedoms during the colonial period.

Since he was a printer, it may not be surprising that Franklin would defend the freedom of the press. Yet, as we shall see, he defended not from any personal advantage so much as for the public good (as John Milton had done before him). He said that ''It is a Principle among Printers, that when Truth has fair Play, it will always prevail over Falsehood; therefore, though they have an undoubted Property in their own Press, yet they willingly allow, that any one is entitled to the Use of it, who thinks it necessary to offer his Sentiments on disputable Points to the Public, and will be at the Expense of it: If what is thus publish'd be good, Mankind has the Benefit of it; If it be bad . . . the more 'tis made publick, the more the Weakness is expos'd, and the greatest disgrace falls on the Author. . . .''[282] Franklin notes also that it removed the occasion for authors to complain that their great ideas are not allowed a hearing. Moreover, to deny an author his services as a printer on the ground that his ideas are unwanted would be to make a printer into a censor.

Franklin's appeal to natural law and natural rights is, however, much clearer in his statement of the position that the legislature has an exclusive right to tax and dispose of public funds in a dispute with the governor of the colony. In the relevant part, Franklin writes: ''we still think, that as every Man has, so every Body of Men have, a natural Right to the Disposition of their own Money, by themselves or their Representatives; and that the Proprietary's Claim of a Voice in the Disposition of Money to which he will contribute no Part, is a Claim contrary to Reason.''[283]

Americans were moving as well toward a belief in free trade, well before they had read Adam Smith on the subject. Franklin deplored in very strong terms the British desire to monopolize all trade by the use of political power. He wrote, ''Nature has put Bounds to your Abilities, tho' none to your Desires. Britain would, if she could manufacture & trade for all the World; England for all Britain;—London for all England;—and every Londoner for all London. So selfish is the human Mind! But 'tis well there is One above that rules these Matters with a more equal Hand. He that is pleas'd to feed the Ravens, will undoubtedly prevent a Monopoly of the Carrion. . . ."[284] Cadwallader Colden, a Scottish born physician whose scientific interests and abilities made him almost an equal with Franklin, wrote on trade from the vantage point of being lieutenant-governor of the colony of New York. His argument was that in the nature of things, as well as because of circumstances, British restrictions on trade from the colonies hurt Britain as well as the colonies. That is to say, he subtly argued for the advantages to all and sundry of freedom of trade. Colden gave several examples in support of his argument, of which the one quoted below is the most succinct:

> It was affirmed, that while the exportation of provisions to neutral ports from the Colonies is absolutely prohibited, great quantities of provisions are openly and with proper clearances carried to the neutral port from Great Britain and Ireland, from whence it was infer'd that the prohibition to the Colonies cannot serve the purposes of the Act, but it's evidently of prejudice to the trade of the Colonies, and in consequence of prejudice to Great Britain; for without freedom in trade the Colonies are not able to pay for the British manufactures consumed in them.[285]

Undoubtedly, Colden was speaking as a colonial, but his argument was nonetheless a brief more generally for free trade.

Nor was liberty only for Englishmen at home or abroad, or white persons only. The logic of both natural law and natural rights was that they were universal, and embraced all peoples and races. Not all Americans who espoused natural law rushed to that conclusion, of course, for Negro slavery was established throughout English America, but many thoughtful Americans understood the logic of the doctrines they embraced. In the Declaration of Independence, Jefferson blamed slavery on British colonial policy. One of the earliest Americans to speak out on this subject was Judge Samuel Sewall (1652–1730) of Massachusetts. In a little tract entitled *The Selling of Joseph: A Memorial,* published in 1700, Sewall wrote: "Forasmuch as Liberty is in real value next unto Life: None ought to part with it themselves, or deprive others of it, but upon most mature consideration. . . . It is most certain that all Men, as they are the Sons of Adam, are Coheirs; and have equal Right unto Liberty. . . . So that Originally, and Naturally, there is no such Thing as Slavery. . . ."[286] By the time the United States Constitution was drawn, many men, including some of the Virginians, had arrived at a similar conclusion, although it could not yet prevail in national councils.

Americans had, by 1765, come to profess and claim a variety of rights, such as the right to property, the right to the produce of his labor, the right to life, freedom of the press, freedom of speech, the right to petition those who governed them, and the like. Above all, they believed that a full grown person should be permitted to manage his own life and direct his own affairs as he would, so long as he did no harm to others. Many, perhaps most, had come to believe in the right of conscience and that in matters of religion people should not be compelled to profess any belief or to attend any church, nor be punished for any failure to do these things. These assorted rights and freedoms, men generally prized as their liberties.

It may be well, then, to conclude this examination of the development of colonial thought with some remarks made by the defense attorney in a famous trial dealing with freedom of the press. They were made by Andrew Hamilton in his closing speech at the trial of John Peter Zenger in 1734. Hamilton rested his case on liberty in general, not simply on freedom of the press. He declared that "The loss of liberty to a generous mind, is worse than death. . . . This is what every man (who values freedom) ought to consider; he should act by judgment, and not by affection or self-interest . . . ; as, on the other hand, the man, who loves his country, prefers its liberty to all other considerations; well knowing that, without liberty, life is a misery. . . ."

Hamilton understood, too, that liberty can only prevail where government is restrained. He put his position this way:

> Power may justly be compared to a great river, which, kept within due bounds, is both beautiful and useful; but when it overflows its banks, it is then too impetuous to be stemmed; it bears down all before it, and brings destruction and desolation wherever it comes. If then this is the nature of power, let us at least do our duty, and like wise men (who value freedom) use our utmost care to support liberty, the only bulwark against lawless power, which in all ages has sacrificed to its wild lust and boundless ambition, the blood of the best men that ever lived. . . .

Then he concluded with a plea to the jury to decide for John Peter Zenger and against those in government who would silence him, and thus lay "a noble foundation for securing to ourselves, our posterity, and our neighbors, That, to which nature and the laws of our country have given us a right,— the liberty—both of exposing and opposing arbitrary power . . . by speaking and writing truth."[287]

Americans were not only growing in their knowledge of liberty but increasingly determined to apply it to their lives as well.

Chapter 7
A Season of Constitution Making

> The Americans are the first people whom Heaven has favoured with
> an opportunity of deliberating upon, and choosing the forms of gov-
> ernment under which they should live. All other constitutions have
> derived their existence from violence or from accidental circum-
> stances, and are therefore more distant from their perfection, which,
> though beyond our reach, may nevertheless be approached under the
> guidance of reason and experience.
>
> —John Jay, 1777

Americans went through quite a season of constitution making from 1775
to 1790, or thereabouts. That is not to say that all constitution making in this
country ended abruptly with the ratification of the First Ten Amendments
(the "Bill of Rights"); it has gone on at a more measured and leisurely pace
since that time. After all, each new state that comes into the union has done
so after constructing and adopting a constitution. And, with the passage of
time, some states have written and adopted new constitutions from time to
time over the years. But the period from 1775 to 1790 was the great era of
constitution making.

Nor did the preparation for and practice in constitution making by Americans begin in 1775. Their preparation for making constitutions harked back
to the Magna Carta and the many succeeding charters in their British background. It went back to the shaping of the structure of the English government in the 14th century: the monarchy, the House of Lords, and the House
of Commons. And it included emendations made to the British constitution
after the settlements had begun in America: the Petition of Right, the British
Bill of Rights, and the Act of Toleration. But they had also practical experience, some of them or their ancestors, in making compacts and charters,
such as the Mayflower Compact, the Fundamental Orders of Connecticut,
the drawing up of company charters, and the like. The habit of constitution
making was firmly ingrained in Americans before they entered upon the
season of constitution making.

They did not, however, rely solely upon their own colonial experience or
even that in their British background. Many American leaders had studied

Ancient, Renaissance, Reformation, and more recent works which probed the nature of government, the forms of government, and analyses of the strengths and weaknesses of these. A generation or so ago, Professor Wilson Ober Clough compiled a list of readings known to many of the Founders, and among them he included selections from Thucydides, Pericles, Demosthenes, Plato, Aristotle, Polybius, Cicero, Epictitus, Epicurus, Lucretius, Seneca, Tacitus, Plutarch, St. Augustine, and Justinian. And these were only the Greek and Roman writers. Among those writers from the Renaissance downward, he included: Sir Thomas More, Thomas Hooker, Richard Hooker, John Milton, James Harrington, Sir Algernon Sidney, Thomas Hobbes, Lord John Somers, Hugo Grotius, Samuel Pufendorf, John Locke, of course, Montesquieu, Jean Jacques Burlamaqui, Anthony Ashley Cooper, Joseph Addison, Lord Bolingbroke, Edmund Burke, and others. Moreover, as has been emphasized in an earlier chapter, Americans had sufficiently mastered natural law philosophy in the 18th century that they could write with confidence in its framework and apply it to particular situations and practices. In sum, Americans were well versed in the great tradition of political thought that came down from the past to them, and awakened and sensitized to the potentialities within it for restraining and limiting government and establishing individual liberty.

a. Declaration of Independence

Strictly speaking, the Declaration of Independence is neither a constitution nor the formal part of any other constitution. Nor are its pronouncements the nature of law that applies to individuals or organizations within the United States. Even so, the document occupied a critical place in the founding of the United States. Even the phrase itself was brought into being by it, for the Declaration, in its last paragraph begins: "We, therefore, the Representatives of the United States of America in General Congress, Assembled . . ." etc. If that was not the first use of the phrase, it was the first in a formal document. Moreover, all the constitutions and governments that followed in its wake depended for their existence upon the independence of either the states or the United States.

The first two paragraphs of the Declaration do set forth some ideas and principles which have not only had considerable impact over many years on American political thought but also have more than a little to do with the foundations of America. Though these paragraphs have never formally been made part of our Constitution, they are probably better known to most Americans than any part of the Constitution itself unless it is the First Amendment. Before discussing these, however, it might be well to give a little background to the document.

The story of the composition and adoption of the Declaration is fairly simple. On June 7, 1776, Richard Henry Lee of Virginia introduced a resolution in the Second Continental Congress that would have proclaimed independence. It was not immediately adopted. Instead, on June 10, Congress decided to delay further consideration of Lee's resolution until July 1, since many delegates were waiting for instructions, or changes of instructions, from their legislatures. Those favoring independence hoped that these instructions would lead all colonies to join the cause. Lee's simple and straightforward resolution would have been for the formal declaring of independence. But America badly needed aid from foreign powers if the appeal to arms was to be successful. Since the British were already making war on the colonies, there was no chance that declaring independence would cause the British to bow out. Thomas Paine had suggested in *Common Sense* that some sort of manifesto be published in order to gain friends with other nations: "Were a manifesto to be published and dispatched to foreign courts, setting forth the miseries we have endured and the peaceable methods which we have ineffectually used for redress; declaring at the same time that . . . we had been driven to the necessity of breaking off all connections . . . —such a memorial would produce more good effects to this continent than if a ship were freighted with petitions to Britain."[288] This was apparently the origin of the idea for a more lengthy justification for declaring independence. In any case, following the determination to delay adopting Lee's resolution, Congress appointed a committee to produce some such document. The committee was composed of Benjamin Franklin, John Adams, Robert Livingston, Thomas Jefferson, and Roger Sherman.

Thomas Jefferson was assigned the task of producing a draft of the proposed declaration. Since Jefferson had only lately acquired a considerable reputation as a writer with his *Summary View of the Rights of British America,* an older better known writer such as John Dickinson might have been given the job, except he was not favorably disposed toward independence at that time. However that may have been, Jefferson's selection turned out to have been one of the happiest decisions ever made by a committee. Some minor changes were suggested by Franklin and Adams, and these were incorporated in the document. Congress also made a few alterations.[289]

Congress acted quickly once the Lee resolution came before it once again on July 1. The next day, it was unanimously approved by 12 colonies, though New York's delegation to the Congress abstained. And then, on July 4, the date which was to be celebrated by posterity, Congress approved the document known as the Declaration of Independence. John Adams thought that the second day of July would be the one celebrated, since that was the day the resolution for independence was adopted. Moreover, he was less than overwhelmed by Jefferson's work, for he later declared that "There is not an idea in it, but what had been hackneyed in Congress for two years before."[290] The remark by Adams was certainly beside the point and probably flavored by sour grapes. Surely, Jefferson was grasping for the sense of Congress (and more broadly, America); he was not trying for originality but essentiality. He got it and produced a masterpiece which has been revered, if not well understood, ever since.

The Declaration can be divided into three parts. The first two paragraphs state the principles which justify the revolt of the former colonies of Britain in America, their break from England, and the taking up of an independent course in the world. The second part is a lengthy list of abuses by Britain which are all blamed directly upon King George III. Then, in the final paragraph, independence is proclaimed and the right of Americans to govern themselves is asserted. From the viewpoint of the Founding of the United States, this last paragraph is probably the crucial one. After all, it is primary that the legitimacy of the governments in the United States depends upon their independence.

It is not, however, that paragraph that has been the focus of attention. Instead, it has been the highly charged opening of the second paragraph of the Declaration, which reads: "We hold these truths to be self-evident that all men are created equal, that they are endowed by their Creator with certain unalienable Rights, that among these are Life, Liberty and the pursuit of Happiness. That to secure these rights, Governments are instituted among Men, deriving their just powers from the consent of the governed. . . ." Jefferson then went on to tie these principles to a justification for the independence of the United States and the erection of a new government.

It is probably not needful to go over here the arguments for the right of revolution, since it has been both alluded to and described in connection with natural-law-natural-rights thought already. Jefferson had, however, introduced two ideas in the above quotation which may need some explanation. One was about *equality* and the other the right to *happiness*. Precisely, Jefferson said that "all men are created equal." The phrase may not have troubled most of Jefferson's contemporaries; some such assertion was usually made by those writing in the natural law framework. It is capable of producing not only quite a deal of confusion and probably trouble but also misunderstanding among those not versed in that framework. To say that all men are created equal in a natural law framework is the rough equivalent of saying that in a "state of nature" all are equal (there being as yet no distinctions introduced). They are equal in rights, in their claims upon the earth, and in rank (no distinctions having as yet been established). According to this view, when men enter into civil societies and form governments, distinctions are introduced, and the full fledged original equality no longer prevails. However, it was also believed (though not universally) that man under government was still entitled to his basic rights and that it was for the protection of these that governments were established. Jefferson was arguing as much here.

The Declaration of Independence was addressed to the "Powers of the earth" out of "a decent respect to the opinions of mankind." Thus, he was saying in the first place, by his reference to equality, that Americans are the equals of Englishmen. No, more than that, he was saying that Americans are the equals of peoples everywhere. In what are they equal of peoples everywhere? They are equal in their right to life, liberty and the pursuit of happiness and to have a government of their own choosing. It may be a logical extension of this to hold that all should be equal before the law, but it was not that in its fullness which Jefferson was affirming in the Declaration of Independence.

Obviously, Jefferson was not saying that we are all the same, nor was he saying that we are all equally gifted, equally physically or mentally endowed, or all fitted out with an equal amount of material goods. Surely, each of us differ from one another in a great variety of ways; the Declaration of Independence was neither addressing these nor supposing they should be other than they are.

The usual way for the natural rights to be summarized was as life, liberty and property. Why Jefferson substituted "happiness" for "property" is not known. It may be that he was looking for a broader and more comprehensive phrase. Happiness had often been named over the years as one of the prime purposes of government or proper objects of political activity. Certainly, the *pursuit* of happiness comprehends the idea of using one's faculties freely for one's own ends or purposes. What property is shorthand for is also comprehended in pursuit of happiness.

Whatever else may be said, it should be clear that the Declaration of Independence was one of the end products of natural law thought.

b. The State Constitutions

The states preceded the United States as political entities. They had been colonies with political identities, many of them going back to the early or mid-17th century. Where they had charters, as most of them did, these had served as constitutions, of sorts. Some of them began contemplating a new basis of government when battles were fought between Britain and the colonials, and once independence was declared, the necessity for new constitutions was apparent more generally. After all, the charters had usually been granted by English kings, and when the colonies broke from Britain they could not base their governments on such grants.

Massachusetts sent a formal letter to the Continental Congress in May, 1775 requesting advice "respecting the taking up and exercising the powers of civil government." At that time, Massachusetts still had a royal governor appointed by the king, but the leaders there were determined to see to it that he did not govern. Congress replied that the colony leaders should "write letters to the inhabitants of the several places which are entitled to representation in Assembly, requesting them to choose such representatives, and that the Assembly . . . do elect counsellors; which assembly and council should exercise the powers of Government" until a satisfactory governor had been appointed.[291] Independence was still a ways off when these events took place, but they were already moving toward the idea of establishing independent state governments. This became clearer during the year as Congress made recommendations to New Hampshire, Virginia, and South Carolina.

In May, 1776, the Continental Congress passed a resolution to the effect that all royal authority should be suppressed or extinguished, "that all the powers of government should be exerted under the authority of the people, and that it be recommended to the assemblies and conventions of the united colonies where no government sufficient to the exigencies of their affairs had been established, to adopt such government as should, in the opinion of the representatives of the people, best conduce to the happiness and safety of their constituents and of America in general."[292]

Conditions in the country were hardly conducive to elaborate constitutional proceedings and calm and lengthy deliberations about the nature of government and what precise forms and substance should be provided in such documents. A Continental Army under the command of General Washington had long since taken to the field. Some of the governments in operation already were little more than revolutionary committees. They were not only contending with Britain but with royal governers, and with a considerable number of Americans who remained loyal to the crown. Pennsylvania was riven by the division between Loyalists and Patriots, and other states were divided to some degree on these as well as other grounds.

Even so, most of the former colonies did go forward with constitution making in 1776–1777. Indeed, two states had adopted brief constitutions before Congress sent out its resolution: New Hampshire in January, 1776 and South Carolina in March. Two states—Rhode Island and Connecticut— had charters of long standing approved by their inhabitants, and they continued to use them until well into the 19th century. During the remainder of 1776 and a part of 1777, all the other states except Massachusetts adopted constitutions. These states went through no extraordinary procedures for drafting and adoption of a constitution. New Jersey, Virginia, and South Carolina did not even hold special elections for the purpose. The revolutionary legislatures simply drafted and adopted their constitutions. "New Hampshire, New York, Pennsylvania, Delaware, Maryland, North Carolina, and Georgia all held special elections for new congresses [legislatures], but these [assemblies] also concerned themselves with legislative matters. In none of the states acting in 1776 and 1777 did the conventions submit their work to the people for approval; rather, they merely proclaimed the new constitution in effect."[293]

The truth was that though American leaders were familiar with the compact theory of the origin of government and believed that the powers of government derived from the people, just how all this should be put into effect was not well developed. On reflection, it should be clear that a separate constitutional convention should be chosen by the voters, should treat only with developing a constitution, and then their handiwork should be submitted to the people for their approval. But that was much clearer after 1787 than before.

Massachusetts followed a different course, one that would serve more of a pattern for later constitution makers. They clearly traced the constitution from the people and received their approval of the final document. Although, considerable care was taken in drawing a constitution in 1777, it was rejected when it was submitted to the people for approval in 1778. Although there were other objections to it, the main one was that it did not have a bill of rights. In 1778, the temporary government asked for a vote as to whether they wanted a new constitution or not. When the voters signified that they did, they were then asked to choose delegates to a constitutional convention. The delegates chosen met in convention in 1779, framed a bill of rights and a constitution. The constitution was approved and put into effect in 1780. The compact theory of the formation was clearly stated in this constitution. It said, in part, "The body politic is formed by a voluntary association of individuals; it is a social compact, by which the whole people covenants with each citizen, and each with the whole people that all shall be governed by certain laws for the common good. . . ." More, "The people alone have an incontestable, unalienable, and indefeasible right to institute government, and to reform, alter, or totally change the same when their protection, safety, prosperity, and happiness require it."[294] Several states did not make provision for amending their constitutions; others like Massachusetts did. When regular elections, popular approval, and power to amend was provided by a constitution, the occasion for revolt against a legal government had been removed.

The state constitutions were very similar to one another in the form of government they provided. Indeed, the new governments were to be similar in form to the ones they had as colonies, which themselves were modeled after the English Parliament. Each of them had a chief executive, but he was no longer a royal governor appointed by the king, he was elected by popular vote or by legislatures, and was styled either "president" or "governor." All but Pennsylvania had a two house (bicameral) legislature, elected by popular vote. The constitutions did not give much power to their governors. They indicated considerable fear of executive power. The terms of governors ranged from one to three years, and if the governor had any power of veto, it was limited rather than absolute. By providing for election of the governor by the legislature, a number of states signified their intent to subordinate him to the legislature.

But Americans of this period were not only concerned about limiting the power of governors, they favored limiting the government power over them as well. Their favorite device for limiting the government were the bills of rights which most state constitutions had, either as a part of them or that

went along with them. One of the more fulsome and among the earliest of
these was the Virginia Bill of Rights. It was drawn by George Mason, and
adopted by a Virginia Convention in June, 1776, about three weeks before
the Declaration of Independence. Undoubtedly, Jefferson was influenced by
it, as the opening paragraph may suggest:

> 1. That all men are by nature equally free and independent, and have
> certain inherent rights, of which, when they enter into a state of soci-
> ety, they cannot by any compact deprive or divest their posterity:
> namely, the enjoyment of life and liberty, with the means of acquiring
> and possessing property, and pursuing and obtaining happiness and
> safety.

This was a general statement of the origin and existence of natural rights, but
some of the later statements get to more particular freedoms. For example,
number 9 reads, "That excessive bail ought not to be required, nor excessive fines imposed, nor cruel and unusual punishments inflicted." Or,
equally familiar, "That the freedom of the press is one of the great bulwarks
of liberty, and can never be restrained but by despotic governments."[295]
Although these were restraints on the state government, that is not so clear
or bluntly stated as in the First Ten Amendments to the United States
Constitution.

The Massachusetts Bill of Rights, drawn mainly by John Adams and
adopted in 1780, was both more extensive and more directly prohibitive than
the Virginia Bill of Rights. Its opening paragraph is a classic statement of
the natural rights doctrine:

> Article I. All men are born free and equal, and have certain natural,
> essential, and unalienable rights; among which may be reckoned the
> right of enjoying and defending their lives and liberties; that of ac-
> quiring, possessing, and protecting property; in fine, that of seeking
> and obtaining their safety and happiness.

It has 30 articles in all, some of them long, and most of them quite explicit
about the rights involved. Here, for example, are excerpts from article X,
which deals at length with the right to property:

> Each individual of the society has a right to be protected by it in the
> enjoyment of his life, liberty, and property. . . . No part of the property
> of any individual can with justice be taken from, or applied to public
> uses, without his own consent or that of the representative body of the
> people. . . . And whenever the public exigencies require that the
> property of any individual should be appropriated to public uses, he
> shall receive a reasonable compensation therefor.

Although the above article is more wordy, it covers some of the ground covered more succinctly in the last two clauses of the Fifth Amendment to the United States Constitution. Article XIV may also have influenced the later national document. It reads, in part: "Every subject has a right to be secure from all unreasonable searches, and seizures of his person, his houses, his papers, and all his possessions. . . . And no warrant ought to be issued but in cases, and with the formalities prescribed by the laws." Most of the very familiar rights are provided for as well. For example, "The Liberty of the press . . . ought not . . . to be restricted in this commonwealth." "The people have a right to keep and bear arms. . . ." "The people have a right, in an orderly and peaceable manner to assemble. . . ."[296] And there are a goodly number of other articles of a similar character to those cited.

The movement toward religious freedom coincided with separation from England. Indeed, in several states it was an almost inevitable consequence. The Church of England was established in several counties in New York, in Maryland, Virginia, the Carolinas, and Georgia. The break from England separated these churches from English control. There were still attempts to retain the establishment of the now independent (of England) Episcopal Church, but they did not succeed. The Congregational church retained some elements of establishment in New England, except for Rhode Island, into the 19th century, but religious toleration was virtually universal from the 1780s onward, and complete religious freedom was waiting in the wings, so to speak. Religious toleration was invoked in the Massachusetts Bill of Rights in these words: "And every denomination of Christians . . . shall be equally under the protection of the law; and no subordination of any one sect or denomination to another shall ever be established by law."

The landmark for the establishment of religious liberty was not in any constitution but rather in the Virginia Statute of Religious Liberty. It was drafted by Thomas Jefferson and passed into law by the Virginia legislature in 1786. It opened with this stirring declaration: "Whereas Almighty God hath created the mind free; that all attempts to influence it by temporal punishments or burthens [burdens], or by civil incapacitations, tend only to beget habits of hypocrisy and meanness, and are a departure from the plan of the Holy author of our religion, who being Lord both of body and of mind, yet chose not to propagate it by coercions on either, as it was in his power to do. . . ." The document goes on to denounce the very notion of the using the power of government to establish what are in effect the opinions of men and to declare that it should not compel either the contribution of money or attendance upon religious services. The crucial passage is in the following paragraph:

> *Be it enacted by the General Assembly,* that no man shall be compelled to frequent or support any religious worship, place or ministry whatsoever, nor shall be enforced, restrained, molested, or [burdened]

in his body or goods, nor shall otherwise suffer on account of his religious opinions or belief; but that all men shall be free to profess and by argument to maintain, their opinion in matters of religion, and that the same shall in no wise diminish, enlarge or affect their civil capacities.

The act contained a concluding paragraph which explained that since this was an ordinary act of the legislature, succeeding legislatures could repeal or change it. But they are warned that in considering whether to do so or not "that the rights hereby asserted are of the natural rights of mankind, and that if any act shall hereafter be passed to repeal the present, or to narrow its operation, such act will be an infringement of natural right."[297]

Most of the state constitutions avowed the principle of the separation of powers, even if they did not always manage to establish them so effectively in practice. Americans generally believed that some separation of powers would tend to make the branches check on the power of one another. In practice, they probably check one another better if their powers are not entirely separate but require concurrent action by two or more branches. This may be most readily accomplished by requiring that both houses of the legislature pass a bill before it becomes a law. That way either house may check the other by refusing to pass the bill. In any case, state constitutions usually required a variety of concurrent actions by different bodies for the governments to act.

Separation of powers ideally might also entail different origins of power for different branches. That way each branch might be truly independent of the others. The British system illustrated this rather well. The monarchy is hereditary. The House of Lords is made up of great nobles, who may have inherited their position or been raised to it by the monarch, and the high churchmen, who attain their rank by merit, election and appointment by other churchmen, as a rule. The House of Commons is elected. If that was ideal, the Americans suffered from the revolutionary bias in attaining it. By and large, they were dead set against hereditary monarchs, nobility whether it was hereditary or appointed, and generally opposed established churches. Both houses of their legislatures were apt to be elective, though some distinctions were made between them. The lower house usually had many more members, was probably chosen in districts determined on the basis of population, had shorter terms of office, and had the authority to originate revenue bills. The upper house would have fewer members ordinarily, might be based on area or region rather than population. If the governor were elected by the people, which quickly became usual, it was by the voters of his whole state, which at least gave him a much broader electorate than individual members of the legislature. Other executive officers, or at least some of them, might be appointed by the governor.

Some of the state constitutions tried to make up for the sameness in the electoral source of their power by making various degrees of wealth required for officeholders. In general, the states required the most wealth or property for governor, the next highest for members of the upper house, and the lowest for the lower house. In Massachusetts, "The Governor was required to have a freehold worth at least £1,000, senators a freehold of £300 or £600 total estate, representatives a freehold of £100 or £200 total estate. . . . These Massachusetts requirements resembled those in North Carolina, where the governor had to have a £1,000 freehold, and members of the upper and lower houses freeholds of 300 or 100 acres respectively."[298]

This may seem strange to Americans today, but it should be made clear that the states generally had property qualifications for voting as well, though not as high as those for office-holding. To vote in Massachusetts, "it was necessary to own real estate worth £3 a year, or real and personal property of a value of £60."[299] Some states had different qualifications for voting for members of the lower house from those of the upper house. Thus, in North Carolina, "every adult freeman of the state received the right to vote for assemblyman. . . . Any resident who owned fifty acres of land enjoyed the right to vote for state senators. . . ." In South Carolina, those who owned fifty or more acres of land could vote.[300] So it went from state to state.

The property qualification for voting was in keeping both with past practice in the colonies and the dominant view after independence was declared. The main reason cited was that those who had a demonstrable interest in society should have the elective franchise and government. The payment of taxes and being a property holder was taken to signify such an interest. If those without property were given the vote, they might well use it to take from those who have to give it to the "have-nots." Most Americans of the time were not levellers; rather than favoring some sort of democracy, they tended to favor some sort of winnowing process. Regarding who should govern, one American wrote, "it is right that men of *birth and fortune,* in every government that is free, should be invested with power, and enjoy higher honours than the people."[301] It is true that natural law theory held that the right to found a government belonged to "the people." And Massachusetts did submit its constitution to male voters twenty-one and over for approval. But generally, that did not occur. Women were nowhere permitted to vote, nor had the notion of that been advanced as yet. Of course, Negro slaves were not permitted to vote, and few, if any, free blacks were franchised.

The thrust in America in the 1770s and especially in the 1780s was toward greater liberty and opportunities. Most of the states north of Maryland freed or made provision for the gradual freeing of the slaves during this period. There was a strong movement as far South as Virginia for the voluntary emancipation of slaves, and some slaveholders provided that upon their death their slaves would be freed. The Northwest Ordinance passed by

Congress under the Articles of Confederation forbade slavery in the North-west Territory (that is, the Midwest). In some of the colonies, the British had imposed quitrents upon land, to be paid to the Crown or to proprietors. These were abolished, of course, with independence, or shortly thereafter. Primogeniture—the requirement or practice that the land go to the eldest son—and entail—the requirement that estates be kept intact—were generally abolished. The effect of this was much greater opportunity to inherit and acquire land and other properties.

c. The Articles of Confederation

The United States of America has had two constitutions: the first was the Articles of Confederation; the second was the Constitution of 1787, which is still in effect. The Articles were the direct result of a resolution passed by the Continental Congress on June 17, 1776, approximately three weeks before the Declaration of Independence, providing for a committee to draw up an instrument for uniting the colonies in a confederation. John Dickinson undertook to provide a draft of such a plan. Franklin had also submitted his Albany Plan with some changes, and it had some influence on Dickinson's work. The committee submitted a plan that was mainly the work of Dickinson the next year, and after making some changes, Congress approved the Articles on November 15, 1877. It was then submitted to the states for ratification, and all the states but Maryland approved it in 1778 and 1779.

Although there was much that might have been questioned about the Articles, Maryland's major objection was that several states laid claims to territory in the west that might go as far as the western boundaries of the United States might extend. These states would dwarf such states as Maryland, which was confined largely to the east coast. The main states involved were New York and Virginia: when they yielded on the western question, Maryland signed, and the Articles were declared ratified and in full effect March 1, 1781. The Articles served as a constitution of the United States for less than eight years. Even so, it is important to take note of some of their features, both for their influence on the making of the Constitution of 1787 and what they tell us about American political ideas at the time.

Although the Articles of Confederation, as a document, is not overly long—there are only 13 articles—, it is verbose, and some of the passages are long winded. Edward Rutledge was of that opinion about Dickinson's draft at the time, and wrote as much in a letter to John Jay of New York: he wrote, "I have been much engaged lately upon a plan of a Confederation which Dickinson has drawn; it has the Vice of all his Productions to a considerable Degree. I mean the Vice of Refining too much." That is, he names too many particulars and goes into too much detail. Rutledge apparently did not appreciate the fact that at least some of this detail was for the purpose of limiting the power of Congress under the Articles, for he went on himself to say, "I am resolved to vest this Congress with no more Power than is absolutely necessary. . . ."[302] In any case, those who worked on the Articles in one way or another were very much aware that the states would only yield power to any central government reluctantly.

The point is driven home in the very first article that deals with the distribution of power, which is Article II. It reads, "Each state retains its sovereignty, freedom, and independence, and every Power, Jurisdiction and right, which is not by this confederation expressly delegated to the United States in Congress assembled."[303] Moreover, the confederation is styled a "league of friendship" in Article III.

Nor could the confederation be considered a full fledged government. It had only one distinct branch, namely, a legislature, which was styled a Congress. It had no separate or distinct executive; the assumption was that such executive powers as might be exercised would be by the Congress or by such committees as Congress might appoint while it was not in session. The judicial powers of the Confederation were limited to settling disputes among the states, to resolving territorial claims of individuals against two or more states, and dealing with discipline and punishing offenses arising out of martial, military, and naval matters, and occurring on the high seas.

As a rule, Congress had no power or authority over the civilian population of the the country, nor did it have either a constabulary to perform the police function nor courts to enforce its will. It had no direct powers of taxation. Since the Confederation, as such, had no sanctions, it was hardly a government at all. As the Articles themselves indicated, most of the substance of sovereignty remained with the states.

In the light of its limitations, the authority and powers of Congress were considerable, supposing that some means could be found to exercise them. Congress was authorized to determine all matters having to do with peace or war with foreign countries. It could make treaties and enter into alliances. Indeed, the most important treaty the United States ever made was the Treaty of Paris of 1783, made under the auspices of Congress under the Articles of Confederation. By it, not only was the War for Independence successfully concluded, but Britain acknowledged the independence of the United States and ceded such territory as Britain possessed from Canada to Florida and all the way west to the Mississippi. It could, of course, declare and make war, and conduct affairs on the High Seas as a full fledged sovereign nation. Congress could establish "rules for deciding in all cases, what captures on land or water shall be legal, and in what manner prizes taken by land or naval forces in the service of the United States shall be divided or appropriated—of granting letters of marque and reprisal in times of peace—appointing courts for the trial of piracies and felonies committed on the high seas and establishing courts for receiving and determining final appeals in all cases of captures, provided that no member of Congress shall be appointed a judge of any of the said courts."

Other powers granted to Congress were those of regulating the content and value of coins issued by either the states or the United States (meaning they would have a common metallic currency), fixing standards of weights and measures, managing Indian affairs not within the bounds of any state, establishing post offices, appointing officers of the land and naval forces in the service of the United States, with certain notable exceptions, to borrow money, to emit bills of credit (that is, to issue what came to be called paper money), to build and equip a navy, and to build such armies as might be required. The Congress was supposed to get money for these activities by levying quotas upon the states, which would presumably be filled by state taxation. Virtually every power granted to Congress required the assent of three-fourths of the states through their Congressional delegations.

It has already been noted that the Confederation could not act upon people directly, except those in the armed forces or otherwise in the employ of the United States or in matters between two or more states. That being the case, it may have been appropriate that only states, not the people, were to be directly represented in the Congress. Each state had only one vote in the Congress, regardless of its size or population. Rhode Island had one vote, and the most populous state of all, Virginia, had one vote. Although each state had only one vote, it was required to have at least two delegates, and might have as many as seven. These would decide among themselves as to how the state's vote would be cast on matters taken up in Congress. The representatives were restricted in that "no person shall be capable of being a delegate for more than three years in any term of six years; nor shall any person, being a delegate, be capable of holding any office under the United States, for which he . . . receives any salary, fees or emolument of any kind." Since he might as a delegate be in position to influence the creation of and appointments as well as the pay for such positions, it was thought improper for delegates to receive such appointments.

A variety of restrictions were placed on the states as well. They had to do mainly with entering into treaties and alliances, going to war, or engaging in relations with foreign countries. If such activities were not absolutely prohibited, they required the approval of Congress. The Articles also provided for the free movement of peoples from one state to another by declaring in Article IV that the "free inhabitants of each of these States, paupers, vagabonds and fugitives from justice excepted, shall be entitled to all privileges and immunities of free citizens in the several States; and the people of each State shall have free ingress and regress to and from any other State, and shall enjoy therein all the privileges of trade and commerce, subject to the same duties, impositions and restrictions as the inhabitants thereof respectively. . . ." Moreover, the Articles require that "Full faith and credit shall be given in each of these States to the records, acts and judicial proceedings of the courts and magistrates of every other State." To support this clause, there is a provision that those who have been convicted of a crime in one state and flee for refuge into another state "shall upon demand of the Governor or Executive power, of the State from which he fled, be delivered up and removed to State having jurisdiction of his offence."

And in the last Article, the document expressed the hope that

> Every State shall abide by the determinations of the United States in Congress assembled, on all questions which by this confederation are submitted to them. And the articles of this confederation shall be inviolably observed by every State, and the Union shall be perpetual; nor shall any alteration at any time hereafter be made in any of them; unless such alteration be agreed to in a Congress of the United States and be afterwards confirmed by the Legislatures of every State.

This last clause probably sealed the fate of the Articles of Confederation. The Union might indeed be perpetual, but it was most unlikely that a constitution which placed such restrictions upon its amendment could long survive. This provision gave every state a veto power over any proposed change in the constitution. This did, of course, protect the basic sovereignty of the states—and in that was consistent with the other parts of the Articles—but it made changes formidable. Before long, other problems were exposing the inherent weaknesses of the Articles of Confederation. And, the season of constitution-making would culminate in its climactic event—the making of the Constitution of 1787. *The* Constitution was much influenced by the Articles of Confederation, but its weaknesses were abandoned for what became the strengths of the Constitution.

d. The Constitution of 1787

Since the provisions of this Constitution have been discussed at considerable length in an earlier chapter, it is not necessary to go over them again here. It is in order, however, to point out the weaknesses and infelicities in the government under the Articles of Confederation that led to a call for a Constitutional Convention, to discuss something of the work of the men at that Convention, and describe the ratification of the Constitution and the immediate actions taken to put the document into effect.

The weakness of the governing power of the confederation extended in several directions. Its greatest weakness lay in its virtual inability to conduct relations with foreign nations effectively. The responsibility devolved upon the Congress, but that body did not have the power to compel the acceptance of its decisions. There was talk that Congress might use force upon states, but such measures would have been war. True, the power had been theoretically granted by the Articles, but the means for enforcing it was lacking.[304]

That Congress was almost impotent in dealing with other nations does not have to be concluded from theory alone; history affords examples enough. Nowhere was the weakness clearer than in relations with England. John Adams became minister to the Court of St. James in 1785. He hoped to obtain a commercial treaty with Britain that would open British colonial ports to American ships. But he found the government there unwilling to make any concessions, almost contemptuous of the usefulness of any agreement with the Confederation, and well satisfied with commercial relations as they stood. Instead of being able to make new agreements, Adams found himself occupied with questions surrounding the terms of and compliance with the Treaty of Paris of 1783.

The British reproached the United States through Adams for not complying with the terms of the treaty. The treaty required Congress to recommend to the states that the rights of Loyalists be restored. (This had been a concession by the United States, since the British were not committed to nor did they make reparations for damages done by their armies or Loyalists in the United States.) Congress did, indeed, make such a recommendation to the states, but some of the states were more inclined to further retaliation, and none of them was favorably disposed to full restitution for Loyalists. Technically, Congress had complied with the terms of the treaty, but the failure of the states to heed their recommendation pointed up the weakness of the Confederation. The treaty also specified that the states would not hamper or impede the collection of debts by British citizens. One history says: "There is no doubt that this article was violated both in letter and spirit. Virginia, where the debts were heaviest . . . , led the way in passing laws hampering the recovery of British debts."[305] Congress was, of course, powerless to do anything about the state recalcitrance.

American compliance with the treaty was made the more pressing, because the British used it as an excuse for failure to comply in the Old Northwest. They had several military posts on the American side of the Great Lakes. Contrary to the treaty provisions, they did not evacuate them; instead, a secret order to hold them indefinitely went out in 1784. Though the posts themselves were peripheral, they provided bases for the British to exercise influence on Indians in American territory and for carrying on a lucrative fur trade.[306] This increased the difficulty of making white settlements in the area and, thus, of the sale of lands by the Confederation.

Difficulties with Spain were, if anything, more pressing than those with Britain. Trading privileges were not at issue, for Spain had opened up her most important colonial ports to America. The major issues were the location of the boundaries between the United States and Spanish territory to the south and west, and navigation and use of the Mississippi and ports on it. The difficulty arose out of differences in claims and designs on the old Southwest between the United States and Spain. Spain had lately reacquired Florida, which included at that time a West Florida extending all the way to the Mississippi. Spain continued its historic claim to the vast territory west of the Mississippi. These territories gave Spain control over the gateway to the Gulf of Mexico. The fact that Britain had ceded territory to the United States did not greatly impress the Spanish, particularly when these same British were clinging to their own posts to the north in defiance of the treaty.

In 1784, Spain concluded treaties with Indians within the territory of the United States. Moreover, Spain held onto a military post at Natchez which had been acquired during the war but which was now within the treaty territory of the United States. Spain also made private agreements with Americans for the use of the Mississippi ports and was working to undermine the allegiance of those west of the Appalachians to the United States. It was the position of both Britain and the United States that navigation of the Mississippi River was free to all, but Spain did not recognize this position. Nor would Spain grant the right of deposit of goods in New Orleans—a right essential to the effective use of the Mississippi—to the United States.

Of course, use of the Mississippi was an absolute requirement for the commercial development of the trans-Allegheny region of America. The expense of transporting freight from the west to the east overland was prohibitive; only lightweight cargo of very high value could even be considered worth transporting in this fashion. Even so, settlers poured into this area in increasing numbers in the 1780's from the older states despite the fact that, as matters stood, they must either switch their allegiance to Spain or be denied the opportunity of developing the country. John Jay conducted negotiations over a considerable period with the Spanish diplomat, Diego de Gardoqui, but the United States had little to offer and the Spanish little to fear from the continuation of the deadlock. Jay saw scant hope for settling the dispute favorably to the United States by negotiation and was entirely unenthusiastic about a recourse to arms. "For," he said in 1786, "unblessed with an efficient government, destitute of funds, and without public credit, either at home or abroad, we should be obliged to wait in patience for better days, or plunge into an unpopular and dangerous war with very little prospect of terminating it by a peace, either advantageous or glorious."[307]

Not all the difficulties of the Confederation were with European countries; those people commonly called the Barbary Pirates along the African coast of the Mediterranean disrupted trade in a particularly distressing way. Several Moslem principalities, or whatever they should be called, had long preyed on shipping in the Mediterranean. Countries who wished to avoid their depredations were expected to pay bribes. Once the Americans cut themselves loose from British protection, they were exposed to these pirates. Algeria went to war with the United States, or so rumor had it, seized two American ships, and enslaved their crews. The enslaved Americans "were forced to carry timber and rocks on long hauls over rough mountainous roads."[308] Congress offered to ransom the sailors, but the amount they could and did offer was too small. A "diplomat" from another principality approached the United States with the proposition that the harassment of shipping would cease if tribute in sufficient amount were paid. As things stood, however, the United States could neither afford to pay tribute nor assemble the necessary force to suppress the pirates.

Many of the Confederation's troubles can be traced to financial difficulties. These were frequently tied in and contributed to the ineffectiveness in dealing with foreign nations. A country that had repudiated its currency at the outset and whose diplomats had to go cup in hand, as it were, to other nations seeking funds was hardly in a good bargaining position. There were, of course, domestic as well as foreign consequences of the financial shambles of the Confederation.

The methods used to finance the war had left not only a debt but also a legacy of inflation through the year of 1780, followed by a drastic deflation. There is no mystery about the cause of the deflation; when the tender laws were removed the Continental paper ceased to circulate as money. Much the same thing happened to the paper money that had been issued by the states during the war. Specie replaced paper as currency, but there was much less of it than there had been of the other. Prices then had to be adjusted downward to make trade feasible in the new currency. "The result was that within a year or two after the war . . . there was a dearth of both paper money and hard money."[309]

A drastic deflation produces, or *is*, what is commonly called a depression. When the amount of currency is drastically reduced, prices must fall. Not only do those who have goods for sale not want the prices of them to fall, but it is especially hard on those saddled with debts of their own, or who have to pay taxes to retire debts accumulated when prices were much higher. As one historian writing about these times said: "Hard is the lot of one who, burdened with taxes and debts and destitute of cash, is beset by falling prices of the things he makes and sells."[310]

Historians differ as to the extent, depth, and impact of the depression of the 1780s. They even differ as to when it was worse: whether in the first part or the middle of the decade. Contemporary observers often gave optimistic reports. For example, Benjamin Franklin wrote in 1786: "America never was in higher prosperity, her produce abundant and bearing a good price, her working people all employed and well paid, and all property in lands and houses of more than treble the value it bore before the war; and our commerce being no longer the monopoly of British merchants, we are furnished with all the foreign commodities we need, at much more reasonable prices than heretofore."[311] George Washington wrote in a similar vein in 1787: "In the old states, which were the theatres of hostility, it is wonderful to see how soon the ravages of war are repaired. Houses are rebuilt, fields enclosed, stocks of cattle which were destroyed are replaced, and many a desolated territory assumes again the cheerful appearance of cultivation."[312] The truth seems to be that some people were in distress while others were prosperous—not an unusual situation. Be that as it may, some people were pressuring governments for action which they thought would benefit them.

These facts are relevant to a mounting crisis in the United States because they were the occasion for pressures on the governments to do something about them. Some of the functions people were accustomed to have government perform were either not being performed or were irregularly performed. Americans not only had a legacy of mercantilism but also one of monetary manipulations. Debts, taxes, and trade regulations plagued the new governments. There was not even a standard currency throughout the United States.

When the Continental and state currencies were repudiated, people used coins primarily for a medium of exchange. There were few minted in America during this period, so that foreign coins circulated mostly: "English, French, Spanish, and German coins, of various and uncertain value, passed from hand to hand. Beside the ninepences and four-pence-ha'-pennies, there were bits and half-bits, pistareens, picayunes, and fips. Of gold pieces there were the johannes, or joe, the doubloon, the moidore, and pistole, with English and French guineas, carolins, ducats, and chequins."[313] In addition to the difficulty of calculating the respective value of each of these coins, there was the complication that coins were frequently worn or clipped. A man who accepted one of the latter at full value might have it discounted when he tried to use it. Americans did not have a medium of exchange; they had media through which exchanges of money for money were almost as precarious as exchanges in goods and they were using coins whose sovereigns could not regulate and over whom Americans had no control.

There was hardly any reason, however, for the citizenry to have any confidence in the monetary actions of the Congress, nor, for that matter, of the legislatures of the states. Not only had the Confederation repudiated its currency, but the debts which it still recognized were poorly serviced. The total debt of the United States at the end of the war, foreign and domestic, was about $35,000,000. Far from being retired, it continued to grow. By way of requisitions from the states, Congress received $2,457,987.25 in the period from November 1, 1781 to January 1, 1786. This was barely enough to pay current expenses for the government.[314] Robert Morris sent along this comment when he resigned as head of the treasury in 1783: "To increase our debts while the prospect of paying them diminishes, does not consist with my ideas of integrity. I must, therefore, quit a situation which becomes utterly insupportable."[315] Those who succeeded him may have had less integrity than he professed, but they were hardly better supplied with money.

It was commonly held that the greatest deficiencies of Congress under the Confederation were the lack of the power to tax and the inability to regulate trade. There should be no doubt that the lack of the power to tax made Congress almost impotent to perform the functions allotted to it. As to trade,

Congress was almost powerless either to regulate or to prevent the states from doing so. Whether trade needed regulating was debatable, but if it did, a strong case could be made against the states doing it. Indeed, some states undertook to set up tariffs and to discriminate against ships of other lands, particularly those of England. But it was exceedingly difficult for states to set rates which would accomplish even those dubious advantages supposed to follow from them. If the tariffs were too high, in comparison with those of surrounding states, goods might come into the state from ports of entry located in other states. If imported goods were finally consumed in another state from the one imposing the tariff, the state was actually levying taxes on citizens of other states.

The regulation of trade by the states worked against a common market for all the United States and threatened to turn some states against others. John Fiske described the situation this way:

> Meanwhile, the different states, with their different tariff and ton-nage acts, began to make commercial war upon one another. No sooner had the other three New England states virtually closed their ports to British shipping than Connecticut threw hers wide open, an act which she followed by laying duties upon imports from Massachusetts. Pennsylvania discriminated against Delaware, and New Jersey, pillaged at once by both her greater neighbours, was compared to a cask tapped at both ends.[316]

Trade discriminations sometimes lead to war. Not only was there the possibility that one American state might go to war against its neighbor but also that discriminations against or by foreign countries might lead some country to go to war against a state. In such a case, the United States would be drawn into the war, for the authority to make war was vested in Congress. To say the least, the situation was anomalous.

It is strange, but true, that the events which finally provoked Americans to do something about the union did not directly involve the Congress and its ineffectiveness. Perhaps it is not so strange on reflection, for Congress rarely did anything. The failure to act may be indictable, but it would be hard to get a jury to convict. Congress presented a low silhouette to its critics. True, it repudiated its currency, could not pay its debts, could not force the states to meet their quotas, could not protect its citizens abroad, and did not do most of the things it was authorized to do with much energy. But, then, it seldom gave offense, and people spread over a vast land were more used to opposing government action than seeking it. It is most probable that if some crisis had swept Congress away it would have gone with a whimper rather than a bang. In our day, we have seen exile governments seeking a country to govern; the United States was an exile country awaiting a government.

It was trouble in New England in 1786–87 that aroused fears which prompted men to action. Paper money, taxes, and debts were the occasion of challenges to some state governments. Most states were under pressure to make paper money issues. Seven had done so by 1788 but, as might be expected, there was considerable opposition to such actions. Rhode Island not only issued paper money but revived harsh methods to try to make it circulate. Faced with fleeing creditors and merchants abandoning the state, the "legislature passed an act declaring that anyone refusing to take the money at face value would be fined £100 for a first offense and would have to pay a similar fine and lose his rights as a citizen for a second."[317] When the act was challenged, the court declared its opinion that the act was unconstitutional. The judges were called before the legislature, interrogated, and some of them dismissed. Rhode Island's government was viewed with contempt by many Americans.

Rhode Islanders would probably have been left to suffer the disadvantages of their own government or get out—the latter was becoming an attractive option—but it was not easy to take so sanguine a view of events in Massachusetts. There was widespread dissatisfaction with the foreclosures on farms and imprisonment for debts. Some of the discontented wanted a moratorium on the collection of debts and/or paper money to be issued. Taxes were also levied in such a fashion as to arouse resistance to their collection. The discontent may have been agitated by British agents; certainly, money was made available for the discontented to use to take action, though who was behind this was never definitely established.

Overt action came when mobs began preventing courts from sitting. Beginning in early September of 1786, a succession of courts were disrupted and prevented from conducting business by large groups of armed men: at Worcester, at Concord, at Taunton, at Great Barrington, and at Springfield. The legislature did not take the desired action, and a rebel force was organized. The climax of these events came in January of 1787. It is known as Shays' Rebellion, taking its name from one of its leaders, Daniel Shays. Massachusetts authorized an armed force to put down the rebellion, and the rebel force was dispersed on January 25. New Hampshire was threatened by a rebel force, but the movement was quickly put down by decisive action by Governor John Sullivan who had been a general during the late war.

Actually, there had been some movement for revision of the Articles of Confederation well before these events transpired. As early as 1780–1781, Alexander Hamilton and James Madison had begun to urge revision. But it took more of a crisis than existed then to stir the states—eager to hold on to all their powers—to approve any convention. The train of events that led to the Constitutional Convention began in 1785. At a Potomac Conference held at George Washington's home in that year, delegates from Virginia and Maryland met to work out agreements for the navigation of the Potomac. Since there were broader navigational and trade problems involving other states, they issued the call for a general conference to be held at Annapolis in 1786.

Meanwhile, it became increasingly apparent that Congress was ineffective, if not impotent. "Between October 1, 1785, and January 31, 1786, Congress had a quorum on only ten days, and never were more than seven states represented. Between October 1, 1785, and April 30, 1786, nine states— the minimum required to do any serious business—were represented on only three days."[318] As mobs began to intimidate courts in Massachusetts, one historian notes that "the Congress had likewise ceased to function."[319]

The Annapolis Convention met in September, 1786, but only five states had sent delegations. Instead of trying to take any action involving the United States, the assembled delegates adopted a resolution proposed by Alexander Hamilton that Congress call a convention in 1787 to render the Articles of Confederation "adequate to the exigencies of the Union." The Congress complied by sending out a call to the states to send delegates to a convention to be held in Philadelphia beginning in May, 1787. This was to be the gathering that is remembered in our history as *the* Constitutional Convention.

Some have described what happened as more than remarkable; it has even been called a miracle. George Washington wrote to Lafayette that it was "little short of a miracle that the delegates from so many different States (which States you know are different from each other), in their manners, circumstances and prejudices, should unite in forming a system of National Government, so little liable to well-founded objections."[320] Miss Catherine Drinker Bowen's recently published book on the convention is called *Miracle at Philadelphia*. Whatever it was, or should be called, all who are open to an examination of the evidence will admit that it was an extraordinary event.

Even so, the convention did not get underway any more auspiciously than did most other assemblages in that age; it was called for May 14, but there was not a quorum to do business until May 25. It was no easy matter to assemble men from over the length and breadth of the United States; delegates from Georgia, say, had a formidable distance to travel, and even an early start did not necessarily lead to a prompt arrival. In any case, promptness was better calculated in weeks than in hours.

The Virginia delegation was the first appointed by a legislature, and its members began to arrive in Philadelphia before other out-of-staters. It was an impressive delegation, including among its members some of that state's leading citizens: George Washington, Edmund Randolph, George Mason, and James Madison. (George Wythe, one of the best legal minds in America, put in an appearance but left shortly to attend his dying wife.) Most of the Pennsylvania delegates did not have to make a journey to get to Philadelphia, so that they were available from the beginning. It was an impressive delegation, for it included Benjamin Franklin, Robert Morris (who, if he was there, remained silent during the debates), Gouverneur Morris, and James Wilson.

The New England states were not only the slowest in appointing delegates but also theirs were among the last to arrive. Rhode Island rejected the invitation to appoint delegates. (The absence of Rhode Islanders was not considered a handicap during the convention, for that state's behavior was so universally deplored that men did not gladly seek the counsel of her citizens.) The New Hampshire delegates were exceedingly late; two of the four appointed finally arrived on July 23. (They could not come earlier because the state had not provided for their expenses.) New York appointed three delegates—Alexander Hamilton, Robert Yates, and John Lansing— rather reluctant ones, we gather, for Yates and Lansing withdrew after a short period of attendance and Hamilton was absent for an extended period. Over all, 12 states had 55 delegates in attendance at one time or another. From most indications, the greatest concern for a stronger general government was among the delegates from the states located from New Jersey southward. The leadership in the convention came mainly from four states, and in this order: Virginia, Pennsylvania, Connecticut, and South Carolina. Two other states' delegations played some considerable role: New Jersey and Massachusetts. Delegates from other states were generally less conspicuous during the debates, though Luther Martin of Maryland and George Read of Delaware would have led if they could have attracted followers.

The delegates were as well qualified as could have been assembled in America, qualified both by experience and training. Among them were 39 who had served at one time or another in Congress, eight who had signed the Declaration of Independence, eight who had helped draw state constitutions, one, John Dickinson, who is credited with the first draft of the Articles of Confederation, seven who had been chief executives of their states, and 21 who had fought in the war. Thirty-three were lawyers, and ten of these had served as judges. About half of them were college graduates, more from Princeton than from any other institution.[321]

Both youth and advanced age were represented at the convention. The youngest delegate was Jonathan Dayton of New Jersey at 26; the oldest, Benjamin Franklin, who was, as he said, in his eighty-second year. The average age was in the low forties. Some of the leaders, however, were rather young: Charles Pinckney of South Carolina was only 29, Gouverneur Morris 35, and James Madison 36. They were counter-balanced by men of middling years and extensive experience, for example: John Dickinson 54, Roger Sherman 66, and John Langdon 67.

George Washington almost did not come, even though his presence at the convention was essential—for it was generally agreed that he was America's first personage. When he was informed of his election, he asked that someone else be appointed in his stead. Friends so earnestly urged him to attend, however, that he changed his mind.

Washington arrived in Philadelphia before the convention was scheduled to begin. It had long since become difficult for him to go anywhere quietly, and there was good reason to publicize this trip. He was met at Chester by a troop of horses which escorted him into Philadelphia where cannon were fired and bells rung. The fact that Washington had arrived gave notice that the convention was important and that laggards should make haste to get there. When the convention was organized, Washington was elected, unanimously (as when was he not), to preside, an office which he took so seriously that he attended each session, though it was the most oppressively hot summer in the memory of Philadelphians. If Washington could endure it, others could and did. He was a man of stern visage, impressive physique, and high seriousness; with him in the chair, the convention could hardly be anything but what it was, a deliberative body which pursued its business in an absence of frivolity and without stooping to personalities. Though Washington did not participate in the debates until the closing days when he made a brief speech, there was no doubt where he stood on the Constitution. He signed it gladly, and took care to let men about the country know that he approved of it.

The men in the convention were aware that when they looked toward the chair, they were gazing at the man who would almost certainly be the first President of the United States. This emboldened those who wanted a strong President to make the office powerful, for they were confident that Washington would not abuse such powers. Gouverneur Morris wrote to Washington a few weeks after the convention to describe the importance of his role:

> I have observed that your name to the new Constitution has been of infinite service. Indeed, I am convinced that if you had not attended the Convention, and the same paper had been handed out to the world, it would have met with a cooler reception, with fewer and weaker advocates, and with more and more strenuous opponents.[322]

Benjamin Franklin was the other most prominent American; his hold on the affections of his countrymen was not so great as that of Washington, but his international fame was such that any gathering which had the benefit of his counsels gained in reputation. Though he was getting old—in fact, was old—his mind was still clear, his vast fund of experience still at his command, and his accomplishments as a raconteur still led men to seek his company. He was not only aged but also infirm. He had to be carried in a sedan chair to the sessions, and he wrote out any but the briefest of remarks so that they could be read to the convention by his fellow Pennsylvanian, James Wilson. Franklin contributed most to the convention by avuncular admonitions to the delegates to compromise, to compose their differences, and to put aside so much of their personal desires as might be necessary to accomplish the object at hand. When the convention appeared to be nearly breaking up over the question of equal or proportional representation, Doctor Franklin said: "When a broad table is to be made, and edges of planks do not fit, the artist takes a little from both, and makes a good joint. In like manner here both sides must part with some of their demands, in order that they may join in some accommodating proposition."[323] At another point, he proposed that the sessions be opened with prayer, for he seemed to think that the influence of religion might link them together in their efforts to arrive at a new system.

His advanced age may have increased the influence of his spirit of accommodation, but he had been adept at the arts of politics and diplomacy long before the contentions of young men tired him.

Though the convention was not a large body, a few men did most of the speaking and a great deal of the other work of hammering out the Constitution. The leaders included: Madison, Mason and Randolph of Virginia, Gouverneur Morris and Wilson of Pennsylvania, Charles Pinckney and Rutledge of South Carolina, Ellsworth and Sherman of Connecticut, King and Gerry of Massachusetts, and, perhaps, Paterson of New Jersey. According to one tabulation, Gouverneur Morris spoke on 173 different occasions; Wilson, 168; Madison, 161; Sherman, 138; Mason, 136; and Gerry, 119.

James Madison has frequently been described as the Father of the Constitution. Certainly, he was one of its principal architects. He was not impressive to look at; judging by his appearance it would have been easy to mistake him for a clerk. He was quite short and thin, "Little Jemmy," they called him, "no bigger than a half cake of soap." Nor was he an orator; he spoke in such a low voice that those keeping journals often missed a part of what he said. He made up for these shortcomings, however, with intellectual acuity, sharp insight, and tenacity in the pursuit of his object. Moreover, he had prepared himself for the task of making a new constitution. Much of his time in the months before the convention had been spent in reading, and mastering, the literature on government. A plea to Jefferson in Paris had brought a plethora of books to augment his supply at home. The Virginia Plan, from which the Constitution emerged, was presented on the floor by Governor Randolph, but Madison had undoubtedly done much of the work on it. He might be said to have mothered the Constitution, too, because he devoted himself to it exclusively during the months of the convention. His recollection was that he not only attended every session but that he was never absent for more than a few minutes, and he was certain that he could not have missed a single speech of any duration. He kept copious notes of the speeches, and they are judged to be the most reliable record of what was said. This was a marathon undertaking itself, but he also spoke frequently, and at length, with a masterful show of erudition.

Gouverneur Morris was, however, the most dazzling speaker in the convention, an orator whose learning and close reasoning gave an irresistible thrust to his forensic skill. He had been maimed both in arm and leg, and stumped about on a wooden leg, but it is difficult to think of him as a cripple, for he was reputed to be quite a lady's man and known as a *bon vivant*. Madison and Morris were men who knew what they wanted, who pressed the convention step by step in their direction, who took care to see that what they had won by their reasoning was not lost in the maneuvers over detail, but who yielded gracefully when they were outvoted.

There must have been many moments of high drama during the convention, but the most eloquent speech fell from Gouverneur Morris. The occasion was the discussion of the counting of slaves for purposes of representation. "He never would concur in upholding domestic slavery." Morris said. "It was a nefarious institution. It was the curse of heaven on the States where it prevailed. . . . Proceed southwardly and every step you take through the great region of slaves presents a desert increasing, with the increasing proportion of these wretched beings. . . . The admission of slaves into the Representation when fairly examined comes to this: that the inhabitant of Georgia and South Carolina who goes to the Coast of Africa, and in defiance of the most sacred laws of humanity tears away his fellow creatures from their dearest connections, damns them to the most cruel bondages, shall have more votes in a Government instituted for the protection of the rights of mankind, than the Citizen of Pennsylvania or New Jersey who views with a laudable horror so nefarious a practice. . . . He would sooner submit himself to a tax for paying for all the negroes in the United States, than saddle posterity with such a Constitution."[324] Aside from his vigorous participation in the debates Morris also contributed by his work on the committee on style, which transformed what survived the debates into the congruous whole we now know as the Constitution with its spare, brief, and potent phrases.

Although the convention was made up of about as impressive an assemblage of men as could have been gathered at any time, there were some prominent Americans not there. Most notably, John Adams and Thomas Jefferson were on diplomatic missions in Europe. Among others not there were Samuel Adams who was not chosen, and Patrick Henry who did not choose to attend. But on the whole, the Convention represented much of the best of America.

The convention was organized so as to proceed about its business without interference from outsiders or without inhibiting full discussion. The sessions were held behind closed doors; no record of what was said or being considered there was to be released without the approval of the convention. There were no galleries to be played to, no press to be placated. Strict rules governing the behavior of members were adopted. For example:

> Every member rising to speak, shall address the President; and whilst he shall be speaking, none shall pass between them, or hold discourse with another, or read a book, pamphlet or paper. . . .

> A member shall not speak oftener than twice, without special leave, upon the same question; and not the second time, before every other, who had been silent, shall have been heard, if he wish to speak.[325]

The convention operated on the rule that no decision on any particular of the constitution should be considered final. This enabled the convention to adjust the parts to one another as alterations were made.

The convention was remarkable both for its orderliness and for the absence of rancor among the members. On the one or two occasions when tempers flared, the strong feeling quickly subsided. Some did appear to be impatient in the last few days from going over ground already covered. Even so, an effort was made in the last days to make changes that might satisfy the few holdouts from signing. It is necessary to read but briefly into Madison's notes to get the feeling that these men were taking very seriously what they were doing, that though their task was urgent everything must be considered with great care. Above all, many were determined to stick with the undertaking until something had been completed to present to the public.

It was well that they were, for their object lay on the other side of a thicket of uncertainties, doubts, and differences. Even what they were supposed to do at the convention was in doubt. The resolution adopted by Congress calling the convention declared that it was to be for the "sole purpose of revising the Articles of Confederation." It was clear enough what Congress had said, but these men were gathered to represent their states and were supposed to act under their instructions, if any. The instructions differed enough one from the other that a good case could be made that the convention could do what its members thought best. Most of those gathered agreed with the idea that their task was to construct a plan for a new system of government, or accepted it without cavil. The few who did not could leave, and some did.

It was only with some difficulty that they agreed on how they would vote. Delegates from several states were bent on having representation in the new government based on population or wealth, as the Virginia Plan provided. They would have the best chance of getting this into a constitution if the states had votes in the convention proportionate to their populations. There was no likelihood, however, that the smaller states might agree to this, so the convention votes were by states, each state having one vote regardless of how many delegates there were, just as in the case of the Congress. If a state's delegation was tied in a vote, that state's vote would not be counted. A majority of the states present and voting was sufficient to any decision.

Sentiment had been building for some time that, if there was to be an effective union of the states, the general government must have the power to use force on individuals. This, as many saw it, was the only way to "render the constitution of the Federal Government adequate to the exigencies of the Union . . . ," as the declaration drawn at the Annapolis Convention the year before had described the need. A man named Stephen Higginson had written to General Knox earlier in 1787 describing precisely what needed to be done: "The Union must not only have the right to make laws and requisitions, but it must have the power of compelling obedience thereto. . . ."[326] Washington had written to Madison in March: "I confess . . . that my opinion of public virtue is so far changed, that I have my doubts whether any system, without the means of coercion in the sovereign will enforce due obedience to the ordinances of a General Government; without which every thing else fails. . . . But what kind of coercion, you may ask. This indeed will require thought. . . ."[327] Washington wrote to John Jay in the following vein: "I do not conceive we can exist long as a nation without having lodged somewhere a power which will pervade the whole Union in as energetic a manner, as the authority of the State Governments extends over the several States. . . ."[328]

There was no way, however, of contriving a general government which could compel obedience without encroaching on the powers of the states. Indeed, any attempt to work out such a plan had major obstacles in the way. Both theory and history militated against divided sovereignty. Theory said it could not be done; history afforded no clear-cut examples of its having been successfully done. If sovereignty could not be divided, if a general government was to have coercive power, then the general government would have to be sovereign and the states become but districts in a nation. There were men at the convention who saw it this way and were ready to grasp the nettle.

But such a plan had little hope of ratification, if any. Madison described some of the difficulty in a letter to Edmund Pendleton before the convention:

. . . The necessity of gaining the concurrence of the Convention in some system that will answer the purpose, the subsequent approbation of Congress, and the final sanction of the States, presents a series of chances which would inspire despair in any case where the alternative was less formidable.[329]

But if Madison had not known beforehand that the states would be jealous of their powers and prerogatives, he would have found out soon enough in the convention. George Mason, his fellow Virginian, expressed his determination to preserve the vitality of the states in calm but measured words: "He took this occasion to repeat, that notwithstanding his solicitude to establish a national Government, he never would agree to abolish the State Governments or render them absolutely insignificant. They were as necessary as the General Government and he would be equally careful to preserve them."[330] Luther Martin of Maryland said that he agreed with Mason "as to the importance of the State Governments. He would support them at the expense of the General Government which was instituted for the purpose of that support. . . . They are afraid of granting powers unnecessarily, lest they should defeat the original end of the Union; lest the powers should prove dangerous to the sovereignties of the particular State which the Union was meant to support; and expose the lesser to being swallowed up by the larger."[331] Doctor Johnson in contrasting the Virginia and New Jersey Plans (the Virginia Plan calling for representation to be apportioned according to wealth and/or population while the New Jersey Plan called for representation by states), brought some of the difficulties out in the open. He noted that James Wilson and James Madison, advocates of the Virginia Plan, did not propose to destroy the states. "They wished," he said, "to leave the States in possession of a considerable, though a subordinate jurisdiction. They had not yet however shewn how this could consist with, or be secured against the general sovereignty and jurisdiction, which they proposed to give to the national Government."[332]

Some held that they were departing from experience even to try to contrive a government which depended upon divided sovereignty. Others argued that the American situation was unique, that history afforded no clear model for it, and that they must innovate. Charles Pinckney summed up the peculiar situation of America in this vigorous exposition:

> The people of this country are not only very different from the inhabitants of any State we are acquainted with in the modern world; but I assert that their situation is distinct from either the people of Greece or Rome, or of any State we are acquainted with among the ancients. . . .
>
> Our true situation appears to me to be this—a new extensive Country containing within itself the materials for forming a Government capable of extending to its citizens all the blessings of civil and religious liberty—capable of making them happy at home. . . .[333]

Reason is the sword of the young; experience the shield of age. Some of the young men at the convention were for casting a new system, but others wanted no such heady innovation. In any case, the states must be preserved.

Some of the proponents of an energetic general government declared that there was little danger to the states to be expected from it. They appealed to the history of confederacies to show that time and again it was the states who had intruded upon and broken up the general government. Others appealed to a broader experience to show that where power was confided in any government it tended to crush all opposing power.

The decision to give the general government power to act directly upon individuals as well as make it the supreme government *in* its realm was accompanied by determined efforts to limit it. There was general agreement that such power should be checked as well. Gouverneur Morris thought the following principles must be introduced:

> . . . Abilities and virtue, are equally necessary in both branches [the legislative and executive]. Something more is now wanted. 1. The checking branch must have a personal interest in checking the other branch, one interest must be opposed to another interest. 2. Vices as they exist must be turned against each other. . . . 3. It should be independent.[334]

James Madison declared that if it "be essential to the preservation of liberty that the Legislative, Executive, and Judiciary powers be separate, it is essential to a maintenance of the separation, that they should be independent of one another." His thought mainly was that they must be independent in their source of power. They accomplished this, so far as they did, by having the House elected directly by the voters, the Senate by the state legislators, the President by an electoral college, and the giving of life terms during good behavior for judges appointed by the President with the advice and consent of the Senate.

Another fateful question was how those who were to govern could be made sufficiently independent of their electors without posing fatal dangers to the liberties of the people. The Founders raised a question which is rarely raised today; namely, whether or not representatives of the people could be trusted not to overstep the bounds of their power and invade the rights of the people. There were those in the Constitutional Convention who thought that could be guarded against by frequent elections. Roger Sherman of Connecticut observed that "Government is instituted for those who live under it. It ought therefore to be so constituted as not to be dangerous to their liberties. Frequent elections are necessary to preserve the good behavior of rulers."[335] Others questioned this principle, for they noted that a too close dependence of the government on the people resulted not in wise and stable government but in the pandering of politicians to the temporary and changing opinions of the populace. Madison had said just prior to Sherman's remarks that the objective of the Constitution was "first to protect the people against their rulers; secondly to protect the people against" their own tendency to err because of "fickleness and passion."[336] Alexander Hamilton pointed out that lately "the Government had entirely given way to the people, and had in fact suspended many of its ordinary functions in order to prevent those turbulent scenes which had appeared elsewhere."[337]

As happened in so many cases, the men at the Convention hit upon a happy compromise between conflicting opinions. The principle of frequent elections was satisfied by having the members of the House stand for election every two years. On the other hand, stability would be the object of having Senate terms run for six years, and having one-third of the Senate stand for election every two years. A further compromise was to have the President's term fall between these extremes. Indeed, there were so many compromises in the course of the making of the Constitution that some historians have gone so far as to describe the document as a "bundle of compromises."

The phrase itself may be apt enough, but not if it be taken to mean that the Founders yielded up their principles on issue after issue to accommodate a welter of narrow interests. It is true that some compromises found no great principle to support them. Thus, it was to accommodate sectional interests that the Constitution prohibits the Congress to stop the slave trade (though the language is more circumspect) before 1808. Nor was there any discernible principle in the provision that slaves should be counted as three-fifths of a person for purposes of representation. Yet a compromise need not be a yielding of principle; it may well be the result of sacrificing narrow interest to the general well being. So it was quite often at the convention at Philadelphia; men advanced one-sided, narrow, or limited views in the debates but arrived at great principles through compromise. The stately, but simple, rhythms of the Constitution as it came from the committee on style captured principle after principle in its verbiage, meshed them together into a symphonic whole, and provided the plan for the government of an empire for liberty. That it could be done appeared most unlikely at the outset of the convention. That it had been done was not so clear at the close. That it was done seems now a miracle.

The state delegations present and voting in the convention at its close gave their unanimous approval to the Constitution. Only a very few individuals, among the delegates, refused to sign the handiwork of the Convention. The document was submitted to the Congress, after which it was to be submitted to the states which were to hold conventions to consider the ratification of it. As the signing was taking place, Benjamin Franklin made the last public remarks recorded for the Convention. James Madison described them this way:

> Whilst the last members signing it Doctor Franklin looking toward the President's Chair at the back of which a . . . sun happened to be painted, observed to a few members near him, that Painters have found it difficult to distinguish in their art a rising from a setting sun. I have, said he often and often in the course of the Session, and the vicissitudes of my hopes and fears as to its issue, looked at that behind the President without being able to tell whether it was rising or setting: But now at length I have the happiness to know that it is a rising and not a setting sun.[338]

All who would having signed, the Convention adjourned *sine die*.

The proposed constitution was then sent to Congress for further action. After some debate by that body, it was decided to submit the proposal to the states according to the conditions required in it. That is, the states would each provide for an election to be held for delegates to its convention. When nine states should approve the Constitution, it would go into effect. (In effect, two-thirds of existing states had to ratify for it to go into effect.) A simple majority in any convention would be sufficient for ratification. Any state that did not ratify could, of course, apply for admission at a later date.

The ratification effort was concentrated in the period from December, 1787 through most of July, 1788. Debates over ratification were most extensive in Virginia, New York, and Massachusetts. Rhode Island refused to hold an election to have a convention, and North Carolina's convention adjourned without ratifying the Constitution. Otherwise, ratification moved along quickly, for that era. Delaware ratified the Constitution December 7, 1787 by a vote of 30-0; Pennsylvania followed 12 December 43-23; New Jersey was unanimous for ratification a few days later, 39-0; Georgia unanimous on January 2, 1788, 26-0; Connecticut overwhelmingly approved, 128-40, on January 9. The vote was close in Massachusetts, but ratification was achieved 187-168 on February 16. The Maryland vote in favor of ratification was not even close; it was 63-11, despite the fact that several Maryland delegates to the Constitutional Convention at Philadelphia opposed it. Those in favor of ratification in South Carolina won handily, 149-73, on May 23; New Hampshire followed on June 21, 1788, 57 to 46.

Nine states had now ratified the Constitution, and legally it could be put into effect. But the chances of it succeeding for long without Virginia and New York were slim. Attention now focused on their conventions. In the Virginia convention which lasted for most of June, both sides were reluctant to take a vote for fear of losing. The debates were thus prolonged, and the examination of the Constitution was most thorough. James Madison was the leading exponent of the Constitution, ably assisted by John Marshall, among others. Patrick Henry was the most tenacious opponent of ratification. When the vote was finally taken, it was 89 to 79. The contest in New York was a heated one. Some of those favoring ratification presented their case at length in a series of newspaper articles. These were later collected and published as *The Federalist;* they endure as the most extensive and authoritative analysis ever made of the Constitution. Though the authors were not originally identified; they are known to have been Alexander Hamilton, James Madison, and John Jay. Even so, when the vote finally came on July 26, 1787, it passed only narrowly, 30-27.

As noted earlier, the most tenacious and widely held objection to the Constitution was that it lacked a bill of rights. Once one had been added by the first ten amendments to the Constitution in 1791, virtually all opposition to the Constitution disappeared. Even before that, the other two states had joined the Union: North Carolina ratified the Constitution in November, 1789, by a vote of 194-77; Rhode Island finally held a convention in 1790 which proceeded to ratify the Constitution by the narrowest possible margin, 34-32. Before these events had transpired, however, the Constitution had been put into operation.

Section III

American Government in the 19th Century

Chapter 8
Introduction

On paper at least, the United States had a constitutionally limited government in 1789. It had a federal system of government with powers divided between a general government and the state governments. The United States was styled a republic, and each of the states was guaranteed a republican system of government by the Constitution. That is to say, both the states and the general governments were based on popular consent and incorporated the representative and majoritarian principle. The United States and the states had a mixed system of government, to some degree at any rate, in that they had a single executive based on the monarchical principle; an upper legislative house, based on at least the relics of an aristocratical principle (government by the few), and a lower house popularly elected, embracing the democratical principle. The executive, legislative, and judicial branches had separate and more or less independent powers, and these powers were so arrayed that they might check one another. Indeed, the federal system provided a check on government also, since the general government might check the states, and vice versa. Moreover, the first ten amendments which were added in 1791 gave the United States a bill of rights which placed further limits on the United States government. All this was on paper, of course, how it would work in practice had not yet been proved.

Even so, the experimental nature of this government should not be over-emphasized. The Constitution may have gone further in limiting the general government than had been done before, but it was based on great political traditions; its principles had been tried both intellectually and in practice, and the learning of the ages could be called to its support. Indeed, much of what has been told thus far has been related to make the antiquity of the political traditions and ideas embraced in American institutions clear. It was not something contrived in the pinch of circumstances, an expedient of the moment. In a sense, the nearly 200 years of colonial experience had been a preparation for this constitution making. The British tradition back of that had helped to prepare the way. So had the Old Testament, the Greeks, the Romans and Christian ideas and beliefs. Nor can what the Americans did be understood at all without understanding the natural law tradition which informed their undertaking. In a very important way, the United States

Constitution was the culmination of two millennia of political thought and practice.

To appearances, at least, the United States Constitution has been a success. It is now more than 200 years old, and the country for which it prescribes the government has grown from a few colonies planted along the eastern coast of North America, remote from the centers of civilization, to a leading world power and the most prestigious nation in the world. Nor has the Constitution been much changed by amendments, which have been rare over the years, if we except the first ten, which were ratified in 1791. The 11th Amendment was added in 1795, but only four more became a part of the Constitution during the whole of the 19th century. Eleven amendments have been joined to the Constitution in the 20th century, though one of these—the 18th Amendment—has since been nullified. By and large, the Constitution as drawn in 1787 still ostensibly holds sway, its original language little altered by the amendments. There are still three branches of government—executive, legislative, and judicial—as the original Constitution prescribed. The national legislature is still divided into two houses, and revenue bills still originate in the House of Representatives. Much else has been but little changed by constitutional amendment.

Yet there have been massive changes in the nature, reach, and activities of the United States government over these two hundred years. Its relations with the state governments have changed as well. Some of these changes have been punctuated by amendments to the Constitution, but most have not. It used to be thought that the great divide in American history was the Civil War. For example, historian John D. Hicks published a two volume history of the United States in the 1940s: the first volume, which ended with the Civil War and Reconstruction, he titled *The Federal Union;* the second, he called *The American Nation.* The thesis which justifies this naming holds that with the Union victory and the imposition of its will upon the South, nationalism triumphed in America. No longer was the United States a union of more or less sovereign states; it was now one nation under one *supreme* government.

While there is more than a little to be said in favor of the above thesis, it is not the one that will be used here. There is no denying that the constitutional amendments which followed in the wake of the Civil War made some impact on the nature of the Union, nor that the Civil War was a major, even cataclysmic, event in our history. But from the present perspective, the great divide in our history was not the Civil War but the one which can be expressed in broad terms as the divide between the 19th and 20th centuries. Actually, the great shift did not clearly begin until 1913, when three major events, big with moment for the future, took place. They were: the passage of the 16th Amendment—income tax amendment—and the 17th Amendment—providing for the direct election of Senators—and the passage of the Federal Reserve Act. But the background for these events was laid earlier, going back even into the 19th century. Indeed, the Civil War had laid the groundwork for the divide between the 19th and 20th centuries. In any case, the divide is not as precise as all that; it is a development which from the perspective of history reveals its character.

There are any number of facts and events which point up the development in one way or another. Take the national debt, for example. It did rise and fall somewhat during the course of the 19th century. The debt amounted to $83 million in 1800 and was slightly over $1¼ billion in 1900. But when the debt was divided by the population of the country it was $15.87 per person in 1800, and had grown to only $16.60 per person in 1900—an insignificant change in the burden of the debt. It has grown by leaps and bounds in the 20th century: it was over $24 billion in 1920, nearly $43 billion in 1940, over $284 billion in 1960, over $900 billion in 1980, over $2.6 *trillion* in 1988, and is now well past $3 trillion. The per capita debt had risen from $16.60 in 1900 to $10,534 in 1988. Many other statistics—such as those for government expenditures, tax receipts, employees, and the like—could be submitted to the same effect. That is, the United States government has grown by leaps and bounds in the 20th century, out of all proportion to the population growth. Something similar could be said about a host of government activities of one sort or another, ranging from government regulation of business to involvement in the affairs of foreign nations around the world.

There is a divide, then, between American government as it was in the 19th century and as it became in the 20th century. The difference is not simply quantitative but qualitative as well. It was not merely the exponential growth and expansion of the government but also the power changes between the United States and the states. Most of the changes do not appear in the written Constitution, which means that they have been made by interpretation. Another way to say it is that the United States government bore a family resemblance to the government provided for in the Constitution in the course of the 19th century (including the last decade of the 18th century). When it moved away from that document, as it did from time to time, it was pulled back toward it by one or another of the branches of government or by the influence of the states. That has not happened in the 20th century, as the government has moved farther and farther away from its authority and its constitutionally prescribed pattern.

The differences between these centuries is so great that it will be useful to treat each of them in a different section of the book. It would be possible, of course, to describe the government as it is in the last decade of the 19th century with little or no reference to how it got that way. If one studied government only for the purpose of operating within its jurisdiction as it now is, that would probably be the way to go about it. But the privileges and duties of citizens in the United States go well beyond conforming to what government decrees, permits, or allows. They extend also to taking part in determining the policies, practices, and course of government behavior. For that we need an understanding of political principles, constitutions, and political ideas, present and past. If the government has slipped its constitutional moorings, as seems apparent, in the 20th century, we need to know how it happened and how to get it on course, if that is possible. In any case, it is never enough simply to know what is; we need also to know as much as possible about what was and what could be.

Chapter 9

Establishing a General Government

What the United States had by way of a government at the beginning of 1789 was a piece of paper, and not much else. The piece, or rather pieces, of paper was the Constitution. As for what else there was by way of government, one scholar has written that when Washington became "the first President under the new Constitution, he took over almost nothing from the dying Confederation. There was, indeed, a foreign office with John Jay and a couple of clerks to deal with correspondence . . . ; there was a Treasury Board with an empty treasury; there was a 'Secretary at War' with an authorized army of 840 men; there was a dozen clerks whose pay was in arrears, and an unknown but fearful burden of debt, almost no revenue, and a prostrate credit. But one could hardly perceive in the winter of 1789 a government of the Union."[339]

The Constitution was undoubtedly an elegant document; it was the work of three months of struggle and concentration of a gathering of many of the best minds in America. But might it not wither away as the Confederation had done? Was it possible to have an effective general government over these states? Would men serve faithfully in and seek offices within it? Would they obey its laws and come to its support when it was attacked? Above all, would those who took office within it have the tenacity and resolution to make it work? Madison's comment after looking over the roll of those elected to the Congress points up some of the difficulty. He said that there were very few members of the new Congress who would take an active part "in the drudgery of the business."[340] That would be done, as usual, by those few committed and industrious people who get things done. Indeed, James Madison was one of those people who made the new government work; he was an indispensable man in the early Congresses.

Perhaps the greatest uncertainty about the new government was whether or not it would become a nation among nations in the world and get the respect of other countries. Certainly, the Confederation had not done that. Neither Britain nor Spain paid much attention to the government under the Confederation. Would the new government fare any better? It was, after all, a republic in a world of monarchies and empires, with a rare exception here and there. As if that were not bad enough, the French Revolution broke out in 1789, and when France became a republic a few years later, it became a symbol of the revolt against monarchy.

Be that as it may, the new government did get underway in 1789, a bit shakily no doubt, but with some fanfare nonetheless. Elections for the House and Senate took place in the states in early 1789 mostly. Congress was scheduled to begin its first session in New York City—the seat of the new government—on March 4, 1789, but events rarely took place with such precision in America at that time. Two weeks after that date, only six Senators had arrived, and two weeks later neither the Senate nor the House had assembled a quorum. There was grumbling that the government might be forgotten before it started with its business. Actually, both houses had a quorum on April 6, and Congress got down to business. Electors for the President and Vice-President had been appointed in January. They had voted unanimously for George Washington for President, and he was inaugurated on April 30. The basics of the new government were in place.

Before proceeding with some description of putting the government into operation, there is another aspect of the undertaking that needs to be mentioned. A number of things are authorized or prescribed in the Constitution without any detail as to how they are to be accomplished. On some matters, the Constitution is entirely silent. For example, what was to be the style of the public appearances and ceremonies of public figures, especially that of Presidents, ambassadors, and the like? Was there to be a great deal of pomp and ceremony, as was customary in monarchical government? The only hint in the Constitution was that titles of nobility were prohibited. Indeed, the whole matter of formal titles rose early on. The question of a title for the President was given attention under the spur of the presiding officer, John Adams. A Senate committee recommended that Washington be addressed as "His Highness, the President of the United States of America, and Protector of their Liberties." Many in the Senate were outraged and under Madison's leadership in the House, that body insisted that he be addressed as the Constitution implies, namely as "the President of the United States," and so he has been ever since.[341]

George Washington may not have aped royalty, but he went in for more than a little formal ceremony. For public appearances on formal occasions, he rode in a stylish coach drawn by four or six horses followed by an entourage in other coaches. Washington also held levees (though he did not enjoy them)—highly formal afternoon receptions, consisting of men only, which followed a precise ritual from beginning to end. Washington's appearance at one of these was described this way. He was dressed in "black velvet; his hair in full dress, powdered and gathered . . . ; yellow gloves on his hands; holding a cocked hat with cockade in it, and the edges adorned with a black feather about an inch deep. He wore knee and shoe buckles; and a long sword, with a finely wrought and polished steel hilt, which appeared at the left hip. . . . The scabbard was white polished leather.'' Washington was also very conscious of rank and position, accepting invitations to dinner from no one, and calling upon no one as President. Both Washington and Adams were very conscious not only of maintaining public dignity and distance in relationships, but also using majesty of surroundings to exact obedience rather than raw power. John Adams declared that ''Neither dignity nor authority can be supported in human minds, collected into nations or any great numbers, without a splendor and majesty in some degree proportioned to them.''[342]

While matters of style were neither prescribed by positive law nor Constitution, it must be noted that from the beginning many Americans disapproved of anything smacking of the trappings of royalty and some ridiculed such formal behavior. As President, Jefferson abandoned virtually all formality and effected a style of ''republican simplicity.'' He is alleged to have hitched his horse in front of the capitol and walked to his inauguration, and he definitely received diplomats at the White House in informal attire.

The absence of guidance in the Constitution, however, may be even better illustrated by other examples. For example, the Constitution confers on the President the power to make treaties, ''by and with the Advice and Consent of the Senate,'' and appoint a variety of other officers in the same fashion. It is clear, especially in the case of treaties, how the Senate is to indicate its concurrence—two thirds of those present must vote for them—, but how he is to obtain their advice is not clear. Washington at first believed that he should get the advice of the Senate on treaties by oral discussion, probably in meetings with the Senate. At any rate, in August, 1789, Washington went to the Senate chamber to get advice on a treaty. Matters did not go his way; a motion was made to submit the matter to a vote. Washington was furious, and when he left he was overheard saying he would not return. Thereafter, he kept the Senate informed of diplomatic missions and negotiations underway, but did not engage in oral exchanges with the Senate. Since that abortive beginning, Presidents have contented themselves generally with written exchanges and informal means of getting advice rather than appearing before the Senate. Washington often obtained information by way of advice, or recommendations, from Senators as well as Representatives regarding appointments, but he never appeared before either house to obtain such information or advice.

In a related matter, Washington set another kind of precedent. Treaties sometimes involve the paying out of funds. The House is authorized to initiate all revenue measures. With this in mind, the House requested the papers having to do with the negotiation of a treaty they were expected to help finance. Washington refused to provide the papers on the grounds that he was not required to provide them and that the validity of a treaty did not depend upon the House of Representatives. The House replied that it could so refuse appropriations for a treaty in accord with its constitutional powers. However, the House then proceeded to pass the requested appropriation, making the question moot until such time as it might be raised again. Actually, Washington had not challenged the constitutional power of Congress in making appropriations. He had simply denied them the record of negotiations and reasserted the terms of a legal treaty. The House does indeed have a check on all matters requiring appropriations.

Washington set one precedent which without constitutional backing lasted over 140 years. During the time when the Constitution was being considered there was considerable concern that a President once elected, might serve for life, by the astute, or corrupt, use of his powers. Washington served two terms and voluntarily, even gladly, retired. Those who followed him and served two terms, did likewise, until Franklin D. Roosevelt decided to run for a third term in 1940. Several years later, what had been a precedent set by George Washington and become a tradition, was made a part of the written Constitution by amendment.

Several of the provisions of the Constitution did not work as expected. The most striking example of this was the electoral college, but discussion of this may be deferred until later on. It seems likely, too, that the office of Vice President has not worked fully as expected. The Vice President was assigned two constitutional roles. One is to succeed the President of the United States upon his death or disability (during the period of his disability). The other is to preside over (be President of) the Senate. That is to say, so long as he remains Vice President, he is constitutionally a part of the Senate, i. e., the upper house of the legislative branch. Constitutionally, then, the Vice President belongs to the legislative, not the executive branch. True, he is authorized to vote only in case there is a tie in a Senate vote, but he is nonetheless the constitutional head of the Senate.

From the very beginning, it seems, Vice Presidents have been overwhelmed by the potentiality of their executive role and underwhelmed by their assigned legislative role. John Adams, the first Vice President, wrote in early 1791: "I find the office I hold . . . so wholly insignificant . . . that I wish myself again at the bar, old as I am." And two years later he wrote to his wife, "my country has in its wisdom contrived for me the most insignificant office that ever the invention of man contrived or his imagination conceived."[343] Nor have later holders of the office had much higher opinions. The basic problem, in this writer's opinion, is that those who have occupied the office either have not tried or could not take advantage of the potential of being head of the Senate. After all, the presiding officer has the power of recognizing whom he will on the Senate floor, thus of delaying or advancing legislation, of determining which side prevails in voice votes, of appointing committees, and of shepherding legislation through the Senate. Undoubtedly, it pleased a succession of Senates over many years to reduce their Presidents (of the Senate) to figureheads, as it has pleased 20th century

Presidents to cuckold, in effect, the Vice Presidents who served with them. In fact, Vice Presidents rarely preside over the Senate; they behave as if they were no more a part of that body than the Queen of England is a part of the government of England. A constitutional power not exercised has withered away.

a. Putting the Government into Operation

The basic business of the new government depended upon the actions of Congress. Without revenue the government would remain at a standstill. The Congress must give the President arms, too, by authorizing departments. The Constitution refers to departments, and department heads, but does not name the departments. In like manner, the Congress would have to provide for the organization of courts.

To provide revenue, Congress, in its first legislative act, passed a Tariff Act on July 4, 1789. This act levied a tax on imports, with the average duty of 8 per cent. Since it was low, as such measures go, it was a tariff for revenue rather than being especially protective. On July 20, Congress passed a Tonnage Act, levying a tax on goods unloaded in American ports: 50 cents a ton on foreign ships, and six cents a ton on domestic ships. Again, the tax was a light one, but it clearly discriminated in favor of American shipping. That the first revenue acts were tariff and foreign trade related turned out to be indicative of things to come, for during much of the 19th century the main sources of revenue for the government was the tariff and the sale of public lands.

Having made provision for revenue, the Congress turned to other matters having to do with getting the government into operation. It provided for three departments, State, War, and Treasury, in that order. Also, Congress authorized a Postmaster General and an Attorney General during that first year, but they did not immediately get departments to head. A Federal Judiciary Act was passed on September 24, 1789, which provided for a Supreme Court with a Chief Justice and five associates. Three circuit courts were authorized, each of which was to have the attention of two Supreme Court justices. Thirteen district courts were also authorized. This latter move was especially important, for Congress made it clear early on that the country would have two different sets of trial courts. There was never any question that the Constitution authorized Congress to create lower courts, but the power was discretionary, not mandatory. Thus, Congress could have left the trial of cases involving Federal law to state courts, but it did not do so. James Madison played a leading role in pressing much of this legislation through the House, as well as in devising and promoting the first ten amendments to the Constitution. As one historian has said: ''In the formulation of the fiscal policies of the new government, James Madison asserted over the

Congress the same high order of leadership that he had exercised over the Constitutional Convention.''[344]

It was now Washington's turn to take the necessary actions to get the government functioning. Men had to be appointed to high offices with the consent of the Senate. Other men had to be appointed to do the more mundane jobs. Washington was finally able to persuade Thomas Jefferson to serve as the first Secretary of State. He persuaded his old comrade at arms, Henry Knox, to become Secretary of War, which for him mainly involved continuing the post he occupied under the Confederation. Hamilton was the first Secretary of the Treasury, a position which quickly became the dominant one in the government, though it is by no means clear whether this was because of the drive and personality of Hamilton or the importance of the office. Edmund Randolph of Virginia was appointed the first Attorney General, and John Jay the first Chief Justice of the Supreme Court.

The Constitution made no provision for a president's council or cabinet. Nor did congressional enactments prescribe that department heads should constitute a cabinet. Rather, they began to be convened as a Cabinet when Washington found it more convenient to have their opinions in concert rather than as individuals on certain matters. In time, of course, the usage was so regularly observed that it became a tradition for department heads to compose a cabinet and be consulted as such from time to time. More precisely, this is a custom which has come to feel as if it were constitutionally prescribed. Even so, it is still the case, as it was in Washington's time, that the Cabinet has only such power and influence as the President accords it. With Washington that was considerable. "He surveyed his Cabinet with justifiable complacency. All were men of ability, and two were men of genius. With such as these, he wrote, 'I feel myself supported by able Co-adjutors, who harmonize well together.' ''[345] This estimate, however, turned out to be too optimistic; the "geniuses" could sometimes behave like *prima donnas,* especially Hamilton, and fundamental differences beset the Cabinet early on.

Early on, it became clear that the department heads were subordinates of the Presidents. They were, in effect, assistants to carry out his policies, not independent of him once they had been appointed, as judges were, for example. Washington explained the role of the department heads this way in a letter to the French minister: "The impossibility that one man should be able to perform all the great business of the State, I take to have been the reason for instituting the great Departments, and appointing officers therein, to assist the supreme Magistrate in discharging the duties of his trust.''[346] Alexander Hamilton had made clear earlier the relationship between the President and his department head, a view which has generally held sway ever since. He wrote:

> . . . The actual conduct of foreign negotiations, the preparatory plans of finance, the application and disbursement of the public mon-

> eys in conformity with the general appropriations of the legislature, the arrangement of the army and navy, the direction of the operations of war—these and other matters of like nature, constitute what seems to be most properly understood by the administration of government. The persons, therefore, to whose immediate management these different matters are committed ought to be considered as the assistants or deputies of the Chief Magistrate, and on this account they ought to derive their offices from his appointment, at least from his nomination, and ought to be subject to his superintendence. . . . [347]

It has generally been held, in support of the President's power, that department heads serve at his pleasure, though the point was controverted during President Andrew Johnson's Administration. Of course, department heads have not been, and hardly could be, minutely superintended in the performance of their numerous duties, but they are expected to support and act in accord with the President's general policies.

As the head of the judiciary—the third branch of the government—the Supreme Court did not have an auspicious beginning. This was so despite the fact that the early court had some distinguished men. John Jay, the first Chief Justice, had a background of government service, had joined with James Madison and Alexander Hamilton in penning the *Federalist Papers,* and was by the 1790s an elder statesman. James Wilson of Pennsylvania had performed yeoman service in both making the Constitution and seeing to its adoption in his home state. Of the other justices on the first court, James Iredell had been attorney general of North Carolina; John Rutledge governor and judge in chancery for South Carolina; William Cushing had been chief justice of the Massachusetts high court; and John Blair was chief justice of the Virginia Court of Appeals.

A part of the problem was that the Supreme Court had very little business to conduct. When it met for its first session on February 1, 1790, no business was brought before it, and it adjourned ten days later for want of anything to do. The same thing happened in its first fall session, and during the first three years hardly anything came before the Supreme Court. That is not to say that the justices were unoccupied. On the contrary, they rode circuits by twos, holding appeal courts joined by the district judge in whatever state they happened to be, to provide a third judge to break ties. Riding circuit hardly contributed to the dignity or the attractiveness of the high position. Several of the early justices, as well as the first two Chief Justices, John Jay and Oliver Ellsworth, retired from the court early to take jobs at the state level rather than serve on the Supreme Court.

Federal courts did set some important precedents and render some important decisions in the 1790s. In several circuit court decisions state laws in violation of national treaties were held invalid. A Rhode Island statute was held to be in violation of the United States Constitution's prohibition against the impairment of contracts. Another circuit court held an act of Congress unconstitutional because it assigned authority to the courts not found in the Constitution. The first weighty decision of the Supreme Court was made in 1793 in *Chisholm vs. Georgia*. It involved a suit brought by two citizens of South Carolina against the state of Georgia for recovery of confiscated property. Georgia refused to appear before the Supreme Court protesting that the exercise of such authority would tend to destroy the sovereignty of the states. The court ruled in favor of Chisholm, but that was not the last word on the matter. In 1794, the 11th Amendment was submitted to the states, and it was finally ratified in 1798. The Amendment provides that "The Judicial power of the United States shall not be construed to extend to any suit in law or equity, commenced or prosecuted against one of the United States by Citizens of another State, or by Citizens or Subjects of any Foreign State." Thus, the Supreme Court had succeeded in having its powers curtailed by the Congress and the states.

The Supreme Court had been heard from in this case and in a very few others, but it had hardly yet emerged as a co-equal with Congress and the President. During the first decade, "the work of the Court was scanty, its judgments few, and the attention of the country was directed to it only at scattered intervals. The turnover of the Justices was heavy, its prestige was limited, and it was only with the reign of Marshall that a weapon was forged powerful enough to influence the political and economic course of the nation in innumerable ways."[348]

b. Setting an Economic Course

Establishing the general government involved more than getting the branches established and operating. It meant also steering a course for the general government within the country, or establishing a direction. Undoubtedly, George Washington as President was the man charged not only with the execution of the laws but also with recommending needful measures to Congress from time to time. Even so, Alexander Hamilton was the man with a plan. From his vantage point as Secretary of the Treasury and a prime adviser to the President, Hamilton took the lead in proposing measures and programs which he hoped, at least, would establish the general government firmly in the affections and interests of the American people. Hamilton had little attachment to state or local government to divert him from his interest in and almost exclusive concern with the national government. He was born in the British West Indies in 1757 and only arrived in the United States in 1772, when he was about fifteen. Thus, he had little American colonial experience and arrived in this country when nationhood was aborning, so to speak. He joined other Americans in their fight for independence and served in the war as a trusted aide to General Washington. His desire for a strong national government had been expressed early in the

1780s, and he was one of the movers for the Constitutional Convention. He produced his greatest writings in *The Federalist*, where he argued effectively for the new government. He was a nationalist, somewhat of a mercantilist at a time when mercantilism was in disfavor, and was sometimes divisive by his vigorous advancement of his ideas.

At any rate, Hamilton conceived a financial program which he hoped would provide the sinews of a nation. His task would have been hopeless enough if he had aimed only to get enough revenue to run the government. Americans were ill disposed toward being taxed, and politicians had shown themselves willing, all too often, to avoid the direct approach of taxation by paper money schemes and the like. He wanted to establish the credit of the United States on a sound basis, when bankruptcy was the obvious outlet. And, he wanted to do so in such a way that he would tie men of wealth and position to the government, influence the people to view the United States government as *the* government, and make it clear that the general government would take care of national concerns. Hamilton presented his program in a series of reports to Congress in 1790–1791. The reports dealt with such matters as the assumption and funding of the debt, the creation of a national bank, the passage of an excise tax on whiskey, and the promotion of manufactures.

The first report, which was on the public credit, was presented to Congress on January 4, 1790. It argued that the domestic debt as well as the foreign debt should be assumed at the full value at which it had been contracted. Many were of the opinion that the domestic debt should be discounted, if it was to be paid at all. After all, many of the obligations were now held by speculators, and, as the argument went, they were men who had bought them at a fraction of their face value and who stood to be greatly enriched if they were paid off at full value. The task at hand, Hamilton held, was not to arrive at some disreputable compromise but to establish the credit of the United States on the highest principles. "By what means," he asked, is the credit of the United States to be established? "The ready answer to which question is," he replied, "by good faith: by a punctual performance of contracts. States, like individuals, who observe their engagements are respected and trusted, while the reverse is the fate of those who pursue an opposite conduct."

> While the observance of that good faith, which is the basis of public credit, is recommended by the strongest inducements of political expediency, it is enforced by considerations of still greater authority. There are arguments for it which rest on the immutable principles of moral obligation. And in proportion as the mind is disposed to contemplate, in the order of Providence, an intimate connection between public virtue and public happiness, will be its repugnancy to a violation of those principles.

This reflection derives additional strength from the nature of the debt of the United States. It was the price of liberty. The faith of America has been repeatedly pledged for it, and with solemnities that give peculiar force to the obligation.[349]

Hamilton's proposal to take on the full national debt was linked in the same bill with an assumption of the state debts contracted during the War for Independence. The argument here was that since these debts had been contracted in support of the war, the general government should undertake to pay them as a national responsibility. There would be considerable inequity involved by such an assumption. Some states had already made some headway in reducing their debts; others had not. Moreover, the debts were hardly proportionate to the population of the states. Hamilton made some adjustments to make the situation more equitable, and gained the support of the Virginia delegation by promising to see that the Federal district prescribed by the Constitution—as the permanent seat of the government—should be located along the Potomac. The bill was then passed.

If Hamilton's proposed mode for funding this considerable debt did not arouse heated controversy at the time, it eventually brought out partisan opposition. The United States issued new securities to replace the old ones, made these securities interest bearing notes, and provided for the setting aside of a fund to retire the debt over the years. Hamilton argued that the debt was thus secured, and that rather than viewing it as something undesirable that it would actually be good for trade and business. The securities could be pledged to gain funds for various enterprises. The Jeffersonians eventually questioned the soundness of such an economic theory.

At the time, however, Hamilton had come forward with a more disturbing proposal. It was for a United States bank to be chartered by the Federal government as a corporation. The government would subscribe 20 percent of the stock, and the remainder would be sold to private investors. This bank was to serve as the depository of Federal funds, and on the basis of these and other funds it was to issue a paper currency which, it was claimed, would become the main currency of the United States. Washington had considerable doubts about the proposal himself and asked the other members of his Cabinet for their views. Both Attorney General Randolph and Secretary of State Jefferson opposed the bank: Randolph because he thought the Constitution did not authorize the making of corporations, Jefferson because of more strenuous constitutional reservations.

In the course of his critique, Thomas Jefferson set forth what amounted to a *strict* construction of the Constitution. He quoted what was at that time on its way to becoming the 10th Amendment to the effect that all powers not delegated to the Federal government were reserved to the states or to the people. Further, he said, "The incorporation of a bank, and powers assumed by this bill, have not, in my opinion, been delegated to the United

States by the Constitution.'' He went on to explore whether it was "necessary and proper" to the carrying out of some power that had been granted. Jefferson observed that the "enumerated powers . . . can all be carried into effect without a bank.'' Jefferson argued that the appropriate definition to attach to necessary was that the power granted would be made of no effect without that particular means of carrying it into effect.[350]

In making his reply to these objections, Hamilton advanced what came to be called a *broad* construction of the Constitution. He argued that the Federal government was sovereign in the exercise of all those powers committed to it, and that it therefore had "a right to employ all the *means* requisite and fairly applicable to the attainment of the ends of such power," if they were not forbidden or immoral. He notes that the government has *implied* powers, even has *resultant* powers, and has the inherent powers belonging to government itself. (On these latter two points Hamilton does appear to have forgotten that the United States has a limited government.) The crux of the broad construction argument, however, is contained in this formulation: "If the *end* be clearly comprehended within any of the specified powers, and if the measure have an obvious relation to that *end,* and is not forbidden by any particular provision of the Constitution, it may safely be deemed to come within the compass of the national authority."[351]

Hamilton's argument swayed President Washington, who had the only vote that counted in the Cabinet, in any case, and he signed into law the charter for the bank to run for 20 years. When the private stock in the bank went on public sale it sold quickly. Neither the bank nor the constitutional issues its chartering had aroused had gone beyond controversy or rejection, however.

Hamilton also proposed new tax measures. He argued that taxes on imports would not suffice for the needs of the government, especially for funding the debt. Nor could they be increased much without discouraging imports, and thus reducing the actual revenues. A tax on manufactures of one sort or another he thought would be necessary. Specifically, a tax on whiskey was passed and put into effect. There was a potential constitutional issue on this one, though not much was made of it at the time. The Constitution says that "No Capitation, or other direct, Tax shall be laid, unless in Proportion to the Census or Enumeration herein before directed to be taken." Whether or not the whiskey tax was a "direct" tax might be debatable. Hamilton said it was an "excise" tax, and it did fall on the manufacturer rather than directly on the people, as a capitation or head tax would.

In any case, the whiskey tax aroused resistance, especially in western Pennsylvania. It almost reached the dimensions of a minor rebellion in 1792 when it was first levied, and did so in 1794. Washington ordered the rebellion suppressed, and government forces brought an end to disorder. Alexander Hamilton accompanied the commander and was pleased to see this demonstration of force by the general government.

Hamilton's most ambitious and extensive program was contained in his Report on Manufactures which he presented in December of 1791. In it, he clothed the argument for government intervention in its most attractive apparel. He held forth a vision of America drawn together in fraternal economic bonds through the interdependence of manufacturers, shippers, and farmers. He pointed out the advantages of the division of labor, the desirability of a lessening of dependence on the rest of the world, and the advantages of drawing immigrants to America, especially those bringing capital for investment. What would bring all this about, he argued, was government aid and assistance to manufacturing. "Such aid must consist of protective duties against competitive foreign manufactures, bounties for the establishment of new industries, premiums for excellence and quality of manufactured articles, exemptions of essential raw materials from import duties . . . , the encouragement of inventions, improvement in machinery and processes by substantial grants . . . , and finally, the construction of roads and canals for a . . . flow of physical goods and materials."[352]

This was a call for a full fledged mercantilist program for young America. Undoubtedly, British mercantilism imposed on America had left a bad taste for it in the mouths of many Americans. Moreover, American thinking was shifting away from government interference in the economy toward free trade and free enterprise. As if that were not enough, where was the authority in the Constitution to spend tax moneys taken from the generality of people for such purposes? Hamilton argued that the power was there in the general welfare clause. If this were so, Madison declared, then "everything from the highest object of state legislation, down to the most minute object of policy, would be thrown under the power of Congress."[353] Therefore, Congress did not see fit to pass legislation putting Hamilton's Report on Manufactures into effect.

Even so, Hamilton had done much to establish the new government on a strong foundation. He had taken major steps toward establishing the credit of the United States by assuming the full burden of the debt, foreign and domestic, by getting Congress to set aside funds to take care of it, stabilized the price of government securities very nearly at face value, and demonstrated the resolve and determination of the general government.

c. Foreign Affairs

The establishment of the government under the Constitution was very much dependent upon establishing the United States as a nation among nations. Above all, Americans were concerned with establishing independence from the rest of the world, especially Europe. American colonial dependence upon Britain had been established by law, policy, and the relations of colony to mother country. America was still very dependent upon continental Europe in breaking the connection with England. The

Franco-American Alliance formed in 1778 was essential to American victory both on land and at sea in the War for Independence. The fact that during a part of that war Britain was at war with other European countries, or had bad relations with them, not only helped in the course of the war but also made it possible for the United States to get much better terms from Britain in the Treaty of Paris which ended the war in 1783.

Technical independence from England did not, however, effect the full independence of America from Europe. The Confederation was still kept afloat in the 1780s by foreign loans. The Franco-American Alliance was still in effect after the war. It committed the United States to the defense of the French West Indies and to not rendering aid to France's enemies. Both Britain and Spain were still very much powers with interests in North America, and they showed scant respect for the United States in the 1780s. What the leaders of the United States generally wanted under the new government was to be freed of political dependence upon and ties with Europe. They wanted to pursue their own course and interests without being entangled in European quarrels and wars.

That was much easier said than done in the conditions that soon existed. Indeed, it took the United States more than twenty-five years after the new government was put into operation before they achieved anything like the independence of Europe they sought. The French Revolution broke out in the very same year, 1789, that the new government in the United States got under way. Many Americans welcomed this event and many of the political changes of the ensuing years. It looked as if France might be following in the path of America, limiting monarchy, ridding itself of the relics of feudalism, and establishing a popular government which might respect the natural rights of people. Things soon turned sour, however. The king and queen were put to death by the gruesome guillotine, and a general bloodletting swept over France during the next two years. France got involved in war with the major powers of Europe in 1793, and a kind of world war— known in history as the Wars of the French Revolution and Napoleon— followed for the next 22 years, with only occasional intervals of uneasy peace. It was, as noted, a world war, with Britain and France most persistently at war against one another, while other countries shifted in and out of the conflict.

Both Britain and France expected to use the United States as they would in the course of their conflict, often as not treating this country as if it were their pawn in their international affairs. Meanwhile, Washington proclaimed the neutrality of the United States shortly after the war broke out in 1793. He warned Americans not to commit hostile acts toward any of the nations at war. The French government, on the other hand, expected that the United States would behave like an ally. A new French ambassador, Citizen Edmond Genet had arrived in Charleston, South Carolina a few days before Washington's proclamation. He proceeded immediately to commission privateers to prey on British shipping along the coast and to make overtures aimed at organizing expeditions against Spanish and British forces in North America. Washington warned Genet that such acts were violations of American sovereignty, and when Genet persisted, Washington moved to request his recall by the French. Meanwhile, a new French government had taken power; it sent a new minister to replace Genet, who was allowed to remain in this country without portfolio. Relations with France deteriorated after that.

Nor did relations with Britain improve after the new Constitution went into effect. Britain continued to occupy posts in American territory in the upper midwest, and the British were suspected of arousing the Indians against the United States. Moreover, when war broke out with France, the British began to interfere with neutral shipping and even went so far as to seize American ships and impress or imprison their crews. The British, on the other hand, complained that Americans had not fulfilled their obligations in paying pre-Revolutionary debts to British merchants or returning the property of Loyalists seized during the war. To settle at least some of these differences, John Jay was sent to England to negotiate with the British. The result was Jay's Treaty, which was presented to the President in 1794. It was finally approved by the Senate in 1795. It provided for the British withdrawal from posts on American territory in the upper midwest, for opening the East Indian trade to the United States, placed British trade with the United States on a most favored nation basis, and for a joint commission to propose a settlement for pre-Revolutionary debts. Nagging questions remained on such matters as neutral shipping and impressment.

Spain continued in the early 1790s to make trouble over American navigation of the Mississippi or use of the prime port of New Orleans, which was at this time under Spanish control. Spain may have been fomenting trouble for the United States with the Indians as well. Thomas Pinckney, the United States minister to Britain, worked out a treaty with Spain in 1795, known generally as Pinckney's Treaty. The treaty recognized American claims as they had been stated in the Treaty of Paris in 1783, namely, territory west to the Mississippi River and north of the 31st Parallel. Spain also recognized the right of the United States to the free navigation of the Mississippi and granted the privilege of depositing goods in New Orleans for trans-shipment for a period of 3 years.

Relations with France went from bad to worse in the following years. While the story of this and even later matters as well take us beyond Washington's presidency, they are still very much a part of the establishment of the new government. The worst difficulties with France occurred during John Adams' Administration (1797–1801). When Charles Cotesworth Pinckney was sent as minister to France in 1796, the French refused to receive him. The Directory, which now headed their government was angered by Jay's Treaty and began interfering with American shipping at sea.

In 1797, President Adams appointed a commission, consisting of Pinckney, John Marshall, and Elbridge Gerry to treat with the French. The French foreign minister Talleyrand did not himself receive the commission. Instead, he sent three obscure men—denominated X,Y, and Z in the commission report, hence the XYZ Affair—to treat with them. These three proposed that if the United States would make a substantial loan to France and pay a bribe of $240,000 that relations between the two countries could be normalized. John Marshall refused flatly (in early 1798), two of the commissioners returned home, and what had transpired was made public. Congress was furious, and the country teetered on the verge of war for the next two years. Congress created a Department of the Navy in 1798, and the United States carried on an undeclared naval war against the French fleet over the next two years. More cordial relations with France resumed following the Convention of 1800, a new treaty which relieved the United States of its defensive alliance with France.

The attempt to establish the independence of the United States on the North American continent from Europe and in the world continued unabated into the 19th century, through most of its first quarter. While the continued story cannot be told in detail here, enough of it can and should be alluded to as will indicate how it went. Jefferson had hardly come to power in 1801 before difficulties with Tripoli came to a head. The Pasha of Tripoli chopped down the United States flag that flew over the American Consulate there in May, 1801. That was his barbaric way of declaring war. Actually, the United States had encountered trouble from these Barbary "Pirates"— as the rulers of these kingdoms on the North African Mediterranean coast were called, including Morocco, Algiers, Tunis, and Tripoli—ever since they lost British protection by declaring independence. These "pirates" demanded bribes from a country in order for its ships to ply their trade in the Mediterranean. Neither Jefferson nor Congress were of a mind to declare war against Tripoli, nor much of a mind to keep paying bribes. Jefferson did, however, order and maintain a naval blockade of the port at Tripoli from 1801 to 1805. At that point, the Pasha came to terms with the United States, agreeing, after exacting compensation from the United States for damages, not to require tribute from our ships any longer. Tribute to the other countries did not entirely end, however, until after the War of 1812.

The Louisiana territory, and especially New Orleans, arose again as a major potential problem in the first years of the 19th century. Louisiana had long been French territory, and New Orleans a French city. But in 1763, at the end of what Americans called the French and Indian War, the French ceded their claims to the territory to Spain. Then, in 1800, by the secret Treaty of San Ildefonso, Spain ceded the territory back to France. Napoleon Bonaparte had become First Consul, in effect dictator, of France in 1799, and he could envision an empire in America. The actual transfer of the territory to France had not taken place yet, but Americans got wind of the change in 1801. In 1802, Spain closed the port of New Orleans by withdrawing the privilege of depositing goods there. Meanwhile, the United States Minister to France, Robert R. Livingston, was asked to inquire about the extent of the territory ceded, and if they might be willing to sell some of it. He learned that East and West Florida had not been acquired and that France was not interested in disposing of the territory.

The Secretary of State, James Madison, sent James Monroe as a special envoy to join Livingston and to try to acquire New Orleans. By the time Monroe arrived, Napoleon had changed his mind. Of a sudden, it seemed, he wanted to be rid of all his American possessions and sell them to the United States. He was about to go to war against Great Britain again, may have needed money, but definitely wanted to improve relations with the United States and cut them off from any alliance with Britain. The American diplomats were astounded; they had no instructions to buy the whole of Louisiana nor any clear idea of how much territory was involved. But the offer was so generous and the price so little that they proceeded. For a total price of approximately $15 million, the United States not only acquired the most crucial port on the Mississippi, but, as it turned out, the whole of the Louisiana territory, which encompassed all of the present states of Louisiana, Missouri, Arkansas, North and South Dakota, Nebraska, Oklahoma, and most of Kansas, Colorado, Wyoming, Montana, and Minnesota. The size of the United States had doubled with this purchase. France was never a threat to the United States on the North American continent again.

It was another matter entirely on the high seas and along the European coast line in the immediately ensuing years. Neither Great Britain nor France inclined to respect the rights of neutrals after the war broke out in Europe again in 1806. From 1804 to 1806, the British gave difficulties especially about trade between the United States and the French West Indies and the impressment of sailors on American ships. In 1806 and the ensuing years troubles with the French and the British mounted. France prohibited neutral trade with Britain. Britain prohibited neutral trade with continental Europe. Ships violating these decrees were to be subject to seizure and confiscation. Then, Napoleon went the British one better in his Milan Decree by declaring that the ships of any country permitting British searches or observing British prohibitions were to be treated as if they were British property and seized and confiscated. It was becoming increasingly difficult for the United States to defend its vessels at sea. How bad things were on the impressment front was illustrated by the *Chesapeake-Leopard* Affair in 1807. The *Leopard*, a British warship, approached the *Chesapeake*, a United States Navy ship, a few miles outside Norfolk, demanding that four alleged British deserters be turned over to them. When the American commander refused to allow a search of his vessel, the *Leopard* opened fire, killing 3 and wounding 18, then boarded the disabled ship and took four men off. From 1807–1811, Congress and the Presidents made a number of moves, including adopting an embargo, and otherwise interdicting trade in various ways.

None of these devices did much good; so far as it stifled American trade, it brought heated resentment from New England and sparked talk of a confederation there. Finally, in 1812, President Madison proposed and Congress declared war on Great Britain. (France had never interfered with trade or shipping to the extent Britain had, and by 1812, Napoleon's main interest had shifted toward Russia.) In asking for a declaration of war, Madison emphasized that the rights of neutrals and other naval matters were at issue. But there were other issues as well. It is well to note that the United States fought an independent war against Britain, sought no allies and had none, though Britain was still at war most of the time against Napoleon. Both the war and the Treaty of Ghent which ended it were inconclusive. The Treaty only provided for peace between Britain and the United States and the restoration of territorial boundaries to the status they had before the war. The United States had shown the willingness, however, to stand up to Britain and fight in defense of the rights of Americans at sea, and General Andrew Jackson won the last contest of the war decisively at the Battle of New Orleans. More, in the course of the war, Indian resistance east of the Mississippi was broken, ending the possibility of most of the intrigue between foreign powers and the Indians. In addition, the United States laid claim through military occupation to the territory then known as West Florida—the southern strip of land extending across what is now south Alabama and Mississippi.

However, Spain still laid claim to West Florida and retained control over East Florida (what is now the state of Florida). The Seminole Indians in Florida still caused trouble along the border with the United States, and Spain exercised little control over them. The United States sent a military expedition into Florida to remove the sources of trouble: one in 1816, and another in 1818 led by General Jackson. Meanwhile, negotiations got underway which concluded with the Adams-Onis Treaty between the United States and Spain in 1819. Spain gave up any claim to West Florida and ceded East Florida. In return, the United States renounced any claim to Texas and agreed to assume any claims of Spanish citizens against the United States to the total amount of $5 million. Spanish forces were now remote from territory claimed by the United States.

During the same period, the United States was working out agreements with Britain about boundaries between Canada and the United States. In the Rush-Bagot Agreement, they worked out a settlement for the virtual disarmament of the Great Lakes. The Convention of 1818 fixed the northern boundary of the United States at the 49th parallel from the Lake of the Woods (northern Minnesota and southwestern Ontario) to the crest of the Rocky Mountains.

With these developments the United States had fully established their independence of Europe (as much as they ever would) and taken their place among the nations of the world. No European nation any longer posed a serious threat to the United States. The United States had survived thirty years under it and the Constitution was no longer an experiment. This section could have gone down to 1825 and the announcement of the Monroe Doctrine, but that document was an attempt to do for the continents of North and South America (as far as force from Europe or the rest of the world were concerned) what had been accomplished by 1819 for the United States.

d. Washington's Farewell Address

Before taking leave of the theme of this chapter on establishing the government, it is appropriate to return to the man who had so much to do with it, namely, George Washington. It is appropriate, too, to conclude this chapter by looking at some vision of a course for the United States. That was provided by Washington in his Farewell Address. Actually, it was not presented as a speech at all; it was presented to the public in 1796 by being printed in a Philadelphia newspaper. Washington had first asked Madison to draw up such a presentation in 1792 when he was thinking about retiring after one term. It was set aside when he decided to serve one more term. As his second term drew to a close, Washington got out the earlier version, and asked Alexander Hamilton to draw up a similar presentation. Washington then combined the two artfully and made it his own.

The overarching theme of his Farewell Address may well have been order and liberty, though that has to be arrived at by reading between the lines, so to speak. Although the word "liberty" occurs several times in the document, it plays mainly a supportive role in what he has to say. The attachment to liberty is assumed, a given if you will, upon which to hinge his arguments. Washington said as much himself: "Interwoven as is the love of liberty with every ligament of your hearts, no recommendation of mine is necessary to fortify or confirm the attachment." But, he says, from first one angle then another, if you would have liberty you must support those things on which it depends.[354]

For example, in recommending a united support for the general government, he declared: "This Government, the off-spring of your own choice . . . , adopted upon full investigation and mature deliberation, completely free in its principles, in the distribution of its powers, uniting security with energy, and containing within itself a provision for its own amendment, has a just claim to your confidence and support." To clinch the argument, he says that these "are duties enjoined by the fundamental maxims of true liberty." In arguing against the involvement of Americans in foreign intrigues, Washington says that by doing so the United States "will avoid the necessity of those overgrown military establishments which, under any form of government, are inauspicious to liberty. . . ."

The word "liberty" occurs frequently throughout the address, by a fairly careful count, however, the word "order" occurs only once. Even that instance is insignificant, however, for the word is used in a phrase, as "in order to" do something or other. It occurs at one point as part of the word "disorders," which, while more significant, is hardly proof of a theme. Yet a sense of order pervades the whole document. It is there in the cadences of the sentences, in the matching of phrase with phrase, in the balance of one tendency against another, in the thrust toward discovering a common bond by piling up references to particular interests. It is clear, if one reads between the lines, that there is an order for men's lives, an order for nations, an order for relations among nations, an order by which parts belong to a whole, and an order by which balance and harmony can be maintained. Government is not the origin of this order, but it is necessary to the maintenance of it, even as it is ever a potential threat to it. Government is made necessary by the bent in man to disrupt order.

The two main sources of disorder to which Washington alludes are these. First, there are those passions in men which incline them to pursue their own particular and partisan designs at the expense of the well-being of others. Washington called it the spirit of party, but we might understand it better as partisanship for causes. (He had in mind the dangers of this to the stability of government, but it does no violence to his idea to apply it to individuals as well as groups.) "This spirit," he said, "unfortunately, is inseparable from our nature, having its roots in the strongest passions of the human mind." Among the dangers of these partisan passions, he declared, are these: "It serves always to distract the public councils and enfeeble the public administration. It agitates the community with ill-founded jealousies and false alarms; kindles the animosity of one part against another; foments occasionally riot and insurrection. It opens the door to foreign influence and corruption. . . . Thus the policy and will of one country are subjected to the policy and will of another."

The other source of disorder, to which Washington alludes, is "that love of power and proneness to abuse it which predominates in the human heart. . . ." It is this power hunger which makes government dangerous, for it prompts those who govern to overstep the bounds of their authority. "The spirit of encroachment," Washington pointed out, "tends to consolidate the powers of all the departments in one, and thus to create, whatever the form of government, a real despotism."

The body of the Farewell Address is devoted to advice and counsel about how to conduct the government so as to maintain order and preserve liberty, and to warnings about holding in check those partisan tendencies and the bent toward consolidating power which endanger them. The following were his main points: (1) Maintain the union; (2) Keep the principles of the Constitution intact; (3) Preserve national independence; (4) Buttress policy and behavior with religion and morality; (5) Cherish the public credit; and

(6) Follow peaceful policies toward all nations. These general principles are not nearly so revealing, however, as his particular recommendations and the arguments he used to support them.

The main device Washington employed to support his advice to maintain the union was to invoke those things the people had in common: the name American, their struggles for independence, their common beliefs, and their common interest. He surveyed the continent, from a mountaintop as it were, and ticked off how north and south, east and west, were bound together.

"The North," he said, "in an unrestrained intercourse with the South, protected by the equal laws of a common government, finds in the production of the latter great . . . resources of maritime and commercial enterprise and precious materials of manufacturing industry. The South, in the same intercourse . . . sees its agriculture grow and commerce expand. . . . The East, in a like intercourse with the West, already finds . . . a valuable vent for the commodities which it brings from abroad or manufactures at home. The West derives from the East supplies requisite to its growth and comfort." This was an economic order which had its roots in the diversities of the regions. Washington warned against the rise of factions seeking to use political power for partisan ends that might disrupt the union and disturb the existing order.

Washington's concern for preserving the Constitution intact was motivated by the belief that a balance had been incorporated in it, a balance in which the national and state governments checked one another, and the branches held one another in check. "The necessity of reciprocal checks in the exercise of political power," he declared, "by dividing and distributing it . . . has been evinced by experiments ancient and modern. . . ." "Liberty itself," he pointed out, "will find in such a government with powers properly distributed and adjusted, its surest guardian." He warned against two things in particular. One was the "spirit of innovation upon its principles." The other was "change by usurpation" of power. That was not to say that the Constitution was perfect as it stood in 1796. But if something needed correction, it should be "by an amendment in the way which the Constitution designates." No man or body of men should assume the power to do so, "for though this in one instance may be the instrument of good, it is the customary weapon by which free governments are destroyed."

Washington hoped that the United States would follow an independent course in world affairs, that it would lend its weight toward an order in which peace would be the norm, but that it would not become entangled with other nations in the quest for power and dominance. His distrust of government did not end at the water's edge, for he believed that foreign governments would, if they could, use the United States for their own ends. He warned "Against the insidious wiles of foreign influence", for "(I conjure you to believe me, fellow-citizens) the jealousy of a free people ought to be constantly awake, since history and experience prove that foreign influence is one of the most baneful foes of republican government.'' Underlying these fears was the belief that in the nature of things, in the natural order, each nation pursues its own interests. Hence, ''There can be no greater error than to expect or calculate upon real favors from nation to nation.'' He cautioned against constant preference for one nation and opposition to others. ''It is our true policy,'' Washington said, ''to steer clear of permanent alliances with any portion of the foreign world. . . .''

The first President had some other recommendations on foreign policy, but before discussing them, it would be best, as he did, to refer to the role of religion and morality. The belief in a natural order, the hope that the American political system had been shaped in accord with it, was not sufficient, in Washington's opinion, to assure the working or continuation of order among men. Man is a creature of unruly passions, as already noted, and the necessary corrective to these is religion and morality.

''It is substantially true,'' Washington commented, ''that virtue or morality is a necessary spring of popular government.'' And, ''Of all the dispositions and habits which lead to political prosperity, religion and morality are indispensable supports. In vain would that man claim the tribute of patriotism who should labor to subvert these great pillars of human happiness. . . . A volume could not trace all their connections with private and public felicity.'' Moreover, ''let us with caution indulge the supposition that morality can be maintained without religion.''

These remarks preceded both his advice on public credit and on peaceful relations with other nations. On cherishing the public credit, he said: ''One method of preserving it is to use it as sparingly as possible . . . .'' Washington expected that there would be occasions for extraordinary expenses, making war came to mind, when it might be necessary for the government to borrow money. But he warned against the ''accumulation of debt,'' declaring that the way to avoid this was ''not only by shunning occasions of expense, but by vigorous exertions in time of peace to discharge the debts which unavoidable wars have occasioned.'' That way, it should be possible to avoid ''ungenerously throwing upon posterity the burthen which we ourselves ought to bear.'' Washington thought his countrymen might be the more inclined to follow these policies if they would keep in mind ''that toward the payment of debts there must be revenue; that to have revenue there must be taxes; that no taxes can be devised which are not more or less inconvenient and unpleasant. . . .'' Not everyone may find the balanced formulations of eighteenth-century sentences pleasant, but it must be admitted that the logic in the above is impressive.

At any rate, the principles discussed in the above two paragraphs provided the framework for his recommendations for maintaining peaceful relations with other nations. To that end, Washington advised this: ''Observe good faith and justice toward all nations. Cultivate peace and harmony with all. Religion and morality enjoin this conduct. And can it be that good policy does not equally enjoin it.'' Above all, ''The great rule of conduct for us in regard to foreign nations is, in extending our commercial relations to have with them as little political connection as possible.''

Any extended political connections—permanent alliances, for example— could only embroil the United States in the conflicts among other nations. Otherwise, ''Harmony, liberal intercourse with all nations are recommended by policy, humanity, and interest. But even our commercial policy should hold an equal and impartial hand, neither seeking nor granting exclusive favors or preferences; consulting the natural course of things; diffusing and diversifying by gentle means the streams of commerce, but forcing nothing. . . .'' That is surely the natural order for trade, and a plausible hope for peace to those who knew of, when they had not experienced, the devastating mercantile wars resulting from the use of force in national commerce.

George Washington reckoned that he had devoted the better part of forty-five years to the service of his country when he retired. He was an unabashed patriot, proud to be called an American, a sturdy friend of the union, and none knew better than he the struggles out of which the United States had been born. He was a man of his time, as are all mortal men, spoke in the phraseology of times past, yet in his Farewell Address he touched upon and elaborated some timeless truths. Further experience has served only to confirm the validity of many of his recommendations. His thoughts on unity, on the love of power, on the impact of partisan strife, on the importance of focusing on our common interests, on avoiding entanglements with other nations, on religion and morality, on the public credit, and on freedom of trade have worn well when they have been observed, and have brought suffering when they have been neglected.

Chapter 10
The Rise of Political Parties

The Constitution made no provision for political parties nor made any reference to them. Nor did the Founders foresee what the existence of political parties might do to the electoral system they had established. The electoral system for the presidency contained a fatal flaw, once political parties came to dominate. It specifies that each elector will have two votes, i. e., may vote for two men, one of whom at least must be from a different state than the elector (though both may be). These are not differentiated as votes for president and vice-president. On the contrary, the Constitution prescribes that when the votes are counted, the man having the largest number of votes shall be President, if it constitutes a majority of the votes cast, and the person receiving the next highest number shall be "Vice President." It does specify that in case of a tie, the election will revert to the House of Representatives, where each state will have one vote in order to break the ties. But the likelihood of ties would be very large if electors voted by party, as indeed soon happened.

In any case, the Constitution was silent on the matter of political parties. George Washington, as has already been noted, hoped the spirit of party would not rise in the country, though he surely was aware that it was taking place before he left the presidency. Probably, he could not see how the necessary unity of the country could be maintained if the presidency became involved in partisan conflicts. The omission from the Constitution did not signify the belief by the Founders that adversarial relationships would not develop in the government. On the contrary, the potentiality for this was built into the system of checks and balances. It was expected that state governments would contend with the United States government when it exceeded its constitutional power, that Presidents would rein in Congress when it acted unconstitutionally, that courts would be called to task, in the final analysis, by impeachment of individual members, and so on. The system both required cooperation among the branches of government for many sorts of action and allowed for the possibility of adversarial positions to restrain power. But this was an adversarial system modified by the necessity for cooperation and a unifying executive. Political parties might be divisive without restraints, at least in theory. Washington said in 1790, "If

241

we mean to support the Liberty and Independence which it has cost so much blood and treasure to establish, we must drive far away the demon of party spirit and local reproach."[355]

No matter, the ink was hardly dry on the Constitution before the seeds of partisan positions were being sown. The first major division was between Federalists, who favored the ratification of the Constitution, and Anti-Federalists, who opposed its ratification without important changes. And in that opposition, some of the Anti-Federalists raised a question that has been an issue from time to time throughout American history. Namely, they pointed to the danger of a strong centralized government to the independence of the states and the liberties of the people. At the very beginning of the Republic, some Anti-Federalists were declaiming that the general government did not have sufficient restraints upon the exercise of its power.

Even so, the Anti-Federalists, as such, did not survive and become a political party. After the Constitution had been ratified, and certainly after the adoption of the Bill of Rights, opposition to the Constitution withered away. Indeed, so far as any strain of Anti-Federalism remained, it was apt to turn up as an insistence upon strict construction of the Constitution as written.

However, a Federalist Party did emerge in the 1790s which at least claimed descent from those determined to have a strong and unifying central government. Washington never accepted or used the tag of being a Federalist. He required no political party to be unanimously elected as President by the electoral college, both in early 1789 and again in 1792. And, though Jefferson was already beginning to oppose the tendencies of Washington's Administration, he still favored him for reelection in 1792. But Washington came to favor more and more some of those we now identify with the emergence of the Federalist Party. After all, Alexander Hamilton was Washington's protege, and he was the prime leader of the Federalists in the early days. Others who should be identified with the Federalists were John Jay, John Adams, and John Marshall. The Federalists were dominant in the legislative and executive branches from the early 1790s to 1801, and much longer in the judiciary, especially the Supreme Court.

An opposition party—generally known as the Jeffersonian Republican Party—emerged in the 1790s. Its formation was provoked by Hamilton's programs while he was Secretary of the Treasury. James Madison was the initial organizer of the party, working from his seat and leadership in Congress. It might have been the Madisonian party if Madison himself had not deferred to and focused on Jefferson during the period when the party was getting underway. In any case, Jefferson was the first person elected President on the Republican ticket, and he did give much time and energy to building the party behind the scenes. As one historian has said, Jefferson "preferred to work through others than to let his hand appear, to write a letter rather than to make a speech, and to remain openly every man's friend rather than to engage openly in quarrels."[356] He wrote numerous letters spreading the Republican ideas and gaining supporters between 1795 and 1800. Indeed, Jefferson had taken a hand in countering Hamilton before he left the State Department. "After Hamilton had encouraged the journalist John Fenno to found an administration paper, the *Gazette of the United States,* Jefferson hired Madison's Princeton classmate, the poet Philip Freneau, as a clerk in the State Department so that Freneau could afford to publish a rival sheet, the *National Gazette.*"[357] The Virginians joined forces with the New Yorkers, George Clinton, Robert R. Livingston, and Aaron Burr in forging the Republican Party.

There was yet another Virginian who played a largely behind the scenes role in the making of the Jeffersonian Republican Party. It was John Taylor of Caroline, often spoken of as the philosopher of Southern agrarianism and Jeffersonian Republicanism. Taylor weighed in early against Hamilton's funding scheme and against various of his other measures in support of banking and manufactures. Like Jefferson, Taylor believed that the hope of a lasting republic lay with having a large number of relatively small, independent farmers. He despised and feared the growth of large scale manufacturing and large cities. And, he looked askance at schemes for expanding the supply of money with a paper currency. His beliefs in a metallic currency have been described this way. "Gold and silver are fairly stable commodities that allow of no sudden increase or diminution, and in consequence a specie currency does not readily lend itself to speculative juggling. But a paper system has no natural limitations. Expanded and contracted at the will of speculators, it subjects the business of the country to the exploitation of the money brokers."[358] His influence on the Jeffersonians and Jacksonians may well have been considerable.

It should be noted at this point that the rise of political parties in America was voluntary. They were not authorized, provided for, nor prohibited by the Constitution. Nor were they provided for nor generally promoted or discouraged by national or state legislative enactments. The 12th Amendment to the Constitution that was adopted in 1804 did in a sense facilitate the role of political parties in the choice of the President, but it neither mentioned political parties nor directly empowered them in any way. The election of 1800 showed what could happen under the existing constitutional rules when the electors were committed to party candidates. Republicans Thomas Jefferson and Aaron Burr each received 73 electoral votes—the highest numbers of any candidates. Though the intention of most of the electors had been that Jefferson would be President and Burr Vice President, there was no way under the Constitution for them to signify that. In consequence, the election was thrown into the House of Representatives which was still controlled by the Federalists, since its composition had not yet been changed by the most recent election. They had no choice except to elect one or the other of these men to the highest office. Instead, the House deadlocked over the matter, and during the winter of 1800–1801, the House balloted again and again without breaking a tie. Finally, through the intervention of Hamilton, the tie was broken, and Jefferson was elected President.

As soon as a new Congress assembled the 12th Amendment was proposed, though it did not get the approval of two-thirds of both houses of Congress until 1803. It was ratified by the states in 1804, before another presidential election was held. The amendment repeats much of the language of the third paragraph of Section 1 of Article II of the Constitution, but alters it by prescribing that electors "shall name in their ballots the person voted for as President, and on distinct ballots the person voted for as Vice-President," and that these distinctions be maintained in the list prepared by states and transmitted to the President of the Senate. Thus was the operation of political parties in electing Presidents, etc., facilitated by an amendment to the Constitution.

Still, political parties retained both their voluntary character as privately run parties past the 19th century, though governments did come to notice their existence on ballots. It has been very important, however, that political parties, as voluntary and largely private organizations have had no power to use force or intimidation either upon voters or to discipline those who have held office. Thus, American officeholders can ignore the recommendations or policies of party leaders, usually with impunity. Political parties cannot apportion their national or state vote among their favorites. Instead, except in presidential elections (and even that has now changed), the voters may vote for candidates by name, though they may be listed by party. This is a major reason that Americans have been largely free of the multiple parties which have plagued many European countries.

Indeed, the United States has had only a handful of major national political parties, which lasted for more than one election. They were: the Federalist, the Jeffersonian Republican, the Democratic, the Whig, and the Lincoln Republican parties. Rarely have there been more than two parties with a substantial national following, and sometimes only one. The winner take-all practice in most elections tends to reduce the likelihood of multiple parties electing candidates. In national elections, by way of example, representatives are elected by districts within states, with only one representative per district elected. Senators are elected by a state-wide vote, but only one seat is ordinarily scheduled to be filled in any one election. And, there are only two offices to be filled by nationwide elections, one President and one Vice President. State elections are often filled as well on a one-winner-take-all basis as well. In fact, the Republican and Democratic parties are so well established now that hardly anyone living can remember a serious outside challenge to them.

A number of issues divided the Federalist and Republican parties in the 1790s. From the outset, they tended to be divided on the interpretation of the

Constitution. The Federalists inclined toward the broad interpretation advanced by Hamilton, while the Jeffersonian Republicans leaned heavily toward a strict construction. That is another way of saying, too, that the Federalists tended to favor a strong and extensive role for the national government. The Jeffersonians, by contrast, insisted upon a limited role for the general government and were much more concerned with preserving the states in their full vigor. In the 1790s, anyway, the Federalists tended to be more favorably disposed toward British influence and the Republicans of the French. These attitudes were exacerbated by developments within the French Revolution. Most Americans were excited by the French Revolution, viewing it favorably, so long as the French were trying to establish a constitutional monarchy. But when they dispensed with monarchy and the terror spread, Federalists were horrified while some of the Jeffersonians continued to hope for the best. The Federalists sought government policies which promoted manufacturing while the Jeffersonians leaned heavily toward free trade and free enterprise. The Republicans generally opposed government intervention in the economy.

Of course, the charges that the Federalists and Republicans leveled at one another often involved exaggerations and distortions. Hamilton was charged with being a monarchist, and Federalists generally were charged with being elitists and having a preference for the trappings of aristocracy. On the other hand, Federalists charged the Republicans with favoring a "mobocracy," and tried to identify them with the terrorists of the French Revolution by calling them "Jacobins." In truth, more often than not, they differed in degree rather than being polar opposites, in emphasis rather than in absolute terms. In fact, Federalists tended to trust government more than did Republicans and to fear the generality of the people, while the Republicans tended to be more trusting of them. Chancellor Kent, who is well identified with the Federalists, said: "there is a constant tendency in the poor to covet and to share the plunder of the rich; in the debtor to relax or avoid the obligations of interest; in the indolent and profligate to cast the whole burden of society upon the industrious and virtuous; and there is a tendency in ambitious and wicked men to inflame those combustible materials."[359] Hence, Federalists were particularly concerned that the vote should be restricted and that government should be strong. By contrast, Jefferson argued that we must trust the people with the government. "Sometimes," Jefferson declared, "it is said that man cannot be trusted with the government of himself. Can he then be trusted with the government of others? Or have we found angels, in the form of kings, to govern him? Let history answer this question."[360] But, as Jefferson pointed out, the differences of opinion which was the stuff of party conflicts often did not amount to differences of principle at all.

Perhaps the issue which led most directly to the decline of the Federalist Party and the triumph of the Jeffersonians came to a head with the persecution of Republican editors under the Sedition Act. This act is one of four acts which have been known collectively as the Alien and Sedition Acts. The acts were passed by Congress in the late spring and early summer of 1798, in the midst of mounting difficulties with the French and on the threshold of an undeclared naval war against them. The tenor of three of the acts was the fear of and determination to restrict, limit, or remove foreigners from the country. The first measure passed was the Naturalization Act, which prescribed a much longer residency than formerly for becoming a citizen, a reporting of activities in detail by aliens, and prohibited an alien who was a citizen of a country with whom the United States was at war from becoming a citizen. The Alien Act gave large and unusual powers to the President which, if exercised, would have taken from aliens the protection of due process of law. The Act declared that "the President of the United States at any time during the continuance of this act [could] *order* all such aliens as he shall judge dangerous to the peace and safety of the United States . . . to depart out of the United States within such time as shall be expressed in such order. . . ." If anyone so ordered should be found in the United States after the time had expired for him to get out, he could be tried and sentenced for up to three years in prison. The President was authorized to ameliorate *his* action, however, if he was convinced by evidence presented to him or those acting for him that the alien posed no danger to the country.

The third measure, the Alien Enemies Act, would go into effect only in case war were declared against some country. In that case, "all natives, citizens, denizens [inhabitants or residents], or subjects of the hostile nation or government, being males of the age of fourteen years and upwards, who shall be within the United States, and not actually naturalized, shall be liable to be apprehended, restrained, secured and removed, as alien enemies." Power was conferred upon the President to determine how all this was to be put into effect. Of course, this act did not go into effect, and President Adams never saw fit to apply the Alien Act. Some French aliens probably left the country for fear of what might happen to them, and others may have applied for naturalization to avoid arbitrary treatment, but except for the Naturalization, none of the above laws were ever exercised.

That was not the case, however, with the Sedition Act. Section 1 might not have met with much resistance, since it dealt with conspiracies and provocations to prevent laws from being put into effect or carried out. Surely, governments were permitted to deal with such matters. But Section 2 dealt with matters that might reasonably have been expected to have been beyond the powers of Congress under the First Amendment. It said "That if any person shall write, print, utter, or publish, or shall cause or procure to be written, printed, uttered or published, or shall knowingly and willingly assist or aid in writing, printing, uttering or publishing any false, scandalous writings or writings against the government of the United States, or either house of the Congress of the United States, or the President of the United

States, with intent to defame the said government, or either house of the said Congress, or the said President, or to bring them, or either of them, into contempt or disrepute; or to excite against them, or either or any of them, the hatred of the good people of the United States. . . .''[361] The Act goes on to name other offenses that are made illegal, but enough has been quoted to indicate that it could be used to squelch political opposition and infringe a clearly recognizable area of free speech or a free press. For those found guilty of violating any of the provisions of this Act, the maximum penalties were a $2,000 fine and two years in prison. Truth was to be allowed as a defense where libel was involved.

The Sedition bill was vigorously contested in the House of Representatives and was only passed by a margin of 44 to 41. Hamilton, surely the leading Federalist, said this about the Sedition Act, that there was much in it that was "highly exceptionable . . . ," and "I hope sincerely the thing may not be hurried through. Let us not establish a tyranny. Energy [argument?] is a very different thing from violence."[362] John Taylor of Caroline wrote this dark assessment of the Sedition Act: "The design of substituting political for religious heresy, is visible in the visage of sedition laws. A civil priesthood or government, hunting after political heresy, is an humble imitator of the inquisition, which fines, imprisons, tortures and murders, sometimes mind, at others, body. It affects the same piety, feigned by priestcraft at the burning of an heretic. . . ."[363]

Two points need to be made here. The first is that both Federalists and Republicans were supported by partisan newspapers, and both sides were given to making shrill charges, *ad hominem* attacks, many of which were libelous, and to playing fast and loose with the truth when it suited their purposes. In the debate over the Sedition bill, Federalist John Allen of Connecticut presented examples of the sort of things being printed by Republican editors and said of them, "Let gentlemen look at certain papers printed in this city [Philadelphia] and elsewhere and ask themselves whether an unwarrantable and dangerous combination does not exist to overturn and ruin the Government by publishing the most shameless falsehoods against the Representatives of the people of all denominations." To which a Republican representative replied that a Federalist paper "contains more libels and lies than any other in the United States."[364]

The other point is that it was only Republican editors who were prosecuted and sometimes it appears, persecuted, under the Sedition Act. The Secretary of State, Timothy Pickering, ordered the district attorney to charge John Daly Burk, editor of the New York *Time-Piece* with sedition. Aaron Burr managed to get the indictment quashed and Burk got away. But others were not so lucky. Matthew Lyon of Vermont, James Thompson Callender, a writer, and Thomas Cooper were indicted shortly after the Sedition act went into effect. In all, about ten editors, writers, or publishers of the Republican persuasion were tried and convicted. Four to six months in prison was the usual penalty, though some were also fined. Some of the judges acted like prosecutors rather than judges, and used their power on the bench to intimidate lawyers, witnesses and juries. The most notorious of such judges was Supreme Court justice Samuel Chase, who sat on several of the cases and acted like nothing so much as a hangman. In the sedition trial of James Thompson Callender at Richmond, Chase made it almost impossible for defense counsel to defend their man. Chase continually intervened when defense counsel tried to examine jurors before they were seated, and demanded that they present him with the written questions for his approval before they questioned witnesses. When the defense tried to introduce witnesses to prove the truth of what Callender had written and for which he was being tried (truth being a specific defense authorized in the very law) Judge Chase refused to allow the witnesses to be heard, declaring that such efforts were "irregular, and subversive of every principle of law; that it had no relation to the issue; that it was a popular argument, calculated to deceive the people, but very incorrect."[365] When the defense argued that the act authorizing the trial was unconstitutional, Chase ruled that it was so, too, constitutional, and when the jury found Callender guilty sentenced him to nine months in prison and fined him as well.

The misbehavior of Federal judges may be more relevant to the success of Jefferson and his Republican followers in the next presidential election than to the constitutional question. It does help to explain the anger and resentment aroused by the Alien and Sedition acts, however. In any case, the constitutional question was raised as soon as could be done after the passage of the acts. Jefferson drafted a resolution which was introduced to the Kentucky legislature and passed as the Kentucky Resolution in November, 1798. James Madison drew up a similar, though much briefer, document, which was introduced by John Taylor of Caroline and passed by the Virginia legislature as the Virginia Resolution in December, 1798. Both argued that the general government of the United States had exceeded its authority under the Constitution by the passage of the Alien and Sedition Acts and that the states ought to act so as to prevent the acts from being put into effect.

Since the Kentucky Resolution is the more thorough and complete of the arguments, and since the argument may have been crucial to the preservation of the federal system of government, it needs to be examined in some detail. It begins by taking the position that the Union was formed by a compact among the states, that the government established by the Constitution was constitutionally limited, "and that whensoever the general government assumes undelegated powers, its acts are unauthoritative, void, and of no force." On the matter of who may decide that the government has exceeded its authority, Jefferson argued in the Kentucky Resolution that the Federal government could not be the sole and final judge of the extent of its powers, "since that would have made its discretion, and not the Constitution, the measure of its powers; but that as in all other cases of compact among parties having no common Judge, *each party has an equal right to judge for itself.* . . ." The crux of the argument here seems to be that since the powers not granted to the United States are reserved to the states (or to the people), the states have a right to intrude or intervene to preserve their powers (or, perhaps, those of the people).

He goes on to make explicit the position that the powers were reserved to the states in regard to the press, and the like. Specifically, Jefferson wrote "that no power over the freedom of religion, freedom of speech, or freedom of the press being delegated to the United States by the Constitution, nor prohibited by it to the States, are reserved to the States, or to the people." Further, he argued that no power over aliens was granted by the Constitution to the general government nor prohibited by it to the States. Moreover, he quotes the Constitution which declared "that the migration or importation of such persons as any of the States now existing shall think proper to admit, shall not be prohibited by the Congress prior to the year 1808." Jefferson's argument then runs to the point that if a state has admitted aliens, they are under its protection and the general government exceeds its powers by intruding into the situation. As if that were not enough, Jefferson notes there are other provisions of the Constitution which make the powers granted to the President under the Alien Acts unconstitutional. After all, the Constitution does say that "no person shall be deprived of liberty without due process of law," and it also provides that in "all criminal prosecutions, the accused shall enjoy the right to a public trial by an impartial jury . . . , to be confronted with the witnesses against him," etc. and etc. Since the Alien Act does not provide these safeguards for those who may be subject to some of its penalties, it "is therefore not law, but utterly void and of no force."

Further, in the Kentucky Resolution, Jefferson attacks the practice of trying to expand the powers of the general government by construing words in the Constitution, words which are explanatory only as granting additional powers. No more does he propose to place great confidence in those who rule that they will not abuse it. "In questions of power," Jefferson said in words that rang down through the years, "let no more be heard of confidence in men, but bind him down from mischief by the chains of the Constitution."

Having said so much, the Resolution ends on a note that is almost surprisingly mild. It requested the Governor of Kentucky to submit copies of the Resolution to the legislatures of the other states in the hope that they "will concur in declaring these acts void and of no force, and each unite with this Commonwealth in requesting their repeal at the next session of Congress."

Without going into nearly so much detail or making extended legal arguments, Madison's Virginia Resolutions arrive at a similar conclusion as the Kentucky Resolutions. They protest against the "infractions of the Constitution in the . . . cases of the 'Alien and Sedition Act,' " which they say tends to subvert the Constitution. That being the case, the Virginia Resolution requests the other states to "concur with this Commonwealth in declaring, as it does hereby declare, that the acts aforesaid are unconstitutional; and the necessary and proper measures be taken by each for co-operating with this state in maintaining unimpaired the authorities, rights and liberties reserved to the states. . . ."[366]

Such state legislatures as elected to reply to one or the other or both the Virginia and Kentucky Resolutions did not concur with them that the Alien and Sedition Acts were unconstitutional. Those from Maryland northward disavowed the views expressed in the Resolutions and generally affirmed the view that the Constitution conferred the power on the Federal judiciary to determine constitutionality of laws passed by the general government. The Rhode Island legislature expressed the view succinctly, saying "That, in the opinion of this legislature, the second section of the third article of the Constitution of the United States, in these words, to wit,—'The judicial power shall extend to all cases arising under the laws of the United States,'—vests in the Federal Courts, exclusively, and in the Supreme Court of the United States, ultimately, the authority of deciding on the constitutionality of any act or law of the Congress of the United States."

Actually, the Constitution does not vest the authority of deciding the constitutionality of laws anywhere, and it certainly does not place it "exclusively" in the Federal judiciary nor "ultimately" in the Supreme Court. The President may veto an act of Congress on the grounds that it is unconstitutional, and though he may be overruled by two-thirds majorities in each of the houses of Congress, his power in this regard shows that constitutionality is not exclusively confided to the judiciary. Ultimately, the power to determine constitutionality lies with those who have the power to amend the Constitution, namely two-thirds of those voting in each of the houses of Congress and three-fourths of the legislatures of the states.

This does not tell us whether the Virginia and Kentucky Resolutions in what they seemed to hint at—that the states could somehow interpose their power between their people and the general government, and rightly do so when there was an attempt to enforce a law reckoned to be unconstitutional—were right or not. No such power is conferred explicitly by the United States Constitution. Nor does the Constitution confirm what Jefferson says, namely, that it is a compact among the states. On the contrary, the Preamble begins with "We the people," and the implication, if any, is that the Constitution derives its authority from them.

Be that as it may, the Kentucky legislature adopted further resolutions in 1799, in reply mainly to those states that had not concurred with their resolution, announcing emphatically: "That the several States who formed that instrument being sovereign and independent, have unquestionable right to judge of the infraction; and, *That a nullification of those sovereignties, of all unauthorized acts done under color of that instrument is the rightful remedy.*''[367] Thus, the word ''nullification'' entered the American language to signify the process by which a state, or some combination of states, might thwart the enforcement of an act believed to be unconstitutional.

Now, such ideas as *nullification* and *interposition* probably were not practical approaches toward limiting the government. Certainly, the Constitution does not provide any mechanism by which this might be done, nor authorize it as a possible course of action. That does not mean that Jefferson and Madison were not on to something in the Virginia and Kentucky Resolutions. In the first place, Jefferson made an excellent point when he said that the Federal government should not be the judge of the extent of its powers. Madison did not go into detail in the Virginia Resolution on the point but he talked about how the Alien and Sedition Acts *"by uniting legislative and judicial powers to those of [the] executive subverts the general principles of free governments. . . ."* What he meant more specifically was that the Acts had given legislative and judicial functions to the President. This may raise an even broader point, namely that under a system of political parties, if all three branches are animated by a partisan bias, the checks and balances may be effectively removed and they may connive to subvert the Constitution. Jefferson and Madison seemed to be saying that there needs to be some way whereby the states can counterbalance such a combination.

It does not dispose of the problem—indeed, the problem has grown more critical from the Civil War down to the present, as those in the Federal government have combined time and again to reduce the states to handmaidens of the general government—, but Jefferson and Madison found an immediate resolution of the problem. They founded the Republican Party and gained control of the legislative and executive branches in 1801. In power, Jefferson stopped all prosecutions under the Sedition Act, allowed the Alien and Sedition Acts to expire, or, if there was no immediate terminal date, had that one repealed. Further, Jefferson pardoned those who had been convicted under the Sedition Act. Moreover, the Jeffersonians, and their successors, the Jacksonian Democrats, went a long way toward establishing their strict construction view of the Constitution, not for all time, of course, but at least down to the beginning of the Civil War.

Chapter 11
Limited Constitutional Government: The Jeffersonian and Jacksonian Way

The election of Jefferson to the Presidency in 1800 was one of the major turning points in American history. It should rank with the election of Abraham Lincoln in 1860 and Franklin D. Roosevelt in 1932, to compare it with two other turning points in history. It was important, in the first place, because Jefferson was the first of an almost unbroken line of Republican and its successor Democratic Party Presidents from 1801 to 1861. Only two men were elected to the office during that period who were not of that lineage: William Henry Harrison in 1840 and Zachary Taylor in 1848. They were both Whigs, died before they finished their terms, were succeeded by John Tyler and Millard Fillmore, respectively, who were technically Whigs, but were not reelected to the office. Congress was usually dominated by the "Republico-Democrats" during this 60 year period, as, to a much lesser extent, was the judiciary.

What makes this so important is that the Jeffersonians and Jacksonians generally advocated and believed in limited constitutional government. Their vision for America was generally commensurate with the Constitution as it was written and could be strictly construed. If they found something that wanted doing but was not authorized in the Constitution, they would most likely suggest a constitutional amendment. For example, Thomas Jefferson thought it would be good to have a nationally financed university, but when he mentioned it in a report on the State of the Union, he noted that he supposed an amendment to the Constitution would be necessary before providing for one by law. Nothing ever came of his proposal. Indeed, only one amendment was added to the Constitution between 1801 and 1861, and that was the 12th, added in 1804. To put the matter another way, the Jeffersonians had no huge plan or program for the country which required the stretching of the Constitution beyond its bounds and expanding its powers by broad and extensive construction. Their vision was of limited government and free men, men freed to fulfill their visions and dreams.

That is not to say that the Democratic-Republicans, as historians have tended to call them, always lived up to those principles and guidelines, did not sometimes try to go beyond what the Constitution prescribed, or were not themselves partisan politicians on many occasions. That was not at all the case. It is rather that they avowed limited government, strict construction of the Constitution, defended the federal system of government in which the states retained their independence and a large measure of sovereignty, and opposed extensive government involvement in the lives of the people.

Undoubtedly, there was a measure of hypocrisy in the lack of universality in the championing of freedom by some of the Jeffersonians and Jacksonians. After all, several of the Presidents, including Jefferson and Jackson, were slaveholders, as were many members of Congress, and the Democratic-Republicans never became an anti-slavery party between 1801–1861. They did pass a law prohibiting the importation of slaves as soon as the Constitution permitted it, but otherwise they generally left matters as they were. They were inconsistent in their attitudes toward chattel slavery, but it would hardly have improved matters to have changed their principles from limited government and free men. If they were wrong, it was their practice that was wrong, not their principles.

a. The Jeffersonians

Thomas Jefferson was not such a man as we would ordinarily expect to be a political leader. Physically, he might have been tall enough, for he was well above the average in height. But he was not a warrior, as Washington had been and Jackson would yet be. Although he was trained in the law, he cared not at all for the harangues and violent exchanges of attorneys in the courtroom. No more did he care for the rough and tumble of political debates, either in legislatures or on the stump. Of course, men did not run for the presidency in his day as they came to do after Jackson's example, and it is most unlikely he would have entered the race if they had. He generally avoided occasions of public speaking, abandoned the early practice of delivering the "State of the Union Address" before Congress, and sent a written message instead. He did like intellectual exchanges, preferably written ones, for he much preferred the quest for truth to the contest of wills for dominance, which most often occurs if three or more people are assembled anywhere.

All that is a way of saying that Jefferson did not enjoy political controversy much. He was not long a member of Washington's cabinet before he was thinking of some way to retire. He wrote James Madison that he had devoted more than 20 years to the public service and that he thought he ought to be able to leave it with a clear conscience, having paid his debt to society, so to speak. He wrote the President in 1792 that he looked forward to retirement "with the longing of a wave-worn mariner, who has at length the land in view and shall count the days and hours which still lie between me and it.''[368]

Yet his retirement from Washington's cabinet did not end Jefferson's political career. Instead, he came storming back in the late 1790s, as we might say, became the leader of a party, and served eight years as a President. However unlikely it may appear, he was a leader of men. He stood out and above most men by his intellect, his ability to discern the genius of the American experience, his devotion to liberty, and his articulation of high principles.

Not only could he articulate them, but he could summarize and state them succinctly and with unusual felicity. Nowhere was this felicity better demonstrated than his First Inaugural Address. Much of its focus was on high principles. Regarding partisan differences, Jefferson said that "every difference of opinion is not a difference of principle." Instead, he said, "We have called by different names brethren of the same principle. We are all Republicans, we are all Federalists." He did not stop with a conciliatory gesture, however, but went on to enumerate the principles. Preparatory to doing that, he pointed out that Americans had much for which to be grateful. After enumerating some of these things, he asked, rhetorically, "what more is necessary to make us a happy and a prosperous people?" His answer: "Still one thing more, fellow citizens—a wise and frugal Government, which shall restrain men from injuring one another, shall leave them otherwise free to regulate their own pursuits of industry and improvement, and shall not take from the mouth of labor the bread it has earned. This is the sum of good government, and this is necessary to close the circle of our felicities."

The following, Jefferson maintained, were the essential principles of our Government:

> Equal and exact justice to all men, of whatever state of persuasion, religious or political; peace, commerce, and honest friendship with all nations, entangling alliances with none; the support of the State governments in all their rights, as the most competent administrations for our domestic concerns and the surest bulwarks against antirepublican tendencies; the preservation of the General Government in its whole constitutional vigor, as the sheet anchor of our peace at home and safety abroad; a jealous care of the right of election by the people—a mild and safe corrective of abuses which are lopped by the sword of revolution where peaceable remedies are unprovided; absolute acquiescence in the decisions of the majority, the vital principle of republics, from which is no appeal but to force . . . , a well-disciplined militia, our best reliance in peace and for the first moments of war, till regulars may relieve them; the supremacy of the civil over the military authority; economy in the public expense, that labor may be lightly

burthened [burdened]; the honest payment of our debts and sacred preservation of the public faith; encouragement of agriculture, and of commerce as its handmaid; the diffusion of information and arraignment of all abuses at the bar of the public reason; freedom of religion, freedom of the press, and freedom of person under the protection of the habeas corpus, and trial by juries impartially selected. These principles form the bright constellation which has gone before us and guided our steps through an age of revolution and reformation. . . .

Jefferson had no equal in the succinct statement of great principles and no superior in keeping to the essentials. His statement on the sum of good government evokes a vision of government limiting itself to the performance of its assigned duty and doing so at the least expense or wasted motion. The longer list has a Jeffersonian spin to it—emphasis on majority rule, encouraging agriculture, subtle opposition to a standing army in the advocacy of the use of the milita in peace time, and the like—but it does encompass many of the features ingrained in the United States government. But principles—however high sounding—are one thing; putting them into practice effectively is sometimes another. The proof of the pudding is in the eating, as the saying goes. To put it another way: how did the Jeffersonians articulate and put their principles into practice? That they did so will become apparent in what follows.

(1) Economy in Government

The Jeffersonians made the first major surge to economy in government in the history of the United States—and the most sustained one.[369] To say this is not to accuse either the Washington or Adams administration, which preceded them, with mismanagement or carelessness toward the economy. It is rather to recognize that the earlier Presidents faced the task of establishing the new government and that much of their business was more immediately pressing than was economy. Moreover, Alexander Hamilton, who occupied so central a role in the early years, tended to subordinate economy in government to his plan for a large role for the general government in the economy. The Jeffersonians, then, inherited a task to their liking, that of setting the government on a rigorous economical course.

They were aided in this undertaking during their first dozen years by an especially talented man from Pennsylvania, Albert Gallatin. He served under Jefferson for two terms and under Madison for one. Gallatin was not only a dedicated economizer, but also one of the most articulate and respected economists in the early years of the Republic.

In his First Annual Message to Congress, Jefferson called for a reduction in taxes. In the same message, he recommended reducing expenditures, but tax reduction was given greater priority. Gallatin had made a strong case for that approach just before the message was sent to Congress. He said that "if this Administration shall not reduce taxes, they never will be permanently reduced. To strike at the root of the evil and avert the danger of increasing taxes, encroaching government . . . , nothing can be more effectual than a repeal of *all* internal taxes, but let them all go, and not one on which sister taxes may be hereafter grafted."[370] In more measured terms, Jefferson declared that "there is reasonable ground of confidence that we may now safely dispense with all the internal taxes, comprehending excise, stamps, auctions, licenses, carriages, and refined sugars. . . ."[371] By the time Jefferson gave his Second Inaugural Address he could proclaim that the internal taxes which had covered "our land with officers" and opened "our doors to their intrusions," thus beginning a "process of . . . vexation which once entered is scarcely to be restrained from reaching successively every article of property and produce" were no more. "What farmer, what mechanic, what laborer," he asked, "ever sees a taxgatherer of the United States?"[372]

It should be clear from the above that Jefferson and Gallatin, in their desire to remove taxes, were concerned with more than the burden which these might be to the taxpayer. They were concerned with the violations of privacy and intrusion into the management of the affairs of citizens involved in some kinds of taxation. They were concerned to inhibit the expansive tendency of government itself, not only the expansion of taxes but also the expansion of government activities. They believed what history tends to prove, that governments will devise means to spend whatever they can take in, and use any established tax on one thing as a basis for taxing whatever may be analogous to it.

In the final analysis, the Jeffersonian thrust to remove taxes was a part of their effort to limit government and free people for the management of their own affairs. This was a goal apparently shared by many members of Congress, not only demonstrated by their willingness to remove taxes but also by their opposition to government regulation of private business. When a committee of the Congress considered legislation to regulate steamboats, it recommended against enactment, declaring that "in a free State, where every one is entitled to cultivate his own vineyard according to the dictates of his own judgment, to require that it should be done in a prescribed form, and with a specific amount of labor, or power, would appear to be an interference with individual discretion, and an encroachment on the rights of the citizen . . . ."[373]

Jefferson coupled his move to reduce taxes with an effort to reduce the expenses of the government. He pointed out in his "First Annual Message" to Congress that there was no need for a vast Federal establishment since "the States themselves have principal care of our persons, our property, and our reputation, constituting the great field of human concerns." That being the case, "we may well doubt whether our organization is not too complicated, too expensive; whether offices and officers have not multiplied unnecessarily and sometimes injuriously to the service they were meant to promote.'' With this in mind he had already begun to reduce the number of personnel, he said. ''The expenses of diplomatic agency have been considerably diminished. The inspectors of internal revenue who were found to obstruct the accountability of the institution have been discontinued. Several agencies created by Executive authority . . . have been suppressed. . . .''[374] In this connection, he recommended that Congress should act to regulate executive authority, so as to restrain Presidents from creating new offices on their own initiative. But since Congress had authorized most of the offices, it alone could reduce them, and Jefferson promised his full cooperation if they wished to review them with that object in view. Clearly, he hoped that it would, for he expressed his fear that otherwise the expense of government would mount as high as the citizens could stand, and ''after leaving to labor the smallest portion of earnings on which it can subsist, Government shall consume the whole residue of what it was instituted to guard.''[375]

To the end that this should not happen, Jefferson proposed that ''it would be prudent'' for Congress ''to multiply barriers'' against spending by doing such things as ''disallowing all applications of money varying from the appropriation in object or transcending it in amount; by reducing the undefined field of contingencies and thereby circumscribing discretionary powers over money, and by bringing back to a single department all accountabilities for money. . . .''[376]

Much of this might have been so much eye wash, and in our day we might cynically expect that it would turn out that way, but there is much evidence that the Jeffersonians took seriously their expressed intentions to keep expenses down. In the Treasury, for example, the number of employees was not only reduced but also held down over the years. In 1801, when Gallatin took over, there were 1,285 employees. In 1826, the total stood at only 1,075. Moreover, one historian has noted that during the Jeffersonian years ''New activities and new objects of expenditure were conspicuously absent.''[377]

How expenses were held down is well illustrated from the attitudes, activities, and reports of Albert Gallatin while he was Secretary of the Treasury. Shortly after Madison took office, Gallatin wrote to Jefferson, ''I cannot, my dear sir, consent to act the part of a mere financier, to become a contriver of taxes, a dealer of loans, a seeker of resources for the purpose of supporting useless baubles, of increasing the number of idle and dissipated members of the community, of fattening contractors, pursers, and agents. . . .''[378]

Not that Jefferson would have suspected him of such a role, for Gallatin had applied himself diligently to economizing for him. He kept a careful watch over the requests for appropriations of all departments. The Navy especially drew his attention, because of what he suspected as lavish requests. In a letter to Jefferson in 1803, Gallatin criticized the Navy's request for $40,000 for contingencies, and reduced it to $10,000. Later that same year, he wrote: "I allow three hundred thousand dollars to the Secretary of the Navy for the equipment of the four additional frigates: he wants four hundred thousand dollars; but that is too much. . . ."[379]

Although it has not been much noticed of late, the United States Constitution is an invaluable ally of those who would economize by keeping the expenses of government down. The Jeffersonians did not often have to appeal to this restraint, at least the Presidents didn't, for Congress was little disposed to adventures in spending either, during this era. There were a few occasions, however, when they had opportunities to show how the Constitution is a barrier.

Most of them had to do with appropriations for internal improvements, specifically, improved roads. It is not clear that the Jeffersonians opposed spending Federal money for internal improvements. Earlier in his career, Jefferson had questioned the advisability of it, but as President he was apparently brought around to Gallatin's view that the government should promote them. Jefferson came to the constitutional question in this way. By 1806, his programs to achieve economy had borne such fruit that he foresaw a continuing and mounting surplus in the Treasury. Rather than remove other taxes (mainly tariffs), he suggested to Congress that the surplus might be well spent for the "great purposes of the public education, roads, rivers, canals, and . . . other objects of public improvement. . . ." However, before these things could be done, he said, "I suppose an amendment to the Constitution, by consent of the States, necessary, because the objects now recommended are not among those enumerated in the Constitution, and to which it permits the public moneys to be applied."[380] No such amendment was forthcoming, and nothing further was done during Jefferson's term in office.

James Madison, however, faced the question of appropriations for internal improvements head on. Just before he left office at the end of his second term he vetoed a bill which would have pledged funds for a general program of road, canal, and navigation improvements. His veto has special significance, for he had played a leading role in drawing up the Constitution and the first ten amendments to it. If anyone understood the intent of the Constitution he should have. Regarding the bill, he said, "I am constrained by the insuperable difficulty I feel in reconciling the bill with the Constitution of the United States to return it with that objection to the House of Representatives, in which it originated."

He explained his reason for the veto this way: "The legislative powers vested in Congress are specified and enumerated in the eighth section of the first article of the Constitution, and it does not appear that the power proposed to be exercised by the bill is among the enumerated powers, or that it falls by any just interpretation within the power to make laws necessary and proper for carrying into execution those or other powers vested by the Constitution in the Government of the United States."[381]

James Monroe drove the point home in his veto of a bill which would have authorized the collection of tolls on the Cumberland Road to keep the road in repair. Since some money from the sale of lands in Ohio had much earlier been applied to the building of the road, it was at least plausible that Congress might now provide for its preservation and repair. Plausible or not, Monroe argued that the exercise of such a power was unconstitutional. He reached that position by inviting Congress to look at the matter whole. "A power to establish turnpikes with gates and tolls," he wrote, "and to enforce the collection of tolls by penalties, implies a power to adopt and execute a complete system of internal improvement." But he denied that Congress had any such far-reaching authority. "If the power exist, it must be either because it has been specifically granted to the United States or that it is incidental to some power which has been specifically granted. If we examine the specific grants of power we do not find it among them, nor is it incidental to any power which has been specifically granted."[382]

Monroe was not satisfied, however, with simply vetoing the measure. Later, he sent to Congress a lengthy paper in which he explored the question from many angles and buttressed with extensive argumentation his conclusions about the constitutional status of the matter. The crux of his argument is found in these words: "If then, the right to raise and appropriate the public money is not restricted to the expenditures under the other specific grants according to a strict construction of their powers respectively, is there no limitation to it? Have Congress a right to raise and appropriate money to any and to every purpose according to their will and pleasure? They certainly have not. The Government of the United States is a limited Government, instituted for great national purposes, and for those only. . . ."[383]

That is the keystone of the Jeffersonian case for economy in government: "The Government of the United States is a limited Government." Above all, it is limited, if it is limited, in its power to tax and to appropriate monies, for it is with these that it may extend its power and sway. The points at which they chose to draw the line may not impress us favorably today, but there should be no doubt that if the line is to be drawn, it must be drawn somewhere. They held that the Constitution fixed the line.

There were two more principles, however, which rounded out their guidelines for economy in government.

The Jeffersonians recognized that there would be occasions when revenue income would not meet extraordinary expenses. Jefferson approved going into debt to make the Louisiana Purchase. Madison accepted the necessity for borrowing for military expenses during the War of 1812. The Monroe administration had to borrow in the wake of the 1819 depression. A balanced budget, in the sense that the term is used today, was no fetish with them. Governments sometimes have to borrow, just as individuals do, and it is neither shameful nor a thing to be avoided at all costs.

Still, they took care that ordinarily income would equal or exceed expenses, and when it did, they considered that they had acquitted their offices well. Usually Jefferson was able to report a surplus in the Treasury at the end of an accounting period. Because of war, Madison was not able to manage so well. Monroe, on the other hand, was able to make mostly successful reports.

Here is a fairly typical report of the financial situation of the government, made by President Monroe to Congress in late 1817: "In calling your attention to the internal concerns of our country the view which they exhibit is peculiarly gratifying. The payments which have been made into the Treasury show the very productive state of the public revenue. After satisfying the appropriations made by law for the support of the civil Government and of the military and naval establishment . . . , paying the interest of the public debt, and extinguishing more than eighteen millions of the principal, within the present year, it is estimated that a balance of more than $6,000,000 will remain in the Treasury on the 1st day of January applicable to the current serving of the ensuing year."[384] The tone of his report suggests the pride he took in good stewardship.

In the early years of the Republic, in the heat of the debates over the funding of the national debt and assumption of certain of the state debts, there were apparently those who advanced the notion that "public debts are public blessings." Indeed, Alexander Hamilton, who was in the forefront of the fight for funding and assumption, believed that the view had been imputed to him. He denied holding any such belief. However, he did maintain that "the funding of the existing debt of the United States would render it a national blessing."[385] He based this claim on the fact that the value of United States securities would and did rise when it became clear that the government was pledged to pay them off upon maturity. From that, he concluded that the actual capital in the country was increased by the debt.

Albert Gallatin went to considerable pains to refute the notion that the debt in any way augmented the capital of the country.[386] In the first place, he pointed out, the war, which had been the occasion for the debt, had consumed an immense amount of potential capital. In the second place, he argued, funding did not increase the total capital of the country. True, those who held or purchased the bonds might experience an increase of capital when the bonds appreciated in value. But that was counterbalanced by the loss of potential capital by taxpayers who would have to pay the debt. More, it would be overbalanced by what would have to be raised by the payment of interest. Far from being enriched by debt, he declared, "every nation is enfeebled by a public debt. Spain, once the first power of Europe . . . , Holland, notwithstanding her immense commerce, still feel the effects of the debts they began to contract two centuries ago, and their present political weakness stands as a monument of the unavoidable consequences of that fatal system. Yet what are those instances when compared with that of France, where the public debt . . . has at last overwhelmed government itself!''[387]

Gallatin was arguing, of course, that government indebtedness should be retired as expeditiously as possible, and avoided, along with war which was the most common occasion for it, whenever practicable. Thus, the Jeffersonians devoted themselves with a right good will to making regular payments on the debt and usually looked forward to its retirement at the earliest possible date. Although the debt was not finally extinguished until the time when Jackson was President, the Jeffersonians pointed the direction and prepared the way.

These, then, were the rules, principles, and guidelines of the Jeffersonians for economy in government: frugal management of public affairs, reduction of taxes, reduction of expenditures, observance of constitutional barriers to undertakings, balance the budget, and retire the debt. Jefferson did not press to put an end to the national bank immediately. However, when its twenty years were up, under Madison in 1811, its charter was not renewed. The story of the United States Bank was not over, however, for a second such bank was chartered in 1816 to run for 20 years. Its course was not so peaceful, however, as we shall see when we examine the Jacksonians. Meanwhile, the Jeffersonians need to be viewed from yet another angle.

(2) Checks and Balances in Practice

Jefferson probably understood better than most of his contemporaries that checks and balances are not the parts of a government machine which will work automatically. They require imagination, determination and the wills of those in the branches of government to protect their interests and assert their prerogatives. There is very little automatic about them. Checks and balances entail tension, an ongoing tension, and men have a tendency to want to resolve tensions. And, since the tension here involves claims to power, men have a tendency to resolve tension among the branches in favor of their own branch. In the 20th century, there has been a major effort to turn over to the Supreme Court the power and authority to remove the tensions over where power resides so far as constitutional interpretation is concerned. The Supreme Court has tended to become for us the ultimate tension resolver. So far as it succeeds in this task, of course, it removes the checks and balances on government power. A trend like this was already underway when Jefferson took office. He was determined to make clear at every opportunity that the judiciary had no monopoly on the interpretation of the Constitution, and that each branch has a role to play in interpreting the

Constitution and in checking the powers of the other branches. All this he considered essential to limited constitutional government.

On the question of whether or not the courts have the ultimate power of interpreting the Constitution, Jefferson answered this question emphatically in answer to a letter raising the question in 1820. "You seem . . . to consider the judges as the ultimate arbiters of all constitutional questions," he wrote to a correspondent. But that, Jefferson said, is "a very dangerous doctrine indeed and one which would place us under the despotism of an oligarchy. Our judges are as honest as other men and not more so. They have with others the same passions for party, for power, and the privilege of their corps. Their maxim is *boni judicis est ampliare jurisdictionem* [i. e., the good judge expands his jurisdiction], and their power the more dangerous as they are in office for life and not responsible, as the other functionaries [i. e., legislative and executive branches] are, to the elective control. The constitution has erected no such single tribunal, knowing that, to whatever hands confided, with the corruptions of time and party its members would become despots."[388]

Who, then, does decide constitutional questions? Jefferson did not believe that the final authority for this had been placed anywhere in the Federal government, or for that matter, in any government. But so far as determinations were made at that level, each of the branches—and in Congress, each of the houses—decides the constitutionality of matters that come before them or lie within their authority. All the branches are independent of the control of the other branches in managing their affairs. He explained how the system of interpretation works this way: "Questions of property, of character and of crime being ascribed to the judges through a definite course of legal proceeding, laws involving such questions belong of course to them, and they decide on them ultimately and without appeal, they of course decide *for themselves*. The constitutional validity of the law or laws again prescribing executive action and to be administered by that branch ultimately and without appeal, the executive must decide for *themselves* also. . . . So also as to laws governing the proceedings of the legislature, that body must judge *for itself* the constitutionality of the law and equally without appeal or control from its co-ordinate branches. And, in general, that branch which is to act ultimately and without appeal on any law is the rightful expositor of the validity of the law, uncontrolled by the opinions of the other co-ordinate authorities."[389]

On first reading of the above it may appear that Jefferson has evaded the issue or begged the question. It may be given that appearance because he used the qualifying phrase, "without appeal," and that may have a legal ring to it, suggesting an appeal to the judiciary. But that was not his meaning, or not his only meaning. Of course, in a case taken and decided in a lower court there may be an appeal to a higher court. But Jefferson was referring to something much broader than this. Many of the powers of the government are jointly exercised by or intertwined with other branches. In that case, usually there is no appeal from a negative decision of one of the other branches. For example, if the Senate refuses to approve an appointment of the President, there is no appeal, and the decision is final.

In order to understand Jefferson's view it is necessary to view it in the context of the constitutional provision of checks and balances and the separation and partial independence of powers, not in the judicial framework to which we have become accustomed. The powers of government are divided among the branches, Jefferson was maintaining, and with that division goes the power of determining the constitutionality of what they do. To put it in its strongest form, none of the branches may force the others to act on its view of the Constitution. Jefferson said, "If the legislature fails to pass laws for a census . . . ; if the President fails to supply the place of a judge . . . , the judges cannot force [them]. . . ."[390]

How these checks and balances work, how each branch interpreting the Constitution for itself limits and restrains government, may best be illustrated with actual examples. When Jefferson became President, he pardoned those who had been convicted under the Sedition Act. He explained his action in letters to Abigail Adams: "I discharged every person under punishment or prosecution under the Sedition Law because I considered, and now consider, that law to be a nullity. . . . The judges, believing the law constitutional, had a right to pass a sentence of fine and imprisonment, because the power was placed in their hands by the Constitution. But the executive, believing the law to be unconstitutional, was bound to remit the execution of it, because that power has been confided to them by the Constitution. That instrument meant that its co-ordinate branches should be checks on one another."[391]

Chief Justice John Marshall also wisely avoided a confrontation with the President by his opinion in the celebrated case of *Marbury vs. Madison*. William Marbury had been appointed justice of the peace by President Adams, but the appointment was so late that the commission was not delivered. James Madison, the incoming Secretary of State, refused to deliver it under orders from Jefferson. Marbury sued in the Supreme Court for a writ of mandamus that would force Madison to deliver the commission.

Marshall held that Marbury was indeed entitled to a commission and force was appropriate, but, unfortunately, by his reading of the Constitution, he had applied to the wrong court. Thus, petition denied, and no mandamus was issued. It was just as well, too, for the general view has been that Jefferson would not have honored it, and the court would have been powerless to enforce it. By Jefferson's interpretation of the Constitution the court could no more force him to act than he could force it to render a decision in accord with his wishes.

Marshall got his opportunity to try force on the President again in the Burr trial for treason in 1807. He issued a subpoena, on motion of defense, for

Jefferson to appear in court. Jefferson declined, though he did send some papers, and gave the court a lecture on the separation of powers.[392] Marshall took no further action.

But before either of these cases came before the courts, Congress had begun to move to rein in and restrain the courts. In 1802, it repealed the Judiciary Act of 1801, taking away a number of new offices. Shortly after, it passed a new act returning Supreme Court justices to riding circuit and restricting the Supreme Court to one session each year. Then, gently prodded by Jefferson, it zeroed in on the most notorious of the judges.

District judge John Pickering, ill famed for his drunken, if not insane, carrying on in court, was impeached by the House and removed from office by the Senate. Supreme Court justice Samuel Chase was impeached by the House for his intemperate behavior in court, but the Senate failed of the two-thirds majority required for conviction. Jefferson was disappointed and thereafter maintained that impeachment was very nearly an empty threat. That was surely an overly pessimistic assessment, however, for it appears that the behavior of judges improved perceptibly for quite a while after the Pickering and Chase cases.

The broader point is this. As Jefferson held, the House of Representatives, the Senate, and the President, as well as the courts, are empowered to act in ways that depend upon interpreting the Constitution. They take oaths to uphold and defend the Constitution, and if its meaning could only be divined by the courts this would amount to nothing more than oaths to obey the courts. Happily, however, the Constitution is written in English, and the other branches have powers that enable them to act upon their own interpretations and even restrain the courts if they get out of line.

All legislative power is vested in the Congress and executive power in the President. If the courts invade the legislative domain of the Congress by their constructions of the Constitution, Congress has the power to set them straight. The Constitution authorizes Congress to define and limit (or expand) the appellate jurisdiction of the courts.

The President can refuse to enforce court orders he believes in conflict with the Constitution. (The courts have no enforcement machinery, i. e., prosecuting attorneys, police, armies, prisons, or electric chairs, of their own.) As Andrew Jackson is alleged to have said, "John Marshall has made his decision; now let him enforce it."

Judges can be impeached and removed from office, though lawyers rail impotently that they can only be removed for indictable crimes. It happens that when the Senate acts as such a high court, there is no appeal from its decisions. As a last resort, Congress can refuse to appropriate money for the operation of the courts. In short, not only can the other branches interpret the Constitution, but they are also in as good position as the courts to make their interpretations stick.

What I have been describing is a system of checks and balances, a system in which no branch has a monopoly of interpretation, in which any branch with a will can work to restrain the others. It is a system of limited government, limited toward the branch which most strictly construes the Constitution. Jefferson hoped that clashes between the branches over the Constitution could be avoided. To that end, he recommended that each branch refrain from approaching too near to the bounds of its powers. That would tend to limit government even more and give room for the liberty of the people, which he thought was the greater end of government.

Jefferson did not believe, however, that all the branches of government together are the final arbiters of constitutionality. Not even the Federal and state governments, to whom he would certainly provide some place, are the ultimate arbiters. Government is too dangerous, too bent on aggrandizing its own powers, to leave to it or them the final decision. "I know of no safe depository of the ultimate powers of the society but the people themselves," he said.[393] In the final analysis, he thought, that was where the power of interpreting the Constitution resides. The people may turn out members of Congress who displease them on constitutional issues. They can refuse the re-election of a President. If all else fails, or if the branches of government cannot agree, the constitution can be amended by the consensual process prescribed.

There is great danger, Jefferson thought, in a court monopoly of the interpretation of the Constitution. Any monopoly would be fearsome, but that of the courts would be the most dangerous. The members of the court are appointed for life, are difficult to remove, and hold perilous power over the populace. Although Jefferson's nose was undoubtedly finely tuned to sniff the threat of despotism in every tainted breeze, he meant no exaggeration when he said that it would be an oligarchic despotism.

Whether the other Jeffersonian Presidents—strictly speaking, Madison and Monroe—agreed fully with Jefferson's view about the full independence of the branches or not, they certainly agreed with him about the desirability of a strict construction of the Constitution. They also took seriously their duty to determine the constitutionality of all bills that came before them, and did veto some on the grounds that they were unconstitutional.

In connection with the presidential review of legislation, it should be noted that much has been made of the so-called judicial review of legislation to determine its constitutionality and applicability. In fact, "judicial review" is a misnomer. Neither Federal courts generally nor the Supreme Court in particular are authorized to review legislation to this end, nor do they do so. The President does review legislation, since he is ordinarily required to sign it before it becomes a law, and he is empowered to veto such laws as he thinks improper or undesirable and to return them to Congress with the reasons for his veto. Each of the houses of Congress reviews the legislation coming from the other house and would have the authority to reject it on grounds of constitutionality or any other, or no, grounds. Courts do not review legislation. Rather, they deal with such cases as come before them involving criminal and civil law, and do on occasion refuse to apply certain laws, or parts of them, that they reckon to be contrary to the Constitution. It is settled practice that they neither review nor pronounce upon the constitutionality of any law until and unless it comes before them in an actual case.

It is the exercise of this power that is commonly referred to as "judicial review," but the phrase is not very apt. It may also provide subtle support to the view that the courts are uniquely and exclusively situated so as to render decisions on the constitutionality of the laws. The Jeffersonians hardly accepted this view, nor did the Jacksonians who came after them.

b. The Jacksonians

Partisan politics waned drastically after the end of the War of 1812; the Federalists ceased to be a national party of consequence, and no new one emerged to contest presidential elections with the Jeffersonians. James Monroe was reelected without opposition in 1820. The presidential election of 1824 was bitterly contested, but the candidates carried no party labels, and no candidate got a majority of the votes for President. The election was thrown into the House of Representatives, where John Quincy Adams was elected, though Andrew Jackson had received the highest number of electoral votes. Henry Clay threw his influence to Adams, thus bringing about the election of Adams and earning the enduring enmity of Jackson.

New party alignments arose out of the contest between Jackson and Adams for President in 1828. Both Adams and Jackson claimed the Republican label coming down from Jefferson, but Adams was reckoned to be a National Republican and Jackson a Democratic-Republican. Jackson was elected President in 1828 and reelected in 1832. By the latter election Jackson's party was on the way to becoming the Democratic Party—a rebirth and more rigorous reincarnation of the old party of Jefferson, more democratic in tendency than Jefferson's had ever been. Otherwise, it was the party of strict construction of the Constitution, defender of the prerogatives of the states within the federal system of government, opposed to a national bank, favored hard money, and eventually opposed a high protective tariff. The new organization which arose to oppose the Democrats in the 1830s was the Whig Party.

The Whigs were the party of Adams and, above all, Henry Clay, who ran on its platform several times for President, but was never elected. Daniel Webster, the great orator from Massachusetts, was also a leading Whig. The Whigs tended to support policies similar to those that had been advanced by Hamilton and the Federalists. They were nationalists, favored the development of manufacturing, advocated a protective tariff, and supported a national banking establishment. Clay advocated what he was pleased to call the American System, a system by which government promoted manufacturing and agriculture by the tariff and capital through a banking system. Thus, as he viewed matters, an American economic system would be developed, and America would be shielded from too great a dependence upon foreign goods or markets. In the main, then, he proposed to keep the home market for American goods by way of a protective tariff. "The importance of the home market," Clay said in 1832, "is among the established maxims which are universally recognized by all writers and all men. However some may differ as to the relative advantages of the foreign and the home market, none deny to the latter great value and high consideration. It is nearer to us; beyond the control of foreign legislation; and undisturbed by those vicissitudes to which all international intercourse is more or less exposed."[394] In his argument, Clay was opposing free traders, which the Democrats tended to be.

The Whigs were a major national party from the early 1830s to the mid-1850s, but they had great difficulties in forging electoral majorities. They only elected two men to the presidency: William Henry Harrison in 1840 and Zachary Taylor, both generals in the army and neither of whom finished their terms in office. Harrison was the first President to die in office, and John Tyler, his Vice President, was the first to succeed a deceased President, Tyler was a misfortune so far as Whig policies were concerned; he had been a Democrat, left the party because he could not abide Jackson, but was not committed to Whig policies. Nor was Millard Fillmore, who succeeded to the presidency on the death of Zachary Taylor, much more apt as a Whig.

The Jacksonians were the leading spirit within the dominant Democratic Party of these years. Historians who have done books on the Jacksonians usually comprehend them within the years 1828–1848. More broadly, however, they see their influence as beginning with the election of Jackson in 1828 and coming to a close with the end of James K. Polk's term in 1849. But the Jacksonian influence lasted much longer than that. Indeed, the Jeffersonian and Jacksonian influences were strong, perhaps dominant, in the Democratic Party down to 1897 at least, that is, to the end of President Grover Cleveland's second term. Their influence was especially strong regarding the interpretation of the Constitution, the nature of the American system of government, the proper role for government in the lives of the people, and matters such as this. True, the Democratic Party was not the dominant party in the United States between 1861 and 1897, since it elected only one President during these years and generally controlled at most one of the houses of Congress during this time. But the Democratic Party was still a strong national party, and the themes of Jefferson and Jackson still had a national voice. The leading Jacksonians in the political arena were: Jackson himself, of course, Martin Van Buren, Thomas Hart Benton, and Roger

B. Taney, whom Jackson appointed to succeed John Marshall as Chief Justice of the Supreme Court. John C. Calhoun, the tough minded South Carolinian, had been a Jacksonian initially, but broke with Jackson in the early 1830s and became his bitter enemy. The political Jacksonians were both attracted to and informed by an assortment of journalists and budding intellectuals such as William Leggett, William Cullen Bryant, and Walt Whitman, among others.

Andrew Jackson was a complex man with a vast store of accomplishments and experience by the time he became President. In his day, and afterward, some thought of him as a barely literate ignoramus, backwoodsman, violent, temperamental, and erratic in behavior. But there was much more substance to him than that. Of his humble beginnings there could be no doubt. He was born in the backcountry of South Carolina, the exact location unknown, had only a bare minimum of schooling, was orphaned in his teens, fought in the War for Independence before he was quite grown, and came to manhood in North Carolina, where he got such legal training as he had. He got an appointment as a judge in what became Tennessee, helped to draw up the constitution of that aborning state, became the first Representative in Congress from Tennessee, was appointed to the Senate, but soon resigned to make his fortune. He put together a plantation, adopted the style and manners of a gentleman planter, which did not keep him from engaging in duels and less mannered brawls. His national fame was acquired during the War of 1812 and the years immediately following it, as an Indian fighter and a general in the United States Army.

Jackson was a frontiersman, a planter, a judge and lawyer, an accomplished military leader, an individualist by training and inclination, self-reliant, enterprising, a democrat in his belief in popular majority rule, a believer in freedom (and a slaveholder, no doubt), and an advocate of equality of rights.

As President, Jackson was more of a Jeffersonian than Jefferson had been, and a constitutionalist *par excellence*. That he was a strict constructionist he meant to make clear in his First Inaugural Address when he said:

> . . . That this was intended to be a government of limited and specific, and not general, powers must be admitted by all, and it is our duty to preserve for it the character intended by its framers. If experience points out the necessity for an enlargement of these powers, let us apply for it to those for whose benefit it is to be exercised, and not undermine the whole system by a resort to overstrained constructions. . . . The great mass of legislation relating to our internal affairs was intended to be left where the Federal Convention [Constitutional Convention] found it—in the State governments. Nothing is clearer, in my view, than that we are chiefly indebted for the success of the Constitution under which we are now acting to the watchful and aux-

iliary operation of the State authorities. . . . I cannot, therefore, too strongly or too earnestly . . . warn you against all encroachments upon the legitimate sphere of State sovereignty. Sustained by its healthful and invigorating influence the federal system can never fall.[395]

By his vetoes and related acts, Jackson made it clear as well that he would construe the powers of the general government strictly. For example, on May 27, 1830, he vetoed the Maysville Road Bill. By way of explanation, he pointed out that the road began and ended in a single state, that it could not thus be justified on the grounds of its national character, nor that it was for the general welfare of the United States. Beyond that, Jackson made clear his doubts about "the expediency of embarking in a system of internal improvements without a previous amendment of the Constitution explaining and defining the precise powers of the Federal Government over it." He pointed out that in view of various opinions that had been given about the constitutional validity of appropriations for internal improvements both by earlier Presidents and by houses of Congress, there was great uncertainty from time to time and place to place as to how and whether to proceed with them. The rule of momentary sentiment and desirability had tended to replace the high ground of constitutionality. "And this will be the case," Jackson declared, "if *expediency* be made a rule of construction in interpreting the Constitution. Power in no government could desire a better shield for the insidious advances which it is ever ready to make upon the checks that are designed to restrain its action."[396]

Jackson went more deeply into the powers conferred on the general government in his veto of the bill by Congress to charter what would have become the Third United State Bank if it had become law. In this veto he explored many matters, including the power of Presidents. On the point that the Supreme Court had earlier ruled the chartering of such a bank to be constitutional, Jackson had this to say:

If the opinion of the Supreme Court covered the whole ground of this act, it ought not to control the coordinate authorities of this Government. The Congress, the Executive, and the Court must each for itself be guided by its opinion of the Constitution. Each public officer who takes an oath to support the Constitution swears that he will support it as he understands it, and not as it is understood by others. It is as much the duty of the House of Representatives, of the Senate, and of the President to decide upon the constitutionality of any bill or resolution which may be presented to them for passage or approval as it is of the supreme judges when it may be brought before them for judicial decision. The opinion of the judges has no more authority over Congress than the opinion of Congress has over the judges, and on that point the President is independent of both. The authority of the Supreme Court must not, therefore, be permitted to control the Congress or the Executive when acting in their legislative capacities, but to have only such influences as the force of their reasoning may deserve.[397]

What Jackson's statement here may bring up is something that has not been directly discussed as yet in this work. It can be approached from the Higher Law perspective. The United States Constitution is neither common law nor the positive law produced by legislative enactments. Since it exists in a specific body of writing, it is not altered or amended by legislative enactments or court decisions or opinions. Whatever the weight of any of these may be, the Constitution still stands to be interpreted in its original language and context, along with such amendments as have been from time to time added. If it were a product of common law, it could of course be changed by the construction that judges put upon it. If it were a legislative enactment, it could be changed by later legislative enactments. Jackson clearly viewed it as a Higher Law, not alterable by these processes and still available to be approached in its own language by those entitled to pronounce upon it.

However, in this instance, Jackson argued that the Supreme Court had by no means pronounced on all questions of the constitutionality of the bank; many of these remained open. Jackson proceeded to explore a number of these in his lengthy veto message. He noted, for example, that the Constitution gave to Congress the power to grant monopolies in only two cases: those of authors to their writings and of inventors to their discoveries. It had, then, exceeded its authority in granting monopolies to the bank under consideration. Jackson explored other angles as well, but enough has been said to show that Jackson used his authority, in practice, to strictly construe the Constitution. It should be noted, too, that in both these cases his vetoes stuck; Congress did not override them.

In his last message before leaving his high office—a "Farewell Address," though neither as succinct or as well known as that of George Washington—, Jackson affirmed once again his belief in a strict construction of the Constitution. He said, on this point, that

> experience would seem to indicate that there is a tendency on the part of this Government to overstep the boundaries marked out for it by the Constitution. Its legitimate authority is abundantly sufficient for all the purposes for which it was created, and its powers being expressly enumerated, there can be no justification for claiming anything beyond them. Every attempt to exercise power beyond these limits should be promptly and firmly opposed, for one evil example will lead to other measures still more mischievous; and if the principle of constructive powers or supposed advantages or temporary circumstances shall ever be permitted to justify the assumption of a power not given by the

Constitution, the General Government will before long absorb all the powers of legislation, and you will have in effect but one consolidated government. From the extent of our country, its diversified interests, different pursuits, and different habits, it is too obvious for argument that a single consolidated government would be wholly inadequate to watch over and protect its interests; and every friend of our free institutions should be always prepared to maintain unimpaired and in full vigor the rights and sovereignty of the States and to confine the action of the General Government strictly to the sphere of its appropriate duties.[398]

Although Jackson was an unabashed champion of the prerogatives of the states, his belief in limited government embraced them as well. That is, the states are limited by the general government. Nor may a state government nullify and refuse to allow a duly passed law to be enforced within a state. Jackson was faced with just such a prospect when South Carolina adopted a Nullification Ordinance in 1832. It declared the Tariff acts of 1828 and 1832 unconstitutional and set in motion plans to prevent their collection in South Carolina. Jackson denounced the moves, ordered military preparations, and asked Congress for authority to use force. Equally important, perhaps, Jackson asked for a lowering of the tariffs. Congress complied on both counts; South Carolina rescinded its Ordinance, and confrontation was avoided. In his Farewell Address, he declared that the preservation of the Union required "that the laws passed by the constituted authorities should be faithfully executed in every part of the country. . . ."[399]

Limited government was not, however, an end in itself for the Jacksonians. It was a means to the end of containing government and freeing men for the management of their own affairs and the seeking of the fulfillment of their individual purposes. William Leggett, a Jacksonian journalist, had this to say on the subject:

As a general rule, the prosperity of rational men depends upon themselves. Their talents and their virtues shape their fortunes. They are therefore the best judges of their own affairs and should be permitted to seek their own happiness in their own way, untrammeled by the capricious interference of legislative bungling, so long as they do not violate the equal rights of others nor transgress the general laws for the security of person and property.[400]

In the *Democratic Review*, initiated in 1837, the author declared:

The best government is that which governs least. No human depositories can, with safety, be trusted with the power of legislation upon the general interests of society so as to operate directly or indirectly on the industry and property of the community.[401]

The Jacksonians linked these ideas of the role of government and free men with what they were pleased to call Democracy. The capital letter may, or may not, have signified that they were talking about the Democratic Party, for they did not distinguish between the partisan variety and some sort of generic democracy. In any case, what they meant by democracy was not simply government by the people in a political sense. They tended to identify it with individual self-government, i. e., mainly, the management of their own affairs by individuals, families, and voluntary groups. Government, properly speaking, in the Jacksonian or Democratic view, was an extension of this self-government to concerns that went beyond these to whole communities, states, and nation. As for looking after themselves, the poet Walt Whitman who hailed this Democracy said: "*Men* must be 'masters unto themselves,' and not look to presidents and legislative bodies for aid."[402]

Martin Van Buren, who became President in 1837, had worked closely with Jackson, and agreed emphatically with him. Jackson had gone far toward driving the despised paper money—issued at the time by state banks mainly—out of circulation by issuing a Species Circular in 1836. A major monetary deflation—often referred to as a depression—followed in 1837. Appeals were made to the national government to do something to improve the conditions in trade, manufacture, and commerce. President Van Buren denied that the government was authorized to engage in such activities. He put it this way:

> All communities are apt to look to government for too much. Even in our own country, where its powers and duties are so strictly limited we are prone to do so, especially at periods of sudden embarrassment and distress. But this ought not to be. The framers of our excellent Constitution and the people who approved with calm and sagacious deliberation acted at the time on a sounder principle. They wisely judged that the less government interferes with private pursuits the better for the general prosperity. It is not its legitimate object to make men rich or to repair by direct grants of money or legislation in favor of particular pursuits losses not incurred in the public service. This would be substantially to use the property of some for the benefit of others. But its real duty—that duty the performance of which makes a good government the most precious of human blessings—is to enact and enforce a system of general laws commensurate with, but not exceeding, the objects of its establishment, and to leave every citizen and every interest to reap under the benign protection the rewards of virtue, industry, and prudence.

. . . If, therefore, I refrain from suggesting to Congress any specific plan for regulating the exchanges of the country, relieving mercantile embarrassments, or interfering with the ordinary operations of foreign or domestic commerce, it is from a conviction that such measures are not within the constitutional province of the General Government, and that their adoption would not promote the real and permanent welfare of those they might be designed to aid.[403]

Nor did these attitudes end with those Democrats directly associated with Jackson or who are identified by historians as Jacksonians. Franklin Pierce, a Democrat from New Hampshire, was President from 1853 to 1857. He said in his Inaugural Address that the "dangers of a concentration of all power in the general government . . . are too obvious to be disregarded. You have a right, therefore, to expect your agents in every department to regard strictly the limits imposed upon them by the Constitution of the United States." Moreover, "If the Federal Government will confine itself to the exercise of powers clearly granted by the Constitution, it can hardly happen that its action upon any question should endanger the institutions of the States or interfere with their right to manage matters strictly domestic according to the will of the people."[404]

He took his duty to decide on the constitutionality of laws seriously before signing them as well. Indeed, Pierce complained to Congress about their habit of putting in his hand large quantities of legislation adjoined to appropriations at the end of their session. This did not give him time to read the legislation before they adjourned, and denied the government funds with which to operate if he exercised his pocket veto. Pierce found occasion in 1854 to veto a bill passed by Congress, a veto which indicates how much he was attending to the question of constitutionality. Congress passed a bill turning Federal lands over to the states for sale to set up funds to provide for the care of the "indigent insane." He said that if Congress had the power to provide for the indigent insane then it had the "power to provide hospitals and other local establishments for the care and cure of every species of human infirmity, and thus to assume all that duty of either public philanthropy or public necessity to the dependent, the orphan, the sick, or the needy which is now discharged by the States themselves or by corporate institutions or by private endowments. . . ." But he denied that any such power had been granted, for he declared that "I can not find any authority in the Constitution for making the Federal Government the great almoner [dispenser] of public charity throughout the United States. To do so would, in my judgment be contrary to the letter and spirit of the Constitution and subversive of the whole theory upon which the Union of these States is founded."[405] That being the case, he vetoed the bill, of course.

His successor, James Buchanan of Pennsylvania, made it clear in his Inaugural Address that he intended to hew closely to the line in interpreting the Constitution. He said, "I desire to state at the commencement of my Administration that long experience and observation have convinced me that a strict construction of the powers of the Government is the only true, as well as the only safe, theory of the Constitution. Whenever in our past history doubtful powers have been exercised by Congress, these have never failed to produce injurious and unhappy consequences. Neither is it necessary for the public service to strain the language of the Constitution, because all the great and useful powers required for a successful administration of the Government both in peace and in war, have been granted, either in express terms or by the plainest implication."[406]

Buchanan got an opportunity to do some strict construing when Congress sent him a bill in 1859 which provided granting public lands to the several states for the establishment of agricultural and mechanical colleges. He pronounced the bill to be both inexpedient and unconstitutional. His main argument for its unconstitutionality was that "Congress does not possess the power to appropriate money in the Treasury, raised by taxes on the people of the United States, for the purpose of educating the people of the respective States. It will not be pretended that any such power is to be found among the specific powers granted to Congress nor that 'it is necessary and proper for carrying into execution' any one of these powers. Should Congress exercise such a power, this would be to break down the barriers which have been so carefully constructed in the Constitution to separate Federal from State authority." Buchanan then explored the question of whether or not money raised from the sale of public lands fell into a different category from that raised directly by taxation. He thought this was a distinction without a difference so far as the powers conferred on Congress were concerned. If Congress could dispose the land money on whatever objects it chose, then it would have "a vast and irresponsible authority. . . . The natural intendment [construction] would be that as the Constitution confined Congress to well-defined specific powers, the funds placed at their command, whether in land or money, should be appropriated to the performance of the duties corresponding with these powers."[407] Only three years later, Congress with the approval of the President ran roughshod over what President Buchanan had seen as a barrier to the general government entering upon the field of public education. This latter event did not mean that Buchanan had been wrong, of course; it meant mainly that neither he nor the Democrats were any longer in power.

Buchanan remained a strict constructionist to the very end of his term as President, which coincided with the end of the long term dominance of the Democrats. In his last Annual Message sent to Congress in December, 1860, at a time when South Carolina had already seceded from the Union, he explored the provisions of the Constitution on this matter. On the one hand, he pointed out, it was clear enough that the Union was intended to be perpetual and that the Constitution provided no means by which a state might secede from the Union or prevent the enforcement of Federal law. Moreover, it is the duty of the President to see to it that laws passed pursuant to the Constitution are enforced. Congress in times past had also authorized the use of military force to put down an "insurgency" within a state when duly appointed officers could not enforce the law.

On the other hand, Buchanan pointed out, the Constitution does not authorize the general government to use force on a state and its government. He said, "I certainly ha[ve] no right to make aggressive war upon any State, and I am perfectly satisfied that the Constitution has wisely withheld that power even from Congress."[408] He did note, however, that force could be used defensively to defend the property of the United States or to aid officers in performing their duties. In the main, however, Buchanan held that every effort should be made to reach some sort of satisfactory compromise, through constitutional amendments, if necessary.

The evidence is abundant, then, that the Jeffersonians, the Jacksonians, and their philosophical descendants in the Democratic Party not only accepted and taught but also showed how a limited government could be maintained by the checks and balances within the Constitution. The Presidents before the Civil War could and did review legislation before they approved it to make sure that it was authorized by the Constitution. Undoubtedly, the Senate and House of Representatives also from time to time, turned back measures they reckoned not to be in keeping with the Constitution. State legislatures, who chose members of the Senate at that time, could convey their displeasure to the Senate when they believed that the general government had exceeded its powers. But it was the courts above all, and the Supreme Court especially, who did the most to make it clear that the Constitution was a Higher Law.

Chapter 12

The Constitution as Higher Law: The Establishment of the Supreme Court

The operation of the Congress was absolutely essential to establishment of a government of the United States. Thus, work began on establishing an effective role for the Congress during its first session in 1789. Since all legislative power was vested in Congress, and all authority to levy taxes and appropriate funds were in its hands exclusively, its preeminent role was fixed by the Constitution, and it could be said the Congress had been more or less fully established and exercising its various powers before the end of its session in 1790. In sum, Congress was established during the two-year duration of the First Congress.

The Presidency, as has already been noted, was established in its premier role in the government during Washington's two terms in office. George Washington gave the office dignity and presence, and the high caliber of many of those who served as department heads signified the importance of the executive branch. The preminence of these two branches was signalled by the magnificence of the capitol building and the White House planned and constructed in the new seat of government in the District of Columbia— first occupied by the Congress and the President in 1800. Indeed, the Capitol which housed Congress and the White House were so magnificent that one Congressman declared they were "much too extravagant, more so than any palace in Europe."[409]

On the other hand, no such structure had been either planned or constructed for the Supreme Court. In fact, the Supreme Court did not have a building or place to meet when the government moved to the city of Washington. As the time drew near for the Supreme Court to hold its sessions, a request was made to the Senate to allow the court to meet in one of its rooms, and the Senate assigned a rather small chamber which the court used for its sessions over the next eight years.

Nor was the Supreme Court held in especially high esteem. When Chief Justice Oliver Ellsworth resigned in 1800, President Adams appointed John Jay, who had earlier held the position, to be Chief Justice. Although the

Senate approved the appointment, Jay, who had not been asked in advance, refused to serve. His main objection was to the fact that the justices had to ride circuit and this tended to undermine their position in public esteem. He said, in declining the appointment: "I left the Bench perfectly convinced that under a system so defective, it [the Supreme Court] would not obtain the energy, weight and dignity which are essential to its affording due support to the National Government, nor acquire the public confidence and respect which, as the last resort of the justice of the nation, it should possess. Hence, I am induced to doubt both the propriety and the expediency of returning to the Bench, under the present system. . . ."[410]

John Marshall was the outgoing President's second choice, but as it turned out, no better selection could have been made, and as Adams himself later observed, "There is no act of my own on which I reflect with more pleasure."[411] At the time of his appointment, however, it was hardly greeted with general acclaim. Some thought Marshall lazy, indecisive, and too dependent upon popular approval. A fellow lawyer in Virginia may have come much nearer to realizing the potential of Marshall, when he described him as no great orator, for "he is inferior in voice and manner, but for talent, he substitutes genius, and instead of talking *about* his subject, he talks upon it. . . . [H]e is superior to every other orator at the Bar of Virginia, in closeness of argument, in his most surprising talent of facing his case in that point of view suited to the purpose he aims at, throwing a blaze of light upon it, and keeping the attention of his hearers fixed upon the object to which he originally directed it. He speaks like a man of plain common sense, while he delights and informs the acute." Another contemporary said that Marshall had the "irresistible cogency and luminous simplicity in the order of his reasoning."[412]

John Marshall was born in Virginia, was of English descent, served as an officer during the War for Independence, attended law lectures at William and Mary for a month or so, was later admitted to the bar. He spent much of the 1780s and 1790s in the practice of law, mainly in Richmond, where he became one of the most prominent lawyers in the state. His political career began in the Virginia legislature (1782–91 and 1795–97); he was a delegate to the Virginia Convention which ratified the Constitution (he was for it), served most of one term as a Representative from Virginia, a brief period as Secretary of State, and from 1801–1835 as Chief Justice of the Supreme Court. He was described in this way shortly after he took his place on the court: "tall, meager, emaciated, his muscles relaxed, and his joints . . . loosely connected. . . . To continue the portrait: his head and face are small in proportion to this height; his complexion swarthy. . . . His voice is dry and hard; his attitude, in his most effective orations, was often extremely awkward. . . ."[413] His less than striking appearance was more than offset, however, by a gentle disposition, by the ability to capture the attention of his audience by the manner of his presentation, and by relying on persuasion rather than dramatics. During his 34 years as Chief Justice he wrote most of the major decisions handed down by the court, and there was rarely a dissent. He achieved this ascendancy by the superiority of his grasp of the issues and his ability to find a resolution in the law—often in the Constitution itself—that compelled assent.

Two public passions moved him over the years and especially his years on the Supreme Court. One was his commitment to the Union, to the United States—to his country and nation. Just looking at Marshall's political career down to 1799, it would be easy to imagine that he might have been a Virginian first, last, and usually. After all, he had been schooled in Virginia, practiced law in that state, had served for years in the Virginia legislature, and represented that state in Congress. But Virginia was old and long established; it could almost be taken for granted. What was new, had come into being in his lifetime and needed nurture and sustaining was the Union— the *United* States. Marshall tended to think of the country as a whole, and in this he resembled another great Virginian, George Washington, who was also his much admired neighbor. Marshall explained his outlook this way: "I had grown up at a time when the love of the Union and the resistance to Great Britain were the inseparable inmates of the same bosom; when the maxim 'United we stand, divided we fall' was the maxim of every orthodox American. And I had imbibed these sentiments so thoroughly that they constituted a part of my being. I carried them with me into the army, where I found myself associated with brave men from different States, who were risking life and everything valuable in a common cause believed by all to be the most precious, and where I was confirmed in the habit of considering America as my country and Congress as my government."[414]

The other passion of Marshall was constitutionalism. Actually both of these great passions were united in the Constitution, for the Constitution is the bond of the Union. He took his text from the Constitution, so to speak, and expounded it in his decisions. He must have been able to do this much more readily because he was unencumbered by any extensive academic training in the law. Had he studied law in England as many of his contemporaries had, or even deeply in some American university, he might have tried to place the Constitution in the broad and nearly comprehensive framework of the common law, as the British Constitution tends to be. Some of his contemporaries tended to do just that, and in the past century it has become increasingly common to treat opinions of the Supreme Court as if they ranked with the Constitution itself. Marshall apparently saw clearly that the Constitution lies outside of and above the common law. The common law, so far as it is applicable, must fit within the frame of the Constitution, not the Constitution within the frame of the common law. The Constitution is a written document which changes only by amendment; the common law evolves, changes, and grows with decisions of the courts.

At any rate, Marshall cast his opinions in the framework of the Constitution. He made it not subsidiary to some great body of law, but a higher law itself. As a 20th century legal authority has said, ''his opinions show that he adhered closely to the words of the Constitution; indeed no one who has attempted to expound that instrument has confined himself more strictly to an examination of the text. In the proper . . . sense he was the strictest of strict constructionists.''[415] Of course, his decisions and opinions did not please everyone. The Jeffersonians were not prepared to be pleased by them, but when they differed with him, they were on their mettle to find grounds in the Constitution for their differences, for those were the chosen grounds of Marshall. It may be that he was assisted in choosing that course by the very fact that the Jeffersonians were avowed strict constructionists, and they were looking over his shoulder, so to speak.

a. Major Decisions of Marshall Court

Despite his great achievements and his eventual historical standing, John Marshall did not join the Supreme Court in 1801 on a triumphal wave. Instead, he came in as the backwash of a defeated Federalist Party and an outgoing President John Adams trying to retain power in the judiciary after losing the executive and legislative branches. In the last major act during the Adams Administration, the Federalists passed the Judiciary Act of 1801. The act eliminated the riding of circuit by Supreme Court justices, reduced the number of justices to five, created 16 new circuit courts to be filled with newly appointed judges, and a variety of other court offices. Adams proceeded to pack these new courts with Federalists and those favorable to them. But all that was backwash, too, and ultimately ineffective.

Jefferson and the Republicans were not only disinclined to allow the outgoing Federalists to get away with such a blatant power move but also bent on curbing the Federal Courts. Jefferson asked for the repeal of the Judiciary Act of 1801 as soon as he took office. It was done in 1802, and a new Judiciary Act passed the next month. This latter restored the number of Supreme Court justices to six, and gave each of them a circuit to ride. The repeal had removed the offices from under a large number of sitting circuit court judges. This precipitated a considerable constitutional debate in the contest over repeal and a potential confrontation between the courts and the Jefferson Administration. Since judicial appointments were for life during good behavior, could they be removed from office by an act of Congress? Or might the courts not declare the repeal unconstitutional on this ground? To delay the time when such a case might be brought to the Supreme Court, the Supreme Court was reduced to holding but one session per year, and the next one would fall in 1803.

Indeed, some Federalists did hold something akin to the 20th century doctrine regarding the power of the courts, that the Supreme Court was the final arbiter of the Constitution. Resolutions were brought in both the House and Senate in favor of submitting to the Supreme Court the question of whether or not they had done right in undercutting the offices of sitting judges. The measure lost by five to fifteen in the Senate and by thirty-five to fifty-seven in the House. Nor were the times propitious for the Supreme Court to have a confrontation with the executive and legislative branches. Many Republicans had heard talk enough and more about the supremacy of the courts. Caesar Rodney of Delaware, talking about the possibility of the judges who had lost their jobs bringing suit in the Supreme Court, wrote: "The Supreme Court will proceed with caution, I should imagine, if the subject be brought before them, which I suspect will be the case. . . . If . . . the Judges of the Supreme Court . . . do assert unconstitutional powers, I confidently trust there will be wisdom and energy enough in the Legislative and Executive branches to resist their encroachments and to arraign them for the abuse of their authority at the proper tribunal. . . . Judicial supremacy may be made to bow before the strong arm of Legislative authority. We shall discover who is master of the ship. Whether men appointed for life or the immediate representatives of the people agreeably to the Constitution are to give laws to the community. . . . I sincerely hope that they may take *wit in their anger.* . . ."[416]

Whether Chief Justice Marshall took "wit in his anger" or not, he was much too cagy to confront Congress and the President at this juncture. At least, he was hardly of a mind to confront Mr. Jefferson in a way to allow Jefferson the opportunity to ignore or disobey the Supreme Court. As noted earlier, Marshall had an opportunity to do that in *Marbury vs. Madison,* which came up in 1803, and did indeed involve some of those late appointments made by Adams who had never been allowed to take office under Jefferson. In theory at least, Chief Justice Marshall, speaking for the Court, could have issued a writ to Secretary of State James Madison—the person being sued—ordering him to deliver the commission to William Marbury, thus filling the post for which he had been appointed. It was as certain as anything can be that never happened that Madison would have ignored any such writ. Indeed, events had already proceeded so far under the Judiciary Act of 1802 that there was no longer any such position to be filled. Be that as it may, Marshall avoided any potential confrontation by ruling that Marbury had come to the wrong court, since the Constitution did not confer original jurisdiction on the Supreme Court in such cases.

Instead, Marshall used the occasion to declare a portion of the Judiciary Act of 1789—that portion under which Marbury had brought his suit directly to the Supreme Court—to be contrary to the Constitution. In sum, he held a portion of an act of Congress unconstitutional, and he did so on the highest possible grounds—that the Constitution was a Higher Law before which ordinary acts must give way when in conflict with it. Much of his argument is worth repeating here. He says that ours is a limited government.

That being the case, "The powers of the legislature are defined and limited; and that these limits may not be mistaken or forgotten, the constitution is written. . . . It is a proposition too plain to be contested that the constitution controls any legislative act repugnant to it; or, that the legislature may not alter the constitution by an ordinary act."

> Between these alternatives there is no middle ground. The constitution is either a superior paramount law, unchangeable by ordinary means, or it is on a level with ordinary legislative acts, and, like other acts, is alterable when the legislature shall please to alter it. . . .
> Certainly all those who have framed written constitutions contemplate them as forming the fundamental and paramount law of the nation, and consequently the theory of every such government must be that an act of the legislature repugnant to the Constitution is void.

Even so, the question that Marshall now addressed was whether the courts had the authority to refuse to apply the legislative enactment or not, i. e., to declare it contrary to the Constitution and hence of no effect. He reasons toward what appears to be the only acceptable conclusion, namely, that the courts must apply the law in the course of their duty and to do so they must determine which of the laws by which they may be controlled they are to apply. Now, follow his argument:

> So if a law be in opposition to the constitution; if both the law and the constitution apply to a particular case, so that the court must either decide that case conformably to the law, disregarding the constitution, or conformably to the constitution, disregarding the law, the court must decide which of these conflicting rules governs the case. This is of course the essence of judicial duty.
> If, then, the courts are to regard the constitution, and the constitution is superior to any ordinary act of the legislature, the constitution, and not such ordinary act, must govern the case to which they both apply. . . .
> It is also not entirely unworthy of observation, that in declaring what shall be the *supreme* law of the land, the constitution itself is first mentioned, and not the laws of the United States generally but those only which shall be made in *pursuance* of the constitution, have that rank.
> Thus, the particular phraseology of the constitution of the United States confirms and strengthens the principle, supposed to be essential to all written constitutions, that a law repugnant to the constitution is void, and that courts, as well as other departments, are bound by that instrument.[417]

Marshall's argument was superbly logical, devastatingly so, as he moved majestically toward his irresistible conclusion: that the Constitution is superior to ordinary law and that the courts are bound by it, as well as the other branches of the government. Neither Jefferson nor his followers could fault Marshall in his reasoning as quoted above, nor in his conclusions. Some of them did, however, disagree with the earlier argument in the decision to the effect that the courts could compel the executive branch to act. But since the decision required nothing out of the executive branch, their opposition was muted.

John Marshall had planted his judicial flag on the highest possible ground in *Marbury vs. Madison,* on the ground of limited constitutional government. And, he had delineated a role for the courts in defending those limits. Operating from that position, Marshall would, over the next three decades, raise the judiciary to the level of the other two branches of government and by his manner of expounding the Constitution establish the United States government as supreme in its realm.

Marshall's dominance of the Court during more than three decades had several grounds. His powers of reason and exposition of the law were undoubtedly superior to those of his colleagues. Second, he tried so far as he could to strengthen the Court by having it speak with one voice. "As a first step in this direction he decided to speak for the Court and to discontinue the practice, as heretofore, of having the Justices give their opinions *seriatum* [one after another]."[418]

Even so, Marshall did not participate in the other court decision dealing with the Judiciary Act of 1802. The case of *Stuart* vs. *Laird* came before the Supreme Court on appeal from a United States Court in 1803. Since Marshall had already heard the case in circuit, he excused himself from taking it on appeal. The decision was written by Justice William Paterson. One of the main issues presented was whether the new Judiciary Act could constitutionally impose circuit riding on the Supreme Court as had been done earlier. The Court held that since the Court had performed that duty for twelve years already, their actions afforded "an irresistible answer, and has indeed fixed the construction. It is a contemporary interpretation of the most forcible nature. This practical exposition is too strong and obstinate to be shaken or controlled. Of course, the question is at rest, and ought not be disturbed."[419] So far as the Act had changed the set up in the lower courts, they validated that portion of it as well, as Justice Paterson wrote, "Congress have constitutional authority to establish from time to time such inferior tribunals as they may think proper; and to transfer a cause from one tribunal to another."[420] The most remarkable thing about this Supreme Court decision is that the justices—Federalists all—though they despised the Jeffersonian Judiciary Act of 1802, nonetheless voted to sustain it. That was at least external evidence that the Court was acting in accord with the Constitution and was not simply asserting the will of the justices.

Again and again Marshall asserted the authority of the courts and of the United States through the supremacy of the Constitution. In *Fletcher vs. Peck,* he declared a state law inoperative, or void, in the case before him. The case involved two issues, as Marshall explained it: (1) whether or not the Court could inquire into the motives of legislators in considering the validity of a law; (2) and did the contract clause of the Constitution apply to activities by state governments or only to contracts between private parties? *Fletcher vs. Peck* arose over acts of Georgia for the sale of land. In 1795, the Georgia legislature passed an act for the sale of large acreages of land to private land companies. In the wake of charges of bribery and corruption, the legislature rescinded the act and the sales of land under it. Meanwhile, however, some of the land had been bought by innocent third parties before the earliest act had been repealed. Thus, a suit to get the land wound its way through the courts and finally reached the Supreme Court in 1810.

Marshall expressed doubts about the propriety of inquiring into the motives of legislators in passing laws. Among other things, he stated, "It may well be doubted, how far the validity of a law depends upon the motives of its framers, and how far the particular inducements . . . to the formation of a contract by that power, are examinable in a court of justice." In any case, he thought it neither desirable nor necessary to go into the motives of the Georgia legislature. The issue could be resolved on constitutional grounds alone. He presented the issue this way in one of the crucial stages of his examination, by noting that it would be doubtful whether it would be lawful for Georgia to rescind a contract unilaterally if the state had all the powers of government. "But," he wrote, "Georgia cannot be viewed as a single unconnected, sovereign power. . . . She is a part of a large empire; she is a member of the American union; and that union has a constitution, the supremacy of which all acknowledge, and which imposes limits to the legislatures of the several states, which none claim a right to pass. The constitution of the United States declares that no state shall pass any . . . law impairing the obligation of contracts."

Marshall goes on to explore whether the clause refers only to contracts between private individuals or those between a state and individuals. He says that "The words themselves contain no such distinctions" and that if states were exempted from the application it would arise from their character and not from the Constitution. In short, he spoke for a majority of the Court in concluding that the state could not rescind a grant after contracts had been made or executed. And the decision was based on the Constitution. A state could not reclaim property it had sold under the guise of repealing a law.[421]

The opinion in *McCulloch vs. Maryland* may well have included some of Chief Justice John Marshall's more nationalistic pronouncements. He was never backward, of course, in his vindications of the supremacy of the United States in its jurisdiction. But in this decision he adopted Hamilton's "broad construction," if not verbatim, certainly in substance. If that were all he did, Marshall's opinion in this case might not have been so important, but he entered a broad field of interpretation in other directions as well. The case would appear to have been simple enough. In 1818, the Maryland legislature imposed a tax on the notes of all banks not chartered by the state. The [second] Bank of the United States had a branch in Baltimore, and the cashier of the bank, by the name of McCulloch, refused to pay the tax. Maryland sued, and the case was decided by the Supreme Court in 1819.

The main questions were: could the United States constitutionally charter a bank; and was a state tax on such a bank constitutional? The Court ruled, with Marshall writing the opinion, that the United States could charter a corporation. Indeed, he noted, that the matter could "scarcely be considered an open question. . . . The principle now contested was introduced at a very early period of our history, has been recognized by many successive legislatures, and has been acted upon by the judicial department. . . ." But it was being challenged once again, so that Marshall would rehearse arguments, many of which had been made before, once again. Before doing that, however, he tackled the thorny question of whether the Constitution was a creature of the states or of the people. He did so, he said, because "the counsel of the State of Maryland have deemed it of some importance, in the construction of the constitution, to consider that instrument not as emanating from the people, but as the act of sovereign and independent States. The powers of the general government, [in that case] are delegated by the States, who alone are truly sovereign; and must be exercised in subordination to the States, who alone possess supreme dominion."

Marshall must have been aching to take on this question, because he got his teeth into it rather well. His position was that the powers granted to the United States were granted by the people, and not by the state governments. In support of his view he made these points. First, he noted some qualifiers: (1) the delegates to the Constitutional Convention were elected by state legislatures; (2) conventions for ratification were held within states. But the state governments did not grant the powers of the United States government or ratify the Constitution. The people did, or so Marshall argued, and submitted facts in support of it. The Constitution, he said, did come from delegates who had been chosen by the states, "But the instrument, when it came from their hands, was a mere proposal, without obligations or pretensions to it. It was reported to the then existing Congress with a request that it might 'be submitted to a convention of Delegates, chosen in each State, by the people thereof . . . for their assent and ratification.' This mode of proceeding was adopted; and by the Convention, by Congress, and by the State Legislatures, the instrument was submitted to the people. They acted upon it . . . by assembling in Convention [that is, the delegates who had been elected by the people did, not the whole people of a state]. . . . Of consequence, when they act, they act in their States. But the measures they

adopt do not, on that account cease to be the measures of the people themselves, or become the measures of the state governments.''

In the following paragraph, Marshall drew his conclusion emphatically:

> From these Conventions the constitution derives its whole authority.
> The government proceeds directly from the people; is "ordained and
> established" in the name of the people. . . . The assent of the States,
> in their sovereign capacity, is implied in calling a Convention, and thus
> submitting that instrument to the people. But the people were at perfect
> liberty to accept or reject it; and their act was final. . . . The govern-
> ment of the Union, then . . . , is emphatically and truly a government
> of the people. In form and in substance it emanates from them, its
> powers are granted by them, and are to be exercised directly on them,
> and for their benefit.[422]

If reason and eloquence, plus a careful marshalling of the relevant facts,
could have established the point, this should have done it. It did not for very
long or for some considerable number of those interested in the question,
however, for there are still those who would argue that the United States
government derives its authority from the states. In fact, both the state
governments and the United States government derive their authority from
the people they respectively govern and by distinct and independent grants.
Thus, it would appear that the states have powers upon which the United
States may not intrude, and the United States has powers upon which the
states may not rightfully intrude. Neither is in that sense dependent upon the
other.

Marshall was, however, making a subsidiary point with the above argument in *McCulloch vs. Maryland.* He was leading to the point that the
United States government is supreme within its jurisdiction and that a state
may not tax its operations as if were a subsidiary of the state. But to do that
he needed to show that the United States Bank had been chartered pursuant
to powers granted in the Constitution. That was not so easy to do. He
admitted, as everyone must, that no specific power had been granted to the
general government either to charter a corporation or to establish a bank.
Marshall argued here that these were means to ends rather than ends themselves, that the Constitution usually describes ends to be sought or accomplished by government and certainly not all the possible means by which the
ends might be achieved. There was a restriction as to means in the Constitution, however, they must be "necessary and proper." Here the old Jef-
ferson-Hamilton debate recurs. What does "necessary" mean? Does it mean
that without the use of this particular means the thing simply cannot be
done? Marshall denied that interpretation. He said, "To employ the means
necessary to an end, is generally understood as employing any means calculated to produce the end." Marshall went on to declare that a "sound

construction of the constitution must allow to the national legislature that descretion, with respect to the means by which the powers it confers are to be carried into execution, which will enable that body to perform the high duties assigned to it, in the manner most beneficial to the people.'' Finally, he lays down this test:

> . . . Let the end be legitimate, let it be within the scope of the constitution, and all means which are appropriate, which are plainly adapted to that end, which are not prohibited, but consist with the letter and spirit of the constitution, are constitutional. . . .

In sum, Marshall concluded, and the rest of the Court unanimously agreed with him that "the act to incorporate the Bank of the United States is a law made in pursuance of the constitution, and is a part of the supreme law of the land. . . ."[423]

Marshall had gone through all of the above to arrive at the issue, which was whether or not the state of Maryland could levy a tax on a branch of the United States bank. Again, the Constitution does not address this issue with any explicit language. There is, of course, the supremacy clause, to which the Chief Justice repaired as soon he had established to his satisfaction the constitutionality of the bank. Then he reasoned to the conclusion that a state could not tax the lawful instrumentalities of the United States. To do so would give a single state control over the activities of government of the whole United States. Thus, he concluded that "States have no power by taxation or otherwise, to retard, impede, burden, or in any manner control, the operations of the constitutional laws enacted by Congress to carry into execution the powers vested in the general government. That is, we think, the unavoidable consequence of the supremacy which the constitution has declared."[424] The Court unanimously declared Maryland's tax unconstitutional and void.

It should be clear from his handling of this case that Marshall was not reticent about plunging into controversies or making the broadest constitutional construction opened by the cases before him. It should be clear, as well, that Marshall was intent on establishing both the authority of the courts, of the Supreme Court especially, and the full power of the United States under the Constitution. Indeed, he stretched that power beyond what could be clearly traced to it, at times. He might well have conceived his role more modestly and contented himself with observing that whatever the merits of particular positions, the Constitution was silent. It must be granted, however, that he reasoned to his conclusions magnificently. It must be repeated, too, that Marshall always took his text from the Constitution, where some constitutional issue was involved, even if he stretched it somewhat in the application.

Chief Justice Marshall handed down another decision in 1819 which is also of interest—*Dartmouth College vs. Woodward*. In 1816, the state of New Hampshire altered the original charter of Dartmouth College issued in 1769 and imposed a new charter and board of trustees on the college. It could be said, indeed, that the state took over at least partial control of what had been a private college, and did so over the objections of those in authority over the college. The suit took up the questions as to whether the charter constituted a contract and, if so, whether it had impaired a contract in violation of the Constitution. In his opinion, he supported both the private property arrangements of corporations and defended private charities so organized from state takeovers and control. The Court held that "the acts of the legislature of New Hampshire . . . are repugnant to the constitution of the United States; and that judgment ought to have been for the plaintiffs. . . ."[425] It was not a unanimous decision, however. Justices Bushrod Washington and Joseph Story gave separate concurring opinions, and Justice Gabriel Duval dissented.

In *Cohens vs. Virginia,* handed down in 1821, Marshall once again asserted the supremacy of the United States within its jurisdiction, and he did so once again on constitutional grounds. This case was simple enough in its character. Cohens was charged with violating Virginia law by selling lottery tickets in that state, found guilty, and fined. Cohens appealed on a writ of error to the Supreme Court of the United States claiming protection under an act of Congress of 1802 which authorized a lottery. The government of Virginia was greatly exercised when the high court agreed to accept the case. Feeling had been mounting for some time in the state at what appeared to some to be a continual expansion of Federal authority by the courts. Thomas Jefferson was one of the sources of this aroused apprehension. In 1820 he wrote, "The Judiciary of the United States is the subtle corps of sappers and miners constantly working underground to undermine the foundations of our confederated fabric. They are construing our Constitution from a coordination of a general and special government to a general and supreme one alone." And, in a letter written in 1821, Jefferson said, "The great object of my fear is the Federal Judiciary. That body, like gravity, ever acting, with noiseless foot, and unalarming advance, gaining ground step by step . . . , is ingulphing [engulfing] the powers of the states. . . ." Along the same lines and at about the same time, the *Washington Gazette* declared editorially, "We have too often had occasion to regret the undefined power of the Judiciary of the United States and the disposition manifested by the Judges to extend their jurisdiction, not only to clashing and conflicting with the Judiciary of the States, but to legislating over the Legislatures of the various States."[426]

It was from this background that the "lawyers for Virginia denied the constitutional authority of the Court to review the finding of the state court."[427] Indeed, they were allowed only to argue the jurisdictional issue, and were instructed that if they lost on this, they should immediately withdraw from the case. The lawyers actually argued two points: "first, that the Court had no jurisdiction on a writ of error to a State Court in a State Criminal prosecution; second, that Congress had no power to authorize a lottery to sell tickets in a State whose law forbade such sale."[428]

Cohens vs. Virginia was not one of Marshall's more cogent or lucid decisions. The arguments were diffuse and often off the point rather than driving it home. Marshall virtually backed into his conclusion. Even so, the decision was rooted in the letter of the Constitution. Virginia was challenging the most basic function of the Court, namely to accept appeals on matters having to do with the authority of the United States. The firmest basis of his decision on the matter of the jurisdiction of the Supreme Court was taken directly from the Constitution, where it reads that "this constitution, and the laws of the United States which shall be made in pursuance thereof . . . , shall be the supreme law of the land; and the judges in every State shall be bound thereby, anything in the constitution or laws of any State to the contrary notwithstanding." The argument becomes diffuse because Marshall had to examine into various nooks and crannies to find if there were some valid exception on which Virginia's argument could stand. What about the 11th Amendment, for example? Well, as Marshall pointed out, that amendment was irrelevant to the case at hand. It only excludes from Federal jurisdiction suits by one state of the United States against another state of the Union, "or by Citizens or Subjects of any Foreign State." Nor could Marshall find any justification for Virginia's case in any other claim; therefore, the Court denied the Virginia motion for dismissal of the case on jurisdictional grounds.

The Virginia lawyers then withdrew, as they had been instructed to do, and the Court considered the case for Cohens on its merits. Cohens lost (and Virginia won). The Court decided that the act of Congress authorizing the lottery applied only in the District of Columbia, that it gave the defendant no right to sell tickets in Virginia, and thus the decision of the Virginia court was affirmed. Was *Cohens vs. Virginia* "much ado about nothing," then? Not at all. It established, so far as a court decision could establish it, the right of appeal in a criminal case from the state courts to the Federal courts where some question falling under the United States authority was concerned.

In *Gibbons vs. Ogden,* Marshall handed down a decision in 1824 which got a very favorable reception. The decision dealt a major blow to interference by the states in commerce and for free trade at large. More specifically, it struck down a state granted monopoly at a time when monopolies were becoming generally to be despised. The legislature of New York had at an earlier time granted to Robert Livingston and Robert Fulton (the inventor of the steamboat) the exclusive privilege to the commercial navigation of the waters of the state of New York. All other steam powered craft were forbidden to navigate the streams of New York, unless they were licensed to do so by Livingston and Fulton. The vessels of violaters could be captured and, in effect, confiscated by these proprietors. (They got a similar grant from the Orleans Territory, the predecessor of the state of Louisiana, in 1811.) New Jersey claimed equal rights to navigation on the lower Hudson, and issued licenses to navigators to enable them to contest New York's claims. At any rate, Aaron Ogden had got a license from Livingston and Fulton to operate exclusively on the Hudson River between New York and New Jersey. Thomas Gibbons, who had a license from the United States under the Coasting Act of 1793, contested Ogden's monopoly over shipping in this area. Gibbons sued first in the state of New York's trial court and the court of appeals, in both of which he ran afoul of the formidable jurist, Chancellor James Kent, and lost. His appeal to the United States Supreme Court turned out much better. The case was heard in February, 1824, and the arguments took four and a half days. The proceedings were enlivened by the appearance of the brilliant lawyer and orator, Daniel Webster, for the appellant, Thomas Gibbons. "Webster opened his argument in broad sweeping terms by contending that the statutes of New York, and by implication all exclusive grants of other states, violated the United States Constitution. 'The power of Congress [he said] to regulate commerce was complete and entire.' Individual states have no concurrent powers in this area; the federal government's domain is exclusive."[429]

Chief Justice John Marshall, who wrote the majority opinion in *Gibbons vs. Ogden*, did not put the matter quite so bluntly, but he tended toward a similar conclusion. As usual, Marshall turned to the language of the written Constitution in an effort to find an answer to controverted questions. The power in question was granted by the Constitution in these words: "congress shall have power to regulate commerce with foreign nations, and among the several states, and with the Indian tribes." The lawyers for Ogden had argued that "commerce" as used in the phrase does not include navigation in its meaning. Marshall rejected this argument as flying in the face of the general experience and common sense of Americans. "All America understands," he wrote, "and has uniformly understood, the word 'commerce' to comprehend navigation. It was so understood, and must have been so understood when the constitution was framed. The power over commerce, including navigation, was one of the primary objects for which the people of America adopted their government, and must have been contemplated in forming it. The [constitutional] convention must have used the word in that sense, because all have understood it in that sense; and the attempt to restrict it comes too late."

Marshall went on to give a broad definition of the power to regulate in the following words:

> We are now arrived at the inquiry, What is this power? It is the power to regulate; that is, to prescribe the rule by which commerce is

to be governed. This power, like all others vested in Congress is complete in itself, may be exercised to its utmost extent, and acknowledges no limitations other than are prescribed in the constitution. These are expressed in plain terms. . . . The power of congress, then, comprehends navigation within the limits of every state in the Union, so far as that navigation may be, in any manner connected with 'commerce with foreign nations, or among the several States, or with the Indian tribes.' It may, of consequence, pass the jurisdiction line of New York, and act upon the very waters to which the prohibition now under consideration applies.

In sum, Marshall had concluded that this power vested in Congress did extend to the waters of the state of New York.

Marshall went on to conclude that the grant of exclusive privileges over navigation of the waters of New York to Livingston and Fulton was contrary to both the action and power of Congress and thus of no effect. He based his conclusion both on the facts and on the supremacy clause of the Constitution, for, as he said, "The nullity of any act inconsistent with the constitution is produced by the declaration that the constitution is supreme law. . . ."

Two other points about this opinion need to be made. One is that in discussing the powers granted under the commerce clause Marshall made the crucial distinction between what we refer to as "interstate commerce" and "intrastate commerce," though he did not use the phrases. He arrived at this distinction by attempting to define what commerce "among" the states means. Marshall wrote, "The word 'among' means intermingled with. A thing which is among others is intermingled with them. Commerce among the states cannot stop at the external boundary-line of each state, but may be introduced into the interior." At this point, Marshall delimited the meaning of the phrase. "It is not intended to say that these words comprehend that commerce which is completely internal, which is carried on between man and man in a state, or between different parts of the same state, and which does not extend to or affect other States. Such a power would be inconvenient and is certainly unnecessary. Comprehensive as the word 'among' is, it may very properly be restricted to that commerce which concerns more states than one. . . . The completely internal commerce of a state then, may be considered as reserved for the state itself."[430] This distinction became so important for American political development that the phrase "interstate commerce" came to refer to that covered by the grant of power in the Constitution, and "intrastate commerce" to that internal commerce within a state not so covered.

The other is that the main impact of the above decision was to limit state interference in interstate commerce and to free it generally from control up until the Civil War, at least. It might appear from the language of the decision that great new powers were vouchsafed to the United States government. That may have been the case, but the powers were not soon utilized extensively. They are discretionary powers, not obligatory ones. That is, Congress could utilize them if it saw fit, but nothing in the Constitution or in the Court opinion required their use. In the latter part of the 19th century, Congress did use and expand the powers on which it legislated under this provision, and in the 20th century it became a kind of catch-all phrase to justify the use of force by the United States.

It should be apparent that Marshall's best known opinions had to do either with affirming the supremacy of the general government or restricting the power of the states. That is true as well of some of his less celebrated opinions. For example, in *Craig et. al. vs. The State of Missouri,* Chief Justice Marshall handed down a majority opinion restricting the states in monetary matters. The decision by the Supreme Court was handed down in 1830, but it dealt with a law passed by the Missouri legislature in 1821. The law authorized the establishment of loan offices which could issue a specified amount of certificates which could be used to pay taxes, debts due to the state, to pay salaries of state employees, and the like. Obviously, these certificates were to serve as or in lieu of money.

The constitutional issue revolved around two clauses in Section 10, Article I of the Constitution. The relevant passage reads, "No State shall . . . emit Bills of Credit; make any Thing but gold and silver Coin a Tender in Payment of Debts. . . ." The state of Missouri's arguments posed little difficulty for Marshall and most of his colleagues, with so clear cut a prohibition to work with. Were the Missouri certificates bills of credit in the constitutional sense? Marshall answered in the affirmative. He said, "To 'emit bills of credit' conveys to mind the idea of issuing paper intended to circulate through the community for its ordinary purposes as money, which paper is redeemable at a future day." He went on to show that this was precisely what the legislation had provided and intended. But, the lawyers argued for Missouri, since these bills were not made legal tender by the legislation, they did not meet the full qualifications of the prohibition. Not so, declared Marshall, for the Constitution prohibits both bills of credit and tender laws in separate phrases [which are separated in the provision by semi-colons, though Marshall does not note this]. "The Constitution, therefore, considers the emission of bills of credit and the enactment of tender laws as distinct operations, independent of each other, which may be separately performed. Both are forbidden." Thus, "a majority of the court feels constrained to say that the . . . [certificates are] against the highest law of the land, and that the note itself is utterly void."[431]

On the other side, it should be pointed out that not all of the decisions of the Supreme Court either advanced the power of the general government or restricted the states. The Court had declared a law passed by Congress unconstitutional in *Marbury vs. Madison.* In *Cohens vs. Virginia,* it affirmed the jurisdiction of the state and restricted the force of a law passed by Congress to the District of Columbia. It should be kept in mind, too, that the Jeffersonians and Jacksonians were in control for most of Marshall's tenure, and they were hardly disposed to extend the role of the general government beyond its constitutional limits. Had they been otherwise disposed, Marshall might have shown himself as equally disposed to limiting the general government to its constitutionally prescribed arena.

In any case, John Marshall had gone far during his thirty-four years on the Supreme Court toward establishing the judiciary branch as of equal importance to that of the legislative and executive branches. The role of the Supreme Court in the interpretation of the Constitution had been vindicated time and again during his tenure. (Nor should the role of his colleague and admirer Justice Joseph Story of Massachusetts be ignored. He served on the Court from 1812–1845, wrote many of the opinions when Marshall didn't, wrote *Commentaries on the Constitution of the United States,* and helped establish Marshall's enduring reputation.) "The greatest task of all," wrote a constitutional historian, "had been the establishment of the Court as the recognized final authority in determining the extent of state powers," but if he did not entirely fail in this effort, neither did he signally succeed, for "almost to the very end of his life he found one state or another denying the Court's authority or even, as in the case of Georgia, flouting it."

Of Marshall's importance, many would no doubt have agreed with a Jeremiah Mason's opinion expressed in letters to Justice Story, in which he said that Marshall's opinions "have done vastly more for the stability and permanency of our system of government than the present generation is aware of." Even Andrew Jackson, who admitted to dissenting from time to time to the Chief Justice's opinions, declared that "In the revolutionary struggles for our National independence, and particularly in the subsequent discussions which established the forms and settled the practice of our system of Government, the opinions of John Marshall were expressed with the energy and clearness which were peculiar to his strong mind, and gave him a rank amongst the greatest men of his age which he fully sustained on the bench of the Supreme Court."[432]

b. The Taney Court

Roger Taney of Maryland served for 28 years as Chief Justice of the Supreme Court, only 6 years less than Marshall. He was born in Calvert county, Maryland in 1777, graduated from Dickinson College, studied law at Annapolis, and became a lawyer. He was successively a state senator, attorney general of Maryland, served as Attorney General of the United States under Jackson, and was appointed Chief Justice of the Supreme Court by Jackson, to succeed Marshall. Though the Jeffersonians and their successors, the Jacksonians, had been in power generally from 1801 to 1835, it was only in the latter year that one of theirs came to head the Supreme Court. Taney had been a Democrat and a loyal follower of Jackson in the years before his appointment to the Court. Jackson had appointed four other members of the Court as well: John McLean of Ohio, Henry Baldwin of Pennsylvania, James M. Wayne of Georgia, and Philip P. Barbour of Virginia. Martin Van Buren finished his work, so far as filling the Court with Southerners, by naming John Catron of Tennessee and John McKinley of Alabama.

So far as the Democrats were concerned, this certainly tended to reduce the tensions between the judiciary and the other branches. Whatever fears the death and replacement of Marshall may have aroused among nationalists and those concerned about a firm government of the Union, they found little justification in the decisions of the Taney Court in the 1830s and 1840s. No frontal assault was made by the Court on the decisions that Marshall and his colleagues had made over the years. Nor were the Whig and other opposition claims that the level of decisions and opinions would decline under the new Chief Justice born out by developments. Indeed, Judge Benjamin R. Curtis of Massachusetts, who served under Chief Justice Taney in the 1850s, said of him that "he was master of all that peculiar jurisprudence which it is the special province of the Courts of the United States to administer and apply. His skill in applying it was of the highest order. His power of subtle analysis exceeded that of any man I ever knew. . . ." Moreover, "the surpassing ability of the Chief Justice, and all his great qualities of character and mind, were more fully and constantly exhibited in the consultation room . . . than the public knew or can ever justly estimate. There, his dignity, his love of order, his gentleness, his caution, his accuracy . . . , were of incalculable importance."[433]

On the other hand, the hopes of some of Jackson's supporters that the appointment of Taney would result in a full-fledged state's rights Court were doomed to some disappointments as well. The Richmond *Enquirer* announced its hope that a new Chief Justice would provide "some opportunity for the good old State-Rights doctrines of Virginia of '98–'99 to be heard and weighed on the Federal Bench. The very profound and brilliant abilities, with which they have been hitherto opposed in the Supreme Court, have only contributed to make us more anxious to bring back the ship to the Republican tack. We believe that Taney is a strong State-Rights man."[434]

While the Court under the leadership of its new Chief Justice was not about to champion the doctrines of the Virginia and Kentucky Resolutions, it wasted little time in demonstrating that it would give a more sympathetic hearing to the claims of state powers and not talk in such absolutist terms as the Marshall Court had frequently done. Three cases awaiting decision by the Court gave Taney and his colleagues an opportunity to illustrate this shift. The first of these, *Charles River Bridge vs. Warren Bridge,* had been before the Court twice before without a decision and was ripe for determination. The issue was the result of this series of events. In 1785 the legislature of Massachusetts incorporated the Charles River Bridge Company authorizing it to build and operate a toll bridge over the Charles River. In 1792, its charter was extended for 72 years. In 1828, the legislature incorporated the Warren Bridge Company to build a competing bridge over the Charles River only a short distance away, a bridge that was to be turned over to the state as soon as the company had recovered from tolls the cost of construction. At that point, passage over the Warren Bridge could be expected to be free. The Charles River Bridge Company sued for an injunction claiming that such action by Massachusetts impaired the contract.

The constitutional issue was whether or not the state had violated the United States Constitution by authorizing the building of a competing bridge. If so, and if the *Dartmouth College* precedent were followed, the Supreme Court might have been expected to grant the injunction. The facts were, of course, different here. There were no provisions in the contract to the Charles River company that had been clearly violated by authorizing another bridge. As Chief Justice Taney said, "It confers on them the ordinary faculties of a corporation, for the purpose of building the bridge; and establishes certain rates of toll, which the company are authorized to take. This is the whole grant. There is no exclusive privilege given to them over the waters of Charles river, above or below their bridge; no right to erect another bridge themselves, nor to prevent other persons from erecting one, no engagement from the State, that another shall not be erected; and no undertaking not to sanction competition, nor to make improvements that may diminish the amount of its income. Upon all these subjects the charter is silent. . . . No words are used from which an intention to grant any of these rights can be inferred."

Having pointed out these facts, the Chief Justice might have concluded his argument at this point with the decision he made, namely, denying the suit. But the lawyers on what was to be the losing side had argued strenuously that the rights for which they were contending were implicit in the charter. Taney denied this, and he did so on the grounds that grants and charters from the states must be strictly construed, especially so in the case of monopolies, for the people are a party to these contracts and they may be severely harmed. Implicit in his argument was the belief that the people generally would benefit from competition, as they so clearly might in the case of these bridges. Moreover, as Taney pointed out, many corporations at the present time engaged in building canals and railroads could be driven out of business on the grounds that turnpikes chartered earlier had implicit rights to provide means for travel and carrying freight. "We shall be thrown back to the improvements of the last century," Taney said, "and obliged to stand still until the claims of the old turnpike corporations shall be satisfied, and they shall consent to permit these States to avail themselves of the lights of modern science. . . ."[435] Taney not only struck a blow for the powers of

Massachusetts but also for the advantages of competition and freedom of enterprise. Justices Story and Thompson dissented, believing, no doubt, that Marshall would have arrived at a different decision.

This case was followed immediately by *New York vs. Miln,* in which the Court vindicated a power of the state exercised over commerce. The state legislature of New York was concerned about the condition of immigrants brought into its port and enacted a law requiring shipmasters to provide information on its passengers to authorities. The suit was brought to the Supreme Court on the grounds that New York was by this action regulating commerce, an activity exclusively within the jurisdiction of the Federal government. "Justice Barbour, speaking for five of the seven justices, held the law valid as a legitimate exercise of the state's police power, since the state's internal welfare was the obvious end purpose of the statute."[436] Some on the Court were not satisfied to ignore the constitutional issue, and took the position that since Congress had not legislated in this field, the state was well within its powers to do so.

The Supreme Court drove this latter point home in the License Cases decided in 1847. These involved the validity of laws passed by the legislatures of Massachusetts, Rhode Island, and New Hampshire regulating the sale of and taxing alcoholic beverages. The suit particularly challenged the power of states to regulate and tax those alcohol products that had been imported into the state on the grounds that such state activity was unconstitutional. There was general agreement on the Court that states might engage in such internal police activity even if it had an incidental impact upon interstate commerce. Taney and several of the justices went further. "It appears to me to be very clear," the Chief Justice wrote, "that the mere grant of power to the general government cannot, upon any just principles of construction, be construed to be an absolute prohibition to the exercise of any power over the same subject by the States . . . In my judgment, the State may nevertheless, for the safety or convenience of trade, or for the protection of the health of its citizens, make regulations of commerce for its own ports and harbors, and for its own territory; and such regulations are valid unless they come in conflict with a law of Congress."[437]

While the above is quoted to show that the Taney Court was more favorably disposed to the powers of the states than the Marshall Court had been, we should not lose sight of the impact of such decisions on people generally. "Police power" has an ominous sound, as well it might, and it was on its way to becoming a catch phrase to justify the state's exercise of power over its inhabitants. Nor was it necessarily beneficial to the citizenry to have two governments exercising power over them in the same general jurisdiction. The object of the federal system of government was not to augment the power either of the general government or of the individual states. The object of the system is to limit government and free men to provide for their own well being. Thus, the focus on "Federal power" and "state's rights" is a focus on means not upon ends. It may be well to note, too, that Taney was concentrating attention less than Marshall had on the Constitution itself and more on earlier court decisions and opinions about it. The subtle shift toward treating the Constitution as in the stream of common law was already under way, tentatively at least.

In any case, the Taney Court did from time to time affirm various powers of the general government. In the *United States vs. Gratiot,* handed down in 1840, the Court affirmed the power of Congress over public lands not only to dispose of them by sale but to lease them as well, even when they were in the bounds of a state. It had been argued by Thomas Hart Benton that Congress had been given power to dispose of the land, not "held by the United States." To give leases, he held, was for the United States to set up tenants within a state. The Court held in favor of the United States, that the tenantry business aroused unnecessary fears, and that Congress had as much right to lease the lands as to sell them.

In the same year, in *Holmes vs. Jennison,* several members of the Supreme Court affirmed the exclusive jurisdiction of the United States government in dealing with foreign nations. Governor Jennison of Vermont had ordered a murderer returned to Canada, though the United States had no extradition treaty at the time with either Britain or Canada. Chief Justice Taney declared that the case "involves an inquiry into the relative powers of the Federal and State governments. . . . It was one of the main objects of the Constitution to make us, so far as regarded our foreign relations, one people and one nation; and to cut off all communications between foreign governments and the several State Governments."[438] In some matters, at least, Taney could be as emphatic about Federal power as Marshall had been.

The Court also affirmed, perhaps extended, the power of the Federal judiciary over executive officers in 1838 in *Kendall vs. United States.* Kendall was Andrew Jackson's Postmaster General, and he had revoked some claims of postal contractors made by his predecessors. Congress referred the matter to the Treasurer for determination, and he held that the claims were valid. When Kendall still refused to pay them, a writ of mandamus was issued by the circuit court of the District of Columbia to compel him to pay. The matter went to the Supreme Court, where Francis Scott Key argued for Kendall that this was an effort to interfere with the executive branch by the courts. Justice Smith Thompson of New York, speaking for the Court, denied that the courts were interfering "in any respect whatever with the rights or duties of the Executive, or that it involves any conflict of powers between the Executive and Judicial Departments of the Government." He distinguished between the ministerial duties of an executive officer which are directed by law and those which are political in character and are directed by the President. In the present case, he held, "the court was simply ordering Kendall to do his duties under the law." Further, Thompson declared that "it would be an alarming doctrine that Congress

cannot impose upon any Executive officer any duty . . . not repugnant . . .
to the Constitution;'' and such duty ''be subject to the control of the law,
and not to the direction of the President.''[439] The Federal courts could be
expected, of course, ordinarily to defend their powers, and win so long as
the matter remained in their hands.

Even so, it could be said with much justice that the Federal judiciary, and
especially the Supreme Court under Chief Justice Taney, continued to gain
in dignity and prestige in the 1830s and 1840s, despite the clamor against
them from time to time by partisans of one cause or another. Highly partisan
Democrats no longer saw the Court as their enemy, and the powers of the
states did sometimes get favorable attention. Certainly, the Court was no
longer bent on a course of continual advancement of the powers of the
general government, if that had ever been its direction. The most prominent
lawyers and orators in the country—such men as Daniel Webster, Thomas
Hart Benton, and even Henry Clay—argued cases before the Supreme
Court, adding to its prestige. The chamber of the High Court had taken on
a new glitter during these years, as a Washington correspondent described it:
''By the bye, this chamber presents just now, in itself, a better look than it
ever did before. A great deal of the furniture is new, the carpets are rich and
beautiful; the desks and chairs of the Judges of a pattern unsurpassed for
beauty and convenience, and the whole appointments of the room, in short,
in excellent taste.''[440] Such a court, in such a setting, could increase its
reputation for impartiality.

A historian of the Court declared that ''In the years 1848–49, the Court
may be said to have reached its height in the confidence of the people of the
country.''[441] Within a few years it would come crashing down. The occasion, of course, was slavery, an issue which could not for much longer lie
dormant, and which was so divisive that it probably lay beyond the power
of a court to resolve. In any case, the anti-slavery movement was gaining in
support, and politicians were becoming more outspoken on the question.
The major question that came into focus for most of the 1850s was that of
the expansion of slavery into the West. Congress had made, not its last
effort, but its last major effort to settle the matter by the Compromise of
1850. But that was so ineffective that yet another effort was made by the
Kansas-Nebraska Act of 1854. But these acts only further unsettled matters
rather than settling them, as Kansas became a battleground between pro- and
anti-slavery forces.

In any case, the Supreme Court plunged into the thicket of the controversy
with its decision in *Dred Scott vs. Sandford*, handed down in 1857. Dred
Scott had been a slave in Missouri, where slavery was recognized. His
owner took him to Illinois and later on to Wisconsin, in both of which
slavery was prohibited. Scott had been taken out of Missouri in 1834 and
brought back in the 1840s. After his return to Missouri, Dred Scott brought
suit against Missouri to obtain his freedom, on the grounds that having lived

in a free state made him free. In the course of getting to the Supreme Court three questions had been raised: whether or not Dred Scott qualified as a citizen for purposes of suing in Federal court; whether his sojourns in Illinois and Wisconsin had rendered him free or not; and the constitutionality of the Missouri Compromise.

Six justices joined Chief Justice Taney in the majority decision, and two justices dissented. Several concurring opinions as well as the dissenting opinions were filed, so divergent were the views of the members of the Court on the case. By reasoning which was circuitous and convoluted, the majority decided that Dred Scott was not a citizen and could not sue in Federal Court. The suit might then have been dismissed without further ado, but the Court had only begun its controversial course. It is conceivable that Chief Justice Taney and a majority of his colleagues believed that they could solve the slavery issue. If so, they badly misread feeling in the country, which is quite possible, since a majority of the Court came from slave states.

At any rate, Chief Justice Taney, speaking for a majority of the Court declared that "the Act of Congress [the Missouri Compromise] which prohibited a citizen from holding property of this kind [slaves] north of the line therein mentioned is not warranted by the Constitution, and is therefore void." This was so, he argued, because slaves were the property of their owners, and Congress is prohibited by the Fifth Amendment to the Constitution to take property without due process of law. "An Act of Congress which deprives a person of the United States of his liberty or property merely because he came himself or brought his property into a particular Territory of the United States . . . could hardly be dignified with the name of due process of law. . . ."[442] The Court had, in effect, ruled out any efforts by Congress to draw any lines separating regions into which slaves could not be carried and presumably worked or otherwise utilized. If this ruling be accepted as the final word on the subject of the constitutionality of slavery, the only route open for limiting and prohibiting slavery was a constitutional amendment.

The reaction to the Dred Scott decision was harsh and often vituperative, especially among abolitionists and Republicans—a recently organized political party which was the political seat of the most vigorous abolitionist sentiment. Republican Congressman Phileomon Bliss of Ohio vented his wrath against the Supreme Court with this pronouncement:

> The spectacle of a gowned conclave, gravely setting aside statutes and Constitutions of States; enforcing powers not granted in the compact, and against the express reservations of the States; with eager zeal reversing the whole current of authority and law, to make universal a local and exceptional despotism; prompting its ministers to mayhem and murder, sure of their illegal shield, never darkened our fathers' vision. Had a tithe of what we stupidly suffer been anticipated by

them, the Federation would have been an impossibility; at least the Court would have been but a Hamilton's dream of a life Executive and Senate. . . .[443]

How far the Court had fallen in esteem in some areas is well illustrated by the Booth case in Wisconsin. Booth was a slave who was arrested by a United States marshall under the Fugitive Slave Act, which had been passed in 1850. The Wisconsin courts repeatedly intervened to free Booth, time and again defying United States courts, including the Supreme Court.

The Taney Court never regained its high standing; indeed, the Federal courts were very much overwhelmed by the executive and legislative branches during the Civil War and Reconstruction. How far matters had gone once war came may be well illustrated by *ex parte Merryman*. It shows, too, that Chief Justice Taney, though now grown old and feeble, could still argue vigorously on the basis of the Constitution. John Merryman, a citizen of Baltimore, Maryland was arrested by military officers and imprisoned at Fort McHenry. Since this had taken place in Taney's circuit, the application for a writ of *habeas corpus* came to him. Taney later wrote that Merryman was not charged with an offence against the laws of the United States; "he appears to have been arrested upon general charges of treason and rebellion, without proof, and without giving the names of witnesses, or specifying the acts, which . . . constituted the crime." General Cadwallader was presented with the writ, but he refused to produce the prisoner, claiming that "he is authorized by the President to suspend the writ of *habeas corpus* at his discretion, and, in the exercise of that discretion, suspends it in this case, and on that ground refuses obedience to the writ." Whereupon, the Chief Justice cited Cadwallader with contempt and made known his reasons in the opinion *ex parte Milligan*.

Taney gave it as his opinion that not only did the President not have the constitutional authority to delegate the power to suspend writs of *habeas corpus*, but he lacked the power to do so himself, without prior authorization by Congress. In fact, as Taney points out, only Congress is authorized by the Constitution to suspend the writ of *habeas corpus*, and there is no presumption in favor of the notion that the power could be delegated to any other branch or body of the government. The only mention of the writ is in the first article of the Constitution, and its mention follows an enumeration of the powers of Congress. The whole reference is in a single sentence, which reads: "The Privilege of the Writ of Habeas Corpus shall not be suspended, unless when in Cases of Rebellion or Invasion the public Safety may require it." No reference to this power occurs at all in listing the powers of the executive or elsewhere in the Constitution.

Taney made it abundantly clear that the President was usurping the power of the legislative branch and infringing upon those of the judiciary. He drives the position home by pointing out, as many had done before him, that the "Government of the United States is one of delegated and limited powers. It derives its existence and authority altogether from the Constitution, and neither of its branches—executive, legislative, or judicial—can exercise powers of government beyond those specified and granted." In support of his conclusion, Taney cites Story's *Commentaries* and an opinion by his predecessor, John Marshall. Marshall said,

> If at any time the public safety should require the suspension of the powers vested by this act in the courts of the United States, it is for the Legislature to say so. That question depends on political considerations, on which the legislature is to decide. Until the legislative will be expressed, this court can only see its duty, and must obey the law.

That is, the court had to issue a writ of *habeas corpus*.

Taney made clear that protections of the United States Constitution were being denied to John Merryman, that they were being denied by military officers who had a preponderance of force, and that the Court was powerless to offer relief in these circumstances. As he put it, "the military authority has, by force of arms, thrust aside the judicial authorities and officers to whom the Constitution has confided the power and duty of interpreting and administering the laws, and substituted a military government in its place. . . . If the military can thus impose its will with impunity, Taney said, "the people of the United States are no longer living under a Government of laws, but every citizen holds life, liberty, and property at the will and pleasure of the army officer in whose military district he may happen to be found."[444] Since Taney was powerless in the face of military force, he directed the clerk of United States Circuit Court of Maryland to send a copy of his opinion to President Abraham Lincoln in the hope that he would restore due process of law. Lincoln was unmoved, but continued on his course of imposing the military over the civil power, as Chief Justice Taney would say.

This case was important because it exemplifies the depths to which the Supreme Court had fallen within a few years. Nor was the Constitution faring much better under Lincoln. Both the standing of the Court and at least some of the standing of the Constitution would be restored, but that awaited the passing of Civil War and Reconstruction.

Chapter 13
Government in the States

Some years back, the present writer was telling an associate that he had been summoned to jury duty in Federal District court. My associate observed that he had earlier served on a jury in circuit court, which is what trial courts dealing with state laws in Alabama are called, but, he said modestly, "I suppose Federal courts are much more important than local state courts?" That would indeed appear to be the case. Certainly, the government of the United States is much larger, more powerful, more prestigious, and presidents outrank governors in the general scheme of things. Indeed, Federal officials generally outrank state officials at comparable hierarchical levels. And, as the Constitution itself says, laws and treaties made under the authority of the Constitution are "the supreme law of the land." It should follow, then, that in dealing with the jurisdiction of authority or power allotted to the Federal government, the Federal courts are superior to state courts.

It does not follow, however, that Federal trial courts are "more important" than state trial courts. For that to be so, it would require that the cases that come before Federal courts deal with graver offenses than do state courts. Or to put it another way, Federal courts would need to deal with those cases which occupy more public attention or excite greater interest than those in state trial courts. In fact, no such situation exists generally and as a rule. The case the present writer sat upon for his Federal jury duty involved a man charged with assisting in the growing of marijuana plants on the lower floor of a vacation home. The only persons who showed interest in the case were those assigned to it, and two or three relatives or friends of the man being tried. In fact, most of the trials that attract widespread interest and attention—with an occasional exception—are tried in state courts. Virtually all trials for murder, rape, assault, robbery, and assorted other villainies are heard in state courts. (It is true that in the latter part of the 20th century an increasing number of cases, such as those involving civil rights violations, and misdeeds of state and national public officials, attract widespread notice and assume considerable importance. But the story of this expanded Federal activity belongs in later chapters.)

There is a broader point to be made along the same lines, namely that the

constitutional allotment of jurisdictions between state and national government left most matters that fall within the warp and woof of the ordinary
lives of people to state and local government. Thus, so far as it was the
concern of government at all, the recording of births and deaths and the
investigation of misdeeds in connection with these was left to state governments. So it was, too, with the recording of business and land and property
transactions, and the usual protections of life and property. States usually
authorized and recorded the existences of assorted corporations, businesses,
charitable, educational, and commercial. So far as such things were done by
government, or when they were, states (and local governments authorized
by them) built and/or maintained roads, maintained places of domicile for or
incarcerated the insane, sometimes provided help for the indigent, for orphans, and the like. When the schooling of children came to be thought of
as the concern of government, states (or local governments) began to provide or support schools. States, of course, provided most prisons, the basic
court system, and enforced the generality of the laws. To put it more broadly
still, for most of the 19th century, and at least a little ways into the 20th
century, the most visible governments, and the ones that had most to do with
the general round of American lives were state and local governments under
their authority.

The Federal government, as was said by many of the Founders and
leaders who came after them, had both limited duties and assignments, and
limited powers with which to perform them. It had the sole authority over
the conduct of relations with other nations, the declaring of war, and the
major authority for maintaining armed forces. The conduct of wars was, of
course, in the hands mainly, if not exclusively, of the Federal government.
It had the authority to regulate commerce with foreign nations and among
the states and with Indian tribes, and it had a few other powers, including
those of taxation and of establishing a court system to enforce national laws.

Even though states do and have performed many of the functions of
government, and most of those close to home, so to speak, it is nonetheless
the case that state governments get short shrift in textbooks and courses in
American government (and will in this one as well). There are some reasons
for this, whether they entirely justify it or not. There are now fifty states,
each with its own constitution and at least some differences in government
from one another. Since people who study American government usually
reside in only one (if any) of the states, they neither have a need to know nor
are likely to have any great interest in the other states. Such interest as
students or others may have probably can be satisfied by studying the
common features of the governments. That can be, and often is, handled
with considerable brevity. But state governments are rarely studied at length
in the schools of particular states. State history is often taught and sometimes required, but rarely, if ever, are courses in state government taught,
except for such as occurs in the history courses.

In fact, state government is frequently played down in the media of communication; state elections often do not draw large numbers of voters, especially not so large as in presidential election years. The national government has become the major focus with the development of radio and television networks. State and local government often seem less dramatic, less interesting, and less important. These developments have been accompanied by a tremendous growth of the general government and loss of relative power by the state governments. This story will be told later, but it needs to be mentioned here to underscore the great importance the states were supposed to have in our federal system of government. The states have obviously declined in public esteem as they have lost their power to perform their counterweight to Federal power.

What will be discussed below will be confined mainly to what state and local governments did and were like in the 19th and the early part of the 20th century. They were neither provinces of the general government nor under its control at that time. Nor were they local distribution points for Federal largess in these early years. The general government neither mandated what they were to provide to the citizenry nor subsidized them in providing it. In general, state and local governments were more independent of the United States government in their operation than it was of them. All these things need to be understood in order to grasp our constitutionally established federal system of government.

a. Government at the State Level

Each state in the United States has a government in its own right with limited sovereignty, as does the United States. It can perform most of the basic functions of government without outside authorization. That is, each state can use force to maintain the peace, make laws binding upon its citizens, tax, spend, perform a variety of functions, and behave in most, if not all, respects as a government. (It is not authorized to make war, but it may defend itself from an invasion or put down an insurrection from within.) Each of the fifty states has its own constitution, as noted earlier, and some states had constitutions before the United States Constitution of 1787.

These constitutions differ considerably from one another. They are generally much longer than the United States Constitution, some running to hundreds of printed pages, while others are relatively much shorter. Some have been amended many times; others less extravagantly. They are apt to go into much greater detail than does the United States Constitution. But however much they differ from one another they have a similar purpose and character. They all authorize a government, grant it powers to act in various ways, and provide for the election, appointment, or choosing of its officials, and the like. These constitutions also limit the powers of the governments they authorize. They do so most obviously by prohibiting the governments to act in certain ways. Generally, the constitutions have bills of rights which limit the government. Some of these rights are familiar from the United States Constitution, but others are different in character. Constitutions formed in the 20th century sometimes contain such alleged "rights" as the "right" to a job. Such provisions are not clearly limitations on government. State constitutions usually profess a belief in the separation of powers in government, and in fact do provide for distinct executive, legislative, and judicial branches.

Most state constitutions have been approved by the direct vote of the electorate in their particular states. "Of the basic documents in effect today [1961] only those of Delaware (1897), Louisiana (1921), Mississippi (1890), South Carolina (1895), Vermont (1793), and Virginia (1902) took effect without first being submitted to the people. Altogether the American states have framed over 130 constitutions since 1776. Excluding the original constitutions and secession documents of the Confederate States, almost ninety per cent of them were popularly ratified."[445] Many of the constitutions also provide for popular approval before an amendment is adopted. Indeed, state constitutions provide for wider direct election of officials than does the United States Constitution. Although state governments still generally depend on the representative principle, and thus are technically republics [a condition supposed to be guaranteed by the United States Constitution], they are much more democratic in tendency than is the general government.

In fact, states have generally extended popular election throughout the government. Not only are governors (and lieutenant-governors) popularly elected, but so also are many of the department heads as well as members of some commissions. The appointive powers of governors are much more limited than those of the President. In consequence, the executive branch is not nearly so unified in the states as it is in the United States. Judges are commonly elected directly by the people in the states; their terms are not for life, of course, but are more apt to be four years than not.

State governments have other governments under them of their own creation, in contrast with the United States government (which has only the government of the District of Columbia under it permanently, and territorial governments temporarily). These include county and municipal governments, as well as any others such as townships, villages and the like. These, and the relations between them and state governments may be spelled out as well in their constitutions. County and city governments have an assortment of officials who must be chosen in some manner for office, be paid in some amount, and serve terms of greater or lesser length. The state constitution or legislation must either define these matters as well as much else, or fix the authority for doing so. This is a field both for constitutional provision and legislative enactments at the state level.

Every state not only has a constitution but also a capital—a city or town which is the seat of the government. So central is this role to the city that its very name becomes entangled with it, as, for example, we say that Albany is the capital of New York state. The capital is sometimes the largest city in the state, e.g., Atlanta of Georgia, Indianapolis of Indiana, and Oklahoma City of Oklahoma, but they were more commonly chosen for their centrality in location within the state and are often located in a small or medium sized city, e.g., Tallahassee in Florida, Austin in Texas, Columbus in Ohio, and Salem in Oregon. Every capital also has a capitol, i.e., a building in which the state legislature meets, although it may also contain offices of other state officials as well. At any rate, the capital as the seat of the government will typically have not only the meeting place of the legislature but also the residence and offices of the governor, the various departments of the government as well as the offices for them, and the highest court in the state. Some departments may have branches spread around the state, as highway departments frequently do, but the headquarters of the department will almost certainly be located in the capital.

(1) The Executive

The governor is the chief executive of the state. His powers and duties are not, however, made clear by that statement. The office had its American origins in the colonial period, where, in royal colonies, the governor was the agent of the king, and generally exercised the power of a king over the colony. The office of the President of the United States was modelled on that of colonial and state governors. And, to round out the picture, in the course of time, the office of governor has tended to be modelled on that of the President. That was not so at first, however. During the early period of constitution-making, Americans were intent on restricting the powers of governors. The legislatures were usually intentionally made the dominant branch. Governors at that time were usually elected by the legislatures and served for only one or two year terms. Consequently, they had little independence. In the course of time, governors did obtain substantive independence of legislatures by direct election. But executive powers remain divided to this day in most states, divided between governors and elective heads of departments, and between these and a variety of "independent agencies" created over the years to perform this or that function. Governors are charged with executing the laws faithfully, but that usually boils down to be such as they can or will execute that are not assigned to others by law.

Governors do have a goodly amount of patronage to hand out to fill an assortment of positions. They can influence legislation by their recommendations and such veto powers as they have. In virtually all the states the governor does have the power of veto, and most states require much larger majorities to override vetoes than to pass legislation which the governor approves. One authority on state government says, "The governor's veto power, and hence his influence on legislation by threatening a veto, is in most states greater than that of the President."[446] The governor can also kill legislation by a "pocket veto"—i. e., by not signing legislation at the end of a session. This is especially effective where the length of a legislative session is constitutionally limited. Some governors also have the power of vetoing items within a bill without vetoing the whole. Governors may also be assigned the duty of submitting budgets, and, where that is the case, they may also influence legislation.

Governors have a number of other duties, responsibilities, and privileges. By the nature of his position, the governor is ceremonial head of the state. Thus, he frequently attends if he does not preside at numerous ceremonies, celebrations, and occasions, ranging from ribbon cutting to ground breaking to the centennials of institutions within the state to Fourth of July barbecues, and the like. He has the power of pardon, by which he may influence the enforcement of the laws. He may not officially command, but he has appointive and directive powers over the police and military force of the state. His is the ultimate authority within the state to maintain the peace, to which end, he has usually been empowered to call out the national guard and direct the state police. If his powers are restricted in certain ways, that may be just as well. Many states do limit the terms of governors, in recognition of the fact that their powers do tend to increase with the length of their time in office.

(2) The Legislature

The power to make laws is vested by the constitutions of states in a legislature, though it is not called by that name in every state. Although there have been rare experiments with a unicameral (one house) legislature, the rule has been that a state legislature, like Congress—and like the British Parliament before it—would be composed of two houses. It is indeed often the case that one of these houses is called the house of representatives and the other the senate, though some are called by other titles. Historically, one house has been based on population, customarily the house of representatives; and the other has been more or less territorially based, ordinarily the senate. Usually, too, the members of one house had longer terms than the other. That is a way of saying, perhaps, that state legislatures were often modelled on the Congress of the United States.

Historically, state legislatures had or have several obligations regarding the operation of the government of the United States. They elected the two United States Senators from their states until the passage of the 17th Amendment in 1913. These Senators were understood to have the special duty of representing state governments nationally. Second, they have a constitutional role in amending the United States Constitution. Ordinarily, approval by three-fourths of the state legislatures is required for ratification of amendments. Congress has the authority, however, to provide for amendment by state conventions instead, but it has rarely availed itself of this option. States may also initiate an application to Congress to call a convention to propose amendments, and when two thirds of them do so, Congress "shall" do so. The legislature of a state may also apply to the United States for aid in dealing with domestic violence. Moreover, the Constitution of the United States specifies that "The Times, Places and Manner of holding Elections for [United States] Senators and Representatives, shall be prescribed in each State by the Legislature thereof; but the Congress may at any time make or alter such Regulations, except as to the Places of chusing [sic] Senators." This last provision might have been changed by the 17th Amendment, but no direct mention was made of it.

It is well to note again at this point that state legislatures are limited in the matters on which they may legislate not only by their constitutions but also by the United States Constitution. Section 10 of Article I contains a list of prohibitions and restrictions on state legislatures and state governments. For example, "No State . . . shall coin Money, emit Bills of Credit; make any Thing but gold and silver coin a Tender in Payment of Debts; pass any Bill of Attainder, ex post facto Law, or Law impairing the Obligation of Contracts, or grant any Title of Nobility." In addition, there are a number of things states are prohibited to do without the consent of Congress, such as "enter into any Agreement or Compact with another State. . . ." It is the case, too, that on any matter in which Congress has legislated in "pursuance of the Constitution" a state may not pass legislation contrary to that.

Still, states have a vast array of matters on which they may, and sometimes must, legislate if government is to be effective. All sorts of violent crimes, such as murder, arson, rape, assault (in many sorts and degrees), harassment, and the like, are subjects for legislation. So are all sorts of non-violent crimes, such as burglary, robbery (in which no force was used or threatened), graft, bribery, and so on. Indeed, every sort of offense that can be conceived, thought of, or remembered, may be subjects of state legislation, except such as may be prohibited by the Constitution or preempted by Congress. Moreover, all sorts of criminal and civil penalties, procedures, and appeals within the state system of courts may be subjects of legislation. In like manner, legislation establishing regulations, requiring licenses, or otherwise dealing with professions, businesses, and other sorts of activities may be dealt with by state legislation. The states may pass requirements and prescriptions for local governments as well. And the most basic business of the state—levying taxes and authorizing expenditures— must be taken care of if the state is to have employees and perform functions. Not all these items must be taken care of at each legislative session, of course, but some of them do, and other pressing matters usually arise.

Even so, legislative sessions, or the number of days legislators are to be paid, are often limited. Indeed, some legislatures meet regularly only every other year. They frequently, even usually, limit the number of working days in a session to 30, 36, 60 days, and the like. There are often other rules and restrictions to try to make legislators get the job done expeditiously, though the usual result is a bundle of legislation on the last day of the session.

(3) State Courts

Historically, the lowest of the state courts is that of justice of the peace. In England, where the office originated, this person was usually prominent and highly respected in the community, not because of his position in the court system but because of his relatively high position in the class system. In the New World, he was appointed by the authorities, and this was continued in the early years of the United States. Since the 1830s, however, he has usually been elected for some district or area. Basically, his task was to settle disputes and enforce laws that did not ordinarily entail imprisonment, i. e., misdemeanors. He was not required to have legal training, and his compensation consisted of fees from those who required his services or were found guilty by him. He could also issue some kinds of warrants and perform marriage ceremonies. He dealt out informal justice without ceremony ordinarily—without lawyers, without a jury, and without a clerk.

While there are other courts at the lower level, they will be dealt with in connection with local governments. The main state court where cases are dealt with initially and decisions are reached are trial courts. They are called by a variety of names in one state or another, such as, circuit courts, district courts, superior courts, and the like. Whatever their name, they are the state equivalent of United States district courts. In Pennsylvania, they are called Courts of Common Pleas, which may best describe them, since virtually all criminal and civil suits may be heard in them. States are divided into districts, which may be counties, combinations of counties, or portions of counties in populous areas for the purpose of such courts. Each of these general trial courts is presided over by a single judge. It is a court of record; its proceedings are recorded and may be examined or reviewed. Trials are ordinarily public, and places for spectators are provided. The state provides a prosecutor, who is usually elected, as is the judge. These judges are trained in the law, and apply statutory and common law, and are bound by oath or affirmation to obey the United States Constitution as well. They may rule on the constitutionality of laws in the course of applying law to cases also. Ordinarily, however, they are not called upon to try cases that fall within the jurisdiction of United States courts. In the scheme of things, there are higher courts than these state district courts, but none which deal with more important matters.

All states have courts of appeal, but many of them have only one level of appeal. Some states do have intermediate courts of appeal, as does the United States, before a case reaches the highest court for the state. These intermediate appeals courts usually have three or more judges, who, depending on state law, may have been appointed or elected. They do not hold trials, and their main job is to review cases appealed to them from general trial courts. Their concern is ordinarily with whether correct procedure was followed and whether the law was properly applied. If a new trial is indicated by the decision, the case will be sent back to the district court for a new trial.

Every state has a highest court of appeal. It is usually called a supreme court, but some states have variations on that title or different names. For example, New York state calls its general trial courts by the title of Supreme Court, and its highest court is called Supreme Court, Appellate Division. The number of judges on the state supreme court, or whatever the highest court happens to be called, ranges from three to nine, with five or seven being usual. They are elected in most states, and appointed by governors or legislatures in others. The man who presides over the state supreme court is usually called a chief justice, for which position he may be either appointed or elected. The chief justice presides over the court and supervises its business activities. Cases are usually argued before the supreme court by lawyers for the opposing sides. They come to the court by way of appeal from a trial court or an intermediate court of appeals. The highest state courts tend to conduct their business in a fashion similar to that of the United States Supreme Court.

It might be well to know, too, that judges have considerable arbitrary power to maintain respect and order in the courtroom. They may order the room cleared if spectators become unruly. Unruly individuals may be removed from the room or held in contempt of court. Lawyers and people being tried may also be held in contempt and fined, jailed, or otherwise punished. In such cases, judges often act as prosecutors, judges, and jurors, as well as witnesses to the offense. Lawyers may object and take exception to rulings of the court, and, if invited by the court, may offer their reasons, but they are well advised not to appear to be arguing with the judge. Judges can not only bark but also bite, and their rulings generally have teeth in them.

Juries also have much power in trial courts. There are two main juries in the American system. They are the grand jury and the petit jury. (The language is from French: *grand* means large; *petit* means small.) The grand jury usually has 18 members who have been chosen by lot from the citizenry in the jurisdiction of the court which they serve. Grand juries, when they are used, usually issue *indictments*. They listen in secret to the evidence against persons accused of crimes. Since they only have to decide whether there is sufficient evidence to warrant a trial, they do not hear the defense. It is sometimes alleged that grand juries are creatures of prosecuting attorneys. That may be the case, sometimes, but grand jurors may ask their own questions of those who testify before them, and they are hardly bound by the

wishes of the prosecuting attorney in voting on whether to indict or not in
any particular case. Grand jurors may also investigate the facilities and
activities of governments in their jurisdiction and make public reports on
them.

Petit juries are usually used in criminal and civil trials, when they are
required or requested. Customarily a petit jury consists of 12 members, who
are selected by lot from among the citizenry. Usually, the duty of a jury
extends to the determination of the facts of a case when they are in dispute.
(If the facts are not at issue, there will not ordinarily be a trial, though judges
may hold a hearing in a legal dispute to determine the law.) In a criminal
case, the jury has the task of determining whether the person is guilty or not
and of what offenses. In civil suits, the jury is supposed to decide questions
of liability, and sometimes what compensation, if any, is to be paid. The
jury may also sometimes determine penalties in criminal cases, or recommend them, at least. Although the official duties of trial duties extend only
to the facts and, sometimes, to the extent of the penalties, they may in fact
find persons not guilty or not liable because they disagree with the law. The
jury meets in secret, and the members are not required to reveal the basis of
their decision.

b. County Government

"The county is the most nearly universal unit of local government in the
United States."[447] Particularly, it generally provides the main local government for rural areas, though most cities fall within or include portions of
counties. Virtually all states are divided into counties, and most of these
have their own governments by provision of the states. They are frequently
administrative units for state governments, and in more recent times sometimes serve the United States government that way as well. While counties
generally have elements of the legislative, executive, and judicial functions,
all these are so limited in their power that the separation of powers has not
been a large concern.

The main governing body of the county is some sort of board, most
commonly called a board of commissioners or supervisors. This board
sometimes acts as a legislature for the county, and at other times acting
either individually or collectively as the executive branch. For example, the
board may be composed of road commissioners who individually have
charge of road work in some district of the county. The powers of the board,
or whatever the governing body is called, are determined by the state constitution and/or the state legislature. Among the powers that the boards
commonly exercise are: levying taxes, borrowing money, making appropriations, setting salaries for employees of the county, licensing businesses,
regulating businesses, looking after county property, such as courthouses,

jails, hospitals, and the like. The county board does not, as a board, ordinarily perform any judicial functions.

Just as the nation and the state have a capital city, so does the county have a seat, ordinarily called the "county seat." It does not have a capitol building, at least not one called by that name, but it does have a central building, commonly called the "county courthouse." Actually, it often does much more than house a court room or court rooms; various county offices may be located there as well as those for judges, court clerks, and district attorneys. The board of commissioners will also have a meeting room in the court house most likely, as well as such other officials as can find room there.

Counties came in the course of time to keep a considerable variety of records, as of births, marriages, deaths, deeds to property, corporate charters (sometimes filed with secretaries of state or at other state offices), mortgages on real property, wills, and the like. They may also distribute an assortment of licenses and permits, such as marriage licenses, driver's licenses, hunting permits, and license plates (such licenses did not exist until sometime after the invention of automobiles, nor did driver's licenses), and the like. Wills must be probated, though that is a court function, when anything other than a formality of making known the existence of the will is involved. All the above functions could be performed in a single office, and sometimes are. In Alabama, most, if not all, of these functions have historically been performed by the Probate Judge and those who assist him. He is the single most important figure in the county, for in addition to serving as recorder and license dispenser for the county, he used to hold court in misdemeanor cases, holds probate court, holds court to commit persons to mental institutions, holds competency hearings, and the like, as well as serving as chairman of the Board of Commissioners. In most states, however, most of these functions are dispersed, and some are even done by state branch offices. Officials who perform these functions may be variously known as recorders, registers of deeds, county judges, ordinaries, licensers, and the like.

The sheriff is one of if not the most important of the county officers. While most county officers are elected, none excites more interest in rural counties than the election of sheriff. That is because sheriffs are usually the chief law enforcement officer in rural counties, and provide virtually the only law enforcement outside city limits. Indeed, the authority of the sheriff usually extends to urban and incorporated areas in his county, but where cities and towns have their own police, the sheriff leaves most law enforcement to them unless called upon for assistance. The sheriff is assisted in his work by *deputies,* who serve by appointment under him. The sheriff has a variety of other duties besides apprehending law violaters. He is an officer of the court in his county, and is required to be present in person or represented by a deputy at all court sessions, to keep the peace, and enforce court orders. He is also responsible for serving summonses, warrants, and sub-poenas. The sheriff holds public sales (auctions) of property ordered to be sold in that fashion, conducts foreclosures, and may evict tenants or tres-passers from private property. He is responsible also for confining those awaiting trial and for securing those convicted until they are presented to prisons. The jail is in his care as well, though jailers may be appointed to run it.

Another important county official in law enforcement is the *coroner*. He may or may not be a physician or surgeon, and he (or she) is usually elected to office. The coroner is called in for cases of violent death or where a person died under peculiar or suspicious circumstances. For example, the coroner will ordinarily be called to the scene of a fatal traffic accident, when there is a shooting death, and when someone dies who was not known to have been ill. Generally speaking, if the coroner can readily decide that no foul play was involved, the investigation ends. If he has difficulty in arriving at a conclusion, he may ask the aid of others, or turn the matter over to police or other investigators. Historically, coroners have sometimes sum-moned a jury to help them in reaching a conclusion. For example, if there is a question of whether a person was accidentally shot, murdered, or com-mitted suicide, a coroner's jury may be called to render a decision.

The *tax assessor* plays a rather obvious role in the county. He assesses, i. e., determines, the amount of tax that is due, on real, personal, and sometimes intangible property. His office keeps records of real property in the county, updates these from time to time, and sends out the bills annually or however they fall due. Some types of notes require that taxes be paid through the financial institution on houses and lots until the mortgage is paid off. In these cases, the householder may pay his taxes monthly in his mortgage payment. In any case, the tax assessor is the person who reckons the amount due in terms of his estimate of the value of the property and the prevailing legal rate of tax on such property.

Of the other county offices, there has been much greater variety. Some counties have had tax collectors who receive funds and pay them out. Some have a treasurer who disburses the funds and may collect them as well. Most have an officer designated as "county clerk," but the functions of those holding the office vary considerably. In some, this officer is custodian of records, administers elections, and issues warrants (authorizations) for pay-ments by the county. In some states, the county clerk may be basically a clerk for the courts of the county. In some, he is also the keeper of records, such as deeds, marriages, and the like. He may also serve as auditor, and may even issue passports and naturalization papers. In short, the clerk's work may be a catchall of jobs for which no other official exists. Counties may also have such functionaries as surveyors, engineers, and auditors. Once public education was established by states, most counties have had a county superintendent of education. Counties may also have a board of

education, whose members are elected, as are a majority of superinten-
dents. Counties now have a varied assortment of boards of this, that, and the
other.

c. Municipal Governments

Cities and incorporated towns usually have more independence of the
state government under which they fall than do county governments. Indeed, and as earlier noted, county governments are for many of their functions administrative units of states. In these functions, and for those prescribed for them, they can neither claim nor have any independence.
Further, counties do not have constitutions or charters of their own; they
exist under the state constitution and enactments of the state legislature. By
at least partial contrast, municipalities do have something more nearly resembling a constitution of their own; it is their corporate charter, which
describes the form of the government, the powers to be exercised, and the
functions to be performed.

Even so, cities are creatures of the state in which they are located (and if
the population extended outward from this city should spread into an adjoining state, its authority still ends at the state line). They are limited to the
powers that have been accorded them by the state. Cities have the following
powers, then, according to one legal authority: "First, those granted in
express words; second, those necessarily or fairly implied in or incident to
the powers expressly granted; third, those essential to the accomplishment of
the declared objects and purpose of the corporation—not simply convenient
but indispensable. . . . Neither the corporation nor its officers can do any
act, or make any contract, or incur any liability, not authorized thereby [by
the charter], or by some legislative act applicable thereto. All acts beyond the scope of the powers granted are void."[448] City governments are no
more sovereign than county or other local governments, regardless of how
populous or large they are.

The historic form of city government in the United States was the mayor-
council. It is the system that was first developed in Britain and brought over
and established in this country, and was generally prevalent until the 20th
century. Under this system, the mayor is usually the leading public figure in
city government. The powers of the mayor are within the framework of the
city charter. He is usually elected by the voters within the city for a specific
number of years. The elections may be partisan or non-partisan, depending
on local practice. Ideally, the mayor is the chief executive officer in the city,
seeing to it that the peace is maintained within the city, that the laws are
enforced, and supervising city employees. Depending on the size of the city,
there may be a hierarchy of supervisors under him to see to the day to day
supervising of the work of the city. The mayor appoints officers, but the
approval of the council may be necessary in some cases. The mayor is also

public head of the city and is expected to address or attend a considerable variety of civic functions.

The mayor may also have legislative powers, along with the council. In the mayor-council system, the council's functions are mainly legislative. Traditionally, members of the council have been elected from districts within the city, although at-large, or city-wide, elections have also been used for some or all members. In almost all cases, the council is a one-house legislature, and it is usually a small body. The mayor is often the presiding officer at council meetings. He may propose legislation, have charge of providing a budget, and veto legislation which he disapproves. The formal acts of the city council are called ordinances, but the council also levies taxes, makes appropriations, and may borrow money, all these within rigorous limitations, as a rule. The city clerk usually serves as clerk of the council as well as looking after a variety of other record keeping duties for the city.

Municipalities carry out a considerable variety of activities, and these have tended to be expanded over the years. The powers of the city generally extend to fire and police protection, street maintenance and construction, the providing of fresh water and sewerage facilities, and the collection and disposal of waste. (Whether or not the city actually provides these services, it will usually have some authority over seeing that they are performed.) In addition to these functions, cities also regulate traffic, health, and businesses located within their bounds. Commonly, cities license those who sell goods and provide services within the city. Cities often have their own school systems as well. They often provide hospitals and such facilities as libraries and recreational centers.

Cities usually have some sort of court under their authority. If for no other reason, if they pass ordinances, they must have a court to enforce them. The counterpart to justice of the peace in rural areas for the city is the magistrate court. These courts deal with misdemeanor cases in general and violations of city ordinances in particular. Sometimes cities have specialized courts, such as traffic or police courts, small claims courts, juvenile courts, and the like. Larger cities often have state and Federal courts located in their bounds as well, but these are not under the control of city governments.

Other varieties of city government than the mayor-council system have been developed in the 20th century. The commission system flourished in the early 20th century, but soon began to lose favor. The executive and legislative powers were combined, since commissioners headed departments within the city (as, for example, police commissioner) and comprised the legislature as well. The city manager system within a mayor-council government has fared somewhat better. In this system, the manager performs the administrative functions of city government, but does not participate in making political decisions.

d. Other Local Governments

There are no other local governments than county and city governments that exist in all states and locales. There are several that are widespread in some states or regions. Perhaps the most unusual of these are the New England town. These governmental units occur and are established generally in Connecticut, Massachusetts, Rhode Island, New Hampshire, Vermont, and Maine. These towns may encompass both urban and rural populations and usually cover 20 to 40 square miles of territory. The town government acts under the authority of a *town meeting* which is a direct democracy made up of the voters within the bounds of the city. A town meeting is held annually and all voters may attend, participate in discussions, and vote.

Many decisions are likely to be made at these town meetings. For example, ordinances may be passed, taxes levied, borrowing, if any, may be authorized, and officers for the town elected for the ensuing year. Any sort of business with which the town is involved may be taken up at town meetings, such as, street lights, building and maintenance of roads, the purchasing of property, the salaries of officials, and the like. The most important office is that of *selectman*. There are usually three such officers, and they may be elected at the annual town meeting or in special elections. Selectmen carry on the business of the town between town meetings, doing such things as, issuing licenses, maintaining streets and sewers, awarding contracts, and conducting elections. The town ordinarily has a clerk, a tax assessor, a law enforcement officer known as a constable, a road commissioner, and such other officials as may be needed. New England towns perform the function performed by counties and cities in other areas.

Some states have a level of government that is referred to as a township. Among the states which have some degree of township government here and there or generally are: New York, Pennsylvania, Ohio, Illinois, Indiana, and New Jersey. A township is a division of a county; if it conforms to a surveyor's measurements it is 36 square miles, but no such precision need be involved. Where a township government exists, there may be township meetings to which all voters are invited. In between these, or if no such general meetings are held, a township board exercises such powers of government as the township has. The township government performs at least some of the functions performed by counties for rural areas or by towns in New England. In fact, the form has fallen into disuse in many places where such governments were once active. They were probably much much more vital before the invention of the automobile.

One other area of local government needs to be mentioned. It is that for which the phrase "special district" may be applied. They exist generally for purposes of providing services for given regions or areas, and usually, though not always, involve the providing of a single service. Customarily, some board looks after the providing of this service, such as a water board, a hospital board, a library board, a sanitation board, and so on. School districts have been common also. These districts are usually created because for one reason or another—including the special character of the service— the established governments do not wish to provide the service. They are not so much distinct governments as semi-formal arms of established governments.

The above survey of state and local governments may give some idea of the variety and extent of governments in the United States. It should remind us, too, that state and local governments provided most of the functions of government for Americans going into the 20th century. A general pattern should also emerge from this survey. Historically, local governments were generally the more popular and democratic of governments. The larger the unit of government, and the remoter it was from the generality of the people, the more it depended upon representation and other electoral and appointive devices. An array of governments, each presumably jealous of its own powers and determined to keep other powers from spreading into its jurisdiction, was believed to be one of the best protections against concentrated power and oppression. It makes sense, too, for people are less likely to oppress their neighbors than those remote from them.

Chapter 14
Civil War and Reconstruction: Constitutional Disruption and Restoration

The Civil War was the first major constitutional disruption in United States history. Historians have generalized much about what the Civil War was about and what its consequences were. To some, it was a contest between the power of industrial capital in the North pitted against the slave-holding gentry of the South. Others have seen it in the light of a life and death struggle between the defenders of chattel slavery and equal rights for all men. Lincoln had said that a "house divided against itself cannot stand." More, "I believe this government cannot endure half slave and half free."[449] It is often seen, too, as the triumph of nationalism. These and other views of the source and results of the Civil War each have their own merits. But the main focus here will be upon the impact of the Civil War and its aftermath upon the Constitution: its content, its meaning, and its application or interpretation.

After all, the proximate cause of the conflict was the nature of the Constitution. One view was that the Union had been formed by the voluntary compact of states (confirmed in conventions held by state governments), and states could in like manner voluntarily withdraw (secede) from the Union. The other view was that the Union was a permanent bond of the people of the United States which could be broken or ultimately sustained only by force. Questions of nullification and secession had been raised from time to time, both in the South and in New England, during the first seventy or so years of the Republic under the Constitution of 1787, but no state had taken the fateful step of actually seceding until South Carolina did so in December, 1860. When other states followed suit and formed the Confederate States of America, the Union was faced with accepting a *fait accompli* or using force. When President Lincoln signaled his determination to use force if necessary and Confederate forces fired on a Union stronghold at Fort Sumter, the die was cast.

The decision to use force in an attempt to preserve the Union hardly resolved all constitutional questions; it raised many others. If the Union was permanent, could the government operate legally in the absence of representatives from many states? Would laws passed in their absence be legal? How could war be made against a portion of the people and states of the Union in accord with the prescribed relations of the Constitution? Could the Constitution survive if one portion of the perpetual Union (the Confederate states) repudiated it (though the Confederate Constitution paid it the sincerest form of flattery by imitating it)? If the Confederate states were out of the Union, could they approve amendments to the Constitution? And if they could not approve amendments, how could they be ratified (as the 13th, 14th and 15th Amendments were)? These and many other questions were there to be examined, though little attention was paid to and few thoughtful answers were given to them. At any rate, the Constitution and how it should be interpreted were very much at issue during and in the aftermath of the Civil War.

Indeed, the dominant forces in the Union generally ran roughshod or trampled under foot opposition views on the Constitution. The war freed many elements in the North from the restraints of strict construction of the Constitution which Southern leaders held the country to as long as they were in the Union. Force tended to replace reason in the midst of a fratricidal war, and the Constitution was virtually eclipsed for sixteen years.

a. Republicans in Power

A major shift in power in the country occurred with the secession of the South and the coming of Civil War. A new party, the Lincolnian Republican Party, was born in the 1850s. It was organized at Ripon, Wisconsin in 1854 and generally opposed slavery expansion and favored free (of slaves)-soil policies in the territories. James C. Fremont was Republican candidate for President in 1856, and he came in second to the Democrat James Buchanan. These events marked the demise of the Whig Party and the move to major party standing of the Republicans. From the outset, leading politicians such as Charles Sumner and Salmon P. Chase were drawn to the Republican Party.

The Republican Party was from the outset a regional party. Unlike the Whigs who had preceded it, the Republican Party had no significant support in the South. Indeed, the Republicans made no effort to gain support in the South. "Their tenets were basically anti-Southern. To conservative business interests they talked of the potentialities of the West as a market to replace the South, of Southern extravagance, of the economic weaknesses of slavery, and of the profits to be gained by Republican tariff and internal improvement policies. . . . Abolitionists like George W. Julian believed that the Republican program contemplated the extinction of slavery; Charles Sumner said that the Constitution gave no protection to that hated institution; and William H. Seward told a Boston audience that Lincoln . . . avows himself . . . a soldier on the side of freedom in the irrepressible conflict between freedom and slavery."[450] Lincoln did not get an electoral vote in the South, but he carried every Northern state except New Jersey. The Democratic Party broke up and did not present a united front in 1860, but had it done so, Lincoln would still have won because of his majorities in the North. Even so, the Democrats still had comfortable majorities in the House and Senate. It could be argued that the election of a Republican President should not have driven the South out of the Union; after all, the political tides could shift again. But that would be to argue in the face of what actually happened, a futile undertaking to say the least.

The main point here is not what might have been but what political changes resulted from the withdrawal of the South from the Union. The South generally dominated national politics from 1801 to 1861, or, at least Southerners did. Indeed, Southerners served for approximately 48 years in the presidency from 1789 to 1861. There were only two Chief Justices of the Supreme Court from 1801 to 1864, John Marshall of Virginia and Roger Taney of Maryland (a slave state though it was unable to join the Confederacy because of its location). Southerners served as Speaker of the House of Representatives for approximately 49 years between 1801–1861.

On the face of it, it may not be clear why Southerners should have been so dominant in the government. From the outset the South had a minority of the population in the country. If disfranchised blacks had not been fractionally counted for electoral purposes in the census, their minority status would have been even more pronounced. It was the prominence of Southerners and of the electoral South in the dominant political parties that gave Southerners their political leverage. The Jeffersonian Republican Party and the Jacksonian Democratic Party which succeeded it, were in control of the government for all but a few years from 1801 to 1861. They probably should not be considered distinct parties, but in any case both were national parties, but the mainstay of their strength was the South. Hence, the national policies followed were such as were acceptable generally to Southerners.

Both the Jeffersonians and Jacksonians had been states' rights parties. Both inclined to oppose government intervention in the economy and favored free trade and free markets. Generally, too, the Jeffersonians and Jacksonians opposed a protective tariff, a national bank, Federal appropriations for internal improvements, and supported hard money. They favored a frugal government, the paying off of debts, and living within their means. The Democratic Party was protective toward the institution of slavery in the 1840s and 1850s.

While the Republican platform of 1860 did not come out in favor of the abolition of slavery, did not even condemn the Fugitive Slave Act or slavery in the District of Columbia, it did reaffirm its opposition to slavery expansion in the territories. It denied that Congress had the authority "to give legal assistance to slavery in the territories," viewed with horror the illegal reopening of the slave trade, and once again demanded the admission of Kansas to the Union as a free state. In contrast to the platform of 1856, it came out in favor of a protective tariff, declaring that duties should be adjusted so as "to encourage the development of industrial interests of the whole country."[451] It opposed any change in the naturalization laws, i. e., favored a liberal immigration policy, and came out for a new homestead law which would make government land available virtually free. Or, as one contemporary newspaper expressed it, the platform offered protection for industry, "economy in the conduct of the government, homesteads for settlers on the public domain . . . , appropriations for rivers and harbors, the admission of Kansas [as a free state], and a radical reform in the government."[452]

The secession of eleven slave states from the United States left the control of the government of the Union in the control of the Republican Party, as their Senators and Representatives returned home. Their control was further consolidated during Reconstruction, mainly by Congressional dictation of the readmission of the Southern states to the Union. Not until 1884 was another Democrat, Grover Cleveland, elected to the presidency, and he was the only one to serve (if Andrew Johnson be excepted) from 1861 to 1913. One or the other houses of Congress was from time to time Democratic, but in general Republicans dominated the government from the Civil War to World War I.

The Republicans in power took full advantage of the absence of Southern representatives during the war. While there is hyperbole in his summation, there is a kernel of truth too in Wilbur Cash's harsh assessment of Northern aims in the following statement: "The Civil War and Reconstruction represent in their primary aspect an attempt on the part of the Yankee to achieve by political means: first, a free hand in the nation for the thievish aims of the tariff gang, and secondly, and far more fundamentally, the satisfaction of the instinctive urge of men in the mass to put down whatever differs from themselves. . . ."[453]

Whether the aims were thievish or not, the Southern representatives were hardly out of Congress before the movement was afoot to adopt a fullfledged protective tariff. It came to fruition in the Tariff Act of 1862, which "increased the rates on articles of non-American production, gave protective increases in the case of many articles which could not be produced at home, and greatly reduced the free list."[454] Tariffs reached a wartime peak after the passage of the Tariff Act of 1864. The average of duties on imports was 47 per cent and some rose as high as 100 per cent.[455]

Nor was Congress any slower in getting around to authorizing the building of a railroad to the Pacific. Federal corporations, subsequently named the Union Pacific and Central Pacific railroads, were authorized to build and operate the roads. Large inducements were offered to the builders of the road, first in 1862, and then by another act in 1864. Among the inducements were the full use of the power of the Federal government to obtain rights of way: the extinguishment of any Indian titles to land along the route, the availability of armed forces to drive off trespassing Indians, the use of eminent domain for acquiring land which could not be bought. In addition, large land grants were made to the railroads and millions of dollars in bonds floated by the government to pay for construction.[456] However, only limited construction took place during the Civil War.

A Homstead Act providing virtual free farmsites on public land was passed in 1862. This action had been in the works for years, but Southern political leaders mostly opposed it and managed to defeat it in Congress. A bill was actually passed in 1860, but was vetoed by President Buchanan. The absence of Southern Congressmen made it possible to pass a new bill, and Lincoln signed it into law in 1862. The act offered 160 acres of surveyed public domain lands to citizen (or those intending to become) heads of household if they would occupy it continuously for five years. The only charge would be a registration fee of approximately $30. The land could be owned free and clear in 6 months of residence for $1.25 per acre, if the occupant so chose.

Another act that had been delayed or turned back earlier by Southerners and Democrats was the Morrill Land Grant Act of 1862. An earlier version had been vetoed by President Buchanan on the grounds that it was unconstitutional, and the attempt failed to pass it over his veto. The act as finally passed called for the granting of Federal lands to the states to be sold to provide a fund to establish and maintain agricultural and mechanical colleges. Each state was to receive 30,000 acres of land for each of its Representatives and Senators, thus the more populous states got the most land. The power of the Federal government was used extensively to influence the character of college education. Republican Presidents of this era concerned themselves less and less about the constitutionality of acts that came before them.

This became much clearer in the methods used to finance the war by the Union. One of these was an income tax law passed in August, 1861. It levied a 3 per cent tax on all incomes in excess of $800. It was about as clear as such things can ever be that this act provided for a "direct tax" in violation of constitutional prescription regarding such an act. Section 9, Article I of the Constitution contains this provision: "No Capitation, or other direct, Tax shall be laid, unless in proportion to the Census herein before directed to be taken." The income tax law did not levy the tax in proportion to the census, but to income. As if that were not sufficiently contrary to the Constitution, by 1864 the tax had become progressive or graduated, ranging from 5 per cent to 7½ to 10 per cent. The thrust of the Constitution was to require uniformity of tax rates, and graduated taxes violated that as well. The tax was never successfully challenged, but it was dropped in 1872.

The tender laws passed in 1862 and afterward were contrary to the understanding of the Constitution that had prevailed until that time. The Legal Tender Act passed in February, 1862, authorized the issuance of $150 million of paper money, known as Greenbacks. These notes were made legal tender for all debts public and private, although they were not redeemable in specie at the time, nor on any day certain in the future. They were, in effect, *fiat* money, i. e., money by government decree. All told, acts of Congress authorized the issue of $450 million in these Greenbacks during the course of the war. The Constitution prohibits the states to make anything but gold and silver legal tender, and does not authorize Congress to pass tender laws or issue paper money. The matter came up at the Constitutional Convention, and the power to do these things was deliberately deleted from the Constitution, and the understanding was that Congress had no such power.

The Supreme Court ruled on the first legal tender case, *Hepburn vs. Griswold* in 1870. Chief Justice Salmon Chase, speaking for a majority of the Court, declared the Legal Tender Act unconstitutional, especially as it applied to contracts entered into before the passage of the act. He focused upon the violation of contracts as the major issue involved. Three justices dissented from the majority opinion. In 1871, following the appointment of two new justices by President Ulysses Grant, justices known to be favorably disposed to the tender laws, the Court reversed itself and declared the laws constitutional by a margin of 5 to 3. Justice William Strong, one of the men appointed by Grant most recently, wrote the majority opinion which relied heavily on the broad construction premises first advanced by Alexander Hamilton and later enunciated by Chief Justice Marshall on the Supreme Court. He argued that if the Legal Tender laws were necessary and proper to carrying out the objects of government, and not otherwise prohibited, they were constitutional. He also advanced the notion of the ongoing civil war as justifying such measures. "It was," he said, "at such a time and in such an emergency that the Legal Tender Acts were passed."

Four justices, including Chief Justice Chase, dissented from the majority decision. Justice Stephen Field, who dissented vigorously, indicated that he resented strongly the intimation that to oppose the tender laws was to oppose the cause of the Union for which they were supposedly passed. "But I do not admit," Field said, "that a blind approval of every measure which they may have thought essential to put down the rebellion is any evidence of loyalty to the country. The only loyalty which I can admit consists in obedience to the Constitution and laws made in pursuance of it."[457] Arguments about the constitutionality of laws in the courts were shifting away from the document itself toward the desirability and practicality of the laws themselves. Indeed, the majority in this case not only did not closely tie the act to any provision of the Constitution but also overturned a precedent of the Court which was only a year old.

As noted earlier, the Jeffersonians had questioned both the desirability and the constitutionality of excises, and, in power, they had either repealed or allowed them to expire. They were now revived with a passion during the Civil War. As one history says, "The internal revenue law of July 1, 1862, has been broadly described as an attempt to tax everything. With regard to a carriage, for instance, the leather, cloth, wood, and metal would be taxed as raw materials; the manufacturer was taxed for selling the carriage; and the purchaser, having paid a price sufficient to cover these various levies, was taxed in addition for its ownership."[458] Indeed, the goods and services taxed ranged from hemp to insurance to telegrams to sheep to pawn brokers to jugglers. The law covered so many items that it went on for over 20,000 words. Unconstitutional or not, the power of the government of the Union was being greatly expanded into new realms.

A national banking system was created during the war. The law that authorized this system was proposed by the then Secretary of the Treasury, Salmon P. Chase, and promoted in the Senate by John Sherman of Ohio. The first of the National Bank Acts was passed in 1863, but it was so unsuccessful in getting a program underway that the law was revised and restated in the National Bank Act of 1864. This act did result in a national banking system, consisting of national banks in various parts of the country chartered by the United States and supervised by the Treasury. They were banks of issue from the outset, that is, they issued national bank notes, which were intended to serve as currency or money. Every bank was required to purchase at least $30,000 of United States bonds, thus providing money for the operation of the government of the Union. The National Banks were authorized to issue bank notes up to 90% of the face value of the United States bonds it held. The maximum amount of National Bank notes in circulation was fixed at $300 million. State banks were invited to join the national banking system, but they did not rush to do so. Then Congress moved in 1865 to make state banking charters much less attractive. It voted to levy a 10% Federal tax on state bank note issues. This tax effectively drove the state chartered banks out of the business of issuing bank notes.

The question of the constitutionality of nationally chartered banks did not agitate the country at this time or later. It probably stood where it had always stood, on the margin of constitutionality. The Supreme Court had earlier ruled that the United States bank was constitutional, not on the basis of any enumerated power, but as a means to achieve ends that were enumerated. The new National Banks might be fitted under this umbrella as well. There were, however, two matters connected with the National Bank acts which did come before the Supreme Court. One was the ten per cent Federal tax on state bank notes. It may be recalled that in our earlier history when Maryland had levied a tax on United States bank notes issued in that state, Chief Justice Marshall, speaking for the Court, had declared the Maryland act null and void and not to be enforced. He had argued that the power to tax is the power to destroy and that an installation of the United States could not be thus taxed. The reverse of that argument might well have been made in defense of state organizations. It was made, at least in part, by arguments before the Supreme Court, but to no avail.

In *Veazie Bank vs. Fenno,* handed down in 1869, Chief Justice Chase, speaking for a majority of the Court, declared the tax to be constitutional. The Court was not greatly moved by the argument that the tax was a direct tax and thus unconstitutional. Chase admitted confusion existed as to exactly what was a direct tax, but had no difficulty in concluding that the tax under consideration "is not, in the sense of the Constitution, a direct tax." He thought that it should, instead, be classed as a "duty," though even a glance at a dictionary should have convinced him otherwise. On the question of whether the tax was so great as to destroy "a franchise of the state," which is how Chase phrased the question, he thought that was beyond the jurisdiction of the Court to determine. He put it this way, "The first answer to this is that the judicial cannot prescribe to the legislative department of the government limitations upon the exercise of its acknowledged powers." He went on to make it appear that it was virtually the duty of Congress in view of its constitutional powers to prevent the circulation of state bank notes. In support of that, he argued that "it is settled by the uniform practice of the government and by repeated decisions, that Congress may constitutionally authorize the emission of bills of credit." This being the case, according to Chief Justice Chase, the Federal government may occupy the field of the issuance of paper money. Two justices dissented from the majority opinion.[459]

The Chief Justice and a majority of the Court had virtually moved out of the frame of the Constitution. Government practice does not determine what is constitutional nor could any number of court decisions prove what is contrary to fact—i. e., that Congress could constitutionally authorize the emission of bills of credit. In fact, state governments are prohibited to issue bills of credit, i. e., paper money, by the Constitution. That being so, they could not authorize banks they chartered to do so. In the second place, the Constitutional Convention deliberately omitted the granting of power to Congress to emit bills of credit, under the understanding it could not then do so. The evidence for this the Court did not bother to examine.

The other matter regarding the national banking acts came before the Supreme Court in the 1880s. Although the Court had already reviewed legal tender cases several times, yet another case came before it under the title *Julliard vs. Greenman.* An act of Congress passed in 1878 required that the Greenbacks issued during the Civil War be kept in circulation as legal tender. The constitutionality of this act was challenged. The Supreme Court announced its opinion without hearing any public arguments on the one side or the other. Justice Horace Gray spoke for the majority of the Court. His conclusion is so broad that it warrants quoting in some detail:

Congress, as the legislature of a sovereign nation, being expressly empowered by the Constitution, "to lay and collect taxes, to pay the debts and provide for the common defense and general welfare of the United States," and "to borrow money on the credit of the United States," and "to coin money and regulate the value thereof and of foreign coin;" and being clearly authorized, as incidental to the exercise of those great powers, to emit bills of credit, to charter national banks, and to provide a national currency for the whole people, in the form of coin, treasury notes, and national bank bills; and the power to make the notes of the government a legal tender in payment of private debts being one of the powers belonging to sovereignty in other civilized nations, and not expressly withheld from Congress by the Constitution; we are irresistibly impelled to the conclusion that the impressing upon the treasury notes of the United States the quality of being a legal tender in payment of private debts is an appropriate means . . . consistent with the letter and spirit of the Constitution. . . .

Justice Field dissented, as well he might. Constitutional historian Charles Warren declared that this decision was "the most sweeping opinion as to the extent of Congressional power which had ever heretofore been rendered." Many members of Congress were so taken aback by the decision that they introduced a number of bills limiting the power of Congress in the matter of legal tender.[460]

The dean of American historians, George Bancroft, though he was eighty-four years old at the time of the decision, wrote a crisp and succinct analysis of evidence to prove that the majority of the Court were wrong. He said that if the interpretation in *Julliard vs. Greenman* were accepted as law, "it would be a death blow to the constitution."[461] Professor Bancroft then proceeded to present the evidence that refutes the 1884 decision. The record, he says, is clear both from the secretary of the Constitutional Convention's minutes and from James Madison's extensive report that the power to emit bills of credit was deliberately deleted from the Constitution to the end that Congress should have no such power. He sums up the matter this way: "Eleven men took part in the discussion; and every one of the eleven, whether he spoke for or against the grant of the power, Gouverneur Morris, Pierce Butler, James Madison, Nathaniel Gorham, George Mason, John F. Mercer, Oliver Ellsworth, Edmund Randolph, James Wilson, George Reed, and John Langdon, each and all, understood the vote to be a denial to the legislature of the United States of the power to emit paper money. . . . The evidence is perfect; no power to emit paper money was granted to the legislature of the United States."[462]

No more does the Constitution contain any grant of power to the Federal government to make any thing legal tender. The power is specifically denied to the states to make anything except gold or silver legal tender. Power is granted to the United States to coin money, but no power was granted or is ordinarily necessary to make the coins circulate. In short, the Supreme Court had gone beyond its authority in reaching its conclusion.

b. Conduct of the War and Presidential Reconstruction

It is undoubtedly the case that the Constitution does not contemplate civil war in the United States nor prescribe rules by which it is to be conducted. It is true also that the Constitution does not contemplate the use of force by the government of the Union against the elected and established government of a state. The Constitution does authorize the declaration of war by Congress, the raising of armed forces, and for the President to be commander-in-chief. Since Congress was authorized to raise armies, probably no sound argument could have been made at the time of the Civil War that Congress could not conscript men to serve in the army. However, it can be reasonably argued that Congress no longer had the power to conscript after December, 1865, when the 13th Amendment was added to the Constitution. The amendment prohibits involuntary servitude, except for convicts, and when a person is forced to serve that is, in the nature of things, involuntary servitude.

Many of those who have written about the Civil War have glossed over many of the questions of constitutionality that the Civil War raised. Some have sided with Lincoln, holding that the Union is insoluable and should be held together by major force, if necessary. Some—many—have believed that the South was wrong and deserved to be overwhelmed and set straight. Or their apologia or justification for the war may have taken some other turn. In any case, they tended to excuse, explain away, justify, or ignore the unconstitutionality of the war and its conduct. Twentieth century writers tend to treat the constitutional questions pragmatically. Thus, they say, or imply, that the consequences were desirable; hence the methods and tactics were justified, much as later Congresses who passed draft laws have ignored the 13th Amendment.

But if the Constitution is the most basic and fundamental law of that land, which is the position being maintained here, acts of the United States government have no justification outside of its authority. The Civil War was, so far as can be determined by examining the Constitution, unconstitutional. Force against a single or combination of state governments is not authorized by it. More, Congress did not declare war against the Confederacy. To have done so would, of course, have been to treat the states of the Confederacy as a foreign nation, and, if that were the case, the Union had been dissolved, and the occasion for using force had been removed. Technically, Lincoln maintained that the states that composed the Confederacy were still in the

Union, though in a state of rebellion. But the people in the states of the Confederacy were not in rebellion against their most fundamental governments—the state. Lincoln was consistent with his most basic premise in maintaining that the states were still in the Union. But his position posed quite difficult problems for the conduct of the war. If the people in the "so-called Confederacy" were still a part of the United States then they deserved the full protection of the United States government in the enjoyment of their rights to life, liberty, and property, in sum, their full constitutional rights. But it is hardly possible to make war on those terms.

War is not, after all, a peaceful, genteel, quiet, and sanitary operation, conducted according to the rules of the Marquis of Queensbury. On the contrary, it is violent, destructive, and at its best a forceful attempt to overcome and overwhelm the enemy. It is indeed possible that war could be conducted against a foreign nation by the United States without too obvious a strain on the Constitution, but Civil War overstepped those bounds drastically and at once, as already noted. It might be supposed, then, that since the very fact of the Union's making war on the Confederacy was so constitutionally questionable, those in control of the government and military power of the Union would make every effort to fastidiously observe the constitutional limit in all other respects during the course of the war. Efforts were undoubtedly made along these lines from time to time in the course of the conflict, but speaking in large, they greatly expanded the reach and extent of Federal power rather than observing the limits. The Constitution was early and late one of the major victims of the war. Moreover, it was ultimately a most uncivil war rather than being a *civil* war. It was the most devastating and destructive war ever fought on the continents of North and South America, so far back as any records go, and the Union military methods in 1864 and 1865 were a foreshadowing of the total wars of the 20th century. That is how remote it became from the limits and restraints of the United States Constitution.

Abraham Lincoln set the pattern of going beyond the bounds of the Constitution and expanding presidential power from the outset. He plunged the United States into war without the aid or guidance of Congress. The attack by the Confederacy on Fort Sumter began on April 12, 1861. On April 15, Lincoln called upon the governors of the states to provide 75,000 troops. On the same day, he called a special session of Congress, but it was not to convene until July 4, which was an unseemly delay, considering the circumstances. Meanwhile, Lincoln went about the business of preparing for and making war. He determined that the Confederate states were in rebellion, proclaimed a blockade of their ports, called up volunteers for three-year terms of service, thus greatly expanding the Army. "He also directed that large additions be made to the regular army and to the navy. He had two million dollars paid out of the federal treasury, and he pledged the government's credit for the unprecedented sum of a quarter of a billion dollars, all without statutory authority."[463] More, he suspended the writ of habeas corpus on his own, as earlier recounted, and used military detention for civilians. And, Lincoln got away with it, too.

Confronted by a *fait accompli* when it did assemble, Congress accepted what Lincoln had done, as well as such justifications as he saw fit to offer. In effect, Lincoln argued that in view of the situation he had not exceeded the powers granted to Congress (an exceedingly strange interpretation of the separation of powers) and trusted they would ratify them at a later date. He further argued that the President being charged with preserving the Constitution could assume whatever powers were necessary to do that. Indeed, Congress did cover Lincoln's actions after the fact on several occasions, by passing tardy laws. A new sort of *ex post facto* law emerged during the war, though such laws are specifically prohibited in the Constitution. The form of such acts was sometimes curious, to say the least. At the special session in 1861, for example, Congress approved an assortment of presidential acts, declaring them "in all respects legalized and made valid, to the same intent and with the same effect as if they had been issued and done under the previous express authority and direction of the Congress."[464]

A great centralization of governmental authority in the government of the United States took place during the Civil War as well as concentration of power in the President. The President used the military extensively, especially in the Border States—i.e., slave states that did not secede from the Union, namely, Missouri, Kentucky, Maryland, and Delaware—to maintain such authority as he wished to be exercised. He also used the military for that purpose in some of the conquered parts of the Confederacy.

One of the more obvious violations of the Constitution was the separation of West Virginia from Virginia. When Virginia seceded from the Union in 1861, representatives from the mountainous section of western Virginia met in convention at Wheeling and organized a Union government. The territory under the control of this government was admitted to the Union as West Virginia in 1863. The Constitution specifically provides that "no new States shall be formed or erected within the jurisdiction of any other State. . . ." No matter, to the Republicans who dominated Congress, or to the President; it was useful to the Union cause to have West Virginia, so it became a state.

Congress passed at least two acts providing for the confiscation of the property of rebels, traitors, and the like. Lincoln himself had grave questions about the constitutionality of the Second Confiscation Act, because it did not provide for due process of law, among other things. But he overcame his qualms and signed it nonetheless. Such laws were rarely enforced during the war, in any case, by civilian courts, because no such courts sat where most of these cases would have been tried. Much more serious was the extensive use of military tribunals for the trial of civilians. This occurred mainly in Border states and occupied territory, but it also extended even into loyal states. The constitutionality of this is highly questionable.

A much more volatile issue at the time, however, was Lincoln's Emancipation Proclamation which was proclaimed to be in effect on January 1, 1863. It began with the statement, after the preliminaries, "That on the 1st day of January, A.D., 1863, all persons held as slaves within any State, or designated part of a State the people whereof shall then be in rebellion against the United States shall be then, thenceforward, and forever free. . . ."[465] First, it should be emphasized that this order then freed slaves only in areas where the Confederates were in power—which is to say, it freed none at the time. Second, he justified it as a war measure for suppressing rebellion. Third, in the last paragraph of the Proclamation, Lincoln declared that it was "an act of justice, warranted by the Constitution upon military necessity. . . ."

So far as can be determined, no actions are authorized in the Constitution under the rubric of "war measures" or "military necessity." In a strict view of the Constitution, slaves were at that time property of their owners, and they were no more subject to be taken or disposed of by the government without just compensation than any other property. Even if such an act were constitutional, Congress had not passed such an act. Indeed, Lincoln did not pretend to have such authority; the Proclamation was a presidential decree in his capacity as commander-in-chief. In fact, Lincoln had expressed himself on many occasions as in favor of compensating the slave owners. In a message to Congress in December, 1862, he had said: "In a certain sense the liberation of slaves is the destruction of property—property acquired by descent or by purchase, the same as any other property."[466] And, as late as February, 1865, when he met with delegates seeking peace from the Confederacy, one biographer says: "Lincoln let it be known that he still favored compensation to owners of emancipated slaves. It had never been his intention to interfere with slavery in the states; he had been driven to it by necessity, he explained. He believed that the people of the North and South were equally responsible for slavery, and if hostilities should cease and the states would voluntarily abolish slavery, he thought the government should indemnify the owners—to the extent, possibly, of $400,000,000."[467] It was not to be, of course; Lincoln's own Cabinet would not support the idea. Whatever his motive for pushing compensation, the result, if achieved, would have provided *ex post facto* justification for his Emancipation Proclamation. That was achieved after his death anyway, by the 13th Amendment.

But the most drastic and sustained violation of the letter and spirit of the Constitution is almost never discussed in that light. It was the vast and expansive destruction of private property in the South. Wars tend to be destructive of property, in any case, and that is especially so in the areas where most of the battles and the war is fought. In fact, virtually all of the battles of the Civil War were fought either in the Border states or the states of the Confederacy. It should not have come as any surprise, then, that the most damage from fighting occurred in the South. There is always incidental damage to civilians and private property in such warfare, too. For example, if troops take refuge in private buildings, artillery and mortar fire may be directed at the buildings to get at the troops. Such destruction is incidental to warfare, unfortunate but understandable, and a just subject for indemnities to be paid to those harmed. But it is neither the destruction incident to warfare nor the fact that territory in the path of battles is apt to suffer the greatest ravages of war that is the focus of attention here.

Rather, it was the deliberate and determined destruction of privately owned civilian property and the taking of private property for public use on a vast scale without compensation that is being described here as done in contempt of the Constitution. Probably, the most direct violations of the Constitution are contained in the prohibitions of the 3rd, 4th, and 5th Amendments. The 3rd says, "No Soldier shall, in time of peace be quartered in any house without the consent of the Owner, nor in time of war, but in a manner to be prescribed by law." The 4th declares, "The right of the people to be secure in their persons, houses, papers, and effects, against unreasonable searches and seizures, shall not be violated. . . ." The 5th says, in part, "No person shall be . . . deprived of . . . property, without due process of law; nor shall private property be taken for public use, without just compensation." It may be that such violations may well occur as incidental to the conduct of war, but it is not these that are the focus of attention here.

The most notorious of these infamous waves of destruction in which virtually everything in the path of advancing armies was laid waste and/or burned was General William T. Sherman's march from Atlanta to Savannah in late 1864 and the subsequent march through South Carolina in early 1865. This was preceded, however, by his forced evacuation of the inhabitants of Atlanta, mostly women and children, and then the burning of the city. His proposal to expel the inhabitants of the city brought horrified responses from the Confederate General John B. Hood, who was in command of the army that had been thereabouts, and Mayor Calhoun of Atlanta. General Hood expressed his horror in a letter to Sherman, saying to him: "You order into exile the whole population of a city; drive men, women, and children from their homes at the point of the bayonet, under the plea that it is to the interest of your Government. . . . You issue a sweeping edict, covering all the inhabitants of a city, and add insult to the injury heaped upon the defenseless by assuming that you have done them a kindness. . . ." The Mayor of Atlanta begged Sherman to reconsider and take into account the fate of these people. He pointed out that as the Union army drove into Atlanta from the north, many of the inhabitants had retreated into Atlanta and then gone farther south, "so that the country south of this is already crowded, and without houses enough to accommodate the people, and we are informed that many are now staying in churches and other outbuildings. This being so, how is it possible for the people still here (mostly women and children) to find any shelter? And how can they live through the winter [it was already the middle of September]—no shelter or subsistence . . . ?''

As for the opinions of General Hood, Sherman said he had no interest in pleasing him. To the Mayor of Atlanta he wrote: "Now you must go, and take with you the old and feeble, feed and nurse them, and build for them . . . proper habitations to shield them against the weather. . . ." After driving the people from their homes in Atlanta, Sherman's army remained until early November, when it embarked on the march to Savannah. But first, whatever had not already been destroyed in the city was burned. As the army departed, "Behind us lay Atlanta, smouldering and in ruins, the black smoke rising high in air, and hanging like a pall over the ruined city."

Before leaving the city, Sherman issued his marching orders. The army was to live off the stores of the inhabitants along the way. Organized foraging parties were to take "corn or forage of any kind, meat of any kind, vegetables, corn-meal, or whatever is needed. . . . Soldiers . . . may be permitted to gather turnips, potatoes, and other vegetables, and to drive in stock in sight of their camps. . . ." Otherwise, foraging was to be left to organized parties. Corps commanders had "the power to destroy mills, houses, cotton gins, etc.," but they should refrain from doing this unless they encountered resistance or sabotage, "then army commanders should order and enforce a devastation more or less relentless, according to the measure of such hostility." Of course, calvary and artillery units and foraging parties could take "horses, mules, wagons, etc., belonging to the inhabitants . . . , freely and without limit," and any "Negroes who are able-bodied and can be of service. . . ." If the officer in command "thinks [it] proper," they can itemize what was taken on paper, "but [give] no receipts. . . ."[468]

These brutal orders to plunder, destroy, and steal the portable goods were modified by various cautions and restrictions, such as not to be abusive toward the inhabitants, but so far as destruction in Georgia or South Carolina, there is little evidence that Sherman or his officers exercised much restraint on their troops. Sherman's army cut a swath from 30 to 60 miles wide along the 300 miles from Atlanta to Savannah. Railroad tracks and stock were systematically destroyed, the rails ripped from the cross-ties, heated, and twisted around trees. Cotton gins and all sorts of machinery and buildings having to do with cotton were destroyed. "Public buildings were often destroyed; foodstores were taken, horses, mules, and livestock were removed. . . . Dwellings were needlessly burned; family plate was seized; wine cellars were raided; property that could not be carried away was wantonly ruined." A newspaper report at the time pictures this condition along Sherman's route: "Dead horses, cows, sheep, hogs, chickens, corn wheat, cotton, books, paper, broken vehicles, coffee-mills, and fragments of nearly every species of property that adorned the beautiful farms of this county, strew the wayside. . . ."[469]

If anything, the attack on property in South Carolina was even more ferocious than in Georgia. A biographer says, "Sherman's boys hit South Carolina like a horde of avenging Goths. . . . Sherman entered Columbia on February 17. That night the city burned. . . . Major James Austin Connolly wrote to his wife in Ohio: 'The army burned everything it came near in the State of South Carolina, not under orders, but in spite of orders. . . . Our track through the State is a desert waste. Since entering North Carolina the wanton destruction has stopped.' ''[470] How the plundering and terror could happen at the home level is told in the following account by a South Carolina lady:

> A crowd has burst in and, disregarding our remonstrances, spread themselves over everything, and from that time until morning a roaring stream of drunkards poured through the house, plundering and raging. . . . Unhappily, they found plenty to plunder, for . . . I had in charge a number of trunks belonging to friends of mine, which were in the house. These they fell upon and tore to pieces. . . .
>
> They generally spoke to us as "lady" and, although they swore horribly, they seldom swore *at us*. Then, too, if a number of men were fighting over a trunk or a closet, spoiling more than they stole, and I would go and stand by, not saying a word, but looking on, they would become quiet, would cease plundering, and would sometimes stop to tell me they were sorry for the women and children but South Carolina must be destroyed.[471]

Sherman's was not the only Union army that was deliberately destructive. The Shenandoah Valley of Virginia was not only the scene of many battles and shifts in military control but also large scale deliberate destruction. The work of destruction was that of General Philip Sheridan, though it was on orders from General Grant. In September, 1864 Grant wrote Sheridan to "Take all provisions, forage, wanted for the use of your command; such as cannot be consumed destroy. . . . The people should be informed that so long as an army can subsist among them recurrences of these raids must be expected, and we are determined to stop them at all hazards." In October, General Stephen D. Ramseur of North Carolina wrote his wife: "The beautiful & fertile valley has been totally destroyed. Sheridan had some of the houses, *all* of the mills and barns, every straw stack & wheat stack burned. We have to haul our supplies from far up the valley."[472] A later historian noted that Sheridan had "burned or carried off so much that he was able to boast that a 'crow flying over the country would need to carry his rations.' ''[473]

But the destruction of property was by no means restricted to Sherman's marches and Sheridan's depredations. Wherever Union armies had gone they had devastated the areas. "Tennessee and Mississippi lay in ruins wherever armies had marched. Alabama claimed destructions amounting to

$300,000,000, and the cane planters alone in Louisiana suffered losses set at $100,000,000. . . . War passed through the streets of Fredericksburg and of Petersburg [in Virginia], and down in Alabama Selma lay in ashes. Over in Mississippi the little college town Oxford had one business house left standing when the Surrender came. And so the story went. . . ."[474] Farming country had been no less devastated; cattle, sheep, and horses had been driven away." The master of one of the best plantations in Mississippi had returned to find only a few mules and one cow left. Houses, fences, and barns, destroyed. . . ."[475]

The point is that the taking of and destruction of property by the Union went far beyond anything incidental to the fighting of the war or that might be occasioned by the exigencies of the war. In any case, such actions were clearly in violation of the Constitution and most of them in violation of the rules of civilized warfare. There can be no talk of the end justifying the means in constitutional terms. The Constitution deals almost exclusively with means; if the end justified the means, the Constitution would be superfluous. Nor was this vast taking and destruction of property ever made even partially right by indemnifying those who had lost property. Instead, the losses were to continue for some during portions of Reconstruction, and new penalties were imposed.

This last might not have occurred much longer if Lincoln had lived or President Andrew Johnson who succeeded him could have had his way. Lincoln's plan for reconstruction had been in place since 1863, and he never wavered from it. In keeping with his concept of an indissoluble Union, Lincoln held that the states had never left the Union. That being the case, all that was needed was to bring them back into a proper relation with the Union. To achieve this, he proposed to give amnesty to Southerners, with some exceptions, who would take an oath of loyalty to the Union. When 10% of those who were eligible to vote in 1860 should take an oath of loyalty, and when the state had authorized the freeing of the slaves, they could then take up their place in the Union as soon as the House of Representatives accepted their representatives. Before Lincoln was assassinated, Loyal governments had been organized in Tennessee, Virginia, Arkansas, and Louisiana, though none had representatives in Congress. Congress had tried to take over direction of reconstruction by the Wade-Davis bill passed in 1864, but Lincoln gave it a pocket-veto. From the outset, Congress tended to favor harder or even harsher terms for reconstruction than did Lincoln, and this attitude was solidified by the assassination of Lincoln.

Johnson was committed to carrying out the main outlines of Lincoln's reconstruction programs. When Congress later balked, he explained the reasoning on which the program was based:

> It is clear to my apprehension that the States lately in rebellion are still members of the National Union. When did they cease to be so?

The "ordinances of secession" adopted by a portion . . . of their
citizens were mere nullities. If we admit now that they were valid and
effectual for the purpose intended by their authors, we sweep from
under our feet the whole ground upon which we justified the war. Were
those States afterward expelled from the Union by the war? The direct
contrary we averred [affirmed] by this Government to be its purpose,
and was so understood by all those who gave their blood and treasure
to aid in its prosecution. It can not be that a successful war, waged for
the preservation of the Union, had the legal effect of dissolving it. The
victory of the nation's arms was not the disgrace of her policy; the
defeat of secession on the battlefield was not the triumph of its lawless
principle. . . .[476]

In some respects, Johnson appeared to be somewhat tougher than Lincoln. His Proclamation of Amnesty in May, 1865, excluded from its provisions all Confederates with a wealth of $20,000 or more. Actually, how-
ever, the program was modelled on that of Lincoln. Congress was not in
session when the war ended and Johnson did not call a special session.
Instead, he proceeded with reconstruction. State conventions were called by
state citizens who had professed their loyalty to the Union. These conventions reversed the procedure of secession, annulled it, abolished slavery, and
in most cases repudiated debts contracted in the fighting of the war. Legislatures were then chosen, and these ratified the 13th Amendment. All the
states but Texas had met these conditions when Congress met in December
of 1865.

Congress proceeded to bring to nought what Johnson had accomplished,
and to impose its harsh program for reconstruction upon the South. Undoubtedly, what Johnson had done lacked legislative authority and had no
Constitutional authorization. Much of what Congress would then do had
even less Constitutional authority, though some of it would have got *ex post
facto* authority in constitutional amendments. Congress and the President
were at loggerheads from 1865 to the end of Johnson's term in 1869.
Historians have speculated that Lincoln would have fared much better had
he lived, but we have no way of knowing that. Johnson certainly had two
strikes against him when he came up to the presidential plate, to use a
baseball analogy. He was born in North Carolina, and his political career
was based in Tennessee. As if that were not bad enough, he was a Democrat
by party. He may have made up for some of this in the eyes of many
Republicans by being a Union man and refusing to join the secessionists. He
had been elected Vice President on a Union ticket with Lincoln, but he was
not a Republican, and he was not a Yankee. Southern Democrats disowned
him, of course, and he was never able to develop a large political base of his
own. In any case, Presidential Reconstruction had failed.

c. Congressional Reconstruction

The Republicans in Congress virtually took over the government in the late 1860s, and their policies drove Reconstruction from 1866 to 1877. They did their best to reduce President Johnson to a functionary, and would have removed him from office if they could. They intimidated the Federal courts, and to all intents and purposes broke the independence of the Southern states. The South was subjected to military occupation during much of the period from 1866 to 1877. The instrument by which Presidential Reconstruction was undone was the refusal to recognize the reconstructed states and their representatives by the House. When the roll of representatives was called in the House, not a single representative from the former Confederate states was called. Presidential Reconstruction could not enable the states to take their place in the Union. That much was constitutional, since Congress has the power to determine the qualification of its members. Much that followed, however, was of doubtful constitutionality, or worse.

The next step in the move toward a takeover by Congress was the formation of a Committee of Fifteen. This was a joint committee to overlook Reconstruction, consisting of 9 Representatives and 6 Senators. All resolutions and bills having to do with reconstruction were to be referred to this joint committee. The committee was made up of Republicans, several of whom were quite radical. Among its members were Thaddeus Stevens, George W. Julian, Benjamin F. Wade, George S. Boutwell, and Benjamin F. Butler. Such a committee almost certainly violated the spirit, if not the letter, of the Constitution, since it tended to forge unity of action by the two houses rather for each of them to act independently as the Constitution provides.

There is no doubt that in the course of 1866 Congress changed the character of the thrust of Reconstruction, changed it from a program of forging the Union anew to a broad-scaled attempt to make over the South. This thrust was the work of men known as Radical Republicans. The strength of the Radicals lay in the fact that they had a purpose and a cause. Theirs was a righteous cause, in their opinion, to avenge the Union soldiers who had died in the war, to punish the South, to not only free the slaves but to elevate them to a condition of equality with whites, and to remake the South so that the rebellious spirit could never again arise there. The Committee of Fifteen funneled the programs through Congress; the Radical Republicans pressed their passage, and the desire to make over the South had intellectual support as well in the North. James Russell Lowell, the poet, thought the South should be "Americanized." "Is it not time," he asked, "that these men be transplanted at least into the nineteenth century, and, if they cannot be suddenly Americanized, made to understand something of the country which was too good for them. . . ."[477] A religious paper declared that the

North would have to "teach the South line upon line, precept upon precept, by military garrisons, by Bureau courts, by Congregational churches, by Northern settlers, by constitutional amendments, by Christian missionaries, by free schools, lectures, newspapers and reading rooms, what be the first principles of social order, political eminence, moral worth and industrial success."[478] Congressman Thaddeus Stevens declared, "It is intended to revolutionize their principles and feelings . . . , to work a radical reorganization in Southern institutions, habits, and manners." And again, Stevens said that the "true doctrine of reconstruction is that defeated rebels have no civil or political rights . . . , and that all loyal men without regard to race or color, are entitled to equal rights as citizens."[479]

Indeed, Thaddeus Stevens was a crucial figure in pushing for an equality reminiscent of the French Revolution. He went much further than most Americans of the time in pushing for social as well as political equality and in his eagerness to use the power of the general government to force this condition on the country. He consistently practiced and pushed for racial equality during much of his life. It may be that his passion for racial equality was heightened by his affection for and dependence on his black housekeeper for many years, Lydia Smith. When he was in Washington, she served as his hostess when he entertained at his apartment; and she lived in his house and took care of it and him at his home in Lancaster, Pennsylvania. It was reported that when he was approached to contribute to a Home for Friendless Children in Lancaster, he refused unless he could be guaranteed that black children would be accepted on equal terms with whites. It should not have been any surprise, as one historian has noted, that Stevens "demanded the immediate enfranchisement of the freedmen, an absolute equality of civil rights, and the confiscation of the land of the Southern aristocrats and its division among the negroes in forty-acre tracts. . . ."[480]

Moreover, Stevens had the leverage during the early years of Reconstruction to push his views. He was Speaker of the House of Representatives, the dominant person on the Committee of Fifteen which controlled reconstruction legislation, and Radical Republican *per excellence.* He was ideally situated to make over the South, if anyone ever was or could.

The difficulty in doing this transcended politics, however; it was and is unconstitutional. The Constitution does not provide for the making over, reconstructing, or revolutionizing of societies and peoples within states, whether what is involved is their beliefs, their practices, their customs and traditions, or their institutions. Such changes produced by force are alien to the very reason for existence of the general government under the Constitution. The United States was founded to protect and secure Americans from foreign intruders and domestic insurrection that would threaten the lives, liberties, and property of the people. The people were the source of authority, not the object of it. To undertake to make over some portion or all of America would be to turn the Constitution upside down.

There is not much evidence that Thaddeus Stevens or Radical Republicans concerned themselves with such constitutional qualms. If the President got in their way, as he did, they would do their best to discredit and drive him from power. If the courts got in their way, they intimidated them. If the Constitution too clearly stood in their path, they amended it. And if Southern whites objected, they disfranchised large numbers of them, and subjected them to military occupation.

In 1867, the Radical Republicans took full control of Reconstruction. They signaled this by getting Congress to pass the First Reconstruction Act in March. It declared that the existing state governments of the former Confederacy, except for Tennessee, were illegal. The ten states involved were divided into five military districts, and the President was ordered to send military forces to each under the command of a general. Responsibility for maintaining order in these regions was under the authority of the military, who were empowered to arrest, try, and enforce sentences against those convicted. The act prescribed that the voters of these states, voting without regard to race or color, should choose delegates to a constitutional convention, which should frame a constitution to be submitted to the voters for their approval. When they had done so, and when they had approved the proposed 14th Amendment, they might then organize governments and take up their place in the Union.

President Johnson returned the bill to Congress with a scorching veto message, declaring that "this measure is in its whole character, scope, and object without precedent and without authority, in palpable conflict with the plainest provisions of the Constitution, and utterly destructive of those great principles of liberty and humanity for which our ancestors on both sides of the Atlantic have shed so much blood and expended so much treasure." His denunciation of the military provisions are especially moving:

> It is plain that the authority here given to the military officer amounts to absolute despotism. But to make it still more unendurable, the bill provides that it may be delegated to as many subordinates as he chooses to appoint, for it declares that he shall "punish or cause to be punished." Such a power has not been wielded by any monarch in England for more than five hundred years. In all that time no people who speak the English language have borne such servitude. It reduces the whole population of the ten States—all persons, of every color, sex, and condition, and every stranger within their limits—to the most abject and degrading slavery. . . .

Then Johnson asked, "Have we the power to establish and carry into execution a measure like this? I answer, Certainly not, if we derive our authority from the Constitution and if we are bound by the limitations which it imposes."[481]

No matter, Congress was bent on a course of rule or ruin, or rule *and* ruin. It passed the measure over Johnson's veto, as it did a succession of bills which followed it and were vetoed, and the Republican leaders determined to impeach and remove him from office. They failed in the effort to remove him from office by the narrowest of margins, but they succeeded in destroying his effectiveness as President. Military rule was used as long as possible to keep the Republicans in power, but the last of it was finally removed in 1877.

d. Constitutional Reconstruction

The period from 1865 to 1870 was a season of major constitutional change. From 1791 to 1865 only two amendments had been added to the Constitution, and after 1870 until 1913 no further amendments were added. By contrast three were added during the years of 1865 to 1870. The 13th Amendment was declared ratified in 1865, the 14th in 1868, and the 15th in 1870. It might be supposed, then, that this was evidence of veneration of the Constitution by the leaders of the time. Hardly, the Congress (and the President in the case of the 13th) showed their contempt of the orderly procedures for amending the Constitution by the manner of the adoption of these amendments.

The 13th Amendment simply abolished slavery and involuntary servitude except for those convicted of crimes. It is probable that by December of 1865, this amendment expressed the will of the great majority of Americans. Most of the slaves had already long since been freed by conquering armies and presidential proclamations. Southerners generally accepted it as a *fait accompli,* and the amendment provided *ex post facto* legal support. There were still legal and constitutional problems with its ratification. By the terms of Presidential Reconstruction, ratification was made a condition of the Southern states' taking up their place in the Union. That may have been tacit coercion. Worse still, the Southern states ratified it, but were then declared not to be in the Union by Congress. Was the Amendment properly ratified? Who can say?

The 14th Amendment's ratification was the most dubious of all, but first its provisions need to be noted. It is a long and complex amendment. Section 1 has had the greatest long term impact. It greatly expanded the power of the Federal government over the states. It reads, in part, "All persons born or naturalized in the United States, and subject to the jurisdiction thereof, are citizens of the United States. . . . No State shall make or enforce any law which shall abridge the privileges or immunities of citizens of the United States; nor shall any State deprive any person of life, liberty, or property, without due process of law; nor deny to any person within its jurisdiction the equal protection of the laws." This section was most directly concerned with giving blacks unquestioned citizenship and an equality of rights, but it is of course general in its provisions and thus greatly extended the reach of the general government. Section 2 sets up a scheme for reducing the representation in Congress of any state which denies the vote to a significant portion of males in a state 21 or older. The 15th Amendment may have made this portion of the 14th moot; at any rate it was not utilized. Section 3 disqualifies a portion of those who served the Confederacy from Federal office-holding. This disability could be and later was removed. The 4th section was punitive in that it prohibited anyone to pay Confederate debts or pay any claim for the loss of slaves by emancipation, "but all such debts shall be held illegal and void." A considerable portion of the wealth of the South was swept away by constitutional decree.

But was it constitutional? When the amendment was submitted in its first version in 1866, it was rejected by all the states of the former Confederacy, except Tennessee, and by Kentucky and Delaware as well. With 12 states rejecting the amendment, it had failed in the bid for ratification. Congress did not bow to defeat, however, it revived the 14th Amendment by providing in the First Reconstruction Act of 1867 that no state could be restored to the Union until it had ratified the amendment and it had become a part of the Constitution. The situation was highly coercive, since ten of the states were under military occupation and could only get out by ratification of the amendment. No principle of law is more venerable than that an agreement entered into by coercion is null and void. No matter, the occupied states ratified the amendment. Even so, Secretary of State Seward was less than certain that it had been properly ratified and noted his doubts in his pronouncement. Ohio and New Jersey had rescinded their ratifications and the standing of some of the Southern states was highly doubtful. That was too uncertain a proclamation in the view of the leaders of Congress, and that body adopted a resolution declaring that three-fourths of the state had ratified the amendment, and the Secretary of State should say so and proclaim it ratified. The controversies were never satisfactorily resolved, but the 14th Amendment was long ago accepted as a part of the Constitution.

The 15th Amendment declares that the right of citizens "of the United States to vote shall not be denied or abridged by the United States or by any State on account of race, color, or previous condition of servitude." By this amendment, the United States entered constitutionally into the determination of who could not be denied the vote for the first time (though hardly for the last). It was an *ex post facto* recognition of what had already been imposed upon the South by military force.

e. Constitutional Restoration

Respect for the Constitution was one of the casualties of the Civil War and especially of Reconstruction. Indeed, the injury to strict construction may well have been terminal. What the Republicans of that era left as a legacy to later generations was that the end justifies the means. The crux of the idea would get a philosophical gloss in William James's Pragmatism and John Dewey's Instrumentalism, but constitutionally the leaders of that era had taught those who came after to stretch the Constitution as far as it would go, evade its restrictions when you could, go ahead and do what could be politically done, and if the Constitution still stood in the way, present the country with a *fait accompli,* and ratify it with constitutional amendments.

Aside from strict construction of the Constitution and respect for it as Higher Law, the other great distortion was the upsetting of the balance of powers. Within the Federal government itself, Lincoln had exercised arbitrary and dictatorial powers, frequently with the *ex post facto* approval of Congress. Temporarily, at least, he greatly expanded the powers of the President. Even more drastically, Congress, pushed by Radical Republicans and guided by the Committee of Fifteen under the thumb of Thaddeus Stevens, intimidated, dwarfed, and dominated the other branches of government during the late 1860s. But the greatest change in the balance of power was between that of the general government and the states. The Union victory in the war put a forceful end to serious claims to state sovereignty. The pounding the states of the former Confederacy took from the Congress and military occupation reduced state governments to puppets of the national government. The spectacle of state legislatures being compelled to ratify constitutional amendments or endure military occupation surely left its mark. Moreover, the Reconstruction Amendments to the Constitution greatly expanded the power of the general government, upsetting the balance achieved at the Convention in 1787 and making it as permanent as constitutional amendments could.

Yet when viewed from the angle of the year 1900, say, the changes in the structure of the government, the Constitution, and law between 1860 and 1875, had made no great impact. True, the slaves had been freed, and their role and status had changed. But otherwise, the balance had been restored as well as it could be, given the constitutional changes. The great zeal that had animated Congress to make over America during Reconstruction had long since played itself out. The driving spirit behind this zeal, Thaddeus Stevens, died in 1868; Charles Sumner ceased to be a factor after 1872; Salmon Chase, Lincoln appointed Chief Justice of the Supreme Court, died in 1873. Congress passed a variety of civil right acts in the early 1870s to protect blacks in the South, especially, but those charged with enforcement eventually wearied of sending in troops and marshals. When President Grant received a request to send troops into Mississippi in 1875, he replied: "The whole public are tired out with these annual autumnal outbreaks in the South and the great majority are ready now to condemn any interference on the part of the Government."[482] The Democrats gained control of the House of Representatives in 1874; such Radical Republicans as remained could no longer control what Congress would do.

The Southern states fell under the control of native whites once Reconstruction ended, and reasserted such independence as they could. Whites regained control of the government of Tennessee in 1869, Virginia and North Carolina in 1870, Georgia in 1871, Arkansas, Alabama, and Texas in 1874, Mississippi 1875, and somewhat later in Louisiana, South Carolina, and Florida. The number of blacks who could vote was drastically reduced in the ensuing years by a variety of subterfuges, the most effective of which was the white Democratic primary. The South became the Solid South in the latter part of 19th century. The white South voted Democratic; blacks were generally excluded from the Democratic primary (on the grounds that it was a *private* party) where the real choice was usually made. And, through leadership in the national Democratic Party, Southern state governments regained some of the lost balance of power. Southerners had lost some of their zeal for strict construction, especially where the 14th and 15th Amendments were concerned.

The Supreme Court, and Federal courts generally, tended by a number of rulings to reduce the import of the 14th Amendment. The High Court reduced that import as early as 1873, when the Slaughter House Cases came before it. One of the questions the majority of the Court dealt with was whether the 14th Amendment protected citizens of the United States from grants of privileges and immunities by the states. The Court denied that it did, and quoted the Amendment in pointing out that it only prohibits the states to abridge the privileges and immunities of citizens of the *United States*. That being the case, the court held, as one history summarizes the case, "that the whole body of traditional rights of the common law and of state bills of rights still remained solely under the protection of the states. The privileges and immunities clause of the Fourteenth Amendment had not placed the federal government under an obligation to protect these rights against state violation."[483] In general, the courts continued with a narrow view of what had been done by the 14th Amendment to the end of the century and beyond.

The balance within the Federal government was generally restored in the latter part of the 19th century. If Congress was still slightly dominant when the Democrat Grover Cleveland came to the presidency in 1885, he did not take long to head it off with his numerous vetoes. In fact, from the 1880s to the end of the century, neither the Congress, the Presidents, nor the courts were especially dominant. In monetary matters, hard money was regaining its earlier position, and the government followed fiscal policies worthy of the first half of the century.

Both the example and the laws of war and reconstruction were still generally on the books as potential for great expansions of power, but during that decade or so there had been a practical constitutional restoration.

Section IV

LEVIATHAN:
American Government
in the 20th Century

Chapter 15
Introduction

While the size and sum of American government has differed greatly and decisively in the 20th century from what it was in the 19th, the difference was barely noticeable from the beginning of 1899 to the end of 1901—to take a two year period for the shift from one century to the next. Nor were there any major changes nationally for the decade from the beginning of 1895, say, to the end of 1904. Actually, some of the changes were in the making as far back as the Civil War and some of them did not reach fruition until the 1930s, or later. Nonetheless, a great change did occur whose major lineaments either appeared fully or became prominent in the 20th century and which distinguished it characteristically from those of the 19th century.

In the most general terms, the great change was from limited and constrained government in the 19th century whose functions and expenditures increased, if at all, in some sort of proportion to the size of the country and its population to an exponentially expansive government in the 20th century whose functions and expenditures increased far beyond the growth of population or territorial size. Indeed, it is apt to describe the government that has emerged in the 20th century as a "Leviathan." The word apparently refers to a huge (imaginary) sea monster. In Job, chapters 40 and 41, there are several references to huge creatures, one referred to as a behemoth, and another as a leviathon. Of the behemoth, it said that "He moveth his tail like a cedar . . . ," that "Surely the mountains bring him forth food. . . ." And again, "Behold he drinketh up a river, and hasteth not: he trusted that he can draw up Jordan into his mouth." Then of the creature called by a different name, "Canst thou draw out leviathan with an hook? or his tongue with a cord which thou lettest down?" Presumably not, for he is a creature of vast size. And it is at least plausible that much larger creatures can and do reside in the sea than on land. At any rate, the term came to be used to refer to an outsized, huge or immense being. Thomas Hobbes called his major work on politics *Leviathan*. In more recent times, the term has been used to refer to overgrown and even totalitarian government. Whether it has become totalitarian or not (it has at least tended in this direction), the United States has certainly grown into an unwieldy monster in this century.

There are many ways to illustrate the growth and spread of this behemoth or leviathan, to use the biblical terms, for it could now, to speak metaphorically, drink the Jordan dry without assuaging its thirst for sustenance. Statistics show in graphic monetary terms how it has grown. For example, the total receipts of the United States government in 1900 were $567 million, or just over one-half billion dollars. They had risen dramatically during the Civil War and had never fallen to their pre-civil war levels. The total receipts had been only $25 million in 1830 and fallen to $20 million in 1840. Still the growth from the Civil War down to 1900 had been, with some fluctuations up and down, steadily but not dramatically upward. They rose drastically during World War I to over $3½ billion in 1918, declined somewhat in the 1920s, and then began a rise in the mid-1930s, and have hardly paused in their drastic upward movement since that time. In 1939, total receipts were over $5.6 billion, in 1950 over $41 billion, in 1960 over $97 billion, in 1970 nearly $210 billion, in 1980 $572 billion, in 1985 over $815 billion, and in 1988 *net* receipts had reached over $908 billion. To put it more dramatically, receipts of the United States government increased from somewhat over $½ billion in 1900 to nearly $1,000 billion (one trillion) in 1988.

Outlays (i. e., expenditures or payments) by the United States government paint an even more lurid picture of the increase in size and activity in the 20th century. The net outlays were $11 million in 1800, $40 million in 1850, $521 million in 1900, over 39 thousand millions (or $39 billion) in 1950, over $326 billion in 1975, and slightly over $1 million millions (or $1,000 billions, or $1 trillion) in 1988. In 1990, just two years later, the outlays had risen another one quarter trillion dollars. The deficit in 1986 was greater than the total outlays of the government (or at least the net outlays) as recently as 1970.

Which brings us to the "public debt" of the United States, which may not exactly be a measure of the growth and spread of the tentacles of the government, but it certainly illustrates the massive growth of fiscal irresponsibility, among other things. For most of the 19th century, the public debt did not loom large in public consciousness or concern. True, the United States accumulated a considerable debt, for the time, in fighting the War for Independence. But the Jeffersonians and Jacksonians often had a surplus in the treasury and were bent on reducing the debt. Indeed, during Jackson's terms the debt was finally paid off. The debt ballooned up during the Civil War, stood at $2.4 billion in 1870, was down to $1.2 billion in 1900, and to $1.1 billion in 1910. It grew swiftly once again during World War I, stood at $24.2 billion, but had been reduced to $16.1 billion in 1930. Those who governed the United States in the 1920s, however, made the last sustained effort to reduce and pay off the debt. The debt began to rise in the 1930s, leaped dramatically during World War II, was reduced slightly in the latter 1940s, but soon proceeded to rise at an ever accelerated pace thereafter. It was $43 billion in 1940, $258.7 billion in 1945; $256.1 billion in 1950;

$284.1 billion in 1960; $370.1 billion in 1970, $907.7 billion in 1980; over $1.8 trillion in 1985 (over 1,800 billion), and had leaped to over $3¼ trillion (over 3,250 billion) by 1990. The public debt of the United States had increased by approximately three thousand times in 1990 over what it had been in 1900.

It is easy enough to demonstrate that these vast increases in the receipts, expenditures, and debt of the United States government, overwhelmingly concentrated in the 20th century, did not significantly reflect increases in population or physical size of the country. The area of the United States in 1800 was 891,364 square miles; the population was 5,308,483 in 1800, and the expenditures of the government were approximately $11 million in 1800. By 1850, the area of the United States had increased to 2,991,655 square miles; the population had increased to 23,191,876, and the outlays of the government to approximately $40 million. The area of the United States was approximately three times what it had been in 1800 by 1850; the population was about 4½ times what it had been; and the outlays of the government was less than four times what it had been. That is a way of saying that the increases in government expenditures from 1800 to 1850 was more or less proportional to the increase of population and size of the country. By 1900, the area of the country had increased to 3,618,770 square miles, the population to over 76 million, and the outlays of the government had risen to $521 million. In area, then, the United States had increased only by 1/5th, the population had not quite tripled, and outlays were thirteen times what they had been in 1850. The outlays were already disproportionate to the other increases in 1900, but nothing compared to what they have become in the 20th century. By 1950, the area of the United States was still the same as it had been in 1900, the population had approximately doubled to about 151 million, but expenditures had increased to $39 billion, which was over 75 times what it had been in 1900. By 1990, the area had risen slightly to 3,787,425 square miles, the population to over 248 million, but expenditures had risen to over $1¼ trillion. In sum, during that most recent 40 year period, the size of the country had only slightly increased, the population was only approximately 1.65 times what it had been, but expenditures had increased greatly, and were 32 times what they had been in 1950. In short, expenditures had increased approximately 19.4 times as fast as population. From 1900 to 1950, the increase had been even greater; expenditures had increased 37.5 times that of population. It should be clear, then, that the vast increases in receipts, in expenditures, and in public debt have been only most remotely related to the increase in population.

Even so, the above must be taken at this point only as symptoms of the behemoth that the United States government has become. The monetary figures exaggerate the extent of the growth, because the value of the money has declined precipitously in the 20th century, particularly from the 1930s on, and especially from the late 1960s into the 1980s. Thus, the monetary figures do not provide anything like a precise index of the growth of government. But since the decline in the value of money is a direct result of the actions of Leviathan, that too is symptomatic of the sway of the Federal government in the 20th century.

There are other ways, of course, to confirm and illustrate the growth of the national government in the 20th century. One is in the increase of cabinet level departments in the government. The Constitution gives Congress the power to establish departments, and it is authorized to do so at will (assuming always that the function to be performed lies within the powers granted to the general government). There was no reasonable doubt about the first three departments established. A Department of Foreign Affairs was authorized by Congress in July, 1789. That the United States government was constitutionally empowered to conduct relations with foreign nations was abundantly clear. The name was changed, however, to Department of State in September, 1789. A War Department was brought into being by act of Congress in August, 1789, and it initially had both the Army and Navy under its authority. The two were separated in 1798, when the Navy Department was set up. Powers were specifically granted in the Constitution for establishing armies and navies. The Treasury Department was authorized by Congress in September, 1789. This department was a logical extension of the monetary powers granted by the Constitution. There was a Postmaster General provided in 1789, but the Post Office Department did not become a fixture until 1795. There was an Attorney General from the outset as well, but the Justice Department was not created until 1870. Since the Constitution authorizes Congress to establish post offices and build post roads, the function of Postmaster General and a department to perform that function had constitutional standing. In similar fashion, since the United States is authorized to make laws and enforce them, an official, and a department, if necessary, to coordinate these functions was in order.

The initial spate of cabinet positions and department making was over by the end of 1798. Nor were the Jeffersonians and Jacksonians much disposed to expanding government or creating new departments. At any rate, it was over fifty years before a new department was established. Congress authorized a Department of Interior in 1849 in the wake of the Mexican War and the territorial expansion of the 1840s. From the outset it was given jurisdiction over the Indians, over the government land offices, over the patent office and an assortment of other functions in the interior of the country. Probably, the initial functions assigned the department were constitutional. For example, the Constitution authorized the issuing of patents, and the conduct of relations with Indians. But the department was a transitional department, nonetheless, for it eventually expanded its functions to making or encouraging Indian dependency on the United States and moved from the sale of public land as a primary function to the development and acquisition of new lands by the government.

The major changes in departments began to occur in the late 19th century, the changes which produced Leviathan. The establishment of the Department of Agriculture marks a signal departure from the past. It was the first department created to cater to and look after a special class, or, in the softer language of our time, an economic interest group—the farmers. It was first established in 1862, as a kind of bureau, but received full cabinet rank as a department in 1889. Its original purpose, as stated in 1862, was "to acquire and diffuse among the people of the United States information on subjects connected with agriculture. . . ." But over the years it became the administrator of a vast assortment of programs by which the Federal government ministered to farmers both as a class deserving aid and requiring direction and control from the government. Such functions were not conceived by the Founders nor embodied in the language of the original Constitution or its amendments. The Bureau of Agriculture was originally established during the time when the defenders of the Constitution had been greatly weakened. By the time the department was raised to cabinet rank, however, class theories were gaining followers, and political parties were on their way to being vehicles for them.

Congress took another major step in this direction by authorizing a Department of Commerce and Labor in 1903. But this apparent effort to reconcile two interest groups with a single department was short-lived, for in 1913 they were separated into a Department of Commerce and a Department of Labor. The Department of Commerce had as its main aim promoting and fostering the development of commerce both within the country and with foreign countries, and the development of mining, manufacturing, shipping, and transportation. If these were proper functions of government at all, they were hardly authorized by the Constitution. As for the Department of Labor, its class interest was transparent. The Department of Labor was expected to advance the welfare of wage earners and has sometimes been a vehicle for the most class conscious of wage workers, those organized into labor unions.

Since World War II, Congress has authorized a variety of departments catering to welfarist and related needs. It created the omnibus Health, Education and Welfare Department in 1953; the Department of Housing and Urban Development in 1965; the Department of Transportation in 1966; and the Department of Energy in 1977. Meanwhile, in 1979 the Department of Health, Education and Welfare was dismantled and reassembled in two distinct departments: the Department of Education, and the Department of Health and Human Services. The whole system was rounded out, perhaps, in 1989 with the addition of a Department of Veterans Affairs. On the other hand, there are many ways of classifying people and things that are not as yet specifically represented by a cabinet rank department in the United States. There is not, for example, a Department of Women, nor, for that matter, a Department of Men, nor even a Department of Children, no

Department of Minorities, and even major racial and ethnic groups do not have departments of their own, and, strange as it may seem, there is no Department of Widows and Orphans, nor any Department of Inhuman or Unhuman Services to give substance to that one for human services. Some, or all, of those may be forthcoming, as well as others not yet dreamed of, but it should be made clear that the Federal government has gone borrowing, taxing, and redistributing wealth on an unprecedented scale in this century. These new government departments created since World War II are mainly concerned with redistribution.

But the growth of Leviathan may be even better illustrated with the proliferation of that strange creature called "independent agencies." The first such agency—the Interstate Commerce Commission—was authorized by act of Congress 1887. The latest listing in *The World Almanac and Book of Facts* for 1992 indicates that there are now 52 such agencies of the United States government. The best known of these are the regulatory agencies, such as the Interstate Commerce Commission, Federal Communications Commission, National Labor Relations Board, Securities and Exchange Commission, Federal Trade Commission, Commodity Futures Trading Commission, Environmental Protection Agency, and Occupational Safety and Health Review Commission. The outstanding feature of these regulatory agencies is that they tend to join together what the Constitution puts asunder. That is, the Constitution separates and generally accords different spheres to the legislative, executive, and judicial functions. These powers tend to be joined in a single body in regulatory agencies. By their interpretations and decisions they make what is now called "administrative law;" they ordinarily enforce—i.e., execute their laws—; and they have courts which perform judicial functions. While these agencies are not entirely independent of the regular government, they nevertheless wield great power without constitutional checks and balances.

But other agencies that are not so much regulatory in character also illustrate the great growth of Leviathan in the 20th century. For example, there is the Central Intelligence Agency, which engages in largely undercover activities on the international scene, the Federal Reserve System which exerts vast power over money and banking in the United States, the Export-Import Bank which plays a major role in finance and trade in the world, the National Aeronautics and Space Administration, the Tennessee Valley Authority with its huge power production and distribution activities, the Government Printing Office, and so on and on. Some of the agencies may be benign enough, such as the Library of Congress, Smithsonian Institution, and the General Accounting Office, but others are more controversial and intrusive, such as the Equal Employment Opportunity Commission, the Farm Credit Administration, and the United States Information Agency.

Much other evidence could be submitted to prove that the United States government has expanded and grown exponentially in the 20th century—that it is a Leviathan. But enough has been given to establish at least a *prima facie* case for it. It has grown so greatly because it has taken on a whole host of new functions and activities. Among the functions that have greatly expanded the powers of the Federal government are the following (by no means an inclusive list): the regulation of rail and other transportation rates, routes, and services; the subsidizing of agricultural prices; the restriction of crop acreages and the paying of farmers to take land out of cultivation; the provision of banking and credit facilities; the creation of currency based on debt; the distribution of farm products through food stamp programs; the making of loans to foreign and domestic governments and institutions; the subsidizing of art and literature; the manipulation of interest rates; the regulation of wages and hours of work, the mediation of labor disputes, setting compulsory "cooling off" periods before strikes, and compelling management to pay back wages when they have committed an "unfair labor practice;" the building of housing projects, subsidizing of rent, providing guarantees for loans to buy homes, and providing for special home loans for Veterans; the providing of old age benefits through Social Security, Medicare for those 65 and older, Medicaid for low income persons, aid to dependent children, and so on and on; fostering hospital building, controlling medicines and drugs, and wielding large influence if not control over hospital, physician and surgical fees; providing all sorts of aid to education from supporting teachers of agriculture and home economics to school lunch programs, to student loans, and the like; the passing of environmental regulations and requirements for construction and building projects to pass; and imposing a host of saving and health regulations. The above is more than the tip of the iceberg of government programs, of course, but it still only provides highlights on the subject and leaves unnamed large numbers of government activities which have made their appearance in the 20th century and contributed to the growth of government.

It is worth noting here, too, that not one of the above programs is directly authorized in the United States Constitution, nor are any of them clearly implied in the powers granted. The Constitution provided for a limited government, limited both by its form, and in substance. It is formally limited by the separation and balance of powers within the Federal government, the dispersion of powers among the Federal and state governments, the differing compositions of the electorate for various elective offices, and the division of the country into relatively small electoral districts. The substantive limitations in the Constitution consist mainly of the enumeration of powers granted and reservation of those not granted to the states or to the people, procedural restrictions, and enumerated prohibitions against certain actions. How all these were evaded, ignored, reconstrued, or otherwise overcome will be a part of the story to be told in what follows in later chapters.

Before proceeding to those, however, it may be well to put the emergence of Leviathan in America in the broadest perspective. The United States has hardly been alone in the expansion and growth of government in this century. Indeed, the phenomenon has been worldwide, and very few places have avoided the trend to extend the sway and activities of government. The motive power behind this expansion and growth is known generically as socialism, though it has been called by many names: social democracy, democratic socialism, Communism, national socialism (Nazism and fascism), democracy, and even liberalism.

The animating idea behind socialism is the belief that the proper role and function of government is to provide for the material well being of the people, including, quite often, the intellectual, artistic, and psychological well being, though not as a rule, the spiritual well being (which socialists have tended to reduce to the psychological or assigned to the private realm). If any people are short of material goods, then government should tend to these "needs," according to this theory. This has spawned large scale redistributions of goods within countries and also on the international scene from country to country. The greatest redistribution effort to other countries has been by the foreign aid programs of the United States since World War II. This same animus has spawned all sorts of government aid and programs for the supposed benefit of their populaces.

This vast activity, materialistic in emphasis, has shifted the theoretical justification of government away from peacekeeping to redistribution of wealth. Government is still charged with its ancient police duties, but these are generally downplayed and poorly performed. Nor is there much emphasis by socialists on the fact that government is that which has a monopoly of the use of force in its jurisdiction. Government tends to be viewed rather as provider and benefactor rather than a potential threat and danger to the populace. A notion that has widespread international currency in this century is that democratic government is benign, and it demonstrates its benign state by its concern for the well being of peoples.

Much of the history of the actual behavior of governments in this century stands in stark contrast to the visionary view of democratic socialists—or just democrats, as they are more commonly known nowadays. The 20th century has been the century of totalitarian governments, of governments relentlessly imposing their wills on peoples under their rule. A major political theme of this century has been dictatorial oppression by tyrants using modern technology to their ends. The most notorious examples have been Adolph Hitler in Nazi Germany and Joseph Stalin in Communist Russia, but lesser tyrants have abounded and less blatantly repressive regimes have been commonplace. In fact, virtually all countries have adopted totalitarian practices to greater or lesser extent in this century, including the United States. Most important, individuals and families have lost control over their possessions, their lives, and their affairs to intrusive governments. The case for limited and restrained constitutional government has never been stronger than in the year 1992, and the United States has never been farther from it.

A contemporary historian has addressed the subject of "Restoring the Republic" in a recent article and has said some wise and important things about it. He wrote, "It is true that we live in a very different world from our [Founding] Fathers and that our solutions cannot always be the same as theirs. But our problem is the same—the harnessing of power." He denies, too, that "Consolidation of power is not so much inherent in our current state as it is the product of choices made and institutions constructed in the past that showed a bias in favor of gigantism over humane scale, centralized control over freedom, and elitism over democratic rule." He says that the way toward doing something about that is by restoring the republic. He notes rightly that the "restoration of the federal republic will not in itself solve all our problems because the ends of human life do not rest in government and because modern society is in deep spiritual crisis. . . . But the restraint of power is a necessary first step for all progress. . . . Leviathan has gotten loose from the harness our forefathers so skillfully fashioned for him. He has knocked over the fence, laid waste our gardens, and waxed fat on our substance. We must begin to look to our husbandry, but first we will have to chain the beast."[484]

Leviathan has indeed knocked over the fence "and waxed fat on our substance." Much of what has been described in this chapter has been a rather abstract discussion of the pillage and destruction. But before any further talk of restoration it is necessary first to get clearly in mind how the fence was knocked down. For that, figurative language will not do; political analysis is necessary.

Chapter 16
Preparation for Leviathan

Leviathan did not spring full grown from the head of Medusa, as her sons did in the Greek myth. The American leviathan did not, anyway. It grew much more slowly and advanced more stealthily than that. The obstacles to the consolidation and concentration of power in the United States government were large. It ran against the temper and beliefs of Americans as expressed in their constitutions and institutions. The Constitution itself dispersed power. Moreover, it limited the taxing power of the general government as well as what fell within its jurisdiction. Even a loose interpretation of the written Constitution would not authorize a massive welfare state attending to the well being of Americans at home and peoples generally around the world. Leviathan could only emerge as the Constitution was changed, evaded, or submerged.

The political groundwork for leviathan was laid during the years from around 1911–1914. Back of that, however, was several decades of changes and developments which prepared the way for Leviathan. The foundations of the constitutional system of limited government were undercut by new ideas, interpretations and persuasions. The doctrines of socialism spread in the United States as elsewhere in the latter part of the 19th century. Major currents of ideas and movements for reform gained sway in the late 19th and early 20th century. All these preceded the major political changes that came with a rush just before World War I.

a. Cutting Away the Foundations

The foundations of American constitutionalism—as well as the Constitution—were philosophical, historical, traditional, rationalistic, and carried with them a substrata of religious sanctions. One of the great insights of Judeo-Christian belief is not only that man is the highest of the animals but also that he exists on a plane both higher and distinct from all others. He is distinct from all other animals intellectually and spiritually. The Bible makes it clear that man is made in the image of God, a little lower than the Angels, according to a traditional formulation, but far above all creation. He was forged from the Divine Fire, so to speak; God breathed life into him, and as Jesus made abundantly clear, man is so akin to God that he may properly address Him as "Father." So long as such a set of beliefs permeates our thought to any extent, it gives gravity, meaning, and insight into ways the works of man can be like unto the works of God.

The Founders of the United States drew on this substrata of religious belief, and it can be shown by numerous expressions of theirs. The possibility of man's being virtuous, honorable, and trustworthy informed their belief in the possibility of liberty and self-government. An ordered universe, created and sustained by God, is an essential for liberty; otherwise, chaos will prevail, and massive government power must maintain order.

American constitutionalism was deeply planted in the natural law tradition. The best of political thought for over 2,000 years was more or less grounded in the natural law tradition. And, the United States Constitution, as well as the state constitutions, was the finest flower of this tradition. Philosophically, this tradition was rooted in the belief in essences and the powers of reason which discovers and sustains them. To put it another way, it was a philosophy whose main focus was on the metaphysical realm. Traditionally, Western philosophers have discoursed in terms of three distincts realms of reality: the physical, the metaphysical, and spiritual. In terms of their durability, the physical is temporary (here today and gone tomorrow, as we say); the metaphysical is enduring (the underlying order or laws whose durability is more or less coextensive with that of the earth), and the spiritual is eternal (from everlasting to everlasting, as is said of God). Knowledge of the physical comes to us by way of the senses, of the metaphysical by way of reason, and of the spiritual by faith or revelation (and perhaps intuition). The natural law tradition in which our Constitution nestles is profoundly based on the metaphysical level of thought.

The foundations of constitutionalism were undermined in the course of the 19th century. The belief in reason was supplanted for many by an emphasis upon feeling. By the end of the 19th century, the focus upon irrationality was pushing reason into the nooks and crannies. Contemporary psychology deals almost exclusively with the irrational and does not appear even to consider the processes of reason to be within its domain. Metaphysics has been hounded out of philosophical court, castigated as if were something vague, insubstantial, and unreal. Natural law has tended to suffer a like fate; nor was it ever likely that belief in it could be sustained without reason and the metaphysical. One who had studied deeply in the natural law theory described what happened to it this way: "The development of natural-law ideas . . . attained its culmination at the end of the eighteenth century. After that time," he continued, "we can begin to trace a process of collapse and disintegration in the natural-law system of thought."[485]

Some thinkers began to attack the very concept of natural law; the utilitarians were generally the most outspoken of these. Jeremy Bentham, a utilitarian if ever there was one, said of those who believe in natural law that they "take for their subject the pretended *law of nature;* an obscure phantom, which in the imaginations of those who go in chase of it, points sometimes to *manners,* sometimes to laws; sometimes to what law is, and sometimes to what it ought to be."[486] Again, he said, *"Natural rights* is simple nonsense; natural and imprescriptible rights, rhetorical nonsense." The natural law philosophy was undoubtedly too complex and diffuse for Bentham. As far as he was concerned, "the sole object of government ought to be the greatest happiness of the greatest possible number of the community."[487] Thus it was said of the utilitarians, in the most common formulation, that they believed in "the greatest good for the greatest number."

The phrase was a kind of "philosopher's stone" for Bentham, the key to all man's endeavors and activities. As one historian has said of it, Bentham "now had a moral imperative of clear import, and a test by which to judge the injunctions of preachers, the exhortations of teachers, the principles of parties, the laws of legislators, the edict of kings. The law must admit no mystical entities like 'rights,' natural, popular, or divine; no revelations from God to Moses or Mohammed or Christ; no punishments for vengeance' sake. Every proposal must answer the question *Cui bono?,* For whose good will it be?—for one, or a few, or many, or all?"[488] Whether he was aware of it or not, Bentham was not only undermining constitutions based on natural law and theism but also preparing the way for unlimited government—by the people. If the greatest good for the greatest number is to be the keystone, then who but the great mass, or at least majority, of the people could determine the political course and action?

John Stuart Mill, another English philosopher, in the line of Bentham, though not quite so single minded, was another utilitarian who attacked the natural law philosophy. He leveled his assault on the very notion of a benevolent and orderly nature (charging nature with cruelties much in the manner that some attack or question God). Mill said, "Nature impales men, breaks them as if on the wheel, cast them to be devoured by wild beasts, burns them to death, crushes them with stones . . . , starves them with hunger, freezes them with cold, poisons them . . . , and has hundreds of other hideous deaths in reserve. . . ." Moreover, "Even the love of 'order' which is thought to be a following of the ways of Nature, is in fact a contradiction of them. All which people are accustomed to deprecate as 'disorder' and its consequences is precisely a counterpart of Nature's ways. Anarchy and the Reign of Terror are overmatched in injustice, ruin, and death, by a hurricane and a pestilence. . . ."[489]

Mill was, of course, dealing with nature in the concrete—not in essence or as underlying law—as the romantics tended to do. Unlike most romantics, however, he did not marvel at the beauty of nature but rather focused on its destructive power, its distemper and disease. His was the nature of tornadoes, hurricanes, earthquakes, plagues of locusts, and the debilitating impact of assorted vermin. The natural law philosophy, as noted, was grounded in the metaphysical realm; nineteenth century thinkers were casting off metaphysics and focusing their attention elsewhere. They did not, of course, disprove either natural law or metaphysics.

After Immanuel Kant, the towering German philosopher of the late 18th and early 19th centuries, most philosophers tended toward *monism,* the belief that there is only one level of reality. They tended to favor the physical level, which made them more or less materialists. Thus, Karl Marx was a *dialectical materialist,* and was in a line of materialists going back to the Greek atomists and through the early 19th century German thinker, Ludwig Feuerbach.

Perhaps the final step in the philosophical undermining of American constitutionalism was the shifting of thought from a focus on the enduring or the eternal to the changing. When change became the primary focus of thought, history tended to replace philosophy as the mode of perception or thinking. The German philosopher who succeeded Kant, G. W. F. Hegel, pushed thought away from the metaphysical plane to the historical plane. Hegel's overweening interest was in what moves and makes change in the world. He believed that ideas were the prime movers, and that change resulted, perhaps even progress, from the contest of ideas. The contest of ideas was, of course, a dialectical process. Marx was greatly influenced by Hegel, but he held that matter, not ideas, was the moving force. The important point, however, was that with these ideas, reality was moving on the historical plane and the shift was being made from the enduring or eternal to the temporal or changing realm.

The most striking development in 19th century thought resulting from the focus on change was the development of evolutionary theories. The great synthetic philosopher, Herbert Spencer, elaborated a theory of universal evolution. Auguste Comte proclaimed a vast philosophy of change which had man going through three stages of development in the course of history. But it was Charles Darwin, the English botanist, who gave at least a scientific gloss to the philosophy of change. To put it another way and get nearer to the truth, he shifted the scientific emphasis to the historical plane, at least in biology. He brought man into the stream of evolution. By the late 19th century, the attention of most thinkers had been drawn away from trying to discover an enduring reality or maintain contact with the eternal. They were no longer looking for the nature of things. Their attention had shifted to seeking the sources of change, growth, and development. Natural law, so far as it dealt with a fixed order in the universe, lost its appeal. So far as there was interest in natural law it was the laws of change. Natural law, in that sense, was a driving force or whatever caused movement and change. For Marx, the motive force was the class struggle over the control over the instruments of production. For Darwin, it was the struggle of living things to sustain life. Determinisms abounded to explain human as well as animal behavior.

Power, force, might, and will moved toward center stage for many. This was especially so in the political realm. What the Germans called *Realpolitik* gained sway in the late 19th and into the 20th century. *Realpolitik* refers to policies based on power rather than upon right or ideals. "Might makes right" is one of the formulations of the concept. "How many troops does the Pope have?," Joseph Stalin was supposed to have asked, a rather blunt statement of the position. The great and destructive wars of this century are a reflection in considerable measure of this attitude. But much else was colored by this outlook: the emphasis upon numbers to determine national courses of action, as in democracy, collectives, labor unions, and so on. Many people who may not have thought about it have come to accept force, might, and power to determine more and more things. Hence, the tremendous growth of governments in the 20th century.

The foundations of constitutionalism were not only eroded by the shifting of reality onto the historical plane, but the traditional role of history was also undercut. The traditional role of history was didactic—that is to provide lessons to guide peoples, groups, and organizations in their behavior. This use has both common sense and philosophical wellsprings. At the common sense level, we learn to avoid dangers and pursue safer courses. For example, a child may learn that a stove is sometimes hot, that it will burn and cause pain, should not be carelessly touched, and so on. Written history is the formalized memory of a people, the record of their experience. It is the public memory of a people, and may serve in general affairs in much the way that an individual's memories of experience serve him—i.e., as a compendium of dangers to be avoided, a depository of successful methods, a storehouse that reveals what the world is like and how to operate in it.

At the philosophical level, the didactic use of history was based upon the existence of an underlying order. It assumed that events, in essence, can recur and that the reason for this is an order in which a given cause will produce a given effect. For example, if political power is concentrated, and not effectively limited, tyranny may be expected to result. This use of history rests upon the view that beneath the surface upon which changes occur there is a substratum which endures—what we are here calling the metaphysical realm. The Founders of the United States believed in such an order and used history didactically. The following are a few examples from the constitution-making era. A Mr. Nason at the Massachusetts convention to consider ratification refers to history to support his fears of a standing army:

A standing army! Was it not with that Caesar passed the *Rubicon*, and laid prostrate the liberties of his country? By this have seven-eights of the once free nations of the globe been brought into bondage! Time would fail me, were I to attempt to recapitulate the havoc made in the world by standing armies.[490]

At the same convention,

> Dr. Willard entered largely into the field of ancient history, and deduced therefrom arguments to prove that where power has been trusted to men, whether in great or small bodies, that thus republics had soon generated into aristocracies. He instanced Sparta, Athens, and Rome. . . .[491]

The Virginia convention was replete with examples from history to show the wisdom of certain courses of action and the folly of others. For example, Edmund Randolph argued for the desirability of union because of the conflicts that were likely to occur among the states otherwise. He said:

> If you wish to know the extent of such a scene, look at the history of England and Scotland before the union; you will see their borderers continually committing depredations and cruelties of the most calamitous and deplorable nature on one another. . . .[492]

Two Viginians spelled out what they were doing in what follows. John Marshall declared,

> We may derive from Holland lessons very beneficial to ourselves. Happy that country which can avail itself of the misfortunes of others—which can gain knowledge from that source without fatal experience.[493]

James Madison added:

> We may be warned by their example, and shun their fate, by removing the causes which produced their misfortunes.[494]

By the early 20th century some historians were even denying that there were any significant lessons to be learned from the past. On this score, Professor James Harvey Robinson wrote:

> It is true that it has long been held that certain lessons could be derived from the past. . . . But there is a growing suspicion . . . that this type of usefulness is purely illusory. The present writer is anxious to avoid any risk of being regarded as an advocate of these supposed advantages of historical study. Their value rests on the assumption that conditions remain sufficiently uniform to give precedents a perpetual

value, while as a matter of fact, conditions . . . are so rapidly altering that for the most part it would be dangerous indeed to attempt to apply past experience to the solution of current problems.[495]

In sum, Robinson was saying that there is no enduring order that would validate historical lessons or make them relevant to the present.

Harry Elmer Barnes, another exponent of the "new history," declared that "the past has no direct lesson for the present in the way of analogies and forecasts." Further, "The newer history . . . holds that few situations in a very remote past will allow of being used as data to test the validity or desirability of measures proposed for present or future application." Why was this the case? Barnes says that the new history "regards civilization as a great organic complex and contends that, as the general cultural setting of events in the past was so vastly different from the present situation, past events can furnish only a very doubtful and unreliable criterion for judging of the wisdom of present policies."[496]

An even better known contemporary of theirs, Charles A. Beard, applied this outlook to cause and effect. He denied that cause and effect could be isolated from the complex events and developments in history. As he put it, no group of complications can "be isolated from surrounding and preceding complications. Even 'simple' events are complex when examined closely. 'George Washington accepted the command of American troops.' What 'caused' that action?"[497] He went on to conclude that it was impossible to draw a conclusion with certainty about the question he posed. He was probably right. The question that he asked did not pose anything about cause and effect. So far as we know, Washington decided to accept the command, may have believed it was his duty to do so, and almost certainly was not "caused" to do so by something external to his own mind, beliefs, and sentiments.

Nonetheless, Beard was right about his conclusion, even if he was not clear about the explanation of it. Given his premises, as well as those of Robinson and Barnes, along with many other thinkers of the early 20th century, it is unlikely they would find cause and effect operating in historical events and developments. They recognized no enduring underlying order that would make it so. History for these historians became not a teacher of lessons but a predictor of the future course of development. For them the pattern of progress for the future grew out of the patterns of the immediate past. Why this should have been so is not entirely clear, but clamorous prophets proclaimed its truth. The important point here, however, is that the Constitution had been undermined by a drastic shift in belief—or unbelief, as the case might be.

The Constitution was more directly undermined as well. The discussion of that point generally will be told further on, but one example, at least, is appropriate here. Charles A. Beard not only subscribed to a view of history that tended to undermine the Constitution but he also used his considerable skills as a writer to undermine it more directly. His best known work along this line was *An Economic Interpretation of the Constitution,* first published in 1913. The thesis of the work was that the makers of the Constitution were men of property and wealth in America and that the document they produced was in their own self-interest. To the extent that his argument was accepted, it would tend to discredit the Constitution. More careful scholars, some of whom were also clearer thinkers, challenged and in considerable measure discredited his thesis, but this was long after much of the damage had been done.

Actually, many of those who worked to undermine constitutionalism were not especially disinterested themselves. They were interested in reducing the extent to which the United States Constitution was an obstacle to political change, reform, and usually some form of socialism. Socialism was not generally popular in the late 19th and early 20th century in the United States. Indeed, it has never been popular under the name of socialism or Communism. Thus, those advancing socialist doctrines and ideas had to do so indirectly. For example, they could not amend the Constitution on the grounds that it would permit the establishment of socialism, for such an amendment would be roundly defeated at every level. Yet socialism did eventually provide the ideological underpinnings of American political life in the 20th century. To see that, the topic must be explored, at least briefly.

b. The Rise of Socialism

Socialism has been the dominant concept driving such practices as government control of or regulation of economies, the redistribution of wealth by government, the efforts to remake man and society, the secularization of life, and the intrusion of law into every area of life. Socialism is the main fount of the notion that the public (i. e., society, government, or whatever organizations there may be) is obligated to provide nourishment for the hungry, better working conditions for the employed, opportunity for those lacking it, and all sorts of goodies for those who need, want, or demand them. Socialism is moved by a vision of utopia which can be achieved if people will only forego their self-seeking and join their efforts in the common quest for well-being. This utopianism is often beneath the surface, but it is nonetheless the impelling vision. Although utopian novels have appeared from time to time in history, the 19th century was the greatest period of their production and the beginning of their great impact.

Our main concern with socialism, of course, is with how it used government and changed political life and the Constitution, especially in the United States. Socialism, as implied above, is the main source of the notion that government is supposed to be the Great Provider for the well being of the populace. That is virtually a new notion, hardly known before the 20th century; it certainly made few inroads on this country until the present century. And, it is this notion that has had most to do with producing Leviathan, or monster-sized, government in this country. There should be no doubt that the notion of government as the Great Provider has long since become widely accepted in this country, nor that politicians regularly run for office on the platform that they will provide more and better goods than their opponents. What is not so well known is that the roots of these notions lie in utopianism and socialism.

Socialism arose in Europe in 19th century in the wake of the French Revolution. The word was unknown and unused in English as recently as the 1820s; it had become commonplace in Europe and America by the middle of the century. Most of the early socialists were French, but before long there was a smattering of them in German speaking countries, in England, and elsewhere. One of the earliest of the French socialists was Henri de Saint Simon. He promoted the idea of some sort of association for the control of productive undertakings by experts or scientists, and the distribution of wealth based on the productive contributions of those who worked. He opposed private ownership of productive property, thought government ought to provide jobs for everyone, and that everyone should work. Opposition to privately owned property was a common tenet of the early socialists. Pierre Joseph Proudhon was not only an early French socialist but also one of the most outspoken opponents of private property. He wrote a book called *What is Property?*, and answered the question succinctly by declaring that ''Property is theft.'' He held that all men have an equal right to the occupation of property and the use of it, that private ownership is simply a means for some people to take from others the fruits of their labor. The thrust of his thought, like that of most 19th century socialists, was toward some sort of common ownership or control over productive property—or perhaps property in general. They were all collectivists, groupists, thinkers in terms of large groups of people rather than of individuals.

Men became socialists, at least in the 19th century, before they had any notion about how socialism might be achieved, if it could be. Most of them did not turn immediately to government as the vehicle for achieving their aims; indeed, they were more likely than not to reject government out of hand as being the proper means. In the middle third of the 19th century, many socialists were communitarians, as the American historian Arthur Bestor called them. They sought to realize their socialist ideal through voluntary communities. One of the earliest of these was Charles Fourier, a French socialist who advanced the communitarian idea by proposing to organize what he called phalanxes. Each phalanx was to have at least 1,500 people, all of whom would live in a common building and share what they produced. Several attempts were made to get his plan underway, with indifferent success. The best known of these efforts was Brook Farm in the United States. Albert Brisbane, an American, came under the influence of

Fourier's ideas, and spread them among American intellectuals. Brook Farm was well known because it attracted a number of literary people, such as Ralph Waldo Emerson and Nathaniel Hawthorne, who put in appearances there, but the project was shortlived.

Etíenne Cabét was another French socialist who tried to found a community for his followers. He published a book called *Voyage to Icarie,* and his followers were called Icarians. He bought a tract of land on the Red River in Texas and sent an expedition of 1,500 followers to America in 1848. The community was shortlived, however, because of quarrels and disagreements among the settlers. Cabét moved the settlement to Illinois, but it fared no better there.

A much more influential socialist and utopian community advocate was the British citizen, Robert Owen. Owen differed from most other socialists in that he was a successful businessman before embarking on his scheme. As a youth, he went into textile management and was so successful that he soon had his own factory. That did not quite fully occupy his mind, however; he was bitten by the reformist bug early on. He conceived the notion that people could be changed, nay transformed, from their self-centered ways toward perfection. It was a time when some men were thinking in terms of "perfectionism" by way of religious belief and practice, but Owen rejected that for secular means. His most famous community was at New Harmony in Indiana. He bought 30,000 acres there and formed a community of such settlers as he could lure to it. He described his purpose this way:

> I am come to this country to introduce an entire new state of society; to change it from the ignorant selfish system, to an enlightened, social system, which shall gradually unite all interests into one, and remove all cause for contest between individuals. . . .
>
> But to change from the individual to the social system; from single families with separate interests, to communities of many families with one interest, cannot be accomplished all at once . . . ; it becomes necessary . . . to proceed, if I may so express myself, to a halfway house on this new journey from poverty to wealth; from ignorance to intelligence; from anxiety to satisfaction of mind; from distrust of all, to confidence in every one; from bad habits and erroneous ideas, to good habits and a correct mode of thinking in all things. . . .[498]

New Harmony was to be such a "halfway house" then. The property was to be owned in common, and decisions were to be made by the community. The community lasted only about three years; the inhabitants were too busy debating what to do to get the necessary work done.

The communitarian effort was a failure, a circumstance that has rarely discouraged socialists for long. By the middle of the 19th century, socialist energy was shifting toward schemes for gaining control of or disposing of governments. Indeed, one of the early French socialists, Louis Auguste Blanqui, thought along these lines. He proposed to achieve socialism by using a minority of workers to seize the power of government and institute socialism. He spent most of his adult life either organizing conspiracies or in prison for his activities. Along at least related lines, Louis Blanc, another French socialist, sought to establish a kind of democratic socialism, with public ownership of productive property, and with workers in control of industry.

Indeed, wherever men were free to do so, socialists and reformists organized a great variety of groups and parties in the latter part of the 19th century, either to get control of government or to promote more or less drastic changes. For example, when a conference of collectivist and socialist organizations was held in England in 1886, there were representatives of 54 such societies present. They came from such organizations as the Socialist League, the Socialist Union, the Fabian Society, the Guild of St. Matthew, the Anarchist Group of Freedom, the Land Restoration Leagues, the Land Nationalization Society, and the National Secular Society. Moreover, the Social Democratic Federation, which was a Marxist organization, was not even present.[499]

The most dramatic of socialist phenomena of the late 19th and early 20th century were the anarchists. Anarchists were, by definition, people who wanted to be rid of government. Radical anarchists believed in taking direct action to be rid of government—that is, to assassinate the rulers. These included, of course, emperors, kings, presidents, prime ministers, and governors, but might be extended to include police, industrialists, and assorted leaders in the prevailing order. Socialist anarchists generally believed that by extreme acts of violence governments might crumble and socialism would take its place wherever there was no government. Among the rulers assassinated by people under the influence of anarchism were: Czar Alexander II of Russia, President Carnot of France, Prime Minister Castillo of Spain, Empress Elizabeth of Austria-Hungary, President William McKinley of the United States, King Umberto I of Italy, and Prime Minister Mendez of Spain. "The year 1892 alone would see over a thousand dynamitings in Europe, over five hundred in the United States."[500] Following the aborted revolutionary attempt in Russia in 1905, two anarchist groups went on a spree. "Gangs, armed with pistols and homemade bombs, profited from the breakdown of Tsarist control by murdering local officials, landlords, and industrial employers."[501]

Anarchists take it as a major premise that man is by nature good and that he has been corrupted by government and the institutions it protects and has foisted upon him. One of the earliest theorists of anarchism was William Godwin, an Englishman. In his book, *An Inquiry Concerning Political Justice,* he said that government by its very nature counteracts the improvement of original mind."[502] The most influential of the anarchists, however, was Mikhail Bakunin, a Russian revolutionary. He taught that all government must be abolished. When it was, communism would immediately replace it, and men would live freely with property in common and have no conflicts. Thus, all forms of political action had to be avoided, including the joining or forming of political parties and voting. He worked with organizations, some secret, some more or less open, to organize anarchists for the overthrow of government, and made several attempts, unsuccessful, at leading revolutions. His anarchist philosophy was particularly influential in Spain, Italy, and Russia.

With exceptions here and there, by the last years of the 19th century two approaches to socialism were moving to occupy the field, which they have generally done in the 20th century: one is revolutionary socialism, and the other is evolutionary (or gradualist or democratic) socialism. Adherents of both varieties generally believe in the necessity of capturing, controlling, and using government. Revolutionary socialists have usually been Marxists in the 20th century, and since the 1920s have gone by the name of Communists. They are called revolutionary because they approve of the violent takeover of political power within countries and drastic changes in society and of social institutions. The state, under Communism, has usually taken over all land and productive property as well as control over all organizations and institutions within the country. Communist governments have usually been leviathons with a vengeance. (Communism originally had a strong streak of anarchism in it. According to Marx, the state would eventually wither away. What withered away under Communism was not the state, however, but all restraints on government power.)

Evolutionary socialism has been the dominant form of socialism in Western Europe, North America, and much of the rest of the world. Extended and covert evolutionary socialism has wrought Leviathon in the United States. Great increases of government action have everywhere accompanied the passage of socialist measures. The most distinctive feature of evolutionary socialism is that it was a program for working within the existing political, economic, and institutional system to change and reform it from within. In even broader terms, evolutionary socialists are *gradualists, democratic*, and *statist*.

They are gradualists in believing that ends of socialism can be achieved by steps and stages within a country, that violent revolution is not essential. To put it another way, they are *reformists,* not revolutionaries. They have generally professed devotion to popular rule and what are commonly thought of as democratic procedures. One of the large myths of socialism is that the bulk of the populace really wants socialism. If that were true, if the people were fully enfranchised and faithfully represented, socialism would be installed. In fact, the generality of people are no more dependably socialists than they are regularly Christian saints—though that parallel should not be pushed very far. In consequence, evolutionary socialists cling to their profession of democracy with eltist tactics when it is to their purpose and by defining democracy to include such ideas as equality, equity, and the like. Evolutionary socialists are statists in that they believe in the use of government to achieve their ends. Unlike the Marxists, who claimed that government would wither away, gradualists apparently believe it will continue to grow and expand indefinitely.

Eduard Bernstein, a German Social Democrat, is sometimes credited with conceiving evolutionary socialism. He did write extensively on the subject and challenge Marx's thesis that wealth would become more and more concentrated in fewer and fewer hands and the oppression of labor would become intolerable. On the contrary, Bernstein presented statistics to show that small businesses continued to emerge. Moreover, he claimed that government initiated reforms were indeed improving the lot of the worker. He wrote:

> In all advanced countries we see the privileges of the capitalist bourgeoisie yielding step by step to democratic organizations. Under the influence of this, and driven by the movement of the working classes which is daily becoming stronger, a social reaction has set in against the exploiting tendencies of capital, a counteraction which, although it still proceeds timidly and feebly, yet does exist, and is always drawing more departments of economic life under its influence. Factory legislation, the democratising of local government, and the extension of its area of work, the freeing of trade unions and systems of cooperative trading from legal restrictions, the consideration of standard conditions of labour in the work undertaken by public authorities—all these characterise this phase of the evolution.[503]

But it was the British Fabian Society who gave currency, at least in the English speaking world, to tactics and methods suited to a gradual movement toward socialism. At least, they succeeded by way of the Labour Party in taking England as far as it has gone toward socialism. The Fabian Society was organized January 4, 1884, and it took its name from the Roman General Fabius, who was famed for his cautious, patient, and stealthy approach to war. First and last, the British Fabians enrolled a large number of British intellectuals of the late 19th and 20th centuries, including: George Bernard Shaw, Sidney Webb, Clement Atlee, Rebecca West, Bertrand Russell, Malcolm Muggeridge, and many, many others.

In contrast to many American intellectuals of a socialist bent, the Fabians never concealed their socialism. In public releases, they proclaimed that "The Fabian Society consists of Socialists." More, they made it clear that they aimed at "the reorganization of Society by the emancipation of land and Industrial Capital from individual and class ownership, and the vesting of them in the community for the general benefit. . . ." More, "The society accordingly works for the extinction of private property in Land. . . . The Society further works for the transfer to the Community of the administration of such industrial Capital as can conveniently be managed socially. . . ."[504] In like manner, the Fabians made it clear that they aimed to use government for their ends. "The Socialism advocated by the Fabian Society is State Socialism exclusively."[505] Above all, though the Fabians were gradualists, they were moving within the existing framework toward whatever measures and programs were in the direction of socialism. They thought that any dependency established by government could be built on to extend the hold of government, and hence of socialism.

Although socialist governments did not gain power anywhere in the world in the 19th century, the ideas were widely spread and the number of socialists was on the increase in many lands. The gradualist route to socialism looked much easier in Britain than the United States. The British Constitution did not have the fixity of the American one. The British were much more accustomed to gradual changes that acquired legitimacy in the course of time than were Americans. Nor were Americans as ready to profess socialism as were the British. Even so, socialist ideas began to gain currency in the late 19th century and socialist political parties even gained some following. A Marxist led party, the Workingmen's Party, was founded in the United States in 1876. More significantly, the name and political orientation of the party was changed in 1877 to the Socialist-Labor Party. Beginning in 1892, the party nominated candidates for the presidency for that and the next two elections. Indeed, the Socialist-Labor Party was only an obscure worker's party until it was taken over by Professor Daniel De Leon in 1890. Even so, it made only a small impact on the country under his leadership, which was mainly in the 1890s.

The opposition to the dictatorial leadership of Daniel De Leon produced a splinter group which led to the only numerically significant Socialist Party the United States ever had. Eugene Debs was one of its leaders and became the perennial candidate during the first two decades of the 20th century. Debs got over 420,000 votes in 1908, more than doubled that in 1912, and over 919,000 in 1920, when he was in prison for activities in opposition to American participation in World War I. The party declined in its following after that, and it became a part of the conventional wisdom that Americans had and would reject socialism by that name.

Many of the basic ideas of socialism, such as that government is responsible for the well-being of the populace and that the government should move toward equality by redistribution of the wealth, had much greater appeal than socialism once they were grafted on to ideas more familiar to Americans. If socialist ideas could be made to appear popular, democratic, and progressive they would have a much better chance in elections, especially if they were advanced through one or the other of the traditional parties. That may not be exactly the way native born American intellectuals

with a bent for socialist programs conceived the matter in advance, but that
was the direction in which they moved.

At any rate, some American intellectuals were developing and spreading
ideas in the late 19th and early 20th centuries that when accepted and
adopted bent Americans toward socialism. One thing they did was to try to
turn Americans away from thinking in terms of the individual to thinking in
terms of society. (If that went far enough it would tend to make socialists of
them.) Lester Frank Ward, a pioneer American sociologist, said:

> The individual has reigned long enough. The day has come for
> society to take its affairs into its own hands and shape its own
> destinies.[506]

And further, along the same lines:

> But society must be looked upon in the light of a conscious indi-
> vidual. Insofar as it is conscious and in proportion to the completeness
> of its consciousness, it does not differ from an individual. . . . Every
> individual is always seeking to benefit himself in every possible way.
> Society should do the same. . . . The extent to which it will do this will
> depend upon the collective intelligence. This is to society what brain
> power is to the individual. . . .[507]

Ward not only taught that society should replace the emphasis on the
individual and viewed society as an organism itself but also made an intellectual link between socialism (or reform) and progress. The idea of
progress was probably the most powerful and attractive idea to gain hold in
the 19th century. Evolution became the mode for progress, particularly for
many Darwinians. The trouble with this notion, for reformers and socialists,
was that evolution was supposed to be a natural and not a man-made phenomenon. If that was the case, it would at best be tinkering to attempt to
make reforms and would at worst change nothing. William Graham Sumner,
an American sociologist sometimes referred to as a conservative Darwinist,
held that it was futile to tinker with social institutions at any stage of their
development. He put it this way:

> The great stream of time and earthly things will sweep on just the
> same in spite of us. It bears with it now all the errors and follies of
> the past, the wreckage of all the philosophies, the fragments of all the
> civilizations, the wisdom of all the abandoned ethical systems, the
> debris of all the institutions, and penalties of all the mistakes. It is only
> in imagination that we stand by and look at and criticize it and plan to
> change it. Every one of us is a child of his age and cannot get out of
> it. He is in the stream and is swept along with it.[508]

Not so, said Lester Frank Ward. Or rather, it may have been so at an earlier stage of evolution, but it was no longer so. He declared that a new stage in evolution had been emerging for millennia, and he held that it was ready to be brought to fruition. This alleged new stage was the "advent with man of the thinking, knowing, foreseeing, calculating, designing, inventing and constructing faculty, which is wanting in lower creatures. . . ." It repealed "the law of nature and enacted in its stead the psychologic law, or law of mind."[509] Thus, in Ward's opinion, men could now take over the direction of social development, and they could shape it to human ends. His work was a call to men to take up their new role in the universe and bring nature and natural law to heel (God had disappeared from his view):

> . . . When nature comes to be regarded as passive, [Ward wrote], and man as active . . . , when human action is recognised as the most important of all forms of action, and when the power of the human intellect over vital, psychic and social phenomena is practically conceded, then, and then only, can man justly claim to have risen out of the animal and fully to have entered the human stage of development.[510]

Whatever the merits of Ward's conception, there should be no doubt that his position was on the winning side, at least for an extended period of American history. Namely, the social reform, and by extension its animating spirit, socialism, came to be reckoned as progressive, i. e., on the side of progress. In fact, it was not only thought of as being progressive but also inevitable, perhaps chosen and instituted by man but driven by the forces undergirding historical change. Thus, an American historian writing about the era of the Franklin D. Roosevelt changes refers to "the *necessity* for the regulation of their affairs by government," "the *need* for control," a "point of view of the problem of relief that was *destined* to be accepted," "the *need* for relief appropriations," and "*justifiable* to meet the *needs* of relief."[511] Socialist ideas, however, began to make their impact more directly on America during the last two decades before World War I.

c. Major Reforms of Progressives

Both of the major political parties shifted toward reformism in the years preceding World War I. The shift of the Democrats may have been more dramatic. In retrospect, it is clear that the change was signaled by the nomination of William Jennings Bryan as Democratic presidential candidate in 1896. The outgoing President, Grover Cleveland, was the last in a line of Democrats that can be traced back to Jefferson and Jackson in their constitutional position. No Democrat has been elected to the presidency in the 20th century, and it is doubtful that one has been nominated, who held to the strict construction of the Constitution. Indeed, the Democrats have generally been at the forefront of those ignoring constitutional restraints and using government to gradually move toward socialism.

Reformist and socialist leaning political action had been advocated by minor parties from the mid-1870s to the mid-1890s. This movement had culminated in the formation of the Populist (People's) Party in the early 1890s. The Populists ran General James B. Weaver for President in 1892 and made a vigorous campaign. They were inflationists, wanted a government printed currency and easy money, government ownership of the railroads (clearly socialist), a graduated income tax, a government mandated shorter working day for industrial laborers, and direct election of Senators. Their candidate got over a million votes, which indicated considerable strength at the time. The important point here, however, is that the Democrats shifted to an inflationist ticket in 1896 when they nominated William Jennings Bryan. They were much more reformist, too, than in the past. Sufficiently so that the Populists nominated Bryan at their convention, and the gold standard Democrats withdrew from the party and nominated their own candidate. The Democrats did not win the election, but they had made a fateful shift toward reformism.

How far the Democrats had moved from strict construction may be suggested by this argument made by Woodrow Wilson in the 1912 campaign. He said:

> The trouble with the theory [of a Constitution based on natural law with checks and balances] is that government is not a machine, but a living thing. It falls, not under the theory of the universe, but under the theory of organic life. . . . Living political constitutions must be Darwinian in structure and in practice. Society is a living organism and must obey the laws of life. . . .
>
> All that progressives ask or desire is permission—in an era when "development," "evolution," is the scientific word—to interpret the Constitution according to the Darwinian principle; all they ask is recognition that a nation is a living thing and not a machine.[512]

In short, Wilson wanted an interpretation of the Constitution in accord with the latest fashion in ideas and beliefs, or at least in accord with his policies. Indeed, the notion did become current in some circles in the 20th century that the Constitution should be so construed as to allow actions they believed to be desirable, though they were more likely to describe them as necessary and even inevitable rather than desirable.

The Republican shift toward reformism came during the presidency of Theodore Roosevelt. Indeed, both Republicans and Democrats were influenced by the ideas that gained a following during the Progressive Era. These may have peaked politically during the election campaign of 1912. Unable to get the Republican nomination for what would have been virtually a third term in the presidency, Roosevelt ran on the Bull Moose ticket, which started the Progressive Party on its ill-fated career. At any rate, in 1912 Roosevelt was clearly designated as a progressive, so was Woodrow Wilson, and so in their own way probably were the other candidates: President William Howard Taft and Socialist Eugene Debs.

Progressivism, as a political ideology, fused together three powerful ideas. It carried with it the belief that progress could be consciously achieved by the aggressive use of government power. Thus, it linked the idea of progress with government instituted reforms. Second, it linked democracy—popular government, extension of the franchise, and making our political institutions more democratic—with progress and reform. John Dewey, the prophet of Progressive Education, was the apostle of democracy. It was for him the philosopher's stone which would transform America. In any case, the notion had taken hold that the United States was a democracy, or was supposed to be, or ideally ought to be, or something of the sort. The idea of democracy was linked with equality, and the notion gained favor of the use of the power of government under democratic control to make people equal. Third, these ideas were linked to nationalism and to the expansion of the role of the central government. Thus, Theodore Roosevelt called his brand of progressivism the New Nationalism in 1912. Less sensibly, Wilson called his the New Freedom.

Undergirding this thrust to reform and transform was a rarely mentioned socialism. Instead, the movement toward it went by less innocuous and more innocent names, such as democracy, progressivism, and eventually liberalism. And, there were American intellectuals pushing what amounted to socialism by gradualist methods. Nowhere was this clearer than in the writings of three men in the years before World War I, three men who helped establish the magazine of opinion, *The New Republic*. They were: Herbert Croly, Walter Weyl, and Walter Lippmann. Although each of these men was clearly thrusting toward establishing some sort of socialism in America, they did not use that word to describe it. As some might say nowadays, they avoided the "S" word. But the socialist vision glistens, or at least glimmers, through their cautious formulations. For example, Lippmann wrote: "Private property will melt away; its functions will be taken over by the salaried men who direct them, by government commissions, by developing labor unions."[513] Croly said that what he was proposing was socialistic "in case socialism cannot be divorced from the use wherever necessary, of the political organization in all its form to realize the proposed democratic purpose."[514] Along similar lines, Weyl wrote: "Today no democracy is possible in America except a socialized democracy, which conceives of society as a whole and not as a[n] . . . assemblage of myriads of individuals."[515]

Their gradualism was even more apparent. Croly described the recommended gradualist tactics this way:

> In the existing condition of economic development and of public opinion, the man who believes in the ultimate necessity of government ownership of railroad road-beds and terminals must be content to wait and to watch. The most that he can do for the present is to use any opening which the course of railroad development affords, for the assertion of his ideas; and if he is right, he will gradually be able to work out, in relation to the economic situation of the railroads, some practical method of realizing the ultimate purpose.[516]

More abstractly, Weyl said "that the surest method of progress is to take one step after another. The first step, often uncontested (*because* it is only one step) leads inevitably to others."[517] These men also favored a gradually changing Constitution, though in fact they viewed the written Constitution as an obstacle to progress. Weyl said, "Our newer democracy demands, not that the people forever conform to a rigid hard-changing Constitution, but the Constitution changes to conform to the people. The Constitution of the United States is the political wisdom of a dead America."[518] Croly, who treated the document somewhat more respectfully, held that the Constitution was generally admirable, "and in most respects it should be left to the ordinary process of gradual amendment by legal construction. . . ."[519] Weyl, too, thought that the changes could be wrought by court interpretation. He said, "It is possible for them [the Supreme Court] by a few progressive judicial decisions to democratize the Constitution."[520]

Croly's book, *The Promise of American Life,* as well as his other writings, are generally believed to have had some considerable impact on political thought at the time. One historian notes that he not only influenced Theodore Roosevelt's thinking but that "Lippmann called his former associate 'the first important political philosopher who appeared in the twentieth century'; Alvin Johnson grants Croly 'the palm of the leadership in the philosophy of the progressive movement' . . . , while Felix Frankfurter credits him with 'the most powerful single contribution to progressive thinking.' "[521] Though utopia may have been in their minds, these men had plotted the course for building Leviathon in America.

(1) Presidential Leadership

A major innovation of progressives was the practice of the President taking the lead in conceiving, promoting, and getting legislation through Congress. Theodore Roosevelt and Woodrow Wilson were at the forefront of asserting this kind of presidential leadership over programs and legislation, though it was Franklin D. Roosevelt who brought the method to fruition in the 1930s. A major device for asserting the leadership was through an elaborated program for reform and change, under some catchy title. Theodore Roosevelt called his program in 1905 a Square Deal. In 1912, he called his Bull Moose program the New Nationalism. In the same election year Woodrow Wilson called his program the New Freedom. Franklin D. Roosevelt called his the New Deal, and some historians claim to have discerned a First New Deal, a Second New Deal, and even the makings of a Third New Deal. It would hardly be surprising since he ran for a third term in office in 1940, and even a fourth in 1944. Harry Truman called his program the Fair Deal; John F. Kennedy called his the New Frontier; and Lyndon B. Johnson ran out the string with his Great Society. The Democratic candidates abandoned programatic titles after the 1960s; no Republican, except Theodore Roosevelt, had ever proposed one.

What such phrases as Square Deal, New Freedom, and New Deal did was enable Presidents to take over the lead in designing legislation, proposing courses of action, and engaging in government planning. It was a way, too, for ideology to guide the government thrust into the future. None of these Presidents professed to be socialist, but such socialist conceptions as social responsibility for the well being of the people, government control over the economy, and redistribution of the wealth, in varying degrees, undergirded these programs.

It was hardly surprising that Theodore Roosevelt should have been a primary examplar in advancing presidential leadership. He was, after all, a man of vast energy and given to vigorous and assertive activity. He had demonstrated well his versatility and vitality before coming to the presidency. By turn, he was a state legislator, member of the Civil Service Commission, head of a police board, Assistant Secretary of the Navy, governor of New York, rancher and vigilante in the Dakotas, historian, biographer, Roughrider in the Spanish-American War, and big game hunter (for whom the Teddy bear was named). Mark Sullivan, a journalist, referred to him as a cross between St. George and St. Vitus. "His every gesture counted," Sullivan wrote, "his every blow went to the mark. . . . Roosevelt in battle—which was Roosevelt most of the time—was a huge personality endowed with energy almost abnormal, directed by an acute intelligence, lightened by a grinning humor, engaged in incessant action."[522]

As President, Roosevelt was soon in the thick of all manner of affairs, domestic and foreign: arbitrating a labor dispute, settling international disputes, trust-busting, intervening in Caribbean countries, launching the Panama Canal project, and conserving natural resources. He had a very generous view of the powers of the President, inclining to the view that he could do whatever the Founders had not had the forethought to forbid. His reformism did not take long to come to the fore after he became President. As one historian said:

>His message to Congress in December, 1904 was significantly with-
>out most of the equivocations of the past. Over half the document was
>given over to proposals for new economic and social legislation.[523]

He called for the Federal government to pass an employer's liability act to
cover its employees and those of contractors employed by government.
There were requests for such things as requiring the use of safety devices on
railroads, regulation of the hours of labor of railroad workers, giving the
Interstate Commerce Commission power to set rail rates, establishing a
Bureau of Corporations to license interstate business, the instituting of numerous reforms in the District of Columbia, and the like. Even if all the
reforms proposed by Theodore Roosevelt had been made, they would have
fallen far short of those of the second Roosevelt's New Deal. But the Federal
government had got its foot in the door and was inching inside.

Woodrow Wilson's avowal and adoption of a strong leadership role for
the President was not so much a matter of personality as was that of
Roosevelt; it was much more cerebral. Roosevelt had been a man of action;
Wilson was an academician, held a Ph.D. in history from Johns Hopkins
University, was a writer and lecturer, became a professor at Princeton and
then president of the university. He had discerned the need for presidential
leadership during his years as a scholar and noted it in this excerpt from a
review of James Bryce's *American Commonwealth*. "It is the separation of
the executive from Congress, a separation which deprives the executive of
all voice in the formation of administrative and financial policy, and which
deprives Congress of such leadership as would give its plans coherency and
make available for its use that special and intimate knowledge of administrative possibilities without which much well meant legislation must utterly
miscarry. . . . Without such legislative leadership [as the European governments have in their ministerial system in which ministers, including their
prime ministers, serve in and lead the legislatures] we remain for long
periods of embarrassment without any solution of some of the simplest
problems that await legislation. . . . The evil consists in slipshod, haphaz-
ard, unskilled and hasty legislation; the good, so far as it may be stated in
a single sentence, consists in delaying the triumphs of public opinion and
thereby, perhaps, rendering them safer triumphs. . . ."[524]

Wilson, as well as Roosevelt, used a unified program under a catchy
title—in this case, the New Freedom—to assert presidential leadership. But
Progressives generally wanted to go further than to assert presidential
leadership. They wanted a dominant role for the Federal government in the
country, and to that end they needed constitutional and other changes. In
the course of 1913, two constitutional amendments and major banking
legislation became law. These changed the potentialities and possibilities of
the exercise of power by the Federal government without restraint by the
states.

(2) The 16th Amendment

The first of these to be adopted was the one known as the income tax amendment. It was proposed by Congress July 12, 1909 and declared ratified by the states February 25, 1913. The amendment is among the simplest and most direct of the amendments. It is composed of a single sentence and reads:

> The Congress shall have power to lay and collect taxes on incomes, from whatever source derived, without apportionment among the several States, and without regard to any census or enumeration.

The amendment was intended to remove the constitutional obstacles to a tax on incomes. The main obstacle is contained in Section 9 of Article I of the Constitution, a section dealing with the limitation of the powers of Congress, and thus of the United States government. The prohibition involved reads:

> No Capitation, or other direct, Tax shall be laid, unless in Propor- to the Census or Enumeration herein before directed to be taken.

Assuming that a tax on incomes is a direct tax—what else could it be?—, this made it virtually impossible for Congress to comply with the prohibition and pass an income tax. True, the waters had been muddied both by earlier action and by reformist partisans of such a tax, who wanted one desperately regardless of what the Constitution might say. Indeed, a tax on incomes had been levied during the Civil War and continued into effect until 1872. That proved little, however, for constitutional restrictions on the Federal government were often ignored during this period. Matters had changed for the better of the Constitution by the 1890s, for when Congress passed a tax on incomes in 1894, the question came before the Supreme Court rather quickly, and in 1895 the Supreme Court declared the tax unconstitutional in the case of *Pollock vs. Farmers' Loan and Trust*. The Court did so on the ground that taxes on income were "a direct tax within the meaning of the Constitution, and, therefore, unconstitutional and void because not apportioned according to representation. . . ."[525] What the Court was saying was that direct taxes to be constitutional had to be apportioned among the states according to their respective populations as is representation in Congress. Practically, there does not appear to be any way to levy such a tax by the Federal government. In sum, it was prohibited by the Constitution.

The 16th Amendment undid that prohibition, of course. More, it opened the way for Congress and the Federal government to avail itself of the income of Americans to as great a degree as they dared. Note, however, that the 16th Amendment did not authorize a graduated or progressive tax on incomes. A graduated tax usually taxes higher incomes at higher rates. For example, net incomes ranging from $10 thousand to $20 thousand might be taxed at a rate of 15%, while those above $20 thousand might be taxed at 28%. In the absence of specific authorization to levy graduated taxes, the assumption should be that a uniform rate would be authorized by the 16th Amendment. That assumption might have been reinforced by the constitutional requirement that all duties, imposts and excises shall be uniform throughout the United States. Neither Congress, Presidents, nor the courts have been deterred by this consideration. They have plunged ahead with levying and accepting graduated taxes with little or no concern for the inequities involved, justifying such taxes on the grounds that people are being taxed according to their ability to pay.

In any case, Progressives were leaning toward the socialist idea of using government to redistribute wealth. The graduated tax was an essential in doing this. The great growth in government, in programs, and in spending was made possible in considerable measure at the Federal level by the income tax.

(3) 17th Amendment

It could be argued that the 17th Amendment was a delayed impact from the Civil War and Reconstruction. Certainly, one of the major thrusts of that war and its aftermath was to undercut and destroy the independence of the states. The 17th Amendment, viewed from that angle, was a *de jure* (legal) recognition of the *de facto* (factual) status of the states and state governments after the war. Even so, as long as the state legislatures elected Senators, they not only retained a modicum of their independence but they also had a major counterweight and restraint on the actions of the Federal government. After all, if the Senate would not approve legislation it could not become law. If it did not set its seal upon presidential appointments, they could not hold office, and if it did not approve treaties they could not become the law of the land. The Senate was the most powerful deliberative body in the United States, and it represented state governments in national councils.

Looked at from another angle, the passage of the 17th Amendment indicated the triumphant sweep of democratization. This democratic urge had got at least partisan support in the Jackson era from the Democratic Party, and the word "democracy" had in the course of the 19th century become fixed in the minds of many as a proper description of what the American political system was, or, at the least, should become. More precisely, what the movement achieved was more widespread *popular* representation in government, not direct democracy, but the two things now became virtually indistinguishable for most people. At any rate, the thrust toward popular representation, democracy, or whatever it should be called, picked up new steam in the last years of the 19th century and the early years of the 20th century. It came from populists, socialists, social democrats, Progressives, and reformers in general. The thrust was toward more popular participation in government in general, not simply for the direct election of Senators. Thus, there were efforts to promote and establish popular initiatives, referendums, and recalls.

The National Progressive Republican League, founded in 1911, illustrates in its stated principles the linkage between radical reform measures and the thrust toward democracy that underlay the 17th Amendment. Those who founded the League declared that its object was the "promotion of popular government and progressive legislation." They declared that as matters stood popular measures for change were being thwarted by special interests. They went on to elaborate the particulars of their indictment of the political system:

> Under existing conditions legislation in the public interest has been baffled and defeated. This is evidenced by the long struggle to secure laws but partially effective for the control of railway rates and services, the revision of the tariff in the interest of the producer and consumer, statutes dealing with trusts and combinations, based on sound economic principles, as applied to modern industrial and commercial conditions; wise, comprehensive and impartial reconstruction of banking and monetary laws, the conservation of coal, oil, gas, timber, waterpower, and other natural resources belonging to the people, and for the enactment of all legislation solely for the common good.

What needed to be done to change these conditions was to have a much more democratic government responsive to the people, according to the Progressive Republican League. They advocated:

(1) The election of the United States Senators by direct vote of the people.

(2) Direct primaries for the nomination of elective officials.

(3) The direct election of delegates to national conventions with opportunity for the voter to express his choice for President and Vice-President.

(4) Amendment to state constitutions providing for the Initiative, Referendum and Recall.[526]

But however variously people were moved, the 17th Amendment was declared ratified by the states in 1913. The Senate, as might have been expected, was the major obstacle to getting a two-thirds majority for an amendment providing for direct election of Senators. The House had several times given the necessary majority for such an amendment, but the Senate was not finally brought around to that view until 1911. State legislatures generally moved with unexpected haste to ratify the amendment, when we consider that they were giving up their representation in Congress.

The main point to keep in mind, however, is that the 17th Amendment entailed a major structural change in the system of federalism and of republican government established by the Constitution. The federal system of government, it should be recalled, provided for a dispersion of the powers of government between the United States government and the states. It was so devised that the Federal government was to limit the states in certain regards, and the states were to limit the central government in its quest for power. Each was to be supreme in its realm—or at least independent of the other. Most of the constitutional leverage by which state governments could limit the United States was by their senatorial representatives in Congress. The 17th Amendment removed that leverage for limiting the Federal government and opened the way for the states to be reduced to appendages and subservient bodies to the United States. The latter did not come with overwhelming force until the 1950s and 1960s.

As for popular participation in government, the Founders leaned strongly toward the republican and away from the democratic side. They believed that government should be based on popular approval at some remove from actual popular participation in government. They not only incorporated the representative principle but also the indirect and filtering principle into their constitutions, both state and national. In general, the Founders accepted the Judeo-Christian view that man is a flawed creature, that he is a sinner, and when given power over others is apt to abuse it. This is true of those who rule as well as those who are ruled. Man was not by nature good, and it followed that when the number of men were multiplied or concentrated in masses their nature and inclinations were not improved. The ruled—i. e., the *people*—needed to be limited and restricted in their use of power just as much as the rulers. This was done in a variety of ways in the state and the United States Constitutions. The electoral franchise was limited in a variety of ways. The power of the people was indirect and filtered on the government. Only the members of the House of Representatives were directly elected by the populace, but even there the popular influence was indirect by representation. The Senate was elected by the legislatures, some or all of whom were directly elected by the voters. And the filtering process was continued by the presidential appointment of judges and other officials with the approval of the Senate, and the choosing of the President by the electoral college, whose members could be either directly elected by the voters within states, or appointed as state legislators might direct. Neither mob rule nor participatory democracy were provided for in the Constitution.

This is not to raise a constitutional objection to a constitutionally ratified amendment. None is permissible. It can only be changed constitutionally by adopting an amendment that supersedes it, and none is in the offing. However, it is appropriate to point out how a constitutional amendment altered the form of government and what its tendencies were. The 17th Amendment facilitated the concentration of power in the central government as well as the exercise of power throughout the Union hardly checked by state legislatures. The states had few enough means for limiting the central government in the original Constitution, and the 17th Amendment removed the main one of those still standing. This amendment, along with other less formal changes that have been made, had reduced the limits on those elected to govern and contributed to the democratizing of the government.

Two other amendments were added to the Constitution by the Progressives. The 18th Amendment was added in 1919, and the 19th Amendment in 1920. The 18th Amendment was surely a venture in using the power of government to make men over into someone's ideal of them. It prohibited "the manufacture, sale, or transportation of intoxicating liquors within, the importation thereof into, or exportation thereof from the United States and all territory subject to the jurisdiction thereof for beverage purposes. . . ." The amendment and the legislation pursuant to it is sometimes called the noble experiment with Prohibition which failed. In any case, the amendment was repealed by the 20th Amendment, ratified in 1933.

The 19th Amendment provides that "The right of citizens of the United States to vote shall not be denied or abridged by the United States or by any State on account of sex." Since the United States government had earlier intruded in the matter of who was entitled to vote in the 15th Amendment, this only extended the prohibition to cover women. The democratization involved was also in keeping with the Progressive emphasis on popular participation in the government. Both the 18th and 19th Amendments, as well as the 15th Amendment, extended the reach of the Federal government at the expense of the powers of the states. Nor should it go unremarked that since women attained the vote, the government has turned decisively toward erecting the welfare state with emphasis on security. It is at least a plausible inference that this emphasis on security may have been influenced by traditional female concerns and the political effort to appeal to the female vote.

Even so, the 16th and 17th Amendments had much more directly to with preparing the ground for Leviathan in the 20th century.

(4) The Federal Reserve System

Of equal importance with the 16th (income tax) Amendment for the expansion and sway of the Federal government was the Federal Reserve Act of 1913. Indeed, it may ultimately have been even more important for tapping the wealth of the country. After all, income taxes can only tap the wealth by being actually levied upon Americans by Congress. By contrast, the Federal Reserve can tap that wealth by the use of credit and debt to inflate and surreptitiously take away the value of the money and appropriate it for political or other purposes. Before looking into that, however, it may be helpful to see what the Act in 1913 did.

The Act authorized up to 12 regional banks (eventually established in Boston, New York, Philadelphia, Richmond, Atlanta, Dallas, Kansas City,

St. Louis, Chicago, Cleveland, Minneapolis, and San Francisco). The purpose of this was to disperse financial centers around the country rather than having finance concentrated in New York City, as was alleged to be the case. They were banker's banks, not banks which serve individuals as do commercial banks, savings and loan associations, and credit unions. A private individual cannot go into a Federal Reserve Bank, make a deposit there, take out a loan there, or conduct any business with it. Only member banks can do that.

The capital stock of the Federal Reserve Banks is subscribed to and owned by member banks. Thus, technically, the banks are owned by member banks. All national banks are required to be members of a Federal Reserve bank, and state banks may belong to the system. Most of the "owners" have been compelled to buy stock, but do not have the usual rights of ownership. The ruling body is the Federal Reserve Board (sometimes referred to as the board of governors), whose members are appointed by the President of the United States and which also includes the Secretary of the Treasury and the United States Comptroller General. True, each Federal Reserve bank has its own governing board composed of nine members, six of whom are chosen by member banks. But only three of them may be bankers; the other three must be from business or agriculture. Furthermore, the remaining three members that make up the nine, are appointed by the central Federal Reserve Board, and executive officers come from these. Thus, while the Federal Reserve banks may be owned by the banks, they are controlled by government appointments and officials. In practice, the centralization of control has become more dominant over the years.

The Federal Reserve banks perform two basic functions as banker's banks: (1) they are banks of issue; (2) they are discount banks. A bank of issue is one which issues currency which is supposed to serve as money. The currency issued by Federal Reserve Banks is Federal Reserve notes. (Indeed, at the present time, Federal Reserve notes are the only legal currency in the United States. That was not so at the time they began to be issued, when there were also gold and silver coins, national bank notes, and, at a later date, there were silver certificates until the late 1960s.) As discount banks, these banks discount commercial paper (i. e., notes which evidence private indebtedness) and agricultural paper (notes indicating farm loans of one sort or another). That is, they enable banks to increase their cash reserves by discounting the notes they have taken for loans they have made. The Federal Reserve Board is empowered to make such discounting more or less attractive by lowering or raising discount rates. The Federal Reserve also can determine the required reserves of member banks and can thus affect the ease of credit and the effective money supply. Federal Reserve notes can be issued to pay for the commercial and agricultural paper they discount. Initially, the Federal Reserve banks were required to back their currency with a 40% reserve of gold.

The Federal Reserve system was supposed to prevent banking panics (and their accompanying depressions) by providing a flexible currency supply. As one account has it (and this has been the generally accepted explanation), "The major problem facing all banks was that the currency supply was inelastic. There was no power, either private or governmental, to expand or contract the money supply to meet the seasonal needs of industry and agriculture or to prevent financial panics."[527] This was a head in the sand attitude with an inflationary bias. One might as well explain drownings on the basis of excess water in swimming pools.

There is no great mystery about bank panics and the depressions that spring from them. The root cause of bank panics is fractional reserve banking. In brief, that is the practice of keeping only a small portion—a fraction—of reserves against the demand deposits of their customers. The fraction may be 10, 15, 20, or whatever per cent, just so that it is any amount significantly less than 100%. In these circumstances, the bank is always potentially bankrupt; all that it takes to turn the potentiality into actuality is for some substantial portion of depositors to demand cash. If the bank cannot accommodate them, the word will quickly spread to its other customers, then to customers elsewhere. The result is a bank panic and its offspring—a *liquidity crisis*. That is the classic process to bank panics, the result of which is a rapid contraction of the money supply—known unpopularly as a depression.

The legal cure for such panics and their unattractive offspring would be to require that all persons (including corporations) who promise to pay on demand have reserves to cover that amount at all times. There is nothing unreasonable about such a requirement. Indeed, the consequence is already prohibited, but the practice is approved and protected for banks. It comes under the "privilege of banking." A hundred per cent, or thereabouts, reserve requirement would drastically alter banking, of course. It would take away most of the power that banks exercise over liquid wealth and its disposition as loans. Above all, it would take away the power of banks to inflate the currency.

It is this last power, the power to inflate, that so attracted Progressives to fractional reserve banking and led them to set up a system of support for banks, and brought most of them more directly under government control. Indeed, if banking in America was not already a government directed and controlled activity, it became one after the passage of the Federal Reserve Act. Private ownership of the Federal Reserve Banks was largely illusory, since the Federal government both set up the system and controlled its operation. Perhaps, the most unconstitutional feature of this arrangement was that Federal Reserve notes were made legal tender. The only power over the money granted to the government of the United States was to coin money. It has no authority to make tender laws nor to print paper money. Even the authority to incorporate national banks was assumed, nor specifically granted. And surely, no power was granted in the Constitution to any government to inflate the currency and take away the value of the money in the hands of the people.

Although the Federal Reserve system did not yet have all the powers it would receive and exercise from the 1930s on, the means was in place after 1913 for the Federal government to exercise both overt and covert control over the liquid wealth of the country. Indeed, the full impact of these developments, amendments, and acts of Congress—the growth of presidential power by way of leadership, the passage of the 16th and 17th Amendments, and the passage by Congress of the Federal Reserve Act—was not felt before the 1930s. The Federal government did concentrate and exercise extraordinary power over Americans during World War I. Indeed, it served as a training ground in the exercise of political power for the New Dealers in the 1930s.

But there was a backing off from the aggressive use of some of these new powers in the 1920s. Neither Presidents Warren Harding nor Calvin Coolidge conceived of ideological programs for America and advanced them as some sort of deal or other. Nor were they disposed to redistribute the wealth by vast taxing or inflationary activities. President Hoover might have been bent a little more in those directions—though he was hardly infatuated with socialism—, but he did not move with dispatch to contrive new programs.

In any case, the next great changes came in the 1930s.

Chapter 17

Breaking the Constitutional Dam

The object of the United States Constitution, it may be recalled, was both to empower a general government and to restrain and limit it within its jurisdiction. It outlined a jurisdiction for the United States, acknowledged a jurisdiction for the states, and recognized that the people retained an assortment of rights. These rights were protected especially by prohibiting or inhibiting the powers of the United States government and/or those of states. The task of enforcing these limits and restrictions was not turned over to any special or particular body. It was not within the jurisdiction of the Supreme Court or Federal courts alone, much contemporary opinion to the contrary notwithstanding. The duty of observing and defending the Constitution falls upon all who serve in significant political offices within the United States.

The Constitution prescribes the language of the particular oath the President is to take when he assumes the powers of that office. On this matter, the Constitution says:

> Before he enter on the Execution of his Office, he [the President] shall take the following Oath or Affirmation:—''I do solemnly swear (or affirm) that I will faithfully execute the Office of President of the United States, and will to the best of my Ability, preserve, protect and defend the Constitution of the United States.''

The more general prescription is found in Article VI of the Constitution, and says:

> The Senators and Representatives before mentioned, and the Members of the several State legislatures, and all executive and judicial Officers, both of the United States and of the several States, shall be bound by Oath or Affirmation, to support this Constitution. . . .

All the officers and legislatures mentioned above have the duty first of all to perform those duties appropriate to their offices, second to observe the constitutional limits on their authority and activity, and third to defend against encroachments either upon their jurisdiction and power or the rights of the people, so far as it is within their power to do so. The line of defense of the Constitution may be thought of as running something like this: from the House of Representatives to the Senate to the President to the Supreme Court or subordinate courts. In fact, violations may begin with any body, and the defense may be in any body or branch of the Federal government or in the states. The main line of the defense of the Constitution by state governments historically was through the Senate. The 17th Amendment removed that line of defense, but the effect was not immediately felt. The state governments may sue in the courts, but that is a weak defense when the courts are the main offenders. The ultimate defense of the Constitution lies with the people in general, but the formal means by which they may act are indirect. The power of numbers can be expressed formally by petition and indirectly by voting. All this is by way of saying that the main lines of defense against violations of the Constitution by the Federal government lie within that government itself, especially since 1913.

So long as each of the branches is acting more or less independently of each other, and individuals and branches are acting honorably by observing the bounds and in their self-interest, then limited government can survive and work in the American system. Indeed, the Constitution worked tolerably well, usually, from 1789 to 1933. Undoubtedly, it had sometimes been bent out of shape—this was certainly the case during Civil War and Reconstruction for a decade and a half, and for a shorter period during World War I. The great danger to the system, and to the liberties of the people, lies in all the branches of government coming under the sway of a common passion, as James Madison observed long ago. A related danger, we might observe with the experience of the 20th century, would be for all the branches to come under the sway of a common ideology. That can wreak havoc when all branches are not only under the sway of an ideology but also controlled under the same political party. Opinion makers and the media of communication have added yet another dimension to the forces and passions which can actuate men in government and lead them to override their limits.

Our Constitution probably had its greatest stress prior to 1933 during wars, especially again, the Civil War. This probably best exemplifies the branches of the government falling prey to a ruling passion, all opposition being overborn, and many of the restraints on government being removed. Even so, as noted already, the Constitution has generally stood well to restrain and limit government. It has served as a great dam to contain the thrusts to power of individuals and branches. To put it another way, men and branches have usually worked as the system provides to hold the government in check. Major breaks in the dam were made in the 1930s.

a. Emergency Used to Justify Action

The United States was in the midst of what has been generally called the "Great Depression" during the national election in November, 1932. Nonetheless, "Happy days" were "here again," at least temporarily, or so the Democrats sang, for they elected a Democratic President, Franklin D. Roosevelt, and both houses of Congress were securely Democratic. The election did not, however, alter the depression, or, if it did, it made it worse. According to most accounts the depression deepened in the winter of 1932–1933.

The length of time between election and inauguration was still quite a while in those days, as it had been since the beginning of the Republic. It was not unusual for it to last four months. This time, the election took place on November 8, 1932; the inauguration did not occur until March 4, 1933, not quite four months. Meanwhile, the old Congress—a "lame duck," as it was said, because a new Congress had already been elected—held its regular legislative session and adjourned. This hiatus between the election and taking over the reins of government might have been of little consequence. After all, the practice was long established, and few had thought to remark or complain about it. There were some differences this time, however. For one thing, the notion was gaining hold that it was the responsibility of the government, especially the Federal government, to deal effectively with the depression. The premises of socialism that had been sown in earlier years were bearing some fruit. For another, President Hoover had at least acted as if the government must take various actions to deal with the economic consequences of the depression. The measures taken probably worsened the situation, but did not still the urge for different government measures. Plus, agencies of the government, such as the Federal Reserve Banks, for one set of them, bore a large measure of responsibility for the worsening banking crisis. More, Roosevelt apparently welcomed the worsening of the crisis, for it afforded him an opportunity to take and advance many emergency measures.

The following is a description by one historian of how Roosevelt refused to take part in Hoover's effort to avert the crisis:

> Meanwhile, President Hoover had been trying to win Roosevelt's approval for policies that would stabilize the financial situation and restore public confidence. In private conference and by letter Hoover exhorted the President-elect to announce that he would balance the budget, maintain the dollar at its current value in gold, and cooperate with the European powers in stabilizing currencies and exchange rates. Roosevelt refused [because these proposals ran counter to his intentions]. . . . Thus irreconcilable difference over policy prevented effective teamwork between the two men. . . .[528]

Roosevelt's formal position was that he could do nothing until he took office. Hoover later maintained that fear of what Roosevelt would do deepened the depression.

However all that may be, the situation did grow worse. Here are some examples of what happened to some stocks between their highs in 1929 to their lows in 1932: "General Motors common, which had been priced at 72¾ at the peak of the Bull Market in 1929 . . . , reached a 1932 low of 7⅝. Radio Corporation common, which had been 101 at the peak . . . , got as low as 2½. And United States Steel, long considered the bellwether of the market, with a 1929 high of 261¾ . . . , sank to 21¼."[529] By March of 1933, according to one account, "The national income was less than half of what it had been four short years before. Nearly thirteen million Americans—about one quarter of the labor force—were desperately seeking jobs. The machinery for sheltering and feeding the unemployed was breaking down everywhere under the growing burden. . . ."[530]

There may have been some exaggeration in the above account, but the arrival of a banking crisis by March of 1933 could not be doubted. There had been large numbers of individual bank failures 1930–1932, but the crisis took on new proportions in late 1932. "The first sign of crisis came on October 31, 1932, when the Governor of Nevada declared a twelve-day banking holiday. . . . On February 4, 1933, Governor Huey P. Long closed the banks of Louisiana; ten days later the Governor of Michigan declared a banking moratorium for a week. Then during the ensuing three weeks, state after state succumbed, until the climax of the crisis came in the early morning of March 4, when Governor Herbert H. Lehman closed the New York banks for two days. By the hour of Roosevelt's inaugural, banks were either closed or doing business under severe restrictions in forty-seven states."[531]

The banking crisis, as well as other problems, were surely grist for Roosevelt's mills. He made clear in his inaugural address that the country was in an emergency and that he was determined to use this as a platform for vigorous action. He said that "the greatest primary task is to put people to work," and that he proposed to do something about it by "treating the task as we would treat the emergency of war. . . ." He emphasized that the country needed leadership and that he was about to "assume unhesitatingly the leadership of this great army of our people. . . ."

He made clear, too, at least in outline, how far he would go in exerting personal power in the emergency. First, he said, he would propose measures to Congress to deal with the emergency. If Congress acted positively in enacting them with such changes as it might make or proposed acceptable measures of its own, he promised to press forward with them.

> But in the event that the Congress shall fail to take one of these two courses, and in the event that the national emergency is still critical, I shall not evade the clear course of duty that will then confront me.
>
> I shall ask the Congress for the one remaining instrument to meet the crisis—broad executive power to wage a war against the emergency as great as the power that would be given me if we were in fact invaded by a foreign foe.[532]

Of course, Congress would have no constitutional authority to grant the President power "to wage a war against the emergency," because no such power exists, either in the Constitution or in the universe. (Wars are waged against men, not abstractions or things.) The Constitution does not, of course, list or recognize any emergency powers belonging either to the President or the Congress. Happily, Mr. Roosevelt did not have to ask for the alleged war powers. He did, however, use the emergency as justification for greatly expanding the powers of the government, many of which are nowhere to be found in the Constitution. He did call a special session of Congress, which met a few days after his inauguration. The Congress did pass quite an array of measures during the hundred or so days of its session, some of which were related to the emergency, and some not clearly so. Emergency was the purported justification for the unprecedented haste with which the measures were passed.

After 1933, great need often vied with emergency as justification for the programs Roosevelt advanced. As late as 1935, however, Roosevelt was proposing that "all emergency public works shall be united in a single new and greatly enlarged plan." And, he preserved the word in speaking of a new "program of public employment. . . ."[533] In his Second Inaugural Address in 1937, he used necessity to justify bold new programs for redistributing the wealth. He said that "I see tens of millions of its [meaning American] citizens—a substantial part of its whole population—who at this very moment are denied the greater part of what the very lowest standards of today call the necessities of life." He spelled out the situation with phrases like the following: "I see millions lacking the means to buy the products of farm and factory and by their poverty denying work and productiveness to many other millions. I see one-third of a nation ill-housed, ill-clad, ill-nourished."[534] For Roosevelt, emergencies and necessities were apparently taking the place of the Constitution as justification for government action.

It is unlikely, too, that when the President takes the leadership in advancing programs and legislation that he will perform his job of defending the Constitution. In theory at least, he might have taken care not to exceed constitutional bounds before he advanced the legislation. There is no evidence that Roosevelt did that. On the contrary, he apparently believed that the Constitution conferred great latitude upon the President and Congress in exercising the powers of Congress. He once offered this as his version of the situation in a "Fireside chat" delivered over the radio in 1937:

I hope that you have re-read the Constitution of the United States in these past few weeks. Like the Bible, it ought to be read again and again.

. . . In its Preamble, the Constitution states that it was intended to form a more perfect Union and to promote the general welfare; and the

powers given to the Congress to carry out those purposes can be best
described by saying that they were all the powers needed to meet each
and every problem which then had a national character and which
could not be met by merely local action.

But the framers went further. Having in mind that in succeeding
generations many other problems then undreamed of would become
national problems, they gave the Congress the ample broad powers "to
levy taxes . . . and provide for the common defense and general
welfare of the United States."[535]

That the phrase in Section 8, Article I of the Constitution which says "to
provide for the common Defence and general Welfare of the United States"
was not a plenary grant of power was pointed out by men who had taken a
hand in making the document several times in the early years of the Republic. Indeed, a much better case can be made that it was a limiting of
power rather than a grant. This is fortified by the fact that the sentence
containing this phrase was followed by a long list of the powers to be
exercised by the government by way of Congress. These would surely have
been superfluous if the phrase in question had been a general grant of power.

In any case, President Roosevelt did not talk like a man who was well
aware of the limits on his powers. He was, instead, busily conceiving
programs and legislation that would vastly increase his powers. Thus, he
was contributing to breaching the dam that restricted and limited the government rather than defending and fortifying.

b. Overwhelming Congress

President Franklin D. Roosevelt came as close to overwhelming Congress—at the worst having it rubber stamp his acts and proposals, or at best
allowing it to approve or disapprove his initiatives, reversing the constitutional relationship prescribed between the President and Congress—as any
Chief Executive ever has. For several years, mostly from 1933 through
1938, he imposed his legislative will over the United States by way of
Congress. He broke what will remained in Congress to observe the limits of
the Constitution and defend it from presidential or judicial encroachments.
It is not too much to say that Congress gave little thought to questions of
constitutionality, hardly raised them, and only individual members gave any
attention to the matter. By the time Congress recovered a modicum of its
former position—in the late 1940s, say—, it was too late in their judgment
to return to constitutional government. The legacy of Roosevelt's dominance lived on until the 1970s at least.

Roosevelt overwhelmed Congress not only with demands for immediate
action to deal with a dire emergency but also with sheer energy and audac-
ity. One historian has described it this way: "In the three months after

Roosevelt's inauguration, Congress and the country were subjected to a presidential barrage of ideas and programs unlike anything known to American history. . . . This was the Hundred Days; and in this period Franklin Roosevelt sent fifteen messages to Congress, guided fifteen major laws to enactment, delivered ten speeches, held press conferences and cabinet meetings twice a week, conducted talks with foreign heads of state, sponsored an international conference, made all the major decisions in domestic and foreign policy, and never displayed fright or panic and rarely even bad temper. His mastery astonished many who thought they had long since taken his measure.[536]

How he overwhelmed Congress needs to be illustrated more directly. Roosevelt was inaugurated on March 4, 1933. On March 5th, he called a special session of Congress. On March 6th, on very dubious authority, constitutional or otherwise, he proclaimed a four day national banking holiday. He also placed an embargo on the export of gold, silver, and the currency. Meanwhile, he put his aids to work fashioning legislation for dealing with the banking emergency. As soon as Congress convened on the afternoon of March 9, the House took up without preliminaries banking legislation prepared by the executive branch. The House of Representatives bypassed all of its arrangements for considering, examining, turning it over to the appropriate committees, holding public hearings, and giving it its place on the calendar. The bill was read aloud to the House of Representatives by the Chairman of the Banking and Currency Committee from the only available copy. Forty minutes was alloted for debate, but before that time was up members were calling for the question (for a vote to be taken). The House passed the Emergency Banking Act unanimously, just four hours after convening. Three and a half hours later the Senate passed it 73–7.

Nor was this a minor piece of legislation. It was some of the most far reaching legislation ever passed, placed virtual dictatorial powers in the hands of the President over banking and financial matters, and authorized the exercise of powers not contemplated in the Constitution. It "gave the President broad discretionary powers over transactions in credit, currency, gold, and silver, including foreign exchange. Gold hoarding and export were forbidden. A maximum penalty of $10,000 fine and ten years in prison was provided. The Act . . . authorized the Secretary of Treasury to call in all gold certificates in the country. . . ."[537]

Whether the power to set the price of gold from day to day was authorized by this or any other act is not clear, but the President proceeded to do so with the major object of raising the price of goods. How he went about doing this was described this way in a book by John T. Flynn:

> Thereafter each day [Henry] Morgenthau [Secretary of the Treasury] and Roosevelt met, with Jesse Jones, head of the RFC, present, to fix the price of gold. They gathered around Roosevelt's bed in the morn-

ing as he ate his eggs. Then "Henny-Penny" [Roosevelt's pet name for Morgenthau] and Roosevelt decided the price of gold for the day. One day they wished to raise the price. Roosevelt settled the point. Make it 21 cents, he ruled. That is a lucky number—three times seven. And so it was done. That night Morgenthau wrote in his diary: "If people knew how we fixed the price of gold they would be frightened."[538]

There was talk of adjourning Congress after it had passed the Emergency Banking Relief Act, but since Congress had passed the first bill with such alacrity, the President proceeded over the next hundred days to present it with legislation to manage and control the economy and to begin redistributing the wealth. The other bills were not pushed through with quite so much inordinate haste as the first bill, nor passed in such a frenzy. Even so what came during these days was a vast extension of Federal powers into areas not considered before, and certainly not in time of peace.

On March 31, a Civilian Conservation Corps was authorized by Congress and approved by the President. It was pushed primarily as providing employment for young men who would work on conservation projects. They lived in camps in a semi-military setting, were provided with food, shelter, and clothing, were paid a small sum of money, a portion of which was sent to their parents. The Federal government had never had such a make-work program before, nor was there any Constitutional program authorizing such activity. On May 12, a much broader Federal Emergency Relief Act was passed. Through this act, the Federal government provided funds to states and municipalities to undertake employment projects.

On the same day, May 12, 1933, Congress passed the Agricultural Adjustment Act. This act assumed vast powers over farm land, farms, farm prices, and agricultural activities. It empowered the Secretary of Agriculture "To provide for reduction in the acreage or reduction in the production for market, or both, of any basic agricultural commodity. . . . To enter into marketing agreements with processors, associations of producers, and others engaged in handling . . ." agricultural commodities. The Secretary was also authorized "To obtain revenue for extraordinary expenses incurred by reason of the national emergency" by levying "processing taxes. . . ." The President was also authorized to create currency called United States notes by having these issued by the Treasury Department. The Constitution does not, of course, authorize the issue of paper money by the United States government. The act further provided that "Such notes and all other coins and currencies heretofore coined or issued by or under the authority of the United States shall be legal tender for all debts public and private."[539] This was a *carte blanche* grant of unconstitutional power to the executive branch of the government.

Congress passed a spate of other acts during these days, the act establishing the Tennessee Valley Authority (which put the Federal Government into the business of making and distributing electricity), the Federal Securities Act, the National Employment System Act, the Farm Credit Act, the Federal Securities Act, the Emergency Railroad Transportation Act, as well as authorizing by legislation such agencies as the Commodity Credit Corporation and the Civil Works Administration, which was a major unemployment relief program.

But far and away the most ambitious program authorized during the Hundred Days of 1933, with only the possible exception of the Agricultural Adjustment Act, was the National Industrial Recovery Act. It was the boldest effort the government had ever made to manage and regulate the industrial side of the American economy. The Act proposed ''to provide for the general welfare by promoting the organization of industry for the purpose of cooperative action among trade groups, to induce and maintain united action of labor and management under adequate governmental sanctions and supervision, to eliminate unfair competitive practices to promote the fullest possible utilization of the present productive capacity of industries . . . , to increase the consumption of industrial and agricultural produces by increasing purchasing power . . . ,'' and so on. All this mind numbing power of regulation and control over private property was justified, according to the words of the Act, by the emergency which was said to exist.

The Act envisioned a series of codes drawn by the companies comprising each particular industry, such as, the automobile industry, the poultry processing industry, and the like. These codes would cover all sorts of practices within the industry as well as the proportions of production and markets for particular companies. The President had the approval of these codes and could impose codes of his own devising if those within an industry could not come up with satisfactory codes. In this connection, the President was given vast discretionary authority. The Act reads, in part:

> . . . The President may, as a condition of his approval of such code, impose such conditions . . . for the protection of consumers, competitors, employees, and others, and in furtherance of the public interest, and may provide such exceptions to and exemptions from the provisions of such code, as the President in his discretion deems necessary to effectuate the policy herein declared.

Moreover, section 7(a) of the National Industrial Recovery Act prescribed that all industrial codes would recognize ''That employees shall have the right to organize and bargain collectively. . . .'' In addition to that, ''employers shall comply with the maximum hours of labor, minimum rates of pay, and other conditions of employment, approved or prescribed by the President.''[540]

Much of this legislation was blatantly unconstitutional, and enough has been told to make clear that Congress was no longer seriously defending the Constitution from serious breaches of its limitations. On the contrary, it had become a willing instrument of the President, conferring on him such powers as no man could effectively exert or oversee and which none would seek if he did not want dictatorial control over the economic activity of the country. It is true that in ensuing years, Congress got its back up from time to time on constitutional matters, but it has generally shown willingness down through the years to go through the openings made by Roosevelt to forge new legislation.

c. Bringing the Courts to Heel

With the President bent on following his agenda with little or no regard to its constitutionality, with Congress overwhelmed and following his leadership, the next line of defense was the courts. The courts, and especially the Supreme Court, did much better in making a stand and defending the Constitution than did Congress. At least the courts held out a while, as might be expected. After all, the courts rarely complete their rounds of decisions under the pressure of particular events. Usually, even if there had been some emergency when the government acted, it will have passed or become less urgent before the courts get cases on appeal and render decisions on them. It was the case, too, that people generally, as well as most lawmakers, had accepted the view that the main responsibility for determining the constitutionality of acts of the government rested with the courts. While this unnecessarily plays down the defensive role of the legislative and executive branches, as well as their responsibilities to observe and defend the Constitution, it did make it more likely that the courts would defend the Constitution.

In any case, two of the major pieces of legislation of the early New Deal were held to be unconstitutional in whole or considerable part: the Agricultural Adjustment Act and the National Industrial Recovery Act. Indeed, between the beginning of 1935 going through the first third of 1936, the Supreme Court decided ten important cases involving New Deal legislation. "Stricken down in succession were Section 9(c) of the National Industrial Recovery Act, the N.R.A. itself, the Railroad Pension Act, the Farm Mortgage law, the Agricultural Adjustment Act, the A.A.A. amendments, the Bituminous Coal Act, and the Municipal Bankruptcy Act. Only two measures, the emergency monetary enactments of 1933 and the Tennessee Valley Authority Act, were given approval in carefully circumscribed and conditional terms. In short, the Court in sixteen months destroyed a very large portion of the Roosevelt program."[541]

Even in the case of some of the legislation that was approved, there were vigorous dissents by some of the justices. A Gold Repeal Joint Resolution had been passed in June of 1933. This cancelled the clauses in all private and public contracts calling for payment in gold. A series of cases, known collectively as the "Gold Clause cases" came to the Supreme Court, and a majority of the Court found them acceptable under the Constitution. Justice James C. McReynolds denounced the decisions in all the gold clause cases, speaking for the three other dissenters as well as himself. He said, "Just men regard repudiation and spoliation of citizens by their sovereign with abhorrence; but we are asked to affirm that the Constitution has granted power to accomplish both." He went on to declare that Congress "really has inaugurated a plan primarily designed to destroy private obligations, repudiate national debts, and drive into the treasury all the gold in the country in exchange for inconvertible promises to pay of much less value." In that case, he cried out in despair, "The Constitution is gone."[542]

The overturning of so much of the New Deal legislation was on constitutional grounds, of course. The first major piece of legislation nullified was the National Industrial Recovery Act, and the basic decision was reached in *Schechter Poultry Corp.* vs. *United States.* This was the landmark decision as well, and Chief Justice Charles E. Hughes gave the majority opinion. He dealt first with the idea that an emergency could provide constitutional justification for legislation. Chief Justice Hughes said:

> . . . Extraordinary conditions do not create or enlarge constitutional power. The Constitution established a national government with powers deemed to be adequate . . . , but these powers of the national government are limited by the constitutional grants. Those who act under these grants are not at liberty to transcend the imposed limits because they believe that more or different power is necessary. Such assertions of extra-constitutional power were anticipated and precluded by the explicit terms of the Tenth Amendment. . . .

These *dicta* were, of course, preliminary to dealing with the act in question. Two main points were made in determining the constitutionality of the act. The first point was the delegation of power to the President to approve and/or prescribe codes for industries. Now the power to legislate is vested in Congress by the Constitution, and the Court ruled, in effect, that it cannot be delegated to any other body to the extent that the other body is actually legislating. "The question," the Chief Justice said, "turns upon the authority which section 3 of the Recovery Act vests in the President to approve or prescribe. If the codes have standing as penal statutes, this would be due to the effect of executive action. But Congress cannot delegate legislative power to the President to exercise an unfettered discretion to make whatever laws he thinks may be needed or advisable for the rehabilitation and expansion of trade and industry."[543] On that ground, the Court declared the code making power was unconstitutionally established by the act.

The other point was the question of justifying the setting of wages and hours under the constitutional authority of the interstate commerce clause of the Constitution. The Court held that the company in question operated within the bounds of a single state, thus providing little constitutional ground for the exercise of congressional authority.

Nor were all the acts found unconstitutional those passed during the special session of Congress in 1933. The Bituminous Coal Act, mentioned in an earlier list, was passed in 1935, and was found unconstitutional by a majority of the Supreme Court in 1936. The majority opinion was read by Justice George Sutherland, and his stirring restatement of the principles of strict construction merit greater attention than the particular arguments in the case. The central paragraph of his restatement is quoted here:

> The ruling and firmly established principle is that the powers which the general government may exercise are only those specifically enumerated in the Constitution, and such implied powers as are necessary and proper to carry into effect the enumerated powers. Whether the end sought to be attained by an act of Congress is legitimate is wholly a matter of constitutional power and not at all of legislative discretion. Legislative congressional discretion begins with the choice of means and ends with the adoption of methods and details to carry the delegated powers into effect. The distinction between these two things— power and discretion—is not only very plain but very important. For while the powers are rigidly limited to the enumerations of the Constitution, the means which may be employed to carry the powers into effect are not restricted, save that they must be appropriate, plainly adapted to the end, and not prohibited by, but consistent with, the letter and spirit of the Constitution. Thus, it may be said that to a constitutional end many ways are open; but to an end not within the terms of the Constitution, all ways are closed[544]

Justice Sutherland went on to show what he was holding to be unconstitutional in the Bituminous Coal Act, but some portion of his purpose was to make clear to the Congress and the President that a majority of the Court was wedded to a strict construction of the Constitution.

By the middle of 1936, it must have been clear the New Deal must either change its course or be put at naught. Nor was the restraint of New Deal measures restricted to the Supreme Court. In "1935–36 federal judges issued some sixteen hundred injunctions preventing federal officers from carrying out federal laws."[545] The Republican Party platform in 1936 declared that the "New Deal Administration has dishonored American traditions. . . ." It further charged:

> The powers of Congress have been usurped by the President.
> The integrity and authority of the Supreme Court have been flouted.

> The rights and liberties of American citizens have been violated. . . .
> The New Deal Administration constantly seeks to usurp the rights reserved to the States and to the people.
> It has insisted on the passage of laws contrary to the Constitution. . . .
> It has dishonored our country by repudiating its most sacred obligations.[546]

Except for a few public comments, Roosevelt kept his own counsel as to what, if anything, he was going to do about the Court's overturning his legislation. The New Deal continued to advance and Congress to pass new measures, some of reenactment of parts of acts already declared unconstitutional on one or more grounds. The Democratic platform of 1936 promised that if they had further difficulty with keeping programs operating because of constitutional difficulties, they would propose constitutional amendments. But none were ever proposed or advanced by President Roosevelt.

He bided his time until after the election of 1936. In the election held on November 3, Roosevelt won an overwhelming landslide victory over his Republican opponent, Alfred M. Landon—27.7 million to 16.6 million for Landon. In the electoral college, Landon got the votes of only Maine and Vermont. It was the most lopsided win since James Monroe's in 1820. Moreover, the Democrats had majorities of 77 to 19 in the Senate and 328-107 in the House.

With majorities like that, Roosevelt believed that he had a mandate behind him to sway and turn the tide in the Court. On his own initiative, Roosevelt submitted a court reorganization plan to Congress. The main feature of the plan was to increase the membership of the Supreme Court from nine to as many as fifteen justices, one new member for each justice who did not retire from the Court after reaching the age of seventy. He also proposed to add 50 judges to the Federal courts. Roosevelt alleged that the courts were not keeping up with their work, and that this was due to the fact that some of the judges were getting too old. Chief Justice Hughes wrote a prominent Senator that the Supreme Court was up-to-date with its work and needed no new members. Roosevelt's major complaint was undoubtedly about the "conservative" justices: Willis Van Devanter, James C. McReynolds, George Sutherland, and Pierce Butler. He was well enough satisfied, no doubt, with the "liberals" on the Court: Louis D. Brandeis, Harlan F. Stone, and Benjamin Cardozo. The two others—Chief Justice Hughes and Justice Owen Roberts—were apt to swing either way on decisions to form a majority.

At any rate, in a radio address of March 9, 1937, Roosevelt launched his most direct attack upon the Supreme Court. He charged the Court with blocking legislation greatly needed to meet conditions in the country, with preventing the government from taking concerted action to meet the needs

of the country, and of asserting its own will rather than obeying precedent
and the Constitution. He said, ''When the Congress has sought to stabilize
national agriculture, to improve the conditions of labor, to safeguard business
against unfair competition, to protect our national resources, and in many
other ways to serve our clearly national needs, the majority of the Court has
been assuming the power to pass on the wisdom of these Acts of the
Congress—and to approve or disapprove the public policy written into these
laws.'' There ''is no basis,'' Roosevelt continued, ''for the claim made by
some members of the Court that something in the Constitution has compelled them regretfully to thwart the will of the people.'' More, ''The Court
. . . has improperly set itself up as a third House of the Congress—a
superlegislature, one of the justices has called it—reading into the Constitution words and implications which are not there, and which were never
intended to be there.'' That being the case, or so the President alleged, a
change was called for:

> We have, therefore, reached the point as a Nation where we must
> take action to save the Constitution from the Court and the Court from
> itself. We must find a way to make an appeal from the Supreme Court
> to the Constitution itself. We want a Supreme Court which will do
> justice under the Constitution—not over it.[547]

No sooner had Roosevelt sent the proposal to Congress than it was denounced as a ''Courtpacking Scheme.'' Roosevelt did not deny the charge;
he only denied that he would expect the men whom he appointed to do his
will without question. But otherwise, he said, ''if by that phrase the charge
is made that I would appoint . . . Justices worthy to sit beside present
members of the Court who understand these modern conditions; that I will
appoint Justices who will not undertake to override the judgment of the
Congress on legislative policy; . . . —if the appointment of such Justices can
be called 'packing the Courts'—than I say that I, and with me the vast
majority of the American people, favor doing just that thing—now.''[548]

For once, however, Roosevelt had misjudged, if not the American people, the reaction in Congress. The Senate Judiciary Committee, to whom the
bill was sent, rejected the proposal as drawn and made an adverse recommendation to the Senate. The Committee concluded, among other things,
about the proposal:

> It would subjugate the courts to the will of Congress and the Pres-
> ident and thereby destroy the independence of the judiciary, the only
> certain shield of individual rights. . . .
> It points the way to the evasion of the Constitution and establishes
> the method whereby the people may be deprived of their right to pass
> upon all amendments of the fundamental law. . . .

Under the form of the Constitution it seeks to do that which is unconstitutional.

Its ultimate operation would be to make this Government one of men rather than one of law, and its practical operation would be to make the Constitution what the executive or legislative branches of the Government choose to say it is—an interpretation to be changed with each change of administration.[549]

With that sterling indictment of the President's purposes before the Congress, the President's proposal, so far as it dealt with packing the Court, was rejected by Congress. It might be supposed, then, that President Roosevelt failed in his attempt to bring the courts to heel, that the Supreme Court retained its independence and continued to defend the Constitution by overturning legislation not sanctioned by it. But that would be to accept the appearances for the reality of what had happened. How deeply the courts had been intimidated by the President's not so subtle assault upon them can never be known. Certainly, it was a fearful thing to have the President appeal to the people over their heads and to send legislation to Congress to straighten out the courts.

What we do know is that after Roosevelt's attack on them the Federal courts, including the Supreme Court, no longer vigorously defended the Constitution from presidential and congressional innovations and intrusions. The President had lost a battle, but he won the war for most legislation that was passed from 1935 onward. The signs of his victory became apparent in 1937 both during the consideration and after the defeat of Roosevelt's Court Reorganization Plan. In March, 1937, the Supreme Court upheld Washington state's minimum wage law, not New Deal legislation but having something of its flavor about it. In April, 1937, the Supreme Court sustained a major piece of new law, the National Labor Relations Act of 1935. In May, the Court upheld the Social Security Act of 1935, and in a following decision declared that the tax on employers and employees for old age benefits was a valid exercise of the taxing power and that Congress could levy such taxes for the general welfare. Meanwhile, the makeup of the court was shifting away from the conservatives. Justice Van Devanter retired in May, 1937, and he was replaced by Senator Hugo Black of Alabama, who was a vigorous supporter of the New Deal in Congress. Justice Sutherland resigned in January, 1938, and he was replaced by Stanley Reed, who had been Solicitor General under Roosevelt and had frequently argued before the courts in favor of New Deal measures being challenged. Pierce Butler died in 1939, and was succeeded by the appointment of Frank Murphy, a New Deal favorite who had been governor of Michigan. Justice McReynolds, the last of the conservatives, died in 1941, and he was replaced by the Attorney General, Robert H. Jackson. The Court had long since become more Rooseveltian than that even would suggest, for such liberals and centrists as had been on the Court had mostly died or resigned to be replaced by Roosevelt's appointees. The most notable example was the replacement of Justice Louis Brandeis by William O. Douglas, who became the liberal bellwether for the next 36 years. Roosevelt's election to a third term in 1940 and a fourth term in 1944 had enabled him to pack the Supreme Court with his appointees without benefit of his Court Reorganization Plan.

Far from vigorously defending the Constitution from usurpation of power by the central government, the Supreme Court was before many years bent on its own aggressive extension of Federal Power.

d. Buying the People

The final defense of the Constitution lies with the states and the people. The most important means they have for defending the Constitution become available when amendments are submitted to the states for approval, or when delegates are chosen by the voters to conventions for the same purposes. It has already been noted, at least, that President Roosevelt never proposed any amendment that would have authorized the expansion of presidential or congressional powers. Indeed, since the 16th Amendment, ratified in 1913, and less certainly the 18th Amendment, ratified in 1919, no amendment has been submitted and ratified extending the powers of the Federal government. The 16th, income tax, Amendment has already been discussed above, and there should be no doubt that it expanded the potential of Federal power. The 18th, the Prohibition, Amendment gave the Federal government power over the manufacture, sale and export of intoxicating liquors, and this was substantial power. But it was subsequently repealed, and the Federal government largely relinquished those powers.

In sum, the great expansions of power by the Federal government and the growth of that government into Leviathon in the 20th century have largely taken place without constitutional amendments. As a rule, the main checks upon that power and its growth by states and the people have been bypassed. Many of the powers have been assumed and usurped by the Congress, the President, and eventually by the courts.

But amendments aside, and even aggressive usurpation aside, it would appear that the electorate have acquiesced in the taking of power by the Federal government. But as a rule, it must be insisted, those who govern have evaded much of the necessity for getting popular approval for their acts. As explained above, most of the expansion of power has never been submitted as amendments for state and popular approval. Two other interrelated devices have been used to get around direct popular approval. One is the dividing of the populace into classes and interest groups and encouraging them to contend against and prey on one another. The other is the buying of their approval and votes.

Divide and conquer—that has been the mode by which the Constitution has been evaded, the people have been seduced, and government has grown to gargantuan size. Those who would govern have divided the population into classes: into capitalist (or "industrialists," or "business") and labor, into farmer and industrialist, into white collar and blue collar, into urban and rural, into black and white, into aborigines, ethnics, and Anglos, into young and old, into Protestant and Catholic, and so on through all those class differences that may be appealed to or cast aspersions on. Thus, the seeds of discord are sown throughout society. Thus, industrial laborers are told that they are exploited by capitalists. Westerners were told they were being taken advantage of by Eastern bankers and manufacturers. Farmers were told that while they were the backbone of the nation the marrow was being sucked out of the their bones by advocates of the gold standard. Tenant farmers were told that they were being exploited by landlords. Blacks were told they were used and abused by whites. Women were told they were maltreated and otherwise discriminated against by men, and so on through all the classes and ranks of society.

It might have been that Americans when confronted with constitutional amendments which posed the question of whether or not to increase the power of Congress, the President, and the Federal courts would have rejected such amendments by considerable majorities. That is not how the questions were posed, however. They were asked if they would like for government to bring social justice to them and punish their adversaries. Everyman cares very much about how his shoes pinch him, and he can sometimes be persuaded that the fault lies with others. Thus, many can be persuaded that it would be good to use government to help them and bring their opponents to heel. So it is, and by way of example, the poor may be persuaded to tax the rich and have their wealth divided among the "needy." Northerners will vote to have Southerners toe the line on the racial issue. Blacks will vote to make white people give them advantages. Farmers will vote to have industrialists give them their "fair share" of the national wealth. The aged will vote to have the young taxed to support them. Parents can often be attracted by the notion of having those without children assist in educating theirs. There is something irresistibly attractive to many people about others being penalized and themselves presumably benefited by government programs.

Thus, the population has been divided into classes and interest groups, and the Constitution has been conquered, so to speak.

Another way to say it is that Americans have been divided into classes and groups and been bought by a host of government programs supposed to benefit them—supposedly at the expense of others. Politicians have bought the American voters with promises of a vast assortment of goodies. The practical problem with this approach—leaving aside morality and ethical questions for the moment—is that the money must be raised by taxation, in one form or another and sooner or later, to pay for this assortment of benefits bestowed by government. Government, as such, has produced no wealth which it can distribute. All the wealth government has must first be taken from those who produced it. Government can distribute wealth, but it does not, as government, produce it.

That is not to say that government is an efficient distributor of wealth. It is not. On the contrary, it is quite costly to use government to distribute wealth. The wealth must first be acquired by the use or threat of force. It must be taken either directly or indirectly from those who produce it. That can be quite costly, because people who produce wealth are ill disposed to having their wealth taken from them by government, and they use various strategems to hold on to it. It also is bad for the economy in general because any very heavy taxation is a disincentive to production. It is difficult to redistribute wealth as well. Categories and classes must be selected to receive the wealth; people must be hired to develop and enforce the rules for distribution.

The main point to be made here, however, is that in the American system of government the redistribution of wealth is a means of buying votes and favors from the people and for the accumulation of more and more power in the government. It is a way of establishing the dependency of whole categories and classes of people on government distributions and handouts. And people in this condition of dependency are hardly likely to insist upon strict observance of the Constitution. After all, these government programs for redistributing the wealth have been passed by evading the restraints on government. The people are not simply powerless; they have been bought.

These programs are not simply methods for redistributing the wealth from the very rich to the very poor. They would have little political impact if that were the case. After all, the number of the very poor is not sufficiently large to subvert the Republic, or undermine the Constitution. Moreover, the very poor are generally the least politically active portion of the population, the least influential, and the least likely to pursue a tenacious course toward some distant end.

In any case, government programs which redistribute the wealth through subsidies, supplements, grants, subsistence payments, and the like are by no means restricted to the poor, the needy, or the unemployed. In one way or another, they reach through to every class and interest group in society, diffusing wealth, establishing expectations, and developing dependencies. How they spread and permeate society is well illustrated by the Social Security program begun in 1935. It is also the bellwether act establishing the Welfare State by making relief payments permanent rather than for some temporary emergency. The Social Security Act had several provisions, including Grants to States for Old Age Assistance, Grants to States for Unemployment Compensation, Grants to States for Aid to Dependent Children, and others, but the main provision, and the one which is usually referred to as "Social Security" by the generality of people is the one which was set up by the Act to provide "Old Age Benefits." The program initially provided for a tax on employers and employees to provide old age benefits to the employees. While the act did not say so directly, the main, if not only, beneficiaries were to be industrial wage workers. The Act specifically excluded agricultural, domestic, and casual workers, as well as all Federal and state government employees. Since only employees would participate in Social Security at this time, self-employed people were automatically excluded, regardless of what their business was.

Over the years, however, more and more people have come under Social Security, including agricultural and domestic workers, the self employed, salaried workers, and eventually virtually all gainfully employed people except Federal employees. Well-to-do—even rich—people may be covered by Social Security, may come under its tax provisions, and receive Social Security payments when they retire. This expansion of coverage has not simply been a political device to get Social Security accepted—though it may also be that—but also a means to finance Social Security. Social Security is, at any given time, a pyramid scheme. That is, it promises to pay out more to people than it takes in. It can only continue to do this by bringing more and more people in, by raising the tax, and by increasing the amount of income that is subject to the tax. As if that were not enough, in the 1960s, Social Security began providing Medicare for all covered people 65 or over. This greatly increased the demand for medical services and soon made the provision of medical services the most rapidly expanding business in the country. Thus, physicians and other providers of medical services and pharmaceuticals were drawn more fully into the web of government programs. In fact, then, Social Security came to be a program to provide aid and sources of income for virtually all Americans, with the exception of Federal employees, who are much more bountifully provided for generally.

That the redistribution of wealth sometimes enriched the wealthy even more than the poor is well illustrated by some of the farm programs. A number of the New Deal programs were devoted to driving prices of various commodities up with price supports, as have programs since that time. One book sums up who got these supports this way: "It has been estimated that the lowest 56 percent of the farmers received only 7 per cent of the subsidies. Most of the aid has gone to the larger commercial farmers, particularly those who produced basic commodities like wheat, corn and cotton. In 1960, 296 cotton growers received more than $30 million in government price supports. The largest amount received by a single producer was $1,236,048, which went to a Mississippi cotton company owned by an English firm."[550] Another has said about the New Deal program, "The AAA brought benefits to almost all commercial farmers. But in limiting acreage and providing the strongest possible incentive for more efficient land use, and thus for better technology, it forced sharecroppers off the land and worsened the plight of farm laborers."[551] It had a similar effect on small farms owned by those who farmed their own land as well.

One more example from another area will show the upscale status of some, if not most, beneficiaries of government programs. This was so of the Urban Renewal program which got underway in the 1950s. The aim of this program was to renew and revive the poorer and more decrepit areas of large (and small) cities. Whatever its intentions, the evidence shows that numerous small businesses were closed and driven out of the inner cities by Urban Renewal, as were many of the dwellers in these locales. The buildings were then torn down, the lots cleared, and the acreage sold to developers to build modern commercial structures and high rise apartments. A sign on a condemned building in Boston told the story with commendable brevity:

> The building in which you now live is located in an area which has been taken by the Boston Redevelopment Authority according to law as part of the Government Center Project. The buildings will be demolished after the families have been relocated and the land will be sold to developers for public and commercial uses, according to the Land Assembly and Redevelopment Plan presently being prepared.[552]

Large numbers of small businesses were driven out of the inner cities to accommodate large developers. A writer describes what happened in East Harlem: "More than 1,300 businesses which had the misfortune to occupy sites marked for housing were wiped away, and an estimated four-fifths of their proprietors ruined. More than 500 noncommercial 'store front' establishments were also wiped away."[553] Many of the poor were "relocated" in other parts of cities where rents were generally higher and less space was available.

The point is not that many programs have not been conceived and carried out that distribute tax money to the poor. Indeed, they have and do. It is rather that peoples from all walks, stations, and financial conditions of life are drawn into the web of government programs, benefit from them, and become more or less dependent upon them. Even when the poorer or less well off are the direct beneficiaries, others may receive important indirect benefits. Thus, medicaid goes mainly, if not entirely, to low income people, but producers of medicine, medical equipment, and providers of medical services receive great proceeds from these programs as well. Government housing projects are presumably built and inhabited by low income persons and families, but builders are often major beneficiaries of such undertakings as well. Pell Grants go to pay the cost of attending college to children of low income families, but they also benefit college professors, textbook publishers, authors, editors, papermakers, pulpwood producers and so on. So it is that Americans have developed a widespread dependency on programs of government aid.

Many, most, if not all, of these programs passed in the 20th century are of quite dubious constitutionality. But the people, the voters, the electorate, have set up no great clamor for their repeal. The reason they have not done so is clear enough. The American people have been bought; they have been bought with their own money—taken by way of taxes, taken by inflation of the currency, and taken by the debts that have been piled upon debts. It may well be that a large majority of Americans lose more through taxes, inflation, and debt, than they gain from the programs. It must be so, for some are considerable gainers on balance, while others are surely losers. But this is very difficult to determine. There are numerous programs with many entitlements and benefits, and even where people may have a net loss, they have become dependent on government programs. We Americans have been corrupted by the goodies handed out by government, and prefer them greatly to the strict construction of the Constitution. That is some of what being bought means.

Chapter 18
Overwhelming the State Governments

The main *coup* of the power of the Federal government over the state governments was delivered in the 1950s and 1960s, though the chokehold of the central government on the states has been maintained down to the present. The way was prepared for this *coup* well before it took place. The backs of the states of the Confederacy, and to a lesser degree some of their neighboring states, had been broken, so to speak during the Civil War and Reconstruction. Even so, the states reasserted their independence after the end of Reconstruction and had recovered most of their earlier position by the beginning of the 20th century.

As noted earlier, the way was prepared in the early 20th century to subordinate the states. The 16th Amendment greatly increased the potential income of the United States government and bypassed the equal taxation provision of the Constitution. The 17th Amendment made Senators representatives of the people rather than state government, thus largely removing both the protection they had afforded to states from Federal intrusion and the influence of the state governments on national policy. The Federal Reserve Act set the stage for the government to greatly expand the currency.

Many developments also contributed to the nationalizing of American attitudes, habits, and outlook. Between the 1840s and 1900 the United States was knit together into a single entity by railroads, the telegraph, and telephone, and was on the verge of much closer cultural links at the beginning of the 20th century by radio, movies, and the automobile. To facilitate the use of the automobile nationally, United States subsidized highways were in the works. The population of the United States was more than a little homogenized by military service in World Wars I and II, as well as the enlarged military force continued after World War II. The development of greatly expanded air passenger service following the introduction of jet-powered aircraft as well as interstate highways for automobiles much increased the mobility of Americans and contributed to the blurring of regional differences and making state lines appear to the casual observer to be anachronisms.

Indeed, the notion began to gain currency in the 20th century that not only were state boundaries outmoded but that nation-states were also. ''One Worlders'' spread the notion that since technology had made virtual instantaneous communication around the world possible and since transportation had placed most of us within a day or two of virtually everyone else in the world, contending nation-states should soon be outmoded. One World should have One Government, a few proclaimed, and many others edged toward their position without openly professing it. This view makes a kind of sense, but for it to do so, it helps greatly to wear intellectual blinders to shield ourselves from unpleasant facts. If government were a benign being, states might indeed be dispensed with in the United States and nation-states in the world. But the notion that government is or can be made benign is contrary to human experience throughout the ages, experience which has been greatly reinforced in the 20th century.

Whatever else government may be, or that men may try to make of it, it remains that body charged with maintaining the peace by the use of force. It is, in the nature of things, that body with a legal monopoly of the use of force within its jurisdiction over grown-ups (a category somewhat broader than is usually included by the term adults). Far from being benign, then, government is the most potentially dangerous of all lawful bodies. It is dangerous not only because the power to use force is subject to abuse but also because men with power tend to seek more power, and the ambitions of the very powerful are often without limits. The problem with government is how to limit and constrain it, and the larger and more centralized the power becomes the more difficult it is to constrain it. That is surely the lesson of this century, where governments tend to become totalitarian by the use of modern technology and rulers become dictators, e. g., the Soviet Union, Nazi Germany, Communist China, Fascist Italy, and so on. Former nations and provinces swallowed up by the Soviet Union are now seeking liberty and independence, not in great empires, but in ever smaller nation states. That may be the lesson that the 20th century should have taught us.

In any case, the contrary notion about smaller political units being made obsolete by technological developments undergirded the assault on the states within the United States. It was also fostered by the thrust to concentrate power in the central government and bolstered by socialist premises about imposing equality, especially in the distribution of wealth.

The overwhelming of the states has been accomplished mainly by two parallel developments. One is by Congress and the executive branch. This development has been two-pronged: one prong is the exertion of the regulatory power of Congress; the other prong is the distribution of wealth to state and local governments. To put it another way, the state and local governments have been bought and then controlled by the Federal government. The other development which has overwhelmed the states has been by the Federal courts, especially the Supreme Court.

a. Buying and Controlling the States

It might be well to notice in advance of the following information that the Constitution does not authorize the granting of funds by Congress to the states. Its power to tax is restricted to the "common Defence and general Welfare of the United States," which is distinguished in what follows from the states themselves. The only joint effort of the states and United States which might entail financing by the United States mentioned in the Constitution is that of the militia (now the National Guard). The Constitution grants to Congress the power "To provide for organizing, arming, disciplining, the Militia, and for governing such Part of them as may be employed in the Service of the United States. . . ." Even in that singular case, there is no reference to granting funds to the states to accomplish a joint purpose.

Even so, there were a few instances of limited grants to states in the 19th century. The Treasury had a surplus in 1836, and there was no debt to absorb it. Congress passed a Deposit Act in that year which authorized the Treasury to make deposits of the surplus in excess of $5 million to the states. Senator Thomas Benton declared of the bill that "It is in name a deposit; in form a loan; in essential design a distribution."[554] He was right, for the money was never repaid. There were some other instances of such distributions of surpluses, though not enough to make it much of an issue. The other main instance was in the provisions of the Morrill Land Grant Act of 1862, which provided for the distribution of lands, or the proceeds from sales, to states for the founding of colleges. This Act, however, was passed when Democrats from the South had withdrawn from Congress, and strict construction of the Constitution was not the order of the day.

In any case, grants from the United States government to the states were limited to treasury surpluses and land grants, and were relatively insignificant in the 19th century. They were hardly calculated to subdue, overwhelm, or subordinate the states to the general government. The independence of the states only began to be compromised by such grants in the 1930s. Several of the New Deal programs provided for grants to be made to the states, but the permanent arrangements under the Social Security Act of 1935 may best illustrate the practice. This Act was chock full of grants to be made to states to get a variety of programs underway and maintain them with Federal assistance. For example, Title I of the Social Security Act provided for "Grants to States for Old Age Assistance." The monthly payments to individuals under this act were often referred to as "pensions" by the recipients and sometimes by the states. The original amount appropriated for this purpose was $49,750,000, but the Act called for appropriations to be made in the following years. The money was to be distributed to those states which had submitted plans that had subsequently been approved by the United States Social Security Board. But the states were not left without guidance as to what should be included in the plan, for there were a list of requirements and prohibitions for the state plans. Examples of requirements were that state plans should "provide for financial participation by the State;" and "provide that if the State or any of its political subdivisions collects from the estate of any recipient of old-age assistance any amount with respect to old-age assistance furnished him under the plan, one-half of the net amount so collected shall be promptly paid to the United States. . . ."

Other grants to states were provided for in the Social Security Act, including those for unemployment compensation, for aid to dependent children, for maternal and child welfare, for public health work, and for aid to the blind. All of them provided for state participation upon approval of plans submitted by the states. All of these Titles laid down more or less rules which state-run agencies were to follow. For example, Title III, dealing with unemployment compensation, provides that state agencies are charged with "making . . . such reports, in such form and containing such information, as the [Social Security] Board may from time to time require, and compliance with such provisions as the Board may from time to time find necessary to assure the correctness and verification of such reports. . . ."[555]

Over the years, all sorts of grants and other aids to state and local government have been made by the Federal government. Among them have been aid to building local hospitals and equipping them, grants for an assortment of local government activities, such as for police equipment, water purification, sanitation, block grants for this, that, and the other, and so on. A good example of how extensive this is can be seen in the programs that might be labeled Federal aid to education in 1990. Virtually all of these are handled through state institutions. There is Federal aid for the educationally disadvantaged, special programs (for the retarded and disabled in one way or another), bilingual education, school assistance in federally affected areas, program development in higher education, Pell grants, work study grants, direct loans for students, special programs for the disadvantaged, higher education facilities, aid for institutional development, vocational education, education for the handicapped (state grant program, preschool grants, special populations, and others), Indian education, and education research and improvement. Over $15 billion was appropriated by the Federal government toward the above educational ends in the fiscal year 1990. Federal aid to states in highway building is another area of huge governmental appropriations.

The first thing that might be emphasized about these 20th century Federal grants is that they are neither a division of surpluses by the United States Treasury nor from revenue income from the sale of land. Far from having a surplus during these years, the Federal government has had a huge and growing debt much of the 20th century, and deficits have been the rule rather than the exception. Thus, these grants have come from tax receipts, other Federal revenues, and loans or other devices by which the debt has been expanded. The notion has sometimes been advanced that the Federal government has greater tax resources than do the states. In proportion to populations, this simply is not so. A state can levy any tax it will (except on Federal installations and undertakings) within its boundaries. The difference between the United States government and the ability of states to raise funds lies in one area only: the United States can expand (inflate) the currency; the state governments cannot. This is a surreptitious power, not authorized by the Constitution, and exercised in a stealthy manner. When the currency is increased by expansion of paper money, the value that the money has in circulation is taken from whatever monetary wealth existed before it was increased. It is by devices such as these that the Federal government makes grants to states and other governments.

Whatever the motives for making these grants may have been or be, they are means for the expansion of the power of the general government and for the subordination of the states to it. In the first place, state and local governments tend to become administrative units of the Federal government in disposing these funds. This is so because the Federal government establishes the purposes for which the funds are to be used and lays down rules for their use. Federal power follows Federal aid, even when it does not accompany it. Secondly, state and local governments become implicated both in the programs and the means used by the Federal government to raise the funds. To put it another way, the state and local governments are bought. Since they are recipients of the grants, and they relish the role of handing out money, they can hardly play their role of defending the Constitution from Federal intrusion.

Third, the states lost their claim to independence by taking Federal aid. They become dependent on the Federal government for its largess. They become participants as well in the buying of the votes of their constituents. Once proud states, proclaiming their sovereignty, have now become mendicants with their hands out for grants from the United States government. It was in this weakened and exposed state that the states came face to face with the compulsion of the Federal Courts in the 1950s and 1960s.

b. States Reduced to Minions
by the Warren Court

The main points in what follows is that the Federal Courts reversed the constitutional role for the judiciary in the 1950s and 1960s and in so doing they reduced the state governments to subordinates of the courts. The independence of the states which had survived the assaults on them during the Civil War and Reconstruction and the New Deal and other welfare programs which had implicated them was finally broken by the courts. It is difficult to keep the focus on these points in relating what follows. Highly controversial and controverted decisions were involved in this subjugation, decisions involving espionage, segregation, prayer in the schools, the treatment of criminals by the police, and so on. It is easy to get drawn off from the constitutional issues into questions of the rightness or wrongness of what was taking place until the Federal courts acted. They may be good questions, but they must be put aside to come to grips with what they did to the Constitution and our system of government generally. George Washington put the case against changing the power relationships in the Constitution by usurpation of one or another branch as well as it could be put in his Farewell Address. He said that ''if in the opinion of the people the distribution or modification of the constitutional powers be in any particular wrong, let it be corrected by an amendment in the way in which the Constitution designates. But let there be no change by usurpation; for though this in one instance may be the instrument of good, it is the customary weapon by which free governments are destroyed. The precedent must always greatly over-balance in permanent evil any transient or partial benefit which the use can at any time yield.'' In what follows, it will be made clear that the Supreme Court, and lower courts, were indeed usurping the powers of the states and making grave alterations in the distribution of powers. The courts were arrogating to themselves powers that had not been bestowed upon them by the Constitution.

These events have sometimes been described as a revolution. The term is not too strong, for a major change in the locus and flow of power occurred. One writer, at least, has called it ''The Warren Revolution.'' The phrase is apt, for Earl Warren was Chief Justice of the Supreme Court from 1953 to 1969, and during these years he either forged or aligned himself with the majority in crucial decisions of these years. If one had been picking the most likely candidates to become revolutionaries, or to lead a revolution, in the early 1960s, it is most doubtful he would have nominated Earl Warren. Warren had been attorney general of California and for ten years governor of the state. He was a Republican, and appointed to head the high court by President Eisenhower, who, whatever else he might have been, was no witting maker of revolutions. The rest of the Court was made up of Democratic appointees, however, five by President Roosevelt—Hugo L. Black, Stanley F. Reed, Felix Frankfurter, William O. Douglas, and Robert H. Jackson—and three by President Truman—Sherman Minton, Harold H. Burton, and Tom C. Clark. These were the nine men—and their successors through 1969, John M. Harlan, William J. Brennan, Charles E. Whitaker, Potter Stewart, Byron R. White, Arthur J. Goldberg, Abe Fortas, and Thurgood Marshall—who made the revolution, if that is the right term for it.

A phrase was eventually coined to describe what was going on during these years—judicial activism. How novel the notion was at the time is now difficult to conceive. The role of the judiciary, both historically and constitutionally, was to apply standing law to particular cases. Historically, they had, as regards the Constitution, primarily a negative role. They could declare legislative enactments null and void. The Constitution is silent about this power, but the Founders generally agreed that it was inherent in their duties as judges. They could not legislate; they could not propose or put laws into effect. They were not supposed to add to or subtract from legislative enactments or constitutional provisions, though they could nullify portions or all of particular legislative acts. For persons bent on making great changes in society, such as reformers, radicals and revolutionaries, serving as a judge must have been more than a little frustrating. Traditionally, the function of the courts was to maintain the existing order as it came to them by way of the standing law.

There was one area of the law that left an opening for changes—the Common Law. Judges could and did sometimes make changes in the common law by landmark decisions, by adjustments to newer conditions, and by bringing it into accord with more recent decisions. Common law might change with social changes, but it could hardly be used to make large or drastic changes in society. Any attempts to do this could be put at naught by legislatures, whose enactments take precedence over common law.

Even so, the Warren Court had some things going for it when it set out on its course of changing America and altering constitutional relationships. The states, which bore the brunt of its decisions, were already the weakened link in the federal system of government. The state legislatures often had a poor press; state governments received relatively little academic attention compared with the national government; and intellectuals often castigated them as obstacles to progress and beneficial change. Indeed, the Federal courts were vigorously supported by the media, the academics, and high churchmen of the old established churches as they began chopping away at state governments. The Federal courts, especially the Supreme Court, had grown in prestige over the years, and the notion had long taken hold that it was the final arbiter, perhaps the only arbiter, of the Constitution. In fact, by the time of the period in question, Supreme Court opinions were coming to be treated as if they were part and parcel of the Constitution itself. As a legal commentater wrote in the mid-1960s: ''Thus, a Supreme Court decision has become equivalent to a provision of the fixed Constitution.''[556]

Courts had for years been treating constitutional law as if it were common law at a higher level. This process was greatly accelerated in the 1950s and 1960s. What it meant, in practice, was that new constitutional law emerged as interpretations based on earlier interpretations led to new interpretations. In effect, if this were the case, the courts could legislate, have their legislation take on the character of being a part of the Constitution, and be indefinitely expanded over the years. Such legislating by the Supreme Court began to appear in the 1950s.

(1) The Segregation Decisions

On May 31, 1955, the Supreme Court gave the following instructions to the lower court in the cases of *Brown vs. Board of Education of Topeka, et. al.*:

> The Courts will require—a prompt and reasonable start toward full compliance—and enter such orders and decrees—as are necessary and proper to admit to public school on a socially non-discriminating basis with all deliberate speed the parties to these cases. . . .

This was to implement a decision reached and announced in 1954 that "racial discrimination in public education is unconstitutional . . . ," and that "All provisions of federal, state or local law requiring or permitting such discrimination must yield to this principle."

There was much that was questionable about the decision in *Brown vs. Board of Education.* It was based on a provision in the 14th Amendment, specifically, as Chief Justice Warren said: "Separate educational facilities are inherently unequal. Therefore, we hold that the plaintiffs and others similarly situated . . . are, by reason of the segregation complained of, deprived of the equal protection of the laws guaranteed by the Fourteenth Amendment." Yet that amendment had been part of the Constitution for nearly a hundred years and had never been applied to schools before. On the contrary, the separate but equal doctrine, announced in the 1890s, had held sway in such cases. The Court now insisted, however, that the intent of the amendment at the time of its adoption was ambiguous, and that, in any case more recently developed psychological knowledge made it clear that separate schools were inherently unequal.

But it is not the overturning of precedent, the lateness of the making of the interpretation, or the giving of constitutional credence to psychological knowledge, that marks the great change involved in this decision. The great innovation lay in the fact that the Federal courts were undertaking to impose integration in the public schools and that doing so entailed taking the management of the schools from the state governments and the local governments which were their creatures. The Court did not simply declare segregation unconstitutional; it proposed to impose integration. If the court had left the matter by declaring segregation to be unconstitutional and declaring all laws imposing segregation to be unconstitutional, it would have been doing the sort of thing Federal courts have done since before *Marbury vs. Madison.* It would have been performing a negative function, negating laws imposing something not authorized by or contrary to the Constitution.

If the Supreme Court had stopped at that point—which was the full extent of its authority—the ball would have been back in the states' court, to use sports terminology. It would have been up to the states to bring their school laws in accord with this new or fuller understanding of the Constitution, or to make whatever changes, adjustments, or dispositions they would in view of these most recent interpretations. In any case, the state governments would still maintain their independence and manage the institutions under them. No orders would have gone out to school districts and no injunctions issued—at least there need not have been.

That is not what happened, of course. The Supreme Court ordered integration in the instant cases, or, more precisely, remanded them to the lower courts for that purpose.

Much of the media and many spokesmen for organizations proclaimed that the Court's decision was the "law of the land." If by that statement, they meant that segregation was unconstitutional and contrary to the law of the land, they were right. But if they meant that the requirement of schools to integrate was the law of the land, the statement could not be substantiated. No such law existed. The Constitution contained no provision requiring either schools or their racial integration. No act of Congress required integration, and all power to legislate for the United States is vested in that body. Nor were there state laws requiring integration in the schools where segregation had been practiced. Neither common law nor statutory law required any such result. The courts have no authority to legislate. At most, they can only determine the law that applies to a particular case and nullify laws that someone else has passed.

In fact, there was no mad rush to integrate schools in the South in the wake of *Brown vs. Board of Education*. It was a decade before most states did much along those lines. Some of the border states did proceed with integration in the 1950s, and Kentucky, Tennessee, and Texas made shows of force, such as bringing out tanks, when integration efforts met with local resistance. Limited integration came to the South generally in the mid-1960s. But it was rarely enough to suit the Federal courts. In consequence, Federal courts took over and managed various school districts, required busing of students from one school to another in vain efforts to achieve racial balance. The state governments were permitted to finance the school, but they increasingly lost control to the courts of determination of how the schools were to be run.

Meanwhile, the courts proceeded to outlaw segregation in transportation, restaurants, hotels, and the like. Where private businesses were concerned, the courts usually justified their decisions on the basis of the interstate commerce clause. By these decisions, the states often lost a portion of their jurisdiction, and owners lost some of their control over private property.

(2) Reapportionment Decisions

The Supreme Court proceeded with an even more direct attack on the powers of the states with its proclamations on reapportioning state legislatures in the 1960s. These decisions were the more astounding for hardly anyone had supposed prior to the 1960s that the Federal courts had any jurisdiction over state legislatures. Indeed, neither did Congress nor the executive branch of the United States. What was at issue in the Federal courts in the early 1960s was the electoral districts for state legislatures. The Constitution does grant power to Congress in the matter of elections to the United States House of Representatives. It says that "The Times, Places, and Manner of holding Elections for Senators and Representatives, shall be prescribed in each State by the legislature thereof; but the Congress may at any time by Law make or alter such Regulations, except as to the Places of chusing [sic] Senators." During a much earlier period the Congress passed a law regarding reapportionment of Congressional districts, but even that law was no longer in effect in the 1960s. In any case, the issue that first came to the Supreme Court in the 1960s did not have to do with Congressional district apportionments.

Instead, *Baker vs. Carr,* which came before the Supreme Court in 1962, concerned the reapportionment of state legislative districts in Tennessee. The case had been brought originally to a United States District court in middle Tennessee, where three judges had dismissed it on the grounds that the court lacked jurisdiction, among other things. It came to the Supreme Court on appeal, where Justice William Brennan, speaking for the majority, declared that the lower court had erred, that the Federal courts did have jurisdiction over apportionment for electing state legislators and that *Baker vs. Carr* had raised the question in a way that made it appropriate for them. In support of this view Mr. Justice Brennan made these observations:

> Article III, Section 2 of the federal Constitution provides that "the judicial power shall extend to all Cases, in Law and Equity, arising under this Constitution, the Laws of the United States, and Treaties made, or which shall be made, under their Authority. . . ." It is clear that the cause of action is one which "arises under" the federal Constitution. The complaint alleges that the 1901 statute effects an apportionment that deprives the appellants of the equal protection of the laws in violation of the Fourteenth Amendment. . . .
>
> Since the complaint plainly sets forth a case arising under the Constitution, the subject matter is within the federal judicial power. . . ."[557]

Having so ruled, the Supreme Court remanded the case to the lower court for adjudication, but with no instructions as to how it was to proceed in providing a remedy if it decided in favor of the plaintiffs.

It may have been "clear" and "plain" to Justice Brennan and the majority who voted with or concurred in his opinion that the issues raised were within the constitutional powers of the Federal courts, but the case was hardly a *prima facie* one, as his language implies. The 14th Amendment does say that "No State shall . . . deny to any person within its jurisdiction the equal protection of the laws." But even supposing that the apportionment for state legislatures came under this prohibition, it is neither "clear" nor "plain" how courts could act upon the matter. The 14th Amendment ends with the following provision. "The Congress shall have power to enforce, by appropriate legislation, the provisions of this article." This proviso confirmed the general rule applying to all such matters, namely, that all legislative power under the Constitution is confided in Congress. Now Congress had passed no laws dealing with apportionment for purposes of electing state legislatures. It had not theretofore been considered within its power to do so, nor was there any considerable body of opinion that the 14th Amendment had changed the situation in that regard. That Congress would certainly have repelled any proposal that it would pass any such laws instructing state governments is clear from the reaction to the Supreme Court's action during these years. In the absence of any legislative enactments, the Federal courts had no law upon which to act regarding state apportionments for purposes of electing their legislatures.

In fact, the Supreme Court was proceeding to act with contempt for the separation of the powers in the United States government, and for the dispersion of powers between the general government and state governments in the federal system of government as they were established by the Constitution. In any case, the Supreme Court did not proceed immediately toward laying down the rules as to how districts should be apportioned in the states for electing legislatures so as to be in accord with the equal protection of the law clause of the 14th Amendment. That is, the high court did not immediately "legislate" in the matter. It grappled for a rule, instead, in *Wesberry vs. Sanders,* which dealt with apportionment for Congressional elections. As noted earlier, Congress had no laws on the books dealing with this question, though there had been such laws earlier, and it was generally conceded that Congress had power to act in this matter. The Supreme Court was not deterred, however, by the absence of such legislation. Speaking for a substantial majority, Justice Hugo Black made this declaration:

> We hold that, construed in its historical context, the command of Art. I, Sec. 2, that Representatives be chosen "by the people of the several States" means that as nearly as is practicable one man's vote in a congressional election is to be worth as much as another's.[558]

Actually, Article I, Section 2 contains nothing to the effect that one man's vote should be "worth" as much as another, nor did Black's rather lengthy meandering through the proceedings of the Constitution turn up any decisive evidence on the subject, his commentary to the contrary notwithstanding. In any case, the power to determine the rules (for reapportionment or whatever) was confided to the state legislatures and the power to alter or govern those was granted to Congress, not to the Federal courts.

However that may be, the probable intent and certain result of Black's excursion into the Constitution in *Wesberry vs. Sanders* was not so much in any change in apportionment for Congressional elections as in those for state legislatures. Justice Black had hit upon the equalitarian rule which the Court proceeded to impose on the states. In *Reynolds vs. Sims,* the Supreme Court ruled in June, 1964 that both houses of the Alabama legislature must be apportioned on the basis of one man, one vote. Not only was the Supreme Court legislating for a state but also intruding its authority into a realm where no power had been conferred on it by the Constitution. If any had been conferred by the 14th Amendment, it had been conferred on Congress, as noted above, not on the Supreme Court.

Beyond that, in regard to the apportionment for the Alabama senate, the Court ruled contrary to practice, tradition, and the different modes prescribed for selecting the United States House of Representatives and Senate. Many states took other factors than population in the selection of one of their houses, where they had bicameral legislatures. The American legislative tradition, as one writer has described it, was that in addition to population, legislative representation might take into account a given area's "historical and cultural attachments, its economic involvements, its geographic configurations, its sense of identity and community . . . , and so on."[559] Chief Justice Warren would have none of this, as he made clear in *Reynolds vs. Sims.* "No, said the Court; neither history, nor area, nor economic interests, nor groups, nor geography, nor political subdivisions nor bicameralism itself can be permitted to warrant deviation from the substantial population equality required of all districts. . . ."[560]

Suppose that the people of a state showed themselves quite willing to base electoral districts for one of its houses strictly on population but wished to use other factors as well in the other house. The matter was not long coming before the Supreme Court. Shortly after *Baker vs. Carr,* Colorado leaders must have astutely read the handwriting on the wall, for they placed alternative reapportionment proposals on the ballot. One amendment would have one house based strictly on population, and the other house on population and other interests. The other amendment would have both houses based strictly on population. The voters by majorities in every county favored differing bases for the houses and rejected the strict population formula for both houses. The case was then taken to Federal Court and eventually made its way to the Supreme Court as *Lucas vs. Forty-Fourth General Assembly of Colorado.* The Supreme Court overturned the state amendments adopted by the people of Colorado. In so doing, Chief Justice Warren said:

> An individual's constitutionally protected right to cast an equally weighted vote cannot be denied even by a vote of a majority of the state's electorate. . . .
>
> A citizen's constitutional rights can hardly be infringed simply because a majority of the people choose to do so.[561]

As the old saw has it,

> What a tangled web we weave,
> When first we practice to deceive.

Or, to apply it more pointedly to the instant case: What a tangled web the Supreme Court has woven from its deceptive "findings" and "plantings" in the Constitution! The only semblance of excuse or justification that the Federal courts had to intervene in apportionment was that state governments were ignoring their own prescriptions for reapportionment. But if there was any constitutional justification for this, in the 14th Amendment or elsewhere, it belonged to Congress, not to the courts. And Congress had not acted. But the early justification went by the boards as soon as the Supreme Court settled on its one-man, one-vote rule. But this rule was neither sanctioned by the Constitution, by custom, by tradition, by Congressional law, nor by state constitutions or laws. It was an invention of the Supreme Court, of Mr. Justice Black and his cohorts.

The saddest part of this high court deception was that in the name of popular government the Supreme Court was hacking away at the very roots of popular government. State and local government lie at the foundation level of popular government; they alone asserted and developed it in the colonial period. Colonies and states made the first constitutions in America; they established the tradition out of which the United States Constitution was formed. If state governments are not significantly independent—and on a large scale—of Federal power, popular government is suppressed at its source. If the edicts of the Supreme Court prevail over Congress, the Presidents, the states, and local government, there is only a smattering of popular government left. After all, the Supreme Court is not popularly elected: its members are appointed by the President by and with the consent of the Senate, and neither the President nor the Senate are chosen by the equally weighted one man, one vote of the Supreme Court. Popular government proclaimed by the Supreme Court is a snare and a delusion.

Nor should there be any doubt that the Supreme Court (followed by other Federal courts) treated the states, their constitutions, their governments, and their people with contempt. These legislative apportionment decisions were not restricted to the states of the Civil War Confederacy, such as Tennessee, Georgia, and Alabama, with Colorado thrown in for good measure. They were made to prevail in states all over the United States, as cases came before the Federal courts. Since that time, Federal courts have not been reluctant to take over state institutions if their decrees were not immediately acted upon. The following is a kind of footnote to one such takeover, which is still in effect in 1992, and illustrates the strange powers which Federal courts have assumed:

> A federal magistrate's recommendation for a state committee with the power to authorize the use of shock treatment goes next to a judge who can accept or reject it.
>
> Vanzetta Penn McPherson, the federal magistrate, recommended that the Extraordinary Treatment Committee include a mental health patient and a relative of the person considered for the treatment.
>
> U. S. District Judge Myron Thompson can accept or reject her recommendation. The recommendation comes in a lawsuit under which Alabama's mental health system was placed under federal control from 1972 to 1986. Under guidelines imposed by then-U. S. District Judge Frank Johnson, Jr., the state Department of Mental Health could administer shock treatment to patients in state hospitals only after getting permission from the five-member Extraordinary Treatment Committee.
>
> In 1991, attorneys for the department and for a class of patients who were involuntarily committed to state mental health facilities asked Thompson to modify the standards.
>
> He approved the proposed standards in May, but asked McPherson to study proposed operating procedures for the panel. She recommended the panel be reduced to a psychiatrist trained in use of shock treatment, a lawyer, a mental health patient and relative of a patient.[562]

Not only have Federal courts taken over areas to which the knowledge and expertise of judges does not extend, but they have undermined the independence of state governments and those duly appointed to their offices. Much of the intervention by Federal courts into state jurisdiction is simply inconceivable under the federal system of government.

Federal judges have freed prisoners from state prisons because the crowded conditions in the prisons allegedly denied the prisoners their constitutional rights. The story is told of Judge Frank Johnson, Jr., mentioned above and one of the more notorious activist judges, that he was named "Realtor of the Year" by the Montgomery Board of Realtors for his changes in the lines of school districts in a vain effort to establish racial balance in Montgomery schools. The result was the scurry of parents to find housing in school districts where the racial imbalance was more to their liking, thus providing a boom in real estate business. It was Judge Johnson, also, who proclaimed that the highway between Selma and Montgomery, Alabama under the authority of the state government should be made available for a march (extended demonstration) by sympathizers with a black registration drive in Selma. Some judges were undoubtedly less imaginative in their usurpation of state and local authority, but the practice has been widespread since the 1960s.

(3) Federal Courts Intervene in Criminal Prosecutions

Most crimes in the United States are violations of state (and local) laws. This is true not only of crimes of violence, such as murder, manslaughter, rape, assault, armed robbery, and the like, but also of extortion, fraud, and many less or non-violent crimes. The prosecutions for a host of such crimes take place in state courts; the apprehension and punishment is also done by the states. All this is carried on under rules established by the states, subject to such restrictions as may be authorized by the Constitution and imposed in accord with laws passed by Congress. (This is not to deny the power of the Federal courts to negate laws reckoned to be contrary to provisions of the Constitution. It is to deny, however, the power of the Federal courts to legislate or exercise executive power.) The Federal courts began to intrude on a large scale in criminal prosecutions by the states in the 1960s. This intervention, once again, entailed loss of independence by the states in these matters, and court legislation as to what procedures should be followed by state officials.

The constitutional questions at issue in these intrusions are found in the 5th and 6th Amendments. The portion of the 5th Amendment involved reads, "No person . . . shall be compelled in any criminal case to be a witness against himself. . . ." And the part of the 6th Amendment reads, "In all criminal prosecutions, the accused shall enjoy the right . . . to have the Assistance of Counsel for his defence." Surely, these are admirable restrictions upon government, and no objection is being raised here to their application to state as well as Federal courts. The first ten amendments to the Constitution were, however, drawn to restrain the general government in view of objections raised during contests over ratification of the Constitution.

What is at issue here is that the Supreme Court gave new meanings to these Amendments and in effect legislated to put them into effect. What the relevant portion of the 5th Amendment prohibition against compulsory self incrimination brings to mind most readily is compelling a person to testify against himself. It may also bring to mind the use of torture to obtain confessions. What it had not generally been reckoned to include were rigorous protections against confession. Most importantly, however, neither state nor Federal law spelled out any such rigorous protections as the Supreme Court now imposed. In general, too, it had been supposed for most of the time since the Bill of Rights had gone into effect that the "right to counsel" was the right of the defendant to utilize such counsel as he could induce to serve him in the court proceedings to act in his defense. That the 6th Amendment required the state to provide defenders for indigents, or others, had not been generally supposed, though there had been a movement in that direction for capital crimes before the 1960s. Such a notion was more than a little illogical. After all, the state prosecutes; if it also defends, it has a conflict of interest in court and is divided against itself. That might not be unconstitutional, but it should raise serious questions about the legality of the state being both the prosecution and the defense.

On the matter of the state's providing attorneys for indigents, the Supreme Court ruled in the case of *Gideon vs. Wainwright* (1963), that Gideon must be retried and be provided with an attorney. This ruling was made retroactive (as were other rulings affecting people in prison), contrary to the rule of law generally. Justice Hugo Black wrote the opinion for the majority in the case. Black argued that precedents as well as "reason and reflection require us to recognize that in our adversary system of criminal justice, any person haled into court, who is too poor to hire a lawyer cannot be assured a fair trial unless counsel is provided. . . . From the very beginning, our state and national constitutions and laws have laid great emphasis on procedural and substantive safeguards designed to assure fair trials before impartial tribunals in which every defendant stands equal before the law. This noble ideal cannot be realized if the poor man charged with crime has to face his accusers without a lawyer to assist him. . . ."[563] Thus, the High Court moved toward prescribing that states should provide counsel to those unable to affort it, on penalty of having their convicted criminals released if they did not.

In 1964, the Supreme Court took a further step in *Escobedo vs. Illinois*. It held that a suspect is entitled to an attorney while he is being interrogated by the police. This was to assure that he not incriminate himself, by confession or otherwise, through ignorance or fear. And finally, in 1966, in *Miranda vs. Arizona*, Chief Justice Earl Warren laid down the rules to be observed by authorities in questioning suspects. This was as clear a case of the Supreme Court's legislating as had occurred. This summary captures what was done in that case:

> To summarize [said Chief Justice Warren], we hold that when an individual is taken into custody or otherwise deprived of his freedom by the authorities in any significant way and is subjected to questioning, the privilege against self-incrimination is jeopardized. Procedural safeguards must be employed to protect the privilege, and unless other fully effective means are adopted to notify the person of his right of silence and to assure that the exercise of the right will be scrupulously

honored, the following measures are required. He must be warned prior to any questioning that he has the right to remain silent, that anything he says can be used against him in a court of law, that he has the right to the presence of an attorney, and that if he cannot afford an attorney one will be appointed for him prior to any questioning if he so desires. Opportunity to exercise these rights must be afforded him throughout the interrogation. [Elsewhere in the opinion, Warren points out that the suspect may decide to remain silent after questioning has begun, and, if so, the interrogation must cease.] After such warnings have been given, and such opportunity afforded him, the individual may knowingly and intelligently waive these rights and agree to answer questions or make a statement. But unless and until such warnings and waiver are demonstrated by the prosecution at trial, no evidence obtained as a result of interrogation can be used against him.[564]

The main concern here is with the Court's legislating and imposing its will over the states or reducing their authority. That was certainly the case in *Miranda vs. Arizona.* Even if it be granted that self incrimination would be entailed in questions before the Court and that the 14th Amendment had applied the 5th and 6th Amendments to the states, it would still only have empowered Congress to lay down rules or legislate. Congress might well have refused, as by omission it had by implication done, to plunge into the thicket of law enforcement, which was mainly the responsibility of state and local governments.

Not only was the Court's venture in the field a usurpation of the legislative powers of the states and of Congress, but it was also infelicitous. The only punishment for failure to comply with court requirements in many instances was for the Federal courts to release prisoners. This was often an illogical action if not an irrational one. This may be best seen, perhaps, in the cases where the Federal courts held that evidence obtained in the prosecution of cases had been obtained in violation of the Constitution. In *Mapp vs. Ohio,* the Supreme Court held that the 4th Amendment rules on searches and seizures applied to the states, and it began vigorously to entertain cases in which investigating police had improperly obtained evidence. The Court might release or order people to be tried again, even when the evidence so seized and used was not necessary to the proof of guilt. The infelicity of this approach was well described by W.H. Parker, Chief of Police of Los Angeles in 1961. Presumably, the criminal is freed to punish the police for their wrongdoing. Yet, the police have no more interest in punishing criminals than others, perhaps even less. "It is the guilty criminal who profits when he is given his freedom on a technicality, and it is the innocent victims of his future crimes who lose," Parker said. "I fail to see how the guilty criminal freed constitutes a personal loss to the police officer who has merely attempted to bring a criminal to justice."[565] The correct approach, if there was wrongdoing in collecting evidence, would be not to suppress the evidence and free the criminal but punish the guilty policeman. But the Supreme Court cannot truly legislate in that fashion, or at least it has not ventured to do so.

The powers of the states in taking care of their responsibilities in law enforcement were circumscribed and restained by these and rulings of the Federal courts.

(4) Driving Religion and Morality out of Public Life

Two general points need to be emphasized here about the first ten amendments to the Constitution, often referred to as the Bill of Rights. The first is that given the context in which they were drawn, submitted, and adopted, they were intended as restrictions on the United States government. However, there is nothing specific in the Fourth through the Ninth Amendments that would suggest that they did not apply to the state governments as well as to the Federal government. The language is general and has the ring of being inclusive so far as governments within the United States are concerned. For example, the Eighth Amendment says:

> Excessive bail shall not be required nor excessive fines imposed, nor cruel and unusual punishments inflicted.

Even so, they were not generally applied to state governments until well into the 20th century, probably because it was understood that they were intended as restrictions on the general government.

When the Federal courts began to apply the Third through the Eighth Amendments (they have generally preferred to ignore the Ninth Amendment, "evade" may be the better term, than to use it to restrain either the general or the state governments), they did so on the grounds that the Fourteenth Amendment had provided for such an application. There was no doubt that the Fourteenth Amendment applied at least a portion of the Fifth Amendment to the states, for it says, "No State shall . . . deprive any person of life, liberty, and property without due process of law . . . ," a phrase lifted literally from the Fifth. As for the other Amendments, there is no specific reference to them or their language in the Fourteenth. It does say that "No State shall make or enforce any law which shall abridge the privileges or immunities of citizens of the United States. . . ." The content of "privileges and immunities" is made clear neither by context nor examples. A phrase similar to this—"rights and immunities"—was used in the original bill to enact the Civil Rights Act of 1866, which was supposed to be authorized by the 14th Amendment. Senator Trumbull of Illinois declared that what was meant by "civil rights" was "the right to make and enforce contracts, to sue and be sued, and to give evidence, to inherit, purchase, sell, lease, hold and convey real and personal property.''[566] Of course, the phrase in the 14th Amendment was less precise and more vague than the one in the civil rights bill. In any case, it is at least conceivable that Amendments three through nine were co-opted into the Constitution by the 14th Amendment. That still would not have justified the Supreme Court's imposing them in the manner of laws, or legislating upon them, which has been one of the main points made thus far.

My second point here, however, is that the language of the First, Third, Ninth, and possibly the Second Amendments could only apply to the United States government. The Third and Ninth are directed to matters which could only be prohibited to the United States: the Third to the quartering of troops and the Ninth of the reservation of powers to the states and to the people and amounts to a restriction on the United States from using any but delegated powers. That brings us to the First Amendment, which is our main concern here. To focus attention on its language, it is quoted in full below:

> Congress shall make no law respecting an establishment of religion, or prohibiting the free exercise thereof; or abridging the freedom of speech, or of the press; or the right of the people peaceably to assemble, and to petition the government for a redress of grievances.

The phrase that governs all the rest of the sentence is "Congress shall make no law. . . ." It is addressed to no other branch of government nor to any other government. If we make some sort of giant leap to the view that the First Amendment was made applicable to the states by the 14th Amendment, it is still not clear what application could be made of it. For, as noted earlier, the 14th Amendment provides that "The Congress shall have power to enforce, by appropriate legislation, the provisions of this article." But how can Congress legislate about matters concerning which the governing phrase is, Congress shall make no law? The obvious answer is that it can't.

There is, and has been ever since the First Amendment was ratified, a way around this apparently insurmountable obstacle. Adopt a constitutional amendment which prohibits the state governments or legislatures to exercise those powers denied to Congress by the First Amendment. None has ever been submitted, passed, or ratified, and in the absence of such action we can conclude that there has never been an intention by the parties concerned, including the voters, to achieve this result. In any case, they were bypassed.

But that aside, and even supposing that the 14th Amendment made the First applicable to the states, there was still no grant of power to the Federal courts to lay down rules as to what constituted an establishment of religion, what state governments might authorize regarding religion, how local governments might celebrate religious occasions, what constitutes obscenity, or issuing decrees about making public property available to protesters. No powers are granted to any branch of government, including Congress, by the

First Amendment. Nor is it clear how any can be read into it. By custom, precedent, and assumption going back to the time of the adoption of the original Constitution, the courts can nullify legislative acts believed to be contrary to the Constitution. Thus, if Congress passed an act which the courts reckoned to be contrary to the First Amendment, the courts could refuse to apply it, and thus eventually nullify it. In like manner, if the state legislatures were reckoned somehow to be under the same restrictions, any acts by them reckoned to be contrary to the First Amendment could be nullified.

For most of American history, including nearly seventy years after the adoption of the 14th Amendment, the courts and just about everybody else believed the First Amendment meant what it said, no more and no less. Then in the late 1930s and early 1940s the Supreme Court made a significant shift in its course—by beginning to apply the First Amendment to state and local governments. This was the Court increasingly under the influence of Roosevelt and the innovative and centralizing tendencies of the New Deal. In 1938, in *Lovell vs. Griffin,* the Supreme Court nullified an ordinance of Griffin, Georgia, which required the permission of the city manager to distribute pamphlets and literature. This was a violation of freedom of the press, according to Chief Justice Hughes. In 1940, in *Cantwell vs. Connecticut,* the Court nullified a Connecticut law requiring prior approval of a government official before making solicitations for religious or charitable contributions. This decision is often cited as a leading one in applying the First Amendment to the states. The violation of the First Amendment was of the free exercise of religion clause. Later decisions were made along the same lines, but so long as they were protecting religious freedom no furor was aroused. Even so, the nose of the judicial camel was under the tent of state authority in the matter of religion and morals, and the control of its own institutions.

The Warren Court made this clear in the early 1960s, if there was any doubt about it, when the Supreme Court began making its rulings about prayer and Bible reading in the schools. This was the opening foray in an ongoing effort by the Federal courts to drive religion out of public life and remove government as a defender of public morals. It was in 1947, however, in an aside not necessary to his ruling, that Justice Hugo Black laid down the rules for governments in relation to religions. He thought the First Amendment required at least the following:

> Neither a state nor the Federal Government can set up a church. Neither can pass laws which aid one religion, aid all religions, or prefer one religion over another. Neither can force or influence a person to go or remain away from church against his will or force him to profess a belief or disbelief in any religion. No person can be punished for entertaining or professing religious beliefs or disbeliefs,

for church attendance or non-attendance. No tax in any amount, large or small, can be levied to support any religious activities or institutions, whatever they may be called, or whatever form they may adopt to teach or practice religion. Neither a state nor the Federal Government can, openly or secretly, participate in the affairs of any religious organizations or groups and vice versa. In the words of Jefferson, the clause against establishment of religion by law intended to erect "a wall of separation between church and state."[567]

This *obiter dictum* had no more standing than a randomly stated opinion, when Justice Black uttered it. No legislation had been passed setting forth these rules. Even so, Justice Black boldly asserted that the First Amendment applied to Federal and state governments alike and spoke confidently about what it meant. The Court might as well have declared these rules to have been legislated, however, for in the ensuing years the courts accepted them as if they had been written in the Constitution.

In 1962, in *Engel vs. Vitale*, the Supreme Court began to get down to cases in applying the First Amendment to state separation of church and state by way of the 14th Amendment. At issue was a prayer recommended by the New York Board of Regents and adopted for their use by the Board of Education of New Hyde Park. The prayer said:

Almighty God we acknowledge our dependence upon Thee, and beg Thy blessing upon us, our parents, our teachers, and our Country.

There was nothing sectarian about the prayer. It was even minimally religious, though it did acknowledge a providential (provider) God. Nor was there to be any overt coercion upon the children. They were free to pray or not to pray, or indeed to withdraw from the room if they so chose. Those who brought the case lost in the New York state trial court and lost also in the New York Court of Appeals. They got a much friendlier hearing in the United States Supreme Court. There, the prayer was declared to be in violation of the establishment clause of the First Amendment.

Justice Hugo Black, speaking for the majority in *Engel vs. Vitale*, declared that "in this country it is no part of the business of government to compose official prayers for any group of the American people to recite as part of a religious program carried on by government." Further, Black claimed that "It is neither sacreligious nor antireligious to say that each . . . government in this country should stay out of the business of writing or sanctioning official prayers and leave that purely religious function to the people themselves and to those the people choose to look for religious guidance."[568]

This decision aroused a considerable furor in the country, and some of this resentment was mirrored in vigorous denunciations in Congress, by governors of the states, and in some of the press. On the other hand, there was some comfort, however luke-warm or cold, that the Supreme Court might only be excluding government composed and officially sanctioned prayers. In any case, that hope was dashed within a year by the Supreme Court's ruling in *School District of Abington vs. Schempp* and *Murray vs. Curlett* (1963). These cases are so similar that they are often discussed in tandem as the *Schempp-Murray* cases. Both cases involved Bible reading and the oral praying of the Lord's Prayer in public schools. Pennsylvania law provided for such exercises, and Abington High School had a 15 minute devotional period each morning. The program was conducted and broadcast over the school's intercom system and consisted of Bible reading by selected students who read ten verses from the Bible (in rotation presumably, from the King James version, the Douay Bible, the Revised Standard, and the Jewish Holy Scriptures) without comment, followed by the repetition of the Lord's Prayer, the making of the Pledge of Allegiance to the United States flag, and assorted announcements. Any students who wished to or whose parents wished them to, could be excused from hearing or participating in the devolitonal service and wait in the hallway near their home rooms until it was over. No matter, Edward Schempp, a Unitarian, brought suit against the Abington School District which eventually came to the Supreme Court. A similar suit, for similar causes, was brought in Maryland by Madalyn Murray and her son, who were militant atheists. Justice Tom Clark found the religious exercises in both cases constitutionally prohibited. He said that they violated "the command of the First Amendment that the Government maintain strict neutrality, neither aiding nor opposing religion."[569]

However, it was Justice William Brennan, in a separate opinion concurring with the majority, who put the Court's case most succinctly: he said that the Pennsylvania and Maryland practices were unconstitutional because they constituted "involvements of religious with secular institutions which (a) serve the essentially religious activities of religious institutions; (b) employ the organs of government for essentially religious purposes; or (c) use essentially religious means to serve governmental ends where secular means would suffice."[570] Justice Potter Stewart protested vigorously that the majority was ignoring the free exercise of religion clause of the First Amendment and that to require neutrality in the schools would contribute to the establishment of religious secularism. He was the lone dissenter in the case.

Other decisions in a similar vein were made by Federal courts in the ensuing years, such as those forbidding the teaching of religion on school property, the saying of prayers at graduation exercises, public prayers at games involving government supported schools, the having of religion related displays by municipal or local governments at Christmas, and so on and on. The tendency of these decisions has been to drive religion and its influence out of public life. Whether these decisions are antireligious or not may be debatable, but there is much about them that surely is not.

That these decisions affecting mainly state and local institutions took the control of further state and local affairs away from state and locally elected officials, and from the people who elected them, is undeniable. That it came about as a result of usurpation of power by the least popular branch of the Federal government is hardly less deniable. More, the High Court and its apologists have attended almost exclusively to the potential effects of these decisions on religion, which they have generally denied would be harmful, and noticed little or any at all the effects of driving religion out of the public square on public respect for government and its officials and servants, or on public behavior and morality in general.

Indeed, government needs religion much more than religion needs government. Religion has prospered greatly in America without substantial aid from government, while government goes ever more deeply in debt and is increasingly weakened in doing its essential job as it has progressively driven religion out of public life. The schools need religion much more than religion needs the schools. Indeed, the more the Courts have driven religion out of the schools the greater has been the disarray in the public schools. There is a reason for this. God is the major premise of effective education. The main business of the schools is learning. Learning is dependent for its significance upon the existence of truth. Truth has its ultimate support in the existence of an all-knowing God in whose knowledge is truth. Without this major premise, there is no fixity to provide us with knowledge worth learning; there are only opinions, and these are relative to one another. Hence, relativism prevails, and opinions, or opinion polls, are what passes for knowledge in the political realm, as well as others, today.

As for morality, it has no firm support once religion is driven out of public life. Of the connection between religion and morality, George Washington captured its essence in his Farewell Address, when he wrote:

> Of all the dispositions and habits which lead to political prosperity, religion and morality are indispensable supports. In vain would that man claim the tribute of patriotism who should labor to subvert these great pillars of human happiness—these firmest props of the duties of men and citizens. . . . And let us with caution indulge the supposition that morality can be maintained without religion. Whatever may be conceded to the influence of refined education on minds of peculiar structure, reason and experience both forbid us to expect that national morality can prevail in exclusion of religious principle.[571]

None of the above is meant to suggest, of course, that God is only or primarily an adjunct to government. Nor does He exist only to substantiate truth. On the contrary, earthly powers and principalities are but adjuncts to God's ultimate purpose for man, and knowledge is finally of God and His purpose for man. Nor is any of the above meant to suggest that God is not concerned about morality. On the contrary, both Judaism and Christianity have evinced a lively concern for public morality. Men imbued with these religions are incomplete and unfulfilled until and unless their religious principles are given a public airing and can be seen to have an impact on public affairs. Religion can indeed survive without government aid, but it is greatly enriched as it informs political life with its high and enduring principles.

(5) Pornography, Vulgarity, and Obscenity

As religion has been progressively driven out of public life, America has been inundated with publicly expressed profanities, vulgarities, and obscenities. A part of this is due to the fact that the Warren Court and other Federal courts were disabling state and lower governments from controlling public obscenities at the same time they were driving religion out of public life. Until the time of the Warren Court, the regulation or prohibition of pornography, obscenity, profanity, public displays of various degrees of undress, observances of the sabbath, and the like were generally left with state and local governments. Such matters had generally been thought to belong to those powers reserved to the states or to the people respectively, as the 10th Amendment says. But as the Supreme Court moved into more and more areas and began to undertake vigorously supervisory powers over the states, it intervened in censorship cases and the like. Once again, it claimed to be enforcing the provisions of the First Amendment by way of the 14th Amendment. Once again, too, the Federal courts moved into areas where neither Congress nor the Executive had ventured theretofore.

In 1957, in a ruling made in *Butler vs. Michigan,* the Supreme Court held a Michigan statute void which prohibited the selling of books which were reckoned to have a bad influence on children. Justice Felix Frankfurter observed wryly that ''The incidence of this enactment is to reduce the adult population of Michigan to reading only what is fit for children.''[572] Thus, the Supreme Court ventured into its new role of monitor of state censorship. That is not to say that the High Court had determined to prohibit all such activity by invalidating laws of that character. On the contrary, less than four months later the Supreme Court sustained a New York statute authorizing the prohibition of obscene written and printed matter in *Kingsley Books vs. Brown.* Again, it is not at all clear how the Court could translate an amendment which says that Congress shall make no law abridging freedom of the press into the position that states could sometimes abridge freedom of the press. Even if the 14th Amendment could perform such alchemy, it still would have only authorized the Congress, not the courts, to legislate on the subject. Actually, the High Court had not yet legislated on censorship by the states in 1957, but that would soon be forthcoming.

In *Roth vs. United States,* the Supreme Court did lay down some rules of a sort. The *Roth* rules, as later refined by Justice William Brennan, went something like this:

> We expressed the view that Federal or State Governments could control the distribution where "three elements . . . coalesce; it must be established that (a) the dominant theme of the material taken as a whole appeals to a prurient interest in sex; the material is patently offensive because it affronts contemporary community standards relating to the description or representation of sexual matters; and (c) the material is utterly without redeeming social value.[573]

The Court had now "legislated," so to speak, or made a stab at it, but it soon discovered that it had done nothing more than open a "can of worms." Indeed, a part of the difficulty lay with judges legislating in the first place. If they could "legislate," so to speak, they could modify, alter, and refine it to their liking. Another part of their difficulty lay in the fact that they had to apply or enforce their "legislation." This was especially onerous in the matter of obscenity, vulgarity, explicit sex, and the like, because ultimately they had to read, view, or listen to the stuff themselves, at least some of it. For example, over a two day period in December, 1965, the court had to listen to cases involving pornographic, vulgar, and explicit books from Massachusetts, New York, and Pennsylvania. "Do we have to read all of them to determine if they have social importance?" asked Chief Justice Warren. "I'm sure that this Court doesn't want to read all the prurient material in the country to determine if it has social value. If the final burden depends on this Court, it looks to me as though we're in trouble." Nor were the attorneys before the Court of a single mind about how the Court should proceed. One suggested that the testimony of experts and authorities should be enough. But another thought that the members of the Court should examine the works individually. To which, Justice William Brennan remarked, "What you are saying is that the Court must look at this stuff and read it." Justice Hugo Black added, "The problem still arises whether this Court can do all this censorship and do anything else and whether it is the one who should do the censoring—if anyone should." And, Justice Douglas protested further, "We are judges, not literary experts or historians or philosophers."[574] Even so, the Court muddled through, making such decisions as it would.

The overall difficulty was that the Supreme Court had long since embarked on a course which led to the above and many other entanglements. There are three functions performed by government: legislative, executive, and judicial. In the American system, these functions are performed by distinct bodies: Congress, the Executive, and the Supreme and lower courts. More, most Americans live under two distinct governments: that of the United States and of the states wherein they reside. Even more, the states have generally conveyed some of their governmental powers to local governments, such as municipalities and counties. By its rulings during the Warren Era, the Supreme Court assumed the powers of the legislature and when it undertook to enforce these rulings it assumed the powers of the executive as well. (More precisely, in so far as these legislative acts by the courts were enforced by the executive, it could be said that the executive branch became subservient to the courts.) But most of the decisions of the Warren Court were not aimed at the Congress or the Executive branch of the United States; rather, they usurped the powers of the states and through them of local governments. It was the state and local governments who would ordinarily perform the censorship of literature, if anyone did, if the Federal courts had left them to their tasks. Thus, it ill behooved the Supreme Court justices to complain about the work when they had brought it upon themselves.

In any case, the Supreme Court continued to wander through the thicket, clinging to the position that there were things so gross they should not be described or depicted and needed censorship, but accepting no one else's views as to what that was. From Mount Olympus, they continued to lay down rules for the "pygmies" below. (To the delight of the increasing number of lawyers who were prospering as never before, as more and more was decided by the courts through litigation, and all the court's modifications and refinements made possible just that much more litigation.) The number of activities or expressions that can be prohibited has declined as the Court has moved further into determining what is and is not obscene. Thus, "Blasphemous or sacrilegious expression is not considered obscene by the court, nor, generally, are scatalogical profanities. Violence has been found obscene only when entangled with sex." As Justice John Marshall Harlan put it in 1971, "Whatever else may be necessary to give rise to the States' broader power to prohibit obscene expression, such expression must be, in some significant way, erotic."[575] But alas and alack, what is erotic to one person may only be disgusting or vulgar to another.

Indeed, the Supreme Court has had great difficulty over the years finding any sort of language or depictions that could be prohibited by state law. It announced in *Redrup vs. New York* in 1967 that it would uphold obscenity convictions only to protect juveniles or unwilling adults from being exposed to obscene materials or pandering. Several years after Earl Warren had retired from the Court, the new Chief Justice, Warren Burger, supposedly gave governments more leeway in controlling obscene materials. He held that states could prohibit "works which depict or describe sexual conduct." But to do so, the works must, "taken as a whole, appeal to the prurient interest in sex, which portray sexual conduct in a patently offensive way, and which, taken as a whole, do not have serious literary, artistic, political or scientific value." The same ruling, *Miller vs. California* (1973), held that the community standard under which local governments might act did not have to be national in scope. "It is neither realistic nor constitutionally sound," Burger wrote, "to read the First Amendment as requiring that the people of Maine or Mississippi accept public depiction of conduct found tolerable in Las Vegas or New York City."[576]

That states or local governments were any freer to control the flood of filth in books, in movies, in videos, on cable television, or in discourse on the streets or other public places has not been apparent since that time. Instead, the Federal courts have gone out of their way to protect scatalogical language on bumper stickers and have proclaimed that the public burning of the United States flag is a form of expression protected by the First Amendment. Most state and local governments are reluctant to venture far into an arena so strewn with vague exceptions and prohibitions.

The Court has lost its ability to distinguish between decency and indecency, between right and wrong, between devotion and profanity, between morality and immorality. It has done so because by its rulings and actions it has cut itself and many of the American people off from the grounds of morality. It has gone far to establish the rule of secularism, moved us into the realm of relativism where the only thing prohibited is any connection between church and state. The Court has erected a *cordon sanitaire* between religion and morality and then flounders around seeking for definitions of obscenity and pornography. It opens the streets and all sorts of public places to the expression of sacrilege, profanity, obscenities, scatalogical language, vulgarity, and proclamations of perversions while forbidding Bible reading and prayer in the schools and religious displays on public property. When the connection between religion and morality is broken, the rest follows.

(6) Abortion

Roe vs. Wade came as a Supreme Court ruling in 1973, four years after the retirement of Chief Justice Earl Warren. Thus, the bold ruling on abortion was not the work of the Warren Court. Not only had a new Chief Justice, Warren Burger, taken over, but President Richard Nixon, a Republican, had named four men, including Burger, to the Court. Moreover, it was one of Nixon's appointees, Justice Harry A. Blackmun, who spoke for the majority in *Roe vs. Wade*. In one sense, this decision was of a piece with the judicial activism that had been characteristic of the Warren Court. Equally important, it signifies that the High Court tended to be activist in the ensuing years, generally extending rather than reducing the role and power of the Court in national affairs. Like the Warren Court decisions discussed above, *Roe vs. Wade* got what justification it could muster from the Bill of Rights made to apply to the states by way of the 14th Amendment. It greatly circumscribed the powers of the states in the matter of abortion. Thus, it belongs with the other matters discussed above.

The ruling itself in *Roe vs. Wade* was simple enough. It nullified a Texas law prohibiting certain types of abortion. In effect, it also declared unconstitutional laws in 46 of the states regulating or prohibiting abortion during the first six months of pregnancy. For purposes of his ruling, Justice Blackmun divided the term of pregnancy into three periods, called trimesters. It was on the basis of this scheme that Blackmun proceeded to "legislate." During the first trimester, he declared, states could not interfere with the "right" of the woman to abort her child-in-embryo. During the second trimester, however, states could regulate the conditions within which abortions could be performed. Justice Blackmun put it this way: "a State may regulate the abortion procedure [during the second trimester] to the extent that the regulation reasonably relates to the preservation and protection of maternal health. Examples of permissible state regulation in this area are requirements as to the qualifications of the person who is to perform the abortion, as to the licensure of that person; as to the facility in which the procedure is to be performed, that is, whether it must be a hospital, or may be a clinic, or some other place of less-than-hospital status; as to the licensing of the facility; and the like."[577] Through the first six months, the only evinced concern of the High Court was for the life and health of the mother, none for the unborn child. So far as the Court was concerned, only two parties were necessary through the second trimester for an abortion to be performed. As Blackmun said, "the attending physician in consultation with his patient, is free to determine without regulation by the State, that, in his medical judgment, the patient's pregnancy should be terminated. If that decision is reached, the judgment may be effectuated by an abortion free of interference by the State." Then, almost as a laconic afterthought, beginning with the third trimester, "If the State is interested in protecting fetal life after viability, it may go so far as to proscribe abortion during that period, except when it is necessary to preserve the life or health of the mother."[578]

It is exceedingly difficult to understand how the Constitution of the United States can be read so as to arrive at the conclusions stated in *Roe vs. Wade*. For more than 180 years after the adoption of the First Ten Amendments, no legislature, chief executive, or High Court had found anything in them warranting Blackmun's conclusions. Nor in the more than 100 years since the announced ratification of the 14th Amendment had a hint of things to come about abortion been found there. Moreover, by reading the Constitution backward and forward, upside down and inside out; no authorization appears for the Supreme Court to prohibit states to regulate or prohibit abortions, much less to lay down rules that amount to legislating.

The only reference to anything in the vicinity of abortion in the Constitution is to "life." There are two signal references to life in the Constitution: the Fifth Amendment says (once again), "No person shall be . . . deprived of life, liberty, or property, without due process of law . . . ;" and the 14th says, "nor shall any State deprive any person of life, liberty, or property, without due process of law. . . ." These are prohibitions against governments, national and state (which includes local ones as well), from taking life without due process of law. If governments are prohibited from taking life, it is a reasonable inference as well that they may not license, condone, or allow people within their jurisdiction to do so. It would be an exceedingly strange approach to restrict governments in the taking of life without due process of law and leave people in general—or, on the other hand, some class of them—free to take life at will. The only reasonable conclusion from the 5th and 14th Amendments is that governments were bound from doing or giving assent or approval in any way to the taking of life without due process of law.

The constitutional exception, "without due process of law," may need some further discussion within this context. The Constitution does acknowledge that governments may justly and properly take the lives of people (war is a special case which should not detain us here). But before doing so, it is bound to observe certain procedures. In practice, a person must ordinarily have been arrested, informed of the charges against him, (ordinarily) indicted by a grand jury, tried by a petit jury before a judge, be present at the trial, be permitted to defend himself by counsel if he so chooses, be afforded the opportunity to compel his witnesses to appear in court, be found guilty of a capital crime, and sentenced to be executed at a particular place and time. In addition to that, he may appeal his conviction and obtain stays of execution until his appeal has been acted upon. Of course, an unborn child cannot be guilty of any crime, and most certainly not a capital one. The due process of law to which the Constitution refers as a condition that must be met before life is taken by government simply cannot be done for an unborn child. It should follow, then, that governments are prohibited to authorize, license, give their assent, or take the life of an unborn child by abortion.

Justice Blackmun did take up the question of life, but he did so only because it was obviously an issue and must be disposed of somehow to make his case. Rather than focusing upon the question of whether and at what stage an unborn child was alive, he focused upon when life began in a fetus. To which he answered, "We need not resolve the difficult question of when life begins. When those trained in the respective disciplines of medicine, philosophy, and theology are unable to arrive at any consensus, the judiciary at this point in the development of man's knowledge is not in a position to speculate as to the answer."[579] That is rather like prohibiting capital punishment because authorities disagree with one another as to the precise instant of death. But surely in criminal executions what matters is that the person dies, just as in the case of unborn children what matters most, for constitutional as well as many other purposes, is that the child is alive when an abortion is performed—otherwise no life is aborted or can be by any procedure.

In any case, Justice Blackmun gave short shrift to the question of life in

the infant and focused instead on the pregnant woman's "right to privacy."
While Blackmun wandered about in trying to locate precisely where this
right could be found in the Constitution, he appears not to have doubted that
it was strong enough to justify her ordering an abortion from a compliant
physician. He notes that "In varying contexts, the Court or individual
Justices have, indeed, found at least the roots of that right in the First
Amendment . . . , or in the concept of liberty guaranteed by the first section
of the Fourteenth Amendment. . . ." The train of his thought, such as it was,
gets virtually lost in a spate of citations, and he never explains just where
these glimmerings are in the First Amendment, or why the reference to
liberty in the first section of the 14th Amendment means anything more than
not in jail, prison, or otherwise confined, which is its obvious meaning. Nor
does Justice Blackmun base the "right to privacy" in the Fourth Amendment which does at least deal with what could reasonably be called the
privacy of persons, houses, papers, and effects from unreasonable searches.
Instead, Blackmun states his case this way:

> This right of privacy, whether it be founded in the Fourteenth
> Amendment's concept of personal liberty and restrictions upon state
> action, as we feel it is, or, as the District Court determined in the Ninth
> Amendments' reservation of rights to the people, is broad enough to
> encompass a woman's decision whether or not to terminate her
> pregnancy.[580]

On this thin reed of constitutional interpretation, the Court rested its case
for nullifying abortion laws in virtually every state in the Union and the
laying down of rules which amount to legislation for giving abortions
throughout the United States. Nor was it a bloodless decision. As one book
reports, "As a result of *Roe v. Wade,* at least 1.5 million babies were
exterminated each year through 'legal' abortion—15 million or more between 1973 and 1983."[581] And the slaughter has continued more or less
apace since that time. Indeed, the Court made clear in the years after *Roe vs.
Wade* that it would brook no interference by state governments with a
woman's unrestrained right to have an abortion during the first six months
of pregnancy. In 1976, the Court ruled that "states could not require the
consent of the husband, or—if the woman was an unmarried minor—the
consent of her parents, as a condition for terminating pregnancy in the first
trimester."[582] The Court sounds like nothing so much as an angry parent
whose child has once again disobeyed its direct command. In fact, *Roe vs.
Wade* had been clear enough that no one was to interfere with the decision
of the pregnant woman to have an abortion in the first three months. This
kind of decision made out of aggravation points up one of the dangers of the
Court acting as a legislator and executive as well as a judiciary in violation
of the separation of powers. The judges become interested parties in en-

forcing their will, in such cases. They cannot be impartial judges when *their* laws are challenged or disobeyed.

Nor has the Supreme Court curbed its penchant for legislating much to the present day. After assessing the High Court's performance for 1992, Judge Robert Bork wrote, "Almost no one these days makes the slightest distinction between the Supreme Court and a legislature. It has become irrelevant to point out that abortion, for example, is one of the multitude of topics to which the Constitution does not speak; that it is, like most issues, left by the Constitution to the moral reflection and then the votes of the American people."[583] He went on to point up that the authority of the Court rests on its impartial interpretation of the actual Constitution, something that it is leaving farther and farther behind.

The overriding point here, however, is that the Federal courts have subjected state governments to their will and have undermined their power to counterbalance the centralizing tendency of the national government.

Chapter 19
Government out of Control

It may not be obvious that the United States government is out of control, and has been for quite some time now. After all, there are many signs that government is in the control of those who are constitutionally chosen to be in charge and going about its business in a reasonably orderly fashion. Presidents are elected in the manner provided by law, inaugurated on the day set for that event, occupy the White House as of yore, make State of the Union addresses, approve and veto legislation, declare an assortment of holidays, appoint those to serve under them and do their bidding and where it is prescribed they do so with the advice and consent of the Senate, and so on and on.

In like manner, the members of Congress—both House and Senate—are chosen in the manner prescribed by the Constitution by their appointed constituencies, assemble in Washington around the time appointed for their sessions, answer roll calls, introduce legislation, engage in debates, hold hearings, and with varying degrees of effectiveness go about the business of being legislators. The sessions have grown longer over the years, the number of clerks and assistants have increased greatly, and the business of Congress has multiplied, but on the surface, at least, Congress is exerting its control over the government by way of legislation.

And, on the face of it, the judiciary, and especially the Supreme Court, have been busily exerting their control over government, especially over state and local governments. Federal judges are still appointed by the President with the advice and consent of the Senate, as they have been since the first government was organized under the Constitution. District Courts hold trials, circuit courts hear appeals, as does the Supreme Court.

Surely, the armed forces of the United States are not out of control. The President, as their constitutionally determined commander-in-chief, is charged with maintaining the most general control over the armed forces. Under him, the Secretary of Defense is appointed to coordinate the branches, and each of these has a civilian secretary in charge. The Joint Chiefs of Staff not only make military co-ordinating decisions for all the armed services but also serve as individual commanders, each for his particular branch. And, in descending order, there are commanders over the largest and smallest units of the Navy, Army, and Air Force. The military commanders accept the authority of the civilians duly appointed over them, and the loyalty and obedience of all ranks is the standard and the norm.

To take a different tack, and speaking now at the surface level, there are many signs that the United States government is fiscally responsible. Particular demands for payments on and redemption of government securities are regularly made. The government meets its payroll regularly. Social Security checks arrive at their destination on their appointed day like clock work. A whole vast system of disbursement is carried on by the government with surprisingly few hitches.

Much, much more could be described along the same line that would serve as evidence that the United States government is apparently under control and functioning more or less as it should, but perhaps the examples given will suffice. After all, the theme of this chapter is not that government is under control but that it is out of control in some highly important ways. Before elaborating on this main theme, however, it is necessary to make the counterpoint, namely, that there are ways that government is apparently *not* out of control. That done, we can now proceed to the main theme.

In the broadest sense, government has been out of control in the United States in the last half of the 20th century (and was headed in that direction for most of the first half) because it is no longer effectively under the control of the Constitution. Formally, of course, the government operates under the Constitution. Most of the forms are rigorously observed, such as, age and residency requirements for various offices, length of terms of elected officers, times for holding elections, and so on. But in substance and spirit, the written Constitution no longer controls by limiting and restricting the government to those powers authorized by it. The Constitution may not be a dead letter, but it has been stretched completely out of shape, ignored, and evaded so as to produce a Leviathan whose justification can be found nowhere in the letter or spirit of the written Constitution.

How the government got out of control has been the burden of most that has been told in this section thus far. In sum, it has been an account of how the Congress, the President, and the Federal judiciary were no longer substantively controlled by the Constitution, and how the restraining powers of the states were wrested from them. It is necessary now only to demonstrate ways in which the government is out of control and the impact of that on Americans. Wherever it is possible, too, that will be shown to be the result of removing or ignoring constitutional restraints.

a. Fiscal Policy and Spending

Nowhere is the fact that government is out of control more easily demonstrated than in the budgetary and spending difficulties of the past decade or so. The government goes through the motions of contriving a budget, but what comes out of it is not a budget in anything but name. By its very nature, a budget is supposed to be a device for holding spending—including payments on interest and retirement of debt—to anticipated income. A government budget would differ from the budget of an individual family, say, not only by its size but also by the fact that governments might well dispense with planning to have something over for savings. An unbalanced budget is not a true budget; it is, instead, a plan for spending more than you take in. Yet that is precisely the character of the "budgets" that Presidents have submitted over the better part of the two past decades and Congresses have activated. Presidents keep announcing that they expect to balance the budget within so many, i. e., 3, 4, 5, 7, or whatever, number of years. But as the appointed time for balancing approaches it is pushed back into the future once again.

Huge deficits occur year after year, and neither Congress nor the President can bring them down. Thus, the deficits (in rounded numbers) were $73 billion in 1976, $53 billion in 1977, $59 billion in 1978, $40 billion in 1979, $73 billion in 1980, $78 billion in 1981, $127 billion in 1982, $207 billion in 1983, $185 billion in 1984, $212 billion in 1985, $221 billion in 1986, $149 billion in 1987, $155 billion in 1988, $153 billion in 1989, and $220 billion in 1990. No more can Congress get a handle on controlling the rapidly mounting national debt. They make futile attempts to control it by setting debt limits from time to time. But these are little more than farce, since as soon as the debt approaches near the limit, the limit is raised once again. Nor do "budgets" make any provision for reducing the debts, as a proper budget should do. No significant reduction in the debt has been made since the late 1940s. The focus has long since shifted from making any effort to reduce the debt to talk about reducing the deficit.

Surely, a government that cannot devise a budget which balances its income with its spending and obligations, continues to run huge deficits year after year, and goes deeper and deeper in debt for more than 50 years, is out of control. With greater precision, perhaps, it can be said that Congress and the President are out of control from one Congress to another and from one President to another. But how is this related to the Constitution? That document does not mandate a balanced budget nor prohibit deficits. Moreover, the Constitution permits Congress to borrow money on the credit of the United States.

Technically, the Constitution has not been violated by the above actions. But if we pose some related questions we can move into view of the evasions of constitutional restraints involved. Why, we can ask, does the Congress persist in authorizing more expenditures than it has income? How can the debt grow from year to year and generation to generation without ever being significantly reduced? The following subheadings will explore these questions and offer some answers to them.

BASIC AMERICAN GOVERNMENT

(1) The Welfare State

One of the major reasons politicians cannot get a handle on spending is the welfare state syndrome. The welfare state grew out the socialistic thrust to equalize wealth by redistributing it, which, in turn, was fueled by the idea that each of us is responsible for all of us. The political translation of these ideas was to buy votes by adopting programs to provide benefits to assorted classes and interest groups. These programs become "entitlements," and the number of beneficiaries increases over the years. Beneficiaries become interest groups to see to it that these programs remain in effect, that the benefits increase with rising prices, and that the qualifications are not stiffened for established recipients. There is a political catch in this situation, however. Established programs do not buy votes as well as new programs do. There is, then, pressure on politicians to expand old and devise new programs. Even without the new programs, however, the established programs often become more and more expensive over the years. The political incentives lie more with increasing spending than in reducing it to balance the budget within the welfare state syndrome.

The welfare state and its drive to mounting spending exists despite the Constitution. The Constitution limits spending to those functions and undertakings covered by it or necessary and appropriate to put them into effect. The myriad programs of redistribution of the welfare state, ranging from crop subsidies to Medicaid to aid to dependent children to aid in building sewers to local government to subsidizing the building of airports to food stamp programs, find no authority in the Constitution. The welfare state, by its nature, provides benefits to special classes, groups, and conditions, not for the general welfare of the United States taken as a whole. Hence, such expenditures are not authorized.

(2) Foreign Aid

The welfare state is a major source of the spending that is out of control. Aid to foreign governments and countries is a lesser source of spending, but it is nonetheless an instructive example of how Federal spending has mounted by eluding or evading the Constitution. Now the United States has always carried on relations with foreign governments, sent and received ambassadors and ministers, maintained embassies in foreign lands, entered into treaties with other nations from time to time, and made efforts to protect its citizens while abroad in other lands. The powers to do these things are provided for in the Constitution, mostly in the powers granted to Presidents, but some of them elsewhere as well. For example, the power of the President to make treaties is shared with the Senate. The power to declare war is vested in Congress, but the President is in command of the armed forces. Congress is empowered "To define and punish Piracies and Felonies committed on the high Seas, and offences against the Law of Nations.'' But most of the initiative for foreign policy and the conduct of relations with other nations is vested in the executive branch of the government. The President is responsible for this activity, but most of the business of the conduct of relations is done by the Department of State.

The Constitution does not, of course, specify what foreign policies shall hold sway nor what matters may be a subject for foreign policy concern. For example, Congress is authorized ''To regulate Commerce with foreign nations . . . ,'' but no particular instructions are found there. Nonetheless, it must be the case that those who govern us are limited in the conduct of foreign affairs as well as domestic. They are, of course, limited by the foreign powers with whom they are dealing. The President is also limited by the Senate and the Congress more generally in his conduct of foreign relations, as Congress is limited by the President. Moreover, both Congress and the President are limited from time to time by their electors, who, if they are displeased, may not return them to office.

There are substantive limits on our government in dealing with other nations as well. Notice that in the first paragraph of Section 8 of Article I of the Constitution there is what should be a major limit on the exercise of such powers. It begins, ''The Congress shall have Power To lay and collect Taxes, Duties, Imposts and Excises, to pay the Debts and provide for the *common Defence and general Welfare of* the *United States. . . .*'' (Italics added.) Let us turn it around to see the relevance of this to foreign relations. There is no authority granted to levy taxes or contract debts to provide for any foreign country. The *United States* is specified alone as the beneficiary for all tax collections.

For most of United States history there was no occasion for raising the question about tax or indebtedness for foreign nations. The situation changed significantly during and after World War I. The United States made large loans to her Allies during the war and some smaller loans especially for relief or to enable countries to acquire American surpluses from the war in Europe. The major debtors were Great Britain, $4½ billion; France, nearly $3½ billion; Italy, over $1.6 billion; and Belgium, over $379 million. The United States never collected on most of these debts, and in the 1930s, there was considerable ill will toward our former Allies over the unpaid debts.

A fairly good case can be made for loans or other aid to allies during the course of fighting a common war. It has been a fairly common practice for such loans to be made during a war, though that is not a constitutional justification for the United States to do so. Such loans could be constitutionally justified, perhaps, as necessary to the defense of the United States. But once the war is over, no further loans could presumably be made under that justification.

In any case, what has come to be called ''foreign aid'' since World War II has been much more extensive than loans prior to that time. Moreover, much of it had only a tangential relation to any fighting war, much less the clear defense of the United States. The first major effort after World War II was relief and rehabilitation to war torn areas of Europe. Between 1945–1947, the United States provided $11 billion in various kinds of aid to Europe through the United Nations Relief and Rehabilitation Administration. Most of this aid went to Eastern Europe, where countries were in the process of being Communized in the presence, quite often, of Red Armies. Western European countries did not seek aid through UNRRA. As it became increasingly clear that the Soviet Union was using the opportunity of their conquest of the Nazis in Eastern Europe, and the devastation of continental Europe generally, as an occasion for expanding their Communist system into Europe, the United States shifted toward unilateral programs for aiding the war torn countries of Europe.

The shift in policy and the focus on Western Europe came in the wake of a speech at Harvard in June, 1947 by Secretary of State George C. Marshall, a speech that became the basis of what was called the Marshall Plan. Marshall emphasized that there had not only been a vast amount of physical destruction in Europe but also the dislocation and disarray of the arrangements and structure of industrial and agricultural economies. These, he claimed, were beyond the powers of the governments and peoples of Western Europe to rebuild on their own in the foreseeable future. "The truth of the matter is," Marshall said, "that Europe's requirements for the next 3 or 4 years of foreign food and other essential products—principally from America—are so much greater than her present ability to pay that she must have substantial help, or face economic, social, and political deterioration of a very grave character." He did not make an argument that such aid would be constitutional, nor, indeed, in any way indicated that there was any constitutional problem. His argument is stated in what follows:

> . . . It is logical that the United States should do whatever it is able to do to assist in the return of normal economic health in the world, without which there can be no political stability and no assured peace. Our policy is directed not against any country or doctrine but against hunger, desperation, and chaos. Its purpose should be the revival of a working economy in the world so as to permit the emergence of political and social conditions in which free institutions can exist. . . .[584]

What Marshall had said was that Europe was in bad shape, that the countries there needed help from the United States to rebuild, and that the United States should provide it. He must have assumed either that the constitutional authority to do such things was there somewhere or that it was best to let sleeping dogs (the Constitution) lie. Even before Marshall spoke, President Harry Truman had embarked on a somewhat different and more pointed course in March, 1947, with his request to Congress for $400 million in economic and military aid for Greece and Turkey. In this, he referred specifically to Communist insurgents in Greece and more broadly to totalitarian aggression generally. Truman said, ''I believe that it must be the policy of the United States to support free peoples who are resisting attempted subjugation by armed minorities or outside pressures.'' And, in a kind of peroration to his request, Truman declared:

> The seeds of totalitarian regimes are nurtured by misery and want. They spread in the evil soil of poverty and strife. They reach their full growth when the hope of a people for a better life has died. We must keep that hope alive. The free peoples of the world look to us for support in maintaining their freedoms.[585]

In providing the aid requested, the Congress merely declared that the ''integrity and survival of these nations are of importance to the security of the United States and of all freedom-loving peoples and depend upon the receipt at this time of assistance. . . .'' That being the case, the Congress proceeded with, ''*Be it enacted,* that notwithstanding the provisions of any other law, the President may from time to time when he deems it in the interest of the United States furnish assistance to Greece and Turkey. . . .''[586] The ''security'' and ''interest'' of the United States are cited as reasons for these programs and acts, but no effort is made to tie that to what is constitutionally authorized.

But aid programs from the United States have gone beyond Europe or the Middle East. Following his reelection in 1948, President Truman announced his Point Four Program for aid to underdeveloped countries around the world. He explained it this way:

> Point Four was aimed at enabling millions of people in underdeveloped areas to raise themselves from the level of colonialism to self-support and ultimate prosperity. . . . In this country we had both the capital and the technical ''know-how.'' I did not see how we could follow any other course but to put these two great assets to work in the underdeveloped areas in order to help them elevate their own standards of living and thus move in the direction of world-wide prosperity and peace. . . .[587]

Mr. Truman gave the following examples of undertakings under the auspices of Point Four:

> A monetary, fiscal, and banking system was introduced in Saudi Arabia. Schools of medicine, public health, and nursing were set up in several countries. A 57,000-acre irrigation project in the Artibonite Valley of Haiti got under way. A great multi-purpose hydro electric

plant was constructed in the Mexican state of Michoacan. Irrigation
projects in Jordan were started to create 120,000 acres of arable land
providing homes and six-and-a-quarter acre tracts for 21,000 families
consisting of 105,000 individuals.[588]

These and other programs like them may have been quite praise-worthy
and may have done a great deal of good, but they pose more than a little
problem for constitutionally limited government. Where was the authority
for the United States government to build an irrigation project in Haiti, for
example? And, if there is such authority, what is its limits and bounds?
What can the United States not do in foreign lands, and to what ends may
taxpayers money not be spent? It is perhaps conceivable that a hydro-electric
plant in Mexico might make Mexicans more prosperous and attached to their
government, and that they might be less attracted to Communism thereby
and less likely to try to overthrow their governments. Indeed, it is conceivable that almost anything that is constructive that could be done would
somehow contribute to the well being of the world and thus to the security
and interest of the United States. But such a concept carries in it no inherent
limits.

In fact, the United States did pour a large amount of money into foreign
aid. For the years 1945–1965, the total for economic and military aid around
the world was over $100 billion. Economic aid to Western Europe amounted
to $23.8 billion, military aid to $16.2 billion; economic aid to the Near East
and south Asia, $15.4 billion, military aid $6 billion; economic aid to the
Far East and Pacific, $14.5 billion, military aid to $12 billion; economic aid
in the Western Hemisphere to $5.6 billion, and military aid to $1 billion.
"Others" received $2.7 billion in economic and military aid.[589] Of course,
foreign aid has continued over the years, though Western Europe is no
longer aided and Africa has become an important recipient. In 1990, total
grants for foreign aid were over $16.2 billion, reduced by credits and returns
to over $11.9 billion. But neither of these figures include "investments" in
international and regional banks and development funds, which came to
about $1.3 billion.[590]

Not only does the above information show another arena in which the
United States government is out of control but it also shows another level of
the growth of Leviathon. The sway of this country in the world has been
greatly extended since World War II. The following is the description by a
political scientist of how extensive that sway became in the decade after
World War II:

> The extent and depth of American commitments in the postwar
> world were staggering. In the decade after the war Americans took the
> lead in the United Nations and American soil became the site of the
> "world's capital." Americans ruled alien peoples in Germany, Aus-

tria, Italy, Trieste, Japan and Korea; and American generals, like Roman generals of old, became world famous as proconsuls. Peacetime "entangling alliances" were made with Asiatics, and with countries as far away as Australia and New Zealand. American spheres of influence arose in Greece, Turkey, and Saudi Arabia, and extended in circular half-moon fashion through the Japanese islands, the Ryukus, Formosa, the Philippines, the Carolines, and the Marshalls. The internal politics not only of Latin American countries but also of European, African, and Asiatic countries turned on American policy.[591]

There have been many changes since 1955, but the American presence remains large in the world, American troops are still stationed in many foreign countries, and American naval bases still dot the globe.

Other examples of fiscal policy and spending could be given that would further illustrate how government is out of control in this area, but it is time now to turn to the matter of how government could continue to spend at ever higher levels, build debt upon debt, and still continue to operate as if it had vast surpluses to dispose at will for every cause and occasion. Where does the money come from? How is government able to do what no private person, or group of them, could ever do?

(3) The Credit Expansion System

The Federal government has financed much of its ongoing spending spree by expanding credit endlessly (as of now), destroying our money, and forcing it's play-like paper money on the American people by legal tender laws. Beyond that, it has used its virtual absolute power over credit and the currency to manipulate and try to control the economy. Its credit has no known limit because the government can expand the credit through instrumentalities that it controls. The Federal government has a monopoly of the power to expand the credit within the bounds of the United States. The states do not have this power, nor do they share in its exercise. Many of the states are now required by their constitutions to balance their budgets for their general expenses, but even if they did not have this requirement they would still be limited in how much they could spend, because they have no credit expansion powers. The resistance in Congress to an amendment to require the Federal government to balance its budget stems mainly from the fear that this would stifle its credit expansion powers. Credit expansion is truly a goose that has laid a fools-gold plated egg for politicians for the better part of three generations now.

Since the above statements stand in need of explanation and substantiation (they are not obviously true), let us delve more into them. Probably, the best way to get some sort of mathematical view of the extent of the ongoing credit expansion is to look at the national debt and its increase over the years. A good place to start is 1930. The national debt was approximately $16.1 billion in 1930. In 1990—sixty years later—it stood at over $3.2 trillion; or, translated into billions and expressed more precisely, it stood at 3 thousand, 233 billion, 300 million dollars. Or, to put the matter in its simplest form, the national debt in 1990 was 200 times what it had been in 1930. Such an increase would only be possible by an ongoing increase of the money supply, or more precisely, drastic expansion of the credit base. That is what has happened.

The credit expansion has been directly related to debt in this way. Credit expansion, *per se*, has taken place by the monetizing of debt. The process can be oversimplified and concretely visualized in this way. A borrower executes a note for a certain amount of money which he proffers to a creditor. The creditor runs off the amount of paper money desired on a printing press and lends it to the debtor. Thus, a debt could be monetized, so to speak. Credit could have been expanded by increasing the supply of the currency. The trouble with the illustration, as noted, is that it makes simple the complicated process by which government has actually expanded credit over the years. In the illustration, the currency would be increased in the same amount as the debt. That need not be and would not usually be the case. The currency would ordinarily need to be expanded for only a fraction of the amount of the debt or credit expansion, if at all. The currency in circulation in the United States—while it can be increased at will today—is usually little more than is needed for cash transactions and holdings, and is only a small fraction of the national debt or credit expansion.

Credit expansion in the United States is done by banks or bank-like institutions. They have exclusive franchises to expand credit by fractional reserve procedures. Although commercial banks—i.e., banks of deposit, are central to this undertaking, an assortment of other banks, public and private, play important roles in it. The lynchpin, or fount, of the credit expansion system is the Federal Reserve system, whose active arms are the regional Federal Reserve banks. These banks can expand credit in a variety of ways, usually by way of commercial and other banking institutions. They can do so by rediscounting notes (for commercial and agricultural short term debts) originally held by banks, thus increasing their cash reserves and lending power. They can raise or lower reserve requirements of member banks, thus expanding or contracting the credit of banks. And, they can buy the securities of the United States, in effect, lend money to the government, and, if cash is wanted, they can issue currency to provide it. In effect, an instrument of the government—the Federal Reserve system—can expand the credit and service the debt of the United States. The dominant power over the Federal Reserve banks is exercised by Federal appointees, so that the government can, in effect, borrow from itself, and the Treasury Department can print the paper money to achieve this, if necessary. That is how the

United States can pile debt upon debt without ever reducing it. It uses its power to monetize debt.

The government accomplished these feats by substituting "play-like" money for our commodity based money (real money, if you like), forcing us to operate with the "play-like" money, and progressively depreciating the value of the currency. The Federal government took away the considerable control people had over their own money supply and greatly increased the power of the government over both the money supply and the people. This was not done overnight, of course. The Federal Reserve system was created, as told earlier, just before World War I. Much of the currency was redeemable in gold still, and it was backed by gold reserves. This was drastically changed in 1933 and 1934. Gold contracts were invalidated, bank notes redeemable in gold were called in and paid for by Federal Reserve notes, and unlicensed Americans were prohibited to own gold except in jewelry or fillings in teeth. There was still a reserve in gold to "back" the currency, but it did so only on foreign markets, since Americans could not own it or demand it. In addition to this roundabout backing by gold, the government issued a limited amount of silver certificates, redeemable in silver.

This done, the government proceeded on a course of credit expansion by inflating the currency. The price of gold was increased from $20 to $35 an ounce, not only increasing the value of gold on hand but also drawing in gold from around the world. Thus, a large base was established to "back" an increased money supply. The most noticed effect of an inflation (increase of the money supply) is the rise in prices of goods. Americans experienced a major rise during World War II, though there was rationing and price controls to hold down prices of many goods. Prices rose after the war and continued a gradual rise in the 1950s and 1960s. Both credit expansion and prices began to rise much more dramatically in the late 1960s and into the 1970s.

It was in this period when all commodity backing of the dollar was removed. The government ceased to back the dollar abroad at a fixed ratio of gold. Silver coins were replaced with cupra-nickel, and a date was fixed after which the silver certificates would no longer be redeemed with silver. By the early 1970s, the United States had full fledged fiat money—money by government decree—or, in short, play-like money. Its true worth is slightly more than the play money that comes with monopoly sets—because the paper is of a higher quality and the printing is more precise.

Why, then, if our paper money is worthless in itself do we still work to be paid in it, sell goods for it, and take such care as we do of it, such as depositing it in banks, to keep it from being stolen? The most direct answer is that we do so because we have no other medium than this to make exchanges. More broadly, we use the paper money because we are accustomed to and greatly benefit from the division of labor, from the specializations by which each of us produces only one or a few things and buys a great variety of goods from others. And we sell our goods for money to effect these exchanges.

The paper money is the only money we have because of the tender laws. Federal Reserve notes—our paper money—bear this legend—"THIS NOTE IS LEGAL TENDER FOR ALL DEBTS, PUBLIC AND PRIVATE." People will not use any other money to settle their debts, because any other money that would be acceptable would have to be more expensive to acquire. Or, as Gresham's Law holds, bad money drives good money out of circulation. (In the absence of tender laws, the opposite would be the case, for people could then determine in what good, commodity, or money they would accept payment.) Thus, no other money can compete with the Federal government's play-like money.

The tendency of this play-like money is to be worth less and less over the years as it comes nearer to reflecting its true value in the market. What has kept it from becoming worthless thus far is that the supply has been limited by government and, as explained above, it is the only money available to us. As the credit expands, as the national debt mounts, as the money supply increases, the money is worth less and less, a fact that is to considerable extent reflected in rising prices. Some random numbers may indicate the rise in prices for selected items. A first class stamp cost 2¢ in 1930 and 29¢ in 1992; a new Chevrolet could be had in 1935 for under $500 and for 15 or more times that in 1992; a haircut in the mid-1930s was 15¢ (the ditty—"Shave and a haircut, two-bits"—was fact then) and is now more likely to be $4–$5 or more; men could be hired to work for a day in some places for $1 in the 1930s, while $35 would almost certainly be the minimum in 1992. Prices are, of course, subject to other variables than changes in the money supply, but they will nonetheless in considerable degree tend to reflect the latter.

In sum, the Federal government is able to spend more and more, increase the debt higher and higher, and neither balance the budget nor make any provision for retiring the debt, because it can expand the credit and print the money to sustain these undertakings. It can do so, however, only by ignoring the restrictions of the Constitution and evading its restraints. There is no authority in the Constitution for the government to expand credit, print money, or make it legal tender. The government of the United States is authorized only to *coin* money and regulate the value thereof. The states are prohibited to make anything *but* gold or silver legal tender, which surely means they are free to make gold and silver legal tender. The Federal government has short-circuited this power by proclaiming that Federal Reserve notes, printed by the United States Treasury, are legal tender.

Thus, the government is out of control because it has evaded and ignored the Constitution, usurped the powers of the states, taken from the people control of the supply of the money, and imposes such controls as it can over the economy. It has depreciated the currency and imposed paper notes, which have only residual monetary functions, upon the economy.

b. Bureaucracy

As effective belief and faith in God has waned in the 20th century and as religion has been increasingly driven from the public square, so to speak, the belief has grown that everything must be controlled by government decreed or passed laws. As many men have ceased to be aware of or believe in God's laws planted in His universe, or natural law as it has been commonly called, they have sought to have man made laws occupy the whole field. More, there has been a great thrust to use the power of government to make over man and society. Those of that persuasion, and it has infected virtually all of us in one way or another, have usually not been satisfied to experiment with such laws at the local or state level, but have above all sought to have the Federal government take over and lay down the rules and laws.

Thus, a vast array of laws have been passed in the United States, both at the Federal and state levels, regulating and controlling all sorts of activities. Many, perhaps most, of these activities are in their nature peaceful, have their own private owners, managers, overseers and the like, to regulate and control them, and even have their own guards and security forces sometimes. No matter, the regulations, laws, and decrees about them have been forthcoming from government. A large number of these laws, regulations and decrees do not go into effect automatically. They require a virtual army of government employees to activate, enforce, and oversee the operation of the rules. These people are the ones who are usually referred to as "bureaucrats," though the term is not all that precise. It most specifically refers to those who work in government bureaus, but the term is expanded to all those in regulatory and control agencies in government at least, and may sometimes be more broadly used than that.

"Bureaucrat" is often used, too, as if were an epithet, and indeed the species does have a bad reputation. Those who have to spend a lot of time dealing with these government workers they dub as bureaucrats often think of them as requiring an endless stream of paperwork, as being evasive, being very slow to get anything done, sometimes haughty, arbitrary, and, all told, difficult and exasperating for those who are trying to accomplish things. But they are a topic for examination here because government is out of control, and one of the reasons that it is out of control is that those with authority to control it find it hard to get a handle on it. A number of Presidents in the 20th century have bemoaned the fact that those who work in the government often go their own way without regard to what those in

454 BASIC AMERICAN GOVERNMENT

the executive branch are trying to do. Some years back, a Congressman complained bitterly that:

> Time and time again, the principles embodied in good legislation are lost by the time the unelected bureaucratic rulemakers publish their regulations. The rules, which really are laws, are now being ground out at the rate of 6,000 per year as compared to about 600 acts of Congress, in the same period.
>
> It is absolutely essential that Congress regain control over this administrative lawmaking process, especially when the violation of these rules—many of which are unreasonable and far beyond, or contrary to, the original purpose of Congress—can result in a citizen's being fined or going to jail just as surely as if he had violated an act of Congress itself.

A part of the problem is that there are so many bureaucrats imposing so many different rules and laws.

(1) The Ubiquitous Bureaucracy

The bureaucracy is almost everywhere that government attempts to regulate, direct, and control. There is an amazing array and variety of Federal bureaus. They range from the Bureau of Outdoor Recreation to Bureau of Apprenticeship and Training to Office of Intergovernmental Affairs to Center for Disease Control. Just how many such bureaus there are—and which are lethal busybodies and which benign record keepers—is well nigh impossible to determine. One reason for this is the variety of names by which they are called: commissions, boards, bureaus, offices, divisions, centers, agencies, administrations, departments, and so on. For example, the Department of Commerce has a Domestic and International Business Administration, Bureau of Census, Economic Development Administration, Planning Division, Technical Assistance Division, Public Works Division, Business Development Division, Technical Support Division, Equal Opportunity Division, Economic Development Representative, National Oceanic and Atmospheric Administration, National Marine Fisheries Service, Office of Audits, and National Weather Service Forecast Office, Minority Business Development Agency, and an office for Consumer Affairs, among others. The Department of Labor has such divisions as, Employment and Training, Employment Standards, Labor Statistics, Labor-Management Standards, Mine Safety & Health, Occupational Safety & Health, and Pensions and Welfare Benefit Programs. Thus, each cabinet level department has its bureaus and other divisions, plus the numerous independent agencies of the government, sampled earlier in this work. In 1991, the Federal government had over 3.1 million civilian employees, most of whom are employed by the

Defense Department and Postal Service, but which still leaves several hundred thousand for the category of bureaucrats.

Of the myriad activities of these bureaus there is no end. In a piece on Federal grants several years ago, newspaper columnist James J. Kilpatrick noted that there were some 975 assistance programs administered by 52 agencies costing more than fifty billion dollars annually. His description of some of their activities deserves to be quoted:

> Each of the 975 assistance programs, it perhaps goes without saying, has its own rules, regulations, application forms, and miscellaneous requirements. These periodically are promulgated, revised, amended, withdrawn, codified, and readvertised in the Federal Register, a paper printed in the city of Washington in type designed to put your eyes out. The Register, which includes a vast deal of other stuff, last year ran to 35,000 pages.[592]

Not only do bureaucracies abound, but they also erect numerous mazes, obstacles, barriers, and roadblocks, so to speak, to constructive activity. It is true what Presidents and Congressmen say, that bureaucrats often go their own way regardless of who is in power and prevent people from doing what they were elected to do, but more important, they often slowdown, hinder, delay, and sometimes punish and drive out those engaged in peaceful activities with beneficial aims. There is talk today of gridlock in government, but the thrust of the bureaucracy is in the direction of bringing gridlock to the country at large.

(2) Bureaucratic Barriers

Several decades ago, there was a cartoon, probably syndicated, which appeared in newspapers. Its heading was, "There ought to be a law," accompanied by a drawing of some common aggravation or difficulty which could presumably be ameliorated by a law. It was more humorous than not, but it does point to a widespread obsession of this century—the notion that the perplexities, problems, difficulties, hardships, disappointments, frustrations, and pains of this life can be dealt with by laws. The counterpart to this obsession is the illusion that when a law has been passed allegedly to deal with some problem, the problem has been solved. There may be matters that can be handled this way—such as prohibiting tractor trailers to use certain named streets—and there may have been times in history when laws were more readily put into effect than in the 20th century. However that may be or have been, it is not the case for a whole range of laws, particularly many of the laws regulating trade, labor, production, and distribution in our time. The tangled webs which are woven from laws in our time is one of the important ways that government is out of control.

Many of the laws passed in this century are only the beginning. They lay down certain general rules or goals, but they also authorize an agency or other type of organization to articulate the rules, apply them to particular cases, and enforce them. The original law, as passed by Congress, may run to a dozen or so pages, but when it is articulated by the agency the resulting rules may become a book of hundreds of pages. Beyond that, the agency sometimes has its own enforcement courts, and these turn out hundreds of thousands of pages of what is known as administrative law. Much of this will likely go far beyond and be remote from or contrary to anything intended by Congress, while meeting few if any of the goals of Congress. Meanwhile, of course, the agency will long since have taken on a life of its own and be buried too deeply in the fabric of government to become the subject of abolition.

In the articulation of laws, bureaucrats often spell out in gruesome detail the rules that apply to particular cases. Congress passed a Truth in Lending Act in the 1970s, in terms of which consumers were supposed to be protected in their credit dealings with companies in a variety of ways. Among these were "Fair Credit Billing Rights." Here are the rules by which these are to be protected, according to a notice sent out to the credit card holders of Sears, Roebuck and Co.:

The Federal Truth in Lending Act requires prompt correction of billing mistakes.

> 1. If you want to preserve your rights under the Act, here's what to do if you think your bill is wrong or if you need more information about an item on your bill:
>
>> a. Do not write on the bill. On a separate sheet of paper write (you may telephone your inquiry but doing so *will not preserve your rights under this law*) the following:
>>
>>> i. Your name and account number.
>>>
>>> ii. A description of the error and an explanation (to the extent you can explain) why you believe it is an error. . . .
>>>
>>> iii. The dollar amount of the suspected error. . . .
>>
>> b. Send your billing error notice to the address on your bill. . . . Mail it as soon as you can, but in any case, early enough to reach Sears within 60 days after the bill was mailed to you.
>
> 2. Sears must acknowledge all letters pointing out possible errors within 30 days of receipt, unless we are able to correct your bill during that 30 days. Within 90 days after receiving your letter, we must either correct the error or explain why we believe the bill was correct. . . .
>
> 3. After we have been notified, neither Sears nor an attorney nor a collection agency may send you collection letters nor take other collection action with respect to the amount in dispute. . . .

4. If it is determined that Sears had made a mistake on your bill, you will not have to pay any FINANCE CHARGES on any disputed amount. If it turns out that we did not make an error, you may have to pay FINANCE CHARGES on the amount in dispute. . . .

5. If our explanation does not satisfy you and you notify us *in writing* within 10 days that you still refuse to pay the disputed amount, we may report you to credit bureaus. . . .

These sound like nothing so much as rules drawn by creditors to discourage debtors from complaining about errors in their bills and get on with paying them. The present writer's rules about errors in bills are much simpler: if the bill has already been paid, do not pay it again; if he did not owe it in the first place, do not pay it at all. If that doesn't satisfy creditors, break off all relations with them. But alas, borrowers can thumb their noses at Truth in Lending acts, but lenders have to at least go through the motions of complying with them.

The Occupational Safety and Health Administration authorized by act of Congress in late 1970 is an example of an agency set up to expand on and enforce rules. Its rules apply to virtually all businesses "affecting" interstate commerce, which has come to mean almost all of them. By June, 1974, its "Safety and Health Standards" ran to 326 triple-columned 8½ × 11 pages in very small print. The examination of just one of its rules, the one having to do with "Ladders, Fixed" will illustrate the lengths to which the rules go as well as their mathematical precision:

a. All fixed ladders shall be designed for a minimum concentrated live load of 200 pounds.

b. All rungs shall have a minimum diameter of ¾ inch, if metal, or 1⅛ inches, if wood. They shall be a minimum of 16 inches in clear length and be spaced uniformly no more than 12 inches apart.

c. Metal ladders shall be painted or treated to resist corrosion or rusting when the location demands.

d. Cages, wells, or ladder safety devices for ladders affixed to towers, watertanks, or chimneys shall be provided on all ladders more than 20 feet long. Landing platforms shall be provided each 30 feet of length, except where no cage is provided for every 20 feet of length.

e. Tops of cage on fixed ladders shall extend 42 inches above top of landing, unless other acceptable protection is provided, and the bottom of the cage shall be not less than 7 feet nor more than 8 feet above the base of the ladder.

f. Side rails shall extend 3½ feet above the landing.

These rules are not, of course, suggestions provided by your friendly government. They are laws to be enforced by punishment. Civil penalties for the violation of these and other like rules can run to as much as $1,000 per day for a failure to comply after a citation by an inspector has been issued. Criminal penalties go as high as $20,000 fine and one year in prison.

In 1972, Congress passed an Equal Employment Opportunity Act. Its enforcement arm is the Equal Employment Opportunity Commission. The act prohibited discrimination on the basis of sex, color, religion, or nationality by most employers of 15 or more persons in their hiring practices. The EEOC proceeded then to spin out what was and what was not permitted under the act. What follows is the Commission's view of what can appear on a job application form as it may refer to sex:

A pre-employment inquiry may ask "Male ____, Female ____;" or "Mr., Mrs., Miss," provided that the inquiry is made in good faith for a non-discriminatory purpose. Any pre-employment inquiry in connection with prospective employment which expresses directly or indirectly any limitation, specification or discrimination as to sex shall be unlawful unless based upon a bona fide occupational qualification.

The Commission has not been prolific in naming "bona fide occupational qualifications" based on sex. Acting roles where a male or female is portrayed would appear to qualify.

The organization with the broadest mandate for dealing with the physical setting of American life was set up in 1970 as the Environmental Protection Agency. It has a wide mandate, according to an information sheet it issued, "The Agency sets and maintains air and water pollution standards, regulates the sale and use of pesticides, sets standards for noise and ambient radiation, develops techniques and procedures for solid waste management, studies toxic substances, conducts research, and demonstrates new pollution control methods and technology." It has gone much farther than that would suggest, however, because it has extensive authority over building, construction, drainage, and earthmoving activities in general.

Regulations, controls, and various forms of government intervention are usually touted at the outset as being put in to promote and advance some public good or to prevent some ill or injustice. They may sometimes do that, but they bring in their train their own ills and injustices. Most of all, however, they set up obstacles to constructive activity and divert much effort into non-productive or unproductive channels.

(3) Oppressions Large and Small

Leviathon—huge and expansive government—has come to America in the 20th century by way of all sorts of laws, government organizations, and agencies announced as beneficial, protective, and for the public good. They operate by bureaus which extend the authority of government into the lives of the people. They proceed by taking away the power and authority of the people over their own lives and property. This has usually been done by ignoring or evading the constitutional restraints on the Federal government and in defiance of the Ninth and Tenth Amendments. The Tenth Amendment has been especially defied by the Presidents, Congress, and the Supreme Court in their march to extend the powers of government in the 20th century. The Tenth says, "The powers not delegated to the United States by the Constitution, nor prohibited by it to the States, are reserved to the States respectively, or to the people." To put it more directly, the powers not delegated to the United States and not granted to individual states are reserved to the people. Time and time again in the twentieth century, as noted in numerous instances above, the United States has usurped powers not delegated to it.

The result has been oppression, some of it small, much of it in larger increments. Probably, not nearly enough has been made of government oppression thus far. Yet that has been the tendency and usual result of evading and ignoring constitutional restraints, violating the Constitution, and acting in defiance of it. The levels of taxation in the United States are oppressive. The taking of powers away from state and local government are oppressive. It is oppressive to cause people to turn in their precious metals for paper money and to nullify their contractual claims to be paid in gold. It is especially oppressive to depreciate the currency by inflation, thereby progressively destroying the value of our money. It is oppressive for government to prescribe the distance between rungs on a ladder, a minimum wage which employers must pay, to restrict the use of mailboxes which householders buy to the United States Postal Service, and to prescribe that employers pay time-and-a-half beyond a certain number of hours worked per week.

The humorist, P. J. O'Rourke has well described some of the oppressions of government, great and small:

> The federal government of the United States of America takes away between a fifth and a quarter of all our money every year. That is eight times the Islamic zakat, the almsgiving required of believers by the Koran; it is double the tithe of the medieval church and twice the royal tribute that the prophet Samuel warned the Israelites against when they wanted him to anoint a ruler. . . .
>
> Our government gets more than thugs in a protection racket demand,

more even than discarded first wives of famous rich men receive in divorce court. Then this government, swollen and arrogant with pelf [money], goes butting into our business. It checks the amount of tropical oils in our snack foods, tells what kind of gasoline we can buy for our cars [unleaded only] and how fast we can drive them, bosses us around about retirement, education and what's on TV; counts our noses and asks fresh questions about who's still living at home and how many bathrooms we have; decides whether the door to our office or shop should have steps or a wheelchair ramp; decrees the gender and complexion of the people to be hired there; lectures us on safe sex; dictates what we can sniff, smoke and swallow. . . .

The government is huge . . . and makes nosy, officious and dangerous intrusions into the smallest corners of life. . . .[593]

This brings us back to the role of bureaucracies in all of this. Much of the bureaucratic activity deals with technicalities and is often petty in detail. No matter, it still infringes on the lives and liberties of Americans. Bureaucrats operate the regulatory agencies, and through them reduce the liberties of those whom they regulate. Bureaucrats are often blamed for this, but it is in fact due to the regulations, the laws that precede them, and the regulating powers. Moreover, every regulation imposed upon society involves a reduction of freedom of action of those to whom it applies; thus, the regulations and those who regulate are generally engaged in an assault on liberty and property.

c. Crime, Punishment, and Litigation

Government is in a sense out of control as indicated by crime, punishment, and litigation in the United States in recent years. More precisely, much of criminal activity is out of control, the courts have at times virtually gridlocked in the trial and punishment of crime, and litigation has reached unprecedented proportions in the United States. Government's most basic business is to maintain the peace—i. e., enforce the law, provide timely trials and decisions, to punish those who disturb the peace by murder, rape, armed robbery, incitement to riot, theft, and spread terror. To put it another way, it is the business of government to maintain order, make communities reasonably safe from violent and intrusive behavior, and protect life and property. When government is ineffective in performing these functions it is not doing its job well.

Facts and analysis will be forthcoming to show ways in which government is or is not performing its functions well in its most basic job, but first it should be made clear how government out of control has its impact on this. Government is out of control in that it has grown massively and spends so much of its energy and attention on nongovernmental or ungovernmentlike functions. In the broadest terms, it has concentrated on making over society and redistributing wealth at home and abroad rather than in dealing with crimes against persons and property. Considerable attention has been given already to this unconstitutional and extra-constitutional government, but at least a summary is in order here.

For two or more generations now, the United States has been under the sway of the notion that society (i. e., people) should be reconstructed, controlled, and directed by government. This notion has now been implemented in thousands, or tens of thousands, of ways. Acts have been passed by legislatures, court orders issued, administrative rules promulgated, and vast bureaucracies set up with the object of making over and regulating Americans. Massive efforts have been made to break up what were called monopolies, to take over and control the money supply, to guarantee savings and deposits in banking institutions, to regulate the operation of businesses, to subsidize businesses, to empower labor unions, to penalize, restrain, and control employers, to regulate transportation, to integrate the races, to provide for the welfare or well being of the indigent, the disabled, the poor, the young, and the old, to regulate the pollution of the environment, to look after the safety and health of employees, to provide hospitalization for the indigent and the aged, to prevent discrimination in hiring on the basis of race, sex, religion, age, or what have you, to compel special treatment for the disabled, to subsidize agriculture, to regulate electricity, stock exchange, radio, television, drugs and foods, national banks and savings and loan organizations, to provide aid for nations around the world, and so on and on. It is hardly surprising, with all that going on, that the apprehension, trial and punishment of criminals may have slowed down somewhat.

That is not exactly what has happened, however. The Federal government has indeed expanded beyond what Congress can oversee and what all the nationally elected officials combined—which are not many—can control, influence, and direct. Thus, government is out of control, as far as the electorate and those who have been elected by them are concerned. No single person can master the budgetary information nor the descriptions of the vast array of government programs and activities, much less control them. The President cannot do so, nor can 535 Representatives and Senators. But that is not the main problem about crime, punishment and litigation.

Most crimes are crimes under state law; most of those arrested for violations of the law in the United are arrested in state jurisdictions by state and local officers and tried in state courts. In like manner, most civil suits begin in state courts. As might be expected, then, most of those serving time in prison are in state penitentiaries, and such executions for capital crimes as have occurred in recent times have all been carried out by state governments. The United States government has, however, entered this field on a large scale over the last thirty-five years. It has done so mainly by way of appeals to the United States Circuit Courts and the Supreme Court. The Federal courts have intervened in and interfered with state law enforcement in a variety of ways during these years. A part of this has already been described in such rulings as *Mapp vs. Ohio, Gideon vs. Wainright, Miranda,* and so on. The Federal courts have prescribed the warnings that must be given before interrogation, set out the necessity for the state to provide counsel, and have made it exceedingly difficult for the state to get or use confessions. They have prescribed the amount of space prisoners must have when confined. They have sometimes released prisoners on a large scale when states did not comply with Federal prescriptions in a timely manner. Even convicted murderers have been released retroactively following the announcement by the Supreme Court of some new rule on the admissability of evidence. In sum, the Federal courts have taken away much of the authority of the states in managing enforcement, but left them with the responsibility for enforcing the law.

Nowhere has this Federal interference been so drawn out as in allowing executions for capital crimes. For ten years, from 1967–1977, the courts permitted no executions. That era ended in 1977, but executions were still difficult for the states to carry out after that. For example, in 1984 there were approximately 1,200 prisoners on death row, but only 5 executed. By 1990, the number on death row had increased to 2,200, but only 23 were executed. During the years of the hiatus in executions, the death penalty had *not* been declared unconstitutional by the Supreme Court, but such obstacles were placed in the way that none were executed. Meanwhile, states that had the death penalty continued to alter and rewrite their laws in a desperate effort to comply with court requirements. Finally, in 1976, the Supreme Court held that the death penalty was *not* unconstitutional—it had never held otherwise—and shortly thereafter executions gradually began to be performed in states which had the death penalty. They are still sufficiently rare, however, that each one is mentioned in newspapers and on television nationally. The delay between conviction and execution is still excruciatingly long, often running ten to twelve years, or even longer. This is because there are a series of mandatory and voluntary appeals which wind their way through the courts, and when all else fails, there will be a series of *habeas corpus* appeals to Federal courts. Some cases have to be tried two or three times to satisfy the courts. The delay between conviction and execution is so long that much, if not all, of the deterrent effect on anyone except the executed person is most likely lost.

The mentality and outlook of the welfare state—with its assorted and various classes of victims to be succored and nourished—took a strange turn as it reached and permeated the Federal courts. Felons, prisoners, and death row inmates were the special class of victims for which judges could show compassion and nourish. They were, according to general sociological lore, the victims of society, which, when translated into the world of courts of appeal, made them more particularly the victims of police, sherrifs, prosecuting attorneys, juries, jailers, and executioners. Granted, these felons may have had their own victims, but these are remote from Federal courts of appeal, where the focus is not on the crimes committed against hapless victims out in real life but rather on the proceedings carried on by the government from the time that arrests are made until people are convicted and punishment, *per se,* begins. This is the stuff with which the United States Supreme Court deals, and the victims here, if any, are the accused felons.

This attitude of the high courts toward felons has undoubtedly had a considerable deterrence effect on state and local law enforcement officials, cutting down on both their zeal and their effectiveness. It is not only reflected in the rising crime rates but also in the contempt of hardened criminals for officers of the law. This syndrome of perpetrators as victims has usually reached its peak in public awareness in riots and open rebellions in cities in the 1960s and 1970s, and most recently in the Los Angeles riots in 1992. In connection with the latter, some of those who were engaging in the rioting, beatings, burnings, and thievery are now apparently marching demanding swifter government aid. In any case, this perverse notion, championed by decisions—though not verbally—by the high courts has had a detrimental impact on law enforcement.

Court rulings of the past several decades have given much aid and comfort as well to the great surge of litigation in recent times. When the courts can make rulings in the absence of positive law, when they can overturn long established interpretations and limitations on their power at will, when they can, in effect, legislate on the basis of their own decrees, they create a setting for the multiplication of lawyers and bountiful litigation. What the Supreme Court, as well as the lower Federal courts—and in the last decade or so the practice is being widely aped by state courts—has done, in effect, is to create a situation in which lawyers can hope with good reason that they can go into court and make their own laws. After all, the rulings of the courts rarely come full grown from the minds of judges. They are first planted and nurtured there by lawyers. Thus, lawyers can bypass the dull business of running for election in some legislative body, spending years rising to a position of influence in the body, and finally being able to put his name and imprint on one or more pieces of legislation. They can simply go into court and get the judge to legislate for them. Much more important for the great growth of litigation is that it becomes less and less clear what the law on any particular matter is. Relativism prevails among intellectuals generally, and in the courts as well. Thus, any argument might get a hearing and any case, however weak, might carry the day. Hence, the great increase in litigation in both civil and criminal matters, and the large increase in lawyers to take care of it.

The statistics compiled by the Federal Bureau of Investigation in the

Crime Index give some indication of the growth and spread of crime. The total number of offenses reported in 1978 was 11,209,000; it had risen to 13,508,700 by 1987. It had grown to 14,475,600 by 1990. Violent crimes had increased much more rapidly, however, than had crimes against property, both of which were contained in the above figures. Reported violent crimes increased from 1,085,550 in 1978 to 1,484,000 in 1987 to 1,820,130 in 1990. Some crimes were increasing much faster than others. For example, forcible rape increased from 67,610 in 1978 to 91,110 in 1987 and to 102,960 in 1990. Aggravated assaults increased from 571,460 in 1978 to 855,090 in 1987.

But to really get the increase of crime in the United States in a broader and more dramatic framework the number of crimes in a considerably earlier year needs to be compared with those in 1987 and/or 1990. The year 1965 will do well enough, since the population of the United States had only increased from around 190,000,000 in 1965 to 248,708,873 in 1990, an increase of only about 24 per cent. The Crime Index total in 1965 was 2,780,015 compared to nearly 14.5 million in 1990, more than 5 times as many crimes in 1990 as in 1965. Violent crimes were about 357,000 in 1965 compared to 1,820,000+ in 1990. The number of murders in 1965 was 9,850 compared to 23,440 in 1990. The number of forcible rapes in 1965 was 22,467 compared with 102,560 in 1990. In sum, serious violent crimes increased by leaps and bounds from 1965 to 1990, 10 to 20 times as fast as the population.[594]

It would give the wrong impression to cite the above statistics as if crimes were evenly spread throughout the United States according to the density of population. That is by no means the case. Much of crime is concentrated in towns and cities, and much more than that in fifty or so of the largest cities in the country. In 1987, the average number of murders per 100,000 population for a total of 7,721 of the larger cities was 10.2. For other cities it was 5 per 100,000; for rural areas it was 6 per 100,000 people. The very largest cities tell a drastically different story (all figures given are averages for murder per 100,000 population): for Baltimore 29.5, for Chicago 22.9, for Detroit 62.8, for Los Angeles 24.3, for San Antonio 18.9, for Washington, D.C. 36.2. Forcible rape was 19 per 100,000 in rural areas, 46 per 100,000 for over 7 thousand of the largest cities, 78 for Baltimore, 125 for Dallas, 126 for Memphis, and 130 for Detroit.

Nor were crimes evenly distributed among races, of which black and white are the major breakdowns available. The following are total figures for arrests for various crimes in 1988: for murder, 7,243 for whites, 8,603 for blacks; for forcible rape, 14,775 for whites, 12,853 for blacks; for robbery, 40,072 for whites, 69,130 for blacks; for burglary, 220,998 for whites, 103,249 for blacks. Blacks are much more numerous in cities than in rural areas or small towns, so that the two sets of figures above about concentration reinforce, if they do not explain, one another.[595]

Some *caveats* are in order about all the above and statistics in general. Statistics give the appearance of a precision and exactness which is rarely true to fact. The Crime Index compiled by the F.B.I. certainly provides numbers which are far less than complete or certain. The F.B.I. reports on only 7 of the more serious crimes, and as one criminologist notes, "in measuring long-term trends the FBI makes an unstated (and untested) assumption that the ratio between Index crimes and other offenses is stable." Further, "A more important source of error derives from the fact that the FBI itself does not collect the data. Instead, it acts as a statistical clearing house for more than 13,000 cooperating law enforcement agencies."[596] Not only may these use different bases for reporting but they may alter their counts sometimes for good or bad reasons. There is a general impression that many crimes are unreported, but that the trends as reported are substantially correct. Indeed, there are all sorts of indications beyond crime statistics for the belief that violent crimes have substantially risen over recent decades, that the streets are unsafe in many vicinities and in large portions of major cities. Prisons are bursting at the seams despite the fact that those people convicted of crimes frequently go on probation instead of to prison, and paroles within a few years are commonplace for major crimes.

Nor do statistics give us the full flavor of what is going on. They are but abstractions from reality, and much less precise ones than they appear to be. Casual crimes seem to be much more common than in times past, the firing of guns from one moving car to another, for example, the firing of guns from passing automobiles into houses, and the killing of innocent bystanders and sometimes small children. The abusive treatment of women by men is substantially on the rise. The killing of whole families by one or the other parent (usually the father, who usually kills himself as well) may not be commonplace, but they happen more than often enough to remind us of the horror. Then, there are serial killings and rapes, the most horrible, perhaps, those of Jeffrey Dahmer a year or so ago.

Any good sized city daily newspaper will give reports on various crimes. Here are some selected items from a newspaper on one day:

> Felipe Cesar . . . died at 2:18 a.m. . . . after receiving multiple stab wounds. . . . He was in his apartment with friends playing cards . . . when the incident took place. . . . According to the report, two of the men playing cards with Cesar got into an argument with him. One held Cesar down while the other stabbed him several times with a steak knife. . . .
>
> The Healthy Way Store . . . was robbed of cash by a gunman who entered the business at 3:15 p.m. Saturday. . . .
>
> Frank Hubbard, 22, found a man breaking into his parked car . . . at 11:30 p.m. Saturday. Hubbard was robbed when the man located [his] pistol in the car and turned it on him. . . . The robber got

away with Hubbard's pistol, cash, credit cards, speakers and a class
ring. . . .
     A young woman was raped at gunpoint late Saturday in a motel . . .
by several men who forced their way into her motel room at
gunpoint. . . .[597]

To see how overwhelmed the legal system is with crime has been well
described by a woman judge in the inner city of Philadelphia. She is inundated with cases, and back of those are many, many more that should have
had an earlier hearing. On a typical day in court, she had three extradition
cases, four applications for bail: one accused of rape, a fourteen year old
accused of the murder of a child in a street rumble, a heroin addict who
killed three strangers, and a middle aged man accused of sodomy; a petition
for a second psychiatric examination by a lawyer for his client, an application for an extension of an extradition warrant, and, as she summarizes,
"The parade of accused muggers, robbers and thieves continues."[598]
     This judge made it clear that courts could only provide a reasonable
approximation of justice and help to restore order if government stopped
trying to do all things and limited itself largely to maintaining the peace. She
put the case this way:

> Equal justice under law is, I believe, a goal worth pursuing. It can
> be achieved only if the legal structure is simplified and made accessible
> to all people, if the courts are limited to the resolution of conflicts and
> disputes within their capacity to decide, and if the aim of justice is to
> treat similarly situated individuals equally is adhered to. *The law
> should abandon its efforts to restructure the economic and social order
> and modify behavior of individuals.* The limited aim of securing equal
> justice is a difficult and taxing goal to attain. It is a task sufficient for
> any single institution. . . . Equal justice cannot be even dimly approx-
> imated if law is utilized in an effort to provide all or a major part of the
> correctives, change and controls required by our complex and diverse
> society.[599]

If one may venture to supplement so eloquent a plea, its direction is this:
Wherever possible, means should be sought to resolve conflicts, inhibit
offenses, and deal with social, economic, and individual difficulties without
recourse to law. Law should be the last resort, and then only on matters with
which it can deal. The law is not suited, for example, to settling labor
disputes, to running businesses, to laying down rules for schools, to redistributing the wealth, or thousands of other things. All the time spent on
matters to which courts (or for that matter law enforcement officers) are not
competent is time taken from establishing justice and maintaining order.
     The rising incidence and increasing severity of crime indicates more than

that government is out of control, however. It signifies as well that an increasing number of people in America are virtually out of control. Maintaining the peace and having order and a law abiding society are only practically possible when most people are engaged in peaceful pursuits, are law abiding most if not all the time, and are on the side of law and order. Some people maintain that the main solution is to hire more police. But that solution has surely been tried. Since the 1950s, police forces have been doubled and tripled, during a period when populations within city limits have often stabilized or even declined. The number of policemen on the New York City force increased from a little under 18,000 in 1950 to just over 31,000 in 1972, to over 36,000 in 1988; the Los Angeles force increased from 4,124 in 1950 to 7,083 in 1972 to 10,023 in 1988. Yet crime rates rose precipitately in these cities during these years.

The problem is not simply, or even particularly, a matter of the number of police. What is missing in many people are belief in and commitment to transcendant moral and religious principles which induce people to avoid violent and illegal behavior. What is missing is that self-control that flows from being taught how to behave and how to live productive lives under these moral restraints. The driving of religion out of the public square has left a vacuum, so to speak. Publicly taught relativism, pragmatism, secularism, and materialism leaves a public vacuum for observing and enforcing rules. The bitter fruit of these doctrines is both government and much of the populace out of control.

d. Potpourri

The government has been out of control in so many directions and so many ways in the latter half of the 20th century that it is not practical to discuss all of them at length or in detail. Thus, what follows is only a mention of this and that to support the thesis and concluding the chapter with a plumbing of the depths.

Medical costs have risen as if they were out of control over the past decade or so. One of the causes of this is the great increase in the cost of medical malpractice insurance, especially for physicians and surgeons and hospitals. This is the direct result of increasing litigation, especially in the area of malpractice and negligence. More generally, the rise in prices reflects an increasing demand for medical services, paid for by private insurance and such government programs as Medicaid and Medicare. New diagnostic and support systems are extremely expensive, as well as such surgical innovations as heart bypass operations and organ transplants. Some of these are incredibly expensive and can easily wipe out a lifetime of savings and other accumulations in short order, in the absence of some sort of insurance. Government programs have contributed much to the demand for these services which have driven prices through the ceiling.

A major symptom of government out of control has been the government efforts to rescue the depositors from failing Savings and Loan institutions. Doing this is supposed to have cost somewhere in the vicinity of $500 billion thus far, or at least it is projected to. This huge outlay was occasioned by the fact that the Federal government undertook by way of the FSLIC to guarantee deposits in Savings and Loan institutions to the tune of $100,000 per depositer. It is rash of government (and would be rash of anyone else if they were fools enough to do it) to guarantee deposits in any fractional reserve situation, and exceedingly rash to do so at the maximum of $100,000 per depositer.

But the Savings and Loan guarantee is only the tip of the iceberg of the far flung guarantees undertaken by the United States. There is, of course, the similar guarantees of commercial bank deposits at the same high level. There is crop insurance for farmers. There are the guarantees of loans to Veterans who purchase homes under the G. I. Bill of Rights, and for the population in general who purchase homes on mortgages guaranteed by the Federal Housing Administration. There are farm loans either made by government or guaranteed under Federal agencies. There are the huge, virtually incalculable, promises of old age benefits under Social Security. There are large guarantees made to international organizations and for loans made to various countries. Efforts are made from time to time by organizations to put dollar amounts on these guarantees and promises, but it may be sufficient to say here that they dwarf the national debt and are in addition to it.

On no single point is it clearer that government is out of control, or at least not in control, than on immigration. The Federal government barely has much of a handle on legal immigration; but it acts as if it were impotent where illegal immigration is concerned. Over the last two decades or so illegal immigrants have poured into the United States in unprecedented numbers. As one writer notes, "During the 1980's, when as many, or nearly as many, immigrants arrived as during any other ten-year period in U. S. history, the number of Hispanics [in the country] grew by fully 7.7 million people . . . , [though] fewer than 54 percent of these additional individuals were immigrants."[600] How many of these entered the country illegally, he does not say. What is known is that large numbers of Mexicans, as well as others from Central America enter the United States illegally by way of its common border with Mexico extending from Texas across the boundary with southern California. Indeed, southern California is a favorite illegal port of entry to the United States.

One writer says, "Many Mexican women come across the border illegally to have their babies." Some return to Mexico having established the baby's claim to U. S. citizenship, but "Others, including entire families, stay here because of the welfare benefits. . . ." Further, "A few years ago, the U. S. Supreme Court ruled that children of illegal aliens are entitled to the same education as an American citizen, and along much of the entire Southern border, the numbers of new students are so high that many school districts should be adding as much as a classroom every day. . . .'' While the following may exaggerate the possible number of illegal aliens, it shows some of their impact: "A judge in Orange County [California] has found that at least 36 per cent of his docket is filled with cases involving illegal aliens who have been arrested for felonies. A recent study in San Diego County found that 41 percent of those arrested for felony crimes are illegals."[601]

Not only are many Hispanics scofflaws, but Federal agents charged with keeping illegal aliens from entering the country are notoriously inadequate to the task. Having failed to perform its assigned job to keep out the aliens, the Federal government passed a law in 1986 making it illegal for American employers to "knowingly" employ illegal aliens. As a further signal that it could not control the situation on the border, the Federal government by the same act, gave amnesty to upward of three million illegal aliens.

One of the greatest weakness of the United States government, as well as governments in general, is in dealing firmly and forcefully with groups. This weakness can be ascribed more specifically to media influence and the prevailing liberal ideology. The elements who purvey this ideology have a great reluctance to use government force on groups. This extends all the way from street riots to making war on nations. The former may have been best illustrated in Los Angeles when the police tactically withdrew from the areas where the rioting was occurring, leaving the streets to gangs, hoodlums, ruffians, and looters. The motive behind this may have been that in the circumstances discretion is the better part of valor. They did not have sufficient numbers to awe the rioters and looters, and they would be so restricted in their use of force that restoring order would be painfully difficult, if not impossible.

At the level of wars among nations, the United States has not declared war on any nation since World War II, though it has been embroiled in two major wars and several smaller ones. It is not simply that declaring war has gone out of style—which it has—but rather that formal war with its rules, its restrictions, its recognition of the essential equality and rights of nations to a continuing lawful existence, has been repudiated. War is no longer acceptable as a civilized undertaking; therefore, it does not occur. Rather than using force, the ideal is to negotiate a settlement. As soon as fighting breaks out, the aim is to get a cease fire, institute talks, begin negotiations, which may go on for days, weeks, months, or however long. A considerable tribe of negotiators for various nations arose after World War II to engage in these long winded negotiations, and when there were not enough cease fires to keep them going, they could be kept busy negotiating arms reduction treaties, which negotiations often lasted even longer than those to settle fighting outbreaks.

Since these cease fire and arms negotiations usually involved Communists, the suspicion arose that Liberals did not wish to have wars with Communists; wanted them to survive, and achieved this through cease fires and negotiations. That may indeed have been the case, but there does appear to be a general animus against conventional warfare (and horror of nuclear warfare) and more broadly against using force against groups. Labor unions have often been allowed to use threats, intimidation, and even persistent violence, without major force of government being brought to bear on them. Where it has been brought to bear, it has been to negotiate. In like manner, students have run amuck sometimes in taking over college buildings and administrators, and have frequently got away with it. Gangs often operate with relative impunity in inner cities. Protesters have been coddled.

All these things, and many more that could be cited, lend color, at least, to the view that there is a prevailing reluctance to use the force of government against groups. It is clear that when the United States goes to war without declaring it that the Constitution is being ignored or evaded. The government is out of control, so far as the Congress is concerned, and the Congress is the body most directly representing the people. It is obviously beyond the control of the state governments. There are serious weaknesses in the reluctance to deal forcefully with groups as well, whether they be protesters, demonstraters, rioters, labor unions, students, or whatever. The business of government is to maintain peace, establish justice, and, if necessary, to impose law and order. Basically, it does so by monopolizing force within its jurisdiction and using it when necessary. It is neither limited to nor committed to negotiation as its mode of operation. Negotiation assumes that those groups who are disturbing the peace are at least partially right in what they are seeking and therefore justified in using threats, intimidation, and disruptive tactics to gain their ends. Whether their cause is just or not should properly be irrelevant to government; if their tactics would be illegal for individuals to use, they should not be tolerated by groups. When government fails to use force to contain and punish disruptive behavior and negotiates instead, somebody is being forced to negotiate against their wills. Groups are so far forth out of control, and government is out of control in joining force with them.

The most profound way in which government is out of control is that it has assumed a role and powers that belong exclusively to God. By vastly extending the reach and range of its powers, by ignoring and evading its constitutional limits, by proposing to provide all manner of goods to all sorts of people and provide them security from all manner of ills, the United States government has intruded upon and taken from them a large realm for freedom and responsibility given and imposed upon them by God, and reduced greatly the voluntary realm in which men may freely serve God. Leviathon itself is proof of the engulfing realm of affairs taken over by the Federal government in the United States. Moreover, the national Leviathon has been joined by the states in many welfarist practices. While the welfare state has gone much beyond what Christians would have thought ought to be done for or to people, it has nonetheless assumed the giving of much help that Christians, along with others generously or charitably disposed, once provided. State governments virtually monopolize elementary and secondary schooling for children, thus taking from parents much of their authority and control over the training and education of their children. College and university training is dominated in most states by the government. The Federal government has intruded itself into schooling as well, as noted above, especially by way of court decisions.

Above all, the United States government has used the weight of its vast power and influence to drive religious teachings out of the schools and much of public life. In the wake of this, it has, wittingly or not, promoted an alien philosophy or ideology to fill the place formerly occupied by religion and morality. How far it has gone in driving religion out of public life is suggested by the following list of recent court decisions reported in a Christian newsletter:

1. A reaffirmation of a complete 100% ban on prayer in public schools, including graduation ceremonies.
2. The reaffirmation of *Roe vs. Wade* on abortion.
3. [Affirming] a law ordering a Denver teacher to remove a Bible from the top of his desk.
4. A law prohibiting a Christian service from being celebrated in a public park.
5. A law prohibiting a university professor from discussing his religious beliefs in class.
6. A law prohibiting two towns from the use of official seals that include minute reproductions of the Cross.
7. A law prohibiting a North Carolina judge from opening his daily courtroom proceedings with prayer for God's Providence.[602]

The alien philosophy which the United States government has been busily promoting by word and by deed is *materialism*. Materialism is the view that matter is primary, that it is what is real, that it is of utmost importance. Materialism, again, is the view, expressed in Biblical terms, that the things of this world matter most. Government teaches this through what it proposes to provide, what its taxes are spent for, and what its politicians promise. By contrast, the Bible teaches that the spiritual is primal and of ultimate importance. Jesus said,

> But the hour cometh, and now is, when the true worshippers shall worship the Father in spirit and in truth: for the Father seeketh such to worship him.
> God is a Spirit: and they that worship him must worship him in spirit and in truth.[603]

On another occasion, Jesus said:

> Therefore I say unto you, Take no thought for your life, what ye shall eat; neither for the body, what ye shall put on.
> The life is more than meat, and the body is more than raiment. . . .
> And seek not ye what ye shall eat, or what ye shall drink, neither be of doubtful mind.
> For all these things do the nations of the world seek after: and your Father knoweth that ye have need of these things.
> But rather seek ye the kingdom of God; and all these things shall be added unto you.[604]

In the first quotation, Jesus was speaking of the nature of the ultimate and he said that God is a spirit. And, in broader terms, these and other Scriptures tell us that reality is ultimately spiritual; it all came from spirit and the goal of man is to return to the spiritual state. In the second quotation, Jesus was speaking of what we now sometimes refer to as priorities, of what should be first and foremost in the scheme of things. He did not say that the things of this earth are not useful and even necessary. He said rather that they are of secondary importance. They are not things to seek after and set your heart upon; they can be depended on to come when your priorities are in order. A philosophy of materialism would put secondary things first.

None of this is any of the business of government. Establishing priorities, whether spiritual or material, is not the business of government. It has no more business providing us with food and raiment than it does to tell us who, how, and when we shall worship. Government's business is to apprehend and punish wrongdoers and thus keep the peace, as the Apostle Paul said. Of good, better, or best—they are beyond government's proper concern.

Leviathan has not observed these bounds and limits, of course. Instead, it has waxed fat and powerful by promising and undertaking to provide all manner of goods to the populace of the United States, and a much lesser amount to chosen nations of the earth. Leviathon has usurped the role of God as Provider of earthly things and has gone much farther than God ever would by making it unnecessary for those who get them to toil and spin. The evidence for this is so bountiful, it is hard to know where to begin to cite some that would show its direction. As usual, Franklin D. Roosevelt's pronouncements will serve well. First, in his annual message to Congress in January, 1941, Mr. Roosevelt announced what he conceived to the ideal situation for every people and nation on earth. They were what he chose to call the "four essential human freedoms." The first was freedom of expression. The second was freedom of religion.

> The third is freedom from want—which translated into world terms, means economic understandings which will secure to every nation a healthy peace time life for its inhabitants—everywhere in the world.

The fourth was freedom from fear.[605] While these were cast in visionary language and were either cliches when he uttered them or so vague they were unlikely to arouse controversy, the "freedom from want" did foreshadow the government-as-provider theme.

Roosevelt drove the point home in his annual message to Congress in January, 1944. He did so with the following propositions:

> In our day these economic truths have become accepted as self-evident. We have accepted, so to speak, a second Bill of Rights [an Economic Bill of Rights, he called it] under which a new basis of security and prosperity can be established for all, regardless of station, race or creed.

Among these are:

> The right to a useful and remunerative job in the industries or shops or farms or mines of the nation;
> The right to earn enough to provide adequate food and clothing and recreation;
> The right of every farmer to raise and sell his products at a return which will give him and his family a decent living.
> The right of every business man, large and small, to trade in an atmosphere of freedom from unfair competition and domination by monopolies at home or abroad;
> The right of every family to a decent home;
> The right to adequate medical care and the opportunity to achieve and enjoy good health;
> The right to adequate protection from the economic fears of old age, sickness, accident and unemployment.
> The right to a good education.[606]

These alleged economic rights differ crucially from the first Bill of Rights found in the first ten amendments to the Constitution. These latter rights arose from restrictions and limitations on government. Whereas, Roosevelt's Economic Bill of Rights would have to be provided by a vast expansion of the powers of government. Who, after all, is going to provide all these goodies: a job for everyone who wants it, the right to earn enough to provide adequate food, etc., the right to a decent home, the right to adequate medical care, etc., and etc.? Only politicians would have the gall to promise such things, and only the maneuverers of government would presume to provide such things, although it is certain that no body on earth could provide them adequately and fully.

In any case, since World War II a massive effort has been made to provide these and other assorted goodies for Americans, and much of this was a continuation of what had already begun in the 1930s. Undoubtedly, Jesus was right that "life is more than meat, and the body is more than raiment." It is undoubtedly more, too, than a job, adequate recreation, a decent living, a decent home, adequate medical care, and a good education, among other things. The United States government, however, has championed materialism on a huge scale. It has told us over and over again that material goods should have top priority. It has supported this view with massive taxation.

And, there is a great deal of evidence that many, many people in America look to government as ultimate provider of these goods. We worship, more than so to speak, at the altar of Leviathon. How far all this has gone was abundantly apparent in the presidential election in 1992. The media proclaimed over and over again that there was one central issue, and that was economics. The leading candidate insisted time after time that the issue in the campaign was economic. Indeed, two of the candidates—"Bill" Clinton and Ross Perot—said it was economics, and if President George Bush disagreed, it was only in trying to maintain that the differences did not lie primarily in the economic. It is economic gospel, so to speak, that it is the business of government to look after and provide for the economic well being of Americans, though they may differ about which sorts of governmental activity are most likely to achieve the result.

It is at this philosophical level that government is most profoundly out of control.

Chapter 20
In Conclusion

The Founders of the United States might not be greatly shocked at what has befallen or been done with their handiwork in the 20th century. They were not so presumptuous as to believe they could build an edifice that could survive intact the universal tendency of earthly things to decay and disintegrate with the passage of time. They were aware, too, that rulers are often corrupted by the temptations of power, that people yield up their principles before the seductive promises of demagogues; they are all too likely, like Esau, to sell their heritage for a mess of pottage. Indeed, the Old Testament is full to overflowing with accounts of the Hebrew people falling away from the teachings of Jehovah into idolatry and licentiousness. What more likely, after all, than that the American Constitution would be subverted by those sworn to defend it, its limits be swept aside, and the powers used to oppress the people, and eat out their substance?

Can the Republic which Benjamin Franklin said they had given America if they could keep it be restored? Can the federal system of government recover its earlier vitality? Can the separate branches restrain one another once more in the exercise of powers? Can the states recover and reassert their independence? Can the American people reclaim their independence and freedom from the numerous regulations and restraints on them? Will the people refuse the goodies proffered them by government but bought with money taken from them? Do they wish to do these things, and, if so, do they have the virtue, the vitality, and the tenacity to recover and restore the Constitution?

This work on American government is intended to be primarily an historical description of the origin, establishment, and development of the state and national governments of the United States, and a political analysis of its institutions in the light of the Constitution. It does not purport to know what Americans in their deepest aspirations and longings want their government to be and do. Nor is it especially a brief on what they should do. It has analyzed and described the emergence of Leviathan in the 20th century, has told how the President and the Congress have broken away from the limits and restrictions of the Constitution and increasingly placed the onus of determining what is constitutional on the courts. It has described and analyzed how the Supreme Court has departed from the confines of the Constitution and turned increasingly from applying the law to making the law. More, this work has shown how the Federal government has grown and how the state governments have progressively lost their independence and any restraining power on the Federal government. They have even lost most of their restraining power by way of their power to approve or disapprove amendments submitted to them. This has been so because many of the vast powers exercised in the 20th century have been assumed rather than acquired by amendment. Thus, both the states and the people have lost much of their control over government.

Much evidence has been submitted that governments, especially the United States government, is out of control in the 20th century. It is out of control, mainly, because it has ignored, evaded and violated the constitutional controls. For those who would like to see the government brought back under control, the way to do so is in one sense seductively easy. Most of what needs doing is simply to see to it that those in government comply with the United States Constitution. After all, much of the original Constitution, which for practical purposes includes the First Ten Amendments, is still intact. And the overwhelming body of evidence from the Founders, their contemporaries, and immediate descendants indicates that they had established a limited government.

Only three amendments have been added since 1791 which significantly altered the limitations on the Federal government. They were the 14th, 16th, and 17th. The 17th Amendment was the most serious structurally, because it took away from state governments their representation in the Senate, and seriously hampers states in any attempts to limit and contain the general government. Any serious attempt to restore their power should probably begin with the repeal of the 17th Amendment. Some limitations on the reach of the 14th Amendment would help to rein in the Federal courts as well as Congress in its lawmaking powers. While it is not necessary to repeal the 16th Amendment to restore the Republic, to do so would reaffirm limits on the government.

In the main, though, the task for those who wish to restore the Constitution lies mainly in getting the President, the Congress, and the Federal courts to observe the constitutional limits on their power. That probably means that the motivations to do so must be fortified and amplified. Today, the rewards for ignoring and evading the constitutional limits are high, and the willingness to do so is politically quite attractive. Presidential candidates have been elected to that high office repeatedly by proposing programs that are not constitutionally authorized. Members of Congress are reelected time and again for their willingness to support programs that are in tacit violation of the Constitution. Judges, legislators, and executives often receive high accolades for their initiative in finding new ways to evade the Constitution, though that language is not usually used to describe what has been done.

By contrast, there are no formal penalties for ignoring, violating, or evading the Constitution. In short, there are no sanctions to protect the Constitution from having its provisions subverted through misinterpretation and overcoming its restrictions by ignoring and evading it. And, without sanctions the power of government cannot be brought to bear to punish offenders.

What about impeachment and removal from office upon conviction? Not only has that sanction never been effectively used to punish constitutional scofflaws, but it is not clear that it could be so used. Article II, Section 4, of the Constitution deals with this sanction, and it reads: "The President, Vice President and all civil Officers of the United States, shall be removed from Office on Impeachment for, and Conviction of, Treason, Bribery, or other high Crimes and Misdemeanors." So far as is known, ignoring, violating, or evading the Constitution is neither treason, bribery, nor any other high crime (felony?) or misdemeanor. In any case, impeachments and subsequent trials in the Senate have been rare occurrences in America, and have not been used to defend the integrity of the Constitution.

Besides which, impeachment is an inner-governmental process and does not include anyone from the broad citizenry who are most concerned with reining in the excesses of government. It would entail considerable hypocrisy in our day for most members of the House to find officers of the United States guilty of violating the Constitution when they are among the more conspicuous violaters themselves. The same goes for Senators who might be called upon to try such an offender. Nor would it be seemly for any Chief Justice over the last half century to preside over such a proceeding.

In any case, the American legal system provides a mode for determining guilt by people not tainted by the crime under consideration. It is the jury system. To bring it into play in this manner would require a constitutional amendment, of course. The amendment would make it a criminal offense for any civil officer of the United States, elective or appointed, to exceed his authority under the *written* Constitution. Those charged by the appropriate authorities would be tried in United States District Courts of the appropriate venue before a jury of 12 citizens of the United States, which would determine the guilt or innocence of the official. Of course, no fact determined by the jury could be elsewhere questioned. The amendment would specify that the penalty for having exceeded his authority by an official would be removal from office, and Congress might then be authorized to pass appropriate legislation to put this amendment into effect. Since Congress might be less than enthusiastic about activating such a provision of the Constitution, the amendment could provide that if Congress did not act within 12 months of the ratification, suits could be brought in the courts for violations, and guilty parties would be removed from office for the term for which they were elected or appointed plus the succeeding term, but in no case more than 12 years.

But the details and particulars of outlawing the exceeding of their authority by officers of the United States need not concern us here. The point is that there need to be penalties which make it unattractive to ignore, evade, or violate the Constitution. There need to be sanctions to discourage and punish behavior which in its cumulative impact undermines the Constitution and removes the obstacles to unlimited and oppressive government. Leviathon needs to be put on a long term diet to reduce this swollen and distended government to a constitutional shadow of its former self. If history has taught us anything, it should be that the Constitution cannot survive without sanctions to preserve its integrity.

Many objections could and may be raised to the above proposal. It is, after all, radical in nature, differing from anything proposed by the Founders, or, indeed, done anywhere in the world, so far as the present writer knows or has heard. It is a proposal to use law in a new and different way, to preserve and maintain constitutional government. It is a proposal for a new application for jury trial. The question immediately arises as to the competence of juries to determine violations of the Constitution. Would this not involve interpretation of the provisions of the Constitution? Yes, in the same sense and to the same degree that juries now interpret myriads of laws, contracts, confusing and contradictory testimony, a large variety of evidence, and so on. In fact, finding a person guilty of exceeding his authority would probably be child's play compared with a similar finding in a complex murder case based on circumstantial evidence. Positive laws, passed by legislatures, are often long, complex, difficult to comprehend, ambiguous, pompous, and hard to interpret. The Constitution, by contrast, is brief, direct, beautifully written, and concise. But above all, the arguments would be made by lawyers, more or less expert in their materials. In sum, juries could make such decisions, at least as well as those made in life and death cases regularly.

But surely, it may be argued, it would be abusive to persons of high rank to penalize them for not attending to all the niceties of their work. What if the courts or the jury wrongly punishes them for allegedly exceeding their authority? Would it not be a miscarriage of justice to remove them from office? Should a President of the United States answer in the dock in a mere district court before ordinary jurors? Such questions are strange ones indeed, if they should indeed be asked. Americans in general are subject to a great array of laws, and potentially subject to much more severe penalties if they are found guilty of violating some of these laws. They are much more likely to be wrongly accused than those in high places and have no more safeguards when it happens. It is a consequence of living under laws that such things may happen. As for Presidents being better than anyone else to be hailed into court, the objection exposes itself as an appeal for the sanctity of inequality before the law.

Again, the point needs to be emphasized that observance of the Constitution is essential to the survival of the Republic and the well being of Americans, their lives, liberties, and property. We now know that if the Constitution is to be faithfully observed it must be protected by sanctions. Those in power must fear the consequences of ignoring, evading, or violating it. They must change their attitude of pressing as far as they can go in extending their power to keeping away from the boundary between what is permitted and not permitted. Members of Congress must not be permitted to wait for the Supreme Court to decide if the Constitution permits the action, they must decide before passing a law whether it is constitutional. Presidents must make the decision about constitutionality before they sign laws. Federal judges must know the bounds of their authority, must come to realize that they do not make laws, or else subject themselves to the penalties of juries. But if district courts and juries not be considered fit bodies to protect the Constitution by Americans generally, Congress could at least pass a law making it a felony for any civil officer of the United States, including the President, the Members of the House of Representatives and Senate, and the justices of the Supreme and lower Federal courts, to exceed the authority granted under the written Constitution. Those who did could then undoubtedly be impeached for commission of high crimes as permitted under the Constitution. Violation of the Constitution is indeed a high crime.

It may be well, in closing, to recall what Thomas Paine said about the possible role of a Constitution for the United States. He said this several months before the Declaration of Independence and before there was a United States. In *Common Sense,* first published in January, 1776, Paine recommended that a "continental conference" be called with representatives from all the colonies. "The conferring members being met," he continued, "let their business be to frame a Continental Charter [constitution] . . . , fixing the number and manner of choosing members of Congress, members of Assembly, with their date of sitting, and drawing the line of business and jurisdiction between them. . . . Securing freedom and property to all men . . . , with such other matter as it is necessary for a charter to contain. . . ." Then, he went into a peroration about the role which the constitution and law should have in the new country, saying:

> But where, says some, is the king of America? I'll tell you friend, he reigns above, and does not make havoc of mankind like the royal brute of Britain [the king]. Yet that we may not appear to be defective even in earthly honors, let a day be solemnly set apart for proclaiming the charter [the constitution]; let it be brought forth placed on the divine law, the word of God [the Bible]; let a crown be placed thereon, by which the world may know that, so far as we approve of monarchy, that in America *the law is king.* For as in absolute governments the

king is law, so in free countries the law *ought* to be king; and there ought to be no other.[607]

But for freedom and property to be protected under constitutional law, the limits of governmental power prescribed by the Constitution must be faithfully observed.

Notes

[1]Keith Hutchison, *The Decline and Fall of British Capitalism* (London: Jonathan Cape, 1951), p. 291.

[2]Alfred F. Havighurst, *Twentieth Century Britain* (New York: Harper and Row, 1962, 2nd ed.), p. 370.

[3]*Ibid.*, p. 384.

[4]Francis Williams, *Socialist Britain* (New York: Viking Press, 1949), p. 98.

[5]Bertrand de Jouvenel, *Problems of Socialist England*, J. F. Huntington, Trans. (London: Batchworth Press, 1949), p. 206.

[6]Quoted in Pittsburgh *Press* (June 19, 1966), Section I, p. 11.

[7]Michael Oakeshott, *Rationalism in Politics and Other Essays* (Indianapolis: Liberty Press, 1991, new and expanded ed.), p. 460.

[8]*Ibid.*, pp. 431–32.

[9]James G. Driscoll, "It's Time for the United States to Work up a New Constitution," Birmingham *News* (January 3, 1991), p. 7A.

[10]*Ibid.*

[11]Alfred C. Cobban, *In Search of Humanity: The Role of the Enlightenment in Modern History* (New York: George Braziller, 1960) pp. 23–24.

[12]Clarence B. Carson, "The Concept of Democracy and John Dewey," *The Fateful Turn* (Irvington, NY: Foundation for Economic Education, 1973), pp. 248–49.

[13]*Ibid.*, pp. 232–33.

[14]Edward Dumbauld, ed., *The Political Writings of Thomas Jefferson* (New York: Liberal Arts Press, 1955), p. 144.

[15]Alexander Hamilton, *et. al.*, *The Federalist Papers* (New York: Arlington House, n. d.), p. 467 (Federalist #78).

[16]*Ibid.*

[17]Henry S. Commager, *Documents of American History*, vol. I (New York: Appleton-Century-Crofts, 1962), pp. 193–94.

[18]Verna M. Hall, ed., *Christian History of the Constitution of the United States* (San Francisco: American Christian Constitution Press), p. 143.

[19]Perry Miller, ed., *The American Puritans* (New York: Doubleday Anchor, 1956), p. 107.

[20]*Ibid.*, p. 95.

[21]*Ibid.*, p. 240.

[22]Dumbauld, *op. cit.*, p. 190.

[23]Richard B. Morris, ed., *Alexander Hamilton and the Founding of the Nation* (New York: Dial, 1957), p. 9.

[24]Hamilton, *et. al.*, *The Federalist Papers*, pp. 230–31.

[25]*Ibid.*, p. 380.

[26]*Ibid.*, p. 378.

[27]*Ibid.*, p. 424.

[28]*Ibid.*, p. 426.

[29]Benjamin F. Wright, ed., *The Federalist* (Cambridge: Harvard University Press, 1960), pp. 280–81.

[30]*Elliot's Debates*, Bk. I, vol. 3, p. 396.

[31]Wright, *op. cit.*, p. 380.

[32]*Elliot's Debates*, Bk. I, vol. 3., pp. 295–96.

[33]*Ibid.*, vol. 1, p. 422.

[34]Vernon L. Parrington, *The Colonial Mind* (New York: A Harvest Book, 1954), p. 317.

[35]*Elliot's Debates*, Bk. I, vol. 2, p. 8.

[36]*Ibid.*, vol. 3, p. 87.

[37]Quoted in Russell Kirk, *The Conservative Mind* (Chicago: Regnery, 1960, rev. Gateway ed.), p. 199.

[38]Wright, *op. cit.*, p. 277.

[39]*Elliot's Debates*, Bk. I, vol. 1, p. 493.

[40]*Ibid.*, vol. 2, p. 8.

[41]*Ibid.*, vol. 3, p. 186.

[42]*Ibid.*, p. 420.

[43]*Ibid.*, p. 37.

[44]Hamilton, *et. al.*, *The Federalist Papers*, p. 322.

[45]*Elliot's Debates*, Bk. I, vol. 2, pp. 257–58.

[46]Wright, *op. cit.*, p. 327.

[47]*Elliot's Debates*, Bk. I, vol. 2, p. 283.

[48]*Ibid.*, vol. 3, p 570.

[49]*Ibid.*, p. 259.

[50]*Ibid.*, p. 301.

[51]*Ibid.*, p. 40.

[52]Hugh Jones, *The Present State of Virginia* (New York: reprinted for Joseph Sabin, 1856), p. 48.

[53]Will and Ariel Durant, *The Age of Reason Begins* (New York: Simon and Schuster, 1961), p. 631.

[54]Will and Ariel Durant, *The Age of Louis XIV* (New York: Simon and Schuster, 1963), pp. 556–57.

[55]James J. Kilpatrick, *The Sovereign States* (Chicago: Regnery, 1957), p. 14.

[56]Quoted in M. J. C. Vile, *The Structure of American Federalism* (London: Oxford University Press, 1961), p. 27.

[57]William Anderson, *The Nation and the States, Rivals or Partners* (Minneapolis: University of Minnesota Press, 1955), p. 14.

[58]John Dickinson, *Letters from a Farmer in Pennsylvania*, Forrest McDonald, intro., *Empire and Interest* (Englewood Cliffs, NJ: Prentice-Hall, 1962), pp. 72–73.

[59]Dumbauld, *op. cit.*, p. 138.

[60]Jack P. Greene, ed., *Colonies to Nation, 1763–1789* (New York: McGraw-Hill, 1967), p. 562.

[61]James Madison, *Notes of the Debates in the Federal Convention of 1787*, Adrienne Koch, intro. (Athens, OH: Ohio University Press, 1966), p. 398.

[62]*Ibid.*, p. 48.

[63]*Ibid.*, p. 53.

[64]*Ibid.*, pp. 76–77.

[65]*Ibid.*, pp. 322–23.

[66]*Ibid.*, p. 332.

[67]Quoted in Moses C. Tyler, *Patrick Henry* (Boston: Houghton Mifflin, 1887), pp. 288–89.

[68]Charles C. Tansill, ed., *Formation of the Union of the American States* (Washington: Government Printing Office, 1927), p. 724.

[69]James D. Richardson, ed., *A Compilation of the Messages and Papers of the Presidents,* vol. II (New York: Bureau of National Literature, 1897), pp. 569–70.

[70]*Ibid.,* p. 712.

[71]*Ibid.,* p. 736.

[72]The discussion, so far as it was preserved in Madison's *Notes,* can be read in Tansill, *op. cit.,* pp. 556–57.

[73]Tansill, *op. cit.,* p. 557.

[74]Alfred Young, ed., *The Debate over the Constitution, 1787–1789* (Chicago: Rand-McNally, 1965), p. 49.

[75]Hamilton, *et. al., op. cit.,* pp. 513–14.

[76]Tyler, *op. cit.,* p. 291.

[77]Dumbauld, *op. cit.,* p. 55.

[78]*Ibid.,* p. xxvi.

[79]Forrest McDonald, *The Formation of the American Republic, 1776–1790* (Baltimore: Penguin Books, 1965), p. 233.

[80]George A. Peek, Jr., *The Political Writings of John Adams* (New York: Liberal Arts Press, 1954), p. 96.

[81]Morris, *op. cit.,* p. 9.

[82]*Ibid.,* p. 13.

[83]Edward S. Corwin, *The Constitution and What It Means Today* (New York: Atheneum, 1963), p. 201.

[84]William Ebenstein, ed., *Great Political Thinkers: Plato to the Present* (New York: Holt, Rinehart and Winston, 1960, 3rd ed.), p. 320.

[85]Proverbs 8:15–16. (This and the following quotations are from the King James Version of the Bible.)

[86]Daniel 2:20–21, 37–38.

[87]John 19:10–11.

[88]I Samuel 8:5.

[89]I Samuel 8:15–18.

[90]I Samuel 10:18–19.

[91]Romans 13:1–7.

[92]See Acts 22–24 *et. passim.*

[93]I Peter 2:13–14.

[94]Psalms 146:3, 5–10.

[95]Matthew 4:8–10.

[96]John 18:36.

[97]Matthew 22:17–21.

[98]George Boas, *Rationalism in Greek Philosophy* (Baltimore: Johns Hopkins Press, 1961), p. 5.

[99]W. T. Jones, *A History of Western Philosophy* (New York: Harcourt, Brace & Co., 1952), pp. 55–56.

[100]Will Durant, *The Life of Greece* (New York: Simon and Schuster, 1966), p. 368.

[101]Eric H. Warmington and Philip G. Rouse, eds., *Great Dialogues of Plato,* trans. by W. H.D. Rouse (New York: New American Library, 1961), pp. 185–86.

[102]Quoted in George H. Sabine, *A History of Political Theory* (Hinsdale, IL: Dryden Press, 1973, rev. ed.), p. 42.

[103]Lawrence C. Walass, *Gettell's History of Political Thought* (New York: Appleton-Century-Crofts, 1953), p. 46.

[104]William Y. Elliott and Neil A. McDonald, eds., *Western Political Heritage* (New York: Prentice-Hall, 1955), p. 131.

[105]*Ibid.*, pp. 136–37.

[106]*Ibid.*, p. 137.

[107]*Ibid.*, p. 170.

[108]Durant, *Life of Greece*, p. 528.

[109]*Ibid.*, p. 525.

[110]Quoted in *ibid.*, p. 532.

[111]Elliott and McDonald, *op. cit.*, pp. 192–93.

[112]Jones, *op. cit.*, p. 236.

[113]Ebenstein, *op. cit.*, p. 76.

[114]*Ibid.*, p. 77.

[115]*Ibid.*, p. 97.

[116]Jones, *op. cit.*, p. 236.

[117]Quoted in *ibid.*, p. 237.

[118]Elliott and McDonald, *op. cit.*, p. 222.

[119]Quoted in Jones, *op. cit.*, p. 239.

[120]Russell Kirk, *The Roots of American Order* (La Salle, IL: Open Court, 1974), p. 97.

[121]Will Durant, *Caesar and Christ* (New York: Simon and Schuster, 1972), p. 27.

[122]Kirk, *op. cit.*, p. 102.

[123]Wilson O. Clough, ed., *Intellectual Origins of American National Thought* (New York: Corinth Books, 1955), p. 51.

[124]Taylor Caldwell, *A Pillar of Iron* (New York: Corinth Books, 1955), p. ix.

[125]*Ibid.*, p. vi.

[126]Clough, *op. cit.*, pp. 58–59.

[127]*Ibid.*, pp. 55–56.

[128]Quoted in Durant, *Caesar and Christ*, p. 425.

[129]*Ibid.*, p. 415.

[130]Quoted in *ibid.*, p. 427.

[131]*Ibid.*, p. 426.

[132]Robert S. Hoyt, *Europe in the Middle Ages* (New York: Harcourt, Brace and Co., 1957), p. 70.

[133]Eugen Weber, ed., *The Western Tradition* (Boston: D. C. Heath, 1959), p. 185.

[134]*Ibid.*, pp. 180–81.

[135]Quoted in James W. Thompson and Edgar N. Johnson, *An Introduction to Medieval Europe* (New York: W. W. Norton, 1937), pp. 645–46.

[136]James B. Ross and Mary M. McLaughlin, *The Portable Medieval Reader* (New York: Viking Press, 1949), pp. 234–35.

[137]Quoted in Hoyt, *op. cit.*, p. 222.

[138]Will Durant, *The Age of Faith* (New York: Simon and Schuster, 1950), pp. 549–50.

[139]Quoted in Thompson and Johnson, *op. cit.*, p. 60.

[140]Quoted in Hoyt, *op. cit.*, p. 65.

[141]*Ibid.*, p. 68.

[142]Quoted in Thompson and Johnson, *op. cit.*, p. 701.

[143]Ross and McLaughlin, *op. cit.*, p. 47.

[144]Quoted in Durant, *The Age of Faith*, p. 952.

[145]Quoted in Jones, *op. cit.*, p. 486.

[146]*Ibid.*, p. 487.

[147]*Ibid.*, p. 484.

[148]Frederick B. Artz, *The Mind of the Middle Ages* (New York: Alfred A. Knopf, 1953), pp. 284–85.

[149]Will Durant, *The Renaissance: A History of Civilization in Italy, 1304–1576* (New York: Simon and Schuster, 1953), p. 8.

[150]*Ibid.*, p. 43.

[151]*Ibid.*, p. 580.

[152]Federico Chabod, "Was there a Renaissance State?" in Heinz Labasz, ed., *The Development of the Modern State* (New York: Macmillan, 1964), p. 37.

[153]Ebenstein, *op. cit.*, pp. 270–71.

[154]*Ibid.*, p. 274.

[155]*Ibid.*, p. 270.

[156]*Ibid.*, p. 275.

[157]*Ibid.*, p. 277.

[158]Franklin L. Van Baumer, ed., *Main Currents of Western Thought* (New York: Alfred A. Knopf, 1964, 2nd ed.), p. 145.

[159]Weber, *op. cit.*, p. 278.

[160]Durant, *The Renaissance*, p. 564.

[161]Quoted in *ibid.*, p. 156.

[162]Quoted in Joyce O. Hertzler, *The History of Utopian Thought* (New York: Macmillan, 1923), pp. 132–33.

[163]*Ibid.*, p. 135.

[164]Quoted in Will Durant, *The Reformation: A History of European Civilization from Wyclif to Calvin, 1300–1564* (New York: Simon and Schuster, 1957), pp. 554–55.

[165]*Ibid.*, p. 361.

[166]*Ibid.*, p. 363.

[167]Durant and Durant, *The Age of Reason Begins*, pp. 552–53.

[168]*Ibid.*, p. 567.

[169]Ebenstein, *op. cit.*, p. 312.

[170]Duncan B. Forrester, "Martin Luther and John Calvin," Leo Strauss and Joseph Cropsey, *History of Political Philosophy* (Chicago: Rand McNalley, 1963), p. 301.

[171]Ebenstein, *op. cit.*, p. 320.

[172]Forrester, *op. cit.*, p. 306.

[173]*Ibid.*

[174]Quoted in *ibid.*, p. 296.

[175]Ebenstein, *op. cit.*, p. 349.

[176]Walass, *op. cit.*, p. 186.

[177]Ebenstein, *op. cit.*, pp. 350–52.

[178]Quoted in Louis L. Snyder, *The Age of Reason* (Princeton, NJ: D. Van Nostrand, 1955), p. 97.

[179]*Ibid.*, p. 102.

[180]*Ibid.*, p. 107.

[181]Quoted in John Herman Randall, Jr., *The Making of the Modern Mind* (Boston: Houghton Mifflin, 1940, rev. ed.) p. 97.

[182]Snyder, *op. cit.*, p. 8.

[183]Preserved Smith, *The Enlightenment, 1687–1776* (New York: Collier Books, 1962), p. 173.

[184]Will and Ariel Durant, *The Age of Voltaire* (New York: Simon and Schuster, 1965), p. 283.

[185]Van Baumer, *op. cit.*, pp. 414–15.

[186]*Ibid.*, p. 416.

[187]*Ibid.*, p. 417.

[188]Quoted in Randall, *op. cit.*, p. 324.

[189]William Bradford, *Of Plymouth Plantation*, Samuel E. Morison, ed. (New York: Modern Library, 1967), p. 25.

[190]Daniel J. Boorstin, *The Americans: The Colonial Experience* (New York: Vintage Books, 1958), p. 21.

[191]*Ibid.*, p. 24.

[192]Jones, *The Present State of Virginia*, p. 48.

[193]Quoted in Boorstin, *op. cit.*, p. 20.

[194]T. Harry Williams, *et. al.*, *A History of the United States* vol. I (New York: Alfred A. Knopf, 1959), p. 34.

[195]Boorstin, *op. cit.*, p. 319.

[196]*Ibid.*, p. 332.

[197]Christopher Brooke, *From Alfred to Henry III, 871–1272* (New York: W. W. Norton, 1961), pp. 218–19.

[198]John J. Wuest and Manfred C. Vernon, eds., *New Source Book in Major European Governments* (Cleveland: World Pub. Co., 1966), pp. 7–8.

[199]George Burton Adams and Robert L. Schuyler, *Constitutional History of England* (New York: Holt, Rinehart and Winston, 1962), p. 110.

[200]George Holmes, *The Later Middle Ages* (New York: W. W. Norton, 1962), p. 82.

[201]*Ibid.*, p. 83.

[202]*Ibid.*, p. 83–84.

[203]Quoted in Norman F. Cantor, ed., *William Stubbs on the English Constitution* (New York: Thomas Y. Crowell, 1966), p. 197.

[204]*Ibid.*, p. 198.

[205]Holmes, *op. cit.*, pp. 87–88.

[206]*Ibid.*, pp. 224–25.

[207]George M. Trevelyan, *A Shortened History of England* (Baltimore: Penguin Books, 1959), p. 203.

[208]W. E. Lunt, *History of England* (New York: Harper & Bros., 1956, 4th ed.), p. 280.

[209]Trevelyan, *op. cit.*, p. 223.

[210]Quoted in *ibid.*

[211]Quoted in George M. Trevelyan, *History of England* vol. II (Garden City, NY: Doubleday, 1953), p. 144.

[212]Christopher Hill, *The Century of Revolution* (New York: W. W. Norton, 1961), pp. 43–44.

[213]Quoted in Lunt, *op. cit.*, p. 387.

[214]Maurice Ashley, *England in the Seventeenth Century* (Baltimore: Penguin Books, 1952), p. 42.

[215]Hill, *op. cit.*, p. 68.

[216]Wuest and Vernon, *op. cit.*, p. 12.

[217]Quoted in Hill, *op. cit.*, p. 73.

[218]*Ibid.*, p. 187.

[219]*Ibid.*, p. 188.

[220]Wuest and Vernon, *op. cit.*, p. 16.

[221]Trevelyan, *History of England*, vol. II, p. 270.

[222]Durant and Durant, *The Age of Louis XIV*, p. 292.

[223]Wuest and Vernon, *op. cit.*, p. 18.

[224]*Ibid.*, p. 19.

[225]*Ibid.*, p. 23.

[226]Trevelyan, *History of England*, vol. II, p. 274.

[227]Quoted in Kirk, *The Roots of American Order*, p. 246.

[228]*Ibid.*, p. 242.

[229]Duncan B. Forrester, "Richard Hooker," Strauss and Cropsey, *op. cit.*, p. 317.

[230]Ebenstein, *Great Political Thinkers*, p. 368.

[231]*Ibid.*, p. 376.

[232]*Ibid.*

[233]Clough, *op. cit.*, p. 125.

[234]*Ibid.*, p. 126.

[235]*Ibid.*, pp. 128–29.

[236]Walter Berns, "John Milton," Strauss and Cropsey, *op. cit.*, p. 404.

[237]Clough, *op. cit.*, p. 141.

[238]Van Baumer, *op. cit.*, pp. 349–50.

[239]Weber, *op. cit.*, pp. 423–24.

[240]*Ibid.*, p. 425.

[241]*Ibid.*, p. 429.

[242]*Ibid.*, p. 427.

[243]Clough, *op. cit.*, p. 156.

[244]Weber, *op. cit.*, p. 434.

[245]Quoted in David L. Jacobson, ed., *The English Libertarian Heritage* (Indianapolis: Bobbs-Merrill, 1965), p. xvii.

[246]*Ibid.*, pp. 108–09.

[247]*Ibid.*, pp. 127–28.

[248]*Ibid.*, p. 128.

[249]Kirk, *The Roots of American Order*, p. 373.

[250]Clough, *op. cit.*, p. 235.

[251]*Ibid.*, p. 237.

[252]Adam Smith, *The Wealth of Nations*, Edwin Cannan, ed. (New Rochelle, NY: Arlington House, n.d.), vol. II, p. 290.

[253]*Ibid.*, vol. I, p. 371.

[254]*Ibid.*, vol. II, p. 30.

[255]*Ibid.*, p. 27.

[256]*Ibid.*, pp. 29–30, 38–39.

[257]Henry S. Commager, ed., *Documents of American History,* vol. I (New York: Appleton-Century-Crofts, 1963, 7th ed.) pp. 9–10.

[258]*Ibid.*, p. 14.

[259]Bradford, *Of Plymouth Plantation*, pp. 75–76.

[260]Commager, *Documents of American History,* pp. 17–18. The spelling has been modernized by the present writer from what it was in the cited source.

[261]*Ibid.*, pp. 23–24.

[262]Beginning with this paragraph and continuing through this section of the chapter, the material appeared in the present author's *The Rebirth of Liberty* (New Rochelle, NY: Arlington House, 1973), pp. 46–54.

[263]Curtis P. Nettels, *The Roots of American Civilization* (New York: Appleton-Century-Crofts, 1963, 2nd ed.), p. 543.

[264]Adams and Schuyler, *op. cit.*, p. 366.

[265]Nettels, *op. cit.*, p. 546.

[266]Quoted in Clinton Rossiter, *The First American Revolution* (New York: Harcourt, Brace and World, 1956), p. 103.

[267]Max Savelle and Robert Middlekauf, *A History of Colonial America* (New York: Holt, Rinehart and Winston, 1964), p. 402.

[268]*Ibid.*

[269]Jack P. Greene, "The Role of the Lower House of Assembly in Eighteenth-Century Politics," *Essays in American Colonial History* (New York: Holt, Rinehart and Winston, 1967), pp. 431–32.

[270]Nettels, *op. cit.*, p. 563.

[271]Rossiter, *op. cit.*, p. 119.

[272]Thomas Paine, *Common Sense and Other Political Writings,* Nelson F. Adkins, ed. (New York: Liberal Arts Press, 1953), pp. 32–33.

[273]Clinton Rossiter, *The Political Thought of the American Revolution* (New York: Harcourt, Brace and World, 1963), p. 78.

[274]The summary which follows is excerpted from the present writer's "Reasoning on the Nature of Things," *The Freeman* (February, 1982), pp. 94–103.

[275]Otto Gierke, *Natural Law and the Theory of Society,* Ernest Barker, trans. (Boston: Beacon Press, 1957), p. 223.

[276]Ernest Barker, "Translator's Introduction," in *ibid.,* p. xi.

[277]Socialists have left much confusion about property in land. They used the very weak argument that since no individual had a greater claim to land than any other at the beginning of society or of man, or whatever, that therefore the land belonged to society, not individuals. Of course, socialists do not accept the doctrine of natural rights, in the first place, nor do they show how either individuals or society could have a legitimate claim to the land. They appear to assume that if the claim of individuals to land could be sufficiently weakened, the claim of society to land would be greatly strengthened. The one does not follow from the other.

[278]Perry Miller, ed., *The American Puritans: Their Prose and Poetry* (Garden City, NY: Doubleday, 1956), pp. 125–26.

[279]*Ibid.,* pp. 127–28.

[280]*Ibid.,* p. 136.

[281]*Ibid.,* p. 138.

[282]Ralph L. Ketchum, ed., *The Political Thought of Benjamin Franklin* (Indianapolis: Bobbs-Merrill, 1965), p. 34.

[283]*Ibid.,* p. 120.

[284]*Ibid.,* p. 169.

[285]Max Savelle, ed., *The Colonial Origins of American Thought* (New York: D. Van Nostrand, 1964), p. 117.

[286]*Ibid.,* p. 124.

[287]*Ibid.,* p. 168.

[288]Paine, *op. cit.,* pp. 43–44.

[289]See John R. Alden, *A History of the American Republic* (New York: Alfred A. Knopf, 1969), pp. 241–42.

[290]Quoted in *ibid.,* p. 243.

[291]Quoted in Andrew C. McLaughlin, *A Constitutional History of the United States* (New York: Appleton-Century-Crofts, 1935), pp. 106–07.

[292]*Ibid.,* pp. 107–08.

[293]Alfred H. Kelly and Winfred A. Harbison, *The American Constitution* (New York: W. W. Norton, 1955), p. 95.

[294]Quoted in John R. Alden, *The American Revolution* (New York: Harper Torchbooks, 1962), p. 153.

[295]Commager, *Documents of American History,* vol. I, pp. 103–04.

[296]*Ibid.,* pp. 107–08.

[297]*Ibid.,* pp. 125–26.

[298]R. R. Palmer, "The American Revolution: The People as Constituent Power," Jack P. Greene, ed., *The Reinterpretation of the American Revolution* (New York: Harper & Row, 1968), p. 352.

[299]*Ibid.,* p. 350.

[300]Nettels, *op. cit.,* pp. 666–67.

[301]Jackson Turner Main, "Government by the People: The American Revolution and the Democratization of the Legislatures," Greene, *op. cit.,* p. 323.

[302]Quoted in McLaughlin, *op. cit.,* p. 119n.

[303]This and the following quotations from the Articles of Confederation are taken from Frances N. Thorpe, ed., *The Federal and State Constitutions,* vol. I (Washington: Government Printing Office, 1909), pp. 9–17.

[304]Most of the treatment of the background to and the Constitutional Convention is excerpted from the present writer's *The Rebirth of Liberty,* cited above, pp. 177–198.

[305]Samuel E. Morison and Henry S. Commager, *The Growth of the American Republic*, vol. I (New York: Oxford University Press, 1942, 3rd ed.), p. 265.

[306]See Andrew C. McLaughlin, *The Confederation and the Constitution* (New York: Collier Books, 1962), pp. 77–78.

[307]*Ibid.*, p. 75.

[308]Curtis P. Nettels, *The Emergence of a National Economy* (New York: Holt, Rinehart and Winston, 1962), p. 67.

[309]Merrill Jensen, *The New Nation* (New York: Vintage Books, 1950), p. 303.

[310]Nettels, *The Emergence of a National Economy*, p. 65.

[311]Quoted in Jensen, *op. cit.*, p. 249.

[312]*Ibid.*, p. 250.

[313]John Fiske, *The Critical Period of American History* (Boston: Houghton Mifflin, 1916), p. 165.

[314]McLaughlin, *The Confederation and the Constitution*, pp. 64–65.

[315]Quoted in *ibid.*, p. 51.

[316]Fiske, *op. cit.*, p. 145.

[317]Jensen, *op. cit.*, p. 324.

[318]McDonald, *The Formation of the American Republic*, p. 140.

[319]*Ibid.*, p. 147.

[320]Quoted in Charles Warren, *The Making of the Constitution* (New York: Barnes and Noble, 1937), p. 737.

[321]See *ibid.*, pp. 55–56.

[322]Quoted in *ibid.*, p. 730.

[323]Madison, *Notes of the Federal Convention*, (Koch edition), p. 227.

[324]*Ibid.*, pp. 411–12. The present writer has taken the liberty of modernizing the spelling and using complete words rather than the abbreviations in the original.

[325]*Ibid.*, pp. 25–26.

[326]Quoted in Warren, *op. cit.*, p. 38.

[327]*Ibid.*, p. 44.

[328]*Ibid.*, pp. 17–18.

[329]*Ibid.*, p. 50.

[330]Madison, *Notes of the Federal Convention*, p. 159.

[331]*Ibid.*, p. 159.

[332]*Ibid.*, p. 163.

[333]*Ibid.*, p. 185.

[334]*Ibid.*, p. 233.

[335]*Ibid.*, p. 195.

[336]*Ibid.*, pp. 193–94.

[337]*Ibid.*, p. 196.

[338]*Ibid.*, p. 659.

[339]Leonard D. White, *The Federalists: A Study in Administrative History* (New York: Macmillan, 1948), p. 1.

[340]Quoted in Nathan Schachner, *The Founding Fathers* (New York: Capricorn Books, 1954), p. 33.

[341]*Ibid.*, pp. 46–47.

[342]White, *op. cit.*, pp. 108–09.

[343]*Ibid.*, pp. 265–66.

[344]John C. Miller, *The Federalist Era* (New York: Harper & Row, 1960), p. 15.

[345]Schachner, *op. cit.*, p. 63.

[346]White, *op. cit.*, p. 27.

[347]Hamilton, *et. al.*, *The Federalist Papers*, pp. 435–36.

[348]Schachner, *op. cit.*, pp. 129–30.

[349]Morris, *Alexander Hamilton and the Founding of the Nation*, pp. 290–91.

[350]Commager, *Documents of American History*, vol. I, pp. 159–60.

[351]*Ibid.*, pp. 156–58.

[352]Quoted in Schachner, *op. cit.*, p. 187.

[353]Quoted in Miller, *The Federalist Era*, p. 66.

[354]What follows from here to the end of the chapter was included in an article by the present writer published as "George Washington on Liberty and Order," *The Freeman* (February, 1983), pp. 70–75.

[355]Quoted in Miller, *The Federalist Era*, p. 99.

[356]*Ibid.*, p. 103.

[357]T. Harry Williams, Richard N. Current, and Frank Friedell, *A History of the United States* (New York: Alfred A. Knopf, 1959), p. 193.

[358]Vernon L. Parrington, *The Romantic Revolution in America, 1800–1860* (New York: A Harvest Book, 1954), p. 18.

[359]Quoted in Miller, *The Federalist Era*, p. 112.

[360]Charles Crowe, ed., *A Documentary History of American Thought and Society* (Boston: Allyn and Bacon, 1965), p. 66.

[361]All of the Alien and Sedition Acts are printed in Commager, *Documents of American History*, vol. I, pp. 175–78.

[362]Quoted in Schachner, *op. cit.*, p. 467.

[363]*Ibid.*, p. 468.

[364]Quoted in *ibid.*, pp. 465–66.

[365]Quoted in *ibid.*, p. 482.

[366]The Kentucky and Virginia Resolutions can be found in Commager, *Documents of American History*, vol. I, pp. 178–83.

[367]*Ibid.*, p. 184.

[368]Adrienne Koch and William Peden, eds., *The Life and Selected Writings of Thomas Jefferson* (New York: Modern Library, 1944), p. 447.

[369]What follows in this section is excerpted from the present writer's article, "Economy in Government, Jeffersonian Style," *The Freeman* (June, 1981), pp. 347–56.

[370]E. James Ferguson, ed., *Selected Writings of Albert Gallatin* (Indianapolis: Bobbs-Merrill, 1967), p. 207.

[371]James D. Richardson, ed., *The Messages and Papers of the Presidents*, vol. I (New York: Bureau of National Literature, 1897), p. 316.

[372]*Ibid.*, p. 367.

[373]Quoted in Leonard D. White, *The Jeffersonians: A Study in Administrative History* (New York: Macmillan, 1951), p. 24.

[374]Richardson, *op. cit.*, vol. I, p. 316.

[375]*Ibid.*, p. 317.

[376]*Ibid.*

[377]White, *The Jeffersonians*, p. 25.

[378]Ferguson, *op. cit.*, pp. 325–26.

[379]White, *The Jeffersonians*, pp. 142–43.

[380]Richardson, *op. cit.*, vol. I, pp. 397–98.

[381]*Ibid.*, vol. II, p. 569.

[382]*Ibid.*, pp. 711–12.

[383]*Ibid.*, p. 736.

[384]*Ibid.*, p. 584.

[385]Morris, *Alexander Hamilton and the Founding of the Nation*, p. 319.

[386]See Ferguson, *op. cit.*, pp. 34–35.

[387]*Ibid.*, p. 40.

[388]Dumbauld, *op. cit.*, p. 153.

[389]*Ibid.*, p. 151, emphasis by Jefferson.

[390]*Ibid.*, p. 153.

[391]*Ibid.*, p. 154.

[392]See Claude G. Bowers, *Jefferson in Power* (Boston: Houghton Mifflin, 1964), p. 410.

[393]Dumbauld, *op. cit.*, p. 154.

[394]Marvin Meyers, Alexander Kern, and John G. Cawelti, *Sources of the American Republic*, vol. I (Chicago: Scott, Foresman and Co., 1960), p. 346.

[395]Richardson, *op. cit.*, vol. II, p. 452.

[396]*Ibid.*, pp. 490–91.

[397]*Ibid.*, p. 582.

[398]James D. Richardson, ed., *The Messages and Papers of the Presidents* vol. III (Washington: Bureau of National Literature and Art, 1897), pp. 298–99.

[399]*Ibid.*, p. 296.

[400]Joseph L. Blau, ed., *Social Theories of Jacksonian Democracy* (New York: Liberal Arts Press, 1954), p. 76.

[401]*Ibid.*, p. 27.

[402]*Ibid.*, p. 131.

[403]Richardson, *op. cit.*, vol. III, pp. 344–45.

[404]James D. Richardson, ed., *The Messages and Papers of the Presidents*, vol. V (Washington: Bureau of National Literature and Art, 1897), p. 201.

[405]*Ibid.*, pp. 248–49.

[406]*Ibid.*, p. 434.

[407]*Ibid.*, pp. 547–48.

[408]*Ibid.*, p. 656.

[409]Quoted in Charles Warren, *The Supreme Court in United States History*, vol. I (Boston: Little, Brown and Co., 1926), p. 169.

[410]Quoted in *ibid.*, p. 173.

[411]Quoted in *ibid.*, p. 178.

[412]*Ibid.*, p. 181.

[413]Quoted in Edward S. Corwin, *John Marshall and the Constitution* (New Haven: Yale University Press, 1919), pp. 39–40.

[414]*Ibid.*, pp. 29–30.

[415]William Draper Lewis, "Marshall" *Encyclopedia Britannica* (1955), vol. XIV, p. 969.

[416]Quoted in Warren, *The Supreme Court in United States History.* vol. I, pp. 228–29.

[417]Commager, *Documents of American History*, vol. I, pp. 193–94.

[418]Charles G. Haines, *The Role of the Supreme Court in American Government and Politics* (New York: Russell and Russell, 1940), p. 226.

[419]Quoted in Warren, *The Supreme Court in United States History*, vol. I, p. 272.

[420]Quoted in Haines, *op. cit.*, p. 257.

[421]All the quotations from *Fletcher vs. Peck* can be found in Commager, *Documents of American History*, vol. I, pp. 206–07.

[422]*Ibid.*, pp. 213–14.

[423]*Ibid.*, pp. 216–18.

[424]*Ibid.*, pp. 219–20.

[425]*Ibid.*, p. 223.

[426]Quoted in Warren, *The Supreme Court in United States History*, vol. I, pp. 546–47.

[427]Andrew C. McLaughlin, *A Constitutional History of the United States* (New York: Appleton-Century-Crofts, 1963), p. 397.

[428]Warren, *The Supreme Court in United States History*, vol. I, p. 547.

[429]Frank Magill, ed., *Great Events from History: American Series*, vol. I (Englewood Cliffs, NJ: Salem Press, 1975), p. 601.

[430]All the quotations from *Gibbons vs. Ogden* are from Commager, *Documents of American History,* vol. I, pp. 239–41.

[431]Commager, *Documents of American History,* vol. I, pp. 252–53.

[432]McLaughlin, *A Constitutional History of the United States,* p. 454; quotations from both Mason and Story can be found in Warren, *The Supreme Court in United States History,* vol. I, pp. 806–07, 813.

[433]Quoted in Charles Warren, *The Supreme Court in United States History,* vol. II (Boston: Little, Brown and Co., 1926), p. 13.

[434]Quoted in *ibid.,* p. 9.

[435]Commager, *Documents of American History,* vol. I, pp. 286–87.

[436]Kelly & Harbison, *op. cit.,* p. 349.

[437]Quoted in *ibid.,* p. 350.

[438]Quoted in Warren, *The Supreme Court in United States History,* vol. II, p. 65.

[439]Quoted in *ibid.,* p. 45.

[440]*Ibid.,* p. 22.

[441]*Ibid.,* p. 206.

[442]Commager, *Documents of American History,* vol. pp. 344–45.

[443]Quoted in Warren, *The Supreme Court in United States History,* vol. II, p. 335.

[444]The above material from *ex parte Merryman* may be found in Commage, *Documents of American History,* vol. I, pp. 398–401.

[445]Russell W. Maddox and Robert F. Fuquay, *State and Local Governments* (Princeton, NJ: D. Van Nostrand, 1962), p. 60.

[446]Thomas H. Eliot, *Governing American: The Politics of a Free People* (New York: Dodd, Mead and Co., 1964), p. 795.

[447]Maddox and Fuquay, *op. cit.,* p. 494.

[448]Quoted in *ibid.,* p. 465.

[449]Quoted in Allan Nevins, *The Emergence of Lincoln,* VOL. II (New York: Charles Scribner's Sons, 1950), p. 361.

[450]Francis Butler Simkins, *A History of the South* (New York: Alfred A. Knopf, 1956), p. 206.

[451]Quoted in James F. Rhodes, *History of the United States,* vol. II (Harper & Bros., 1893), p. 464.

[452]Quoted in Louis M. Hacker, *The Triumph of American Capitalism* (New York: Columbia University Press, 1947), p. 338.

[453]Wilbur J. Cash, *The Mind of the South* (Garden City, NY: Doubleday Anchor Books, 1954), p. 113.

[454]J. G. Randall and David Donald, *The Civil War and Reconstruction* (Boston: D. C. Heath, 1961), p. 287.

[455]See *ibid.*

[456]*Ibid.,* pp. 288–89.

[457]Quoted in McLaughlin, *A Constitutional History of the United States,* p. 694.

[458]Randall and Donald, *op. cit.,* p. 345.

[459]Commager, *Documents of American History,* vol. I, pp. 508.

[460]*Ibid.,* pp. 563–66.

[461]George Bancroft, *A Plea for the Constitution* (Spencer Judd Pubs., 1982), p. 2.

[462]*Ibid.,* p. 44.

[463]Kelly & Harbison, *op. cit.,* p. 424.

[464]Quoted in *ibid.,* p. 427.

[465]See Commager, *Documents of American History,* vol. I, pp. 420–21.

[466]*Ibid.,* pp. 403–05.

[467]Benjamin P. Thomas, *Abraham Lincoln* (New York: Alfred A. Knopf, 1952), p. 502.

[468]Meyers, Kern and Cawelti, *Sources of the American Republic,* vol. I, pp. 422–25.

[469]Randall and Donald, *op. cit.*, pp. 428–29.

[470]Quoted in Thomas, *op. cit.*, p. 505.

[471]Quoted in Randall and Donald, *op. cit.*, pp. 431–32.

[472]Quoted in Thomas, *op. cit.*, p. 446.

[473]Simkins, *op. cit.*, p. 245.

[474]E. Merton Coulter, *The South During Reconstruction* (Baton Rouge: Louisiana State University Press, 1947), pp. 2–3.

[475]Claude G. Bowers, *The Tragic Era: The Revolution after Lincoln* (Cambridge: Riverside Press, 1929), pp. 46–47.

[476]Marvin Meyers, Alexander Kern, and John G. Cawelti, *Sources of the American Republic*, vol. II (Chicago: Scott, Foresman and Co., 1961), p. 22.

[477]Quoted in Paul H. Buck, *The Road to Reunion* (Boston: Little, Brown and Co., 1937), p. 23.

[478]Quoted in Coulter, *op. cit.*, p. 80.

[479]Quoted in Avery Craven, *Reconstruction: The Ending of the Civil War* (New York: Holt, Rinehart and Winston, 1969), pp. 126–27.

[480]Bowers, *Tragic Era*, p. 83.

[481]Commager, *Documents of American History*, vol. I, pp. 481–85.

[482]Quoted in Simkins, *op. cit.*, p. 289.

[483]Kelly and Harbison, *op. cit.*, p. 504.

[484]Clyde Wilson, "Restoring the Republic," *Chronicles: A Magazine of American Culture* (June, 1992), p. 17.

[485]Gierke, *op. cit.*, p. 223.

[486]Quoted in John Bowle, *Politics and Opinion in the Nineteenth Century* (New York: Oxford University Press, A Galaxy Book, 1964), p. 66.

[487]Quoted in Ludwig von Mises, *Human Action* (Chicago: Henry Regnery Co., 1963, 3rd rev. ed.), p. 175.

[488]Durant and Durant, *The Age of Napoleon*, p. 406.

[489]Quoted in Henry Hazlitt, *The Foundations of Morality* (Los Angeles: Nash Publishing Co., 1972), pp. 204–05.

[490]*Elliott's Debates*, Bk. I, vol. 2, p. 136.

[491]*Ibid.*, pp. 68.

[492]*Ibid.*, vol. 3, p. 75.

[493]*Ibid.*, p. 225.

[494]*Ibid.*, p. 311.

[495]James H. Robinson, *The New History* (New York: Macmillan, 1912), p. 252.

[496]Harry E. Barnes, *The New History and the Social Studies* (New York: The Century Co., 1925), p. 588ff.

[497]Charles A. Beard, *The Discussion of Human Affairs* (New York: Macmillan, 1936), p. 90.

[498]Quoted in Samuel L. Blumenfeld, *Is Public Education Necessary?* (Old Greenwich, CT: Devin-Adair, 1981), pp. 75–76.

[499]See A. M. McBriar, *Fabian Socialism and English Politics* (London: Cambridge University Press, 1962), p. 23.

[500]Eugen Weber, *A Modern History of Europe* (New York: W. W. Norton, 1971), p. 723.

[501]Roderick Kedward, *The Anarchists* (New York: American Heritage, 1971), p. 45.

[502]"William Godwin," *Encyclopedia Britannica* (1955), vol. X, p. 465.

[503]Weber, *The Western Tradition*, p. 663.

[504]Fabian Tract #7.

[505]Fabian Tract #70.

[506]Lester F. Ward, "Sociocracy," Perry Miller, ed., *American Thought: Civil War to World War I* (New York: Rinehart, 1954), p. 113.

[507]Lester F. Ward, *Applied Sociology* (Boston: Ginn and Co., 1906), pp. 38–39.

[508]William G. Sumner, "The Absurd Effort to Make the World Over," Miller, *American Thought*, p. 104.

[509]Quoted in Henry S. Commager, *The American Mind* (New Haven: Yale University Press, 1954), p. 206.

[510]Lester F. Ward, "Mind as a Social Factor," Gerald N. Grob and Robert N. Beck, eds, *American Ideas*, vol. II (New York: Free Press of Glencoe, 1963), p. 129.

[511]See Dexter Perkins, *The New Age of Franklin D. Roosevelt* (Chicago: University of Chicago Press, 1957), chapter 1.

[512]Woodrow Wilson, *The New Freedom*, William E. Leuchtenburg, intro. and notes (Englewood Cliffs, NJ: Prentice-Hall, 1961), p. 42.

[513]Walter Lippmann, *Drift and Mastery*, William E. Leuchtenburg, intro. (Englewood Cliffs, NJ: Prentice-Hall, A Spectrum Book, 1961), p. 49.

[514]Herbert Croly, *The Promise of American Life*, Cushing Strout, intro. (New York: Capricorn Books, 1964), p. 209.

[515]Walter E. Weyl, *The New Democracy* (New York: Macmillan, 1912), p. 162.

[516]Croly, *op. cit.*, p. 377.

[517]Weyl, *op. cit.*, pp. 265–66.

[518]*Ibid.*, p. 13.

[519]Croly, *op. cit.*, p. 351.

[520]Weyl, *op. cit.*, p. 317.

[521]Charles Forcey, *The Crossroads of Liberalism* (New York: Oxford University Press, 1961), pp. 5–6.

[522]Meyers, Kern and Cawelti, *Sources of the Republic*, vol. II, p. 102.

[523]George E. Mowry, *The Era of Theodore Roosevelt* (New York: Harper, 1958), pp. 108–09.

[524]Ray Allen Billington, Bert James Loewenberg, Samuel Hugh Brockunier, and David S. Sparks, eds., *The Making of American Democracy* (New York: Holt, Rinehart and Winston, 1962, rev. ed.), pp. 209–10.

[525]Commager, *Documents of American History*, vol. II, pp. 608–09.

[526]Billington, *et. al., op. cit.*, pp. 217–18. There is evidence, too, that at least some of the Senators did serve as a bulwark against radical reformist legislation. See Kelly & Harbison, *op. cit.*, p. 620.

[527]Frank N. Magill, ed., *Great Events from History*, vol. III (Englewood Cliffs, NJ: Salem Press, 1975), pp. 1432–33.

[528]Arthur S. Link, *American Epoch* (New York: Alfred A. Knopf, 1955), p. 384.

[529]Frederick L. Allen, *The Big Change* (New York: Bantam Books, 1952), pp. 130–31.

[530]Arthur M. Schlesinger, Jr., *The Coming of the New Deal* (Boston: Houghton Mifflin, 1959), p. 3.

[531]Link, *American Epoch*, p. 384.

[532]Commager, *Documents of American History*, vol. II, pp. 240–42.

[533]Meyers, Kern and Cawelti, *Sources of the American Republic*, vol. II, p. 328.

[534]Franklin D. Roosevelt, *Nothing to Fear*, Ben D. Zevin, ed. (New York: Popular Library, 1961), p. 105.

[535]Edwin C. Rozwenc and Thomas T. Lyons, eds., *Presidential Powers in the New Deal* (Lexington: D. C. Heath, 1964), pp. 23–24.

[536]Schlesinger, *The Coming of the New Deal*, pp. 20–21.

[537]Richard B. Morris, ed., *Encyclopedia of American History* (New York: Harper & Bros., 1953), p. 342.

[538]John T. Flynn, *The Roosevelt Myth* (New York: Devin-Adair, 1956, rev. ed.), p. 57.

[539]Commager, *Documents of American History*, vol. II, pp. 243–45.

[540]*Ibid.*, pp. 272–74.

[541]Kelly & Harbison, *op. cit.*, pp. 728–29.

[542]Quoted in *ibid.*, pp. 731–32.

[543]Commager, *Documents of American History*, vol. II, pp. 278–83.

[544]*Ibid.*, pp. 347–48.

[545]Arthur M. Schlesinger, Jr., *The Politics of Upheaval* (Boston: Houghton Mifflin, 1960) p. 447.

[546]Commager, *Documents of American History*, vol. II, p. 354.

[547]Rozwenc and Lyons, *op. cit.*, pp. 24–26.

[548]Commager, *Documents of American History*, vol. II, p. 386.

[549]*Ibid.*, p. 391.

[550]Gilbert C. Fite and Jime E. Reese, *An Economic History of the United States* (Boston: Houghton Mifflin, 1965, 2nd ed.), p. 665.

[551]Paul K. Conkin, *The New Deal* (New York: Thomas Y. Crowell, 1967), p. 42.

[552]Quoted in Martin Anderson, *The Federal Bulldozer* (Cambridge: M.I.T. Press, 1964), p. 1.

[553]Jane Jacobs, *The Death and Life of Great American Cities* (New York: Random House, 1961), p. 312.

[554]Quoted in Fite and Reese, *op. cit.*, p. 148.

[555]Commager, *Documents of American History*, vol. II, pp. 326–34.

[556]L. Brent Bozell, *The Warren Revolution* (New Rochelle, NY: Arlington House, 1966), p. 30.

[557]Commager, *Documents of American History*, vol. II, p. 725.

[558]Quoted in Bozell, *op. cit.*, p. 85.

[559]*Ibid.*, pp. 80–81.

[560]G. Theodore Mitau, *Decade of Decision: The Supreme Court and the Constitutional Revolution* (New York: Charles Scribner's Sons, 1967), p. 95.

[561]Quoted in Lyman A. Garber, *Of Men and Not of Law* (New York: Devin-Adair, 1966), p. 74n.

[562]Birmingham *News* (September 18, 1992), p. 3B.

[563]Wallace Mendelson, ed., *The Supreme Court: Law and Discretion* (Indianapolis: Bobbs Merrill, 1967), pp. 235–36.

[564]Leon Friedman and Fred L. Israel, eds., *The Justices of the United States Supreme Court*. vol. IV (New York: R. R. Bowker, 1969), p. 279.

[565]Quoted in Garber, *op. cit.*, p. 183.

[566]Quoted in Bozell, *op. cit.*, p. 44.

[567]Quoted in Kelly & Harbison, *op. cit.*, p. 814.

[568]Quoted in Mitau, *op. cit.*, pp. 123–24.

[569]*Ibid.*, p. 131.

[570]Quoted in *ibid.*, p. 133.

[571]Commager, *Documents of American History*, vol. I, p. 173.

[572]Quoted in Edward S. Corwin, *The Constitution and What It Means Today* (New York: Anteneum, 1963), p. 265.

[573]Leon Friedman and Fred L. Israel, eds., *The Justices of the United States Supreme Court*, vol. V (New York: R. R. Bowker, 1978). p. 260.

[574]Quoted in John D. Weaver, *Warren: The Man, The Court, The Era* (Boston: Little, Brown and Co., 1967), pp. 277–78.

[575]Elder Witt, ed., *Guide to United States Supreme Court* (Washington: Congressional Quarterly, 1979), p. 428.

[576]*Ibid.*, p. 429.

[577]Friedman and Israel, *op. cit.*, vol. V, p. 43.

[578]*Ibid.*

[579]Quoted in William F. Buckley, Jr., *Execution Eve* (New York: G. P. Putnam's Sons, 1975), p. 447.

[580]Friedman and Israel, *op. cit.*, vol. V, p. 38.

[581]Laurel Hicks, *et. al.*, *American Government and Economics* (Pensacola: A Beka Book, 1984), p. 219.

[582]Witt, *op. cit.*, p. 645.

[583]Robert H. Bork, "Beside the Law," *National Review* (October 19, 1992), p. 44.

[584]Commager, *Documents of American History*, vol. II, p. 532.

[585]*Ibid.*, pp. 525–26.

[586]*Ibid.*, p. 526.

[587]Harry S. Truman, *Memoirs*, vol. II, *Years of Trial and Hope* (Garden City, NY: 1956), p. 232.

[588]*Ibid.*, p. 237.

[589]See Donald B. Cole, *Handbook of American History* (New York: Harcourt, Brace and World, 1976), p. 287.

[590]See *The World Almanac and Book of Facts, 1992* (New York: Pharos Books, 1991), p. 831.

[591]Clarence B. Carson, *The World in the Grip of an Idea* (New Rochelle, NY: Arlington House, 1979), p. 435.

[592]Quoted in Clarence B. Carson, "The Bureaucratic Incubus," *The Freeman* (January, 1976), p. 11.

[593]P. J. O'Rourke, *Parliament of Whores* (New York: Atlantic Monthly Press, 1991), pp. 3–4.

[594]The figures for crime in 1965 were taken from *The Challenge of Crime in a Free Society*, A Report by the President's Commission on Law Enforcement (Washington: Government Printing Office, 1967), p. 18; the Crime Index, 1982–1987 taken from *Crime in the United States*, Uniform Crime Reports from the Federal Bureau of Investigation (Washington: Government Printing Office, 1987), p. 41; and for 1990 from *The World Almanac and Book of Facts, 1992*, p. 954.

[595]The statistics for the above two paragraphs come from *The 1990 Information Please Almanac* (Boston: Houghton Mifflin, 1990), pp. 822–23.

[596]Charles E. Silberman, *Criminal Violence, Criminal Justice* (New York: Random House, 1978), p. 447.

[597]"Crime Reports," Birmingham *News* (October 27, 1992), p. 2B.

[598]Lois G. Forer, *The Death of the Law* (New York: David McKay, 1975), p. 92.

[599]*Ibid.*, pp. 335–36, emphasis added.

[600]Richard Estrada, "The impact of Immigration on Hispanic Americans," *Chronicles* (July, 1991), p. 24.

[601]Barbara McCarthy, "Letter from San Diego," *Chronicles* (February, 1992), p. 36.

[602]Quoted in James L. Sauer, "Free Press," *The New American* (November 16, 1992), pp. 30–31.

[603]John 4:23–24.

[604]Luke 12: 22–23, 29–31.

[605]Commager, *Documents of American History*, vol. II, p. 449.

[606]*Ibid.*, pp. 482–83.

[607]Paine, *Common Sense and other Political Writings*, p. 32.

Glossary

Abolitionist—one who is determined to abolish or put an end to something. In the United States, the term was applied to those who advocated or worked to end or abolish slavery. They were generally uncompromising in their position toward slavery.

Absolutism—the possession of absolute power by a government. The government is not constrained by a constitution or tradition, and is not controlled by those who are governed by it. It may also be referred to as an autocratic government.

Alienation—a separation from something or barrier between two beings, as a man separated from his property, his family, his kin, his country, or from God.

Amnesty—a general pardon for a particular class of offenders by a government. For example, those who fought against a government may be pardoned by an amnesty proclamation.

Aristocracy—a form of rule by a few. It commonly refers to an hereditary class of rulers, as a nobility. Such aristocrats may share ruling powers with a monarch who may be a noble himself, but of higher rank.

Attainder, Bill of—an extended form of punishment for a person guilty of some grave offense, such as murder, regicide, treason, highway robbery, and the like. He may be attainted by having to forfeit lands, houses, inheritances, and his civil rights, and sometimes working corruption of blood, i. e., extending the punishment to his heirs and descendants. Bills of attainder are prohibited in the United States Constitution, and are unknown to American law.

Belligerent—a nation at war. Different international rules apply to a nation at war and one that is not, and the distinction is made public by such categories.

Bicameral—in politics, a legislature that has two chambers or houses. The practice is so widespread that it is sometimes referred to as bicameralism.

Bolshevik—a member of a faction which resulted from a split in the communist party in Russia in the early 20th century. This faction claimed to be a majority, which is what Bolshevik means. At any rate, it was the party of V. I. Lenin which brought off the October (Bolshevik) Revolution in Russia in 1917.

Border States—those states on the periphery of the Southern Confederacy, i. e., Maryland, Kentucky, Missouri, and Delaware, where slavery was established, but were divided over joining the Confederacy or remaining in the Union. The phrase is still used sometimes to describe states on the periphery of the South.

Bounty—a reward paid by government for producing some good or disposing of pests. For example, a government might pay a bounty for each rattlesnake killed to reduce their numbers, or it might pay a bounty for each pound of magnesium mined.

Broad Construction—to interpret a document, such as the United States Constitution, so as to give those who govern the greatest latitude for action possible within the range of the language of the Constitution. It may also be stated this way, to give the government the latitude to do those things which are by any reasonable interpretation permitted in that they are not otherwise prohibited. The Federal government has gone far beyond these bounds in the 20th century.

Cabal—a small group of plotters who form a conspiracy to achieve some secret, illegal, or immoral purpose.

Capital (economics)—wealth used in the production of goods, esp., machinery, equipment, tools, raw materials, seed, motive power, buildings, and any liquid wealth used to pay rents, wages, and salaries—that is, expenses not yet being defrayed by the sale of goods being produced.

Capital (government)—the town or city in which the seat of government is located, for examples, Washington is the capital of the United States, and Raleigh is the capital of North Carolina.

Capitalism—a system or ideology of preference for capital over the other elements of production, i. e., land and labor, in the production of goods. Karl Marx appears to have concocted the term and conceived the ideology, but he looked forward to the demise of the practice. Others, however, describe it simply as a system in which private ownership of property holds sway and freedom of enterprise is the rule. But if it is nothing more than a brief for the private ownership of property, there would appear be little reason to call that position capitalism. In fact, it is a term entangled in the disputes between socialists and their opponents and might better be avoided in favor of more specific and descriptive language.

Capitation Tax—also called a head or poll tax. A direct tax levied on each person,

made difficult for the United States to use because of constitutional restrictions. The "poll tax" levied in some states in order to qualify to vote, was not a true capitation, head, or poll tax. At any rate, it has now been prohibited by the 24th Amendment.

Central Government—the general government of a nation, kingdom, empire, such as the Federal government of the United States. It is usually the dominant government within a country, and sometimes all government power is concentrated in it.

Communism—an ideology devised by Karl Marx in the 19th century, and imposed on the remains of the Russian Empire—renamed the Soviet Union—in 1917–1918 by V. I. Lenin and his followers. Thereafter, Communism tended to be what was advocated, instituted or done in the Soviet Union by the Communist Party. The dominant features of what happened were the taking over of virtually all property by the Soviet government and the establishment of a totalitarian state in which all power came from the government.

Concentration of Power—the practice of concentrating all governmental power in the central government. In the United States, the tendency toward such concentration has proceeded by taking power away from the states and those governments under them and locating it within the Federal government.

Confederation—a union, league, or organization of nations or city-states for some limited purpose, such as defense against enemies or making war. The nations or states within a confederacy usually keep all their powers over their citizenry and may reassume their complete independent status at some later date. There have been many confederacies in the course of history, but they have not usually been longlived.

Credit Expansion—credit is expanded to accommodate more and more debt for a nation by issuing paper money against debt instruments, or increasing the money supply in other ways.

Deflation—a major decline in the money supply signalled by a widespread and general drop in prices. Although there may be other causes, the most common cause of a drastic decline in the money supply would be a bank panic and widespread bankruptcies. This could be triggered by or related to such an event as a stock market crash. Economic recessions or depressions often reflect or are identical with deflations.

Demagogue—an orator, agitator, or a politician who arouses the passions of those who will pay attention to him by appealing to their ignorance and prejudices. An example of such demagoguery would be for a politician to attack persons of wealth, and promise to tax the rich to pay for goodies for the poor.

Democracy—a much abused and misused concept in our time. It means, literally, rule by the people, and was historically associated with a people assembling and taking political action directly, such as occurred in Ancient Athens and in colonial (and later) New England. Some now use the term to refer to what occurs when the people elect representatives, such as in the United States. This is called "representative democracy." The Founders, however, thought of it as an aspect of republics.

Depression—a decline in business activity of some duration, usually brought on by deflation following in the wake of a prolonged inflation. Any significant business slowdown used to be described as a depression, but since the Great Depression of the 1930s, which was prolonged for ten years by drastic government interventions, business downturns are described as recessions.

Despot—an absolute or autocratic ruler, usually one person who uses his power arbitrarily and tyrannically. Roman and Byzantine rulers were often described as despots. The term was employed in Ancient times much as people in the 20th century refer to dictatorships.

Dialectical Materialism—the theory expounded by Karl Marx which gave the impetus to Communism. It is the theory that the moving force behind events and developments in this world is material; who controls the instruments of production rules the land. In Marx's view true history is the story of the struggle for the control of these instruments of production, a struggle that will culminate in the victory of the working class and the end of history.

Dialectical Method—a mode of reasoning aimed at arriving at clarity of beliefs and truths by the assertion of opposing ideas and allowing the better ideas to win out. Plato may have best exemplified this approach in his dialogues, though Socrates was the dominant person in most of them.

Dictatorship—rule by one man, usually by way of his control of a ruling party. This mode of rule was introduced by Lenin with his control over the Communist Party in the Soviet Union, and was imitated in Italy by Mussolini, by Hitler in Germany, and in other lands as well. Joseph Stalin developed this mode of rule as far as it could probably go. What was new about this was not one man rule, of course, but rule by way of an ideologically activated party.

Dyarchy—rule by two persons, rather than by one, as in monarchy. If two heads are better than one, this form of rule should have triumphed, but it did not. In fact, it appears that rule by one person is the most effective rule, not necessarily, however, the best.

Economy—the thrifty or frugal management of resources; achieving the maximum produce with a minimum input of the land, labor, and capital mix. The term has been "thingified," i. e., treated as if it were a thing instead of a method, in the 20th century by using it to describe the dominant economic system in a country. Thus, we hear references to the "American economy," "British economy," "French economy," when what is being referred to may not be economy at all but whatever sorts of economic doings are going on in these countries.

Edict—a public announcement of a rule, decision, or act having the force of law. The term is more apt to be used figuratively or by way of editorial comment than literally in the 20th century.

Elector—one who is qualified to vote in a given election or for candidates for certain offices. Thus, all registered voters are potential electors in the those elections in which they may vote. On the other hand, members of the electoral college are electors of the President of the United States.

Elitism—an ingrained preference for or ideology of rule by a selected few. While there have been theories in other eras justifying rule by an elite, they are not much referred to in the 20th century by those who appear to be attached to elitism. The idea evinces itself in the covert claim that there are those who know better what's good for people than they do themselves. Thus, they seek to use government to provide what we presumably would not provide. Public schools are a prominent example, but there are many, many more.

Emancipation—the freeing of persons bound to servitude. It has usually been done by the owner, and not by the government. Abolition is the name for the forced freeing of slaves by the government. Lincoln confused all that with his "Emancipation Proclamation."

Empire—a kind of super-state which rules over an assortment of peoples, often of different religions, languages, cultures, and historical backgrounds. The rulers of empires have not usually attempted to wipe out all these differences; instead the cultural, territorial and political arrangements may be permitted to survive in the framework of the empire.

Entitlements—government welfare programs to which recipients are "entitled" because they meet the government requirements to receive them.

Eviction—the process by which a landlord can secure the force of government to remove a tenant from his property. Trespass, failure to pay rent, or the harboring of criminals, would be occasions for eviction.

Excise Tax—a tax levied on particular goods prior to their retail sale. Since it is usually added to the sale price, it is called a hidden tax upon the consumer.

Ex Post Facto Law—a law passed after an act was done to punish a person for doing something which was not prohibited when he did it. The passage of such acts are prohibited in the Constitution.

Faction—a term which meant approximately the same thing to the Founders that "interest group" does to us. Washington feared that factions might gain control of the general government and use it for selfish ends. Madison argued in *The Federalist* #10 that in a country as extensive as the United States, any ruling group would have to be so broadly based that it would embrace many general interests.

Fascism—an ideology justifying a military regime bent on territorial expansion. Benito Mussolini imposed such a system on Italy in the 1920s and 1930s. More broadly, the term was used to castigate any dictatorial anti-Communist government, especially by Communists.

Federalism—a system of government in which there is a general government having limited authority over the whole country, and several state, principality, or provincial governments having independent authority over their territorial divisions within the country. Americans invented this system by the modifications they made in the traditional confederation.

Felony—a crime of such a serious nature that a person found guilty of it may be sentenced to prison for more than a year and have his civil rights curtailed. Manslaughter, murder, armed robbery, rape, arson, and the like, are felonies.

Feudalism—a system of political rule based on authority over land. The rulers were bound together in a network of personal allegiances ordered in a hierarchy of lords and vassals. The material base of this system was the landed estate on which the serfs provided the wealth to support a warrior. The spiritual leaven and counterpoint to this system was provided by the Roman Catholic Church.

Fiat Money—currency that circulates because government has made it legal tender. It has no commodity value, nor is it redeemable in a fixed amount of anything of value. It is usually paper currency—money by government decree.

Foreclosure—a process by which a creditor calls in a loan on which payments are in arrears (behind) on real property. The creditor claims the property pledged by mortgage in support of the loan.

Franchise—in politics, the privilege of voting. It is also referred to as the elective franchise, and to say that one has the franchise is to say he is qualified to vote. It is that which makes him an elector in whatever capacity he has.

Freehold—real estate that is owned outright, in "fee simple," as lawyers say. That is, you pay for it, and the land belongs to you.

Gradualism—the gradual approach to socialism. It was an approach advanced by British socialists, who perceived no prospect of a revolutionary overthrow of the government and made a virtue of necessity by thrusting for power within the system. Americans imbued with socialistic ideas generally took an even more covert approach; they did not avow their socialism but rather claimed to be "progressives" or "liberals."

Habeas Corpus, **writ of**—an order from a court to the jailer to produce the body of the person being held or charge him with the violation of some standing law and be ready to produce the evidence in support of the charge. The availability of such a writ is a major weapon against arbitrary arrest and confinement.

Hierarchy—the arrangement of persons or things in ranked or graded orders. In politics, it refers to the ranking of those wielding power and authority. This may be best exemplified, perhaps, by the grades through which military power may be exercised. It begins at the lowest level with non-commissioned officers; in the armies of the past it was customarily a corporal, goes through the various grades of sergeant through first sergeant or sergeant major, through the ranks of officers from lieutenant to captain to major to lieutenant colonel to colonel through the various ranks of generals from brigadier to general-of-the army (if any) to the secretary of the army to the Secretary of Defense to the President of the United States. All those who govern exist somewhere within a hierarchy, though it is not always as rigorous or extended as that of the military.

Homestead—a dwelling place occupied by the owner and the land it is situated on and that surrounding it. This land and buildings, up to a certain value, may be exempt from taxation and from seizure and sale for the payment of debts.

Idea of Progress—the idea or notion that mankind or civilization or a particular country or people are making progress generally. People have not always believed this and may not generally do so today. The much more obvious belief would be that things are deteriorating, decaying, running down, and coming apart. Nonetheless, the idea that progress is taking place began to take hold in the 18th century, and has been given great impetus since that time by evolutionary theories and technological developments.

Ideology—a complex of ideas which purports to explain either all of reality or all of social reality, and especially the end toward which things should be or are moving. (Ideologies are more or less utopian and even the least utopian tend to be dragged in that direction by the temper of the times.) With the breakdown of philosophy in the 19th century and the decline in the sway of Christian beliefs, ideologies abounded, i.e., communism, capitalism, democratism, liberalism, and the like.

Induction—in logic, a means of arriving at general laws, principles or conclusions from the relevant evidence found in many instances. It is known as inductive reasoning, and it is familiarly described as the scientific method.

Inflation—an ongoing increase of the money supply. It does generally result in widespread price increases, and many people refer to the price increases themselves as inflation. This obscures the cause, however, for the cause is the increase of the money supply. Governments are now, and always have been, the main sources of the inflation, because of their penchant for taking control of the money supply and manipulating it to their ends.

Initiative—in politics, a procedure whereby voters can get proposals for laws, constitutional amendments, or ordinances on the ballot to vote on them. Some states provide for procedures to do that, and they usually involve getting sufficient (the minimum number provided by law) signatures of registered voters on a petition for some measure(s) to go on the ballot.

Insurgent—a person who attempts to overthrow lawful authority, who rebels against the government. By analogy, the term is also used in a much less drastic sense, to refer to a revolt against the establishment in a political party.

Intangible Property—that which has no substantive value in itself but stands for something of value, as notes, mortgages, good will (of a business), stocks of corporations, and the like.

Interdict—to forbid or prohibit, a punishment imposed by the Roman Catholic Church in the Middle Ages to secure obedience from temporal rulers. If a land was laid under interdict, it would usually mean that the inhabitants would be denied some or all of the good offices of the Church until those who were disobedient submitted to the authority of the Church.

Interstate—that which goes between and within two or more states. For example, interstate commerce is commerce that crosses the boundaries of two or more states. Interstate highways enter or go through two or more states. The concept is important because it helps to interpret both the powers and their limits of the United States government under the Constitution.

Intervention—to intrude or meddle in the affairs of another. Thus, individuals may intervene in someone else's business; one country may intervene in another country; and governments may intervene in the affairs of citizens. It is always a questionable practice, and it usually provokes resentment and sometimes retaliation.

Intrastate—that which goes on within the bounds of a single state. Intrastate commerce does not cross state lines. The distinction developed in the 19th century that the authority of the United States did not extend to the regulation of intrastate commerce. This distinction has been broken down both by the Federal courts and the interstate character of so much business activity in the 20th century.

Irrepressible Conflict—the notion that the American Civil War was unavoidable. It may be of some use to raise the question whether it was or not in order to explore what was going on, but there can be no absolute certainty as to what might have been.

Judicial Activism—the taking of an active role by the courts in overturning precedents, propounding new rules, and extending their authority into more and more areas. It has been well said that courts should apply the laws to cases, not make the laws. When courts proceed to make the law, in effect, they are engaged in judicial activism.

Judicial Review—a misleading phrase to describe what courts do when they determine the constitutionality of government acts. In fact, courts do not review—i. e., examine all acts of government—to determine their constitutionality. They do so only when some case comes before them that raises the question of the constitutionality of something done by government.

Jurisdiction—the arena within which particular governmental, judicial, or police authority extends. In the United States, most people fall within the jurisdiction of at least two governments, but on any particular only one government will have jurisdiction.

Letters of Marque and Reprisal—authorizations to captains of vessels to seize and deal with enemy ships at sea.

Liberalism—an ideological or political outlook whose meaning has changed over the years, at least in the United States. It arose in the 19th century as a political movement favoring individual liberty, limited constitutional government, free trade and extension of the elective franchise to more of the people. In the 20th century, it has been claimed by those who favor big government looking after the material and intellectual well-being of people.

Liquidity Crisis—a general shortage of cash to meet on-demand payments. Such crises are the product of ongoing credit expansions and tend to produce runs on banks, bankruptcies, drastic drops in prices, and recessions or depressions.

Lords Spiritual—the high churchmen who have seats in the British House of Lords.

Lords Temporal—the nobles who have seats in the British House of Lords.

Loyalists—Those Americans who remained loyal to Britain and King George III during the War for Independence. Their numbers tended to fluctuate with the fortunes and nearness of British armies.

***Mandamus*, writ of**—an order from a court to a government official or judge of a lower court to perform some act which is among his proper duties.

Manifesto—a public statement or declaration of the intentions, purposes or positions of a government, private organization, or group. It may not be an official document of any organization but it tends to take on that character by its very name.

Mercantilism—a politico-economic system that is nationalistic, usually involves a tacit alliance between rulers and merchants or tradesmen, who seek to use government to achieve a "favorable" balance of trade, and one of its main operating principles is that a nation's wealth consists of its holdings in precious metals. Protective tariffs, subsidies, and bounties to manufacturers are examples of mercantilist practices.

Metaphysics—the study of the underlying and enduring order of things, an order that is beyond the physical and short of the spiritual. It is an order that must be for things and men to be and happen as they do. Thus, it is available to and can be known by reason.

Middle Ages—that period of time between the Ancient Age of Greece and Rome and the modern era in European history, the customary dates being A.D. 476 and 1453, i. e., from the traditional date for the fall of the Roman Empire to the Germans until the fall of Constantinople to the Moslems.

Misdemeanor—a relatively minor offense, punishable by less than a prison sentence of more than one year. It is nonetheless illegal behavior and is a crime.

Mixed Government—one which has within it two or more of the forms of government. The basic forms are: monarchy—rule by one—, aristocracy or oligarchy—rule by a few—, and democracy—rule by the many. Ancient writers tended to favor a mixed government, and the United States has one.

Monarchy—literally, rule by one, as might be the case with an hereditary monarch. If there are no fixed limits it might be described as an absolute or autocratic monarchy. If the monarch is legally limited, the system might be described as a constitutional monarchy. Thus, King George III of England was a constitutional monarch.

Monism—the philosophy that holds that all of reality springs from a single substance. There is only one order or level of reality. This view is achieved by downplaying or ignoring indications of more than one level, hence, it is reductionist. Examples of monism are materialism, spiritualism, humanism, and rationalism.

Monolithic Rule—a way of describing one party rule headed by a dictator—all other parties being outlawed. The party speaks with one mind and one voice, as if it were a single unit. It is a figure of speech drawn from such objects as a large block of stone, obelisk, or anything large and of one piece.

Nationalization—the process of taking control of private businesses by government. For example, if a government seizes or gains control of all the newspapers in a country, it thereby "nationalizes" them. The practice of nationalization of industry stems from socialism and has been carried out in varying degrees by an assortment of tactics in many countries in the 20th century.

Nation-States—the independent nations which emerged in Europe at the end of the Middle Ages, such as France, England, and Spain. They differed from city-states in that they were basically countries not simply cities, from empires in that their population was of one culture and language rather than being diverse, and from medieval kingdoms in that they were ridding themselves of their feudal ties.

Naturalization—the process by which someone of foreign birth obtains the rights and privileges of a citizen.

Natural Law—those laws imbedded in the nature of things. These laws cannot be sensed themselves by our five senses, but they can be reasonably ascertained. For example, the law of the uniform acceleration of freely falling bodies is a natural law. It is a natural rule, as well, that men tend to be corrupted by the quest for and holding of power. It is a natural law, as well, that bad money drives good money out of circulation.

Natural Rights—the natural law doctrine that man is endowed by God through nature with certain rights, that these rights are the right to life, liberty, to acquire and hold property, and to manage his affairs and look after himself.

Nazism—an ideology professed by Adolf Hitler and his Nazi Party in the 1930s and during World War II. Nazi was short for National Socialist German Worker's Party. It had a nationalistic, expansionist, racist, and totalitarian theory which helped to provoke World War II.

Nominalism—a species of philosophical skepticism which holds that there are no general or universal truths. There are only particular objects, things, and individuals. What appear to be universals are only names which we have invented.

Nullification—the theory that a state could rightfully prohibit the enforcement of national law held to be unconstitutional within its boundaries. South Carolina came the closest to testing this theory in practice during Andrew Jackson's presidency. A protective tariff was the issue, but South Carolina rescinded its nullification before force was applied to the state.

Obiter Dictum—incidental remarks made by a judge in reaching a decision, hence having no binding authority on the instant or later cases.

Old Northwest—the territory in the Midwest acquired by the United States in the Treaty of Paris of 1783. It consisted of Ohio, Indiana, Illinois, Michigan, and Wisconsin. It was the territory to which the Northwest Ordinances applied.

Oligarchy—rule by a few, not necessarily because they are the best equipped or have inherited their positions but because they have somehow come to power.

Participatory Democracy—means by which the individual can take part more or less directly in government decisions, as in public hearings, town meetings, signing petitions, initiatives, recalls, and referenda.

Petit Jury—a small jury, usually of 12 people, which tries civil and criminal cases to determine the facts as to the guilt or blame of persons and sometimes to recommend the penalty as well. In the United States, juries made up of the generality of citizens make the final decisions about life, liberty, and property.

Physiocrats—a school of economists which arose in the last half of the 18th century in France. They believed there was a natural order for economy, advocated free trade and enterprise, and thought that land was the ultimate source of wealth.

Pocket Veto—a veto accomplished by inaction by the executive after the close of a legislative session. Any of the legislation passed in the closing days of the session that the executive does not approve, he does not have to take any action, because he cannot return a veto to the legislature. The legislation is simply allowed to die without his approval.

Polity—a Greek concept meaning a just and successful political organization of a community. In a more general sense, it refers to the manner in which a community or country is organized for governing.

Pragmatism—a relativist philosophy advocated by the American, William James, among others. It holds that there are no absolute truths—no fixities in the universe. The test of the validity of any idea or proposition is whether or not it produces the desired result. Translated into political terms by advocates of democracy, it means little more than that whatever the people want is good and valid. It is a pagan philosophy, to say the least.

Primogeniture—the practice or requirement that the inheritance of an estate goes to the oldest son in the family. This requirement was generally removed when the American colonies broke from England, and thereafter property was generally disposed by the will of the owner, or if he died intestate, by division among the heirs.

Progressive—one who claims that the policies and programs that he advocates will produce progress. Progressives in the United States in the early 20th century linked social reform and/or socialism with the idea of progress. Reformist measures were advanced as the latest and best thing, in a word, as being progressive. It followed that it was backward or reactionary to oppose them. Since people generally believed that progress was good and desirable, they were often induced to vote for those who claimed to be progressive.

Puppet Regime—a government by figureheads, people who pretend to make the decisions and govern but who are actually controlled by secret or foreign powers.

Quitrent—a payment on land made to the grantor, such as a colonial proprietor or the king of England. It was an encumbrance on land that was everywhere removed by American independence from Britain.

Radical Republicans—those Republicans during and after the Civil War who were not only bent upon punishing the white South but also in making over these people and their ways. They wanted and got revenge on the South.

Realpolitik—a German phrase to describe political action based on power rather than right. A corollary of this view is that might makes right. It was a part of the mix of ideas that provided the framework for the total wars of the 20th century.

Real Property—land, buildings and other fixtures. By its nature it is ordinarily not movable, and is thus distinguished in law and practice from movable property.

Recall—an electoral device for removing an elected official from office. The usual procedure is for a specified minimum number of voters to petition for a recall election. Then, if an election is held, and the vote is in favor of a recall, the official is removed from office.

Referendum—referring a question or decision to the electorate. The voters are offered the opportunity to vote on some question, such as a school bond issue, whether or not to have a government run lottery, or the like. This could be called direct democracy; it is a way to get around lobbyists and assorted other organized interests. It has not been so widely used yet as to threaten representative government, though in recent years California has appeared to be heading in that direction.

Reformism—a kind of ideology of reform. Reform and change appear to be good in

and of themselves regardless of the results they produce or the damage they do.

Relativism—a belief that what is true, good, desirable, beautiful, or whatever, is relative to the viewer, the situation, conditions, and what people in general prefer or want. To the relativist, there is, in fact, no truth; there are only opinions. The relativism prevalent in this era is mirrored in the numerous public opinion polls.

Republic—a government based on popular approval, rule by representatives, no monarch, no aristocracy, no church bodies represented by participating in governing. Republics abound in the 20th century, but the term has lost its glitter to democracy.

Revolution—the overthrow of a government and replacing it with another one. It is any successful revolt against a reigning authority. Socialists have expanded the scope of revolution, if they have not entirely changed the meaning. They speak of all sorts of revolutions, i. e., social, cultural, economic, and so on, but somewhere along the way they also expect that in a revolution there will be an overthrow of political authority.

Scholasticism—the method of reasoning in the schools and universities of the Middle Ages. It proceeded by presenting the pros and cons on some proposition, the citing of authorities on both sides of an issue, and the statement of a conclusion about or resolution of the dispute. It was probably at its most effective as a means of mastering the learning of the past.

Secession—the theory that a state may withdraw from the United States by the reverse of the procedure by which it joined the Union. The Constitution neither describes nor authorizes such a procedure, nor does it otherwise contemplate the dissolution of the Union. Neither, however, does it authorize the use of force against a legally constituted state government.

Separation of Powers—the doctrine or principle that the legislative, executive, and judicial powers of government should be vested in different branches and exercised by different persons, and that those serving in different branches should ideally be selected by different electors.

Ship Money—a tax levied on ports in time of war for the building of ships.

Social Compact or Contract—a part of the natural law doctrine having to do with the fundamental agreement holding a society together. The social contract may be conceived of in two ways. One is that it need not be, or is not, a formal agreement at all, but rather consists of a tacit agreement which is essential to a just and peaceful society. It is, in effect, an agreement about those rights, duties, and responsibilities without which a peaceful society could not exist. It can also be conceived of as a formal compact, such as the Mayflower Compact.

Socialism—the generic term for the belief in the primacy of society, considered collectively, over the individual. Socialists tend to favor the vesting of control of productive activities and wealth in government, to favor government redistribution of wealth, to oppose war, to favor negotiation of all struggles between or among all recognized groups. Socialists prefer the collective to the individual approach for doing anything, and claim to favor democratic methods.

Solid South—a phrase to describe the dominance of the Democratic Party in the South from the late 19th century until after World War II. The key to this dominance was the White Democratic Primary election in which only whites were permitted to vote. The Democratic Party was so dominant in the South that primary nomination was tantamount to (virtually the same as) election. The whites maintained a lock on their control of politics in this way. Other devices, such as the poll tax, were used,

but none had the longtime effectiveness of the White Primary.

Sovereignty—the supreme power over a particular territory. Kings were once said to be sovereign, and the concept itself smacks of government absolutism.

Specie—coined money; the actual coins, usually made of precious metals such as gold or silver.

Standing Army—an army made up of regulars, a professional army, an army maintained by a government in times of peace as well as war.

State—the term has two distinct usages. The most common usage in the United is to refer to those geo-political units which make up the United States. These states have governing powers distinct from those of the government of the Union, but they do not carry on relations with foreign nations. The other usage means roughly the same thing as a nation or country. It means a territory with its own sovereign power, one which conducts relations with foreign countries as equals. Thus, France is a state; Sweden is a state; Japan is a state; and even the United States may qualify in this sense as a state.

Statists—people who favor using the power of government to impose their views within a society. They are sometimes said, also, to be state worshippers. At the least, they tend to look to the state as the provider of their preferred goods.

State of Nature—a natural law concept which holds that we learn the nature of things by conceiving of them in their natural state, i. e., the state of nature. To attain such an understanding, it is necessary to strip away—mentally—all that has been added to persons or things to distinguish them from all others of their kind.

Statute—a legislative act, written law, and a portion, at least, of positive law.

Stoicism—a philosophical substitute for religion originated by the philosopher Zeno. He taught that people should strive to be free of passion, learn to accept without complaint the misfortunes of life, and give way neither to ecstasy nor to grief. The "philosopher-kings" of the late Roman Empire inclined to Stoicism.

Strict Construction—to construe a document such as the United States Constitution in terms of its language as understood when it was written and adopted.

Subpoena—a court order compelling a witness to appear and give testimony in a trial. Those witnesses who will not voluntarily appear are subpoenaed.

Summons—an order to appear before a court or a judicial official for some stated purpose.

Syllogism—a formal device for illustrating the deduction of a particular conclusion from a general principle. It has three parts: a major premise, a minor premise, and a conclusion, usually preceded by "therefore." It is an example of deductive reasoning.

Synod—an assembly or council of churchmen gathered for some purpose. It could also be a council of noblemen.

Totalitarian—a political system in which government claims authority over all aspects of the lives of a people. A totalitarian government dominates the people not only by secret police, militia, and armies but also by education, training, propaganda, and its control over the organizations and institutions of a country and the means of travel and communication. In effect, these governments make continual war on their people to control and transform them. Totalitarianism is a 20th century phenomenon, but it had antecedents in the despotisms of other times and places.

Triarchy—rule by three, occurs when there are three rulers over a people.

Tyrant—a ruler who uses his power arbitrarily and oppressively, any absolute ruler. The Greeks used the term to apply to a person who seized power without a legitimate claim on it.

Utopia—an imaginary land where all the social and political and economic ills that have beset man have been removed or resolved by beneficent laws. It is a perfect society in which perfect justice and equity prevail. It is the vision which helped to draw contemporary peoples toward the approval of socialistic proposals for reforming and perfecting society.

Vassal—a term used in the Middle Ages to signify the subordination of a property-holder to his feudal lord. In rank, a vassal might be anything from a knight to a king, or even an emperor, since it was held, at the time, that every man should have an overlord. A vassal owed allegiance to his overlord.

Vestry—a committee that looks after the business of the church in the Church of England and Episcopal church. The vestry members are chosen by the congregation. Serving on the vestry was one of the ways Americans got political experience during the colonial period.

Welfare State—a phrase that came into use to describe a nation in which the government undertakes to look after the material and intellectual well being of a people. "Welfare" was probably chosen because the phrase "general welfare" occurs twice in the United States Constitution, and its use might make it appear that the Constitution authorized such redistribution programs.

Western Civilization—the civilization which emerged in lands around the Mediterranean, was given cohesion and a measure of intellectual unity by the Greeks during the Hellenistic era, was more or less physically unified by Rome, and was Christianized in the Middle Ages. It became European Civilization in the Modern era.

DOCUMENTS

Declaration of Independence

IN CONGRESS, JULY 4, 1776

THE UNAMINOUS DECLARATION OF THE THIRTEEN UNITED STATES OF AMERICA

When in the Course of human events, it becomes necessary for one people to dissolve the political bands which have connected them with another, and to assume among the Powers of the earth, the separate and equal station to which the Laws of Nature and of Nature's God entitle them, a decent respect to the opinions of mankind requires that they should declare the causes which impel them to the separation.

We hold these truths to be self-evident, that all men are created equal, that they are endowed by their Creator with certain unalienable Rights, that among these are Life, Liberty and the pursuit of Happiness. That to secure these rights, Governments are instituted among Men, deriving their just powers from the consent of the governed, That whenever any Form of Government becomes destructive of these ends, it is the Right of the People to alter or to abolish it, and to institute new Government, laying its foundation on such principles and organizing its powers in such form, as to them shall seem most likely to effect their Safety and Happiness. Prudence, indeed, will dictate that Governments long established should not be changed for light and transient causes; and accordingly all experience hath shown, that mankind are more disposed to suffer, while evils are sufferable, than to right themselves by abolishing the forms to which they are accustomed. But when a long train of abuses and usurpations, pursuing invariably the same Object evinces a design to reduce them under absolute Despotism, it is their right, it is their duty, to throw off such Government, and to provide new Guards for their future security. Such has been the patient sufferance of these Colonies; and such is now the necessity which constrains them to alter their former Systems of Government. The history of the present King of Great Britain is a history of repeated injuries and usurpations, all having in direct object the establishment of an absolute Tyranny over these States. To prove this, lets Facts be submitted to a candid world.

He has refused his Assent to Laws, the most wholesome and necessary for the public good.

He has forbidden his Governors to pass laws of immediate and pressing importance, unless suspended in their operation till his Assent should be obtained; and when so suspended, he has utterly neglected to attend to them.

He has refused to pass other Laws for the accommodation of large districts of people, unless those people would relinquish the right of Representation in the Legislature, a right inestimable to them and formidable to tyrants only.

He has called together legislative bodies at places unusual, uncomfortable, and distant from the depository of their Public Records, for the sole purpose of fatiguing them into compliance with his measures.

He has dissolved Representative Houses repeatedly, for opposing with manly firmness his invasions on the rights of the people.

He has refused for a long time, after such dissolutions, to cause others to be elected; whereby the Legislative Powers, incapable of Annihilation, have returned to the People at large for their exercise; the State remaining in the mean time exposed to all the dangers of invasion from without, and convulsions within.

He has endeavoured to prevent the population of these States; for that purpose obstructing the Laws for Naturalization of Foreigners; refusing to pass others to encourage their migration hither, and raising the conditions of new Appropriations of Lands.

He has obstructed the Administration of Justice, by refusing his Assent to Laws for establishing Judiciary Powers.

He has made Judges dependent on his Will alone, for the tenure of their offices, and the amount and payment of their salaries.

He has erected a multitude of New Offices, and sent hither swarms of Officers to harrass our People, and eat out their substance.

He has kept among us, in times of peace, Standing Armies without the Consent of our legislature.

He has affected to render the Military independent of and superior to the Civil Power.

He has combined with others to subject us to a jurisdiction foreign to our constitution, and unacknowledged by our laws; giving his Assent to their Acts of pretended Legislation:

For quartering large bodies of armed troops among us:

For protecting them, by a mock Trial, from Punishment for any Murders which they should commit on the Inhabitants of these States:

For cutting off our Trade with all parts of the world:

For imposing Taxes on us without our Consent:

For depriving us in many cases, of the benefits of Trial by Jury:

For transporting us beyond Seas to be tried for pretended offences:

For abolishing the free System of English Laws in a neighbouring Province, establishing therein an Arbitrary government, and enlarging its Boundaries so as to render it at once an example and fit instrument for introducing the same absolute rule into these Colonies:

For taking away our Charters, abolishing our most valuable Laws, and altering fundamentally the Forms of our Governments:

For suspending our own Legislatures, and declaring themselves invested with Power to legislate for us in all cases whatsoever.

He has abdicated Government here, by declaring us out of his Protection and waging War against us.

He has plundered our seas, ravaged our Coasts, burnt our towns, and destroyed the Lives of our people.

He is at this time transporting large Armies of foreign Mercenaries to compleat the works of death, desolation and tyranny, already begun with circumstances of Cruelty & perfidy scarcely paralleled in the most barbarous ages, and totally unworthy the Head of a civilized nation.

He has constrained our fellow Citizens taken Captive on the high Seas to bear Arms against their Country, to become the executioners of their friends and Brethren, or to fall themselves by their Hands.

He has excited domestic insurrections amongst us, and has endeavoured to bring on the inhabitants of our frontiers, the merciless Indian Savages, whose known rule of warfare, is an undistinguished destruction of all ages, sexes and conditions.

In every stage of these Oppresions We have Petitioned for Redress in the most humble terms: Our repeated Petitions have been answered only by repeated injury. A Prince, whose character is thus marked by every act which may define a Tyrant, is unfit to be the ruler of a free People.

Nor have We been wanting in attention to our British brethren. We have warned them from time to time of attempts by their legislature to extend an unwarrantable jurisdiction over us. We have reminded them of the circumstances of our emigration and settlement here. We have appealed to their native justice and magnanimity, and we have conjured them by the ties of our common kindred to disavow these usurpations, which would inevitably interrupt our connections and correspondence. They too have been deaf to the voice of justice and consanguinity. We must, therefore, acquiesce in the necessity, which denounces our Separation, and hold them, as we hold the rest of mankind, Enemies in War, in Peace Friends.

We, therefore, the Representatives of the United States of America, in General Congress, Assembled, appealing to the Supreme Judge of the world for the rectitude of our intentions, do, in the Name, and by Authority of the good People of these Colonies, solemnly publish and declare, That these United Colonies are, and of Right ought to be Free and Independent States; that they are Absolved from all Allegiance to the British Crown, and that all political connection between them and the State of Great Britain, is and ought to be totally dissolved; and that as Free and Independent States, they have full Power to levy War, conclude Peace, contract Alliances, establish Commerce, and to do all other Acts and Things which Independent States may of right do. And for the support of this Declaration, with a firm reliance on the Protection of Divine Providence, we mutually pledge to each other our Lives, our Fortunes and our sacred Honor.

John Hancock

New Hampshire

Josiah Bartlett,	Matthew Thornton.
Wm. Whipple,	

Massachusetts Bay

Saml. Adams,	Robt. Treat Paine,
John Adams,	Elbridge Gerry.

Rhode Island

Step. Hopkins,	William Ellery

Connecticut

Roger Sherman,	Wm. Williams,
Sam'el Huntington,	Oliver Wolcott.

New York

Wm. Floyd,	Francis Lewis,
Phil. Livingston,	Lewis Morris.

New Jersey

Richd. Stockton,   John Hart,
Jno. Witherspoon,   Abra. Clark.
Fras. Hopkinson,

Pennsylvania

Robt. Morris,   Jas. Smith,
Benjamin Rush,   Geo. Taylor,
Benja. Franklin,   James Wilson,
John Morton,   Geo. Ross.
Geo. Clymer,

Delaware

Caesar Rodney,   Tho. M'Kean.
Geo. Read,

Maryland

Samuel Chase,   Charles Carroll of
Wm. Paca,   Carrollton.
Thos. Stone,

Virginia

George Wythe,   Thos. Nelson, Jr.,
Richard Henry Lee,   Francis Lightfoot Lee,
Th. Jefferson,   Carter Braxton.
Benja. Harrison,

North Carolina

Wm. Hooper,   John Penn.
Joseph Hewes,

South Carolina

Edward Rutledge,   Thomas Lynch, Junr.,
Thos. Heyward, Junr.,   Arthur Middleton.

Georgia

Button Gwinnett,   Geo. Walton.
Lyman Hall,

Virginia Bill of Rights

ARTICLE I
BILL OF RIGHTS

A declaration of rights made by the representatives of the good people of Virginia, assembled in full and free convention; which rights do pertain to them and their posterity, as the basis and foundation of government.

1. That all men are by nature equally free and independent, and have certain inherent rights, of which, when they enter into a state of society, they cannot, by any compact, deprive or divest their posterity; namely the enjoyment of life and liberty, with the means of acquiring and possessing property, and pursuing and obtaining happiness and safety.

2. That all power is vested in, and consequently derived from, the people; that magistrates are their trustees and servants, and at all times amenable to them.

3. That government is, or ought to be, instituted for the common benefit, protection, and security of the people, nation, or community; of all the various modes and forms of government, that is best which is capable of producing the greatest degree of happiness and safety, and is most effectually secured against the danger of maladministration; and that when any government shall be found inadequate or contrary to these purposes, a majority of the community hath an indubitable, unalienable, and indefeasible right to reform, alter, or abolish it, in such manner as shall be judged most conducive to the public weal.

4. That no man, or set of men, are entitled to exclusive or separate emoluments or privileges from the community, but in consideration of public services; which, not being descendible, neither ought the offices of magistrate, legislator, or judge to be hereditary.

5. That the legislative and executive powers of the state should be separate and distinct from the judiciary; and that the members of the two first may be restrained from oppression, by feeling and participating the burthens of the people, they should, at fixed periods, be reduced to a private station, return into that body from which they were originally taken, and the vacancies be supplied by frequent, certain, and regular election, in which all or any part of the former members to be again eligible or ineligible, as the law shall direct.

6. That elections of members to serve as representatives of the people in assembly ought to be free; and that all men having sufficient evidence of permanent common interest with, and attachment to the community, have the right of suffrage, and cannot be taxed or deprived of their property for publick uses, without their own consent, or that of their representatives so elected, nor bound by any law to which they have not, in like manner, assented for the public good.

7. That all power of suspending laws or the execution of laws by any authority, without consent of the representatives of the people, is injurious to their rights, and ought not to be exercised.

8. That in all capital or criminal prosecutions a man hath a right to demand the cause and nature of his accusation, to be confronted with the accusers and witnesses, to call for evidence in his favor, and to a speedy trial by an impartial jury, of his vicinage, without whose unanimous consent he cannot be found guilty; nor can he be compelled to give evidence against himself; that no man be deprived of his liberty, except by the law of the land or the judgment of his peers.

9. That excessive bail ought not to be required, nor excessive fines imposed, nor cruel and unusual punishments inflicted.

10. That general warrants, whereby an officer or messenger may be commanded to search suspected places without evidence of a fact committed, or to seize any person or persons not named, or whose offence is not particularly described and supported by evidence, are grievous and oppressive, and ought not be granted.

11. That in controversies respecting property, and in suits between man and man, the ancient trial by jury is preferable to any other, and ought to be held sacred.

12. That the freedom of the press is one of the great bulwarks of liberty, and can never by restrained but by despotic governments.

13. That a well-regulated militia, composed of the body of the people trained to arms, is the proper, natural, and safe defence of a free State; that standing armies in time of peace should be avoided as dangerous to liberty; and that in all cases the military should be under strict subordination to and governed by the civil power.

14. That the people have a right to uniform government; and,

therefore, that no government separate from or independent of the government of Virginia ought to be erected or established within the limits thereof.

15. That no free government, or the blessings of liberty, can be preserved to any people but by a firm adherence to justice, moderation, temperance, frugality and virtue, and by a frequent recurrence to fundamental principles.

16. That religion, or the duty which we owe to our Creator, and the manner of discharging it, can be directed only by reason and conviction, not by force or violence; and, therefore, all men are equally entitled to the free exercise of religion, according to the dictates of conscience; and that it is the mutual duty of all to practise Christian forbearance, love, and charity towards each other.

Appendix D

Articles of Confederation

TO ALL TO WHOM THESE PRESENTS SHALL COME, WE THE UNDERSIGNED
DELEGATES OF THE STATES AFFIXED TO OUR NAMES SEND GREETING.

Whereas the Delegates of the United States of America in Congress assembled did on the fifteenth day of November in the Year of our Lord One Thousand Seven Hundred and Seventyseven, and in the Second Year of the Independence of America agree to certain articles of Confederation and perpetual Union between the States of NewHampshire, Massachusetts-bay, Rhodeisland and Providence Plantations, Connecticut, New York, New Jersey, Pennsylvania, Delaware, Maryland, Virginia, North-Carolina, South-Carolina and Georgia in the Words following, viz.

> "Articles of Confederation and perpetual Union between the States of Newhampshire, Massachusetts-bay, Rhodeisland and Providence Plantations, Connecticut, New-York, New-Jersey, Pennsylvania, Delaware, Maryland, Virginia, North-Carolina, South-Carolina and Georgia.

ARTICLE I. The stile of this confederacy shall be "The United States of America."

ARTICLE II. Each State retains its sovereignty, freedom and independence, and every power, jurisdiction and right, which is not by this confederation expressly delegated to the United States, in Congress assembled.

ARTICLE III. The said States hereby severally enter into a firm league of friendship with each other, for their common defence, the security of their liberties, and their mutual and general welfare, binding themselves to assist each other, against all force offered to, or attacks made upon them, or any of them, on account of religion, sovereignty, trade, or any other pretence whatever.

ARTICLE IV. The better to secure and perpetuate mutual friendship and intercourse among the people of the different States in this Union, the free inhabitants of each of these States, paupers, vagabonds and fugitives from justice excepted, shall be entitled to all privileges and immunities of free citizens in the several States; and the people of each State shall have free ingress and regress to and from any other State, and shall enjoy therein all the privileges of trade and commerce, subject to the same duties, impositions and restrictions as the inhabitants thereof respectively, provided that such restrictions shall not extend so far as to prevent the removal of property imported into any State, to any other State of which the owner is an inhabitant; provided also that no imposition, duties or restriction shall be laid by any State, on the property of the United States, or either of them.

If any person guilty of, or charged with treason, felony, or other high misdemeanor in any State, shall flee from justice, and be found in any of the United States, he shall upon demand of the Governor or Executive power, of the State from which he fled, be delivered up and removed to the State having jurisdiction of his offence.

Full faith and credit shall be given in each of these States to the records, acts and judicial proceedings of the courts and magistrates of every other State.

ARTICLE V. For the more convenient management of the general interests of the United States, delegates shall be annually appointed in such manner as the legislature of each State shall direct, to meet in Congress on the first Monday in November, in every year, with a power reserved to each State, to recall its delegates, or any of them, at any time within the year, and to send others in their stead, for the remainder of the year.

No State shall be represented in Congress by less than two, nor by more than seven members; and no person shall be capable of being a delegate for more than three years in any term of six years; nor shall any person, being a delegate, be capable of holding any office under the United States, for which he, or another for his benefit receives any salary, fees or emolument of any kind.

Each State shall maintain its own delegates in a meeting of the States, and while they act as members of the committee of the States.

In determining questions in the United States, in Congress assembled, each State shall have one vote.

Freedom of speech and debate in Congress shall not be impeached or questioned in any court, or place out of Congress, and the members of Congress shall be protected in their persons from arrests and imprisonments, during the time of their going to and from, and attendance on Congress, except for treason, felony, or breach of the peace.

ARTICLE VI. No State without the consent of the United States in Congress assembled, shall send any embassy to, or receive any embassy from, or enter into any conference, agreement, alliance or treaty with any king, prince or state; nor shall any person holding any office of profit or trust under the United States, or any of them, accept of any present, emolument, office or title of any kind whatever from any king, prince or foreign state; nor shall the United States in Congress assembled, or any of them, grant any title of nobility.

No two or more States shall enter into any treaty, confederation or alliance whatever between them, without the consent of the United States in Congress assembled, specifying accurately the purposes for which the same is to be entered into, and how long it shall continue.

No State shall lay any imposts or duties, which may interfere with any stipulations in treaties, entered into by the United States in Congress assembled, with any king, prince or state, in pursuance of any treaties already proposed by Congress, to the courts of France and Spain.

No vessels of war shall be kept up in time of peace by any State, except such number only, as shall be deemed necessary by the United States in Congress assembled, for the defence of such State, or its trade; nor shall any body of forces be kept up by any State, in time of peace, except such number only, as in the judgment of the United States, in Congress assembled, shall be deemed requisite to garrison the forts necessary for the defence of such State; but every State shall always keep up a well regulated and disciplined militia, sufficiently armed and accoutred, and shall provide and constantly have ready for use, in public stores, a due number of field pieces and tents, and a proper quantity of arms, ammunition and camp equipage.

No State shall engage in any war without the consent of the United States in Congress assembled, unless such State be actually invaded by enemies, or shall have received certain advice of a resolution being formed by some nation of Indians to invade such State, and the danger is so imminent as not to admit of a delay, till the United States in Congress assembled can be consulted; nor shall any State grant commissions to any ships or vessels of war, nor letters of marque or reprisal, except it be after a declaration of war by the United States in Congress assembled, and then only against the kingdom or state and the subjects thereof, against which war has been so declared, and under such regulations as shall be established by the United States in Congress assembled, unless such State be infested by pirates, in which case vessels of war may be fitted out for that occasion, and kept so long as the danger shall continue, or until the United States in Congress assembled shall determine otherwise.

ARTICLE VII. When land-forces are raised by any State for the common defence, all officers of or under the rank of colonel, shall be appointed by the Legislature of each State respectively by whom such forces shall be raised, or in such manner as such State shall direct, and all vacancies shall be filled up by the State which first made the appointment.

ARTICLE VIII. All charges of war, and all other expenses that shall be incurred for the common defence or general welfare, and allowed by the United States in Congress assembled, shall be defrayed out of a common treasury, which shall be supplied by the several States, in proportion to the value of all land within each State, granted to or surveyed for any person, as such land and the buildings and improvements thereon shall be estimated according to such mode as the United States in Congress assembled, shall from time to time direct and appoint.

The taxes for paying that proportion shall be laid and levied by the authority and direction of the Legislatures of the several States within the time agreed upon by the United States in Congress assembled.

ARTICLE IX. The United States in Congress assembled, shall have the sole and exclusive right and power of determining on peace and war, except in the cases mentioned in the sixth article - of sending and receiving ambassadors - entering into treaties and alliances, provided that no treaty of commerce shall be made whereby the legislative power of the respective States shall be restrained from imposing such imposts and duties on foreigners, as their own people are subjected to, or from prohibiting the exportation or importation of any species of goods or commodities whatsoever - of establishing rules for deciding in all cases, what captures on land or water shall be legal, and in what manner prizes taken by land or naval forces in the service of the United States shall be divided or appropriated - of granting letters of marque and reprisal in times of peace - appointing courts for the trial of piracies and felonies committed on the high seas and establishing courts for receiving and determining finally appeals in all cases of captures, provided that no member of Congress shall be appointed a judge of any of the said courts.

The United States in Congress assembled shall also be the last resort on appeal in all disputes and differences now subsisting or that hereafter may arise between two or more States concerning boundary, jurisdiction or any other cause whatever; which authority shall always be exercised in the manner following. Whenever the legislative or executive authority or lawful agent of any State in controversy with another shall present a petition to Congress, stating the matter in question and praying for a hearing, notice thereof shall be given by order of Congress to the legislative or executive authority of the other State in controversy, and a day assigned for the appearance of the parties by their lawful agents, who shall then be directed to appoint by joint consent, commissioners or judges to constitute a court for hearing and determining the matter in question: but if they cannot agree, Congress shall name three persons out of each of the United States, and from the list of such persons each party shall alternately strike out one, the petitioners beginning, until the number shall be reduced to thirteen; and from that number not less than seven, nor more than nine names as Congress shall direct, shall in the presence of Congress be drawn out by lot, and the persons whose names shall be so drawn or any five of them, shall be commissioners or judges, to hear and finally determine the controversy, so always as a major part of the judges who shall hear the cause shall agree in the determination: and if either party shall neglect to attend at the day appointed, without showing reasons, which Congress shall judge sufficient, or being present shall refuse to strike, the Congress shall proceed to nominate three persons out of each State, and the Secretary of Congress shall strike in behalf of such party absent or refusing; and the judgment and sentence of the court to be appointed, in the manner before prescribed, shall be final and conclusive; and if any of the parties shall refuse to submit to the authority of such court, or to appear or defend their claim or cause, the court shall nevertheless proceed to pronounce sentence, or judgment, which shall in like manner be final and decisive, the judgment or sentence and other proceedings being in either case transmitted to Congress, and lodged among the acts of Congress for the security of the parties concerned: provided that every commissioner, before he sits in judgment, shall take an oath to be administered by one of the judges of the supreme or superior court of the State where the cause shall be tried, "well and truly to hear and determine the matter in question, according to the best of his judgment, without favour, affection or hope of reward:" provided also that no State shall be deprived of territory for the benefit of the United States.

All controversies concerning the private right of soil claimed under different grants of two or more States, whose jurisdiction as they may respect such lands, and the States which passed such grants are adjusted, the said grants or either of them being at the same time claimed to have originated antecedent to such settlement of jurisdiction, shall on the petition of either party to the Congress of the United States, be finally determined as near as may be in the same manner as is before prescribed for deciding disputes respecting territorial jurisdiction between different States.

The United States in Congress assembled shall also have the sole and exclusive right and power of regulating the alloy and value of coin struck by their own authority, or by that of the respective States, - fixing the standard of weights and measures throughout the United States, - regulating the trade and managing all affairs with the Indians, not members of any of the States, provided that the legislative right of any State within its own limits be not infringed or violated - establishing and regulating post-offices from one State to another, throughout all the United States, and exacting such postage on the papers passing thro' the same as may be requisite to defray the expenses of the said office - appointing all officers of the land forces, in the service of the United States, excepting regimental officers - appointing all the officers of the naval forces, and commissioning all officers whatever in the service of the United States - making rules for the government and regulation of the said land and naval forces, and directing their operations.

The United States in Congress assembled shall have authority to appoint a committee, to sit in the recess of Congress, to be denominated "a Committee of the States," and to consist of one delegate from each State; and to appoint such other committees and civil officers as may be necessary for managing the general affairs of the United States under their direction - to appoint one of their number to preside, provided that no person be allowed to serve in the office of president more than one year in any term of three years; to ascertain the necessary sums of money to be raised for the service of the United States, and to appropriate and apply the same for defraying the public expenses - to borrow money, to emit bills on the credit of the United States, transmitting every half year to the respective States an account of the sums of money so borrowed or emitted, - to build and equip a navy - to agree upon the number of land forces, and to make requisitions from each State for its quota, in proportion to the number of white inhabitants in such State; which requisition shall be binding, and thereupon the Legislature of each State shall appoint the regimental officers, raise the men and cloath, arm and equip them in a soldier like manner, at the expense of the United States; and the officers and men so cloathed, armed and equipped shall march to the place appointed, and within the time agreed on by the United States in Congress assembled: but if the United States in Congress assembled shall, on consideration of circumstances judge proper that any State should not raise men, or should raise a smaller number of men than the quota thereof, such extra number shall be raised, officered, cloathed, armed and equipped in the same manner as the quota of such State, unless the legislature of such State shall judge that such extra number cannot be safely spared out of the same, in which case they shall raise, officer, cloath, arm and equip as many of such extra number as they judge can be safely spared. And the officers and men so cloathed, armed and equipped, shall march to the place appointed, and within the time agreed on by the United States in Congress assembled.

The United States in Congress assembled shall never engage in a war, nor grant letters of marque and reprisal in time of peace, nor enter into any treaties or alliances, nor coin money, nor regulate the value thereof, nor ascertain the sums and expenses necessary for the defence and welfare of the United States, or any of them, nor emit bills, nor borrow money on the credit of the United States, nor appropriate money, nor agree upon the number of vessels of war, to be built or purchased, or the number of land or sea forces to be raised, nor appoint a commander in chief of the army or navy, unless nine States assent to the same: nor shall a question on any other point, except for adjourning from day to day be determined, unless by the votes of a majority of the United States in Congress assembled.

The Congress of the United States shall have power to adjourn to any time within the year, and to any place within the United States, so that no period of adjournment be for a longer duration than the space of six months, and shall publish the journal of their proceedings monthly, except such parts thereof relating to treaties, alliances, or military operations, as in their judgment require secresy; . . . and the delegates of a State, or any of them, at his or their request shall be furnished with a transcript of the said journal, except such parts as are above excepted, to lay before the Legislatures of the several States.

ARTICLE X. The committee of the States, or any nine of them, shall be authorized to execute, in the recess of Congress, such of the powers of Congress as the United States in Congress assembled, by the consent of nine States, shall from time to time think expedient to vest them with; provided that no power be delegated to the said committee, for the exercise of which, by the articles of confederation, the voice of nine States in the Congress of the United States assembled is requisite.

ARTICLE XI. Canada acceding to this confederation, and joining in the measures of the United States, shall be admitted into, and entitled to all the advantages of this Union: but no other colony shall be admitted into the same, unless such admission be agreed to by nine States.

ARTICLE XII. All bills of credit emitted, monies borrowed and debts contracted by, or under the authority of Congress, before the assembling of the United States, in pursuance of the present confederation, shall be deemed and considered as a charge against the United States, for payment and satisfaction whereof the said United States, and the public faith are hereby solemnly pledged.

ARTICLE XIII. Every State shall abide by the determinations of the United States in Congress assembled, on all questions which by this confederation are submitted to them. And the articles of this confederation shall be inviolably observed by every State, and the Union shall be perpetual; nor shall any alteration at any time hereafter be made in any of them; unless such alteration be agreed to in a Congress of the United States, and be afterwards confirmed by the Legislatures of every State.

And whereas it has pleased the Great Governor of the world to incline the hearts of the Legislatures we respectively represent in Congress, to approve of, and to authorize us to ratify the said articles of confederation and perpetual union. Know ye that we the undersigned delegates, by virtue of the power and authority to us given for that purpose, do by these presents, in the name and in behalf of our respective constituents, fully and entirely ratify and confirm each and every of the said articles of confederation and perpetual union, and all and singular the matters and things therein contained: and we do further solemnly plight and engage the faith of our respective constituents, that they shall abide by the determinations of the United States in Congress assembled, on all questions, which by the said confederation are submitted to them. And that the articles thereof shall be inviolably observed by the States we re(s)pectively represent, and that the Union shall be perpetual.

In witness whereof we have hereunto set our hands in Congress. Done at Philadelphia in the State of Pennsylvania the ninth day of July in the year of our Lord one thousand seven hundred and seventy-eight, and in the third year of the independence of America.

The Federalist, No. X

TO THE PEOPLE OF THE STATE OF NEW YORK:

Among the numerous advantages promised by a well-constructed Union, none deserves to be more accurately developed than its tendency to break and control the violence of faction. The friend of popular governments never finds himself so much alarmed for their character and fate, as when he contemplates their propensity to this dangerous vice. He will not fail, therefore, to set a due value on any plan which, without violating the principles to which he is attached, provides a proper cure for it. The instability, injustice, and confusion introduced into the public councils, have, in truth, been the mortal diseases under which popular governments have everywhere perished; as they continue to be the favorite and fruitful topics from which the adversaries to liberty derive their most specious declamations. The valuable improvements made by the American constitutions on the popular models, both ancient and modern, cannot certainly be too much admired; but it would be an unwarrantable partiality, to contend that they have as effectually obviated the danger on this side, as was wished and expected. Complaints are everywhere heard from our most considerate and virtuous citizens, equally the friends of public and private faith, and of public and personal liberty, that our governments are too unstable, that the public good is disregarded in the conflicts of rival parties, and that measures are too often decided, not according to the rules of justice and the rights of the minor party, but by the superior force of an interested and overbearing majority. However anxiously we may wish that these complaints had no foundation, the evidence, of known facts will not permit us to deny that they are in some degree true. It will be found, indeed, on a candid review of our situation, that some of the distresses under which we labor have been erroneously charged on the operation of our governments; but it will be found, at the same time, that other causes will not alone account for many of our heaviest misfortunes; and, particularly, for that prevailing and increasing distrust of public engagements, and alarm for private rights, which are echoed from one end of the continent to the other. These must be chiefly, if not wholly, effects of the unsteadiness and injustice with which a factious spirit has tainted our public administrations.

By a faction, I understand a number of citizens, whether amounting to a majority or a minority of the whole, who are united and actuated by some common impulse of passion, or of interest, adverse to the rights of other citizens, or to the permanent and aggregate interests of the community.

There are two methods of curing the mischiefs of faction: the one, by removing its causes; the other, by controlling its effects.

There are again two methods of removing the causes of faction: the one, by destroying the liberty which is essential to its existence; the other, by giving to every citizen the same opinions, the same passions, and the same interests.

It could never be more truly said than of the first remedy, that it was worse than the disease. Liberty is to faction what air is to fire, an element without which it instantly expires. But it could not be less folly to abolish liberty, which is essential to political life, because it nourishes faction, than it would be to wish the annihilation of air, which is essential to animal life, because it imparts to fire its destructive agency.

The second expedient is as impracticable as the first would be unwise. As long as the reason of man continues fallible, and he is at liberty to exercise it, different opinions will be formed. As long as the connection subsists between his reason and his self-love, his opinions and his passions will have a reciprocal influence on each other; and the former will be objects to which the latter will attach themselves. The diversity in the faculties of men, from which the rights of property originate, is not less an insuperable obstacle to a uniformity of interests. The protection of these faculties is the first object of government. From the protection of different and unequal faculties of acquiring property, the possession of different degrees and kinds of property immediately results; and from the influence of these on the sentiments and views of the respective proprietors, ensues a division of the society into different interests and parties.

The latent causes of faction are thus sown in the nature of man; and we see them everywhere brought into different degrees of activity, according to the different circumstances of civil society. A zeal for different opinions concerning religion, concerning government, and many other points, as well of speculation as of practice; an attachment to different leaders ambitiously contending for pre-eminence and power; or to persons of other descriptions whose fortunes have been interesting to the human passions, have, in turn, divided mankind into parties, inflamed them with mutual animosity, and rendered them much more disposed to vex and oppress each other than to co-operate for their common good. So strong is this propensity of mankind to fall into mutual animosities, that where no substantial occasion presents itself, the most frivolous and fanciful distinctions have been sufficient to kindle their unfriendly passions and excite their most violent conflicts. But the most common and durable source of factions has been the various and unequal distribution of property. Those who hold and those who are without property have ever formed distinct interests in society. Those who are creditors, and those who are debtors, fall under a like discrimination. A landed interest, a manufacturing interest, a mercantile interest, a moneyed interest, with many lesser interests, grow up of necessity in civilized nations, and divide them into different classes, actuated by different sentiments and views. The regulation of these various and interfering interests forms the principal task of modern legislation, and involves the spirit of party and faction in the necessary and ordinary operations of the government.

No man is allowed to be a judge in his own cause, because his interest would certainly bias his judgment, and, not improbably, corrupt his integrity. With equal, nay with greater reason, a body of men are unfit to be both judges and parties at the same time; yet what are many of the most important acts of legislation, but so many judicial determinations, not indeed concerning the rights of single persons, but concerning the rights of large bodies of citizens? And what are the different classes of legislators but advocates and parties ot the causes which they determine? Is a law proposed concerning private debts? It is a question to which the creditors are parties on one side and the debtors on the other. Justice ought to hold the balance between them. Yet the parties are, and must be, themselves the judges; and the most numerous party, or, in other words, the most powerful faction must be expected to prevail. Shall domestic manufactures be encouraged, and in what degree, by restrictions on foreign manufactures? are questions which would be differently decided by the landed and the manufacturing classes, and probably by neither with a sole regard to justice and the public good. The apportionment of taxes on the various descriptions of property is an act which seems to require the most exact impartiality; yet there is, perhaps, no legislative act in which greater opportunity and temptation are given to a predominant party to trample on the rules of justice. Every shilling with which they overburden the inferior number, is a shilling saved to their own pockets.

It is in vain to say that enlightened statesmen will be able to adjust these clashing interests, and render them all subservient to the public good. Enlightened statesmen will not always be at the helm. Nor, in many cases, can such an adjustment be made at all without taking into view indirect and remote considerations, which will rarely prevail over the immediate interest which one party may find in disregarding the rights of another or the good of the whole.

The inference to which we are brought is, that the causes of faction cannot be removed, and that relief is only to be sought in the means of controlling its effects.

If a faction consists of less than a majority, relief is supplied by the republican principle, which enables the majority to defeat its sinister views by regular vote. It may clog the administration, it may convulse the society; but it will be unable to execute and mask its violence under the forms of the Constitution. When a majority is included in a faction, the form of popular government, on the other hand, enables it to sacrifice to its ruling passion or interest both the public good and the rights of other citizens. To secure the public good and private rights against the danger of such a faction, and at the same time to preserve the spirit and the form of popular government, is then the great object to which our inquiries are directed. Let me add that it is the great desideratum by which this form of government can be rescued from the opprobrium under which it has so long labored, and be recommended to the esteem and adoption of mankind.

By what means is this object attainable? Evidently by one of two only. Either the existence of the same passion or interest in a majority at the same time must be prevented, or the majority, having such coexistent passion or interest, must be rendered, by their number and local situation, unable to concert and carry into effect schemes of oppression. If the impulse and the opportunity be suffered to coincide, we well know that neither moral nor religious motives can be relied on as an adequate control. They are not found to be such on the injustice and violence of individuals, and lose their efficacy in proportion to the number combined together, that is, in proportion as their efficacy becomes needful.

From this view of the subject it may be concluded that a pure democracy, by which I mean a society consisting of a small number of citizens, who assemble and administer the government in person, can admit of no cure for the mischiefs of faction. A common passion or interest will, in almost every case, be felt by a majority of the whole;

a communication and concert result from the form of government itself; and there is nothing to check the inducements to sacrifice the weaker party or an obnoxious individual. Hence it is that such democracies have ever been spectacles of turbulence and contention; have ever been found incompatible with personal security or the rights of property; and have in general been as short in their lives as they have been violent in their deaths. Theoretic politicians, who have patronized this species of government, have erroneously supposed that by reducing mankind to a perfect equality in their political rights, they would, at the same time, be perfectly equalized and assimilated in their possessions, their opinions, and their passions.

A republic, by which I mean a government in which the scheme of representation takes place, opens a different prospect, and promises the cure for which we are seeking. Let us examine the points in which it varies from pure democracy, and we shall comprehend both the nature of the cure and the efficacy which it must derive from the Union.

The two great points of difference between a democracy and a republic are: first, the delegation of the government, in the latter, to a small number of citizens elected by the rest; secondly, the greater number of citizens, and greater sphere of country, over which the latter may be extended.

The effect of the first difference is, on the one hand, to refine and enlarge the public views, by passing them through the medium of a chosen body of citizens, whose wisdom may best discern the true interest of their country, and whose patriotism and love of justice will be least likely to sacrifice it to temporary or partial considerations. Under such a regulation, it may well happen that the public voice, pronounced by the representatives of the people, will be more consonant to the public good than if pronounced by the people themselves, convened for the purpose. On the other hand, the effect may be inverted. Men of factious tempers, of local prejudices, or of sinister designs, may, by intrigue, by corruption, or by other means, first obtain the suffrages, and then betray the interests, of the people. The question resulting is, whether small or extensive republics are more favorable to the election of proper guardians of the public weal, and it is clearly decided in favor of the latter by two obvious considerations:

In the first place, it is to be remarked that, however small the republic may be, the representatives must be raised to a certain number, in order to guard against the cabals of a few; and that, however large it may be, they must be limited to a certain number, in order to guard against the confusion of a multitude. Hence, the number of representatives in the two cases not being in proportion to that of the two constituents, and being proportionally greater in the small republic, it follows that, if the proportion of fit characters be not less in the large than in the small republic, the former will present a greater option, and consequently a greater probability of a fit choice.

In the next place, as each representative will be chosen by a greater number of citizens in the large than in the small republic, it will be more difficult for unworthy candidates to practice with success the vicious arts by which elections are too often carried; and the suffrages of the people being more free, will be more likely to centre in men who possess the most attractive merit and the most diffusive and established characters.

It must be confessed that in this, as in most other cases, there is a mean, on both sides of which inconveniences will be found to lie. By enlarging too much the number of electors, you render the representatives too little acquainted with all their local circumstances and lesser interests; as by reducing it too much, you render him unduly attached to these, and too little fit to comprehend and pursue great and national objects. The federal Constitution forms a happy combination in this respect; the great and aggregate interests being referred to the national, the local and particular to the State legislatures.

The other point of difference is, the greater number of citizens and extent of territory which may be brought within the compass of republican than of democratic government; and it is this circumstance principally which renders factious combinations less to be dreaded in the former than in the latter. The smaller the society, the fewer probably will be the distinct parties and interests composing it; the fewer the distinct parties and interests, the more frequently will a majority be found of the same party; and the smaller the number of individuals composing a majority, and the smaller the compass within which they are placed, the more easily will they concert and execute their plans of oppression. Extend the sphere, and you take in a greater variety of parties and interests; you make it less probable that a majority of the whole will have a common motive to invade the rights of other citizens; or if such a common motive exists, it will be more difficult for all who feel it to discover their own strength, and to act in unison with each other. Besides other impediments, it may be remarked that, where there is consciousness of unjust or dishonorable purposes, communication is always checked by distrust in proportion to the number whose concurrence is necessary.

Hence, it clearly appears, that the same advantage which a republic has over a democracy, in controlling the effects of faction, is enjoyed by a large over a small republic,—is enjoyed by the Union over the States composing it. Does the advantage consist in the substitution of representatives whose enlightened views and virtuous sentiments render them superior to local prejudices and schemes of injustice? It will not be denied that the representation of the Union will be most likely to possess these requisite endowments. Does it consist in the greater security afforded by a greater variety of parties, against the event of any one party being able to outnumber and oppress the rest? In an equal degree does the increased variety of parties comprised within the Union, increase this security? Does it, in fine, consist in the greater obstacles opposed to the concert and accomplishment of the secret wishes of an unjust and interested majority? Here, again, the extent of the Union gives it the most palpable advantage.

The influence of factious leaders may kindle a flame within their particular States, but will be unable to spread a general conflagration through the other States. A religious sect may degenerate into a political faction in a part of the Confedracy; but the variety of sects dispersed over the entire face of it must secure the national councils against any danger from that source. A rage for paper money, for an abolition of debts, for an equal division of property, or for any other improper or wicked project, will be less apt to pervade the whole body of the Union than a particular member of it; in the same proportion as such a malady is more likely to taint a particular county or district, than an entire State.

In the extent and proper structure of the Union, therefore, we behold a republican remedy for the diseases most incident to republican government. And according to the degree of pleasure and pride we feel in being republicans, ought to be our zeal in cherishing the spirit and supporting the character of Federalists.

The Constitution

We the People of the United States, in order to form a more perfect Union, establish Justice, insure domestic Tranquility, provide for the common defence, promote the general Welfare, and secure the Blessings of Liberty to ourselves and our Posterity, do ordain and establish this *Constitution* for the United States of America.

ARTICLE I

SECTION 1. All legislative Powers herein granted shall be vested in a Congress of the United States, which shall consist of a Senate and House of Representatives.

SECTION 2. The House of Representatives shall be composed of Members chosen every second Year by the People of the several States, and the Electors in each State shall have the Qualifications requisite for Electors of the most numerous Branch of the State Legislature.

No person shall be a Representative who shall not have attained to the Age of twenty five Years and been seven Years a Citizen of the United States, and who shall not, when elected, be an Inhabitant of that State in which he shall be chosen.

Representatives and direct Taxes shall be apportioned among the several States which may be included within this Union, according to their respective Numbers, which shall be determined by adding to the whole Number of Free persons, including those bound to Service for a Term of Years, and excluding Indians not taxed, three fifths of all other Persons. The actual Enumeration shall be made within three Years after the first Meeting of the Congress of the United States, and within every subsequent Term of ten Years, in such Manner as they shall by Law direct. The Number of Representatives shall not exceed one for every thirty Thousand, but each State shall have at Least one Representative; and until such enumeration shall be made, the State of New Hampshire shall be entitled to chuse three, Massachusetts eight, Rhode Island and Providence Plantations one, Connecticut five, New York six, New Jersey four, Pennsylvania eight, Delaware one, Maryland six, Virginia ten, North Carolina five, South Carolina five, and Georgia three.

When vacancies happen in the Representation from any State, the Executive Authority thereof shall issue Writs of Election to fill such Vacancies.

The House of Representatives shall chuse their Speaker and other Officers; and shall have the sole Power of Impeachment.

SECTION 3. The Senate of the United States shall be composed of two Senators from each State, chosen by the Legislature thereof, for six Years; and each Senator shall have one Vote.

Immediately after they shall be assembled in Consequence of the first Election, they shall be divided as equally as may be into three Classes. The seats of the Senators of the first Class shall be vacated at the Expiration of the second year, of the second Class at the Expiration of the fourth Year, and of the third Class at the Expiration of the sixth Year, so that one-third may be chosen every second Year; and if Vacancies happen by Resignation, or otherwise, during the Recess of the Legislature of any State, the Executive thereof may make temporary Appointments until the next Meeting of the Legislature, which shall then fill such Vacancies.

No Person shall be a Senator who shall not have attained to the Age of thirty Years, and been nine Years a Citizen of the United States, and who shall not, when elected, be an Inhabitant of that State for which he shall be chosen.

The Vice President of the United States shall be President of the Senate, but shall have no Vote, unless they be equally divided.

The Senate shall chuse their other Officers, and also a President pro tempore, in the Absence of the Vice President, or when he shall exercise the Office of President of the United States.

The Senate shall have the sole Power to try all impeachments. When sitting for that Purpose, they shall be on Oath or Affirmation. When the President of the United States is tried, the Chief Justice shall preside: and no Person shall be convicted without the Concurence of two thirds of the Members present.

Judgment in Cases of Impeachment shall not extend further than to removal from Office, and disqualification to hold and enjoy any Office of honor, Trust or Profit under the United States: but the Party convicted shall nevertheless be liable and subject to Indictment, Trial, Judgment and Punishment, according to Law.

SECTION 4. The Times, Places and manner of holding Elections for Senators and Representatives, shall be prescribed in each State by the Legislature thereof; but the Congress may at any time by Law make or alter such Regulations, except as to the Places of chusing Senators.

The Congress shall assemble at least once in every Year, and such Meeting shall be on the first Monday in December, unless they shall by Law appoint a different Day.

SECTION 5. Each House shall be the Judge of the Elections, Returns and Qualifications of its own Members, and a Majority of each shall constitute a Quorum to do Business; but a smaller Number may adjourn from day to day, and may be authorized to compel the Attendance of absent Members, in such Manner, and under such Penalties as each House may provide.

Each House may determine the Rules of its Proceedings, punish its Members for disorderly Behaviour, and, with the Concurrence of two thirds, expel a Member.

Each House shall keep a Journal of its Proceedings, and from time to time publish the same, excepting such Parts as may in their judgment require Secrecy; and the Yeas and Nays of the Members of either House on any question shall, at the desire of one fifth of those Present, be entered on the Journal.

Neither House, during the Session of Congress, shall, without the Consent of the other, adjourn for more than three days, nor to any other Place than that in which the two Houses shall be sitting.

SECTION 6. The Senators and Representatives shall receive a Compensation for their Services, to be ascertained by Law, and paid out of the Treasury of the United States. They shall in all Cases, except Treason, Felony and Breach of the Peace, be privileged from Arrest during their Attendance at the Session of their respective Houses, and in going to and returning from the same; and for any Speech or Debate in either House, they shall not be questioned in any other place.

No Senator or Representative shall, during the Time for which he was elected, be appointed to any civil Office under the Authority of the United States, which shall have been created, or the Emoluments whereof shall have been encreased during such time; and no Person holding any Office under the United States, shall be a Member of either House during his Continuance in Office.

SECTION 7. All Bills for raising Revenue shall originate in the House of Representatives; but the Senate may propose or concur with Amendments as on other Bills.

Every Bill which shall have passed the House of Representatives and the Senate, shall, before it become a Law, be presented to the President of the United States; If he approve he shall sign it, but if not he shall return it, with his Objections to that House in which it shall have originated, who shall enter the Objections at large on their Journal, and proceed to reconsider it. If after such Reconsideration two thirds of that House shall agree to pass the Bill, it shall be sent, together with the Objections, to the other House, by which it shall likewise be reconsidered, and if approved by two thirds of that House, it shall become a Law. But in all such Cases the Votes of both Houses shall be determined by yeas and Nays, and the Names of the Persons voting for and against the Bill shall be entered on the Journal of each House respectively. If any Bill shall not be returned by the President within ten Days (Sundays excepted) after it shall have been presented to him, the Same shall be a Law, in like Manner as if he had signed it, unless the Congress by their Adjournment prevent its Return, in which Case it shall not be a Law.

Every Order, Resolution, or Vote to which the Concurrence of the Senate and House of Representatives may be necessary (except on a question of Adjournment) shall be presented to the President of the United States; and before the Same shall take Effect, shall be approved by him, or being disapproved by him, shall be repassed by two thirds of the Senate and House of Representatives, according to the Rules and Limitations prescribed in the Case of a Bill.

SECTION 8. The Congress shall have Power to lay and collect Taxes, Duties, Imposts and Excises, to pay the Debts and provide for the common Defence and general Welfare of the United States; but all Duties, Imposts and Excises shall be uniform throughout the United States;

To borrow Money on the credit of the United States;

To regulate Commerce with foreign Nations, and among the several States, and with the Indian Tribes;

To establish an uniform Rule of Naturalization, and uniform Laws on the subject of Bankruptcies throughout the United States;

To coin Money, regulate the Value thereof, and of foreign Coin, and fix the Standard of Weights and Measures;

To provide for the Punishment of counterfeiting the Securities and current Coin of the United States;

To establish Post Offices and post Roads;

To promote the Progress of Science and useful Arts, by securing for limited Times to Authors and Inventors the exclusive Right to their respective Writings and Discoveries;

To constitute Tribunals inferior to the supreme Court;

To define and punish Piracies and Felonies committed on the high Seas, and Offences against the Law of Nations;

To declare War, grant Letters of Marque and Reprisal, and make Rules concerning Captures on Land and Water;

To raise and support Armies, but no Appropriation of Money to that Use shall be for a longer Term than two Years;

To provide and maintain a Navy;

To make Rules for the Government and Regulation of the land and naval Forces;

To provide for calling forth the Militia to execute the Laws of the Union, suppress Insurrections and repel Invasions;

To provide for organizing, arming, and disciplining, the Militia, and for governing such Part of them as may be employed in the Service of the United States, reserving to the States respectively, the Appointment of the Officers, and the Authority of training the Militia according to the discipline prescribed by Congress;

To exercise exclusive Legislation in all Cases whatsoever, over such District (not exceeding ten Miles square) as may, by Cession of particular States, and the Acceptance of Congress, become the Seat of the Government of the United States, and to exercise like Authority over all Places purchased by the Consent of the Legislature of the State in which the Same shall be, for the Erection of Forts, Magazines, Arsenals, dock-Yards, and other needful Buildings; - And

To make all Laws which shall be necessary and proper for carrying into Execution the foregoing Powers, and all other Powers vested by this Constitution in the Government of the United States, or in any Department or Officer thereof.

SECTION 9. The Migration or Importation of such Persons as any of the States now existing shall think proper to admit, shall not be prohibited by the Congress prior to the Year one thousand eight hundred and eight, but a Tax or duty may be imposed on such Importation, not exceeding ten dollars for each Person.

The Privilege of the Writ of Habeas Corpus shall not be suspended, unless when in Cases of Rebellion or Invasion the public Safety may require it.

No Bill of Attainder or ex post facto Law shall be passed.

No Capitation, or other direct, tax shall be laid, unless in Proportion to the Census or Enumeration herein directed to be taken.

No Tax or Duty shall be laid on Articles exported from any State.

No Preference shall be given by any Regulation of Commerce or

Revenue to the Ports of one State over those of another: nor shall Vessels bound to, or from, one State, be obliged to enter, clear, or pay Duties in another.

No Money shall be drawn from the Treasury, but in Consequence of Appropriations made by Law; and a regular Statement and Account of the Receipts and Expenditures of all public Money shall be published from time to time.

No Title of Nobility shall be granted by the United States: And no Person holding any Office of Profit or Trust under them, shall, without the Consent of the Congress, accept of any present, Emolument, Office, or Title, of any kind whatever, from any King, Prince, or foreign State.

SECTION 10. No State shall enter into any Treaty, Alliance, or Confederation; grant Letters of Marque and Reprisal; coin Money; emit Bills of Credit; make any Thing but gold and silver Coin a Tender in Payment of Debts; pass any Bill of Attainder, ex post facto Law, or Law impairing the Obligation of Contracts, or grant any Title of Nobility.

No State shall, without the Consent of the Congress, lay any Imposts or Duties on Imports or Exports, except what may be absolutely necessary for executing it's inspection Laws: and the net Produce of all Duties and Imposts, laid by any State on Imports or Exports, shall be for the Use of the Treasury of the United States; and all such Laws shall be subject to the Revision and Controul of the Congress.

No State shall, without the Consent of Congress, lay any Duty of Tonnage, keep Troops, or Ships of War in time of Peace, enter into any Agreement or Compact with another State, or with a foreign Power, or engage in War, unless actually invaded, or in such imminent Danger as will not admit of delay.

ARTICLE II

SECTION 1. The executive Power shall be vested in a President of the United States of America. He shall hold his Office during the Term of four Years, and, together with the Vice President, chosen for the same Term, be elected, as follows:

Each State shall appoint, in such Manner as the Legislature thereof may direct, a Number of Electors, equal to the whole Number of Senators and Representatives to which the State may be entitled in the Congress: but no Senator or Representative, or Person holding an Office of Trust or Profit under the United States, shall be appointed an Elector.

The Electors shall meet in their respective States, and vote by Ballot for two persons, of whom one at least shall not be an Inhabitant of the same State with themselves. And they shall make a List of all the Persons voted for, and of the Number of Votes for each; which List they shall sign and certify, and transmit sealed to the Seat of the Government of the United States, directed to the President of the Senate. The President of the Senate shall, in the Presence of the Senate and House of Representatives, open all the Certificates, and the Votes shall then be counted. The Person having the greatest Number of Votes shall be the President, if such Number be a Majority of the whole Number of Electors appointed; and if there be more than one who have such Majority, and have an equal Number of Votes, then the House of Representatives shall immediately chuse, by Ballot one of them for President; and if no Person have a Majority, then from the five highest on the List, the said House shall in like manner chuse the President. But in chusing the President, the Votes shall be taken by States, the Representation from each State having one vote; A quorum for this Purpose shall consist of a Member or Members from two thirds of the States, and a Majority of all the States shall be necessary to a Choice. In every Case, after the Choice of the President, the Person having the greatest Number of Votes of the Electors shall be the Vice President. But if there should remain two or more who have equal Votes, the Senate shall chuse from them by Ballot the Vice-President.

The Congress may determine the Time of chusing the Electors, and the Day on which they shall give their Votes; which Day shall be the same throughout the United States.

No person except a natural born Citizen, or a Citizen of the United States, at the time of the Adoption of this Constitution, shall be eligible to the Office of President; neither shall any Person be eligible to that office who shall not have attained to the Age of thirty five Years, and been fourteen Years a Resident within the United States.

In Case of the Removal of the President from Office, or of his Death, Resignation or Inability to discharge the Powers and Duties of the said Office, the Same shall devolve on the Vice President, and the Congress may by Law provide for the Case of Removal, Death, Resignation or Inability, both of the President and Vice President, declaring what Officer shall then act as President, and such Officer shall act accordingly, until the Disability be removed, or a President shall be elected.

The President shall, at stated Times, receive for his Services, a Compensation, which shall neither be encreased nor diminished during the Period for which he shall have been elected, and he shall not receive within that Period any other Emolument from the United States, or any of them.

Before he enter on the Execution of his Office, he shall take the following Oath or Affirmation: -"I do solemnly swear (or affirm) that I will faithfully execute the Office of President of the United States, and will to the best of my Ability, preserve, protect and defend the Constitution of the United States."

SECTION 2. The President shall be Commander in Chief of the Army and Navy of the United States, and of the Militia of the several States, when called into the actual Service of the United States; he may require the Opinion, in writing, of the principal Officer in each of the executive Departments, upon any Subject relating to the Duties of their respective Offices, and he shall have Power to grant Reprieves and Pardons for Offences against the United States, except in Cases of Impeachment.

He shall have Power, by and with the Advice and Consent of the Senate, to make Treaties, provided two thirds of the Senators present concur; and he shall nominate, and by and with the Advice and Consent of the Senate, shall appoint Ambassadors, other public Ministers and Consuls, Judges of the supreme Court, and all other Officers of the United States, whose Appointments are not herein otherwise provided for, and which shall be established by Law: but the Congress may by Law vest the Appointment of such inferior Officers, as they think proper, in the President alone, in the Courts of Law, or in the Heads of Departments.

The President shall have Power to fill up all Vacancies that may happen during the Recess of the Senate, by granting Commissions which shall expire at the End of their next session.

SECTION 3. He shall from time to time give to the Congress Information of the State of the Union, and recommend to their Consideration such Measures as he shall judge necessary and expedient; he may, on extraordinary Occasions, convene both Houses, or either of them, and in Case of Disagreement between them, with Respect to the time of Adjournment, he may adjourn them to such Time as he shall think proper; he shall receive Ambassadors and other public Ministers; he shall take Care that the Laws be faithfully executed, and shall commission all the Officers of the United States.

SECTION 4. The President, Vice President, and all civil Officers of the United States, shall be removed from Office on Impeachment for, and Conviction of, Treason, Bribery, or other high Crimes and Misdemeanors.

ARTICLE III

SECTION 1. The Judical Power of the United States, shall be vested in one supreme Court, and in such inferior Courts as the Congress may from time to time ordain and establish. The Judges, both of the supreme and inferior Courts, shall hold their Offices during good Behaviour, and shall, at stated Times, receive for their Services, a Compensation, which shall not be diminished during their Continuance in Office.

SECTION 2. The judicial Power shall extend to all Cases, in Law and Equity, arising under this Constitution, the Laws of the United States, and Treaties made, or which shall be made, under their Authority;--to all Cases affecting Ambassadors, other public Ministers and Consuls;--to all Cases of admiralty and maritime Jurisdiction;--to Controversies to which the United States shall be a Party;--to Controversies between two or more States;--between a State and Citizens of another State;--between Citizens of different States,--between Citizens of the same State claiming Lands under Grants of different States, and between a State, or the Citizens thereof, and foreign States, Citizens or Subjects.

In all Cases affecting Ambassadors, other public Ministers and Consuls, and those in which a State shall be Party, the supreme Court shall have original Jurisdiction. In all the other Cases before mentioned, the supreme Court shall have appellate Jurisdiction, both as to Law and Fact, with such Exceptions, and under such Regulations as the Congress shall make.

The Trial of all Crimes except in Cases of Impeachment, shall be by Jury; and such Trial shall be held in the State where the said Crimes shall have been committed; but when not committed within any State, the Trial shall be at such Place or Places as the Congress may by Law have directed.

SECTION 3. Treason against the United States, shall consist only in levying War against them, or in adhering to their Enemies, giving them Aid and Comfort. No Person shall be convicted of Treason unless on the Testimony of two Witnesses to the same overt Act, or on Confession in open Court.

The Congress shall have Power to declare the Punishment of Treason, but no Attainder of Treason shall work Corruption of Blood, or Forfeiture except during the Life of the Person attained.

ARTICLE IV

SECTION 1. Full Faith and Credit shall be given in each State to the public Acts, Records, and judicial Proceedings of every other State. And the Congress may by general Laws prescribe the Manner in which such Acts, Records and Proceedings shall be proved, and the Effect thereof.

SECTION 2. The Citizens of each State shall be entitled to all Privileges and Immunities of Citizens in the several States.

A person charged in any State with Treason, Felony, or other Crime, who shall flee from Justice, and be found in another State shall on Demand of the executive Authority of the State from which he fled, be delivered up to be removed to the State having Jurisdiction of the Crime.

No person held to Service or Labour in one State, under the Laws thereof, escaping into another, shall, in Consequence of any Law or Regulation therein, be discharged from such Service or Labour, but shall be delivered up on Claim of the Party to whom such Service or Labour may be due.

SECTION 3. New States may be admitted by the Congress into this Union; but no new State shall be formed or erected within the Jurisdiction of any other State; nor any State be formed by the Junction of two or more States, or Parts of States, without the Consent of the Legislatures of the States concerned as well as of the Congress.

The Congress shall have Power to dispose of and make all needful Rules and Regulations respecting the Territory or other Property belonging to the United States; and nothing in this Constitution shall be so construed as to Prejudice any Claims of the United States, or of any particular State.

SECTION 4. The United States shall guarantee to every State in this Union a Republican Form of Government, and shall protect each of them against Invasion; and on Application of the Legislature, or of the Executive (when the Legislature cannot be convened) against domestic Violence.

ARTICLE V

The Congress, whenever two thirds of both Houses shall deem it necessary, shall propose amendments to this Constitution, or, on the Application of the Legislatures of two thirds of the several States, shall call a Convention for proposing Amendments, which, in either Case, shall be valid to all Intents and Purposes, as Part of this Constitution, when ratified by the Legislatures of three fourths of the several States, or by Conventions in three fourths thereof, as the one or the other Mode of Ratification may be proposed by the Congress; Provided that no Amendment which may be made prior to the Year One thousand eight hundred and eight shall in any Manner affect the first and fourth Clases in the Ninth Section of the first Article; and that no State, without its Consent, shall be deprived of its equal Suffrage in the Senate.

ARTICLE VI

All Debts contracted and Engagements entered into, before the Adoption of this Constitution, shall be as valid against the United States under this Constitution, as under the Confederation.

This Constitution, and the Laws of the United States which shall be made in Pursuance thereof; and all Treaties made, or which shall be made, under the Authority of the United States, shall be the supreme Law of the Land; and the Judges in every State shall be bound thereby, any Thing in the Constitution or Laws of any State to the Contrary notwithstanding.

The Senators and Representatives before mentioned, and the Members of the several State Legislatures, and all executive and judicial Officers, both of the United States and of the several States, shall be bound by Oath or Affirmation, to support this Constitution; but no religious Test shall ever be required as a Qualification to any Office or public Trust under the United States.

ARTICLE VII

The Ratification of the Conventions of nine States, shall be sufficient for the Establishment of this Constitution between the States so ratifying the Same.

Done in Convention by the Unanimous Consent of the States present the Seventeenth Day of September in the Year of our Lord one thousand seven hundred and Eighty seven and of the Independence of the United States of America the Twelfth IN WITNESS whereof We have hereunto subscribed our Names,
G⁰: Washington—Presidt.
and deputy from Virginia

Attest William Jackson Secretary

Articles in addition to, and amendment of, the Constitution of the United States of America, proposed by Congress, and ratified by the legislatures of the several States, pursuant to the fifth article of the original Constitution.

FIRST AMENDMENT [First ten amendments ratified December 15, 1791]

Congress shall make no law respecting an establishment of religion, or prohibiting the free exercise thereof; or abridging the freedom of speech, or of the press; or the right of the people peaceably to assemble, and to petition the government for a redress of grievances.

SECOND AMENDMENT

A well regulated militia, being necessary to the security of a free State, the right of the people to keep and bear arms, shall not be infringed.

THIRD AMENDMENT

No soldier shall, in time of peace be quartered in any house, without the consent of the owner, nor in time of war, but in a manner to be prescribed by law.

FOURTH AMENDMENT

The right of the people to be secure in their persons, houses, papers, and effects, against unreasonable searches and seizures, shall not be violated, and no warrants shall issue, but upon probable cause, supported by oath or affirmation, and particularly describing the place to be searched, and the persons or things to be seized.

FIFTH AMENDMENT

No person shall be held to answer for a capital, or otherwise infamous crime, unless on a presentment or indictment of a grand jury, except in cases arising in the land or naval forces, or in the militia, when in actual service in time of war or public danger; nor shall any person be subject for the same offense to be twice put in jeopardy of life or limb; nor shall be compelled in any criminal case to be a witness against himself, nor be deprived of life, liberty, or property, without due process of law; nor shall private property be taken for public use, without just compensation.

SIXTH AMENDMENT

In all criminal prosecutions, the accused shall enjoy the right to a speedy and public trial, by an impartial jury of the State and district wherein the crime shall have been committed, which district shall have been previously ascertained by law, and to be informed of the nature and cause of the accusation; to be confronted with the witnesses against him; to have compulsory process for obtaining witnesses in his favor, and to have the assistance of counsel for his defense.

SEVENTH AMENDMENT

In suits at common law, where the value in controversy shall exceed twenty dollars, the right of trial by jury shall be preserved, and no fact tried by a jury shall be otherwise reexamined in any court of the United States, than according to the rules of the common law.

EIGHTH AMENDMENT

Excessive bail shall not be required, nor excessive fines imposed, nor cruel and unusual punishments inflicted.

NINTH AMENDMENT

The enumeration in the Constitution of certain rights shall not be construed to deny or disparage others retained by the people.

TENTH AMENDMENT

The powers not delegated to the United States by the Constitution, nor prohibited by it to the States, are reserved to the States respectively, or to the people.

ELEVENTH AMENDMENT [January 8, 1798]

The judicial power of the United States shall not be construed to extend to any suit in law or equity, commenced or prosecuted against one of the United States by citizens of another State, or by citizens or subjects of any foreign State.

TWELFTH AMENDMENT
[September 25, 1804]

The electors shall meet in their respective States, and vote by ballot for President and Vice President, one of whom, at least, shall not be an inhabitant of the same State with themselves; they shall name in their ballots the person voted for as President, and in distinct ballots, the person voted for as Vice President, and they shall make distinct lists of all persons voted for as President and of all persons voted for as Vice President, and of the number of votes for each, which lists they shall sign and certify, and transmit sealed to the seat of the government of the United States, directed to the President of the Senate;—The President of the Senate shall, in the presence of the Senate and House of Representatives, open all the certificates and the votes shall then be counted;—The person having the greatest number of votes for President, shall be the President, if such number be a majority of the whole number of electors appointed; and if no person have such majority, then from the persons having the highest numbers not exceeding three on the list of those voted for as President, the House of Representatives shall choose immediately, by ballot, the President. But in choosing the President, the votes shall be taken by States, the representation from each State having one vote; a quorum for this purpose shall consist of the member or members from two thirds of the States, and a majority of all the States shall be necessary to a choice. And if the House of Representatives shall not choose a President whenever the right of choice shall devolve upon them, before the fourth day of March next following, then the Vice President shall act as President, as in the case of the death or other constitutional disability of the President. The person having the greatest number of votes as Vice President shall be the Vice President, if such number be a majority of the whole number of electors appointed, and if no person have a majority, then from the two highest numbers on the list, the Senate shall choose the Vice President; a quorum for the purpose shall consist of two thirds of the whole number of Senators, and a majority of the whole number shall be necessary to a choice. But no person constitutionally ineligible to the office of President shall be eligible to that of Vice President of the United States.

THIRTEENTH AMENDMENT
[December 18, 1865]

SECTION 1. Neither slavery nor involuntary servitude, except as a punishment for crime whereof the party shall have been duly convicted, shall exist within the United States, or any place subject to their jurisdiction.

SECTION 2. Congress shall have power to enforce this article by appropriate legislation.

FOURTEENTH AMENDMENT [July 28, 1868]

SECTION 1. All persons born or naturalized in the United States, and subject to the jurisdiction thereof, are citizens of the United States and of the State wherein they reside. No State shall make or enforce any law which shall abridge the privileges or immunities of citizens of the United States; nor shall any State deprive any person of life, liberty, or property, without due process of law; nor deny to any person within its jurisdiction the equal protection of the laws.

SECTION 2. Representatives shall be apportioned among the several States according to their respective numbers, counting the whole number of persons in each State, excluding Indians not taxed. But when the right to vote at any election for the choice of electors for President and Vice President of the United States, representatives in Congress, the executive and judicial officers of a State, or the members of the legislature thereof, is denied to any of the male inhabitants of such State, being twenty-one years of age, and citizens of the United States, or in any way abridged, except for participating in rebellion, or other crime, the basis of representation therein shall be reduced in the proportion which the number of such male citizens shall bear to the whole number of male citizens twenty-one years of age in such State.

SECTION 3. No person shall be a senator or representative in Congress, or elector of President and Vice President, or hold any office, civil or military, under the United States, or under any State, who having previously taken an oath, as a member of Congress, or as an officer of the United States, or as a member of any State legislature, or as an exective or judicial officer of any State, to support the Constitution of the United States, shall have engaged in insurrection or rebellion against the same, or given aid or comfort to the enemies thereof. But Congress may by a vote of two thirds of each House, remove such disability.

SECTION 4. The validity of the public debt of the United States, authorized by law, including debts incurred for payment of pensions and bounties for services in suppressing insurrection or rebellion, shall not be questioned. But neither the United States nor any State shall assume or pay any debt or obligation incurred in aid of insurrection or rebellion against the United States, or any claim for the loss or emancipation of any slave; but all such debts, obligations, and claims shall be held illegal and void.

SECTION 5. The Congress shall have power to enforce, by appropriate legislation, the provisions of this article.

FIFTEENTH AMENDMENT [March 30, 1870]

SECTION 1. The right of citizens of the United States to vote shall not be denied or abridged by the United States or by any State on account of race, color, or previous condition of servitude.

SECTION 2. The Congress shall have power to enforce this article by appropriate legislation.

SIXTEENTH AMENDMENT
[February 25, 1913]

The Congress shall have the power to lay and collect taxes on incomes, from whatever source derived, without apportionment among the several States, and without regard to any census or enumeration.

SEVENTEENTH AMENDMENT
[May 31, 1913]

The Senate of the United States shall be composed of two senators from each State, elected by the people thereof, for six years; and each senator shall have one vote. The electors in each State shall have the qualifications requisite for electors of the most numerous branch of the State legislature.

When vacancies happen in the representation of any State in the Senate, the executive authority of such State shall issue writs of election to fill such vacancies: *Provided,* That the legislature of any State may empower the executive thereof to make temporary appointments until the people fill the vacancies by election as the legislature may direct.

This amendment shall not be so construed as to affect the election or term of any senator chosen before it becomes valid as part of the Constitution.

EIGHTEENTH AMENDMENT*
[January 29, 1919]

After one year from the ratification of this article, the manufacture, sale, or transportation of intoxicating liquors within, the importation thereof into, or the exportation thereof from the United States and all territory subject to the jurisdiction thereof for beverage purposes is thereby prohibited.

---

*Repealed by the Twenty-first Amendment.

The Congress and the several States shall have concurrent power to enforce this article by appropriate legislation.

This article shall be inoperative unless it shall have been ratified as an amendment to the Constitution by the legislatures of the several States, as provided in the Constitution, within seven years from the date of the submission hereof to the States by Congress.

NINETEENTH AMENDMENT
[August 26, 1920]

The right of citizens of the United States to vote shall not be denied or abridged by the United States or by any State on account of sex.

Congress shall have the power to enforce this article by appropriate legislation.

TWENTIETH AMENDMENT
[January 23, 1933]

SECTION 1. The terms of the President and Vice President shall end at noon on the 20th day of January, and the terms of Senators and Representatives at noon on the 3rd day of January, of the years in which such terms would have ended if this article had not been ratified; and the terms of their successors shall then begin.

SECTION 2. The Congress shall assemble at least once in every year, and such meeting shall begin at noon on the 3rd day of January, unless they shall by law appoint a different day.

SECTION 3. If, at the time fixed for the beginning of the term of President, the President-elect shall have died, the Vice President-elect shall become President. If a President shall not have been chosen before the time fixed for the beginning of his term, or if the President-elect shall have failed to qualify, then the Vice President-elect shall act as President until a President shall have qualified; and the Congress may by law provide for the case wherein neither a President-elect nor a Vice President-elect shall have qualified, declaring who shall then act as President, or the manner in which one who is to act shall be selected, and such person shall act accordingly until a President or Vice President shall have qualified.

SECTION 4. The Congress may by law provide for the case of the death of any of the persons from whom the House of Representatives may choose a President whenever the right of choice shall have devolved upon them, and for the case of the death of any of the persons from whom the

Senate may choose a Vice President whenever the right of choice shall have devolved upon them.

SECTION 5. Sections 1 and 2 shall take effect on the 15th day of October following the ratification of this article.

SECTION 6. This article shall be inoperative unless it shall have been ratified as an amendment to the Constitution by the legislatures of three-fourths of the several States within seven years from the date of its submission.

TWENTY-FIRST AMENDMENT
[December 5, 1933]

SECTION 1. The Eighteenth Article of amendment to the Constitution of the United States is hereby repealed.

SECTION 2. The transportation or importation into any State, Territory, or possession of the United States for delivery or use therein of intoxicating liquors in violation of the laws thereof, is hereby prohibited.

SECTION 3. This article shall be inoperative unless it shall have been ratified as an amendment to the Constitution by conventions in the several States, as provided in the Constitution, within seven years from the date of the submission thereof to the States by the Congress.

TWENTY-SECOND AMENDMENT
[March 1, 1951]

No person shall be elected to the office of the President more than twice, and no person who has held the office of President, or acted as President, for more than two years of a term to which some other person was elected President shall be elected to the office of the President more than once.

But this article shall not apply to any person holding the office of President when this article was proposed by the Congress, and shall not prevent any person who may be holding the office of President, or acting as President, during the term within which this article becomes operative from holding the office of President or acting as President during the remainder of such term.

This article shall be inoperative unless it shall have been ratified as an amendment to the Constitution by the legislatures of three-fourths of the several States within seven years from the date of its submission to the States by the Congress.

TWENTY-THIRD AMENDMENT
[March 29, 1961]

SECTION 1. The District constituting the seat of Government of the United States shall appoint in such manner as the Congress may direct:

A number of electors of President and Vice President equal to the whole number of Senators and Representatives in Congress to which the District would be entitled if it were a State, but in no event more than the least populous State; they shall be in addition to those appointed by the States, but they shall be considered, for the purposes of the election of President and Vice President, to be electors appointed by a State; and they shall meet in the District and perform such duties as provided by the twelfth article of amendment.

SECTION 2. The Congress shall have power to enforce this article by appropriate legislation.

TWENTY-FOURTH AMENDMENT
[January 23, 1964]

SECTION 1. The right of citizens of the United States to vote in any primary or other election for President or Vice President, for electors for President or Vice President, or for Senator or Representative in Congress, shall not be denied or abridged by the United States or any State by reason of failure to pay any poll tax or other tax.

SECTION 2. The Congress shall have power to enforce this article by appropriate legislation.

TWENTY-FIFTH AMENDMENT
[February 10, 1967]

SECTION 1. In case of the removal of the President from office or of his death or resignation, the Vice President shall become President.

SECTION 2. Whenever there is a vacancy in the office of the Vice President, the President shall nominate a Vice President who shall take office upon confirmation by a majority vote of both Houses of Congress.

SECTION 3. Whenever the President transmits to the President pro tempore of the Senate and the Speaker of the House of Representatives his written declaration that he is unable to discharge the powers and duties of his office, and until he transmits to them a written declaration to the contrary, such powers and duties shall be discharged by the Vice President as Acting President.

SECTION 4. Whenever the Vice President and a majority of either the principal officers of the executive departments or of such other body as Congress may by law provide, transmit to the President pro tempore of the Senate and the Speaker of the House of Representatives their written declaration that the President is unable to discharge the powers and duties of his office, the Vice President shall immediately assume the powers and duties of the office as Acting President.

Thereafter, when the President transmits to the President pro tempore of the Senate and the Speaker of the House of Representatives his written declaration that no inability exists, he shall resume the powers and duties of his office unless the Vice President and a majority of either the principal officers of the executive departments or of such other body as Congress may by law provide, transmit within four days to the President pro tempore of the Senate and the Speaker of the House of Representatives their written declaration that the President is unable to discharge the powers and duties of his office. Therupon Congress shall decide the issue, assembling within forty-eight hours for that purpose if not in session. If the Congress, within twenty-one days after receipt of the latter written declaration, or, if Congress is not in session, within twenty-one days after Congress is required to assemble, determines by two-thirds vote of both houses that the President is unable to discharge the powers and duties of his office, the Vice President shall continue to discharge the same as Acting President; otherwise, the President shall resume the powers and duties of his office.

TWENTY-SIXTH AMENDMENT
[June 30, 1971]

SECTION 1. The right of citizens of the United States who are eighteen years of age or older to vote shall not be denied or abridged by the United States or by any State on account of age.

SECTION 2. The Congress shall have power to enforce this article by appropriate legislation.

TWENTY-SEVENTH AMENDMENT [1992]

No law, varying the compensation for the services of the Senators and Representatives, shall take effect, until an election of representatives shall have intervened.

Washington's Farewell Address

Friends and Fellow-Citizens:

The period for a new election of a citizen to administer the Executive Government of the United States being not far distant, and the time actually arrived when your thoughts must be employed in designating the person who is to be clothed with that important trust, it appears to me proper, especially as it may conduce to a more distinct expression of the public voice, that I should now apprise you of the resolution I have formed to decline being considered among the number of those out of whom a choice is to be made.

I beg you at the same time to do me the justice to be assured that this resolution has not been taken without a strict regard to all the considerations appertaining to the relation which binds a dutiful citizen to his country; and that in withdrawing the tender of service, which silence in my situation might imply, I am influenced by no diminution of zeal for your future interest, no deficiency of grateful respect for your past kindness, but am supported by a full conviction that the step is compatible with both.

The acceptance of and continuance hitherto in the office to which your suffrages have twice called me have been a uniform sacrifice of inclination to the opinion of duty and to a deference for what appeared to be your desire. I constantly hoped that it would have been much earlier in my power, consistently with motives which I was not at liberty to disregard, to return to that retirement from which I had been reluctantly drawn. The strength of my inclination to do this previous to the last election had even led to the preparation of an address to declare it to you; but mature reflection on the then perplexed and critical posture of our affairs with foreign nations and the unanimous advice of persons entitled to my confidence impelled me to abandon the idea. I rejoice that the state of your concerns, external as well as internal, no longer renders the pursuit of inclination incompatible with the sentiment of duty or propriety, and am persuaded, whatever partiality may be retained for my services, that in the present circumstances of our country you will not disapprove my determination to retire.

The impressions with which I first undertook the arduous trust were explained on the proper occasion. In the discharge of this trust I will only say that I have, with good intentions, contributed toward the organization and administration of the Government the best exertions of which a very fallible judgment was capable. Not unconscious in the outset of the inferiority of my qualifications, experience in my own eyes, perhaps still more in the eyes of others, has strengthened the motives to diffidence of myself; and every day the increasing weight of years admonishes me more and more that the shade of retirement is as necessary to me as it will be welcome. Satisfied that if any circumstances have given peculiar value to my services they were temporary, I have the consolation to believe that, while choice and prudence invite me to quit the political scene, patriotism does not forbid it.

In looking forward to the moment which is intended to terminate the career of my political life my feelings do not permit me to suspend the deep acknowledgment of that debt of gratitude which I owe to my beloved country for the many honors it has conferred upon me; still more for the steadfast confidence with which it has supported me, and for the opportunities I have thence enjoyed of manifesting my inviolable attachment by services faithful and persevering, though in usefulness unequal to my zeal. If benefits have resulted to our country from these services, let it always be remembered to your praise and as an instructive example in our annals that under circumstances in which the passions, agitated in every direction, were liable to mislead; amidst appearances sometimes dubious; vicissitudes of fortune often discouraging; in situations in which not unfrequently want of success has countenanced the spirit of criticism, the constancy of your support was the essential prop of the efforts and a guaranty of the plans by which they were effected. Profoundly penetrated with this idea, I shall carry it with me to my grave as a strong incitement to unceasing vows that Heaven may continue to you the choicest tokens of its beneficence; that your union and brotherly affection may be perpetual; that the free Constitution which is the work of your hands may be sacredly maintained; that its administration in every department may be stamped with wisdom and virtue; that, in fine, the happiness of the people of these States, under the auspices of liberty, may be made complete by so careful a preservation and so prudent a use of this blessing as will acquire to them the glory of recommending it to the applause, the affection, and adoption of every nation which is yet a stranger to it.

Here, perhaps, I ought to stop. But a solicitude for your welfare which can not end but with my life, and the apprehension of danger natural to that solicitude, urge me on an occasion like the present to offer to your solemn contemplation and to recommend to your frequent review some sentiments which are the result of much reflection, of no inconsiderable observation, and which appear to me all important to the permanency of your felicity as a people. These will be offered to you with the more freedom as you can only see in them the disinterested warnings of a parting friend, who can possibly have no personal motive to bias his counsel. Nor can I forget as an encouragement to it your indulgent reception of my sentiments on a former and not dissimilar occasion.

Interwoven as is the love of liberty with every ligament of your hearts, no recommendation of mine is necessary to fortify or confirm the attachment.

The unity of government which constitutes you one people is also now dear to you. It is justly so, for it is a main pillar in the edifice of your real independence, the support of your tranquillity at home, your peace abroad, of your safety, of your prosperity, of that very liberty which you so highly prize. But as it is easy to foresee that from different causes and from different quarters much pains will be taken, many artifices employed, to weaken in your minds the conviction of this truth, as this is the point in your political fortress against which the batteries of internal and external enemies will be most constantly and actively (though often covertly and insidiously) directed, it is of infinite moment that you should properly estimate the immense value of your national union to your collective and individual happiness; that you should cherish a cordial, habitual, and immovable attachment to it; accustoming yourselves to think and speak of it as of the palladium of your political safety and prosperity; watching for its preservation with jealous anxiety; discountenancing whatever may suggest even a suspicion that it can in any event be abandoned, and indignantly frowning upon the first dawning of every attempt to alienate any portion of our country from the rest or to enfeeble the sacred ties which now link together the various parts.

For this you have every inducement of sympathy and interest. Citizens by birth or choice of a common country, that country has a right to concentrate your affections. The name of American, which belongs to you in your national capacity, must exalt the just pride of patriotism more than any appellation derived from local discriminations. With slight shades of difference, you have the same religion, manners, habits, and political principles. You have in a common cause fought and triumphed together. The independence and liberty you possess are the work of joint councils and joint efforts, of common dangers, sufferings, and successes.

But these considerations, however powerfully they address themselves to your sensibility, are greatly outweighed by those which apply more immediately to your interest. Here every portion of our country finds the most commanding motives for carefully guarding and preserving the union of the whole.

The *North,* in an unrestrained intercourse with the *South,* protected by the equal laws of a common government, finds in the productions of the latter great additional resources of maritime and commercial enterprise and precious materials of manufacturing industry. The *South,* in the same intercourse, benefiting by the same agency of the *North,* sees its agriculture grow and its commerce expand. Turning partly into its own channels the seamen of the *North,* it finds its particular navigation invigorated; and while it contributes in different ways to nourish and increase the general mass of the national navigation, it looks forward to the protection of a maritime strength to which itself is unequally adapted. The *East,* in a like intercourse with the *West,* already finds, and in the progressive improvement of interior communications by land and water will more and more find, a valuable vent for the commodities which it brings from abroad or manufactures at home. The *West* derives from the *East* supplies requisite to its growth and comfort, and what is perhaps of still greater consequence, it must of necessity owe the secure enjoyment of indispensable *outlets* for its own productions to the weight, influence, and the future maritime strength of the Atlantic side of the Union, directed by an indissoluble community of interest as *one nation.* Any other tenure by which the *West* can hold this essential advantage, whether derived from its own separate strength or from an apostate and unnatural connection with any foreign power, must be intrinsically precarious.

While, then, every part of our country thus feels an immediate and particular interest in union, all the parts combined can not fail to find in the united mass of means and efforts greater strength, greater resource, proportionably greater security from external danger, a less frequent interruption of their peace by foreign nations, and what is of inestimable value, they must derive from union an exemption from those broils and wars between themselves which so frequently afflict neighboring countries not tied together by the same governments, which their own rivalships alone would be sufficient to produce, but which opposite foreign alliances, attachments, and intrigues would stimulate and imbitter. Hence, likewise, they will avoid the necessity of those overgrown military establishments which, under any form of government, are inauspicious to liberty, and which are to be regarded as particularly hostile to republican liberty. In this sense it is that your union ought to be considered as a main prop of your liberty, and that the love of the one ought to endear to you the preservation of the other.

These considerations speak a persuasive language to every reflecting and vertuous mind, and exhibit the continuance of the union as a primary object of patriotic desire. Is there a doubt whether a common government can embrace so large a sphere? Let experience solve it. To listen to mere speculation in such a case were criminal. We are authorized to hope that a proper organization of the whole, with the auxiliary agency of governments for the respective subdivisions, will afford a happy issue to the experiment. It is well worth a fair and full experiment. With such powerful and obvious motives to union affecting all parts of our country, while experience shall not have demonstrated its impracticability, there will always be reason to distrust the patriotism of those who in any quarter may endeavor to weaken its bands.

In contemplating the causes which may disturb our union it occurs as matter of serious concern that any ground should have been furnished for characterizing parties by *geographical* discriminations--*Northern* and *Southern, Atlantic* and *Western*--whence designing men may endeavor to excite a belief that there is a real difference of local interests and views. One of the expedients of party to acquire influence within particular districts is to misrepresent the opinions and aims of other districts. You can not shield yourselves too much against the jealousies and heartburnings which spring from these misrepresentations; they tend to render alien to each other those who ought to be bound together by fraternal affection. The inhabitants of our Western country have lately had a useful lesson on this head. They have seen in the negotiation by the Executive and in the unanimous ratification by the Senate of the treaty with Spain, and in the universal satisfaction at that event throughout the United States, a decisive proof how unfounded were the suspicions propagated among them of a policy in the General Government and in the Atlantic States unfriendly to their interests in regard to the Mississippi. They have been witnesses to the formation of two treaties--that with Great Britain and that with Spain--which secure to them everything they could desire in respect to our foreign relations toward confirming their prosperity. Will it not be their wisdom to rely for the preservation of these advantages on the union by which they were procured? Will they not henceforth be deaf to those advisers, if such there are, who would sever them from their brethren and connect them with aliens?

To the efficacy and permanency of your union a government for the whole is indispensable. No alliances, however strict, between the parts can be an adequate substitute. They must inevitably experience the infractions and interruptions which all alliances in all times have experienced. Sensible of this momentous truth, you have improved upon your first essay by the adoption of a Constitution of Government better calculated than your former for an intimate union and for the efficacious management of your common concerns. This Government, the off-spring of our own choice, uninfluenced and unawed, adopted upon full investigation and mature deliberation, completely free in its principles, in the distribution of its powers, uniting security with energy, and containing within itself a provision for its own amendment, has a just claim to your confidence and your support. Respect for its authority, compliance with its laws, acquiescence in its measures, are duties enjoined by the fundamental maxims of true liberty. The basis of our political systems is the right of the people to make and to alter their constitutions of government. But the constitution which at any time exists till changed by an explicit and authentic act of the whole people is sacredly obligatory upon all. The very idea of the power and the right of the people to establish government presupposes the duty of every individual to obey the established government.

All obstructions to the execution of the laws, all combinations and associations, under whatever plausible character, with the real design to direct, control, counteract, or awe the regular deliberation and action of the constituted authorities, are destructive of this fundamental principle and of fatal tendency. They serve to organize faction; to give it an artificial and extraordinary force; to put in the place of the delegated will of the nation the will of a party, often a small but artful and enterprising minority of the community, and, according to the alternate triumphs of different parties, to make the public administration the mirror of the ill-concerted and incongruous projects of faction rather than the organ of consistent and wholesome plans, digested by common counsels and modified by mutual interests.

However combinations or associations of the above description may now and then answer popular ends, they are likely in the course of time and things to become potent engines by which cunning, ambitious, and unprincipled men will be enabled to subvert the power of the people, and to usurp for themselves the reins of government, destroying afterwards the very engines which have lifted them to unjust dominion.

Toward the preservation of your Government and the permanency of your present happy state, it is requisite not only that you steadily discountenance irregular opposition to its acknowledged authority, but also that you resist with care the spirit of innovation upon its principles, however specious the pretexts. One method of assault may be to effect in the forms of the Constitution alterations which will impair the energy of the system, and thus to undermine what can not be directly overthrown. In all the changes to which you may be invited remember that time and habit are at least as necessary to fix the true character of governments as of other human institutions; that experience is the surest standard by which to test the real tendency of the existing constitution of a country; that facility in changes upon the credit of mere hypothesis and opinion exposes to perpetual change, from the endless variety of hypothesis and opinion; and remember especially that for the efficient management of your common interests in a country so extensive as ours a government of as much vigor as is consistent with the perfect security of liberty is indispensable. Liberty itself will find in such a government, with powers properly distributed and adjusted, its surest guardian. It is, indeed, little else than a name where the government is too feeble to withstand the enterprises of faction, to confine each member of the society within the limits prescribed by the laws, and to maintain all in the secure and tranquil enjoyment of the rights of person and property.

I have already intimated to you the danger of parties in the State, with particular reference to the founding of them on geographical discriminations. Let me now take a more comprehensive view, and warn you in the most solemn manner against the baneful effects of the spirit of party generally.

This spirit, unfortunately, is inseparable from our nature, having its root in the strongest passions of the human mind. It exists under different shapes in all governments, more or less stifled, controlled, or repressed; but in those of the popular form it is seen in its greatest rankness and is truly their worst enemy.

The alternate domination of one faction over another, sharpened by the spirit of revenge natural to party dissension, which in different ages and countries has perpetrated the most horrid enormities, is itself a frightful despotism. But this leads at length to a more formal and permanent despotism. The disorders and miseries which result gradually incline the minds of men to seek security and repose in the absolute power of an individual, and sooner or later the chief of some prevailing faction, more able or more fortunate than his competitors, turns this disposition to the purposes of his own elevation on the ruins of public liberty.

Without looking forward to an extremity of this kind (which nevertheless ought not to be entirely out of sight), the common and continual mischiefs of the spirit of party are sufficient to make it the interest and duty of a wise people to discourage and restrain it.

It serves always to distract the public councils and enfeeble the public administration. It agitates the community with ill-founded jealousies and false alarms; kindles the animosity of one part against another; foments occasionally riot and insurrection. It opens the door to foreign influence and corruption, which find a facilitated access to the government itself through the channels of party passion. Thus the policy and the will of one country are subjected to the policy and will of another.

There is an opinion that parties in free countries are useful checks upon the administration of the government, and serve to keep alive the spirit of liberty. This within certain limits is probably true; and in governments of a monarchical cast patriotism may look with indulgence, if not with favor, upon the spirit of party. But in those of the popular character, in governments purely elective, it is a spirit not to be encouraged. From their natural tendency it is certain there will always be enough of that spirit for every salutary purpose; and there being constant danger of excess, the effort ought to be by force of public opinion to mitigate and assuage it. A fire not to be quenched, it demands a uniform vigilance to prevent its bursting into a flame, lest, instead of warming, it should consume.

It is important, likewise, that the habits of thinking in a free country should inspire caution in those intrusted with its administration to confine themselves within their respective constitutional spheres, avoiding in the exercise of the powers of one department to encroach upon another. The spirit of encroachment tends to consolidate the powers of all the departments in one, and thus to create, whatever the form of government, a real despotism. A just estimate of that love of power and proneness to abuse it which predominates in the human heart is sufficient to satisfy us of the truth of this position. The necessity of reciprocal checks in the exercise of political power, by dividing and distributing it into different depositories, and constituting each the guardian of the public weal against invasions by the others, has been evinced by experiments ancient and modern, some of them in our country and under our own eyes. To preserve them must be as necessary as to institute them. If in the opinion of the people the distribution or modification of the constitutional powers be in any particular wrong, let it be corrected by an amendment in the way which the Constitution designates. But let there be no change by usurpation; for though this in one instance may be the instrument of good, it is the customary weapon by which free governments are destroyed. The precedent must always greatly overbalance in permanent evil any partial or transient benefit which the use can at any time yield.

Of all the dispositions and habits which lead to political prosperity, religion and morality are indispensable supports. In vain would that man claim the tribute of patriotism who should labor to subvert these great pillars of human happiness--these firmest props of the duties of men and citizens. The mere politician, equally with the pious man, ought to respect and to cherish them. A volume could not trace all their connections with private and public felicity. Let it simply be asked, Where is the security for property, for reputation, for life, if the sense of religious obligation *desert* the oaths which are the instruments of investigation in courts of justice? And let us with caution indulge the supposition that morality can be maintained without religion. Whatever may be conceded to the influence of refined education on minds of peculiar structure, reason and experience both forbid us to expect that national morality can prevail in exclusion of religious principle.

It is substantially true that virtue or morality is a necessary spring of popular government. The rule indeed extends with more or less force to every species of free government. Who that is a sincere friend to it can look with indifference upon attempts to shake the foundation of the fabric? Promote, then, as an object of primary importance, institutions for the general diffusion of knowledge. In proportion as the structure of a government gives force to public opinion, it is essential that public opinion should be enlightened.

As a very important source of strength and security, cherish public credit. One method of preserving it is to use it as sparingly as possible, avoiding occasions of expense by cultivating peace, but remembering also that timely disbursements to prepare for danger frequently prevent much greater disbursements to repel it; avoiding likewise the accumulation of debt, not only by shunning occasions of expense, but by vigorous exertions in time of peace to discharge the debts which unavoidable wars have occasioned, not ungenerously throwing upon posterity the burthen which we ourselves ought to bear. The execution of these maxims belongs to your representatives; but it is necessary that public opinion should cooperate. To facilitate to them the performance of their duty it is essential that you should practically bear in mind that toward the payment of debts there must be revenue; that to have revenue there must be taxes; that no taxes can be devised which are not more or less inconvenient and unpleasant; that the intrinsic embarrassment inseparable from the selection of the proper objects (which is always a choice of difficulties), ought to be a decisive motive for a candid construction of the conduct of the Government in making it, and for a spirit of acquiescence in the measures for obtaining revenue which the public exigencies may at any time dictate.

Observe good faith and justice toward all nations. Cultivate peace and harmony with all. Religion and morality enjoin this conduct. And can it be that good policy does not equally enjoin it? It will be worthy of a free, enlightened, and at no distant period a great nation to give to mankind the magnanimous and too novel example of a people always guided by an exalted justice and benevolence. Who can doubt that in the course of time and things the fruits of such a plan would richly repay any temporary advantages which might be lost by a steady adherence to it? Can it be that Providence has not connected the permanent felicity of a nation with its virtue? The experiment, at least, is recommended by every sentiment which ennobles human nature. Alas! is it rendered impossible by its vices?

In the execution of such a plan nothing is more essential than that permanent, inveterate antipathies against particular nations and passionate attachments for others should be excluded, and that in place of them just and amicable feelings toward all should be cultivated. The nation which indulges toward another an habitual hatred or an habitual fondness is in some degree a slave. It is a slave to its animosity or to its affection, either of which is sufficient to lead it astray from its duty and its interest. Antipathy in one nation against another disposes each more readily to offer insult and injury, to lay hold of slight causes of umbrage, and to be haughty and intractable when accidental or trifling occasions of dispute occur.

Hence frequent collisions, obstinate, envenomed, and bloody contests. The nation prompted by ill will and resentment sometimes impels to war the government contrary to the best calculations of policy. The government sometimes participates in the national propensity, and adopts through passion what reason would reject. At other times it makes the animosity of the nation subservient to projects of hostility, instigated by pride, ambition, and other sinister and pernicious motives. The peace often, sometimes perhaps the liberty, of nations has been the victim.

So, likewise, a passionate attachment of one nation for another produces a variety of evils. Sympathy for the favorite nation, facilitating the illusion of an imaginary common interest in cases where no real common interest exists, and infusing into one the enmities of the other, betrays the former into a participation in the quarrels and wars of the latter without adequate inducement or justification. It leads also to concessions to the favorite nation of privileges denied to others, which is apt doubly to injure the nation making the concessions by unnecessarily parting with what ought to have been retained, and by exciting jealousy, ill will, and a disposition to retaliate in the parties from whom equal privileges are withheld; and it gives to ambitious, corrupted, or deluded citizens (who devote themselves to the favorite nation) facility to betray or sacrifice the interests of their own country without odium, sometimes even with popularity, gilding with the appearances of a virtuous sense of obligation, a commendable deference for public opinion, or a laudable zeal for public good the base or foolish compliances of ambition, corruption, or infatuation.

As avenues to foreign influence in innumerable ways, such attachments are particularly alarming to the truly enlightened and independent patriot. How many opportunities do they afford to tamper with domestic factions, to practice the arts of seduction, to mislead public opinion, to influence or awe the public councils! Such an attachment of a small or weak toward a great and powerful nation dooms the former to be the satellite of the latter. Against the insidious wiles of foreign influence (I conjure you to believe me, fellow-citizens) the jealousy of a free people ought to be *constantly* awake, since history and experience prove that foreign influence is one of the most baneful foes of republican government. But that jealousy, to be useful, must be impartial, else it becomes the instrument of the very influence to be avoided, instead of a defense against it. Excessive partiality for one foreign nation and excessive dislike of another cause those whom they actuate to see danger only on one side, and serve to veil and even second the arts of influence on the other. Real patriots who may resist the intrigues of the favorite are liable to become suspected and odious, while its tools and dupes usurp the applause and confidence of the people to surrender their interests.

The great rule of conduct for us in regard to foreign nations is, in extending our commercial relations to have with them as little *political* connection as possible. So far as we have already formed engagements let them be fulfilled with perfect good faith. Here let us stop.

Europe has a set of primary interests which to us have none or a very remote relation. Hence she must be engaged in frequent controversies, the causes of which are essentially foreign to our concerns. Hence, therefore, it must be unwise in us to implicate ourselves by artificial ties in the ordinary vicissitudes of her politics or the ordinary combinations and collisions of her friendships or enmities.

Our detached and distant situation invites and enables us to pursue a different course. If we remain one people, under an efficient government, the period is not far off when we may defy material injury from external annoyance; when we may take such an attitude as will cause the neutrality we may at any time resolve upon to be scrupulously respected; when belligerent nations, under the impossibility of making acquisitions upon us, will not lightly hazard the giving us provocation; when we may choose peace or war, as our interest, guided by justice, shall counsel.

Why forego the advantages of so peculiar a situation? Why quit our own to stand upon foreign ground? Why, by interweaving our destiny with that of any part of Europe, entangle our peace and prosperity in the toils of European ambition, rivalship, interest, humor, or caprice?

It is our true policy to steer clear of permanent alliances with any portion of the foreign world, so far, I mean, as we are now at liberty to do it; for let me not be understood as capable of patronizing infidelity to existing engagements. I hold the maxim no less applicable to public than to private affairs that honesty is always the best policy. I repeat, therefore, let those engagements be observed in their genuine sense. But in my opinion it is unnecessary and would be unwise to extend them.

Taking care always to keep ourselves by suitable establishments on a respectable defensive posture, we may safely trust to temporary alliances for extraordinary emergencies.

Harmony, liberal intercourse with all nations are recommended by policy, humanity, and interest. But even our commercial policy should hold an equal and impartial hand, neither seeking nor granting exclusive favors or preferences; consulting the natural course of things; diffusing and diversifying by gentle means the streams of commerce, but forcing nothing; establishing with powers so disposed, in order to give trade a stable course, to define the rights of our merchants, and to enable the Government to support them, conventional rules of intercourse, the best that present circumstances and mutual opinion will permit, but temporary and liable to be from time to time abandoned or varied as experience and circumstances shall dictate; constantly keeping in view that it is folly in one nation to look for disinterested favors from another; that it must pay with a portion of its independence for whatever it may accept under that character; that by such acceptance it may place itself in the condition of having given equivalents for nominal favors, and yet of being reproached with ingratitude for not giving more. There can be no greater error than to expect or calculate upon real favors from nation to nation. It is an illusion which experience must cure, which a just pride ought to discard.

In offering to you, my countrymen, these counsels of an old and affectionate friend I dare not hope they will make the strong and lasting impression I could wish-that they will control the usual current of the passions or prevent our nation from running the course which has hitherto marked the destiny of nations. But if I may even flatter myself that they may be productive of some partial benefit, some occasional good--that they may now and then recur to moderate the fury of party spirit, to warn against the mischiefs of foreign intrigue, to guard against the impostures of pretended patriotism-this hope will be a full recompense for the solicitude for your welfare by which they have been dictated.

How far in the discharge of my official duties I have been guided by the principles which have been delineated the public records and other evidences of my conduct must witness to you and to the world. To myself, the assurance of my own conscience is that I have at least believed myself to be guided by them.

In relation to the still subsisting war in Europe my proclamation of the 22nd of April, 1793, is the index to my plan. Sanctioned by your approving voice and by that of your representatives in both Houses of Congress, the spirit of that measure has continually governed me, uninfluenced by any attempts to deter or divert me from it.

After deliberate examination, with the aid of the best lights I could obtain, I was well satisfied that our country, under all the circumstances of the case, had a right to take, and was bound in duty and interest to take, a neutral position. Having taken it, I determined as far as should depend upon me to maintain it with moderation, perseverance, and firmness.

The considerations which respect the right to hold this conduct it is not necessary on this occasion to detail. I will only observe that, according to my understanding of the matter, that right, so far from being denied by any of the belligerent powers, has been virtually admitted by all.

The duty of holding a neutral conduct may be inferred, without anything more, from the obligation which justice and humanity impose on every nation, in cases in which it is free to act, to maintain inviolate the relations of peace and amity toward other nations.

The inducements of interest for observing that conduct will best be referred to your own reflections and experience. With me a predominant motive has been to endeavor to gain time to our country to settle and mature its yet recent institutions, and to progress without interruption to that degree of strength and consistency which is necessary to give it, humanly speaking, the command of its own fortunes.

Though in reviewing the incidents of my Administration I am unconscious of intentional error, I am nevertheless too sensible of my defects not to think it probable that I may have committed many errors. Whatever they may be, I fervently beseech the Almighty to avert or mitigate the evils to which they may tend. I shall also carry with me the hope that my country will never cease to view them with indulgence, and that, after forty-five years of my life dedicated to its service with an upright zeal, the faults of incompetent abilities will be consigned to oblivion, as myself must soon be to the mansions of rest.

Relying on its kindness in this as in other things, and actuated by that fervent love toward it which is so natural to a man who views in it the native soil of himself and his progenitors for several generations, I anticipate with pleasing expectation that retreat in which I promise myself to realize without alloy the sweet enjoyment of partaking in the midst of my fellow-citizens the benign influence of good laws under a free government--the ever-favorite object of my heart, and the happy reward, as I trust, of our mutual cares, labors, and dangers.

Jefferson's First
Inaugural Address

Friends and Fellow-Citizens.

Called upon to undertake the duties of the first executive office of our country, I avail myself of the presence of that portion of my fellow-citizens which is here assembled to express my grateful thanks for the favor with which they have been pleased to look toward me, to declare a sincere consciousness that the task is above my talents, and that I approach it with those anxious and awful presentiments which the greatness of the charge and the weakness of my powers so justly inspire. A rising nation, spread over a wide and fruitful land, traversing all the seas with the rich productions of their industry, engaged in commerce with nations who feel power and forget right, advancing rapidly to destinies beyond the reach of mortal eye—when I contemplate these transcendent objects, and see the honor, the happiness, and the hopes of this beloved country committed to the issue and the auspices of this day, I shrink from the contemplation, and humble myself before the magnitude of the undertaking. Utterly, indeed, should I despair did not the presence of many whom I here see remind me that in the other high authorities provided by our Constitution I shall find resources of wisdom, of virtue, and of zeal on which to rely under all difficulties. To you, then, gentlemen, who are charged with the sovereign functions of legislation, and to those associated with you, I look with encouragement for that guidance and support which may enable us to steer with safety the vessel in which we are all embarked amidst the conflicting elements of a troubled world.

During the contest of opinion through which we have passed the animation of discussions and of exertions has sometimes worn an aspect which might impose on strangers unused to think freely and to speak and to write what they think; but this being now decided by the voice of the nation, announced according to the rules of the Constitution, all will, of course, arrange themselves under the will of the law, and unite in common efforts for the common good. All, too, will bear in mind this sacred principle, that though the will of the majority is in all cases to prevail, that will to be rightful must be reasonable; that the minority possess their equal rights, which equal law must protect, and to violate would be oppression. Let us, then, fellow-citizens, unite with one heart and one mind. Let us restore to social intercourse that harmony and affection without which liberty and even life itself are but dreary things. And let us reflect that, having banished from our land that religious intolerance under which mankind so long bled and suffered, we have yet gained little if we countenance a political intolerance as despotic, as wicked, and capable of as bitter and bloody persecutions. During the throes and convulsions of the ancient world, during the agonizing spasms of infuriated man, seeking through blood and slaughter his long-lost liberty, it was not wonderful that the agitation of the billows should reach even this distant and peaceful shore; that this should be more felt and feared by some and less by others, and should divide opinions as to measures of safety. But every difference of opinion is not a difference of principle. We have called by different names brethren of the same principle. We are all Republicans, we are all Federalists. If there be any among us who would wish to dissolve this Union or to change its republican form, let them stand undisturbed as monuments of the safety to combat it. I know, indeed, that some honest men fear that a republican government can not be strong, that this Government is not strong enough; but would the honest patriot, in the full tide of successful experiment, abandon a government which has so far kept us free and firm on the theoretic and visionary fear that this Government, the world's best hope, may by possibility want energy to preserve itself? I trust not. I believe this, on the contrary, the strongest Government on earth. I believe it the only one where every man, at the call of the law, would fly to the standard of the law, and would meet invasions of the public order as his own personal concern. Sometimes it is said that man cannot be trusted with the government of himself. Can he, then, be trusted with the government of others? Or have we found angels in the forms of kings to govern him? Let history answer this question.

Let us, then, with courage and confidence pursue our own Federal and Republican principles, our attachment to union and representative government. Kindly separated by nature and a wide ocean from the exterminating havoc of one quarter of the globe; too high-minded to endure the degradations of the others; possessing a chosen country, with room enough for our descendants to the thousandth and thousandth generation; entertaining a due sense of our equal right to the use of our own faculties, to the acquisitions of our own industry, to honor and confidence from our fellow-citizens, resulting not from birth, but from our actions and their sense of them; enlightened by a benign religion, professed, indeed, and practiced in various forms, yet all of them inculcating honesty, truth, temperance, gratitude, and the love of men; acknowledging and adoring an overrruling Providence, which by all its dispensations proves that it delights in the happiness of man here and his greater happiness hereafter—with all these blessings, what more is necessary to make us a happy and a prosperous people? Still one thing more fellow-citizens—a wise and frugal Government, which shall restrain men from injuring one another, shall leave them otherwise free to regulate their own pursuits of industry and improvement, and shall not take from the mouth of labor the bread it has earned. This is the sum of good government, and this is necessary to close the circle of our felicities.

About to enter, fellow-citizens, on the exercises of duties which comprehend everything dear and valuable to you, it is proper you should understand what I deem the essential principles of our Government, and consequently those which ought to shape its Administration. I will compress them within the narrowest compass they will bear, stating the general principle, but not all its limitations. Equal and exact justice to all men, of whatever state or persuasion, religious or political; peace, commerce, and honest friendship with all nations, entangling alliances with none; the support of the State governments in all their rights; as the most competent administrations for our domestic concerns and the surest bulwarks against antirepublican tendencies; the preservation of the General Government in its whole constitutional vigor, as the sheet anchor of our peace at home and safety abroad; a jealous care of the right of election by the people—a mild and safe corrective of abuses which are lopped by the sword of revolution where peaceable remedies are unprovided; absolute acquiescence in the decisions of the majority, the vital principle of republics, from which is no appeal but to force, the vital principle and immediate parent of despotism; a well-disciplined militia, our best reliance in peace and for the first moments of war, till regulars may relieve them; the supremacy of the civil over the military authority; economy in the public expense, that labor may be lightly burdened; the honest payment of our debts and sacred preservation of the public faith; encouragement of agriculture, and of commerce as its handmaid; the diffusion of information and arraignment of all abuses at the bar of the public reason; freedom of religion; freedom of the press, and freedom of persons under the protection of the habeas corpus, and trial by juries impartially selected. These principles form the bright constellation which has gone before us and guided our steps through an age of revolution and reformation. The wisdom of our sages and blood of our heroes have been devoted to their attainment. They should be the creed of our political faith, the text of civic instruction, the touchstone by which to try the services of those we trust; and should we wander from them in moments of error or of alarm, let us hasten to retrace our steps and to regain the road which alone leads to peace, liberty, and safety.

I repair, then, fellow-citizens, to the post you have assigned me. With experience enough in subordinate offices to have seen the difficulties of this the greatest of all, I have learnt to expect that it will rarely fall to the lot of imperfect man to retire from this station with the reputation and the favor which bring him into it. Without pretensions to the high confidence you reposed in our first and greatest revolutionary character, whose preeminent services had entitled him to the first place in his country's love and destined for him the fairest page in the volume of faithful history, I ask so much confidence only as may give firmness and effect to the legal administration of your affairs. I shall often go wrong through defect of judgment. When right, I shall often be thought wrong by those whose positions will not command a view of the whole ground. I ask your indulgence for my own errors, which will never be intentional, and your support against the errors of others, who may condemn what they would not if seen in all its parts. The approbation implied by your suffrage is a great consolation to me for the past, and my future solicitude will be to retain the good opinion of those who have bestowed it in advance, to conciliate that of others by doing them all the good in my power, and to be instrumental to the happiness and freedom of all.

Relying, then, on the patronage of your good will, I advance with obedience to the work, ready to retire from it whenever you become sensible how much better choice it is in your power to make. And may that Infinite Power which rules the destinies of the universe lead our councils to what is best, and give them a favorable issue for your peace and prosperity.

Index